How to Critique
Authoritarian Populism

D1563587

Studies in Critical Social Sciences Book Series

Haymarket Books is proud to be working with Brill Academic Publishers (www.brill.nl) to republish the *Studies in Critical Social Sciences* book series in paperback editions. This peer-reviewed book series offers insights into our current reality by exploring the content and consequences of power relationships under capitalism, and by considering the spaces of opposition and resistance to these changes that have been defining our new age. Our full catalog of *SCSS* volumes can be viewed at https://www.haymarketbooks .org/series_collections/4-studies-in-critical-social-sciences.

HOW TO CRITIQUE AUTHORITARIAN POPULISM

Methodologies of the Frankfurt School

EDITED BY
JEREMIAH MORELOCK

Haymarket Books
Chicago, IL

First published in 2021 by Brill Academic Publishers, The Netherlands
© 2021 Koninklijke Brill NV, Leiden, The Netherlands

Published in paperback in 2022 by
Haymarket Books
P.O. Box 180165
Chicago, IL 60618
773-583-7884
www.haymarketbooks.org

ISBN: 978-1-64259-767-7

Distributed to the trade in the US through Consortium Book Sales and
Distribution (www.cbsd.com) and internationally through Ingram Publisher
Services International (www.ingramcontent.com).

This book was published with the generous support of Lannan Foundation and
Wallace Action Fund.

Special discounts are available for bulk purchases by organizations and
institutions. Please call 773-583-7884 or email info@haymarketbooks.org for more
information.

Cover design by Jamie Kerry and Ragina Johnson.

Printed in the United States.

10 9 8 7 6 5 4 3 2 1

Library of Congress Cataloging-in-Publication data is available.

Contents

Acknowledgements

Thanks are extended to the following publishers: to *Logos* journal, for permitting the publication of an updated version of Dan Krier's "Behemoth Revisited: National Socialism and the Trump Administration" from Volume 16, Issues 1–2, 2017, at http://logosjournal.com/2017/behemoth-revisited-national-socialism-and-the-trump-administration/; to *Radical Philosophy Review*, for permitting the publication of "Mobilization of Bias Today: The Renewed Use of Established Techniques; A Reconsideration of Two Studies on Prejudice from the Institute for Social Research" by Peter-Erwin Jansen and translated by Charles Reitz, from Volume 16, Issue 1, pages 169–186, 2013; and to Harvard University Press for permitting the publication of a page from the graphic novel *Unflattening* by Nick Sousanis, 2015 (also thank you to Nick Sousanis for giving his permission for use of the page and supplying the image). Thanks are also extended to Artists Rights Society for permission to publish an image of Jose Clemente Orozco's painting "Christ Destroying His Cross." Thanks are also due to Joanne Chapman Morelock, Lucy Morelock, Cherylann Silva, Amy Cardoso, Christine A. Payne, Michael J. Roberts, Critical Theory Research Network, and everyone who contributed to this volume.

Illustrations

Figures

Table

Notes on Contributors

Robert J. Antonio
is a Professor of Sociology at the University of Kansas. He specializes in social theory, but also teaches and works in the areas of globalization, political economy, and environment. He is currently working on multiple projects related to contemporary capitalism's crisis tendencies, especially concerning the intersection of increased economic inequality, ecological risk, and democratic and authoritarian responses. Among his earlier publications related to themes in his essay in this collection are "Immanent Critique as the Core of Critical Theory" (*British Journal of Sociology* 32(3): 330–345) and "After Postmodernism: Reactionary Tribalism" (*American Journal of Sociology* 106(1): 40–87).

Stefanie Baumann
is currently a contracted researcher at CineLab/IFILNOVA (New University of Lisbon, Portugal). She obtained her Ph.D. in philosophy in 2013, and has taught philosophy, aesthetics, and contemporary art theory at University of Paris VIII (Paris, 2007–10), Ashkal Alwan (Beirut, 2013), ALBA – the Lebanese Academy of Fine Arts/University of Balamand (Beirut, 2012–15), and the Maumaus Study Program (Lisbon, since 2016). She also worked with the artist Esther Shalev-Gerz as personal assistant from 2005 to 2010 and collaborated with video artists Marie Voignier and Mounira Al Solh.

Christopher Craig Brittain
is Dean of Divinity and Margaret E. Fleck Chair in Anglican Studies at Trinity College in the University of Toronto. He is interested in political theology and the writings of the early Frankfurt School on religion and theology. His publications include: "Racketeering in Religion: Adorno and evangelical support for Donald Trump," *Critical Research on Religion* 6(3) (2018), *The Anglican Communion at a Crossroads: The Crisis of a Global Church, Religion at Ground Zero: Theological responses to times of crisis* (Continuum, 2011), and *Adorno and Theology* (T&T Lark, 2010).

Dustin J. Byrd
is an Associate Professor of Philosophy and Religion at Olivet College (Michigan). He earned his Ph.D. in political and social philosophy at Michigan State University (2017), where he specialized in the Frankfurt School's Critical Theory of Religion, as well as modern Islamic thought. He is the author of

numerous books, including *Critical Theory of Religion: From the Frankfurt School to Emancipatory Islamic Thought* (Ekpyrosis Press, 2020), and *Islam in a Post-Secular Society: Religion, Secularity, and the Antagonism of Recalcitrant Faith* (Brill 2016; Haymarket Books, 2017). He has co-edited numerous books, including those on the subject of Malcolm X, Ali Shariati, and Frantz Fanon. He is the Editor-and-Chief of *Islamic Perspective Journal,* published by the London Academy of Iranian Studies, as well as the Editor-and-Chief of Ekpyrosis Press, which he founded in 2020. He is currently studying the intersection of Far-Right populism and Islam in Europe, as well as palingenetic ultra-nationalism in the United States.

Mariana Caldas Pinto Ferreira

is a Ph.D. Candidate at Pontifícia Universidade Católica do Rio de Janeiro (PUC-Rio). She holds a Master's degree in law, and worked as an Associate Researcher at the Truth Commission of Rio de Janeiro between 2014 and 2015. She was a Visiting Researcher fellow of the Department of War Studies, King's College London during 2018 and 2019. Her research aims to discuss violence in the field of critical security studies by engaging with its representation along with aesthetics literature and privileging lived experience of suffering expressed in works of art, specifically with Brazilian art.

Panayota Gounari

is Professor and Chair of the Department of Applied Linguistics at the University of Massachusetts Boston. She has published extensively on the politics of language & bilingualism, the discourse of financial crises, authoritarian discourse, language policy, and critical pedagogy. Her most recent books include *Liberatory and Critical Education in Greece: Historical Trajectories and Perspectives* (Gutenberg, 2016, co-authored with G. Grolllios) and the edited volume *A Reader in Critical Pedagogy* (Gutenberg, 2010).

Peter-Erwin Jansen

is the editor of six volumes of previously unpublished writings from the Marcuse papers and responsible for new publications from the Leo Loewenthal Archive. Both held at the Archivzentrum of the Goethe University in Frankfurt. He currently teaches social science and social work at the University of Applied Sciences, Koblenz, Germany. During his university studies in Frankfurt, he did research on Marcuse's social philosophy under Jürgen Habermas and Axel Honneth. Most recent books in English include *Ecology and the Critique of Society Today. Five selected papers for the current context,* co-edited with Herbert Marcuse, S. Surak and Ch. Reitz (independently published, 2019) and *Transvaluation of Values & Radical Change. Five Lectures 1966–1976*, edited by Herbert Marcuse (CreateSpace Independent Publishing Platform, 2017). Both books are sponsoring the International Herbert Marcuse Society (IHMS). In German Jansen recently co-edited with L. Doppler/A. Doppler-Neupert Herbert Marcuse: *Kapitalismus und Opposition. Vorlesungen zum eindimensionalen Menschen. Paris, Vicennes 1974* (zu Klampen Verlag, 2017) and "Die irrationale Rationalität des Fortschritts. Herbert Marcuses weitsichtige Technologiekritik", in *Zeitschirft für Kritische Theorie*, 48/49 (11/ 2019): 232–251.

Imaculada Kangussu

is professor at the Instituto de Filosofia, Artes e Cultura of the Universidade Federal de Ouro Preto, Brasil. She is the author of *Sobre Eros* [*About Eros*] (Skriptum, 2007), *Leis da Liberdade* [*Laws of Freedom*] (Ed. Loyola, 2008), and *A Fantasia e as Fantasias* [*The Fantasy and the Fantasies*] (2020, forthcoming). Among her edited volumes are *Katharsis* (C/Arte, 2002), *Theoria Aesthetica* (Escritos, 2005), *O Cômico e o Trágico* (7 Letras, 2008), and *Estéticas Moderna e Contemporânea* (Relicário, 2017). Kangussu is the treasurer of the Brazilian Committee for the Reunification of the Parthenon Sculptures. She serves on the board of the International Herbert Marcuse Society.

Douglas Kellner

is George Kneller Chair in the Philosophy of Education at UCLA and is author of many books on social theory, politics, history, and culture. His most recent books are *American Nightmare: Donald Trump, Media Spectacle, and Authoritarian Populism* (Springer, 2016) and *The American Horror Show: Election 2016 and the Ascendency of Donald J. Trump* (Springer, 2017). Kellner's website is at https:// pages.gseis.ucla.edu/faculty/kellner/ which contains several of his books and many articles.

Dan Krier

is Professor of Sociology at Iowa State University where he specializes in critical social theory, political economy, and comparative-historical sociology. His books include *Capital in the Mirror* (co-edited with MP Worrell, SUNY, 2020); *The Social Ontology of Capitalism* (co-edited with M. P. Worrell, Palgrave Macmillan, 2017); *NASCAR, Sturgis and the New Economy of Spectacle* (with W. Swart, Brill, 2016), and *Capitalism's Future: Alienation, Emancipation and Critique* (co-edited with M. P. Worrell, Brill, 2016). He is currently completing *Economic Theology: The Religious Foundations of Capitalism* (under contract with Brill, to be published in the Studies in Critical Social Sciences Series).

Lauren Langman

received his Ph.D. from the University of Chicago Committee on Human Development He has since been a Professor of Sociology at Loyola University of Chicago. His work is in the tradition of the Frankfurt School of Critical Theory, with a focus on relationships between culture, identity, ideology and politics/ political movements. His latest books are on American Character: *God, Guns, Gold and Glory* (Brill, 2016) and *Inequality in the 21st C: Marx, Piketty and beyond* (Brill, 2018), and *Mobilization for Dignity* (Routledge, forthcoming).

Claudia Leeb

is an Associate Professor in political theory at Washington State University. She works at the intersection of early Frankfurt school Critical Theory, feminist theory, and psychoanalysis to address questions of power and socio-political change. Here recent books are *The Politics of Repressed Guilt* (Edinburgh University Press, 2018), and *Power and Feminist Agency in Capitalism* (Oxford University Press, 2017). She has published in numerous journals, including *Political Theory, Theory & Event, Perspectives on Politics, Constellations, Social Philosophy Today, Philosophy & Social Criticism*, and *Radical Philosophy Review*. She has also contributed several book chapters to anthologies on Frankfurt School Critical Theory.

Gregory Joseph Menillo

is a composer and Ph.D. candidate at the Graduate Center of the City University of New York, where he also holds a certificate in Critical Theory specializing in the work of Theodor W. Adorno. His doctoral dissertation focuses on Adorno's aesthetic theory and its relationship to post-war American modernist music, specifically the work of Elliott Carter. He is an adjunct lecturer at both Manhattan College and Lehman College, where he teaches courses in the aesthetics of music, music theory and analysis, and music history.

Jeremiah Morelock

is an instructor of sociology at Boston College. In his research, he analyzes populism, authoritarianism, and illness narratives in media and popular culture. He is the editor of *Critical Theory and Authoritarian Populism* (University of Westminster, 2018), and co-author (with Felipe Ziotti Narita) of *O Problema do Populismo* (Paco, 2019). He is also author of *The Society of the Selfie* (University of Westminster, forthcoming), and *Pandemics, Authoritarian Populism and Science Fiction: Tribalism, Militarism, Medicine and Morality in American Film* (Routledge, forthcoming). Morelock is co-editor (with Felipe Ziotti Narita) of a forthcoming special issue of *Theoretical Practice*. He serves as a reviewer for the journals *TripleC: Capitalism, Communication and Critique, Cadernos CIM-EAC,* and *Fast Capitalism,* and, is founder and director of the Critical Theory Research Network.

Felipe Ziotti Narita

received a postdoctoral training in the social sciences at the University of São Paulo (USP) and Federal University of São Carlos (UFSCar), as well as a Ph.D. from the São Paulo State University (UNESP). He is a lecturer in public policy at UNESP and associate researcher in the social sciences at the São Paulo Research Foundation (FAPESP). Ziotti Narita was an invited researcher at the inauguration of the Forschungskreis Gregor Girard at the University of Fribourg (Switzerland), associate editor of *Theoretical Practice* (Adam Mickiewicz University, Poland), and a member of Historiar: Identity Narratives, Concepts, Language (a research group supported by the National Council for Scientific and Technological Development of Brazil, CNPq).

Michael R. Ott

is an Emeritus Associate Professor of Sociology at Grand Valley State University, Allendale, Michigan, from which he retired in 2014. He received his Master of Divinity degree from Princeton Theological Seminary in 1975 and his Ph.D. in sociology from Western Michigan University in 1998, where his focus was on the development of the Critical Theory of Religion and Society (CTRS) under the direction of Dr. Rudolf J. Siebert. Ott is also an ordained minister of the United Church of Christ, having served the church as a full-time pastor for 25 years prior to his becoming a university professor. Although now retired from his institutional professions, he continues his research, writing and public discourses on the dialectical relationship between the Sacred and the Profane, Religion and Reason, Faith and Science as critique of the increasing antagonisms of modernity in the theoretical and practical pursuit of creating a more reconciled, just, humane, and peace-filled future society wherein subjective freedom and universal solidarity prevail.

Charles Reitz

is the author of *Ecology and Revolution: Herbert Marcuse and the Challenge of a New World System Today* (Routledge, 2018); *Philosophy and Radical Pedagogy: Insurrection and Commonwealth* (Peter Lang Publishing, 2016); *Crisis & Commonwealth: Marcuse, Marx, McLaren* (Lexington Books, 2015), and *Art, Alienation and the Humanities* (State University Of New York Press, 2000).

Avery Schatz

will be graduating in the Fall of 2020 with her bachelor's degree in sociology from Loyola University. She has worked alongside Lauren Langman as a Research Assistant. At Charles University in Prague, she studied women's oppression under capitalism. Her research interests include social psychology, gender inequality and Marxist Feminism.

Rudolf J. Siebert

Rudolf J. Siebert was born in Frankfurt am Main, on October 1, 1927. He has studied history, philosophy, psychology, sociology, social work, and theology at the Universities of Frankfurt, Mainz, Münster, and Catholic University of America, Washington DC. Siebert created and is a specialist in the Critical Theory of Religion and Society (CTRS), or Dialectical Religiology (DR). He has taught, lectured, and published widely in Western and Eastern Europe, the United States, Canada, Israel and Japan. He is Professor Emeritus of Comparative Religion, and founder and director of the Center for Humanistic Future Studies, at Western Michigan University. He is also the founder and director of the international courses in Croatia and Crimea. The most recent of his over 30 books is *The Evolution of the Critical Theory of Religion and Society: Union, Disunion, and Reunion of the Sacred and the Profane (1946–2020)* (SANBUN Publishers, 2020).

William M. Sipling

works in the non-profit industry in the field of digital media and education and is an independent scholar. Previously, he held fellowships at the University of St. Thomas within the Department of Catholic Studies and the School of Law. He has earned master's degrees in religion from St. Thomas and Dallas Theological Seminary, and his research interests are in social and political theory, mythological and theological studies, and communication and linguistic theory.

David Norman Smith

(Ph.D., Wisconsin) teaches sociology at the University of Kansas. He is the author of books on Marx's *Capital,* George Orwell, and class analysis, and his papers have appeared in *Sociological Theory, Current Perspectives in Social Theory, Sociological Quarterly, American Psychologist, Rethinking Marxism, Critical Sociology,* and other journals and books. His recent articles include several ("The Anger Games", in *Critical Sociology* 44(2):195–212; "The Heart of Whiteness: Patterns of Race, Class, and Prejudice in the Divided Midwest" with Eric Hanley, in *Political Landscapes of Donald Trump,* edited by Barney Warf, Routledge, 2020; and "Authoritarianism Reimagined", in *The Sociological*

Quarterly 60(2): 210–223) which report findings drawn from authoritarianism scales that the American National Election Study included at his recommendation. With past support from the National Endowment for the Humanities, he is editing *Marx's World: Global Society and Capital Accumulation in Marx's Late Manuscripts* for Yale University Press (forthcoming).

Daniel Sullivan

is an Assistant Professor of Psychology at the University of Arizona. He received a Ph.D. in psychology from the University of Kansas and a BA in German studies from the University of Arizona. His research concerns cultural differences in how individuals and groups experience and defend against psychological threats, including the psychology of enemyship, scapegoating, and conspiracy theories. He is the author of *Cultural-Existential Psychology* (Cambridge University Press, 2016).

AK Thompson

got kicked out of high school for publishing an underground newspaper called *The Agitator* and has been an activist and social theorist ever since. He is currently a Professor of Social Movements and Social Change at Ithaca College, his publications include *Sociology for Changing the World: Social Movements/ Social Research* (Fernwood Publishing, 2006); *Black Bloc, White Riot: Anti-Globalization and the Genealogy of Dissent* (AK Press, 2010); *Keywords for Radicals: The Contested Vocabulary of Late-Capitalist Struggle* (AK Press, 2016); *Spontaneous Combustion: The Eros Effect and Global Revolution* (SUNY Press, 2017), and, most recently, *Premonitions: Selected Essays on the Culture of Revolt* (AK Press, 2018). Between 2005 and 2012, he served on the Editorial Committee of *Upping the Anti: A Journal of Theory and Action.*

Introduction: Frankfurt School Methodologies

Jeremiah Morelock and Daniel Sullivan

The current surge in authoritarian populism is an urgent situation that requires dedicated attention inside and outside of the academy. In the United States, the notion of fascism as largely an historical anomaly, that "we" had somehow surpassed this kind of prejudice and brutality, was the status quo until the past several years. Now, with far-right parties raging across Europe and the Americas, it is more than clear that, however idiosyncratic the experiences of countries like Germany and Italy in the 1930s and 1940s, whatever larger social forces stood behind the emergence of right-wing extremism then, still have their corollaries today. Far from disappearing, authoritarian populism has been reinvigorated, and the scope of its appeal far surpasses its spread in the inter-war era. If social science is intended to help society, then any social scientist should be aware today of the pressing need to understand authoritarian populism, to help society overcome it.

Yet authoritarian populism is no simple object of analysis. It is very complex, and while every instance is unique, many characteristics are shared between far-right parties in Europe and the Americas. To understand it necessitates a potent social science. Such social science maintains the ability to use theory that stretches above the "middle range," theory that addresses head on large questions, to allow space for theoretical speculation that is not confined religiously to the immediate facts. It requires the capacity for rigorous empirical research, and the willingness both to "operationalize" variables for statistical analysis, and to look beyond statistical generalizations and the fetishism of already established quantitative methods with their underlying labyrinthine algebras. It should employ an analytical sophistication that can see the particularities of historical instances, rather than subsuming them within hastily applied "grand narratives," and yet this sophistication should be willing to see broad patterns and even to consider large historical *forces*, rather than being religiously confined to unassuming interpretation of idiosyncratic personal narratives under a dogma of postmodern-era relativism.

Under a positivist framework and under a relativist framework, there is no solid footing to stand on to ground one's research in outright critique of forms of domination such as found in movements of the far-Right. So, the problem is not only that the dominant frameworks are intellectually disempowering, they are also normatively disempowering. For the positivist, research should be "value-free," and for the postmodern-era relativist, one can only speak about perspectives and interpretations.

In recent years there has also been a resurgence of interest in the writings of the early Frankfurt School. This trend has occurred in correlation with – and no doubt in reaction to – the rise of authoritarian populist movements in Europe and the Americas. There is good reason for this. No other school of thought has focused so thoroughly on understanding and critiquing the way authoritarian movements come to be embraced within liberal democracies. Yet Frankfurt School Critical Theory remains a rogue element in the academic social sciences, belonging to the margins rather than to the mainstream. The embrace of the Frankfurt School on the basis of their forceful critiques – however powerful and intuitively compelling – is not enough to earn those critiques a strong position in 21st century academic social sciences; a position not just as an artifact of historical curiosity, but as a living practice of scholarly inquiry.

To earn a robust footing as a continued area of scholarly practice in the social sciences today, Critical Theory requires not just political appeal, but also steadfast attention to its methodological salience. This would include a renewed reception of the multiple, extensive empirical studies of authoritarianism and contemporary capitalism performed by the early Institute for Social Research (ISR). There are at least three major impediments to this.

First, the boldness of their social and political critiques is so strong that Critical Theory earns both advocates and detractors on this basis, methodological considerations typically falling into the background or out of discussion. Second, the ISR's empirical approach was truly beyond the boundaries of disciplines. Hence it can be harder to justify within the methodological orthodoxies of particular social sciences – and most social science research is conducted within university departments dedicated to particular academic fields. Being interdisciplinary or transdisciplinary by nature, this approach is moreover not typically incentivized either in discipline-specific (i.e. most) doctoral training programs or in top tier scholarly journals. In order to dialogue with the current academic literature in multiple disciplines simultaneously, work inspired by early Critical Theory also requires wider background knowledge than discipline-specific work. Third, and relatedly, the ISR was not definitively interpretivist or positivist. It was however, strongly rooted in both philosophy and empirical research. Thus, work like theirs requires an additional level of methodological flexibility beyond the binary alignment to either social constructionist approaches or statistical analysis, or the typically contrasting predilections of philosophers vis-à-vis researchers.

Likely for these reasons, the early works of the ISR and critical theory have received a fractured reception in social science and the humanities. While the former tends to consecrate *The Authoritarian Personality* (Adorno et al. 2019 [1950]), the latter does the same to *Dialectic of Enlightenment* (Horkheimer and Adorno 2002 [1947]. Scholars in either area hardly ever encounter the "tomes" locked in the opposite tower. As a result, the interconnected, transdisciplinary effort of the early ISR has hardly ever been historically experienced.

The present volume is offered in response to this relative defection toward deep engagement with the methodologies of the Frankfurt School. And the material is very rich methodologically, owing both to the ingenuity of the ISR and to their transdisciplinary reach. This introductory chapter provides a broad outline of ISR methodologies. These revolve around three axes which may be analytically distinguished, but that throughout much of their work were dedicatedly combined: philosophy, empirical research, and aesthetics.[1]

The chapter is structured as follows. First, we describe the methodological malaise plaguing much contemporary sociology and social psychology, in our era of the lackluster contrasting poles of positivism[2] and postmodernism, and the new wave of what we will refer to as "lazy pragmatism." Against this background, we then explain the approaches promoted and practiced by the early Frankfurt School. Here we discuss their definitions for "Critical Theory," and three dialectical tensions that they highlighted as intrinsic in the combined terrain of social theory and science, and which they sought to preserve and harness rather than reduce or reconcile. Along the way, in broad strokes, we will discuss their philosophical methodologies – namely, their use of dialectic as critique – outline their major empirical studies on authoritarianism

---

1   The relative focus of Horkheimer, Adorno, Marcuse and others on this or that axis differs, and so do their methodological preferences. Yet as a general movement, and especially when considered under the joint leadership of Horkheimer and Adorno, there is much consistency, and in this respect we will often refer to the group as a singular entity (the ISR) and to their intellectual movement in a singular sense (Critical Theory). We discuss variation between thinkers, and yet a general contour to the school of thought is also outlined.

2   As has long been noted (Meehl 1986), virtually no currently practicing social scientists identify with the fundamental tenets of logical positivism as outlined by the Vienna Circle, and indeed one of the ironies of the "positivism dispute" is that none of the disputants – including Popper – identified as "positivist." The term positivism as used here – and throughout the writings of Critical Theorists – might be more accurately replaced by others they frequently used, e.g., "technocratic" or "administrative" research (Habermas 1987; Marcuse 1964). Nevertheless, we will retain the term due to its rhetorical force and frequency in Critical Theory epistemology, and the fact that certain basic assumptions of logical empiricism dating back to the 1930s still ground the "mainstream view" of empirical social science, particularly in psychology (Gergen 1982, 6–11; Sullivan 2020).

and explore their inclusion of non-rational or aesthetic elements within social critique.

1   The Contemporary Detente: Positivism, Postmodernism, and Lazy Pragmatism

Historically, positivist epistemology is an inheritance from one of the first debates in modern social science: that between advocates of a view that science should focus on causal explanations and minimize the role of researcher values and bias, and advocates of a view that science should strive to understand individuals in the complex context of their historically determined environments and beliefs (Cole 1996; Dallmayr and McCarthy 1977).

1.1   *Positivism*

The positivist or logical empiricist position in this debate has certain defining characteristics. This view is grounded in the logic of fallibilism (Popper, 1934/2005): theories can only be considered valid insofar as they generate hypotheses which can in principle be falsified. A closely related criterion is that of replicability: any individual should be able to repeat the crucial falsification test (Derksen 2019). In order to satisfy the criteria of fallibilism and replicability, most contemporary positivist theories are also embedded in logics of quantification and statistical objectivity (Freese and Peterson 2018; Leonelli 2018). Quantitative social scientists tend to be obsessed with empirical operationalizations (Green 1992), as well as the pursuit of systematic harmony in theoretical models. They are wary of research that appears too "applied" or too "political." Positivist social scientists assume that their propositions "hit bedrock" when they can be converted into quantifiable variables (e.g., a Likert-type scale for a construct; the presence or absence of an experimental condition). Behavioral, quantifiable demonstrations of phenomena under controlled conditions are often considered the holy grail of the positivist approach.

Positivist epistemology produces a strong tendency to subsume theory to research, rather than the other way around (Greenberg et al. 1988). Indeed, as Horkheimer (1947) realized long ago, positivist social scientists tend to subordinate theory to method: From this perspective, philosophy is only valuable in the guise of epistemology, as a handmaiden to scientific methods. For all these reasons, positivist theories tend to be universalizing and ahistorical. Social theories are constructed to fit the rigid methods and conditions of an experimental worldview ultimately derived from physics. For this fitting to work, complex interrelationships and temporal stochasticity must be hacked apart or ignored.

1.2   *Postmodernism*

On the other side of the divide is the skeptical outlook of postmodernism (broadly construed). This orientation toward truth has distant antecedents in ancient skepticism and sophistry, and close antecedents in figures such as Nietzsche, Heidegger and Wittgenstein. While there is no clear or definitive postmodern "anti-truth" statement, in works such as Lyotard's *The Postmodern Condition* (1984) and Foucault's *The Order of Things* (2012), scientific truth and other forms of "master narrative" are shown to be historically contingent, and losing their grip in the contemporary period.

The primary posited alternative – more common in sociology and anthropology than in other social sciences – is the wedding of social constructionist epistemology to qualitative research methods, a movement that has retained a deep infusion of postmodern thought since the 1980s (e.g., Lincoln and Guba 2000). Here there is a turning away from principles and generalization (Hammersley 1992). Most contemporary work here falls between the interpretation of meaning in discourse – avoiding any claims about a reality beyond language – and the phenomenological exploration of idiosyncratic lived experience. This camp also has diverse origins, reaching into phenomenology as well as the two different semiotic traditions embodied in American pragmatism and French structuralism.

Especially during the 1980s and 1990s, postmodernism rose to present a formidable challenge to the domination of positivism in the academy, and to cultural dogmatism in the broader society. Some of the challenges shared kinships with ideas from the early Frankfurt School, such as criticism of the fascistic effects that monopolistic scientific rationality can have in society, despite its ostensibly liberating purposes. Yet, the postmodern movement went further than the Frankfurt School in eschewing rationality, raising skepticism and relativism to dogmatic principles themselves – in effect echoing the same dialectical contradiction that plagues the fetishism of scientific reason. The sides – postmodernism and positivism – were essentially incommensurable Kuhnian paradigms, and their mutual rejection has never been resolved. Instead, academia grew tired of their sparring. The "paradigm wars" ended "not with a bang, but a whimper." Quantitatively fixated positivism and qualitatively fixated postmodern-era relativism retired to their proverbial rooms, where they learned to coexist to some degree, but not to work out their problems.[3]

---

3   An ironic and pathetic update to the paradigm wars can be observed in their recent resurrection in a series of polemics against the Humanities and their alleged cardinal sins of "grievance studies" and "identity politics" (e.g., Pinker 2018; Pluckrose and Lindsay 2020). What is ironic about these polemics in the present context is that their authors often mindlessly

1.3   *"Lazy" Pragmatism*

Against this backdrop, "pragmatism" has been on an upswing for several years now, both as a "research paradigm" – especially in relation to mixed-methods (Maxcy 2003) – and as a general open-minded/uncritical attitude about the relationship between theory and research. Notwithstanding philosophical pragmatism's rich and varied intellectual tradition, the adoption of pragmatism as a research paradigm in the academy is a different beast. Instead of offering a new robust guide to research, [lazy] pragmatism has provided a philosophical justification for not thinking critically about the philosophical presuppositions or implications of social research. Perhaps because philosophical pragmatism is so varied, when viewed as a murky whole, it can befriend positive science in the vein of Charles Sanders Peirce, as well as the relativism of William James and the anti-epistemology of Richard Rorty. No actual stance needs to be taken – simply do "whatever works."[4]

There are benefits to this mood taking root in the academy, within limits. Surely qualitative content analysis and structural equation modeling both have their place, and the slinging of dogmatic arrows is often a waste of time and energy (or, viewed alternatively, a means of establishing distinctions and triage factors in an increasingly growing, competitive, and specialized academic job market; Calhoun and VanAntwerpen 2007). Yet without limits, the pragmatism that leaps across or sidesteps such distinctions degrades into an even more severe relativist dogma than that of postmodernism. Here, however, instead of eschewing truth claims within research, it eschews normative claims about research. If postmodernism was a threat to the hegemony of scientific reason, pragmatism is a threat to the reflexive dialogue that actively promotes quality in academic work by assessing the criteria of judgement and establishing standards. With a prohibition against such philosophical interrogation, we are not left without standards. We are left with a murky stew of various trends and dogmas, preferences and customs that rule the day niche by niche and journal by

---

incorporate Frankfurt School critical theory into the long list of offenders, despite the fact that Critical Theory epistemology arose exactly as a response to the impasse of naïve objectivism and relativism (Horkheimer 2014 [1935]; Morrow and Brown 1994). The damage done by such polemics over the years should not be underestimated; as noted above, popular assimilation of the Frankfurt School to simple political positions has played a key role in circumventing a more widespread and comprehensive reception of their scientific work.

4   While few scholars would probably label their own epistemology 'lazy pragmatism,' the view we are describing is essentially what is referred to in psychology as either "perspectivism" or "evolutionary epistemology" (Rosenthal and Rosnow 2008); more broadly, these views would probably be described by the majority of social scientists who embrace them as "postpositivist" (Lincoln and Guba 2000).

journal. This jambalaya is the perfect recipe for academia to suffer a legitimation crisis, and that is certainly happening, along with a general anti-intellectualism that dovetails with authoritarian populism (Morelock 2017; Burston 2020).

This sort of lazy pragmatic epistemological stalemate was perhaps not so alarming to many inside and outside of the American academy during the Obama presidency. Epistemology was a stodgy old irrelevant notion to be saved for the classicists, the intellectual historians, and the most tedious analytic philosophers. But during this time the mojo of postmodernism continued to subside, while rejection of science continued to grow – notably on the Right among evangelicals and climate change deniers, but also among the Left among new agers and decriers of the Eurocentric cannon. Surrounding the election of Donald Trump, the situation changed. The rejection of Western scientific reason surged, particularly among the far-Right, who grew in power and (evident) numbers. The Left, who had championed postmodern skepticism and relativism in decades prior, were suddenly hit with the reality of how debilitating such stances truly can be. When real world problems become very pressing, submerging them in notions of linguistic indeterminacy seems dangerously miscalculated. And the pragmatist love-and-let-live attitude towards paradigms, value systems and truth claims does nothing to help, except to facilitate a return to positivism.

And this is the current popular trend among many on the Left today, in response to the "post-truth" condition that allows basic ignorance of empirical reality to have an honored place in public and political discourse. Donald Trump's famous "alternative facts" remark really branded the moment. The torches of skepticism and relativism were passed to the far-Right as an excuse for ignoring truth claims, and the popular Left leapt back toward the arms of positivism, that bedrock of dogma and one-dimensionality[5] With the aid of rampant "pragmatism," postmodernism could simply be ignored – sidestepped instead of contended with. Rather than having a serious dialogue concerning the philosophical and political limitations of skepticism and relativism, rather than attempting to work through the postmodern challenge and come out the other side in a robust, Hegelian "determinate negation," the dominant trend has been just to ignore postmodern critiques because they can be annoying

---

5   It is interesting (and tragic) to see how this has played out in the coronavirus response. The Left has blindly embraced the positivism of public health recommendations and "model projections," for the most part ignoring their impact on the broader political economy (which is exactly what the positivist prophets have been trained to ignore); and the Right, of course, has sworn against listening to the medical scientific 'elites,' which of course is at best a very dangerous stance in a time of global pandemic. As always, the disenfranchised classes are the worst victims of these quarrels, in terms of unemployment, desperation, sickness and death.

and inconvenient. If there is such a thing as progress in human understanding, this move is a regression; and ironically enough, an expression of postmodern culture. Only in postmodern conditions, where philosophical paradigms are treated as language games, are such lateral moves permissible.

At this moment it is vital to recognize that Horkheimer (2014 [1935], 1947) developed Critical Theory exactly in response and as an alternative to the versions of positivism and pragmatism practiced in his day. He presciently recognized an affinity between these traditions that has only solidified as they have more-or-less merged in the last three decades of mainstream social scientific practice. Despite lip services paid by positivism to the Truth, and by lazy pragmatism to socially desirable aims, these twin epistemologies operate in their contemporary, neutered versions as a foundation for the continual ascendancy of subjective (as opposed to objective) reason. (Horkheimer 1947) Both abandon intellectual activity to the dictates of historical contingency, whether these materialize as the whims of passing method-fetishisms or the call of contemporary sociopolitical initiatives. Both abet the reduction of empirical qualitative differences – between the opposing experiences of rich and poor, between the conflicting political aims of Left and Right, etc. – to quantified and neutralized equilibria. Embrace of lazy pragmatism fits smoothly with a naïve positivist conviction that the "data will speak for themselves," culminating in rigidified trust of statistical objectivity and calls for the total abolition of theory in the wake of Big Data (Anderson 2008).

Of course, superficially equivalent data can be marshalled for either side of any argument when value-laden interpretations are shackled and eco-historical context is walled off by method limits; and so the end result is that banally nihilistic scientists justify all perspectives (especially those attached to the longest purse-strings), rallying to the cause of political "moderation," that ultimate abettor of neoliberal exploitation. As Horkheimer (2014 [1935], 1947) saw all too clearly, positivism and lazy pragmatism are the twin epistemologies for a reified world, the inhabitants of which cannot imagine an alternative to their current mode of existence and don't like to dwell on questions of its origin and purpose; and for those few who are unwilling to submit, postmodernism offers a dazzling but ultimately illusory escape room. But there are other options.

2   Options from the Early Frankfurt School: Critical Theory as a New Vision for Social Science

The term "Critical Theory" cannot be defined in an airtight way. Back in the days of the early Frankfurt School, it meant different things to different ISR members. Yet, as Adorno would attest, "defining" the term is not the point. Rather, we should witness this object "Critical Theory" in its full multiplicity. And yet the early ISR was under the directorship of Horkheimer and Adorno, who shared a deep intellectual comradery and complementarity, and who wrote most early Frankfurt School essays dedicated specifically to philosophy of science. Thus, to understand early Critical Theory as a singularity is not so far-fetched either. Here, we will do a little of both.

2.1 *Horkheimer's Vision of Critical Theory*

In 1922–1924, Felix Weil, the politically active son of a wealthy capitalist, created an endowment to establish an independent research center (to be affiliated with the University of Frankfurt) dedicated to the promotion of Marxist scholarship. The Institute for Social Research was thus born, under the directorship of Carl Grünberg. Karl Korsch and Georgy Lukács were very prominent members of the institute in these early years, producing a wealth of writings for the ISR's journal. In *Marxism and Philosophy* (1923), Korsch railed against the economistic "vulgar Marxism" that characterized the Second International, insisting that it had become rigidly scientific-materialist, which defies the truly dialectical extent of Marx's thought. Marx was not just an economist, he was a philosopher greatly influenced by Hegel, and this aspect of his thought needs to be recognized and preserved, against the dogmatisms and oversimplifications of the Comintern. Lukács agreed, expressed powerfully in his essay "What is Orthodox Marxism?" and displayed in his essay "Reification and the Consciousness of the Proletariat," both included in his collection *History and Class Consciousness*. An important part of this turn to Hegelian-Marxism was really investigating the "superstructure," the realm of ideas, culture, philosophy, art, and so on. The turn was profoundly influential for the ISR overall. In particular, the investigation of culture and psychology in their specific historical-material embeddedness would provide a lasting epistemological center. Karl Korsch (1938) stressed the centrality of the "principle of historical specification" in Marxist criticism: "Marx comprehends all things social in terms of a definite historical epoch. He criticizes all the categories of the bourgeois theorists of society in which that specific character has been effaced" (n.p.).

Less than a decade later after the founding of the Institute for Social Research, Max Horkheimer, an academic with a passionate interest in the plight and revolutionary potential of the working class, assumed leadership of the Institute for Social Research with primary assistance from his friend Friedrich Pollock, a political economist (Jay 1973). Under Horkheimer's early leadership, the ISR developed an idiosyncratic method of "interdisciplinary materialism" that cross-pollinated Marxist thought, Enlightenment philosophy, and empirical research. Retaining Marx and Engels' interest in the economic determinants of culture and the nature of political false consciousness, the ISR crafted a transdisciplinary approach integrating psychology – to show how individual minds mediated economic factors and the cultural superstructure – and philosophy – to discern a progressive path for society that would not neglect the needs of the individual (Held 1980). The syntheses of Marx and Freud by Wilhelm Reich and Erich Fromm – much like the turn to Hegelian-Marxism by Korch and Lukács – proved central to this and remained foundational for the Frankfurt School long after. Horkheimer established scholarly credentials in 1931 by creating an independent journal, *Zeitschrift für Sozialforschung*, to which all of the ISR inner circle contributed and where Horkheimer published central methodological treatises of interdisciplinary materialism and its descendant Critical Theory (Jay 1973; Horkheimer 1972).

Of import was Horkheimer's 1936 essay "Egoism and Freedom Movements," which exhibited a Marxist approach to the subject of "philosophical anthropology," i.e. philosophical beliefs about human nature, and hence drew on the ideas about historical specificity of Korsch and others. Horkheimer looked at the philosophical beliefs that animated bourgeois revolutions as concrete expressions of bourgeois character as it was shaped in different material/social circumstances over time. Fromm and Maccoby's (1970) much later case study of *Social Character in a Mexican Village* is an excellent example of using ethnographic methods within a theoretical framework consistent with Horkheimer's approach in the Egoism essay.

As outlined in Max Horkheimer's (1937) "Traditional and Critical Theory," Critical Theory is an alternative to the logical positivist view of the place of theory in social science. Horkheimer was concerned that the dominant epistemology shackled theory, preventing the formulation of broader or social-critical claims through a myopic focus on empiricism. In contrast, Critical Theory links philosophy and history with more micro-level data about the relationship between society and the individual. In Horkheimer's vision, Critical Theory includes theory and empirical research operating together, checking each other, and informing one another. This involves a commitment to deep interdisciplinarity as well as a fundamentally historical approach to establishing causality (as opposed to the experimental, deductive-nomological model of causality embraced by positivists). Critical Theory must expose the present as a moment within historical process and be informed by the experience of real sociopolitical struggles. There is also a key *critical* aspect, involving commitments to reflexivity and the philosophical consideration of value-laden aims. Critical Theory must be committed to emancipation, to overcoming domination.

2.2   Marcuse, Adorno, and the "Ends" of Theory

Marcuse, in his essay "Philosophy and Critical Theory" of the same year, frames Critical Theory in different terms, this time very consonant with Lukács, who in works such as *History and Class Consciousness* had extended Marx's critique of philosophy as alienated bourgeois ideology back into more Hegelian dialectics – namely to see science, philosophy and art all through the lens of expressive totality. In Lukács' famous reification essay, the ascendance of formal rationality in the administration of society, coupled with the profound alienations of class-divided capitalist society, was also expressed in the form that philosophy took in the modern era: the ascendance of formal logic and scientific reason, and a celebration of "pure" reason, abstracted from concrete reality, and – in Kant – segregated from the *thing-in-itself*; a fundamental form of alienation as a truth below all thought and experience. For Lukács, "philosophy" as such reaches its final stage in the form of Marxism. Yet it is a specific, pragmatic vision of Marxism that Lukács advocates. In a grand reconciliation, philosophy would disappear into material life when the proletariat assumed dictatorship. Philosophy's highest truth is that is in an expression of class relations, and thus when class divisions disappear, so would philosophy.

Marcuse's essay carries this argument on, although he places Critical Theory where Lukács had placed proletarian class-consciousness. Like Horkheimer, Marcuse's characterization of Critical Theory here includes situating the present in historical process. But for Marcuse, envisioning future potentialities is a very important element. Critical Theory helps us see how far the present reality strays from what the future reality could be, and this understanding helps emancipate us from a myopia which fixates on facts, on *what is*. Critical Theory helps us see more than just facts – in historical context, including an understanding of *what could be*, we are more informed. But Critical Theory, oriented as it is toward a future society, aims ultimately at its own destruction. Once a better society is created, there will be no need for it. It will merge into daily life, rather than being a separate, bourgeois, abstract enterprise.

Adorno's *Negative Dialectics*, which a few decades later temporarily enjoyed the status of popularly defining Critical Theory as such, was presaged in its basic purpose in an essay Adorno wrote in 1931, several years before Horkheimer's seminal essay described above. In this essay, titled "The Actuality of Philosophy," Adorno advocates that philosophy destroy itself. Rather than articulating fundamental axioms, first principles, immutable truths, and so on, and then proceeding to build a self-supporting philosophical "system" (as in Kant and the German Idealists), Adorno advocates using philosophic thinking in a process of shifting configurations, where questions are answered in a flash which also contains their annihilation. While Lukács and Marcuse advocated a disappearance of philosophy accompanying a revolutionary, utopian social transformation, Adorno advocated the disappearance of philosophy's attempt to capture truth – not the annihilation of philosophic thinking. Instead, he proposed using philosophy – dialectical philosophy in particular – in several different ways: a) to "liquidate" philosophical idealism by destroying all its questions, b) in moving configurations, c) as invention, and d) as interpretation. Adorno thus set out a program for philosophy to continue, made *more* robust by the abandonment of its unrealistic pretensions.

As practiced decades later in *Negative Dialectics*, Adorno's philosophical style and method was infused throughout by *immanent critique*, a process of drawing out the contradictory essences behind appearing objects, or in the case of philosophical objects, drawing out the antinomies implicit within them. Instead of transcendent critique – where antagonistic concepts would be brought to philosophical objects from the outside – in immanent critique that which is implicit in the logic of the object itself is brought out to manifest tension. Whereas in Hegel, dialectical tensions are always reconciled through unity on another level (this moment of reconciliation sometimes called the "second negation" or the "negation of the negation"), in Adorno dialectical tensions are not to be resolved. There is continuous movement, but not upwards towards a totalizing system. Adorno's rejection of the second negation was a very significant element in his philosophy, and really the key element that separated his from Hegel's dialectical method.

Adorno's attempt to save philosophy by taking it beyond itself carries a different tenor from the end-of-philosophy prophesies of Lukács and Marcuse. Yet he also criticized philosophical universals that took no influence from empirical particulars. He insisted on the "priority of the object," but this priority was far from a narrow empiricism or particularism, far from the ontology that all that exists are individual material "objects," and any abstraction above the meticulous reporting of these "facts" should be vanquished from social inquiry. Adorno's dialectical approach to sociology and philosophy was exclusively opposed to any stance toward reality that prematurely precluded answers, be it through an ideological dogmatism oblivious to observation or a methodological fetishism that ruled out areas of inquiry as "beyond reach" (Benzer 2011).

Like positivism, the Critical Theory approach also considers theory accountable to data, but in a very different sense. It sees the purpose of theory as offering the scholar a *thorough and actionable account* of the data, these latter being the actual, historically situated manifestation of social phenomena at a given point in history (rather than single "cases" testifying to universal laws). Further, it is the bridge from observation to philosophy that allows the social researcher to "go beyond" the data in synthetic and value-laden interpretations of the social condition. Horkheimer's "anthropological" approach was a seminal embodiment of this style of attention to the particular *and* theoretical, and it resonates with the complex relation between particular and universal that Adorno promoted for philosophy.

3   Epistemological Underpinnings of Critical Research

In 1961, at a conference of the German Sociological Society in Tübingen, Adorno and philosopher of science Karl Popper gave competing papers on research methodology. Adorno elaborated the Critical Theory approach, and Popper explained his critical rationalism that would have profound impact on modern empiricism. The debate spanned a decade-long series of exchanges on methodology, in which Habermas was a prominent participant, confirming both him and Adorno as the rear-guard of the Critical Theory approach Horkheimer had first formulated in the 1930s (Adorno et al. 1976; Wiggershaus 1994). While Habermas would for decades continue the attempt to develop a total theory of society by integrating critiques of "technocratic" research and oppressive late capitalism, it was in the context of the 1960s "positivist dispute" and the twilight of the early ISR that Adorno summarized and expanded upon the philosophical underpinnings of social research in the spirit of Critical Theory.

The following is an explication of Adorno's late vision of the aims, epistemology, and methods of critical research. The ISR generated an approach to social research characterized by the consistent attempt to include together elements and techniques typically kept separate: social theory and empirical research; qualitative and quantitative methods; and individual and societal levels of analysis. Most unique about this methodological commitment is its practitioners' insistence on juxtaposing these elements *despite* a profound skepticism that they are in any way reconcilable or reinforcing. Whereas lazy pragmatism preserves philosophical contradiction by downplaying the importance of deep engagement with theoretical issues, ISR methodology could be summarized as the effort to *leverage* dialectical tension to unmask truths about society. In this respect, Adorno's revision of Hegelian dialectics was implicit at the base of the ISR's empirical work.

3.1   *The Antinomy of Empirical Research: Tension between Interpretive Philosophy and the Data of Science*

Horkheimer (1995) called for an interdisciplinary materialism through which philosophy would be

> capable of giving particular studies animating impulses, and at the same
> time [remain] open enough to let itself be influenced and changed by
> these concrete studies. (10)

The ISR was deeply concerned with what they called the antinomy of empirical research – namely, the tendency for scientific methods and the "disinterested" pursuit of truth to become a fetish (Frankfurt ISR 1972 [1956]).
They took objection to the fact that research ultimately replaces "the actual
object of interest with one defined in 'operational terms'" (Pollock, Adorno
et al. 2011: 30), a process which "sanctions the primacy of the method over the
object, and ultimately sanctions the arbitrariness of the scientific enterprise
itself" (Adorno 1976: 73). These concerns form the logical core of the ISR's argument against positivism as discussed above. They proposed that the alleged
objectivity of standard research simply reproduces or reifies, in symbolic-
textual form, the objectivity of a late capitalist society in which individuals are
themselves reduced to objects. At best, this form of research is paralyzed and
incapable of improving society; at worst, it is a tool in the hands of elites who
treat subjective human concerns as malleable objects of technical intervention (Marcuse 1964).

From the perspective of the ISR researchers, the phenomena unearthed by
empirical study are not to be taken at face value, chronicled and catalogued.
Rather, they serve alternately as ending and starting points for the act of interpretation, which "requires both increased exactness of empirical observation
and the force of theory" (Adorno 1976: 32–33). The ISR's method involves dialectical movement between the focused investigation of concrete empirical
phenomena and interpretations that illuminate those phenomena in light of
a theoretical and historical understanding of the society in which they take
place. Horkheimer (1989 [1940], 1972) repeatedly insisted that individual social
psychological constructs and events can only be adequately interpreted in
terms of their broader historical context. This is the method Adorno (1976)
came to describe as "social physiognomy" (Buck-Morss 1977; Mele 2015).

> It is an essential, a central moment of sociology to interpret social phe-
> nomena as an expression of society, much as one may interpret a face as
> an expression of the psychological processes reflected in it. One might
> say, more precisely, that the dimension of interpretation in sociology
> lies primarily in the fact that history is stored up in phenomena which
> are seemingly at rest, which seem to be something given and entirely
> momentary. The faculty for interpretation is essentially the ability to per-
> ceive that which has become, or the dynamic arrested within phenomena

> ... just as it is one of the essential faculties of a critical theory of society
> to grasp things which purport to be existent and thus given by nature in
> terms of their having come to be.
>
> ADORNO 2000 [1968]: 146

ISR researchers were convinced that theory and research must inform one
another to overcome the limitations of fetishizing research methods, the solip-
sism of ungrounded philosophical systematizing, *and* the unhelpful arbitrariness of relativism. They were as skeptical of anti-rationalist developments in
philosophy and the humanities (e.g., Heidegger's existential phenomenology)
that would eventually give rise to postmodernism as they were of positivism.
"Therefore critical reflection about empirical social research is necessary, and
also an incisive familiarity with its results" (Frankfurt ISR 1972 [1956]: 119).

Yet just as they opposed the strict demarcation of theoretical and empirical endeavors, the ISR simultaneously denied the notion that these two forms
of understanding could be easily reconciled. Indeed, part of their critique of
the standard model of scientific thinking was that it separated the domains of
discovery and justification, of theory-generation and hypothesis-testing, in an
artificial manner that allowed both forms of thought to be controlled and contradictions nullified (Horkheimer 1972). In part because they saw deep fault
lines running between concrete elements in society (e.g., individuals) and the
totality in which they were enmeshed, the ISR researchers believed that the
findings of particular studies would often appear contradictory to the view of
society provided by theory. They were staunchly opposed to efforts to gloss
over such contradictions through accommodative tinkering with theory or
passive anticipation of the day when "sufficient data" would be gathered to
clarify the paradox.

> The empirical and the theoretical cannot be registered on a continuum
> ... It is not a question of smoothing out such divergences and harmoniz-
> ing them ... Instead, the tensions must be brought to a head in a fruitful
> manner.
>
> ADORNO 1976: 70

3.2 *The Aporia of Sociology: Tension between Quantitative and Qualitative Methods*

Adorno (2000 [1968]) referred repeatedly to the fact that quantitative methods, for the sake of obtaining "universal" reliability and generalizability, sacrifice the deeper validity regarding historical experience offered by qualitative

methods. To address this aporia, the ISR consistently employed both quantitative and qualitative techniques in their studies. The researchers clearly appreciated the role of quantification in furthering knowledge. Their studies sought global views of complex phenomena that would permit systematic comparison between extremes, whether it be the multiple polarizing forces that fatefully coalesced in a single personality factor (the Berkeley studies) or the fractious ideological groups and personality types that constituted the Weimar working class. Such studies would have fallen far short of their goals if the ISR researchers were not committed to the quantification (and hence reduction and standardization) of data. Yet consistent with their aim of illuminating the social totality made manifest in individual objects of study, ISR researchers used qualitative interpretation as a complement to quantitative analyses.

The ISR made a strong case for qualitative research as a corrective to the more reifying aspects of quantitative empiricism. In particular, the researchers (Frankfurt ISR 1972 [1956]; Pollock et al. 2011) attacked the prevailing methods of quantitative attitude surveys as simply providing a "subjective reflection" of the total society. When individuals are demanded to have an opinion about topics which they may only understand through socially filtered preconceptions and presented with a preselected "cafeteria" array of responses, the results often simply confirm dominant ideologies, since the latter were built into the inquiry from the outset. In contrast, "the nature of qualitative analysis is to tease out types of attitudes and opinions, not their distribution ... What our qualitative analysis can bring to light are webs of meaning, ideological syndromes" (Adorno 2010: 50–56).

Interestingly, the ISR asserted that interpretations of qualitative data permit researchers to go both "deeper" and "broader" than conventional empiricism; to probe the psychological tensions of individual subjects, and to link quantitative findings to broader social trends. Thus, from the earliest ISR studies, researchers like Fromm were employing psychoanalytic interpretations of open-ended participant responses to reveal repressed tendencies. Later, in the Berkeley studies and *Gruppenexperiment*, Adorno used interpretive methods to show how individual responses as well as quantitative trends could be understood as particular instances of broader social "facts," syndromes, and types, illuminating how "the social manifests itself through the individual" (Adorno 2000 [1968]: 74).

Qualitative methods grant studies an element of critical reflexivity foreclosed by strictly quantitative research. The ISR researchers could utilize bold interpretations of their qualitative data to question the rigid patterns composed by counts of participant responses. This reflexive foothold avoided the reduction of qualitative differences to quantitative equilibria. The ISR viewed inflexible procedures of standardization and replication in quantitative research as inevitably leading to a stagnant condition of knowledge (Adorno 2010). This wariness is echoed in the concern that a demarcation of quantitative and qualitative study as separate domains of inquiry would subsequently sanction an artificial harmonizing of these two domains. For instance, to interpret interview data as simply reinforcing the findings of a survey is "to posit as separate two moments which in reality are inextricably intertwined, and to create the illusion that they can be added together" (Adorno 2000 [1968]: 74).

3.3   The Dialectical Investigation of Society: Tension between Individual and Societal Levels

Throughout their work the ISR scholars emphasized the nature of the individual-social mediation, taking pains to distinguish their position from either methodological individualism or the sociological holism associated with Durkheim (Adorno 2000 [1968]). Presciently sidestepping a narrow focus on agency or structure, the ISR researchers worked with an understanding of society as socially constructed and yet exerting a certain "objective" resistance to the actions and desires of particular individuals, in no small part through phenomena of false consciousness. The object of the ISR's empirical studies was never

> the isolated individual nor ... a sum-total of individuals ... [but] rather a definite individual in his real relation to other individuals and groups, in his conflict with a particular class, and, finally, in the resultant web of relationships with the social totality and with nature.
>
> HORKHEIMER 1972: 211

Reflecting this broad aim, the ISR methods always sought to combine sociology and psychology (Adorno 1967). However, the researchers were equally insistent that this combination not give rise to the illusion that individual and society are seamlessly connected. Dialectical tension between the struggling individual and the alienating social environment was at the heart of the ISR studies, and attempts to "harmonize" this tension, as in Talcott Parsons' systems approach, were fiercely criticized.

> The separation of sociology and psychology is both correct and false. False because it encourages the specialists to relinquish the attempt to know the totality ... and correct in so far as it registers more instransigently the split that has actually taken place in reality than does the premature unification at the level of theory. Sociology in the strict sense ...

never loses sight of the objective moment of the social process. But the more rigidly it disregards the subject and his spontaneous impulses, the more ... [it becomes] sociology minus society, the replica of a situation in which people have lost contact with themselves. The accumulation of particulars which would begin to disclose their meaning only in the total social context blocks that context from view.

ADORNO 1967: 78

In order to avoid smoothing over the tensions between individual and society, and to approximate the theoretical goal of "not equating society as subject with society as object" (Adorno 2000 [1968]: 138), the ISR researchers developed methods that permitted close analysis of mediating levels: culture, the development of personality, the small group. At the same time, the combination of quantitative and qualitative methods allowed them to go beyond the unit of empirical analysis and interpret the quantified facts in light of their connection to the social totality. "Induction in social theory ... should seek the universal within the particular, not above or beyond it, and, instead of moving from one particular to another and then to the heights of abstraction, should delve deeper and deeper into the particular and discover the universal law within" (Horkheimer 1989 [1940]: 266). Through these means, they avoided the twin traps of reifying society as a set of natural, universal, and immutable arrangements (as in structural-functionalism) or liquidating the objectivity of social structure through naïve methodological individualism (as in phenomenology).

Importantly, from the very beginning the ISR's aim in incorporating individual psychology was *not* to account for the agency of the individual *contra* a naïve historical materialism. Quite the opposite, the researchers wanted to understand how irrational social structures could be maintained through the irrational psychologies in which they were mirrored. Depth psychology, and psychoanalysis in particular, proved crucial to this endeavor from the ISR's earliest studies. By viewing individuals as subject to unconscious anxieties that required rationalization at the conscious level, ISR researchers were able to explain "how the economic situation is transformed into ideology via man's drives" (Fromm 1970 [1932]: 127). The methodological result was that the ISR studies consistently sought to measure not only manifest, but more importantly *latent* individual attitudes. The goal was always to unearth the notorious "cement" (Fromm 1970 [1932]) of repressed fears and desires that determined "why a society functions in a certain way, why it is stable or dissolves," due to the "tenacity" of "certain attitudes" arising from "the fact that men cling to them passionately" (Horkheimer 1972: 54–65).

Rather than separately examining the individual and society and succumbing to the functionalist illusion that they interrelated seamlessly, the
ISR progressively shifted their focus on various sites of mediating tension. In
keeping with their Marxist- psychoanalytic assumptions, these were understood to be the bulwarks of false consciousness binding individuals to the
social system. In their earlier works, *culture* often played this mediating role,
viewed classically as a superstructure that committed individuals to irrational
hierarchies (Horkheimer 1972). The ISR subsequently moved toward a more
developmental-psychological framing of *personality* as "an agency through
which sociological influences upon ideology are mediated" (Adorno et al. 2019
[1950]: 6). Personality was formed by early experience of the patriarchal *family*,
understood to operate as a microcosm of societal authority structures. In their
final years of active research, the ISR centered increasingly on the *group* or
organization as a mediating level (Pollock et al. 2011).

4   The ISR's Innovations in Empirical Methodology

Common narratives hold that the inner circle of the early ISR all but abandoned empirical research in their later years, and that it always played second
fiddle to their philosophical endeavors. Yet such simple accounts and the fractured reception of their work has obscured the fact that the early ISR carried
out an astoundingly productive program of empirical research – focusing on
trends in late capitalist society and culture that encouraged authoritarianism
and fascism – from the year of Horkheimer's inauguration in 1929 through
the end of the 1950s. The researchers first carried out a massive questionnaire
study of the *Working Class in Weimar Germany* in 1929–1931, largely guided by
Fromm with a strong focus on the social psychology of authoritarianism. At this
time there were almost no previous examples of social scientific quantitative
surveys obtaining direct data on culture and personality on this scale (Smith
1998). Although data collection was completed, the Fascist takeover drove the
ISR scholars from Germany in 1933, and the results of their first comprehensive
study of authoritarianism were not finally published and translated until the
1970s (Fromm 1984).

    Horkheimer miraculously managed the financial and scholarly continu-
ation of the Institute in the United States, first in affiliation with Columbia
University and later with Berkeley in the 1940s. During their exile, Horkheimer
and his inner circle turned with increased urgency to the problem of authoritarian tendencies in the middle and working classes. The resulting interdisciplinary work *Studien über Autorität und Familie* (1936) synthesized many of the

methodological innovations of critical research and summarized the ISR's first wave of investigations into the false consciousness of the proletariat. As historians have noted (Wheatland 2009; Ziege 2009), loss of financial autonomy in the 1940s – which had allowed the ISR to develop its unique character in the 1930s – led to a period of "professionalization" during U.S. exile. The work of this time had more in common with "positivist" social scientific techniques than at any other period in the group's output, and largely for this reason it remains the only widely recognized empirical work of the Frankfurt School in positivist circles.

A turning point occurred when the relocated ISR received funding from the American Jewish Committee to finance investigations inspired by Horkheimer and Adorno's growing theoretical interest in the relationships between anti-Semitism, authoritarian psychology, and administrative-consumerist society. It was clear from the outset that prejudice, and anti-Semitism in particular, should be the focus of the work, but in keeping with the principles of critical research, a broad multi-method approach was adopted (Worrell 2009). The fortuitous result was a collaboration between Horkheimer, Adorno, Löwenthal, Pollock, political scientist Paul Massing, psychologist Else Frenkel-Brunswik, and colleagues in public opinion research at Berkeley. This produced the interdisciplinary five-volume series *Studies in Prejudice*. All the studies sought understanding of fascism's psychological appeal in the Weimar era, and to translate this into means for fighting the American public's susceptibility to fascism. Representing the closest collusion of the ISR with "positivist" empirical methods, *The Authoritarian Personality* (AP) – an investigation of the psychological structure of latent prejudice – would exert the widest influence. But during this time the ISR also researched anti-Semitic propaganda and anti-Semitism in U.S. labor unions (Worrell 2009).

When, in 1950, Horkheimer was able to re-establish the Institute in post-war Frankfurt with the support of the U.S. occupying force, he, Adorno, and Pollock trained a new generation of German social scientists while further applying Critical Research to the investigation of contemporary false consciousness (Wiggershaus 1994). This final wave of the early ISR's critical research program on authoritarianism was characterized by further methodological innovation and mature critical engagement with empirical social science as it took shape in the mid-century. Horkheimer's growing interest in the domination of individual by (organizational) group consciousness in modern society, and Adorno's confrontation of U.S. quantitative and public opinion research (Jennemann 2007), provided the impetus for a novel "group experimental" method to investigate public opinion. Going beyond AP's observations of individual psychology, the *Gruppenexperiment* (GE; Pollock et al. 2011) shifted the ISR's critical research toward the *in vivo* study of false consciousness as it emerges dynamically in face-to-face social interaction. Several themes in this study and the subsequent "organizational climate" investigations – the dominance of propagandistic group consciousness, the importance of language as an indicator thereof, and the suppression of individual rationality in pursuit of conformist solidarity – provided the essential backdrop for the work of Jürgen Habermas, a young ISR associate who worked on the group experiment before becoming the clear leader of the Frankfurt School's "second generation" (Wiggershaus 1994). Habermas advanced these themes in new directions in the early 1960s, both in a critical research project on the political attitudes of German college students (Habermas et al. 1969 [1961]) and in his treatise on the history of the "public sphere" in Euro-American culture (Habermas 1989 [1962]).

What is perhaps most remarkable in this empirical research program – and what will form a primary focus of the present volume – is the wealth of largely undiscovered methodological innovations it produced. Table 0.1 (at the end of this Introduction) provides an overview of the several empirical methods utilized by the early ISR in these studies, almost all of them either invented wholesale by the researchers or heavily adapted from extant methods. While these methodologies, and the fascinating historical and psychological data they gleaned, will be discussed in more detail in subsequent chapters, for the moment it is well worth pausing to take stock of the extent and ingenuity of the ISR's approach to social science. Several of these methods anticipated approaches that would be "reinvented" to popularity decades hence, while some have never even been utilized outside of the original ISR investigations. Considered as a whole, and in comparison to predominant contemporary quantitative and qualitative methods, these techniques offer several potential advantages to the current researcher, most notably the ability to achieve a multilevel perspective on interlocked societal and individual phenomena, as well as insights into defensive, non-conscious psychological processes. The ISR methodologies deserve not only to be holistically engaged with for the first time, but to come alive once more in the hands of practicing social scientists willing to combat authoritarian populism.

5   Beyond One-dimensional Social Theory

In *One-Dimensional Man*, Marcuse contrasts dialectical logic with formal logic, tying the former to Plato and the latter to Aristotle and contemporary one-dimensional thought. Aristotle's tendency to categorize, ossify, and rule out contradiction, is to Marcuse the forerunner of the tendency for thought to close off connections and possibilities beyond the immediate facts. One-dimensional philosophy leads us to a rigid empiricist pragmatism, where we can't see beyond our noses; and because we consider the only truth to be what is immediately apparent, we treat the world beyond the nose as if it were non-existent. In a sense the heart of philosophy is wiped out – creative speculation, values, dreams, and so on, are treated as antiquated, as philosophy becomes rationalized and reified along with the rest of society (à la Weber and Lukács). Marcuse believed that dialectical logic keeps open space rather than closing it down, and yet he in no sense advocated relativism or lazy pragmatism. The point is not to close off theory by nailing it to rigid empiricism and formal logic, nor to degrade it by having no standards, letting it float in any and every direction with no serious deliberation. Rather, for Marcuse, philosophy should be active, potent, and meaningfully interwoven with life.

In recent years, the newer generations of theorists from the Frankfurt School and those inspired by them have argued for bringing a normative foundation to social research. This is in line with rejecting the notion of "value-free" social science (as positivism would have it), and it is also a way of trying to get beyond the dogmatic relativism that emerged from the postmodern movement. Much of this can be traced to Habermas' universal pragmatics, which includes the claim that a normative dimension is intrinsic to all communication. In Habermas' theory of "discourse ethics," a universal normative framework for undistorted deliberation can be discerned from the nature of communication itself. Because, he claims, the search for undistorted consensus is an implicit presupposition in all communication, a moral position against social conditions that lend obstacles and distortions to the project of consensus-building can be considered a universal truth. In a Habermasian way, the researcher could analyze whether social phenomena contribute to or inhibit undistorted communication, appealing to this normative foundation. Honneth (1996) has offered a different universal normative theory – that all humans seek "recognition" and that struggles over recognition are at the heart of social conflict in general. Again, with this, a researcher could adopt the position of critiquing obstacles to recognition as rooted in objective, universal truth about humanity.

Whether or not this new trend is an expression of wishful thinking, it is not the only way to get beyond the paralysis of rigid positivism and dogmatic relativism. Another way, which fits with early Critical Theory, is to recognize that norms and aims are indeed behind all research, but rather than trying to claim pure universality or pure particularity, owning one's own aims and debating them openly is an intrinsic part of social research. This is one way in which pragmatism almost hits the mark. *Philosophical* pragmatists argue that it is essential to keep one's *aims* – normative or otherwise – in mind when evaluating the functionality of a theory (Cudd 2005; Laudan 1986, 1996). Aims are integral to the value of the theory, scientific or otherwise. In simple terms, a theory is only valuable if and when it helps you do something you are actually trying to do. There are two areas here that can be evaluated: the aims, and the theory's functionality for the aims. Competing theories must be tested in the court of rational, informed public opinion and objective reason; this is the only viable model for adjudicating theories in the spirit of Critical Theory. In this sense, philosophical pragmatism has plenty to offer as a meta-theoretical perspective, provided "whatever works" does not translate into "anything goes." The trouble with pragmatism as a paradigm is that it offers no guidance in itself. It is an open door, and often a deference to 'common sense,' which at its best is a veiled term for either naïve empiricism (subservience to what is immediately *there*) or relativism (what people agree upon), and at its worst is a total rejection of rigorous intellectual engagement with complex social realities. When 'pragmatism' means 'common sense,' it slips into a pseudonym for anti-intellectualism and shirking the big questions. As a 'research paradigm,' this is insufficient – unless, of course, as seen through the smug, stultifying blinders of lazy pragmatism. Nietzsche's (1997 [1874]: 171) summary assessment describes all too well the epistemological environment of many contemporary social scientific specialists: "A mole-tunnel is the right place for a mole."

There is no impartial meta-discourse or Archimedean point from which to adjudicate aims. Any such perspective would itself be grounded in certain presupposed aims, which could only be justified tautologically, which of course is a very flimsy basis for belief. Instead, even assuming a Habermasian 'Ideal Speech Situation,' at unwritten points in the rational deliberation process it is up to interpreting persons to cognitively exit rational deliberation and place investment in this or that aim or method on the basis of what Adorno referred to as mimesis – an experience of direct aesthetic resonance; or as he put it in 1931 regarding the question of any particular constellations of concepts, "they must be produced by human beings and are legitimated in the last analysis alone by the fact that reality crystallizes around them in striking conclusiveness" (131). This is certainly not to abort rationality entirely, but only to acknowledge that mimetic moments are intrinsic to even the most rational analysis. Or in Nietzsche's terms, an 'aesthetic comportment' is involved in the depths of all linguistic representation – all language is metaphor. And of course, rational deliberation takes place through language, through metaphor.

This might seem like an argument for postmodern-era relativism, but it does not have to be, in the sense that relativism is a mono-normative stance positioned against the elevating of any position (other than itself) above other

positions. A position which articulates truth as partial or rooted in perspective does not *intrinsically* thereby prohibit conviction, persuasion, scientific
experimentation, or the use of empirical evidence. It simply means that there
is no controlling system of thought which can legislate or guarantee what people will choose to care about.[6] What people care about and how they orient
their research and adjudicate claims can only be shaped by human actors as
the course of history plays out.[7] Neither is this an invitation to lazy pragmatism. It is an invocation to engage deeply with empirical observations, ask
the big questions, and keep hashing it out with dedication and honesty. As
Horkheimer wrote:

> Recognition of the conditional character of every isolated view and
> rejection of its absolute claim to truth does not destroy this conditional
> knowledge; rather, it is incorporated into the system of truth at any given
> time as a conditional, one-sided and isolated view. Through nothing but
> this continuous delimitation and correction of partial truths, the process
> itself evolves its proper content as knowledge of limited insights in their
> limits and connection ... The truth is advanced because the human beings
> who possess it stand by it unbendingly, apply it and carry it through, act
> according to it, and bring it to power against the resistance of reactionary,
> one-sided points of view.
>
> HORKHEIMER 2014 [1935]: 63–70

In light of such considerations of truth's perspectival nature, we would be participating in a long series of silences if we failed to make any remarks concerning the relevance – or lack thereof – of critical theory to postcolonial
thought, which many contemporary scholars would see as the correct "way
out" of the impasse of '90s postmodernism. The relationship between these
domains of inquiry has often been fractious at best, in no small part because
of the "Eurocentrism" of the early ISR's theoretical heritage and research foci
(Allen 2016; Mignolo 2011). By advocating a renewal of the ISR's approach to

---

6 Persuasion is still fair game, one just has to own one's own aims, and hope others will adopt
   them, rather than attempting (and failing) to convince by defining one's aims as rationally
   unassailable.

7 This is both description and prescription, and while it might seem disempowering, it is really
   not so much. Our guess is that in all of human history relatively few – if any – disagreements
   in perspective have been overcome by one side asserting: "my perspective is objectively correct, and all are inherently obligated to adopt it." A side with more power might use this claim
   as rationalization, such as in cases of colonization and Western expansion; but between
   equals, the claim is particularly *unconvincing* in most situations.

research, are we simply encouraging the ongoing use of methods that ought to have been long since "de-colonized?"

While this issue is too complex to fully address here, we hope that efforts such as the present volume will instead have the opposite effect and facilitate better cross-pollination between the critical and decolonial strains of contemporary thought. First, scholars should recognize that, regardless of the specific content of their empirical and aesthetic studies, the early Frankfurt School bequeathed to us a powerful toolbox of methodologies that could be powerfully utilized in service of decolonizing aims. Techniques such as the group experimental method, for instance, can be leveraged either to denaturalize the taken-for-granted perspectives of populations in the Global North, or, if used in collaboration with more marginalized populations, to indigenize knowledge by observing how it is spontaneously constructed in local contexts (see Adams et al. 2019). We also hope that a more careful and holistic reception of the ISR's work will reveal that, while it undoubtedly centered on the European-American context, it can nevertheless contribute to contemporary efforts to understand how "internal" colonization (of the poor and disenfranchised) in Europe interlocks historically with "external" colonization (of the Majority World; see Alliez and Lazzarato 2018). For example, the ISR's studies of prejudice – particularly "Antisemitism among American Labor", The Authoritarian Personality, and Guilt and Defense – contain extensive historical documentation of the complex relationship between prejudice against Jewish people and against people of color (e.g., the trope employed in postwar Germany that Nazi crimes were "not as bad" as acts of lynching in the United States).

While such points increase our optimism, we fully acknowledge that much work needs to be done to expand our understanding of truth and normativity claims beyond the Eurocentrism of early critical theory. But such a project seems fully in line with the epistemology developed by the early ISR (Allen 2016). Moreover, we by no means claim that Frankfurt School methodologies are beyond criticism and the only way to go. That would be ridiculous. We do, however, see in the early Frankfurt School a great example of deep engagement with truth and normativity claims, and various innovative approaches to theory and research which can still be leveraged today. In some ways, despite their massive influence, the Frankfurt School were ahead of their time, and the full potential of their contributions to scholarship has yet to be excavated. And in a time where informed understandings about authoritarian populism, rather than kneejerk reactions, are direly needed, the frequent focus of the ISR on just these issues makes them an especially pertinent group of minds to consult in the present historical moment. Philosophy and empirical social science need each other in equal measure; certainly, despite their own limitations, no group of thinkers before the Frankfurt School understood and acted upon this principle so thoroughly, and none has since.

6   The Aesthetic Dimension

So far, we have discussed the philosophical and empirical methods of the Frankfurt School, but their aesthetic theories and strategies were also very significant and have also been enormously influential in the humanities. From literature to music to popular film, Kracauer, Bloch, Benjamin, Adorno, Löwenthal and Marcuse submitted many aesthetic objects to ideology critique in a variety of ways. When considered together, the Frankfurt School approach to art takes on a discernible, overall shape: As Marxists, these thinkers treated art under capitalism as commodified, and as part of the superstructure, as 'ideology' which serves to mask or excuse objective relations of domination, exploitation and alienation.[8] As Hegelians, they viewed art as part of an expressive totality, as embodying objective historical conditions and their social contradictions. And as Freudians, they viewed art as having not just manifest content but latent or covert social-psychological meanings with political ramifications. As Weberians, they were concerned with the withering away of non-rational artistic experience under the progressive rationalization of modernity. Despite their famous political pessimism, embodied most explicitly in Adorno's essay "Resignation," they generally held out a hope that non-rational or "autonomous" art could supply instances of cognitive escape from the otherwise hegemonic logics of exchange value and instrumental reason (Adorno 1997; Marcuse 1979). Sometimes, as in Marcuse's (1969) "An Essay on Liberation," they held out hope that aesthetic experiences could contribute to the creation of a better society.

Lukács' early work *The Theory of the Novel* is essentially a Hegelian treatise on the types of narrative form in literature, tying these forms into their historical contexts. Lukács read these forms as expressing the state of society in its grappling with self-alienation, and in its hopes – or lack thereof – for utopic reconciliation. Siegfried Kracauer, a friend, mentor and colleague to the Frankfurt School, took influence from Lukács, and wrote highly influential works on film theory. Most significant for the present book is his early study of German film during the Weimar era *From Caligari to Hitler*. He advocated

---

8   Bloch's approach to ideology critique is more complex, however. While Bloch acknowledged this mystifying, oppressive aspect of ideology, he also identified a positive aspect: latent longings for utopia (Kellner n.d.).

investigating 'surface-level,' apparently unimportant objects and images in films and in other art as 'visual hieroglyphs,' that could be decoded to reveal the unconscious of society. For instance, Kracauer analyzed manifest objects, themes and characters in German films, showing how they expressed latent mentalities of the German 'collective soul' that eventually fed the rise to power of Nazism.

In addition to his work on fiction films of the Weimar era, Kracauer wrote "Propaganda and the Nazi War Film," closely analyzing how Nazi propaganda techniques worked in documentary films such as Leni Riefenstahl's *Triumph of the Will*. Here he specifically identified uses of commentary, visuals, and sound, playing off one another to convey meanings to the audience without acknowledging them as such. The effect is to ostensibly maintain a pretension of neutrality or objectivity, yet to put the viewer through a holistic experience rich with politically loaded insinuation. Benjamin (2008) warned as well of the "aestheticization of politics" so common in fascism. Essentially, the viewer is struck on a non-rational level by romantic messages and imagery associated with fascism, the viewer's critical faculties bypassed or shut down.

Unlike Kracuaer, who considered films to be collective productions and hence reflective of society rather than the vision of a specific author, Leo Löwenthal was interested in the psychology of the specific authors of literary works. "More or less consciously, usually less, the author is a manipulator who tries to get over certain messages that reflect his own personality and personality problems" (Löwenthal 1984: 281). For instance, in his study of Hamsun's work, he uncovers the author's fascist leanings, metaphorically expressed through his anti-humanistic reverential framing of nature.

Adorno analyzed a variety of artistic and entertainment media – music, literature, film, television, etc. – in a comparable way. Like a Liebnizian 'monad,' the work of art expresses the contradictions of the social totality. The contradictions embodied in the artwork-as-monad should not be simply laid out in a rational, linear fashion that would somehow define the work or delimit its incontrovertible meaning. Instead, Adorno advocated the use of dialectical models or 'constellations' of theoretical concepts that could illuminate different dimensions of the work of art, in its internal contradictions as well as its contradictory relationships with its environment – the social totality. His essay "How to Look at Television" expresses a Freudian approach very reminiscent of dream interpretation and the early Kracauer's film interpretation, again describing the need to see manifest content as displacement and condensation of latent thoughts, desires, and so on.

True to their expansive, dialectical *modus operandi*, the Frankfurt School not only treated aesthetics from a theoretical point of view, but also treated theory with an aesthetic sensibility. As Nietzsche once said: "To be mistaken about the rhythm of a sentence is to be mistaken about the very meaning of that sentence."[9] Superseding the modern separation and hyper-specialization of disciplines and domains of life, Frankfurt School thinkers such as Adorno, Benjamin and Kracauer often wrote poetically.[10] And Adorno stated outright at times that philosophic understanding should take influence from aesthetic experience, from the "mimetic" experience where one intuitively syncs with the work of art and *feels* (Adorno 2014).[11] If they believed that the non-rational was an irreplaceable part of our humanness, and that knowledge should be a transformative affair, not a matter of acquisition (Adorno 1993 [1959]; Morelock 2017; Fromm 2013), then it was consistent that their philosophy should venture out where it could convey meaning through form, style, expressiveness, poetics.

The tendency is most pronounced in Kracauer, Benjamin and Adorno. To some degree, analyzing in rational language their supra-rational aesthetic maneuvers would miss the point. Yet we will note a few things here. Most broadly, we can reasonably name a certain shift toward incorporation of what might be called "literary" qualities. These thinkers did not merely explain theory to you. They expressed it in a way that might resonate with and in the reader's experiences and perceptions. It is a move toward a kind of philosophical writing that *expresses* rather than merely explains. This is perhaps one reason why their writings have been so compelling and remain a source of inspiration to this day. They hit the receptive reader not just on the rational level, but on the aesthetic level, encouraging a kind of mimetic recognition and identification. They do not just explain but show the world to you, and you instantly recognize what you already knew but were previously unable to articulate.

One reason for the notorious difficulty of some of Adorno's texts is that his writing often incorporates dialectic, in the sense that his exposition is structured according to dialectical rather than formal logic. This means that he willingly contradicts himself, and his concepts *move*. He provides explanations that develop and change, rather than define any sort of static entity or claim. This is perhaps the clearest in his *Minima Moralia: Reflections from a Damaged Life* (2005) and in the "philosophical fragments" he and Horkheimer included

---

9   From Nietzsche's *Beyond Good and Evil*, quoted in Kristeva (1982: 133).
10   Wilhelm Reich exhibited this tendency in some of his later works as well, such as *The Murder of Christ* and *Listen, Little Man!*.
11   He also suggests taking a more philosophical approach to art, beyond simply this surface level of sensation and beauty, symmetry, etc. The fuller theory of art and its dialectical 'truth content' is elaborated in *Aesthetic Theory*.

with *Dialectic of Enlightenment* (1972 [1944]). Adorno is also prone to argue by means of homology, meaning he will describe something and compare it to something else, demonstrating familial relations by means of the similar shape or logic these objects display. Without rationally articulating or defending his connections, he presents them for the reader to intuit. The connection can be almost fable-like, such as his and Horkheimer's comparison of the story of Odysseus and the Sirens to the modern bourgeois individualist and entrepreneur, who welcomes their own implicit domination in the service of their own explicit power and liberation. It is a method of juxtaposing philosophical images, to generate the reader's own experience of their homology, and thus a kind of truth of their relation.[12]

Juxtaposition of images is at the heart of Benjamin's notion of 'constellations,'[13] as well as his related methodological legacy: the dialectical image. In Benjamin's "Epistemo-critical Prologue" to *The Origin of German Tragic Drama* he introduces the notion of 'constellations,' claiming: Ideas are to objects as constellations are to stars" Benjamin (2009 [1963]: 34). Understanding Benjamin's affinity for juxtaposition in the dialectical image, we might interpret his notion of constellations this way: A constellation, as we experience it, is a collection of independent images (stars), which, when viewed in proximity to other images (stars), combine to participate in a synthetic image in the viewer's eye. Hence, his comparison might mean that concepts, when "viewed" together in proximity, generate a synthetic idea in the thinker's mind. The stars are not epistemologically primary to the constellation, nor are they reducible to what the constellation makes of them in conjunction.

The dialectical image is rooted in this notion of juxtaposition and emergence and is the guiding methodology Benjamin uses in his unfinished opus *The Arcades Project.* Broadly stated, the technique involves the juxtaposition of two "images" from different points in time – usually one from the past and one from the present. When viewed or comprehended together, the images participate in a synthetic understanding of the images as connected moments in the historical process, and in turn this implicates the present as part of a historical process leading toward the future, which is unknown. It is a kind of broadening and hence liberating of perception from the domination of the immediate facts of the present. In this way, Benjamin's style makes his writing as much art as theory. It is an aesthetic intervention into the reader's experience and

---

12   In this regard, Adorno's philosophical and pedagogical style was not so far removed from that of his early sparring partner, Søren Kierkegaard; see Gordon (2016).

13   To some degree this style of juxtaposition is also preserved in Adorno's 'constellation' methodology – although the latter is more complex.

perception, intended to metaphorically awaken the reader from a dream – the mystifications of capital, the hypnotic myopia to only see what is immediately apparent (Gelley 2014).

The use of art to widen or liberate perception figured in a different way in Brecht's "alienation effect," which he promoted as part of his 'dialectical theatre' or 'epic theatre'[14] approach. Rather than aiming to be convincing, i.e. giving the audience the sense – almost the illusion – that the play and its characters are real, Brecht wanted to give the audience an experience of alienation from what was being portrayed, partly due to the self-alienation of the portrayal. He wanted "no illusions that the player is identical with the character and the performance with the actual event" (Brecht 1964: 195). Essentially the technique is one of denaturalization: "A representation that alienates is one which allows us to recognize its subject, but at the same time makes it seem unfamiliar" (8).

For the Frankfurt School, intellectual activity was always framed within the hopes of somehow creating a better world. For the most part, they offered no direct, programmatic suggestions over how to do this. They were not activists, although Marcuse had an affinity for the student protests of the 1960s. Their project hinged on the tacit assumption that any real social overcoming of the spell of capital – in whatever way, on whatever scale – would require raised human awareness and understanding. All their projects – from surveys and group interviews with thousands of participants to philosophical reflections on isolated films, books, or news articles – were directed toward unmasking and overcoming domination, superseding the hegemony of exchange value and instrumental reason, and fending off fascist tendencies. In many ways, their legacy today is a massive, powerful, multi-dimensional, transdisciplinary collection of methodologies to aid in the ongoing struggle against authoritarianism and authoritarian populism in late capitalist society.

7   Outline (of This Book)

7.1   *Part 1: Dialectics*
The first section of this book is dedicated to philosophical methodologies and foundations. Robert J. Antonio begins the section by discussing the methodology of immanent critique, in his essay "When History Fails Us: Immanent Critique of Capitalism to the New Right and Beyond." Antonio explains that

---

14   It is more commonly referred to as 'epic theatre' which is what Brecht called it for most of his career, but in his later years he adopted the term 'dialectical theatre.'

Marx applied immanent critique to capitalism in order to identify: a historical basis for normative criticism with emancipatory intent; contradictory social conditions that made emancipation possible; and a collective agent that could direct history toward realizing this end. Failure of his scenario to eventuate shaped the agenda for later critical theorists. Those operating in Marx's tracks used his method to assess facets of capitalism that prevented revolutionary transformation and to illuminate emergent conditions offering new possibilities for emancipation. Responding to the rise of Fascism, Stalinism, and Fordism, World War II-era critical theorists shifted focus from capitalism to Enlightenment culture and argued that sociocultural changes neutralized immanent critique. Later twentieth century theorists made a 'linguistic and cultural turn' that hardened this move and pluralized 'critical theory.' They argued that Marxism and class politics were moribund and superseded by new cultural politics. Others held that the new mediatized culture neutralized the capacity to distinguish ideology from reality and adopted strictly deconstructive methods. Recognizing and attempting to move beyond these various developments and impasses, this chapter explores the decoupling of capitalism and democracy. This decoupling undercuts the neoliberal regime's capacity to engage its contradictions, generating legitimacy crises and opening the way for ethnoracial nationalist "alternatives." Ultimately, a return to immanent critique of capitalism is favored.

In "A Dialectical Constellation of Authoritarian Populism in the United States and Brazil," Jeremiah Morelock and Felipe Ziotti Narita aim to articulate Theodor Adorno's critical methodology of dialectical models or 'constellations,' and to develop a model of 'authoritarian populism' in the Americas, focusing on the United States and Brazil. Rather than being pinned to a definition, in Adorno's approach the object is experienced in a process of dialectical exposition. The chapter follows this basic structure, moving through dialectical moments that illustrate dimensions of the complex, abstract object that is authoritarian populism. A constellational skeleton composed of dialectical movements is constructed based on a model of the overlapping domains of 'authoritarianism' and 'populism,' as well as the complex and conflictual dichotomy between the 'people' and the 'non-people.' The skeleton is expressed within a filled out fleshy exterior of more specific contemporary trends and empirical examples. Instead of subsuming many elements into an imposed unity, the chapter outlines a multidimensional sociopolitical rationality of authoritarian populism that deals with the dissonances and contradictions of the conceptual moments of this object.

David Norman Smith takes us back to the Frankfurt School's first decade in "Capital Fetishism and the Authoritarian Personality: Critical Theory in the Weimar Years." This period, which coincided with the rise and fall of the Weimar Republic, was germinal for the Frankfurt Institute both politically and theoretically. In the years from 1923 to 1933, and under the influence of Lukács and Korsch, the Institute broke new ground on the terrain of Marxism and psychology. Lukács and Korsch were both concerned with reinvigorating the Hegelian aspects of Marx's thought, in opposition to the reductive, economistic, 'vulgar' Marxism of the Second International and the Comintern. In this sense they were central figures in the creation of what is often referred to as 'Western' or 'Hegelian' Marxism. Many activist-scholars who are now obscure or overlooked – Hilde Weiss, Felix Weil, Boris Roniger and Kurt Mandelbaum, among others – contributed signally to what can justly be regarded as the founding decade of critical theory. In this chapter, two themes from that germinal phase are highlighted: capital fetishism and characterological authoritarianism. Neither concept had been intensively elaborated before the 1920s. Both remain exceptionally relevant.

In the final chapter of this section, "Mythology, Enlightenment, and Dialectic: Determinate Negation," Rudolf J. Siebert, Michael R. Ott, and Dustin J. Byrd explain the Hegelian dialectical methodology of "determinate negation" used by the Critical Theory of Religion and Society [CTRS] in its critique of the increasing crises of Modernity. These are rooted theoretically in the "dialectic of Enlightenment" and the modern antagonism between the realms of the Sacred and Profane, Religion and Science, Faith and Reason. The CTRS emerged out of the Critical Theory of Society of the Frankfurt School, having been inspired particularly by the works of Max Horkheimer, Theodor W. Adorno, Walter Benjamin, Herbert Marcuse, Erich Fromm, et al. This chapter explains the CTRS's development of determinate negation methodology by drawing on the Frankfurt School as well as the critical political theology of J.B. Metz. While the Frankfurt School focused its critique on the increasing class war crises of modern secular society, the CTRS focuses first on the critical, emancipatory substance of religion within this society and emphasizes its potential for the revolutionary creation of a more reconciled, humane and peace-filled future society. In this struggle, the CTRS determinately negates the mythological *form* of religion as it translates the theological liberating, prophetic, Messianic, and eschatological *substance* of religion into rational, revolutionary secular theory and praxis of societal change.

7.2   Part 2: Psychoanalysis

The second section focuses on various ways that the Frankfurt School use psychoanalytic theory, and how many of their concepts and strategies are still important for understanding and overcoming authoritarian populism today. Lauren Langman and Avery Schatz begin the section by arguing for a critical and psychoanalytic approach to understanding why many people today uncritically accept wildly irrational empirical claims, especially various forms of political discourses from conspiracy theories to outright fabrications. In their chapter "The Dialectic of Unreason: Authoritarianism and the Irrational," they argue that to understand the persistence of irrationality, we need note how authoritarianism underpins perceptions and understandings. Elucidating the extent to which authoritarian characters accept certain views of reality requires investigating the emotional and motivational impacts of authoritarianism on perception and understanding. Aggression is projected toward perceived collectively threatening 'enemies,' typically elite 'traitors' and/or weak marginal groups who allegedly pose economic, political or cultural threats to the 'real people.' Times of crisis evoke powerful emotional responses such as fear, 'extinction anxiety,' anger, *ressentiment*, and shame disposing more authoritarian groups – typically lower middle classes who feel victimized – to embrace various rightwing populist leaders and ideologies. Given motivated reasoning, dogmatism, and binary thinking, there is little ability to deconstruct or critique what is clearly irrational. Consider how at the time of the COVID-19 pandemic, many believed it was developed in a Wuhan lab to be used as a biological weapon, or that it is simply a flu, or a leftwing hoax to gain power.

In "Adorno and Freud Meet Kazuo Ishiguro: The Rise of the Far-Right from a Psychoanalytic Critical Theory Perspective," Claudia Leeb combines insights of early Frankfurt school critical theory, in particular those of Theodor W. Adorno, with insights from Freudian psychoanalytic theory to grasp the rise of the far-Right that plagues us today. She shows that understanding the psychoanalytic mechanisms of ego-ideal replacement and introjection, as well as the narcissistic love-relationship between the leader and her followers, is central to comprehending why millions of people respond to the failure of neoliberal capitalism by voting in far-Right leaders. Leeb analyzes Kazuo Ishiguro's book *The Remains of the Day* as an example of how the theoretical framework works in practice. She shows that Mr. Stevens gains his moral self-worth through replacing his ego-ideal with that of his employer, Lord Darlington. Via ego-ideal replacement, the supposedly "great deeds" of his employer generate his own view of himself as a 'great professional.' As a result of his narcissistic love-relationship with his employer, he fails to question his employer's unethical deeds in his involvement with Hitler's Germany. Indeed, further assisted by his incapacity for genuine feelings, Mr. Stevens actively contributes to such deeds. The outlined psychoanalytic mechanisms help explain why followers continue to support far-Right leaders despite the mounting critiques of their politics.

Imaculada Kangussu explains how Marcuse's approach to Freud is particularly useful when it comes to dealing with contemporary authoritarian populism in her essay "Marcuse and the Symbolic Roles of the Father: Someone to Watch over Me." According to Freud's hypothesis on the primal father, the figure of the savior father – who has solutions to all problems and subjugates everyone – belongs to the personal story of most people as well as to the archaic past of human beings. The desire for this figure can be seen as the ontogenesis and phylogenesis of authoritarian populism. For Kangussu, the symbolic value of this story lies at the moment the sons dethroned the father and established the power of the brotherhood. It is the moment of emancipation. However, Freud also remarks that the brothers' new order once again was based on dominance and control. Liberation failed, as have so many revolutions in history. However, Marcuse says the libidinal basis of society is pliable: the instinctual apparatus is biological, but *highly modifiable*. The plasticity of the instincts makes it possible to imagine a distinct aftermath in the wake of the brothers' liberation. Marcuse considers economic conditions as one of the primary modifying factors, and because these are historical, he historicizes Freud's concepts in order to make it clear that libidinal forces, the cement of social structures, can also be dynamite. Marcuse's framework has a practical, experiential truth value, regardless of its lack of empirical foundation. It teaches us that to liberate society from domination, rational political programs are not enough. People need to be reached, inspired, and transformed on the level of their drives. And this is not impossible. Marcuse's framework, and his prescription for social change that he based upon it, offers an indispensable perspective for building a non-repressive – and non-authoritarian – society.

Gregory Joseph Menillo outlines the psychoanalytic framework that Horkheimer and Adorno use to link the culture industry with fascism in his essay " 'Variation within a Single Paradigm': The Latent Authoritarian Dynamics of the Culture Industry." For Adorno, fascism was an historical manifestation of latent authoritarian tendencies already present within modern capitalist society. Adorno also observed that modern, mass consumer culture is similarly animated by certain latent authoritarian dynamics. He therefore viewed the outcome of WWII as not only the Allies' victory over Germany, but also as the triumph of the 'culture industry' over Nazism, better understood, after Jameson (1990: 140), as *"variation within a single paradigm,* rather than the victory of one paradigm over another." An examination of Adorno's work on the social psychology of fascism provides insight into the latent authoritarianism he perceived in mass consumer culture. Menillo traces two closely related concepts – *standardization* and *pseudo-individualization* – in Adorno's work on fascism in order to show that these are the same mechanisms at the core of his work on the culture industry. The chapter discusses the 'authoritarian personality,' the historical decline of the individual, and the rise of the authoritarian leader to show how pseudo-individuality replaces the autonomous subject under fascism. Menillo then applies this framework to Adorno's culture industry and concludes with a conceptual schema that situates both fascism and the culture industry in proper theoretical relation to one another.

To close the section, in his chapter "What Would Jesus Do? Christianity as Wish Image and Historical Bloc," AK Thompson explains that although Christianity is currently a central component of the historical bloc now galvanized around the Republican Party, the religion itself remains internally riven and politically ambivalent. Thompson offers a strategic and psychoanalytic suggestion about how this bloc might be smashed and its constituent elements gathered around a new socialist core. Drawing on Antonio Gramsci's conception of the historical bloc and Walter Benjamin's conception of the wish image (and showing how they can be combined and operationalized), the essay unearths and analyzes American Christianity's contradictions and tensions so that they might be leveraged in the struggle to unsettle existing power relations. Concretely speaking, this means exacerbating the factional schisms underlying the only apparent unity of the current Christian bloc, while revealing how the desires that lead believers to become cathected to Christian doctrine cannot be resolved within the terms set out by Christianity itself.

7.3   *Part 3: Human Subjects*

In the third section we turn in a more empirical direction. First, in "Mobilization of Bias Today: The Renewed Use of Established Techniques; a Reconsideration of Two Studies on Prejudice from the Institute for Social Research," Peter-Erwin Jansen, translated by Charles Reitz, discusses how the classic, five-volume series Studies in Prejudice, undertaken by Max Horkheimer and others in the Frankfurt School, furnishes a critical foundation for intelligent analysis and societal intervention in the face of the resurging racial animosities being mobilized today by rightwing voices in the US media. The mobilization of bias with regard to historical anti-Semitic abuses was seen by the Frankfurt School to depend in definite ways upon an authoritarian type of personality structure. Herbert Marcuse strengthened the analysis by emphasizing that prejudice formation must also be understood within concrete socioeconomic conflicts and the requirements of repressive political forces.

Taking a longitudinal view, Daniel Sullivan outlines the variety of the Frankfurt School's empirical studies in his chapter "From 'False' to 'Reified' Consciousness: Tracing the ISR's Critical Research on Authoritarianism." He reviews the three-wave critical research program on authoritarianism that the 'inner circle' carried out almost over their entire working lives – from the 1930s study of the Weimar working class, through the 1940s authoritarian personality and anti-Semitism research, and into the 1950s *Gruppenexperiment* and *Betriebsklima* studies. While focusing on systematic explication of the methods utilized throughout the innovative research program, Sullivan also demonstrates that it makes an important scientific contribution to understanding how social factors contributed to authoritarianism in the 20th Century. Further, the co-dependence of research and theory in the work of the ISR is attested to by tracing parallels between the 1940s 'pivot' in inner circle theorizing and the unfolding results of the studies. Sullivan concludes by making a case for the ongoing (but neglected) relevance of ISR theory, research, and methods for contemporary studies of authoritarianism in social psychology.

Next, Dan Krier brings us to the work of Franz Neumann, in "Franz Neuman's *Behemoth* and Trumpism: Comprehending the Beast of Bad Government." Krier asks: Is Trump a new Hitler, and is Trumpism a new form of Nazism as suggested by many critics? Rather than making simple assertions about similarities and differences between these two illiberal movements, this article approaches these questions with a (re) reading of the most detailed analysis of the rise of Hitler, the Nazi Party and the Nazi state: Franz Neumann's (1944) *Behemoth: The Structure and Practice of National Socialism, 1933–1944*. Comparing the Trump administration to Neumann's portrait of National Socialism, it is apparent that the aging, clownish, dilettante Trump is a rather pathetic Führer. Because his moment on the world stage will soon pass, attention and concern should focus much more on comparisons between Trumpism and National Socialism. In less than four years, the new hybrid Trumpist-Republican party has followed the National Socialist playbook closely and has laid the groundwork for a complete "movement state" in the Nazi manner. The US may be only a single 'state of exception' away from the transformation of the country into something approximating National Socialism.

The success of Donald Trump's 2016 presidential election, and the subsequent support he was able to maintain while in office, has baffled many commentators. Numerous observers have been struck by the seemingly contradictory support Trump has received from white Evangelical Christians, and to a lesser degree, from white Roman Catholics. In "Donald Trump and the Stigmata of Democracy: Adorno and the Consolidation of a Religious Racket," Christopher Craig Brittain draws from sociological studies of right-wing populist movements that were conducted by Theodor W. Adorno in the 1940s, 50s, and 60s to help explain the attraction Trump has among those who vote for him. Brittain demonstrates that Christian support for Trump is appropriately described as a religious 'racket' that functions as 'social cement.' He demonstrates Adorno's general approach with reference to a dispute within the evangelical movement over an editorial published in *Christianity Today* in early 2020. The resulting analysis stands in contrast to scholarly literature that emphasizes cultural over economic factors to explain support for Trump. Brittain supports his position with reference to emerging ethnographic studies conducted among white evangelicals and Roman Catholics who have continued to support Donald Trump since 2016.

7.4   *Part 4: Media Discourse*

In the fourth and final section, we examine strategies for interpreting different types of media artifacts and discourses. For popular cinema, in "Siegfried Kracauer and the Interpretation of Films" Jeremiah Morelock outlines a methodology in a broad tradition that runs from Siegfried Kracauer to Douglas Kellner. This 'film-as-dream' interpretation is modelled after Freud's theory of dream interpretation, which states that the manifest content of a dream is an expression of displacement and condensation of latent thoughts that the dreamer harbors at the time of the dream. In the case of popular films, their content expresses the thoughts, attitudes, desires, and fears characteristic of society – in Kracauer's language, society's 'collective soul' – at the time of the film. Building on Kellner's argument for 'multiperspectivalism,' Morelock argues the importance of considering the different significations and resonances that film themes and imagery may have for different social groups, such as those differentiated by race, gender and class. He suggests popular films can be investigated as harboring "overdetermined" forms that may metaphorically speak differently to different subject positions simultaneously, through displacement and condensation. Kracauer's interest in looking at popular film in terms of latent, broad thoughts and attitudes that led toward the rise of Hitler, can be taken up again today to uncover deep authoritarian elements in the collective multiperspectival soul.

Next, Stefanie Baumann turns to documentaries. In "How to Mediate Reality: Thinking Documentary Film with Adorno and Horkheimer," she explains that documentary formats have recently entered prominently into the realm of the culture industry, especially since Hollywood and Netflix started to invest in costly productions addressed to the mainstream. Many of these documentaries claim to show reality in its immediacy ('as it really is'), to reveal that which is obscured, or to critically assess societal evils. They use aesthetic strategies that reinforce the appearance of authenticity, while concealing the mediation of what they represent, and the authoritarian stances they presuppose. This turns them into powerful instruments for diffusing authoritarian and populist ideologies. Their political impact on society, their performative power of opinion-shaping, and their subliminal influence on how we perceive and understand reality call urgently for critical assessment. Horkheimer and Adorno's critique of the culture industry, along with their philosophical, sociological, and aesthetic writings, provide a constructive starting point. This essay aims to mobilize their critical theory to problematize documentary films in terms of their dialectical relation to society.

Switching gears, in "One-dimensional Social Media: The Discourse of Authoritarianism and the Authoritarianism of Discourse," Panayota Gounari says the analysis of right-wing authoritarianism as manifested through language and discourses, in its contemporary iteration in social media, has a lot to gain from revisiting Critical Theory. More specifically, Critical Discourse Studies (CDS) analyzing authoritarianism in social media can find important theoretical, conceptual, and analytical tools in Theodor Adorno et al.'s *The Authoritarian Personality* as well as in Herbert Marcuse's work, particularly *One-Dimensional Man*. Marcuse's work, however, remains largely unexplored in the CDS field. The chapter explores existing connections in the bibliography between the Frankfurt School's CT and CDS. Gounari discusses Marcuse's work related to discourse in order to draw theoretical, conceptual and analytical tools that can support and enrich inquiry into right-wing authoritarian discourse. The chapter thus aspires to a framework that will address current needs for scholars working on authoritarianism in social media.

In "Applying and Extrapolating *Prophets of Deceit*: Heuristics of 'Agitator' Identification through Löwenthal and Guterman's Analysis," William M. Sipling provides a thorough synopsis of Löwenthal and Guterman's work on authoritarian populist orators or "agitators," and makes a bid for their framework to continue to inform work on contemporary agitators, importantly including their online discourse. Sipling extracts five categories of criteria from Löwenthal and Guterman for assessing agitator-like communication: anti-Semitic, narrative, adversarial, in-group-ing, and concealment. These criteria categories, says Sipling, provide a useful and flexible heuristic that can be used to identify agitator-like qualities in statements and texts from anywhere within the political landscape, rather than sticking purely to popular far-right orators. Löwenthal and Guterman's psychoanalytic approach for qualitative content analysis also allows the investigation of pertinent social dynamics that cannot be accounted for within more surface-level, empiricist sociological approaches.

Finally, in the last chapter, "Dialectical Images and Contemporary Times: Thinking Critically about Authoritarian Populism," Mariana Caldas Pinto Ferreira introduces Walter Benjamin's concept of the dialectical image. She argues this concept is an attempt to re-think traditional historiography,

TABLE 0.1   Novel empirical methods used in the ISR's Program of Critical Research on Authoritarianism and Anti-Semitism

Method	Description	Analytical approaches	Aim
Interpretative questionnaire - *The Working Class in Weimar Germany* (see also "Projective Questions," Ch. xv, in *Authoritarian Personality*)	In survey format, participants given several open-ended or list/rank questions (e.g., "Who are the great people in history?")	Surveys analyzed in entirety to develop image of a participant; Responses categorized and quantified for psychoanalytic themes	Indirectly assess and quantify latent attitudes or personality traits; Accessing political attitudes through "nonpolitical" items
Screened interview - "Anti-Semitism Among American Labor"	"Participant interviewers" (workers) trained to engage fellow workers in conversation and covertly record responses to questions	Responses categorized and quantified for attitudes/themes; Qualitative analysis of categories of prejudice	Indirectly determine the extent and nature of prejudice (anti-Semitism) in a large worker sample
Latent disposition questionnaire - *The Authoritarian Personality*	Likert-style questionnaire ("F-Scale") iteratively developed through factor analysis and corresponding interviews	Responses summed/averaged and compared to interview results or correlated with other "manifest" attitude measures	Translate depth-psychological assessment of latent attitudes to a generalizable, quantifiable method
Depth psychological interview - *The Authoritarian Personality*	Single-session 90-180 min. guided interviews based on schedule of "manifest" (direct) and "underlying" questions of interest	Responses coded and quantified for correlation with other methods (e.g., scale responses); Qualitative content analysis of socio-political themes	Validate and develop the latent disposition questionnaire while gaining deeper insight into life-historical and sociocultural factors

TABLE 0.1   Novel empirical methods used in the ISR's Program of Critical Research on Authoritarianism
and Anti-Semitism (*cont.*)

Method	Description	Analytical approaches	Aim
Propaganda content analysis - *Prophets of Deceit* (see also *The Psychological Technique of Martin Luther Thomas's Radio Addresses*)	Samples of propagandistic radio speeches content-analyzed	Strategies for emotionally affecting listeners categorized and analyzed in terms of their interrelationship and likely psychological effects	Identify and enumerate the tactics employed by agitators to channel authoritarian aggression for political aims
Cultural product content analysis - *Stars Down to Earth*	Daily astrological forecasts in a newspaper over a multi-month period content-analyzed	Strategies for emotionally affecting readers categorized and analyzed in terms of their interrelationship and likely psychological effects; Some content also quantified	Identify and enumerate the tactics through which culture-industrial products engender further psychological attachment to totally socialized society
Group discussion method - *Gruppenexperiment, Betriebsklima*	Groups of 10-15 strangers/coworkers prompted to engage in moderated discussion after exposure to a threatening or thematic stimulus	Transcribed discussions qualitatively analyzed for common themes; Individual responses coded, quantified, and categorized	Indirectly assess latent attitudes on sensitive topics (German guilt, work conditions) through provocation; Observe *in situ* development of public opinion

insofar as Benjamin intended to understand how media and cultural expression correspond to the modes of perception of each historical moment. Perception plays an important role because it informs both how we see things and our embeddedness in history. The dialectical image generates a moment of consciousness, in which different temporalities and narratives, contradictory as they might be, appear together in relationship. It is a moment when one looks at reality differently, such as becoming newly aware of violent discourses, which is especially important considering the recent resurgence of authoritarian populism. Dialectical images help us be more attentive to how various social and discursive contradictions appear in the way we understand the world around us. Having elaborated this concept, Ferreira presents the Adorno-Benjamin debate on aesthetics and dialectics and explains why the methodology of the dialectical image is relevant for criticising authoritarian populist movements. The dialectical image concept offers a critical approach that can heighten awareness of our political and social conditions during the ongoing onslaught of authoritarian populism.

References

Adams, Glenn, Sara Estrada-Villalta, Daniel Sullivan, and Hazel Markus. 2019. "The Psychology of Neoliberalism and The Neoliberalism of Psychology." *Journal of Social Issues* 75: 189–216.

Adorno, Theodor W. 1993. "Theory of Pseudo-Culture (1959)." *Telos* 1993(95): 15–38.

Adorno, Theodor W. 1967. "Sociology and Psychology." *New Left Review* 46: 67–97.

Adorno, Theodor W. 1977. "The Actuality of Philosophy." *Telos* 1977(31): 120–133.

Adorno, Theodor W. 2005. *Minima Moralia: Reflections on a Damaged Life*. New York: Verso.

Adorno, Theodor W. 1973. *Negative Dialectics*. London: A&C Black.

Adorno, Theodor W. 1997. *Aesthetic Theory*. London: A&C Black.

Adorno, Theodor W. 2000 [1968]. *Introduction to Sociology*, ed. C. Gödde and trans. E. Jephcott. Cambridge: Polity Press.

Adorno, Theodor W. 2010. *Guilt and Defense*, ed. and trans. by Jeffrey K. Olick and Andrew J. Perrin. Cambridge: Harvard University Press.

Adorno, Theodor W. 2014. *Lectures on Negative Dialectics: Fragments of A Lecture Course 1965/1966*. Hoboken, NJ: John Wiley & Sons.

Adorno, Theodor, Else Frenkel-Brenswik, Daniel J. Levinson, and R. Nevitt Sanford. 2019 [1950] *The Authoritarian Personality*. New York: Verso Books.

Adorno, T. W., G. Adey, and D. Frisby. 1976. *The Positivist Dispute in German Sociology*. London: Heinemann.

Allen, Amy. 2016. *The End of Progress: Decolonizing the Normative Foundations of Critical Theory*. New York: Columbia University Press.

Alliez, Éric and Maurizio Lazzarato. 2018. *Wars and Capital*, trans. Ames Hodges. Cambridge: MIT Press.

Anderson, Chris. 2008. "The End of Theory: The Data Deluge Makes the Scientific Method Obsolete." *Wired*. At https://www.wired.com/2008/06/pb-theory/.

Benjamin, Walter. 1969. *Illuminations*. New York: Random House.

Benjamin, Walter. 2009 [1963]. *The Origin of German Tragic Drama*. New York: Verso.

Benjamin, Walter. 1999. *The Arcades Project*. Harvard University Press.

Benjamin, Walter. 2008. *The Work of Art in The Age of Its Mechanical Reproducibility and Other Writings on Media*, trans. Edmund Jephcott. Cambridge: Harvard University Press.

Benzer, M. 2011. *The Sociology of Theodor Adorno*. New York: Cambridge UP.

Brecht, Bertolt. 1964. *Brecht on Theatre: The Development of an Aesthetic*. London: Macmillan.

Buck-Morss, Susan. 1977. *The Origin of Negative Dialectics: Theodor W. Adorno, Walter Benjamin, and the Frankfurt Institute*. New York: Free Press.

Burston, Daniel. 2020. *Psychoanalysis, Politics and The Postmodern University*. London: Palgrave Macmillan.

Calhoun, Craig, and Vanantwerpen, J. 2007. *Orthodoxy, Heterodoxy, And Hierarchy: "Mainstream" Sociology and Its Challengers*. In *Sociology in America: A History*, ed. Craig Calhoun, 367–410. Chicago: University of Chicago Press.

Cole, M. 1996. *Cultural Psychology*. Cambridge: Harvard University Press.

Cudd, A. E. 2005. "How to Explain Oppression: Criteria of Adequacy for Normative Explanatory Theories." *Philosophy of the Social Sciences* 35: 20–49.

Dallmayr, Fred R., and Thomas A. Mccarthy. 1977. *Understanding and Social Inquiry*. Notre Dame: Notre Dame University Press.

Derksen, M. 2019. "Putting Popper to Work." *Theory and Psychology* 29: 449–465.

Fichte, J. G. 1982. *The Science of Knowledge: With the First and Second Introductions*. Cambridge University Press.

Frankfurt Institute for Social Research. 1972 [1956]. *Aspects of Sociology*. Boston: Beacon Press.

Freese, J., and Peterson, D. 2018. "The Emergence of Statistical Objectivity: Changing Ideas of Epistemic Vice and Virtue in Science." *Sociological Theory* 36: 289–313.

Foucault, Michel. 2012. *The Archaeology of Knowledge*. Vintage.

Fromm, Erich. 1970 [1932]. "The Method and Function of An Analytic Social Psychology: Notes on Psychoanalysis and Historical Materialism." In Erich Fromm, *The Crisis of Psychoanalysis*, 110–134. New York: Rinehart.

Fromm, Erich. and Maccoby, M. 1970. *Social Character in A Mexican Village*. Piscataway, NJ: Transaction Publishers.

Fromm, Erich. 1984. *The Working Class in Weimar Germany: A Psychological and Sociological Study*. Oxford, UK: Berg Publishers.

Fromm, Erich. 2013. *To Have or To Be?* London: A&C Black.

Gelley, Alexander. 2014. *Benjamin's Passages: Dreaming, Awakening*. New York: Fordham Univ Press.

Gergen, Kenneth. J. 1982. *Toward Transformation in Social Knowledge*. New York: Springer.

Gordon, Peter E. 2016. *Adorno And Existence*. Cambridge: Harvard University Press.

Green, C. D. 1992. "Of Immortal Mythological Beasts: Operationism in Psychology." *Theory and Psychology*: 291–320.

Greenberg, Jeff, Sheldon Solomon, Tom Pyszczynski, and Lynne Steinberg. 1988. "A Reaction to Greenwald, Pratkanis, Leippe, and Baumgardner. (1986): Under What Conditions Does Research Obstruct Theory Progress?" *Psychological Review* 95: 566–571.

Habermas, J. 1987. Toward A Rational Society: Student Protest, Science, and Politics. Tr. J. J. Shapiro. Cambridge: Polity Press.

Habermas, Jürgen. 1989 [1962]. *The Structural Transformation of The Public Sphere*, trans. T. Burger and F. Lawrence. Cambridge: Polity.

Habermas, Jürgen, Ludwig Von Friedeburg, C. Oehler, and F. Weltz. 1969 [1961]. *Student Und Politik: Eine Soziologische Untersuchung Zum Politischen Bewusstsein Frankfurter Studenten*. Berlin: Luchterhand.

Hammersley, M. 1992. *What's Wrong with Ethnography? Methodological Explorations*. New York: Routledge.

Held, David. 1980. *Introduction to Critical Theory: Horkheimer To Habermas*. Berkeley, CA: University of California Press.

Honneth, Axel. 1996. *The Struggle for Recognition: The Moral Grammar of Social Conflicts*. Cambridge: MIT Press.

Horkheimer, Max. 1947. *Eclipse of Reason*. New York: Oxford University Press.

Horkheimer, Max. 1972. *Critical Theory: Selected Essays*. London: A&C Black.

Horkheimer, Max. 1989 [1940]. "Notes on Institute Activities." In *Critical Theory and Society*, eds. Stephen Eric Bronner and Douglas Kellner, 264–266. New York: Routledge.

Horkheimer, Max. 1995. *Between Philosophy and Social Science: Selected Early Writings*. Cambridge, MA: The MIT Press.

Horkheimer, Max. 2014 [1935]. "On the Problem of Truth." In *Subject and Object: Frankfurt School Writings on Epistemology, Ontology, and Method*, ed. R. Groff, 55–90. New York: Bloomsbury. Original Work Published 1935.

Horkheimer, Max and Theodor W. Adorno. 2002 [1947]. *Dialectic of Enlightenment*. New York: Seabury Press.

Institut für Sozialforschung. 1936. *Studien uber Autorität und Familie*. New York: Ifs.

Jameson, Fredric. 1990. *Late Marxism: Adorno, or, the Persistence of the Dialectic*. New York: Verso.

Jay, Martin. 1973. *The Dialectical Imagination: A History of The Frankfurt School and The Institute of Social Research*, 1923–1950. University of California.

Jennemann, D. 2007. *Adorno In America.* Minneapolis: University of Minnesota Press.

Kellner, Douglas. "N.D. Ernst Bloch, Utopia, and Ideology Critique." *Illuminations: The Critical Theory Project.* At https://pages.gseis.ucla.edu/faculty/kellner/illumina%20 folder/kell1.htm.

Korsch, Karl. 1938. *Karl Marx.* At https://www.marxists.org/archive/korsch/1938/karl-marx/index.htm.

Korsch, Karl. 2013. *Marxism And Philosophy.* New York: Verso.

Kracauer, Siegfried. 1995. *The Mass Ornament: Weimar Essays.* Cambridge: Harvard University Press.

Kracauer, Siegfried. 2019 [1947]. *From Caligari To Hitler: A Psychological History of The German Film.* Princeton, NJ: Princeton University Press.

Kristeva, Julia. 1982. *Powers of Horror: An Essay on Abjection.* New York: Columbia University Press.

Laudan, Larry. 1986. *Science and Values: The Aims of Science and Their Role in Scientific Debate.* Berkeley: University of California Press.

Laudan, Larry. 1996. *Beyond Positivism and Relativism: Theory, Method, And Evidence.* Boulder: Westview Press.

Leonelli, S. 2018. "Rethinking Reproducibility as A Criterion for Research Quality." In *Research in The History of Economic Thought and Methodology, Vol.* 36B, eds. L. Fiorito, S. Scheall, and C. E. Suprinyak, 129–146. Bingley: Emerald.

Lincoln, Y., and Guba, E. G. 2000. "Paradigmatic Controversies, Contradictions, and Emerging Conflicts." In *Handbook of Qualitative Research*, eds. N. K. Denzin and Y. Lincoln, 163–188. Thousand Oaks, CA: SAGE.

Löwenthal, Leo. 1984. *Literature and Mass Culture. Communication in Society*, Vol. 1. Piscataway, NJ: Transaction Publishers.

Lukács, Georg. 1971. *Theory of The Novel.* Cambridge, MA: The MIT Press.

Lukács, Georg. 1972. *History and Class Consciousness: Studies in Marxist Dialectics.* Cambridge: MIT Press.

Lyotard, Jean-François. 1984. *The Postmodern Condition: A Report on Knowledge.* Minneapolis: University of Minnesota Press.

Marcuse, Herbert. 1964. *One-Dimensional Man.* Boston: Beacon Press.

Marcuse, Herbert. 1969. *An Essay on Liberation.* Boston: Beacon Press.

Marcuse, Herbert.1979. *The Aesthetic Dimension.* London: Macmillan.

Marcuse, Herbert. 2009. *Negations: Essays in Critical Theory.* London: Mayflybooks.

Maxcy, Spencer J. 2003. "Pragmatic Threads in Mixed Methods Research in The Social Sciences: The Search for Multiple Modes of Inquiry and The End of The Philosophy of Formalism." In *The Handbook of Mixed Methods in Social and Behavioral Research*, eds. Abbas Tashakkori and Charles Teddlie, 51–90. Thousand Oaks, CA: SAGE.

Meehl, P. E. 1986. "What Social Scientists Don't Understand." In *Metatheory in Social Science: Pluralisms and Subjectivities*, eds. D. W. Fiske and R. A. Shweder, 315–338. Chicago: University of Chicago Press.

Mele, Vincenzo. 2015. "At the Crossroad of Magic and Positivism. Roots of an Evidential Paradigm Through Benjamin and Adorno." *Journal of Classical Sociology* 15: 139–153.

Mignolo, Walter. 2011. "Decolonizing Western Epistemology/Building Decolonial Epistemologies." In *Decolonizing Epistemologies: Latina/O Theology and Philosophy*, eds. A. Isasi-Díaz and E. Mendieta, 19–43. New York: Fordham University Press.

Morelock, Jeremiah. 2017. "Authoritarian Populism Contra *Bildung*: Anti-Intellectualism and The Neoliberal Assault on The Liberal Arts." *Cadernos CIMEAC* 7(2): 63–81.

Morelock, Jeremiah, Ed. 2018. *Critical Theory and Authoritarian Populism*. London: University of Westminster.

Morrow, R. A., and Brown, D. D. 1994. *Critical Theory and Methodology*. Thousand Oaks, CA: SAGE.

Nietzsche, Friedrich. 1997 [1874]. "Schopenhauer As Educator." In *Untimely Meditations*, ed. D. Brezeale, 125–194. Cambridge: Cambridge University Press.

Penny, S. 2009. "Rigorous Interdisciplinary Pedagogy: Five Years Of ACE." *Convergence* 15(1): 31–54.

Pinker, S. 2018. *Enlightenment Now*. New York: Viking.

Pluckrose, H., and Lindsay, J. A. 2020. *Cynical Theories*. Durham, NC: Pitchstone Publishing.

Pollock, Friedrich, Theodor W. Adorno and Colleagues. 2011. *Group Experiment and Other Writings: The Frankfurt School on Public Opinion in Postwar Germany*. Cambridge: Harvard.

Popper, Karl. 2005 [1934]. *The Logic of Scientific Discovery*. New York: Routledge.

Rosenthal, R., and Rosnow, R. L. 2008. *Essentials of Behavioral Research: Methods and Data Analysis* (3rd Ed.). Boston: Mcgraw-Hill.

Smith, David Norman. 1998. "The Ambivalent Worker: Max Weber, Critical Theory, and the Antinomies of Authority." *Social Thought & Research* 21: 35–83.

Sullivan, D. 2020. "Social Psychological Theory as History: Outlining the Critical-Historical Approach to Theory." *Personality and Social Psychology Review* 24: 78–99.

Turner, S. 1994. "The Origins Of 'Mainstream Sociology' and Other Issues in The History of American Sociology." *Social Epistemology* 8: 41–67.

Wheatland, Thomas. 2009. *The Frankfurt School in Exile*. Minneapolis: University of Minnesota Press.

Wiggershaus, Rolf. 1994. *The Frankfurt School: Its History, Theories, And Political Significance*. Cambridge: MIT.

Worrell, Mark P. 2009. *Dialectic of Solidarity: Labor, Antisemitism, And the Frankfurt School*. Leiden: Brill.

Ziege, Eva-Maria. 2009. *Antisemitismus Und Gesellschaftstheorie: Die Frankfurter Schule Im Amerikanischen Exil*. Frankfurt: Suhrkamp.

PART 1

Dialectics

∴

When History Fails Us: Immanent Critique of Capitalism to the New Right and Beyond

Robert J. Antonio

Frankfurt School theorists took varied positions in every phase of their history, made dramatic shifts at different historical moments, and critically engaged and borrowed from other traditions. A chief characteristic has been their "aversion to closed philosophical systems" said Martin Jay (1973: 41). Concluding a comprehensive history of the Frankfurt School, Rolf Wiggershaus asserted that it went through "many forms and phases" and "never corresponded to any uniform phenomenon." He added that the Frankfurt School belongs to a wider "critical theory" tradition initiated by Karl Marx, whom it has variously updated, revised, and departed. Wiggershaus (1994: 657–59) held, however, that the tradition "still has a recognizable face." Many years ago, I argued that critical theory's "definable core" originated from Marx's revision of Hegelian *immanent critique*. This essay revisits that argument at a very different historical moment. Applied in critical analyses of capitalism, Marx believed that his method could identify a historical basis for normative criticism with emancipatory intent, contradictory social conditions that make emancipation possible, and a collective agent that can direct a sociopolitical course toward realization of that end (Benhabib 1986: 1–143; Antonio 1981, 2017; Becker 2018).

Marx believed the rise and development of capitalism to be the most consequential social change in human history. In the *Communist Manifesto*, Marx and Engels held that the capitalist ruling class transformed productive forces and overall culture so radically and attained so much power that they would soon globalize the capitalist system. Having eliminated the status orders of feudal and ancient societies, Marx and Engels held, capitalism intensified, simplified, and made transparent the bourgeois ruling class's efficient, brutal extraction from proletarian direct producers and would soon spread this extractive regime worldwide (Marx 1948 [1848]: 9–14). They argued that the proletariat was being immiserated and leveled by modern industry and was organizing itself as a class capable of overthrowing the bourgeoisie and seizing the political apparatus (Marx and Engels 1948: 14–31). Even after acknowledging major political

setbacks and unanticipated problems, Marx still embraced the vision of proletarian revolution and creation of socialism, and claimed, at key junctures, that
they were "inevitable." Although sometimes speaking with too much certainty
about these hopes, Marx took account of impactful historical vicissitudes and
sociocultural changes that sidetracked his original emancipatory hopes.

Failure of the optimistic emancipatory scenario to eventuate shaped the
agenda for later critical theorists. Those operating in Marx's tracks employed
immanent critique to assess changes of the capitalist system that blocked
revolutionary transformation and identify emergent conditions that offered
fresh possibilities for emancipatory change. However, leading World War
II-era critical theorists shifted focus from capitalism to Enlightenment culture and argued that sociocultural changes neutralized immanent critique.
The late twentieth century "linguistic turn" and "cultural turn" hardened this
move and increased pluralization of "critical theory." These theorists shifted
away from a critique of capitalism when postwar "Fordism" was collapsing,
and neoliberal globalization was becoming hegemonic.[1] They argued that
Marxism and class politics were moribund and superseded by the new cultural theories and cultural activism. Postmodern theorists held that the new
mediatized culture obliterated the capacity to distinguish ideology from
reality and adopted strictly negative, deconstructive methods. My analysis
of the break from immanent critique aims to illuminate conditions leading
to a decoupling of capitalism and democracy that undercut the neoliberal
regime's capacity to engage its contradictions, generated legitimacy crises, opened way for ethnoracial nationalist "alternatives," and today favors
renewed immanent criticism of neoliberalism and capitalism per se, as we
have known it.

---

1   The Frankfurt School did *not* employ the term "Fordism," which Antonio Gramsci originated.
    Later twentieth century social theorists used the term to refer to the rise of managerial cap-
    italism, discussed by Horkheimer and other critical theorists. Fordist capitalism emerged in
    the 1920s, matured in the post-World War II era, and neoliberalism supplanted it in the 1980s.
    Fordism had large, vertically integrated, managerial firms, national unions, and an interven-
    tionist regulatory and welfare state. It employed Keynesian economic policy and forged a
    "capital-labor accord." Fordism flourished until slowed growth, a profit squeeze, and other
    problems eroded its legitimacy. Neoclassical and Austrian School economists and conser-
    vative political theorists and public intellectuals revived "market-liberal" or "free-market"
    ideas justifying creation of the neoliberal regime of accumulation by corporate and political
    elites. Neoliberalism flourished in English speaking capitalist heartland nations. Although
    unevenly developed in different regions of the world, neoliberal governance still dominated
    globalized capitalism for nearly forty years.

1   Immanent Critique: The Hegelian-Marxian Root of Critical Theory

> From idealism ... I arrived at the point of seeking the idea in reality itself.
> If previously the gods dwelt above the earth, they now became its center.
> MARX 1976 [1837]: 18

The quoted passage above was from young Marx in a letter to his father about
his conversion to Hegelianism. Hegel's immanent criticism stressed judging
historical moments by their own internal norms and employing them to frame
one's critical standpoint. Marx had joined the leftwing, "Young Hegelians,"
who attacked religion and the state for undermining freedom and rationality.
They opposed rightwing Hegelians, who claimed that the Prussian state had
already culminated human progress and ended history. Hegel contended that
humans produce themselves and their sociocultural worlds, suffer estrangement by treating their own creations as alien objects beyond their knowledge
and control, and overcome this alienation and attain self-conscious agency in
progressive stages. Humanity drives this upward pathway by criticizing and
overcoming contradictory sociocultural conditions, negating their limiting
facets, and preserving favorable ones in higher syntheses that culminate eventually in "Absolute Spirit" or total knowledge and freedom. Marx broke with
Hegelianism's idiom of spirit and consciousness but incorporated centrally in
his "materialist" position its historicist idea of self-constitutive labor and consequent capacity to transcend existent conditions that truncate our potential
as a species.

Criticizing Hegel's "idealism," Marx portrayed humanity as a "corporeal,"
"sensuous," "objective," "*natural being*" with "*needs*." His naturalistic turn radically historicized Hegel's anti-dualist philosophy. Paralleling Darwin, Marx
predicated his position on the idea that our surviving and flourishing, like
other living things, depend on effective and sustainable utilization of resources
from the biophysical environment (Marx 1964 [1844]: 180–82). Marx held that
our morphology and sociality, which distinguish our "species being," generate
human intelligence and other distinctly human capabilities first manifested
in simple cooperative arrangements and primitive tools and later language,
enhanced productive powers, complex cooperative and sociocultural systems,
large concentrated populations, and massive built environments. He argued
that when productive forces advance, generate surplus, and reduce need for
subsistence labor, a class division arises between subordinate "direct producers," who carry out both "necessary labor" and "surplus labor" yet receive only
subsistence, and superordinate "ruling classes," who exert effective control
over productive forces, appropriate "surplus product," and govern politically

and culturally. In Marx's view, these two fundamental classes are locked in continual struggle (peaceful and violent), which determines how labor duties and product are distributed and ultimately the overall shape of society and culture.

Marx contended that productive force development shapes class structure and the consequent "mode of production"[2] determines the ruling ideas (ideology), polity, and law, and leaves a substantial imprint on the overall social formation (Marx and Engels 1970 [1845–46]: 35–95). He declared, however, that the relationship between ruling classes and direct producers "reveals the hidden basis of the entire social structure ..."[3] Averting a narrow mechanistic position, Marx (1967b: 792) held that "the same economic basis" could be "due to innumerable different empirical circumstances" and manifest "infinite variations and gradations in appearance, which can be ascertained only by analysis of the empirically given circumstances." Driven by intelligent human agency and mediated by class struggles, Marx argued, productive force development and subsistence levels progressed in the long run. He held that advances have been episodic, uneven, and slow until capitalism ignited unparalleled revolutionary expansion of productive forces. Marx acknowledged social progress attained by the capitalist working class of direct producers (driven by emergent organized labor and social reformers) but warned that exploitation rates were increasing sharply and that underemployed people and especially those falling below subsistence were growing rapidly with capitalist production and accumulation.

In the "Preface" of the fortieth anniversary publication of the *Manifesto*, Engels (1949 [1888]: 6–7) asserted that, although Marx's naturalistic analytical framework was still "correct," historical conditions and capitalism had changed and altered prospects for the revolutionary scenario they outlined four decades earlier. For example, Engels contended that the proletariat could not simply seize the state apparatus and "wield it for its own purposes." He said that he left the *Manifesto* unchanged to respect its status as a "historical document." However, many of their followers treated it as a catechism. Consequently, Engels (1959 [1890–1894]: 396–97, 399–400) criticized younger

---

2 A "mode of production" includes the distinctive array of productive forces (tools, labor power, natural resources, cooperative organization, and knowledge) and social relations that determine effective control over them and over the distribution of product and usage of surpluses.

3 Marx (1967b [1894]: 791–92) explained, "The specific economic form, in which unpaid surplus-labor is pumped out of direct producers, determines the relationship of rulers and ruled, as it grows directly out of production itself and, in turn, reacts upon the determining element. Upon this, however, is founded the entire formation of the economic community which grows up out of the production relations themselves, thereby simultaneously its specific political form."

"Marxists" for applying their framework too mechanistically and producing "the most amazing rubbish." In response to these versions of "Marxist orthodoxy," Marx allegedly declared, "All I know is that I am not a Marxist ..." Engels reported.[4] He admitted, however, that Marx and he sometimes exaggerated "the economic side" in battles with political opponents and consequently were partly responsible for the ahistorical versions of their position. By contrast, Engels argued that their analytical framework stresses simply the centrality of "the production and reproduction of real life" and is only "a guide to study" that requires constant attention to ongoing historical change and new economic, sociocultural, and political conditions. Critical theorists opposed later orthodox Marxists for deploying Marx's "materialist" analytical framework ideologically, insisting dogmatically on the inevitability of socialism, and misrepresenting authoritarian communist regimes and parties as emancipatory agents.

Marx's optimism about the transparency of exploitation and imminence of revolution waned after the failed 1848 revolutions. In response to restored dictatorship in France, Marx (1963 [1852]: 15) declared famously that, "Men make their own history, but they do not make it just as they please; they do not make it under circumstances chosen by themselves, but under circumstances directly encountered, given and transmitted from the past. The tradition of all the dead generations weighs like a nightmare on the brain of the living." Speaking of modern industrial capitalism, Marx asserted, "The semblance of simplicity disappears in more advanced systems of production" (1987 [1859]: 276). He held that high finance made commodity production and the extractive process opaquer and more complex and shrouded it in mystification. He aimed *Capital* to demystify justifications of capitalist extraction by the voluntary labor contract and other facets of market-liberal ideology. His theory of value pointed directly to systematic exploitation of wage labor as a hidden driver of fluctuating prices and profits. He also held that proliferation of intermediate classes fragment class interests and undercut the linear class split that he and Engels portrayed in the *Manifesto* (1967a: 71–83; 1967b: 885–86) and that splits plagued the communist movement (e.g., Marx 1989a [1875]). Although sometimes speaking of "inevitable" revolution and socialism, Marx analyzed blockages to these possibilities and grasped their uncertainty. Agonizing over

---

4 A long debate ensued over how strictly and comprehensively Marx saw the determination exerted by productive forces and class structure over the rest of social life. Critical theorists rejected rigid determinist interpretations of Marx's "materialism" and especially mechanistic Soviet-era "dialectical materialism" ("Diamat"). Marxian oriented critical theorists usually have embraced a less comprehensive, multi-causal interpretation of materialism that stresses the "relative autonomy" of culture and politics (McMurtry 1978; Shaw 1978; Larrain 1986).

multiple drafts of a letter to Russian revolutionary Vera Zasulich, elderly Marx (1989b [1881]) acknowledged that capitalist development, which he held generates the precursory productive and class conditions for socialism, advanced much more slowly and unevenly than he originally expected and may not ever extend beyond Europe. Although Marx's faith wavered at times, he never gave up hope in the proletariat nor abandoned his relentless critique of capitalism and search for possible triggers of emancipatory struggle.

Marx turned the capitalist class's market-liberal claims about expanding freedom, justice, and democracy against lived conditions of workers and critically expanded on counterclaims by working-class movements and social reformers. His immanent criticism followed what he saw to be contradictions and potentialities of capitalism, and he extrapolated from emergent potentially progressive social structural and normative conditions. Socialism inhered in capitalism's cooperative system, reform movements, and state intervention he contended.[5] The "socialized" complex cooperation of modern industry and capacity to produce socially shared "real wealth" contradicted private accumulation of moneyed "abstract wealth" by the capitalist ruling class. He saw the capitalist class to be "revolutionary," because they spurred and directed productive force development that generated enormous material progress, which a new socialized political economic regime could redirect to reduce vastly human drudgery and misery and greatly increase free time for cultural activities that enhance human flourishing. Growth of the "reserve army" of underemployed and impoverished along with productive power and concentrated wealth was a primary rift that intensifies class conflict Marx thought. Globalization, he predicted, would increase competition and drive automation that diminishes demand for "living labor" (the ultimate source of profit and capital accumulation he held), cause profit rates to fall, stir massive growth of the reserve army, and generate emancipatory proletarian solidarity and struggle. He saw *capitalist* productivism to be socially and environmentally destructive but held that modern industrial science and technology could be liberating if redirected from capitalist accumulation to shared abundance, free time for self-development, and other humane, sustainable ends.

Marx (1977 [1845]: 30) said famously he aimed to change the world, not merely interpret it. To serve that end, he practiced at least four styles of immanent critique of capitalism.[6] One illuminated the contradiction of ideology

---

5 Marx (1967b: 436) even argued that the development of "stock companies" and early signs of emergent managerial capitalism were "social undertakings" that constituted "the abolition of capital as private property within the framework of capitalist production itself."

6 I do not claim that Marx formulated these as distinct strategies or that the four are all-inclusive.

(e.g., market-liberal claims about freedom and plenty) and reality (e.g., worker poverty and underemployment). Another exposed the contradiction of reality (e.g., capitalism's revolutionary advances of productive forces, shared grossly unequally) and potentiality (e.g., socially shared abundance and free time). A third stressed contradictions between actualities (e.g., the enhanced productivity of capitalist cash crop agriculture and exhaustion of the soil).[7] A fourth strategy focused on contradictions between ideologically distorted meanings (e.g., wage labor as "free labor") and their "actual" lived meanings (e.g., "exploited labor").[8] These different variants all distinguish distorted surfaces from depth realities and illuminate emancipatory possibilities. Marx understood that workers' capacity to "see" such potentials and execute collective action to realize them depend on the vicissitudes of history as well as their talents. However, the contradictions of industrial capitalism were so glaring, and expansion of the working class was so rapid, that his belief in proletarian revolution never faded.

Later critical theorists held that historical catastrophes, which Marx did not imagine, eradicated the "two-dimensional" culture that enables emancipatory agents to distinguish depth realties and determinants from distorted surfaces, and identify and mobilize resources for social change. In these deeply pessimistic moments, critical theorists employed an array of strategies. Aiming to overcome myopia and quiescence, critical theorists sometimes employed a fifth type of immanent critique that pits the past against the present. They reclaimed historical cultural resources employed by previous exemplary agents of emancipatory change to overcome blockages in parallel situations and illuminate ideologically occluded or hard to identify contradictions and potential agents. However, many prominent critical theorists opted for purely negative criticism devoid of emancipatory possibilities. Others pinned their emancipatory hopes on claims about biologically based aesthetic impulses, transcendental norms, and evolutionary progress. At best, these moves turn their emancipatory ideal into a *Flaschenpost* or "message in a bottle" for future generations when conditions may favor change. Yet, they arguably manifest the ahistorical universalism or ethical formalism that critical theorists originally aimed to supersede.

---

7 See Marx's (1967a [1867]: 504–07) argument about "metabolic rift," later elaborated, expanded, and applied to current global ecological problems (e.g., Foster and Clark 2020).

8 Marx (e.g., 1976 [1865]: 42–43) saw market-liberal claims that direct producers were "freed" (because they enter voluntary contracts with employers) when capitalist wage labor replaced serfdom and slavery to conceal their exploitation (i.e., a ruling class still expropriates their surplus product and they continue to suffer from immobility, poverty, and coercive force).

2   From Marx to Dialectic of Enlightenment: Critical Theory as
         Negation

> There are times when faith in the future can be kept alive only through
> absolute resistance to the prevailing responses of men. Such a time is the
> present.
>
> HORKHEIMER 1971 [1941]: 280

> The traditional transcendent critique of ideology is obsolete.
>
> ADORNO 1981 [1967]: 33

In the classic essay "Traditional and Critical Theory" marking the seventieth
anniversary of Marx's *Capital*, Max Horkheimer (1972b [1937]) distinguished
the historically oriented, critical theoretical practices of the Frankfurt School
version of Marxism from Orthodox Marxist "Diamat" and empirical, social scientific "traditional theory." These other approaches, he argued, take for granted
the era's reified domination systems and serve the new administrative states.
He also elaborated then emergent political economic and sociocultural realities that precluded Marx's revolutionary scenario. He contended that the rise of
more centralized, concentrated monopoly capitalism and state-centered managerialism replaced the market-liberalism that Marx criticized. Horkheimer
held, however, that Marx's method of immanent critique, analytic framework,
and normative vision were still needed tools to analyze and criticize capitalism, because its fundamental extractive process and basic economic logic were
unchanged.[9]

Although embracing theoretically Marx's goals of identifying capitalism's
contradictory features, normative directions to transform the regime, and collective agents who can implement the changes, Horkheimer argued that new
sociocultural conditions blocked realization of the second and third aims. He
held that the nexus of economic and political power in ascendant "authoritarian states" neutralized "ideology," eliminated "cultural factors" having "positive
value," drove the "general intellectual level of the 'great masses' " into steep,
rapid decline, destroyed autonomy and agency of workers, and made them
prey to "charlatans." In his view, profound mystification distorted the mentality

---

9   Horkheimer stressed anchoring critical theory in a Marxian immanent critique of capital-
    ism, but he referred generally to Marx's thought without engaging specifically his materialist
    theory of history or labor theory of value. It is unlikely that Horkheimer or Adorno stud-
    ied *Capital* or Marx's overall corpus closely. See Smith (2017), on the Frankfurt School and
    Marxism.

of even those parts of the masses "bent on truth," undercut their capacity to distinguish depth from surface, and thereby sapped their political independence. Although stressing the primacy of economic drivers, Horkheimer held that culture, authority, and family mediated them and facilitated the ready compliance demanded by administrative domination (Horkheimer 1972a [1936], 1972b: 234–38, 242). In another essay pointing to factors conditioning ultimate economic drivers, Horkheimer (1972a [1936]) employed Nietzschean and Freudian ideas to analyze authority and the family and stress irrational forces that evoke blind obedience. Horkheimer (1972c [1941]: 278–79) later argued that commodified mass culture evaporates art's oppositional powers and its capacity to inspire imagined worlds transcending the actual one. Following Frederick Pollock and Herbert Marcuse, he considered fascism to be a political form arising from advanced "monopoly capitalism" (Horkheimer 1972b). In an essay on the "authoritarian state," Horkheimer (1973 [1942]) held that monopoly capitalism was being transformed into "state capitalism" and that its "integral statism" was displacing the market, emerging as a dominant feature of Fordist America, and developing even more fully in centralized, totalitarian fascist regimes and the Soviet Union.

Marx believed that the proletariat could be readily educated, generate leaders from its own ranks, and exert collective agency. By contrast, Horkheimer held that proletarians of his time could not grasp their conditions, interests, and possibilities and that an overly reverent attitude toward them by their political allies would only deepen their blindness and weakness. Bombarded with lies, he argued, they are "following their leaders with their eyes tight shut." He and other Frankfurt School theorists rejected orthodox Marxist and Communist Party claims to carry on Marx's project, represent the proletariat's "objective interests," and "build socialism." However, Horkheimer (1972b: 213–16) maintained that critical theorists still aspire to illuminate "from historical analysis ... the goals of human activity" and a "reasonable organization of society" that meets the needs of all community members and is "immanent" in the organization of labor. Although implying that capitalism still had depth attributes with emancipatory potential, he believed that the new managerial states negated such possibilities and threatened the "darkest barbarism." He argued that consequent social conditions, which obstructed transcendent vision, limited critical theory to a "negative formulation" opposing injustice. He speculated that "truth" may reside in "hardly noticed" small circles "who may become leaders at the decisive moment" because of their depth of understanding. Departing Marx's hope to unify theory and practice, Horkheimer addressed a moment when fascism and Stalinism were ascendant and Fordist managerialism, commercial culture, and wartime mobilization appeared to preclude emancipatory aspirations in capitalist nations (Horkheimer 1972b: 234, 240–43; Dubiel 1985: 39–67).

In *Dialectic of Enlightenment*, Horkheimer and Adorno (1972a [1944]) deepened the break with earlier critical theory. They still stressed total commodification and the extraordinary power of political economic elites, but no longer embraced Marx's analytical framework or claimed that an emancipatory alternative inhered in a labor regime. Rather, they traced then current sociocultural and political catastrophes to Enlightenment culture. By contrast to Marx's hopes about the emancipatory potential of science and technology, Horkheimer and Adorno stressed nearly exclusively their employment in sweeping domination of people and nature and consequent cultural "regression," atrophied imagination, "total schematization," and creation of obedient human fodder. Rather than liberation, they held, "the fully enlightened earth radiates disaster triumphant" (Horkheimer and Adorno 1972a: 3, 35–37). They argued that the "culture industry's" mass consumption and mass entertainment produce "manufactured need" and "mass deception." Inspired by Nietzsche and de Sade, they contended, means-dominated instrumental rationality reifies existent realities and produces irrational, destructive consequences so extreme that its raw factuality becomes "myth." Horkheimer and Adorno (1972a: 4, 18, 126) suggested a radical sociocultural rupture (e.g., "power and knowledge is synonymous," "sign and image" are split, "real life" becomes "indistinguishable from the movies") that anticipated and influenced later postmodernist broadsides that declared the total exhaustion of rational culture and social progress. "Totalitarian capitalism" and its fascist and Stalinist offspring, they claimed, manifest Enlightenment culture's single-minded pursuit of instrumentally rational "self-preservation" and "domination." Twenty-five years later, Horkheimer and Adorno (1972b [1969]: 10) held that this declinist trend toward "total integration" and a totally "administered world" had not abated.

Describing immanent critique, Horkheimer (1974 [1947]: 178, 182) spoke of employing a society's "highest values" to assess itself, with awareness that they merely reflect the "taints of reality." Ideas opposing "the social systems that bore them" and the "contradiction between existent and ideology," he declared, drive "all historical progress." He held that cultural conditions once allowed critical theorists to contrast market-liberal values of "justice," "equality," and 'freedom' with capitalist realities, expose their reified elements, and reconstruct them to draw out their immanent possibilities for serving emancipatory human flourishing. However, Horkheimer (1974: 96) argued that ruling instrumental reason elevates "reality to the status of an ideal," blunts critical sensibilities, and commands adjustment to the status quo. This forgery of ideals, identified

WHEN HISTORY FAILS US

and experienced seamlessly as existent unfreedom, precludes critical theorists from generating immanently critical norms and emancipatory visions of alternative regimes. Attacking positivism and pragmatism, Horkheimer contended that the liberal reformism of the Fordist regime conflates critique with "planning" and "social engineering." Because "constructive philosophies" cannot come to terms with the "cultural debacle," he argued, critical theory must employ the "method of negation" to simply denounce what "mutilates" us and impedes our "free development," especially what we now call "reason" (187).

In *Prisms*, Adorno (1981: 19–34) portrayed a similar neutralization of immanent criticism driven by extreme commodification of consumer capitalism and engulfment of critics in reified culture. This totally integrated society, Adorno held, is an "open-air prison" governed by "the absolute rule of that which is" (34). He held there are no more authentic ideologies that we can turn against the societies they represent. Rather they are "only advertisements for the world" that reproduce it and command silence. Adorno asserts that immanent criticism "is dragged into the abyss by its object" – the ruling ideas so closely identify with existent society that the contradiction between ideology and social reality vanishes. The "immanent method," he held, cannot provide critical theorists normative direction or help them envision emancipatory change. Under these cultural conditions, they can at most illuminate the "absolute reification" and pseudo-harmonious nature of the status quo that they could not yet overcome or reimagine.

In *One-Dimensional Man*, Herbert Marcuse (1964) described the "absorption of ideology into reality" and into "the process of production itself."[10] He contended that Fordist managerial capitalism and its "welfare-warfare state" integrated the working class into the system and that "stupefication" from meaningless work, cheap entertainment, wasteful consumption, and a false sense of security produce "comfortable, smooth reasonable democratic unfreedom," "repressive desublimation," and "euphoria in unhappiness," which suffocate "needs that demand liberation" (Marcuse 1964: 1, 5, 7). Employing "advanced industrial society" to refer to capitalist and communist regimes, Marcuse stressed convergent trends toward increased affluence and "total administration" that neutralize critical thought and opposition. Marcuse's (1971 [1958]) immanent critique of Soviet Marxism pointed to glaring contradictions between ideology and reality, but he held that the method could not illuminate possible emancipatory alternatives or collective agents capable of bringing one into being. Marcuse (1964: 254) held that critical theory's "greatest weakness" is

---

10   Marcuse (1964: 11) cites Adorno's *Prisms* as an inspiration for these ideas.

its inability to illuminate "liberating tendencies *within* the established society."
Remaining closer to the spirit of Marx than Adorno and Horkheimer, however,
he provided enthusiastic support to the New Left. He identified radical students, hippies, ghetto inhabitants, and Third World peoples as possible revolutionary subjects.[11] He argued that emancipatory alternatives and agents
emerge in the process of struggle and we cannot foresee them in advance via
an immanent critique of capitalism as Marx held. Borrowing from Freud and
Nietzsche, Marcuse (1968, 1969) contended that desire for a pleasurable, liberated collective existence and resistance to domination have universal aesthetic and biological roots providing wellsprings for transcendent alternatives
when history fails. He consequently breaks with Hegelian-Marxist historically
based immanent critique.

Jürgen Habermas argued that critical theorists' identification of
Enlightenment reason exclusively with domination and coercion undercuts
their appeals to reason and claims to have deployed it in their own analyses
and critiques.[12] Contra *Dialectic of Enlightenment* pessimism, he defended
the rational "unfinished project of modernity" and sought to restore critical
theory's constructive thrust and emancipatory vision by way of a linguistic
turn. However, he retained facets of the earlier generation's critique of one-
dimensional culture and affirmed their rejection of Marx's claim that emancipatory possibilities are immanent within the organization of labor. Asserting
that, "bourgeois consciousness has become cynical" and "bourgeois ideals have
gone into retirement," Habermas (1979 [1976]: 97) held that "there are no norms
and values to which an immanent critique could appeal with [the expectation of] agreement." His distinction between "labor" (coordinated by technical
rules, controls, and routines necessary for economic production and bureaucratic governance) and "interaction" (guided by social norms, reciprocity, and
communicative intent) signify distinct social realms with divergent differentiation processes, which are "decoupled" and contradictory within modern societies.[13] Emancipatory potential thus arises from cultural evolution not from the
organization of labor he held; i.e., communicative rationalization generates

---

11   A literary symbol of the New Left, the first edition of *One-Dimensional Man* sold more
      than 300,000 copies. Marcuse's written work, speeches, and public statements influenced
      late 1960s and early 1970s radical student, antiwar, and countercultural politics (Aronson
      2014). Horkheimer and Adorno were scathingly critical of these movements.
12   See Jay (1973: 63–64; 2016: 145–63) on the undertheorized conception of reason in critical
      theory and effort by Habermas to resolve the problem.
13   Rather than labor and interaction, Habermas (1987a [1981]: 153–97) employed "system"
      (i.e., social organization governed by instrumental rationality and the media of power

capacities for post-conventional morality, heightened reflexivity, and increased autonomy and responsibility. By contrast, rationalization of labor, or system, he contended, serves political economic and bureaucratic coordination and domination. Although instrumental rationalization of organizational modernity has undisputed socio-material benefits, Habermas held, its power and money "colonize" interaction and stem democratic potentialities of communicative rationalization. He argued that tensions between the two domains spur "defensive" social movements aimed to resist colonization (Habermas 1987a: 332–403).[14]

Habermas (1987a: 383) explained that his critical theory proceeds "reconstructively that is unhistorically" – it no longer draws on "concrete ideals immanent in traditional forms of life." He held that normative resources reside in a "transcendental site" in the lifeworld, which provides a warrant for critical reason outside history (Habermas 1987a: 126). He argued that his normative foundation for critical theory is anchored in presuppositions of everyday speech – i.e., that expressed ideas are factually true, sincere, and ethically right and that speakers who can contribute are permitted to participate, have equal chances to do so, and can speak freely without coercion. We often violate these tacit norms, he acknowledged, but we can activate them to criticize distorted or coerced communication and resist domination and coercion. He also implied that communicative rationalization and consequent ascendance of deliberative democratic culture and institutions calls forth their usage. In his view, activation of these norms in rational argument and its good reasons can be decisive in resolving disagreements and affirm voluntary consensus and discursive democracy. However, this linguistic turn departed Hegelian-Marxian immanent critique or historically based analysis of publicly shared values embedded in bourgeois ideology and capitalism. Habermas (1987a: 332–73) rejected Marx's labor theory of value and his view that unequal extractive relations and struggles between producers and capitalists are the fundamental driving forces of social modernity's dynamics, catastrophes, and potentialities.[15]

---

and money) and "lifeworld" (i.e., background consciousness shaping ability to reach uncoerced understandings) in his later theory of communicative action. Also see Habermas (1984 [1981]). See Antonio (1989) on Habermas's evolutionary normative justification and other problems of his framework, and Browne (2008) for a different viewpoint about Habermas and immanent critique.

14 Habermas (1987a: 393–94) held that "feminism" is today's "offensive" social movement, i.e., it has redemptive emancipatory qualities that once characterized the "American civil rights movement" and earlier "bourgeois-socialist liberation movements."

15 Habermas still considered economic inequality to be a fundamental ethical and social problem and source of tension and supported strongly egalitarian social policy and the welfare state.

Editor Paul Piccone and his circle at *Telos* contributed enormously to bringing first generation critical theory and critical Continental sociopolitical thought to English speakers. *Telos* published essays by leading second generation, critical theorist Habermas, reviews of his books, interviews with him, and critical and interpretive commentaries about his theory. However, Piccone (1985) attacked mercilessly Habermas' work and sympathetic interpretations of it – "What we have here is English analytic philosophy plus American functionalism jargonized into German and repackaged as critical theory." He added that it is "the biggest joke since the Playboy [Magazine] Philosophy or Sade's 'Philosophy of the Bedroom. ...'" Piccone (1987) argued that Habermas' academic formalism, bland universalism, and "lame, contentless, liberal" thrust impoverished his work. He charged that Habermas provided intellectual and political support for the progressive liberal "New Class," who managed the Fordist Welfare State and exerted power via bureaucratic legislation, regulation, and administration. He charged that these "apparatchiks" fashioned a human rights agenda and social reforms that domesticate left ideals, liquidate sociocultural particularity, and greatly accentuate the homogenization and regimentation signified by first generation critical theory's conception of "total administration." He held that "Great Society" era capitalism foreclosed radical change from the exhausted left.

Piccone contended that a new age of "artificial negativity" had dawned. Dialectic of Enlightenment critical theory held that one-dimensional society's evaporation of the ideology and reality distinction precluded identification of transcendent possibilities and limited critique to negation, or the Marcusean "Great Refusal" (Marcuse 1964: 257). Piccone held that Fordist New Class politics domesticated that radical impulse and generated lockstep sociocultural integration that exceeded that described by the one-dimensionality thesis (Piccone 1978; Luke 1978). He argued that the New Left and new social movements supported by Habermas and Marcuse serve the administrative state. Artificial negativity simulates dynamism, Piccone held, but hardens and totalizes bureaucratically coordinated regulation, expands state power, produces "cretinized" people incapable of critical thought, and thereby neutralizes critical theory, as we have known it and its method of negation. He wanted critical theorists to scuttle their abstract idea of emancipation and seek "the kind of broad popular base previously ruled out by earlier formulations of the theory itself" (Piccone 1977: 37, 1980). The search for "organic negativity" led Piccone and his circle eventually to bring Carl Schmitt, the French New Right, the Italian Northern League, and "postmodern populist" theory to their readers.

The *Telos* circle anticipated today's critique of globalization from the populist right, which they have influenced.[16]

3   Market Liberalism Returns: Neoliberal Dedemocratization

> ... neoliberalism assaults the principles, practices, cultures, subjects, and institutions of democracy understood as rule by the people.
>
> BROWN 2015: 9

In the 1980s, the regulatory and redistributive welfare state and expansive middle classes of post-World War II Fordism were declining, identity politics were supplanting labor-centered politics, and culture was becoming the topic of pitched battles between ascendant cultural conservatives and an increasingly diverse, fragmented left. Habermas was a much-debated figure in the broader linguistic and cultural turn in social theory. Advocates of the new linguistically oriented "postmodern" and "poststructuralist" versions of "critical theory" attacked Habermas for staying too close to Marx, defending Enlightenment rationalism, and underemphasizing cultural difference (e.g., Lyotard 1984).[17] Their deconstructive substitutes for negative dialectics held that immanent critique was moribund. Radical postmodernists portrayed a mediatized one-dimensionality (i.e., a flattened hyperreal, aleatory flow of signifiers and images) that dissolves the reality principle per se – it erases contradictions between ideological surfaces and structures and processes said

---

16   Piccone's publication of a special issue on Schmitt, populist drift, and vocal disregard for Habermas' theories of communicative action and discursive democracy were the source of sharp splits among the *Telos* circle that led to departures of core staff and writers in the late 1980s. See Antonio (2011) for comprehensive discussion of *Telos* during the Piccone editorship and of his artificial negativity thesis and its contribution to the journal's populist turn.

17   Postmodernist theories were rooted largely in 1960s French philosophy and social theory but spread globally in the late 1970s through the 1990s. In the United States, these approaches had substantial impacts in the humanities (especially in the languages and continental philosophy) and less extensive impacts in the social sciences. "Postmodernist" or "poststructuralist" approaches ignited intense splits within disciplines and departments. Although participating in the linguistic turn, Habermas (1987b [1985]) embraced the modern social theory tradition and criticized postmodernists and poststructuralists for anti-rationalism and "conservatism." They in turn portrayed Habermas along with Marx as chief representatives of the bankrupt, repressive Enlightenment tradition. On postmodern theories and debates, see Antonio (1998).

to underlay and determine the mystifications (e.g., Baudrillard 1983a, 1983b). Postmodern simulation, they held, neutralizes "depth models" that iden- tify social drivers (e.g., labor theory of value) shaping cultural surfaces (e.g., prices and profits) (Jameson 1984: 61–62). The splitting of sign and image, and blurring of media fantasy and "real life," which Adorno and Horkheimer had warned about forty years before now prevailed totally postmodernists claimed.

Lambasting these new "cultural theories" and postmodern cultural trends, center-right thinkers portrayed them as causes of sociocultural and political malaise and products of an exhausted left and spent social liberalism (e.g., Bell 1976; Bloom 1987; Fukuyama 1989). Center-left critics decried the "end of left and right" or "end of alternatives" (e.g., Giddens 1994; Bobbio 1996). Mediating political economic drivers, Marxists held, postmodern culture undercut immanent critique, emancipatory vision, and progressive resis- tance (e.g., Jameson 1984; Harvey 1989; Offe 1996). Most importantly, they argued that postmodernism and identity politics was oblivious to the return of market-liberalism with its much sharper class divisions cutting across divergent sociocultural groupings, reduced welfare provision, and increased precarity and insecurity for low wage and middling workers. English speak- ing, core neoliberal nations and especially the United States eliminated countervailing power and political alternatives. *New Left Review* editor, Perry Anderson (2000: 17) said that there is no collective agent, "that can match the power of capital ... on the horizon" and that "the first time since the Reformation, there is no longer any significant oppositions – that is sys- tematic rival outlooks – within the thought-world of the West; and scarcely any on the world scale either." He implied despairingly what Margaret Thatcher and her allies celebrated about neoliberal hegemony – "There is no alternative!"

Market-liberal theorists argued from the start that the state is *the* source of repressive coercive power and that rule based on the market's economic sig- nals is efficient and benign. Forerunner neoliberal, Friedrich Hayek (1944: 69– 71, 1978) advised not to make a "fetish of democracy," and held that autocracies can sometimes enjoy more "cultural and spiritual freedom" than democracy. Hayek endorsed autocratic state power when needed to uphold market-lib- eralism and stem redistribution and regulation by democratic plebiscites.[18] Revived market liberalism became the dominant policy framework of the new

---

18   Hayek advised the brutal Chilean Pinochet dictatorship because it preserved economic "liberty." Milton Friedman and his students also aided the Pinochet regime.

global regime of accumulation.[19] In a bestselling encomium about neoliberal globalization and its deregulated financial markets, Thomas L Friedman
(2000: 103–06) held that their "Golden Straightjacket" shrinks politics to grow
the economy and reduces political choices to "Pepsi and Coke." He argued that
online financial traders (enabled by new information technologies and deregulation, financialization, and securitization) replaced political electorates as
the decisive force shaping public policy and "blew away all the major ideological alternatives to free-market capitalism." Making capital accumulation
the *sine qua non* of public policy, "market fundamentalists" rolled back unions,
regulation, and progressive taxation, and slashed the state's health, education,
and welfare arms. "Supply-side" tax cuts for the "investor class" or "one percent"
and austerity politics for lower strata sharply increased economic inequality,
and led to warnings about a new immobile Gilded Age in which one's fate
depends on family and inheritance (Piketty 2014; Milanovic 2016; Stiglitz
2018).[20] According to Wendy Brown (2015: 201, 207), neoliberal "economiza-
tion of political life and usurpation of *homo politicus* by *homo œconomicus*"
has undermined belief that the "demos should rule" and spurs "antidemocratic
authoritarianism."

Earlier aligned with postmodern sensibilities, Richard Rorty (1998) criticized
them sharply as well as left-leaning thinkers who made the linguistic turn and/
or contended that identity politics (politics of recognition) had replaced class
politics as sole basis of emancipatory hope. Skyrocketing economic inequality and gentrification under neoliberalism led him to attack the academic left
for stressing textual deconstruction and identity and ignoring class polarization and the rise of a twenty percent society in which only the professional
middle class (including the tenured professoriate) and the wealthy have the
resources to exercise full citizenship. Rorty (1999: 255–61) called for a "return
to class politics" on the American Left but understood that a realizable vision
of a democratic alternative and collective agent to bring it into being would
have to be fashioned anew. Engaging in an immanent critique, Rorty discussed

---

19   Despite divergence in ultimate beliefs, market liberals and cultural conservatives allied
      politically in the Republican Party, which was decisive in forging neoliberal hegemony in
      the United States. "New Democrats," especially Bill Clinton, contributed to the neoliberal
      policy shift, but usually opposed the Republican Party's draconian economic and cultural
      policies.

20   Long before Piketty, Bennett Harrison and Barry Bluestone (1988) analyzed incisively the
      nascent, political-economic "Great U-turn"-the neoliberal drift away from the egalitar-
      ian policies of social-liberalism toward reduced union power, polarized labor markets,
      increased economic insecurity, middle-class squeeze and decline, and much sharper dis-
      parities of income and wealth.

Walt Whitman and John Dewey and other progressive intellectual and political advocates of the later nineteenth and early twentieth century, American
"Reformist Left," who animated substantial sociocultural and sociopolitical change
against formidable market-liberal elites. Rorty posed sociopolitical resources
embedded in cultural and political history against one-dimensional neoliberal
culture. Rather than turning back the clock, he aimed to rediscover, reconstruct,
and redeploy progressive culture to illuminate nascent contradictions of neoliberal capitalism and to inspire a mobilization for regime change. His immanent
critique appealed to historically specific facets of the American progressive tradition to illuminate the class contradictions obscured by excessive pessimism of
one-dimensional neoliberal culture, which ruled imperiously. Presciently, Rorty
warned that continued failure to acknowledge and mitigate the gross inequities of
neoliberal austerity would motivate return of "Weimar-like," extreme rightwing,
authoritarian forces who would mobilize growing class resentment of the "non-
suburban [white] electorate" by blaming liberal elites and minorities for the economic decline and making them public enemies (Rorty 1998: 88–91).

4   New Right Populism: The Alternative to Neoliberalism?

> We advocate the primacy of politics over economics.
>
> FRIBERG 2015: 30

The aforementioned late 1980s turn to Carl Schmitt and populist New Right
in the 1990s by the *Telos* circle aimed to elaborate theoretical resources and
nascent political forces that could revive organic negativity and reverse the
depoliticization cheered by Friedman and criticized by Brown.[21] Although
bitterly opposed to the neoliberal reduction of politics to economics, Piccone
rejected just as scathingly social-liberal egalitarianism and statism, and thus
concurred with substantial facets of market-liberal critiques of redistribution,
regulation, and the state (Piccone 1993). He thought that populism's "organic"
politics and sociocultural solidarity could displace neoliberal economism and
globalism and insure terminal demise of the moribund left. In retrospective

---

21   The *Telos* circle's turn to Schmitt began with a special section in *Telos* Number 71
      (Spring 1987) followed by an entire issue Number 72 (Summer 1987) devoted to him. See
      Bendersky (2018) on *Telos'* long, substantial, and continuing engagement with Schmitt.
      They introduced the French New Right to English language readers in a special double
      issue Numbers 98–99 (Winter 1993-Spring 1994). The journal published much more on
      the topic in later issues along with coverage of other right-wing populist and federalist
      movements, such as Italy's *Lega Nord*.

reflection about *Telos'* direction after 100 issues, Piccone (1994) declared that the course had been set nearly two decades earlier by his artificial negativity thesis, which portrayed the sociopolitical damages of extreme one-dimensionality and cultural homogenization and identified the social-liberal New Class as the collective subject who orchestrated the declinist shift. He advocated a populist "vindication of particularity" via disempowerment of the New Class and eradication of Fordist leveling forces – multiculturalism, egalitarian ideals, universal human rights, and liberal democracy. Concurring with Piccone, paleoconservative Schmittean, Paul Gottfried (1994: 172) and *Telos* Editorial Associate asserted, in his "After Liberalism," that the journal's "towering contribution" has been its exposure of liberal democracy as flagrantly undemocratic. This "illiberal" assessment resonates with the populist right today.[22]

The Schmitt revival was underway before the *Telos* special issues and diverse thinkers and venues around the globe have engaged his work and stressed its relevance for contemporary politics. Although his critique of market-liberalism influenced some left-leaning thinkers, his ideas have been much more impactful among rightwing populists and ethnoracial nationalists.[23] He earlier influenced authoritarian facets of Hayek's thought (Scheuerman 1984; Mirowski 2009: 442–46). Schmitt conceived of the world as a "multipolar pluriverse" of distinct national cultures grouped into spatially and culturally proximate "great spaces."[24] He thought that ethnically rooted national cultures are incommensurable, and that communication cannot bridge highly divergent cultural communities. Schmitt (1996 [1932]) argued that market-liberal possessive individualism, liberal-democratic pluralism, and multiparty politics produce a cacophony of discordant voices that undermine national solidarity and collective identity, and consequently "depoliticize" and "demilitarize" culture. Liberalism subordinates the state to the market and disempowers it he contended.[25] He held that a fundamental *friend-enemy* dichotomy animates

---

22 Gottfried's (1999) later book provided a Schmittean critique of social-liberal theory and "New Class" managerialism and advocated for a New-Right populist alternative.

23 On the influence of Schmitt, see Müller 2003; and for treatment of the wider movement of thought of which Schmitt has been a part, see Pels 1998. For divergent views of Schmitt, see Gottfried (1990); Wolin (1990); Agamben (2005); Mouffe (2006); Strong (2012: 218–62).

24 On states, spatial politics, blocs (*Grossraum* or great space), and the world order (Nomos), see, Schmitt (2003 [1950]); Benoist (2013: 90–107); Minca and Rowan (2015); Spector (2017).

25 Schmitt was more critical of market liberalism than Piccone. However, the New Right, which almost universally opposes domestic multiculturalism, cultural and political

all genuine politics and democracy – it unifies a nation by cultivating inexorable opposition to "others" or "strangers," who are "existentially something different and alien" (Schmitt 1996: 27). "The high points of politics are simultaneously the moments in which the enemy is, in concrete clarity, recognized as the enemy..." declared Schmitt (1996: 67). Enemies stir shared feelings of "passionate attachment" to one's group along with intense enmity toward the other who threatens them (Johnson 2011). Trump rally theatrics and chants of "lock her up," "build that wall," and "send them back" seem designed to stir these emotions. Thus, critics claim that the President "channels" Schmitt without having read him (Kolin 2017; Weiner 2018)

Schmitt formulated his conception of friend-enemy politics while Nazism was on the rise, and he served in the Hitler regime.[26] His illiberal vision of democracy stressed national solidarity animated by common cultural identity, hostility toward public enemies, and consequent mass submission to the political leadership. Schmitt held that a politicized nation, with citizenry keenly aware of their shared identity, are always prepared to mobilize and even die to defend their culture against enemies who threaten it. He argued that political leaders are empowered to declare a "state of exception" suspending law and instituting dictatorial rule in the name of the people (Schmitt 1996: 69–79). In contrast to liberal versions of democracy, he contended that "actual democracy" requires cultural "homogeneity" and restrictive citizenship that subordinate or eradicate the "foreign and unequal." Schmitt asserted that that no democracy has extended full citizenship or equal rights to all those they governed. In his view, democracy is simply identity of the ruler and the ruled, which is "not palpable reality," but can be forged by "acclimation" or "taken for granted" and manifested in the "power of democratic feeling." Dictatorships that generate such solidarity are in his view "democratic" (Schmitt 1988 [1923–26]: 6–17, 24–27).[27]

---

globalism, and open immigration, vary widely in their views of market liberalism, markets, and capitalism per se.

26   Theorists have debated the depth and duration of Schmitt's commitment to the Nazi regime. However, he joined the Nazi Party in 1933, expressed anti-Semitic views, intellectually justified the regime, served Hitler directly (e.g., defending the legality of the "Fuhrer's" murder of political opponents and purging Jews from the German legal system), and served as an important jurist in the early years of the regime (Lilla 1998; Müller 2003: 1–47; Vinx 2019).

27   From a Schmittean perspective, the adulation Hitler received from the crowd at the 1933 Nuremberg Rally and, after the German annexation of Austria, from the masses cheering his entry into Vienna in an open car are *prima facie* evidence of democracy by acclimation.

A sophisticated intellectual and creative theorist, Schmittean Alain de Benoist helped found the New Right movement in late 1960s France. He led GRECE (i.e., "Research and Study Group for European Civilization"), composed of hard-right French thinkers who combined ideas from Weimar Era, proto-Fascist Conservative Revolutionaries, including Schmitt[28] with New Left ideas about cultural struggle influenced by Western Marxist Antonio Gramsci. They aspired to be right-wing versions of Gramscian "organic intellectuals" and operate a center and journal paralleling the style of the early Frankfurt School. The group gained international attention in the late 1970s and early 1980s (O'Meara 2004: 14–56). Interest in Benoist's work spread to the English-speaking world in the late 1980s and 1990s, when he wrote regularly for *Telos* and to the "Alt Right" in the 2010s via internet.[29] Benoist deploys Schmittean ideas widely and meshes them with extreme rightwing theories and with other approaches, such as postmodernism and communitarianism (Müller 2003: 207–18; Sunic 2011: 83–90, passim; Benoist 2003, 2013).

Schmitt's influence is transparent in Benoist and Champetier's (2012 [1979]) coauthored manifesto for the French New Right. They depicted a profound sociocultural crisis characterized by commodification, homogenization, and depoliticization, and portrayed "liberalism" as the "main enemy." Advocating a "right to difference," Benoist and Champetier (2012) maintained that strong identities are cultivated by a Schmittean, global "pluraversum" of culturally unified nations bound by local and regional traditions and hierarchies and liberated from market-liberal individualism and social-liberal universalism and egalitarianism. While stopping short of forced mass deportations, they opposed immigration and implied that *ethnos* should be the basis of citizenship. They asserted that biology differentiates ethnoracial groupings and the genders and that denial of these intrinsic differences is racist and sexist. They contended that universal human rights level these particularities and liquidate culture and politics. They deployed Schmittean ideas against neoliberal globalization's economically subsumed politics, individualism, human rights,

---

28   Conservative Revolutionaries aimed to create an intellectual vanguard to provide a third-way alternative to what they believed to be the failed Left and failed market-liberalism.

29   Overlapping the New Right, Alt Right refers primarily to revived white nationalism that arose in the second decade of the twenty-first century (Neiwert 2017). They rally people against social-liberal and leftwing "political correctness" and "social justice warriors," Alt-Right conspiracy theories and propaganda are pervasive on internet and sometimes reach broader publics via Fox News, Breitbart News, Rush Limbaugh, and other AM Radio and media sites. President Trump and some of his advisors have been receptive to Alt-Right conspiracy theories and have deployed them politically. Alt-Right ideas, media sites, and groups have spread globally.

multiculturalism, and especially mass immigration from the Islamic world and Global South. Benoist and Champetier advocated "participatory democracy" but *sans* liberal democratic mechanisms designed to insure citizen participation, rule of law, and individual and minority rights. They implied convergence with the Schmitt's view that the identity of ruler and ruled, cultivated by homogeneous ethnoracial citizenship and by reproduction of local authority and traditions, constitutes democracy. Many others on the European New Right have been much more explicit about their "identitarian," ethnoracial nationalism, which Benoist's theories has helped inspire and legitimate. Claiming to oppose Fascism, racism, and nationalism and to embrace democratic communitarianism, Benoist today aims to broaden his audience and expand the New Right political base (O'Meara 2004; Sunic 2011; Williams 2017; Versluis 2014).

In "The Charlottesville Statement," American Alt-Right leader Richard Spencer (2017) expresses emphatically the white nationalist version of New Right politics. He has read and draws on the works of Carl Schmitt.[30] Seeing racial differences to be the "foundation of identity," Spencer holds that America is a White-Christian nation and that European ancestry should be the basis of citizenship. He argues that Jews are an "ethno-religious people," who are biologically differentiated from European peoples and who cannot be assimilated. In his view, heredity is the foundation of individual, group (gender, race, ethnic), and national differences (and distinguish the European family of nations). The sociocultural reproduction of nations and civilizations depend on preserving their biologically based order Spencer believes. He holds that higher education should be limited to those gifted by superior biology and that women are fated by their biology to be "mothers and caregivers." He attacks liberalism, multiculturalism, and globalism for deracinating and destroying identity and culture. Daniel Friberg's (2017) manifesto for the European Alt Right parallels Spencer's views and both borrow heavily from Benoist and Schmitt.[31] Friberg contends that ethnic identity is the "natural point of departure for political organization" and that parliamentary processes "can never be more than complements

---

30   Spencer was a leading figure in the 2017 spring and summer white supremacist protests in Charlottesville, Virginia. Spencer coined the term Alt Right, heads the National Policy Institute, a white supremacist think tank, founded altright.com, and is a leading white supremacist (Wood 2017). Spencer worked and coedited a book with aforementioned Schmittean Paul Gottfried (*Telos* Editorial Associate), who disavows antisemitism and racial politics.

31   A leading Swedish New Rightest inspired by Alain de Benoist, Friberg founded far-right Arktos Media and Motpol think tank, cofounded the Altright Corporation with Richard Spencer, and was a cofounder and serves as the European Editor of altright.com (Stavrou 2017).

to broader cultural and political work." Following Benoist's (1993–1994) vision of a Schmittean "great space" or *Grossraum*, Freiberg envisions a new Europe like ancient empires, with federated nations that base citizenship on group rights rooted in shared ethnicity, culture, history, language, and biological difference. The New Right and Alt Right envision "organic democracy" to be an "ethnically homogenous and culturally cohesive community." Shared values, habits, and sentiments would be the basis of participation, rather than liberal democratic processes and bureaucracy (O'Meara 2004: 194–97). Schmittean "democracy by acclamation" lurks here.

Spencer (2017) sees the left as "an ideology of death" that must be crushed politically. Following Benoist, however, he and other Alt-Right theorists contend that they are practicing "metapolitics" inspired by Western Marxist Antonio Gramsci's views about engaging in cultural warfare to overcome and attain "cultural hegemony." Alt-Right thinkers argue that Frankfurt School critical theorists won the Fordist era culture war that produced the social-liberal Great Society. They see the works of Adorno and Horkheimer, which I have described above as pessimistic and no longer Marxist, to be the font of "Cultural Marxist" ideas that shaped New Class thought, inspired their triumphant cultural war, and perpetuated their hegemony thereafter (Surtrson 2017). They contend that critical theorists inspired the New Class takeover of higher education, government bureaucracy, mainstream media, and other important sociocultural venues (e.g., see O'Meara 2004: 43–56; Freiberg 2015; Benoist 2019). They portray critical theorists as a kind of brain trust for the New Class, which still rules the centers of cultural power and "Deep State." This conspiracy theory is rooted in historical anti-Semitic currents still embraced by many on the Alt Right and often expressed on their social media. They point to the Jewish origins of second-generation critical theorists to imply or express directly anti-Semitic views. They see themselves as *the* cultural vanguard struggling to reverse the "Great Replacement" engineered by the New Class, who subverted formerly hegemonic, traditional White European, gentile values and institutions. We can trace this argument about cultural Marxism back at least to the 1990s, but the Alt Right revived, embellished, and spread it widely via internet. Alt-Rightists refer to it casually and often.[32] This conspiracy even reached a receptive President Trump in a

---

32   The idea of Marxists subverting culture goes back to Nazism and before, but today's Alt-Right versions likely originated in the circle of the mercurial radical and seven-time presidential candidate Lyndon Larouche (see Minnicino 1992). Paleoconservatives William S. Lind and Pat Buchanan later wrote apocalyptic novels that that treated Cultural Marxists as the enemy and have regularly propounded on the Cultural Marxist threat. Andrew Breitbart helped spread this narrative in his writings and via Breitbart News and

National Security Council memo alleging that deep state Cultural Marxists and their New Class agents have orchestrated the subversive war against Trump and his Administration.[33] Conspiratorial and racist ideas of the Alt Right, pervasive on internet, penetrate wider circles of public life and blur the borders between what people once deemed unacceptable and legitimate public discourse.

5   History Opens Again: Crises of Capitalism and Immanent Critique Redux

... we are living in the throes of an epochal crisis of capitalism...[34]

NANCY FRASER 2018

Our house is on fire![35]

GRETA THUNBERG 2019

Michael Thompson (2016: 1–38, 196) argues that Habermas' effort to escape the cul-de-sac of negative dialectics via his linguistic turn "domesticated" critical theory by breaking with the critique of capitalism and anchoring it in "linguistically mediated intersubjectivity." Former Habermas assistant and successor to his Chair in Frankfurt, Axel Honneth revised his mentor's approach by rooting critical theory in "recognition," but this revision still decoupled it from capitalism and "from the concrete foundations of social power nested in economic life..." Thompson (2016: 64) argues.[36] He holds that they made this theoretical

---

other media. On this conspiracy narrative, see Jay (2011); Huyssen (2017); Ross (2016); Jamin (2018); Moyn (2018); Hanebrink (2018); and Wilson (2019). On the critical theory and rightwing populism, see Abromeit (2016).

33   The President reportedly loved the May 2017, 3500-word memo, which may have influenced his resistance to condemn the Charlottesville White Nationalist marchers in August of that year. The memo writer, Rich Higgins was later fired by the National Security Council (POTUS and Political Warfare 2017; Winter and Groll 2017; Heer 2017). Many rightwing thinkers refer to the Cultural Marxist conspiracy. For example, Swedish mass murderer Anders Brevick rants about it in his ethnonationalist manifesto. Other politicians and cultural critics, such as Rand Paul and Jordan Peterson, have alleged Cultural Marxist debasement of mainstream liberal culture and politics. Brazilian President Jair Balsonaro's Foreign Minister Ernesto Araújo has portrayed climate change as a Cultural Marxist plot (Watts 2018).

34   See Fraser and Jaeggi (2018: 10).

35   See Workman (2019), for the quotation and statement by Greta Thunberg.

36   One of only two scholars who passed their Habilitation with Habermas. Honneth aimed to continue Habermas' general trajectory (Müller-Doohm 2016: 195, 228, 317, 336).

shift when neoliberalism was arising, becoming hegemonic, and recreating capitalist political economic and cultural contradictions paralleling earlier versions of market liberalism prior to Fordist rule. Convergent with Thompson's criticism, Moishe Postone (2017: 139) contends that Habermasians and others, who concurred in part with Horkheimer and other earlier pessimistic critical theorists that cultural conditions neutralized immanent critique of capitalism, presupposed Fordist political-economic reality. Postone (2017: 160–61) argues that "supersession of the 'Fordist' accumulation regime" by "neoliberal global capitalism" calls for reviving "the critical theory of capitalism." He holds that capitalist society today retains its "two-dimensional" or "contradictory character" so that immanent critique and depth models are still viable, necessary tools for critical theory.

Rahel Jaeggi asserts, "For a long time, capitalism had been largely absent from political and intellectual debates. It was even absent from the agenda of 'critical theory'. ... But now the interest in capitalism is surging" (Fraser and Jaeggi 2018: 1). Nancy Fraser agrees with Jaeggi but qualifies that critical theory should not be exclusively economic. She says it should engage "capitalist society," because the crisis is "also ecological, political and social" (Fraser and Jaeggi 2018: 10).[37] Fraser and Jaeggi (2018: 10–12, 138–64) contend that envisioning emancipatory alternatives today must start with immanent criticism of capitalism. Revived Hegelian-Marxian immanent critique need not pit political economy against theories and movements that illuminate other forms of domination and cruelty. Critical theorists engage sociocultural injustice (e.g., racial, gender, immigrant, ecological) as well as its economic forms. Income polarization and casualization of work cuts across almost all racial, ethnic, and religious groups. Critical theorists, who engage these intersections and identitarian ethnoracial politics, anchor their criticism, at least implicitly, in an immanent normative ethos stressing the need to secure a just distribution of the means of participation, recognition, and human flourishing and their necessary biophysical, socioeconomic, and

---

37   Following Fraser's advice does not necessitate a singular, totalizing theory of capitalist society, which would risk oversimplification or excessive complexity. For example, a critical theory focusing explicitly on the economic features of neoliberal globalization and closely related sociocultural conditions that enable it does not foreclose space for other domain-specific critical theories. If critical theory is to engage forms of domination and cruelty that are part of capitalist society but have causal mechanisms largely or completely independent of capitalist economic relations, they call for their own specific theories, analytical strategies, languages, and social movements. All belong to the *plural* practice of critical theory if they share its emancipatory intent and employ its method of immanent critique.

cultural foundations. This standpoint calls for protecting, reimagining, and radically reconstructing liberal democratic institutions, eroded by plutocracy and under attack by ethnoracial demagoguery. Meshing "class politics" with "politics of recognition" means seeking societal-wide democracy and a transnational culture capable of reducing economic inequality and cruelty and averting growing threats of political economic and ecological catastrophe.[38]

By depleting the political-economic and sociocultural substructure of liberal democracy, neoliberals attenuated its substantive meaning for everyday life and opened way for globally resurgent ethnoracial nationalism (Brown 2015; Milanovic 2016: 204–11; Neiwert 2017; Mounk 2018: 53–131; Antonio 2019). Right-wing populists exploit the failure of mainstream political parties to address the contradictions of neoliberalism. President Trump's mantras "make America great again" and "build that wall" played on economic fears, resentment, and precarity entwined with ethnoracial hostility.[39] Critical theorist, Wolfgang Streeck (2017: 14) argues that we are in an "interregnum" or "a period of uncertain duration in which an old order is dying, but a new one cannot yet be born."[40] He contends that income inequality, financial instability, institutional failure, and the "post-factual politics" of rightwing populists has created legitimacy problems for the neoliberal regime. In the Covid-19 pandemic, the staggering policy failures of the Trump Administration dwarf the mismanagement of the Hurricane Katrina and the 2008–09 financial crisis. The exceptional institutional failure and enormous loss of life and economic devastation caused by the pandemic in the United States illuminated the incapacities and limits of the neoliberal structure of accumulation and could lead to a terminal crisis of regime (Packer 2020). Prior to the pandemic, Jaeggi argued that decades of neoliberal political economic and sociocultural depletion of democracy call for "a form of immanent critique that finds its starting point not 'positively,' in already shared values, but in the immanent crises and contradictions inherent

---

38   Misunderstood by most first generation Frankfurt School theorists, recent critical theorists (e.g., Habermas and Fraser) have shown increased appreciation of John Dewey's thought. Dewey (e.g., 1989 [1939]) held that only forging an egalitarian, deliberative democracy could preserve what was left of liberal democratic institutions and stem the rising tide of Fascism and Stalinism.

39   On the role of economic stagnation and insecurity motivating Trump supporters, see Mounk (2018: 151–60). See Smith and Hanley (2018), on ethnoracial hostility motivating Trump's base.

40   Antonio Gramsci originally employed the term to describe interwar war period when market-liberal hegemony eroded, but the successor regime had not yet been determined. See Stahl (2019).

in the dynamic of forms of life" (Fraser and Jaeggi 2018: 10). That should start by addressing two profoundly dangerous crises made more transparent by the Covid-19 pandemic.

First, neoliberal capitalism reversed the mid-twentieth century trend toward increased economic equality. Leading advocate and implementer of the neoliberal regime, the United States is the most economically unequal rich nation. In 1978, the bottom 50 percent of the American income pyramid received 20 percent of national income and the top 1 percent about 10 percent. Those figures have nearly reversed. The 2019 income of about 122 million adult lower-half earners averages only $18,500 before taxes and transfers. The 2.4 million top 1percent earners average $1.5 million. The 400 richest Americans own more wealth than 150 million bottom 60 percent earners, whose share of national wealth dropped from 5.7 in 1987 percent to 2.1 in 2014 (Saez and Zucman 2019: 4–7; Ingraham 2019). Economists tracking increased inequality warn that the United States is becoming an immobile plutocracy, where inheritance and luck determines one's fate rather than merit (Piketty 2014; Milanovic 2016). Economic inequality has increased in other rich countries, but most sharply in the neoliberal heartland nations (Zucman 2019). Globalization improved well-being for many in some parts of the world, but inequality has grown sharply, and immense numbers of casual workers suffer precarity. Immiseration of low-wage workers and immobility and insecurity of middling earners is grist for populist demagogues. Americans have record levels of public and private debt (Egan 2019), which COVID-19 economic contraction has made profoundly problematic and even perilous.[41]

A second crisis arises from a massive expansion of the global economy relative to the biosphere, which has vastly increased resource throughput and waste production (Daly 2015). The postcommunist consolidation of global capitalism and relentless neoliberal growth imperative accelerated this trend and put natural systems and vital ecological services in peril. The feedback effects between global ecological problems make this degradation increasingly unpredictable and potentially catastrophic. A recent major report holds that likely consequences are so severe that, "Urgent action at an unprecedented scale is necessary to arrest and reverse the situation" (UN

---

[41] Just prior to the Covid-19 crisis, President Trump declared repeatedly that he had led the creation of "the greatest economy ever." At that time, 39 percent of American adults could not cover an unexpected $400 expense with cash, a check, or credit card; 17 percent could not meet their monthly expenses; 25 percent could not afford and had to skip necessary medical care; 25 percent had no savings or pension for retirement (Federal Reserve Board 2019: 1–4).

Environment 2019: 4, 8).[42] Climate change is the most dangerous, fast moving ecological problem. Policymaking elites resist addressing its main driver – the neoliberal policy regime's pursuit of unregulated, exponential economic growth (Anderson and Bows 2012). The Rio Declaration, signed by more than 175 nations in 1992, enumerated necessary measures to avoid catastrophic impacts, but policymakers have been unable to agree on binding rules to achieve the goals. Powerful political economic interests, disinformation machines and, publics unwilling to accept the costs block collective action. A one-degree Celsius increase in global temperatures above its preindustrial levels has already caused irreversible melting of glaciers, destabilization of the West Antarctica and Greenland Ice Sheets, substantial sea level rise and coastal flooding, forced migrations from floods and droughts, extreme heat waves, and other problems. The most devastating impacts of climate change have been in poor nations that have the least capacity to adapt to it and have contributed least to its drivers. Leading climate scientists contend that averting catastrophe requires restricting the global temperature rise to 1.5 degree Celsius (IPCC 2018). "Business as usual," however, will likely produce more than a 4-degree rise. Even if implemented, current global mitigation plans have only a fifty percent chance of limiting the temperature rise to 3 degrees, which many climate scientists argue insure widespread global catastrophic consequences (Committee on Climate Change: 2019).

Although an alternative regime is not in sight, mitigating global economic inequality and ecological devastation require global cooperation, planning, and redistribution. These needs provide a departure point for rethinking capitalism, as we have known it. With remarkable eloquence and moral clarity, 16-year old Greta Thunberg told the neoliberal policy elite at the World Economic Forum that climate crisis calls for "transformational action" of this sort.[43] She

---

42 "Key actions include reducing land degradation, biodiversity loss, and air, land and water pollution; improving water management and resource management; climate change mitigation and adaptation; resource efficiency; addressing decarbonization, decoupling and detoxification; and the prevention and management of risk and disasters. Those all require vastly more ambitious and effective policies, including sustainable consumption and production, greater resource efficiency and improved resource management, integrated ecosystem management, and integrated waste management and prevention" (UN Environment 2019: 4).

43 Thunberg is a powerful voice in a wave of global youth oriented social movements that cut across national boundaries, race, gender, and other identities. Struggles of young people against neoliberal austerity and authoritarianism have been intensifying along with street protests against repressive illiberal regimes (e.g., in Lebenon; Chile; Hong Kong). The latest UN greenhouse gas emissions report portrays its findings as "bleak" but sees young climate and ecological protestors as a hopeful sign of a possible political awakening (UNEP 2019: iv).

asserted that policy elites know we must reduce greenhouse gas radically or face catastrophe for humanity and for other living things with which we share the planet. We know what we must do but lack the "political will" she asserts (Workman 2019). Her call for immediate collective action echoes UN Environmental Programs (2019: 19) scientists. The neoliberal regime ultimately undercuts the social and biophysical bases of economic growth and threatens civilization and life, as we have known them, and upholds Marx's worst fears about out of control capitalism generating a cruel, unequal society in which poverty grows amongst affluence and disrupting profoundly the "metabolic interaction" between humans and the planet. The "full world" and ecological wall preclude exponential unplanned growth from continuing to be the alleged solution for nearly all problems. The crisis conditions of the neoliberal regime are rooted in capitalism per se, as we have known it. There is no sustainable way back to the alleged postwar fusion of capitalism and democracy, which was reliant on the growth imperative. The looming specter of illiberal capitalism propelled by authoritarian ethnoracial nationalism obliterates the wistful vision of a liberal democratic "end of history," which neoliberals claimed to usher in, and makes formulation and creation of a sustainable deliberative democratic alternative an urgent task. The historical conditions and resources for critical theorists exercising immanent criticism of capitalism to theorize and possibly help motivate this democratic reconstruction are at hand.

Acknowledgements

For my teacher Pasquale Caracciolo. Thanks to Jeremiah Morelock for his excellent criticism of an earlier draft, which contributed substantially to this essay.

References

Abromeit, John. 2016. "Critical Theory and the Persistence of Right-Wing Populism." *Logos*. At http://logosjournal.com/2016/abromeit/(accessed June 9, 2019).

Adorno, Theodore W. 1981 [1967]. *Prisms*. Cambridge: The MIT Press.

Agamben, Giorgio. 2005. *State of Exception*. Chicago: University of Chicago Press.

Anderson, Kevin and Alice Bows. 2012. "A New Paradigm for Climate Change." *Nature Climate Change* 2(9): 639–40. https://doi.org/10.1038/nclimate1646.

Anderson, Perry. 2000. "Renewals." *New Left Review* (Second Series) 1: 5–24.

Antonio, Robert J. 1981. "Immanent Critique as the Core of Critical Theory: Its Origins in Hegel, Marx and Contemporary Theory." *British Journal of Sociology* 32(3): 330–45.

Antonio, Robert J. 1989. "The Normative Foundations of Emancipatory Theory: Evolutionary Versus Pragmatic Perspectives." *American Journal of Sociology* 94(4): 721–748.

Antonio, Robert J. 1998. "Mapping Postmodern Social Theory," ed. Alan Sica, 22–75. *What is Social Theory?* Malden, MA: Blackwell.

Antonio, Robert J. 2011. "Absolutizing Particularity." In *A Journal of No Illusions*, eds. Ben Agger and Tim Luke, 23–46. New York: Telos Press.

Antonio, Robert J. 2017. "Immanent Critique and the Exhaustion Thesis: Neoliberalism and History's Vicissitudes." In *The Palgrave Handbook of Critical Theory*, ed. Michael J. Thompson, 655–76. New York: Palgrave Macmillan.

Antonio, Robert J. 2019. "Ethnoracial Populism: An Alternative to Neoliberal Globalization?" *Social Epistemology* 35(4), October: 280–97. https://doi.org/10.1080/02691728.2019.1638984.

Aronson, Ronald. 2014. "Marcuse Today." *Boston Review* (November 17). At http://webcache.googleusercontent.com/search?q=cache:Oo2GjwbpYVwJ:bostonreview.net/books-ideas/ronald-aronson-herbert-marcuse-one-dimensional-man-today&hl=en&gl=us&strip=1&vwsrc=0.

Baudrillard, Jean.1983a. *Simulations*. New York: Semiotext(e).

Baudrillard, Jean. 1983b. *In the Shadow of the Silent Majorities*. New York: Semiotext(e).

Becker, Michael E. 2018. "On Immanent Critique in Hegel's *Phenomenology*." *Hegel Bulletin* (June 20): 1–23. https://doi.org/10.1017/hgl.2018.8.

Bell, Daniel. 1976. *The Cultural Contradictions of Capitalism*. New York: Basic Books.

Bendersky, Joseph W. 2018. "On the Road to Damascus: The *Telos* Engagement with Carl Schmitt." *Telos* 183: 69–94.

Benhabib, Seyla. 1986. *Critique, Norm, and Utopia*. New York: Columbia University Press.

Benoist, Alain de. 1993–1994. "The Idea of Empire." *Telos* 98–99: 81–98.

Benoist, Alain de. 2003. "Schmitt in France." *Telos* 126: 133–52.

Benoist, Alain de. 2013. *Carl Schmitt Today*. London: Arktos.

Benoist, Alain de and Charles Champetier. 2012 [1979]. *Manifesto for a European Renaissance*. London: Arktos.

Benoist, Alain de. 2019. "Antonio Gramsci." *Arktos* (May 2). At https://arktos.com/2019/05/02/antonio-gramsci/.

Bloom, Alan. 1987. *The Closing of the American Mind*. New York: Simon and Schuster.

Bobbio, Norbeto. 1996. Left & Right. Chicago: University of Chicago Press.

Brown, Wendy. 2015. *Undoing the Demos*. Brooklyn: Zone Books.

Browne, Craig. 2008. "The End of Immanent Critique." *European Journal of Social Theory* 11(1): 5–24. https://doi.org/10.1177/1368431007085285.

Daly, Herman. 2015. "Economics for a Full World." *Great Transition Initiative* (June). At https://greattransition.org/images/Daly-Economics-for-a-Full-World.pdf.

Dubiel, Helmut. 1985. *Theory and Politics*. Cambridge: The MIT Press.

Eagan, Matt 2019. "Americans Now Have a Record $14 Trillion in Debt." *CNN Business* (November 13). At https://www.cnn.com/2019/11/13/business/household-debt-student-loans-fed/index.html.

Engels, Friedrich. [1888] 1948. "Preface." In *The Communist Manifesto*, 3–7. New York: International Publishers.

Engels, Friedrich. 1959 [1890–1894]. "Letters on Historical Materialism." In *Marx and Engels: Basic Writings on Politics and Philosophy*, ed. Lewis S, Feuer, 395–412. Garden City: Anchor Books.

Federal Reserve Board. 2019. *Report on the Economic Well-Being of U.S. Households in 2018* (May). At https://www.federalreserve.gov/publications/files/2018-report-economic-well-being-us-households-201905.pdf.

Foster, John Bellamy and Brett Clark. 2020. *The Robbery of Nature: Capitalism and Ecological Rift.* New York: Monthly Review.

Fraser, Nancy and Rahel Jaeggi. 2018. *Capitalism: A Conversation in Critical Theory.* Cambridge, UK: Polity.

Friberg, Daniel. 2015. *The Real Right Returns.* London: Arktos.

Friberg, Daniel. 2017. "Ideological Principles of for the European Alt-Right." *AltRight. com.* At https://altright.com/2017/10/03/ideological-principles-for-the-european-alt-right/(accessed September 29, 2019).

Friedman, Thomas L. 2000. *The Lexus and the Olive Tree.* New York: Anchor Books.

Fukuyama, Francis. 1989. "The End of History?" *The National Interest* 16: 3–35.

Giddens, Anthony. 1994. *Beyond Left and Right.* Stanford: Stanford University Press.

Gottfried, Paul Edward. 1990. *Carl Schmitt: Politics and Theory.* Westport: Praeger Publishers.

Gottfried, Paul Edward. 1994. "After Liberalism." *Telos* 101: 169–72.

Gottfried, Paul Edward. 1999. *After Liberalism.* Princeton: Princeton University Press.

Habermas, Jürgen. 1979 [1976]. *Communication and the Evolution of Society.* Boston: Beacon Press.

Habermas, Jürgen. 1984 [1981]. *The Theory of Communicative Action: Reason and the Rationalization of Society*, Vol. 1. Boston: Beacon Press.

Habermas, Jürgen. 1987a [1981]. *The Theory of Communicative Action: Lifeworld and System: A Critique of Functionalist Reason*, Vol. 2. Boston: Beacon Press.

Habermas, Jürgen. 1987b [1985]. *The Philosophical Discourse of Modernity.* Cambridge: The MIT Press.

Hanebrink, Paul. 2018. *A Spector Haunting Europe.* Cambridge: Harvard University Press.

Harrison, Bennett and Barry Bluestone. 1988. *The Great U-Turn.* New York: Basic Books.

Harvey, David. 1989. *The Condition of Postmodernity.* Cambridge: Basil Blackwell.

Hayek, Friedrich. 1944. *The Road to Serfdom.* Chicago: University of Chicago Press.

Hayek, Friedrich. 1978. *Law Legislation and Liberty Vol. 2 The Mirage of Social Justice.* Chicago: University of Chicago Press.

Heer, Jeet. 2017. "Trump's Racism and the Myth of 'Cultural Marxism.'" *The New Republic* (August 15). At https://newrepublic.com/article/144317/trumps-racism-myth-cultural-marxism.

Horkheimer, Max. 1972a [1936]. "Authority and the Family." In *Critical Theory: Selected Essays*, ed. Max Horkheimer, 47–128. New York: Herder and Herder.

Horkheimer, Max. 1972b [1937]. "Traditional and Critical Theory." In *Critical Theory: Selected Essays*, ed. Max Horkheimer, 188–243. New York: Herder and Herder.

Horkheimer, Max. 1972c [1941]. "Art and Mass Culture." In *Critical Theory: Selected Essays*, ed. Max Horkheimer, 273–90. New York: Herder and Herder.

Horkheimer, Max. 1973 [1942]. "The Authoritarian State." *Telos* 15: 3–20.

Horkheimer, Max. 1974 [1947]. *Eclipse of Reason*. New York: Seabury Press.

Horkheimer, Max and Theodor W. Adorno. 1972a [1944]. *Dialectic of Enlightenment*. New York: Seabury Press.

Horkheimer, Max and Theodor W. Adorno. 1972b [1969]. "Preface to the New Edition, ix-x." *Dialectic of Enlightenment*. New York: Seabury Press.

Huyssen, Andreas. 2017. "Breitbart, Bannon, Trump, and the Frankfurt School." *Public Seminar* (September, 28). At http://www.publicseminar.org/2017/09/breitbart-bannon-trump-and-the-frankfurt-school/.

Ingraham, Christopher. 2019. "Wealth Concentration Returning to 'levels Last Seen in the Roaring Twenties,' According to New Research." *Washington Post* (February 8). At https://www.washingtonpost.com/us-policy/2019/02/08/wealth-concentration-returning-levels-last-seen-during-roaring-twenties-according-new-research/.

IPCC. 2018. "Summery for Policymakers." Global Warming of 1.5°C. October. At https://www.ipcc.ch/site/assets/uploads/sites/2/2019/05/SR15_SPM_version_report_LR.pdf.

Jameson, Fredric. 1984. "Postmodernism, or the Cultural Logic of Late Capitalism." *New Left Review* 146: 53–92.

Jameson, Fredric. 2003. "Future City." *New Left Review* 21: 65–79.

Jamin, Jérôme. 2018. "Cultural Marxism: A Survey." *Religion Compass* 12(1–2). At https://onlinelibrary.wiley.com/doi/pdf/10.1111/rec3.12258.

Jay, Martin. 1973. *The Dialectical Imagination*. Boston: Little, Brown and Company.

Jay, Martin. 2011. "Dialectic of Counter-Enlightenment: The Frankfurt School as Scapegoat of the Lunatic Fringe." *CISA* (December 22). At http://canisa.org/blog/dialectic-of-counter-enlightenment-the-frankfurt-school-as-scapegoat-of-the-lunatic-fringe.

Jay, Martin. 2016. *Reason after its Eclipse*. Madison: University of Wisconsin Press.

Johnson, Greg. 2011. "Reflections on Carl Schmitt's *Concept of the Political*." *Counter-Currents Publishing* (February 24). At https://www.counter-currents.com/2011/02/reflections-on-carl-schmitts-the-concept-of-the-political/.

Kolin, Andrew. 2017. "Politics above Law: How Trump Channels Far Right icon Carl Schmitt Without Knowing it." *Informed Consent* (September). At https://www.juan-cole.com/2017/09/politics-channels-schmitt.html.

Larrain, Jorge. 1986. *A Reconstruction of Historical Materialism*. London: Allen & Unwin.

Lilla, Mark 1997. "The Enemy of Liberalism." *New York Review of Books* (May 15). At https://www.nybooks.com/articles/1997/05/15/the-enemy-of-liberalism/8.

Luke, Tim. 1978. "Culture and Politics in the Age of Artificial Negativity." *Telos* 35: 55–72.

Lyotard, Jean-François. 1984. *The Postmodern Condition: A Report on Knowledge*. Minneapolis: University of Minnesota Press.

Marcuse, Herbert. 1964. *One-Dimensional Man*. Boston: Beacon Press.

Marcuse, Herbert. 1968. *Negations*. Boston: Beacon Press.

Marcuse, Herbert. 1969. *An Essay on Liberation*. Boston: Beacon Press.

Marcuse, Herbert. 1971 [1958]. *Soviet Marxism: A Critical Analysis*. Harmondsworth Middlesex: Penguin Books.

Marx, Karl. 1963 [1852]. *The 18th Brumaire of Louis Bonaparte*. New York: International Publishers.

Marx, Karl. 1964 [1844]. *The Economic and Philosophic Manuscripts of 1844*, ed. Dirk J. Struik. New York: International Publishers.

Marx, Karl. 1967a [1867]. *Capital: A Critique of Political Economy*, Vol. l: *The Process of Capitalist Production*. New York: International Publishers.

Marx, Karl. 1967b [1894]. *Capital: A Critique of Political Economy*, Vol. 3: *The Process of Capitalist Production as a Whole*. New York: International Publishers.

Marx, Karl. 1975 [1837]. "A Letter from Marx to his Father." In Vol. 1 of *Karl Marx and Frederick Engels: Collected Works*, 10–21. New York: International Publishers.

Marx, Karl. 1976 [1865]. "Value, Price, and Profit." In *Wage-Labor and Capital & Value, Price, and Profit*, 1–62. New York: International Publishers.

Marx, Karl. 1977 [1845]. "Theses on Feuerbach" In *Karl Marx and Frederick Engels: Selected Works: In One Volume*, 28–30. New York: International Publishers.

Marx, Karl. 1987 [1859]. "A Contribution to the Critique of Political Economy." In Vol. 29 of *Karl Marx and Frederick Engels: Collected Works*, 257–417. New York: International Publishers.

Marx, Karl. 1989a [1875]. "Marginal Notes on the Programme of the German Worker's Program." In Vol. 24 of *Karl Marx and Frederick Engels Collected Works*, 81–99. New York: International Publishers.

Marx, Karl. 1989b [1881]. "Drafts of the Letter to Vera Zasulich." In Vol. 24 *Karl Marx and Frederick Engels Collected Works*, 346–371. New York: International Publishers.

Marx, Karl and Frederick Engels. 1948 [1848]. *The Communist Manifesto*. New York: International Publishers.

Marx, Karl and Frederick Engels. 1970 [1845–1846]. *The German Ideology*, ed. C. J. Arthur. New York: International Publishers.

McMurtry, John. 1978. *The Structure of Marx's Worldview*. Princeton: Princeton University Press.

Milanovic, Branko. 2016. *Global Inequality*. Cambridge: Belknap Press of Harvard University Press.

Minca, Claudio and Rory Rowan. 2015. "The Question of Space in Carl Schmitt." *Progress in Human Geography* 39(3): 268–289. https://doi.org/10.1177/0309132513517989.

.Minnicino, Michael. 1992. "The New Dark Age: The Frankfurt School and Political Correctness." *Fidelio* 1. At https://archive.schillerinstitute.com/fid_91-96/921_frankfurt.html.

Mirowski, Philip. 2009. "Postface: Defining Neoliberalism." In Philip Mirowski and Dieter Plehwe. 2009 *The Road from Mont Pelerin*, 417–55. Cambridge: Harvard University Press.

Mouffe, Chantal. 2006. *The Return of the Political*. London: Verso.

Mounk, Yascha. 2018. *The People versus Democracy*. Cambridge: Harvard University Press.

Moyn, Samuel. 2018. "The Alt-Right's Favorite Meme is 100 Years Old." *New York Times* (November 13). At https://www.nytimes.com/2018/11/13/opinion/cultural-marxism-anti-semitism.html.

Müller, Jan-Werner. 2003. *A Dangerous Mind*. New Haven: Yale University Press.

Müller-Doohm, Stefan. 2016. *Habermas: A Biography*. Cambridge, UK: Polity.

Neiwert, David. 2017. *Alt-America*. London: Verso.

Offe, Claus. 1996. *Modernity and the State*. Cambridge: MIT.

O'Meara, Michael. 2004. *New Culture, New Right*. Bloomington: 1stBooks.

Packer, George. 2020. "We Are Living in a Failed State." *The Atlantic* (June [Special Preview]). At https://www.theatlantic.com/magazine/archive/2020/06/underlying-conditions/610261/.

Pels, Dick. 1998. "Fascism and the Primacy of the Political." *Telos* 110: 39–70.

Piccone, Paul. 1978. "The Crisis of One-Dimensionality." *Telos* 35: 43–54.

Piccone, Paul. 1977. "The Changing Function of Critical Theory." *New German Critique* 12: 29–37.

Piccone, Paul. 1980. "The Future of Critical Theory." *Current Perspectives in Social Theory* (Vol. 1), eds. Scott G. McNall and Gary N. Howe, 21–30. Greenwich, CT: JAI Press.

Piccone, Paul. 1985. "The Telos Public Sphere" (Newsletter) (December 10). 1–21.

Piccone, Paul. 1987. "The Telos Public Sphere" (Newsletter) (October 19). 1–8.

Piccone, Paul. 1993. "Scapegoating Capitalism." *Telos* 97: 85–96.

Piccone, Paul. 1994. "From the New Left to the New Populism." *Telos* 101: 173–208.

Piketty, Thomas. 2014. *Capital in the Twenty-First Century*. Cambridge: Belknap Press of Harvard University Press.

Postone, Moishe. 2017. "Critical Theory and the Historical Transformations of Capitalist Modernity." In *The Palgrave Handbook of Critical Theory*, ed. Michael J. Thompson, 137–63. New York: Palgrave Macmillan.

POTUS & Political Warfare. 2017. (National Security Council Memo) (May). At https://assets.documentcloud.org/documents/3922874/Political-Warfare.pdf.

Rorty, Richard. 1998. *Achieving Our County*. Cambridge: Harvard University Press.

Rorty, Richard. 1999. *Philosophy and Social Hope*. London: Penguin Books.

Ross, Alex. 2016. "The Frankfurt School Knew Trump Was Coming." *The New Yorker* (December 5). At https://www.newyorker.com/culture/cultural-comment/the-frankfurt-school-knew-trump-was-coming.

Saez, Emmanuel and Gabriel Zuchman. 2019. *The Triumph of Justice*. New York: Norton.

Scheuerman, William E. 1984. "The Unholy Alliance of Carl Schmitt and Friedrich A. Hayek." *Constellations* 4(2): 172–88. https://doi.org/10.1111/1467–8675.00047.

Schmitt, Carl. 1988 [1923–26]. *The Crisis of Parliamentary Democracy*. Cambridge: The MIT Press.

Schmitt, Carl. 1996 [1932]. *The Concept of the Political*. Chicago: University of Chicago Press.

Schmitt, Carl. 2003 [1950]. *The Nomos of the Earth*. New York: Telos Press.

Shaw, William H. 1978. *Marx's Theory of History*. Stanford: Stanford University Press.

Smith, David Norman. 2017. "Theory and Class Consciousness." In *The Palgrave Handbook of Critical Theory*, ed. Michael J. Thompson, 369–423. New York: Palgrave Macmillan.

Smith, David Norman and Eric Hanley. 2018. "The Anger Games: Who Voted for Donald Trump in the 2016 Election and Why." *Critical Sociology* 44(2): 195–212. https://doi.org/10.1177/0896920517740615.

Spector, Matthew. 2017. "*Grossraum* and Geopolitics: Resituating Schmitt in an Atlantic Context." *History and Theory* 56(3): 398–406. https://doi.org//10.1111/hith.12028.

Spencer, Richard. 2017. "What it Means to be Alt-Right." *AltRight.com* (August 11). At https://altright.com/2017/08/11/what-it-means-to-be-alt-right/.

Stahl, Rune Møller. 2019. "Ruling in the Interregnum: Politics and Ideology in Nonhegemonic Times." *Politics and Society* 47(3): 333–60. https://doi.org/10.1177/0032329219851896.

Stavrou, David. 2017. "How Sweden Became a Thriving Base of neo-Nazi Ideology" (December 30). At https://www.haaretz.com/world-news/europe/.premium.MAGAZINE-how-sweden-became-a-thriving-base-of-neo-nazi-ideology-1.5629892.

Stiglitz, Joseph. 2018. "The American Economy Is Rigged." *Scientific American* (November 1). At https://www.scientificamerican.com/article/the-american-economy-is-rigged/.

Streeck, Wolfgang. 2017. "The Return of the Repressed." *New Left Review* 104: 5–18.

Strong, Tracey B. 2012. *Politics Without Vision*. Chicago: University of Chicago Press.

Sunic, Tomislav. 2011. *Against Democracy and Equality*. London: Arktos.

Surtrson, Jossur. 2017. "Identitarianism and the Great Replacement." *AltRight.Com*. At https://altright.com/2017/05/12/identitarianism-and-the-great-replacement/ (accessed September 30, 2019).

Thompson, Michael J. 2016. *The Domestication of Critical Theory*. London: Rowman & Littlefield.

UN Environment. 2019. "Summary for Policymakers." Global Environmental Outlook-GEO6. Nairobi. https://doi.org/10.1017/9781108639217.

UNEP. 2019. "Emission Gap Report 2019." *Executive Summary*. United Nations Environmental Programme. At https://newclimate.org/wp-content/uploads/2019/11/EGR19ESEN.pdf.

Versluis, Arthur. 2014. "A Conversation with Alain de Benoist." *Journal for the Study of Radicalism* 8(2): 79–106.

Vinx, Lars, "Carl Schmitt." 2019. *The Stanford Encyclopedia of Philosophy*, ed. Edward N. Zalta. At https://plato.stanford.edu/entries/schmitt/.

Watts, Jonathan. 2018. "Brazil's New Foreign Minister Believes Climate Change is a Marxist Plot." *Guardian* (November 15). At https://www.theguardian.com/world/2018/nov/15/brazil-foreign-minister-ernesto-araujo-climate-change-marxist-plot.

Weiner, Mark S. 2018. "Trumpism and the Philosophy of World Order." *Project Syndicate* (July 23). At Trumpism and the Philosophy of World Order by Mark S. Weiner – Project Syndicate (project-syndicate.org).

Wiggershaus, Rolf. 1994. *The Frankfurt School*. Cambridge: MIT.

Williams, Thomas Chatterton. 2017. "The French Origin of 'You Will Not Replace Us.'" *New Yorker* (November 27). At https://www.newyorker.com/magazine/2017/12/04/the-french-origins-of-you-will-not-replace-us.

Wilson, Jason. 2019. "'Cultural Marxism': A Uniting Theory for Rightwingers Who Love to Play the Victim." *Guardian* (May 6). At https://www.filmsforaction.org/articles/cultural-marxism-a-uniting-theory-for-rightwingers-who-love-to-play-the-victim/.

Winter, Jana and Elias Groll. 2017. "Here's the Memo that Blew Up the NSC." *Foreign Policy* (August 10). At https://foreignpolicy.com/2017/08/10/heres-the-memo-that-blew-up-the-nsc/.

Wolin, Richard. 1990. "Political Existentialism and the Total State." *Theory and Society* 19(4): 389–416.

Wood, Graeme. 2017. "His Kampf." *The Atlantic* (June). At https://www.theatlantic.com/magazine/archive/2017/06/his-kampf/524505/.

Workman, James. 2019. "Our House is on Fire; 16 Year-old Greta Thunberg Wants Action." *World Economic Forum* (January 25). At https://www.weforum.org/agenda/2019/01/our-house-is-on-fire-16-year-old-greta-thunberg-speaks-truth-to-power/.

Zucman, Gabriel. 2019. "Global Wealth Inequality." *Annual Review of Economics* 11: 109–38.

CHAPTER 2

A Dialectical Constellation of Authoritarian Populism in the United States and Brazil

Jeremiah Morelock and Felipe Ziotti Narita

We are long past the expansion of liberal democracy enjoyed in the middle to late 20th century. In the wake of uncertainties following the 2007–2008 economic crisis, and deep crises of representation in contemporary politics, the current conjuncture is rife with uncertainty regarding the fates and promises of democratic regimes. Today, authoritarian populism poses a daunting challenge. "Toxic straws" (De Kadt 2019), "anti-pluralism" (Galston 2018), "cultural backlash" (Norris and Inglehart 2019), and "new authoritarianism" (Bugaric 2019) are some terms associated with these emerging illiberal movements, where established institutions and formal procedures are stretched, side-stepped, or overturned to make way for "free" autocratic action.

However, the contemporary combinations of authoritarianism and populism reach beyond political offices and formal institutions. They involve many elements in the social terrain. The cultural war of the populist authoritarian revolt (Weiß 2017) is not only about taking control of the state, but also about attaining cultural hegemony. Polarization, empowerment of 'the people,' anti-pluralism, charismatic performance, vituperation of multicultural societies and scapegoating of subpopulations are only some of the components of populist mobilization in the contemporary authoritarian genre. Critical social theory might be useful to grasp the issue in a way that preserves its subtleties, contradictions and multiplicities, without collapsing into pure description. Rather than squeezing and cropping authoritarian populism so that it can fit into a reductive, general theoretical overlay, and rather than fetishizing the particular so that no coherent dynamics or transferable tendencies are permitted voice, we seek to map out subtleties spread throughout the social terrain (inside and outside of formal channels), articulating them into broader contexts of ideological twists and historical transformation.

Our aim is to transpose Theodor Adorno's formulations concerning dialectics and constellations into contemporary socio-political scenarios in order to construct a broad critique of authoritarian populism. Adorno's constellation methodology is useful for illuminating the complex contexture (Kaufmann 2000) of objects like authoritarian populism. Attending to multiple theoretical angles, allowing discovered contradictions to sit rather than avoiding them or stretching to synthesize them, a dialectical constellation presents a development of conceptual moments (a process) that composes a larger view of objects instead of imposing unity. Adorno's argument about the lack of equivalence between concept and object is not purely negative – it is a claim that phenomena *can* be *approached* – rather than contained – by understanding. Adorno's constellation methodology consists of the juxtaposition of dialectically connected conceptual elements in which one element might shed light on the limitations of the other. Instead of pinning the object to a definition, the object is experienced in a process of dialectical exposition. This sort of directed yet non-systemic theorizing is especially useful for drawing connections between closely related yet differently constituted developments in different parts of the world. Instead of avoiding terms such as populism because of the many variations they refer to, constellations afford us the opportunity to name and explore a proposed class of phenomena – an abstract object – without confining ourselves to narrow, limiting designations. The choice between atheoretical empirical description on the one hand, and myopic conceptual oversimplifications on the other hand, is not necessary. This is one of the brilliances of Adorno's invention.

The argument will be voiced from various angles that this kind of decentered analysis introduces an anarchistic lack of accountability into the project of social theory. If concepts are no longer bound by limits nor by the prohibition of internal contradiction, then in theory anyone could invent any constellation just to give theoretical voice to their prejudices. But we argue that this is nothing new. Social theory must fit the "real world" enough to be illuminating, but beyond this vague stricture, we always evaluate it according to some combination of the impersonal dictates of logic and the personal/social dictates of resonance. Adorno incorporates both elements. The constellation is an expressive portrait structured by dialectical logic.

In our exploration here, we pull back some from Adorno's expressive emphasis and style. Our constellation is structured along dialectical lines, but instead of our theoretical thought "whirling" around our object, we move slower in order to explain more and illustrate with examples. Our sympathies are with Adorno, and we hold what he did in great esteem. But even if we wanted to and were able to, and even if somehow our publisher and peer reviewers were amenable, as a general rule the academic world is nowhere close to accepting theoretically dense, artful and expressive constellations as legitimate sources of knowledge – so it would be bogus and irresponsible of us to claim that constructing full-blown constellations in the style of Adorno is a working strategy to move social theory and research forward today. Yet it does have a very powerful 'backbone,' in the use of dialectics to unravel complex, abstract objects without apology. In this sense our analytical animal consists of a constellational skeleton under more familiar and orthodox flesh and skin. We *do* claim *this is* a working strategy to move social theory and research forward today.

Our analysis follows this basic structure – we move through dialectical moments that illustrate dimensions of the complex, abstract object authoritarian populism. There is no teleology or golden thread. Our exposition is part narrative, part socio-psychological. In describing authoritarian populism as a narrative phenomenon, we borrow from articulation theory (Hall 2018; Laclau and Mouffe 1985). While we find the theory of articulation to be a powerful and quite adept basis for critiquing the inflamed identity politics of authoritarian populism, we agree with Gandesha (2018) that the approach of Laclau and Mouffe is incomplete; staying on the level of discourse, it is bereft of social psychology. This limits both its explanatory scope and its insight into human motivation and experience.[1]

To frame our description of the socio-psychological dynamics that surround social articulations, we focus on recognition and power. Somewhat like our take on Laclau's theory of articulation, we see recognition theory (Taylor 1997; Honneth 1996) as very important yet incomplete. Honneth's elevation of recognition to an overarching and defining principle of all social struggle understates inequalities of power (Allen, 2010; Bader 2007) and wealth (Fraser and Honneth 2003; Fraser 2009), prematurely subsuming them when they might be more appropriately represented using a more pluralist approach (Bader 2007). These different domains of inequality can define themselves,

---

1   As for whether a discursive theory of articulation can be combined with theoretical social psychology in a way that is epistemologically sound (enough), our answer is "yes." The connecting link between the two can be summed up in the 'Thomas theorem' that "if men define situations as real, they are real in their consequences." (Thomas and Thomas 1928). For our purposes, we might emphasize that "if people articulate social divisions as real, they are real in their socio-psychological consequences." There remain many open questions about distinctions and relationships between discourse, experience and the unconscious. We reject the strong postmodernist stance that it is "discourse all the way down." Discourse is not the whole of human experience, but it is impossible to extract it from the non-discursive parts of ourselves. When Kristeva posits the intermingling of prerational, preverbal 'semiotic' cognition with rational, verbal, 'symbolic' cognition (McAfee 2004), this points in a very important direction. We suggest that this murky area of distinctions and relationships between discourse, experience and the unconscious is central to human existence, and yet we can only offer tentative observations and hypotheses. We should not ignore this area because of its murkiness. Its significance outweighs its difficulty. Any theory worthy of its salt contains speculation and risks error (Morelock 2019). It is up to each reader to decide if and to what extent what we present seems resonant and fitting.

so to speak, even as they inevitably overlap and intertwine. We assume that authoritarian populist political mobilization is generated from experienced deprivations and threats concerning recognition and power, in various combinations. And we view these developments through a specifically dialectical methodology. For instance, we say experienced disrespect generates desire for attaining recognition. And experienced political domination generates desire for political liberation. We posit recognition and domination as separate yet intrinsically intertwined issues. The full extent of their relations requires much more elaboration, and so is outside our scope here. Instead, we will present suggestions about how they operate together in different ways throughout our dialectical constellation.

To complicate this a little further, we emphasize that these threats and deprivations, and the social movements targeted against them, occur in both discursive and structural dimensions of social life. In other words, empirical conditions are interpreted discursively, and discourse always refers back to empirical conditions. Narratives influence [empirical] social action, and changes in [empirical] social relations influences popular discourse. The connections we draw are influenced threefold: empirical trends, social theories, and dialectical logic. Although Adorno disliked empirical examples because using them falsely implies that particulars can be subsumed within the logic of general categories, we construct a model of critique in which examples are intended in illustrative rather than denotative spirit, to clarify and lend support to the theoretical exposition.

We frame authoritarian populism as the meeting of two domains: authoritarianism and populism. This logical and analytical separation of two domains is important because it avoids the deterministic reduction of one domain to the other (as if every populist movement would be condemned to be authoritarian), yet in many places they overlap or intertwine, making a strict separation of them difficult if not impossible. In our discussion, we will treat them in this separate-but-related fashion – as forces or tendencies that merge in the 'object' of our analysis. In each domain considered separately, one can identify dialectical movements that pertain to power or recognition. In the domain of authoritarianism arise relationships between power and resistance, domination and freedom, since we understand authoritarianism as an attempt at imposing unity in heterogeneous societies. In the domain of populism are the drawing of social distinctions and conflicts over recognition between 'the people' and what we will call the "non-people," the latter including elites and outsiders. 'the people' operate as non-elites when contrasted with elites, and as insiders when contrasted with outsiders. The people are often articulated as an actual or potential authentic community, pitted against the alienated establishment.

In our constellation, these dialectical elements often overlap, mix and merge as the domains of authoritarianism and populism run together.[2] Finally, in the meeting of the two domains, other elements frequently emerge, namely the association of authenticity with decisionism and the myth of recreating a lost golden age. We also discuss some social and narrative dialectical dynamics in the emergent trends.

1   Dialectical Constellations

In the 1960s, when Adorno published his most important theoretical work, *Negative Dialectics*, he was also interested in political issues in general and German politics in particular. He was perfectly aware of latent regressions in democratic political systems and the intimate relationship between capitalist modernization and far-right extremism. His 1967 public lecture on the presence of the far-right in post-war German politics, for example, pointed to the failures of modern democracies in light of class societies vulnerable to declassification (*Deklassierung*), the aggressive defense of lost privileges and crisis of representation within bureaucratic apparatuses (political system) as the preconditions (*Voraussetzungen*) of (neo)fascist movements and authoritarian revolt against the established institutions (Adorno 2019 [1967]). Instead of a linear history of progress in which democracy would be the reconciliation of enlightenment premises, Adorno warned that new forms of domination and barbarism become latent in contemporary societies.

It is well known that Adorno was a pessimist. He saw no grand political solution, as his essay on "resignation" attested. His lamentation in *Minima Moralia* that "wrong life cannot be lived rightly" (Adorno 2003 [1951]: 43) speaks of the negative core of his "melancholy science," as well as of a similar temperament if not assessment as his broad historical diagnosis of Enlightenment turning to myth, this time applied to everyday experience in late capitalism. And yet, one could argue that Adorno had an unshakeable faith in humanity. Despite all his pessimistic assessments, he continued to write and to theorize, to critique forms of domination. Believing that philosophy was falling into ruin, he invested astounding intellectual resources in composing his *Negative Dialectics* – a venture intended to rescue philosophy from its demise

---

2   The mixing of authoritarianism and populism is not a determinate negation; this step is synthetic, not dialectical. Yet when the two domains are combined, their respective internal contradictions interface, for example in dialectics of domination and freedom of insiders and outsiders.

by helping it move beyond itself. On the one hand, for Adorno there could be no poetry or metaphysics after Auschwitz. Hegel's optimistic dictum that the real is the rational and the rational is the real had become indefensible, and "any appeal to the idea of progress would seem absurd given the scale of the catastrophe" that had already taken place in the course of capitalist history (Adorno 2006 [1965]: 14). The early twentieth century socialist liberation movements found their consummation in authoritarian regimes, e.g., under Stalin in the Soviet Union. On the other hand, in the face of the proliferated dogmatic and determinist "vulgar Marxism" – which converted dialectics into a "thoughtless theory" (Adorno 2007 [1963]: 79) – administrated by the socialist bureaucracy of the Eastern bloc, Adorno forged on to work out his own "modified version of dialectics." The importance of Adorno's work goes well beyond his persistence, his finesse with dialectics, and his iconoclasm. Adorno also offers a powerful positive vision (Sherratt 2002) of how philosophy can outgrow its straitjacket. Rather than skepticism, Adorno offers us a way forward without illusions.

For Adorno, dialectics must deal with objects not simply as given and final truths. Dialectics needs to take into account the conceptual contexture of objects: "because the entity [*Seiende*] is not immediate, but only through [*durch*] and via [*hindurch*] the concept," it would be useful "to begin with the concept and not with the mere datum" (Adorno 2003 [1966]: 156). As a contradictory relationship between the dynamic parts and the whole, the fundamental ontological concepts always require their opposites and their mediations to constitute the contours of the process (Adorno 2007 [1963]: 82). In other words, Adorno's *démarche* might be useful to make explicit the contradictory trends that underlie the appearance of unity imposed by any concept in its effort at producing an immediate identity between reason and effective reality (*Wirklichkeit*). Adorno's dialectic is a process in which the confrontation between the concept and the object implies that "a contradiction in reality [*Realität*] is a contradiction against reality." In this sense, he states:

> But such dialectics is no longer compatible [*sich vereinen*] with Hegel. Its motion [*Bewegung*] does not tend to the identity in the difference between each object and the concept; on the contrary, this dialectics turns the identical suspect [*beargewöhnt*]. Its logic is one of disintegration [*Zerfall*]: disintegration of the constructed [*zugerüsteten*] and objectified image [*Gestalt*] of the concept that the cognitive subject faces immediately [*unmittelbar*].
>
> ADORNO 2003 [1966]: 148

Adorno does not seek to subsume objects under a dialectical reason that covers them absolutely. Against the "strong form of identity" (Jameson 1990, 20) that subsumes dissonances and conflicts under a concept, Adorno advocates the consistent consciousness (*Bewußtsein*) of nonidentity between concepts and the objects they refer to. For Adorno, there is no absolute equivalence between concepts and their objects because concepts cannot exhaust (*aufgehen*) the complexities of the objects they point toward (Adorno 2003 [1966]: 17).[3] In other words, the differences cannot be reconciled into a homogeneous whole, but rather co-exist as differences and contradictions (Stone 2014), that is, the whole is not prior to its parts.

Instead of being a blockade to the thought, contradiction is the very motion of critical theory since it depicts (*herrstellen*) the barriers that lead to a trans-formation of the concept without losing its determinations (*Bestimmungen*) (Adorno 2010 [1958]: 18). Adorno's negative dialectic is not merely a dialectical logic without the rational moment of synthesis, but rather a consistent theo-retical rearrangement within Hegelian idealist assumptions in which Adorno rejects any positive identity that falsely reconciles the heterogeneous concep-tual moments under a synthetic, unitary "construction [*Aufbau*] against the disintegration [*Zersetzung*]" of the concept (Adorno 2003 [1966]: 158). This implies that

> Objectively, dialectics means to break the forced identity,[4] and to break it through the energy stored in that compulsion and congealed in its objectifications[5] ... Since the concept is experienced [*erfährt*] as non-identical, as inwardly in motion [*in sich bewegt*], it is no longer purely itself; in Hegel's terminology, it leads to its otherness without absorbing [*aufzusaugen*] that otherness. It is defined by that which is outside it, because on its own it does not exhaust itself [*sich erschöpft*].
>
> ADORNO 2003 [1966]: 159

Adorno's effort is put in motion via the liberating potential of determinate negation and the critique of the immediate adequacy of identitarian reason.

---

3 Adorno also says that particular objects cannot account for the formal, general and abstract qualities that are intrinsic to concepts. This assertion is important in the sense that Adorno's methodology cannot be collapsed into an empiricism that rejects theoretical concepts in favor of pure particularity. Adorno preserves the sense found in Hegel that concepts and objects constitute one another. The key difference is that Adorno sees the relationship as inherently dissonant.

4 [*Identitätszwang*].

5 [*Vergegenständlichungen*].

This approach is far from falling into unproductive pessimism or any kind of *naïve* irrationalism, as it appears in the critique expanded by the late Georg Lukács (1973: 218–219) against Adorno, in the sarcastic conclusion of the 1962 preface to *The Theory of the Novel*, arguing that Adorno's philosophy flirted with the "abyss of nothingness," that is, "the disconsolate background of the vainness [*Sinnlosigkeit*] of existence," which lifts theory "above the wretched mob [*Pöbl*] that is shortsighted enough to fight and to suffer [*leiden*] for a betterment of social conditions." Rather, the force of the negative is productive to the extent that treating concepts and their opposites on their own, liberated from the positive moment of Hegelian reconciliation (the negation of the negation), avoids any temptation to soften (*glätten*) determinate negation, which Adorno understood as the indissoluble expression of nonidentity in dialectical logic (Adorno 2003 [1966]: 162).

The theoretical exposition turns the constant (*ständigen*) confrontation between the concept and the thing (*Sache*) into the potency of an immanent critique committed to unveil the "movement of the concept" (Adorno 2010 [1958]: 18–19), according to determinate historical situations, remaining always open to heterogeneous elements with no teleological horizon nor hierarchies grounded in progressive casual chains. In this sense,

> The unifying moment survives without a negation of negation, but also without delivering itself to abstraction as a supreme principle. It survives because there is no step-by-step progression [*fortgeschritten*] from the concepts to a more general cover concept [*Oberbegriff*]. Instead, the concepts enter into a constellation. The constellation sheds light on the specificity [*Spezifische*] of the object, that is, the element that is either a burden or indifferent to a classifying procedure.
>
> ADORNO 2003 [1966]: 164

The "overarching sensibility" (Pensky 1997) of the dialectical constellation points out that the effort at unifying complex social phenomena through concepts is always a tense conflict to redeem the particular and the nonidentical. The moments and the parts of the constellation are used as simultaneous categories that constantly affect each other and modify themselves. Rather than synthesis, the critical task of social theory is to deal with the contradictory process. Constellations are discontinuous (Buck-Morss 1977, 94–95), since the logic of disintegration liberates every element and sublates causal hierarchy, leaving the parts are unimpaired. As a methodological tool (Buck-Morss 1977: 102), thus, two movements are important to the dialectical process of constructing constellations: one is conceptual-analytical (breaking apart the primeval phenomenon by isolating its elements and mediating them by means of concepts), and the other is representational, that is, the effort at bringing the elements together in an exposition of social contradictions.

2   Populism and Authoritarianism

Over the last several years, the rise of far-right parties and governments, with strong populist and authoritarian trends, gained momentum in the Americas with the election of Donald Trump in 2016 (United States) and Jair Bolsonaro in 2018 (Brazil). Besides public speeches, the massive use of social media by those governments, especially Twitter and Facebook, offers lots of empirical data to analyze, and points to the political significance of information technologies and the reconfiguration of sociotechnical and communication structures that they ushered in. This is true in terms of understanding both the place of social media in 'manufacturing consent' and in the ways that new masses are incorporated into populist politics (Morelock and Narita 2018). Especially when looked at together, both cases – Brazil and the United States – illustrate how 'authoritarian populism' comprises a constellation of elements that calls for the expansion of the mainstream definition of populism (e.g., the conflictual and moral divide between 'the people' and 'the elites') in order to grasp the nuances and contradictory moments underlying the construction of 'the people' vis-à-vis the non-people, outsiders and so on.

2.1   *Typology of Populist Narratives*
In authoritarian populism, the people self-articulate in contrast to the non-people, the latter comprising elites and outsiders. 'the people' can only narratively exist in such contrasts and is defined as 'the people' by virtue of its negative relation to the non-people. There are several overlapping dialectical relations here. We will classify three types of populist narrative: people/elite (liberation), people/outsiders (nationalism), and people/non-people. The performative rhetoric of far-right leaders can embody these experiences and motivations, appealing to and further solidifying support from 'the people,' defining reality in terms that simultaneously speak to these mentalities and promote authoritarian measures. For example, in February 2019, Trump framed the alleged need to build a wall along the U.S./Mexico border as a "National Emergency" (Baker 2019).

2.1.1   People/Elite

Elites can only narratively exist if the people are articulated as non-elites, and so in this narrative, the importance of the people is in their *non-elite* status. Here, the story is that *elites* have too much power, and perhaps have recently increased their power, decreasing the people's power and recognition. The coherence and solidarity of the people grows with experience of alienation from elites, especially in light of the polarization grounded in social resentment due to a sense of growing inequalities, political exclusion, and injustice. The people want to overturn this alienated, disempowered and disrespected state, and to shrink if not erase the distance that separates them from the elite center. This can be seen across all varieties of populism – left and right, democratic and authoritarian. Concerns about power are at play here, but strategies of empowerment can be many, and so authoritarianism per se is possible but not preordained. It is essentially a revolutionary logic. Every consummated revolution requires a moment of the transfer of power that necessarily implies the forceful removal or suppression of the powerful persons or systems of the old regime. Because of this, every revolution contains at minimum what we might call an "authoritarian moment," which is also the moment that liberation is achieved, and every revolutionary movement includes the anticipation of this moment. But the size, duration, and severity of this authoritarian moment can vary widely, as can the degrees and qualities of freedom and democracy in envisioned and enacted post-revolutionary societies. It could mark far more than just a "moment;" it could rather mark a *slip* into establishing a new authoritarian regime. And yet it also could be quite fleeting, disappearing more or less instantaneously.

2.1.2   People/Outsiders

Outsiders can only exist to the extent that the people are articulated as insiders, and so in this narrative, the importance of the people is in their *insider* status. Here, the story is that *outsiders* have grown in power and recognition by growing in numbers relative to the people, impoverishing the power and recognition of the people as their relative numbers shrink. The coherence and solidarity of the people grows with its experience of dis-alienation (e.g., sharing of space) from outsiders. Their experience of *difference* from outsiders makes their dis-alienation from outsiders more threatening the closer or more prominent they become; the people want to be further from the outsiders, must reject outsiders, and ultimately want to stay entirely distinct from outsiders. This one has a more implicitly authoritarian flavor, as it is prone to involve scapegoating and implies that the road to empowerment of the people is through [forceful] exclusion of outsiders. Yet without specifying a strategy of empowerment and exclusion, it is not inherently authoritarian per se. It is essentially a nationalist logic of populist mobilization. The whole affair surrounding the "immigrant caravan" approaching the U.S./Mexico border was a clear case of this narrative, using the symbol of encroaching outsiders to argue for a need to protect the people from them with increased force.

2.1.3   People/Non-people

This is a combination of the other two narratives and *is* specifically authoritarian. It comes in two basic variations: a) infiltration – outsiders are or have become elites; b) betrayal – elites are aligned with outsiders more than with the people. Also possible are c) mixed – especially when there are multiple types of outsider groups. The people/non-people narrative is also a fertile soil for paranoia and conspiracy theory. Once again, far-right leaders will echo these various narratives in their rhetoric and public displays. One example of the mixed type is Trump's accusation of Somali American and Muslim congresswoman Ilhan Omar of supporting al-Qaeda (Rizzo 2019). The accusation of betrayal is clear, but infiltration is also implied, due to Omar's ethnic background, which marks her as an outsider to far-right America's articulation of 'the people.' Another example of the mixed type is Trump's frequent use of the issue of immigration to portray Democrats (elites) as caring more about immigrants (outsiders) than they do the rest of the country (Barabak and Levey 2019). In the United States today, 'outsiders' are generally immigrants or ethnic minorities. But in principle outsider status can accrue to any sub-population simply by not being narrated in the category of 'real' or 'pure' people.

With the electoral victory in Brazil, 2018 of the conservative far-Right via Jair Bolsonaro, we can analyze an interesting example: due to its peripheral integration into the modern world-system, immigration is not a key concern in Brazilian populism. Brazil is far from attracting immigrants like the United States or Western Europe. In Brazil, mass migration and border crises play a minor role in public debate. In populist mobilizations of peripheral countries like Brazil, outsider status falls on successful political opponents, their parties and the established institutions of liberal democracy. In Brazil, the people/non-people narrative (variation b) is the rule. The establishment is associated with "corrupted" liberal elites (centrist and center-left groups that embrace political correctness and the progressive agenda) and the center-left Worker's Party, which ruled the country from 2003 to 2016. A cultural tension is aesthetically expressed with the intensive public use of national symbols and green and yellow colors by supporters of the far-right government and/or the supporters of anti-establishment movements (Biller 2019). Despite the strong nationalist rhetoric, populism in Brazil is an internal dispute over political cleavages within the population – in other words, 'the people' is a nationalist – but not nativist – designation.

2.2   *Dialectics of Authoritarian Populism*

2.2.1   Power and Liberation

'The people,' under the experienced threat of disempowerment from the 'non-people,' (the elites and outsiders) look toward strengthening their power. The people feel disempowered due to expanded power and presence of non-people. Empowerment is, for the people, understood as *liberation* from this disempowerment. The people/elite narrative states that the elites have power *over* the people, and that the people should rise to liberate and reclaim their alienated *power-to*. One example is Bolsonaro's campaign for liberating the use of firepower to defend "our liberty": he states that "the people must have the right to arms to defend themselves against those who dare to take away their freedom," since he stands "for individual weaponry for our people so that temptations will not pass over the heads of rulers by taking power absolutely. We have examples in Latin America. We don't want to repeat it" (his examples are leftist governments) (Twitter – Jair Bolsonaro @jairbolsonaro, June 17, 2019). Another example is Trump's executive order concerning freedom of speech on college campuses in March 2019. The freedom of speech argument is likewise generally touted by the political Right in response to left-wing pressures for "political correctness." During the Black Lives Matter protests in the summer of 2020, right wing voices used terms like "mob rule" to refer to them. One article in *The Federalist* donned a subheading: "BLM Isn't Interested in Free Speech, It Wants Power" (Davidson 2020). At the same time, the response to the protests under Trump included tear gas, rubber bullets, the National Guard, and Trump's praise for "overwhelming force" and "domination" (Phelps and Gittleson 2020). During this same period of time, Trump responded to Twitter's fact-checking his posts by claiming it to be a violation of his first amendment rights. He threatened to shut down social media sites and signed an executive order to pull back legal protections for them – allegedly to defend free speech (Bort 2020; Wong 2020).

It should be obvious that guns are tools for power – to force others' lives to end, to physically debilitate them, or to force their actions under the threat of death or debilitation. Yet "freedom of speech" against "political correctness" and freedom of the market against government regulation also contribute to other dominations. In the freedom of speech case, the curbing of discourse to adopt new terms for minority populations, new terms that do not carry the baggage of immediate and explicit or historical and implicit prejudice, is an attempt in the interests of liberating minority populations from a cultural tyranny of the majority.[6] When embodied in policy, "politically correct" movements achieve new freedoms for oppressed populations. For example, legalization of same-sex marriage can be understood as liberation for sexual minorities from subordinate legal status. Yet some argue that this is not properly liberation, because it involves the assimilation of sexual minorities to the norms of straight society, and the institutionalized regulation of queer coupledom by the state (Robson 2002; Butler 2004; McCormick 2018).

In our era of neoliberalism, liberation discourse is also used to refer to liberation of the market from government regulation. For instance, the far-right caucus in the American government, called the "Freedom Caucas," are aligned with the *libertarian* Tea Party. In class terms, neoliberal reforms empower the capitalist class and social accumulation at the expense of workers. This might not be the case were available jobs to outnumber workers. But – as Karl Marx (2008, 665–667) indicates in his theory of the reserve army of labor – with a surplus of unemployed persons, workers are pressed to accept whatever working conditions are allotted. The more free choices the capitalist class has, the more their whims exert power over the working class. As John Bellamy Foster emphasizes, in the case of "externalities" such as pollution and its impacts on the environment and human health the capitalist class has the 'freedom' to toxify the natural world, which all humans – never mind all species – live in (Foster 1999; Foster and Burkett 2018). The greater freedom of the capitalist class from environmental regulations means the greater powerlessness of workers (and non-humans) against the whims of the capitalists.

2.2.2   Alienation, Authenticity, and Agitation
When considered as a whole, the non-people have an ambivalent status for the people. As insiders, the people push against outsiders to increase distance, but as non-elites, the people push against elites to decrease distance. This is not just about controlling the establishment, although that plays in. There is also a fantasy of punching through the establishment, of dismantling and recreating it with less structure, less compromise, and more connection to the lifeworld of the people. As people are further alienated from the establishment, 'the people' emerges as a self-conscious collective subject, its members representing to themselves an authentic community antithetical to the alienated establishment. There is a rejection of the alienated apparatus of government,

---

6 Marcuse wrestles with this dialectic extensively in his essay "Repressive Tolerance" (Wolff, Moore and Marcuse 1966). Marcuse's thesis, which supports the suppression of intolerant ideologies, was criticized heavily at the time of its publication due to its direct call to limit some [hate] speech. Recently it has gained much popularity again (Fopp 2007, 2010).

bureaucracy, and formal procedure – which in contemporary society are not altogether different from an alienating cultural decomposition process where the individual is pitted against a largely anonymous 'system world' (Calhoun 1988) which the elites uphold and in which the elites are entrenched. The wheels of the liberal democratic system are large, and often a disappointingly small amount of action comes out of a deeply divided congress where heels are dug in on both sides of the divide.

The mobilization of popular resentment can play a key role in this case. In April and May 2020,[7] in popular rallies that advocated a military coup and blamed liberal democracy for the corruption and crisis, Bolsonaro expressed the authoritarian content of populist agitation. Amidst popular calls to close the congress and the federal court, he attacked the established elite: "everyone in Brazil is subjected to the will of the people. The era of rascality is over; now it is the people in power. I am here because I trust you [the people]" (Portal G1, 2020). Between 2014 and 2018, alongside deep socioeconomic deterioration, a juridical crusade against corruption scandals, a crisis of representation of traditional political parties (materialized in the street protests between 2013 and 2015) and an institutional crisis (with an impeachment in 2016), the election of Bolsonaro in 2018 and his promises of a "new politics" promoted a constant conflict with constitutional powers.

More than just assembling and mobilizing the people, populist rationality is grounded in polarization and the presupposition of conflict without end. It thrives on antagonism and agitation, or the stoking of social divisions through political rhetoric (Morelock and Narita 2019b). The people, self-consciously alien from elites, amplify this alienation through polarizing rhetoric, aided by damnations from non-people. When the leader galvanizes anti-establishment rhetoric, democracy is jeopardized twofold. To explain the first by example: when Bolsonaro supports street protests as "spontaneous manifestations of the people" against instituted powers like the congress or the supreme court (Twitter – Jair Bolsonaro @jairbolsonaro, May 26, 2019.), he posits the people and its purity not only against the corrupt (entrenched in those institutions), but more broadly: against the checks and balances limiting Executive power (Estadão 2019). Second, polarization is grounded in scapegoating leftists as enemies that represent not only degradation of the political order, but

---

7 These rallies took place during the COVID-19 pandemic, which infected 121,600 and killed 8,128 Brazilians (official data from Johns Hopkins University in May 6, 2020). The populist agitation of Bolsonaro has been carried out in support of right-wing protestors against social distancing and the political elite in the congress, the Supreme Court and governors that follow the measures of the World Health Organization.

moral decay associated with political correctness, multiculturalism and cultural menaces against the conservative *Weltanschauung* grounded in Western Christianity and the bourgeois family. Democracy is only meaningful if there are differences of opinion that are held to legitimate arbitration. It requires a willingness to compromise and to cooperate with persons who hold views that you do not agree with. Polarizing rhetoric is a move directly in contrast to this. When political differences are framed as irreconcilable cleavages, refusal to cooperate with the non-people may be framed as necessary and even honorable. Explicitly, it may be framed as 'resistance' to their tyranny. But implicitly, this refusal, which takes the shape of political agitation, is also a refutation of liberal democracy, and by extension an endorsement of authoritarian rule.

2.2.3   Emergent Elements I: Decisionism

All the oppositional naming and dividing by the people seeks reconciliation with the establishment, to rebirth it. In the people's move to be closer to the establishment, the establishment comes closer to the people. Like Odysseus in the territory of the Sirens, the people tie themselves to their Homeric mast (Horkheimer and Adorno 2002). The thirst is like this: rather than ossified processes and negotiations, the authentic will of those in command should be experienced fresh, with minimal mediation from leader's mind to people's lives. The total, voluntary submission of the people to the ruler, animated by the experience of identity with the ruler, united by the all-encompassing "will of the people," constitutes true democracy, according to Nazi political theorist Carl Schmitt (Schmitt 1988 [1923–26]).[8] The leader, the spokesperson for the authentic people's will, must be *free* of bureaucracy, to command as he sees fit, by his own decisions.

Here, Trump and Bolsonaro share a common strategy: they flood the Congress with measures, executive orders and decrees in order to show the people they are trying to carry out their promises (Odilla 2019; Turollo Jr. and Cancian 2020) Congressional resistance is taken up as a kind of political alibi to justify autocratic action and agitate the people against the established institutions. In this case, the threat to liberal democracy does not come from a coup d'état, nor from a violent overthrow of the regime, but rather from normative alterations that can progressively corrode liberal counterchecks via autocratic legalism (Scheppele 2018).

Trump's penchant for executive orders (like the 2019 stratagem for the construction of the US/Mexico border wall), and his refusal for his inner circle

---

8   See Antonio, this volume.

to comply with congressional subpoenas during his impeachment inquiry, exhibit a clearly decisionist style. The justification for withholding subpoenaed documents and keeping subpoenaed witnesses from testifying before congress was couched in the Republican Party line during the proceedings, which included the insinuation that Trump's defiance of congress was a patriotic act in the name of freedom. The Republicans echoed in a seemingly unified voice throughout the proceedings the accusation that the Democratic Party was acting in an authoritarian manner via the impeachment process. The justification for the dictatorial undermining of the separation of powers in the act of Trump's defiance of Congress was a narrative of resistance to tyranny. In a letter from Trump to Democratic Speaker of the House Nancy Pelosi, Trump described his impeachment as an "attempted coup" and an "unprecedented and unconstitutional abuse of power" (Shear 2019; Stahl 2019). These quotes are especially interesting considering the charges of his impeachment: abuse of power, and obstruction of congress.

During the COVID-19 pandemic, Trump spoke in support of right-wing protestors against social distancing, who framed their resistance in terms of freedom, with signs like "give me liberty of give me death" and "social distancing = communism." An advisor to Trump even compared the protestors to African American civil rights protestor Rosa Parks, who famously refused to give up her seat on the bus to a white person in 1955 (Steib 2020). And yet during this same period he boasted at a press conference that his "authority is total," when discussing the issue of states letting up on social distancing measures (John 2020).

2.2.4 Emergent Elements II: The Construction of the Charismatic Leader

Leadership is not an existent; it is constructed in the political correlation of forces. The assertive behavior and political decisionism of the authoritarian populist are predicated on their construction as a leader, which in turn is dependent on there being a base of followers who are under the spell of the leader's charismatic appeal. Charisma is not properly sympathy nor courtesy, that is, it is not the product of education nor an individual skill. Max Weber (1976: 124) points out that charisma is a *political relation* and a form of domination (*Herrschaft*) that depends both on the personal (*Persönlichkeit*) appeal and the recognition (*Anerkennung*) of the individual as a leader (*Führer*). The construction of the leader, thus, implies the agitation of the affects and the social resentments of their audience, as well as the audience's trust in the leader's personal abilities. The leader's intentions aside, the sense of 'authenticity' or spontaneity of a charismatic leader, rebelling against status quo mores and political processes, is implicitly deceptive. It can only persist on condition that a) there still is still an alter political establishment to rebel against, b) the charismatic movement or community is relatively unstructured and unpredictable, and c) the charismatic leader is still alive. In all these cases, any power gained by the charismatic leader must be transformed to survive into some sort of formal political structure. In Weber's language, charisma must be 'routinized' (*Veralltäglichung*) in directions either 'traditional,' 'rational-legal,' or both (Weber 1976: 140–141). With the spectacle – that is, the political exhibition of the leaders via images, voices and social media (Morelock and Narita 2021) – the routinization of charisma counts on the dematerialization of the leader itself. The mirage of the leader's 'direct' contact with the people (with followers, likes, etc.) and the ordinary language that says things straightly produces the effect of connecting the people with the former alienated establishment.

The long secularization of political institutions since the beginning of the Modern era has produced a new kind of devotion: the secular authority of the state does not impose only outward obedience, but also a sincere inner devotion to the personal capacities of the leader. In this sense, charisma calls for obedience to the leader not because of his useful functions, but because of his alleged superhuman gifts (Neumann 1943: 83). The only way for individuals to find full, empowered expression within a collective unit, is for the individuals to become empty, disempowered expressions of the collective unit. No "authentic" nation could function as a collective unit unless morally united under a dictator or sacrosanct or cause. Upon electoral victory, this 'freedom'-seeking people loses its position of 'resistance' and becomes a force explicitly for unfreedom. Every "liberation" from the stultifying democratic architecture increases the unchecked domination of the new leader.

2.2.5   Emergent Elements III: Mythological Uses of the Past

This break from the past is also ostensibly a return to the past before society's fall from grace. In the absence of any seemingly viable future utopian visions, the impulse toward 'retrotopia' (Bauman 2019) is more prominent. It is expressed in Trump's "Make America Great Again" slogan, and in Bolsonaro's echo "Make Brazil Great Again." The desire to return to paradise is a common one, possibly even deeply rooted in human experience. In the Judeo-Christian tradition, the Fall of Adam and Eve opens the saga of humanity. Other very common examples are the religious notions of rejoining an infinite, divine consciousness in death or nirvana. Bolsonaro's constant refrain of admiration toward the 1970s Brazilian and the Chilean military dictatorships combines visions of retrotopia with attacks against liberal democracy. This rhetoric serves to reinforce decisionism and the privileging of the Executive will over the Congress and the Justice, which he characterizes as entrenched with corruption. In this case, conservative values fit with authoritarian slips (Morelock and Narita 2018), as blame is placed on human rights, multiculturalism and liberal democracy for the fall of the moral order of the past. A particular use of the past underlies this assertion: historical process is understood as the erosion of an idealized past that must be re-enacted and imposed via conservative cultural hegemony.

There are homologous moments to the biblical Fall in the psychic life of each person, for instance in the traumatic experience of birth (Rank 1999) and in the early development of an individuated sense of self with the induction into the symbolic order (Lacan 1988; Kristeva 1982). What 'great' refers to is of course unspecified in both cases. This masks the fact that the past that was 'great' for some was still *terrible* for others. In the case of the United States, the romanticized past is in the immediate past-WWII era, when the country assumed status of global capitalist hegemon and enjoyed its greatest period of economic prosperity. Of course, this was *before* the successes of the civil rights movement, second wave feminism, and protests over the Vietnam War. In other words, it was a short and transient period, where middle class straight white men may have had it 'great,' but many others certainly did not. Perhaps some of the wives and mothers in the successful American Dream families had it 'great,' and certainly there were benefits to the children of these families during the Baby Boom era, when patriotic optimism and affluence ran high and the tumult of the 1960s had not yet hit. And yet this selective memory might seem perfectly appropriate to a large portion Trump's base, considering the prevalence of older white men among his supporters (Cole 2019).

It is perhaps more effective that the designation 'great' is left at least denotatively open in this way, since as a floating signifier its vagueness facilitates the power and universality of the impulse that is tapped – for Laclau (2005), it is desire that seeks Lacan's (2018) empty and impossible "*objet petit a*," but which can be collapsed into drive for a 'partial object,' something – a symbol, a slogan, a social movement, a charismatic leader – that is very real and historically specific, but which is treated as a conduit for the infinite *jouissance*. The evangelical notion that Trump's presidency is an expression of God's will is a case in point. In other terms, the retrotopic slogan can be like the manifest content of dreams, operating as a source of wish-fulfillment for these deep, universal longings for completeness through returning to God or the womb. The nostalgia of the authoritarian populist is an allegiance to pretense. Whether delusion or manipulation, the "authentic" community is united under a lie, that is, under the political construction and ideological use of the past.

3   Concluding Notes

In this exposition we applied a constellation methodology to contemporary authoritarian populism as object. Consistent with Adorno's approach, we do not look at the object as a whole that subsumes its parts. On the contrary, our attempt is to articulate the nuances and the contradictory moments that organize the constellation. We dialectically unfolded the conceptual moments and suggested the possibility of a critical social theory committed to the analysis of the current sociopolitical scenario in the Americas. The rise of the populist far-Right in the 2010s produced and expressed major social, economic and political shifts by giving voice to new right-wing factions and movements, which are different from the traditional Republican Party (à la George W. Bush) in the US and the neoliberal and conservative parties of the 1990s and 2000s in Brazil. Besides the impact on liberal democracy and the correlation of political forces and parties, authoritarian populism spreads and brings together multiple resonances in the social terrain.

Our point of departure is the mainstream definition of populism as the antagonism between the people and the elite, but we argue that this must be expanded. In this sense, the dialectical constellation is useful for shedding light on the elements that participate in populism and its concept, as well as how the elements interact and generate contradiction and movement. Especially with the encounter of two political domains – populism and authoritarianism – we present this dialectical constellation as a diagnostic sketch of the historical horizon of contemporary American democracies. As an expression of multiple crises – uneven recoveries from the 2008 crisis and deep crises of representation in traditional parties and political systems – authoritarian populism is not properly an accidental detour in an inevitable destination of post-Cold War societies toward liberal democracy. As Adorno remarked in the 1960s, authoritarian regression is intrinsic to the capitalist whirlwind of crises.

References

Adorno, Theodor. 2019 [1967]. *Aspekte des neuen Rechtsradikalismus: ein Vortrag*. Frankfurt am Main: Suhrkamp.

Adorno, Theodor. 2010 [1958]. *Einführung in die Dialektik*, ed. Christoph Ziermann – Nachgelassene Schriften, 2/IV. Frankfurt am Main: Suhrkamp.

Adorno, Theodor. 2006 [1965]. *History and Freedom: Lectures 1964–1965*, trans. Rodney Livingstone. London: Polity.

Adorno, Theodor. 2003 [1951]. *Minima Moralia: Reflexionen aus dem beschädigten Leben*. Frankfurt am Main: Suhrkamp.

Adorno, Theodor. 2003 [1966]. *Negative Dialektik/Jargon der Eigentlichkeit*. Frankfurt am Main: Suhrkamp.

Adorno, Theodor. 2007 [1963]. *Três Estudos sobre Hegel*, trans. Ulisses Vaccari. São Paulo: São Paulo State University Press.

Allen, Amy. 2010. "Recognizing Domination: Recognition and Power in Honneth's Critical Theory." *Journal of Power* 3(1): 21–32.

Bader, Veit. 2007. "Misrecognition, Power, and Democracy." *Recognition and Power: Axel Honneth and the Tradition of Critical Social Theory*, eds. Bert van den Brink and David Owen. London: Cambridge University Press.

Baker, Peter. 2019. "Trump Declares a National Emergency, and Provokes a Constitutional Clash." *The New York Times* (February 15). At https://www.nytimes.com/2019/02/15/us/politics/national-emergency-trump.html.

Barabak, Mark and Noam Levey. 2019. "Are Democrats Helping Trump by Promising Healthcare to Undocumented Migrants?" *Los Angeles Times* (July 9).

Bauman, Zygmunt. 2019. *Retrotopia*. London: Premier Parallèle.

Biller, David. 2019. "Brazilian Politics Stain the Famous Yellow and Green Jersey." *Bloomberg* (July 7).

Bort Ryan. 2020. "Trump Threatens to Shred First Amendment to Defend 'Free Speech.'" *Rolling Stone* (May 28). At https://www.rollingstone.com/politics/politics-news/trump-twitter-mail-in-voting-free-speech-1005629/.

Buck-Morss, Susan. 1977. *The Origin of Negative Dialectics*. London: Macmillan.

Bugaric, Bojan. 2019. The Two Faces of Populism: Between Authoritarian and Democratic Populism. *German Law Journal* 20(2): 390–400.

Butler, Judith. 2004. *Undoing gender*. London: Routledge.

Calhoun, Craig. 1988. "Populist Politics, Communications Media and Large Scale Societal Integration." *Sociological Theory* 6(2): 219–241.

Cole, Nicki Lisa. 2019. "Meet the People Behind Donald Trump's Popularity: Survey Research Reveals Stark Trends in Voters and Values." *Thoughtco* (June 29). At https://www.thoughtco.com/meet-the-people-behind-donald-trumps-popularity-4068073 (accessed December 19, 2019).

Davidson John Daniel. 2020. "If You Don't Support Black Lives Matter, You're Fired." *The Federalist* (June 11). At https://thefederalist.com/2020/06/11/if-you-dont-support-black-lives-matter-youre-fired/.

De Kadt, Raphael. 2019. "The End of the Liberal Democratic Era?" *Journal of the Helen Suzman Foundation* 2(84): 3–10.

Editorial note: "Bolsonaro e o Povo." *Estadão* (May 23, 2019).

Fopp, Rodney. 2007. "Herbert Marcuse's 'Repressive Tolerance' and His Critics." *Borderlands* 6(1).

Fopp, Rodney. 2010. "'Repressive Tolerance': Herbert Marcuse's Exercise in Social Epistemology." *Social epistemology* 24(2): 105–122.

Foster, John Bellamy. 1999. "Marx's Theory of Metabolic Rift: Classical Foundations for Environmental Sociology." *American Journal of Sociology* 105(2): 366–405.

Foster, John Bellamy, and Paul Burkett. 2018. "Value Isn't everything." *Monthly Review* 70(1): 1–17.

Fraser, Nancy. 2009 *Scales of Justice: Reimagining Political Space in a Globalizing World.* New York: Columbia University Press.

Fraser, Nancy, and Axel Honneth. 2003. *Redistribution or Recognition? A Political-philosophical Exchange.* New York: Verso.

Galston, William. 2018. *Anti-Pluralism: The Populist Threat to Liberal Democracy.* New Haven: Yale University Press.

Gandesha, Samir. 2018. "Understanding Right and Left Populism." *Critical Theory and Authoritarian Populism*, ed. Jeremiah Morelock. London: University of Westminster Press.

Hall, Stuart. 2018. "Popular Culture, Politics and History." *Cultural Studies* 32(6): 929–952.

Honneth, Axel. 1996. *The Struggle for Recognition: The Moral Grammar of Social Conflicts.* Cambridge: The MIT Press.

Horkheimer, Max and Theodor W. Adorno. 2002. *Dialectic of Enlightenment.* Redwood City: Stanford University Press.

Jameson, Fredric. 1990. *Late Marxism: Adorno, or, the Persistence of the Dialectic.* New York: Verso.

John, Arit. 2020. "Does Trump Have 'Total Authority' During the Coronavirus Outbreak, or Any Other Time?" *Los Angeles Times* (April 18). At https://www.latimes.com/politics/story/2020-04-18/trump-governors-coronavirus-authority-reopen-states.

Kaufmann, David. 2000. "Correlations, Constellations and the Truth: Adorno's Ontology of Redemption." *Philosophy and Social Criticism* 26(5): 62–80.

Kristeva, Julia. 1982. *Powers of Horror.* New York: Columbia University Press.

Lacan, Jacques. 1988. *Freud's Papers on Technique, 1953–1954.* New York: WW Norton & Company.

Lacan, Jacques. 2018. *The Four Fundamental Concepts of Psychoanalysis.* London: Routledge.

Laclau, Ernesto. 2005. *On Populist Reason.* New York: Verso.

Laclau, Ernesto, and Chantal Mouffe. 1985. *Hegemony and Socialist Strategy: Towards a Radical Democratic Politics.* New York: Verso.

Lukács, Georg. 1973. *Die Zerstörung der Vernunft: Irrationalismus zwischen den Revolutionen.* Darmstadt: Luchterhand Verlag.

Marx, Karl. 2008. *Das Kapital: Kritik der politischen Ökonomie.* Berlin: Dietz. Vol. 1.

McAfee, Noëlle. 2004. *Julia Kristeva.* London: Routledge.

McCormick, Tracey Lee. 2018. "Why Same-Sex Marriage is Not the Ultimate Tool for Queer Liberation." *The Conversation* (October 14). At https://theconversation.com/why-same-sex-marriage-is-not-the-ultimate-tool-for-queer-liberation-103702.

Morelock, Jeremiah. 2019. "Resuscitating Sociological Theory: Nietzsche and Adorno on Error and Speculation." *Nietzsche and Critical Social Theory: Affirmation, Animosity, and Ambiguity*, eds. Michael Roberts and Christine Payne. Leiden: Brill.

Morelock, Jeremiah and Narita, Felipe Ziotti. 2018. "Public Sphere and World-System: Theorizing Populism at the Margins." *Critical Theory and Authoritarian Populism*, ed. Jeremiah Morelock. London: University of Westminster Press.

Morelock, Jeremiah and Narita, Felipe Ziotti. 2019a. *O Problema do Populismo: Teoria, Política e Mobilização*. São Paulo: Paco, São Paulo State University.

Morelock, Jeremiah and Narita, Felipe Ziotti. 2019b. "Populism and Political Agitation in Late Capitalism: Research Notes". *3rd International Seminar on Public Policy and Social Development*, ed. Alexandre Mendes. Franca: São Paulo State University Press.

Morelock, Jeremiah and Narita, Felipe Ziotti. 2021. *The Society of the Selfie: Social Media and the Crisis of Liberal Democracy*. London: University of Westminster Press. (under contract).

Neumann, Franz. 1943. *Behemoth*. London: Victor Gollancz.

Norris, Pippa and Ronald Inglehart. 2019. *Cultural Backlash: Trump, Brexit and Authoritarian Populism*. Cambridge: Cambridge University Press.

Odilla, Fernanda. 2019. "Dos EUA ao Brasil, Como Presidentes Tentam Governar Sem Congresso." *BBC News*, London, 17 June.

Pensky, Max. 1997. "Adorno's Actuality." In *The Actuality of Adorno: Critical Essays on Adorno and the Postmodern*, edited by Max Pensky. Albany: State University of New York Press.

Phelps, Jordyn and Ben Gittleson. 2020. "Trump Praises 'Overwhelming Force' and 'Domination' in DC Morning After Peaceful Protest Broken Up for Photo Op." *ABC News* (June 3). At https://abcnews.go.com/Politics/trump-praises-overwhelming-force-domination-dc-morning-peaceful/story?id=71.

Portal G1. 2020. "Bolsonaro Discursa em Brasília para Manifestantes que Pediam Intervenção Militar" (April 19). At https://g1.globo.com/politica/noticia/2020/04/19/bolsonaro-discursa-em-manifestacao-em-brasilia-que-defendeu-intervencao-militar.ghtml.

Rank, Otto. 1999. *The Trauma of Birth*. London: Psychology Press.

Rizzo, Salvador. 2019. President Trump Accuses Rep. Omar of supporting al-Qaeda. *Washington Post*, July 17.

Robson, Ruthann. 2002. "Assimilation, Marriage, and Lesbian Liberation." *Temp. L. Rev* 75: 709.

Scheppele, Kim. 2018. "Autocratic Legalism." *The University of Chicago Law Review* 85(2): 545–580.

Schmitt, Carl. [1923–26] 1988. *The Crisis of Parliamentary Democracy*. Cambridge: MIT.

Shear, Michael D. 2019. "Trump Diatribe Belittles Impeachment as 'Attempted Coup' on Eve of Votes." *The New York Times* (December 17). At https://www.nytimes.com/2019/12/17/us/politics/trump-impeachment.html.

Sherratt, Yvonne. 2002. *Adorno's Positive Dialectic*. Cambridge: Cambridge University Press.

Stahl, Chelsea. 2019. "Trump Impeached by the House on Both Articles." *NBC News: Live Blog/Live Updates* (December 19). At https://www.nbcnews.com/politics/trump-impeachment-inquiry/live-blog/live-updates-house-votes-impeachment-president-trump-n1103576/ncrd1104536#liveBlogHeader.

Steib, Matt. 2020. "Trump Adviser Stephen Moore Compares Social-Distancing Protesters to Rosa Parks." *Intelligencer* (April 20). At https://nymag.com/intelligencer/2020/04/trump-advisor-compares-coronavirus-protesters-to-rosa-parks.html.

Stone, Alison. 2014. "Adorno, Hegel and Dialectic." *British Journal for the History of Philosophy* 22(6): 1118–1141.

Taylor, Charles. 1997. "The Politics of Recognition." *New Contexts of Canadian Criticism* 98: 25–73.

Thomas, William I., and Dorothy S. Thomas. 1928. *The Child in America*. New York: Alfred P. Knopff.

Turollo Jr., Reynaldo and Cancian, Natalia. 2020. "Supremo Blinda Congresso de Medidas de Bolsonaro que Atropelam Legislativo." *Folha de São Paulo* (January 6).

Weber, Max. 1976. *Wirtschaft und Gesellschaft: Grundriss der verstehenden Soziologie*. Vol. 1. Tübingen: Mohr.

Weiß, Volker. 2017. *Die autoritäre Revolte: Die neue Rechte und der Untergang des Abendlandes*. Stuttgart: Klett-Cotta.

Wolff, Robert Paul; Moore, Barrington and Marcuse, Herbert. 1966. *A Critique of Pure Tolerance*. Boston: Beacon Press.

Wong, Queenie. 2020. "Trump vs. Twitter: Here's What You Need to Know About the Free Speech Showdown." *CNET* (June 2). At https://www.cnet.com/news/trumps-social-media-executive-order-faces-lawsuit/.

CHAPTER 3

Capital Fetishism and the Authoritarian Personality: Critical Theory in the Weimar Years

David Norman Smith

1   Introduction

Stereotypes about the Frankfurt School abound. One of the most misleading is the claim – often, simply an assumption – that the Frankfurt Institute for Social Research was mired in traditionalism until it moved to New York not long after Max Horkheimer became the Institute's second director in 1930. Critical theory, transcending traditionalism, is said to have sprung, Athena-like, from reflection about the disasters that drove the Institute into exile. The Institute's first decade, from 1923 until Hitler's *Machtergreifung* in 1933, is viewed as an era of dogmatic, uncritical, pedestrian Marxism.

Critics and admirers alike have construed Horkheimer's circle in New York – above all, Theodor Adorno and Herbert Marcuse – as the heralds of a new form of post-enlightenment critique. Georg Lukács did not intend it as a compliment when he called Adorno *et al.* refugees in the "Grand Hotel Abyss, ... with every comfort, on the edge of an abyss, of nothingness, of absurdity," enjoying subtle comforts and empty meditations (1962: 219). But even that famous barb, which echoes in the titles of two histories of the Frankfurt School, places the accent on novelty and sophistication.[1] Historians have not seen the Institute's Weimar period – "the Frankfurt School in Frankfurt" – in the same light.[2]

I see matters differently. The Institute's early Marxism was sharply at odds with traditional Marxism, in precisely the spirit of Horkheimer's call for critical theory – theory, that is, which does not take class consciousness for granted and risks alienation from left-wing and labor orthodoxy.[3] Much of what the Institute ultimately achieved, empirically and philosophically, was prefigured

---

1   See Jeffries (2017) and Reijen and Noerr (1988). A novel and a journal now share this title, too.

2   Jay said in so many words (1982: 134) that "the Frankfurt School ... actually came into existence on Morningside Heights," that is, at Columbia University. This Frankfurt School, he said, orbited around a nucleus composed of Max Horkheimer, Theodor Adorno, Erich Fromm, Leo Lowenthal, and Herbert Marcuse.

3   See Smith (2017).

by projects in the 1920s. Indeed, in several respects, the early Institute posed questions that went beyond what Horkheimer's circle attempted or achieved. That was true, most notably, in the realm of commodity and authority fetishism.

Capital and authority were both challenged in radically new ways in the tumult after World War 1. Germany was suspended between revolution and counter-revolution, between hope and despair. The Institute was conceived, in the words of the original 1922 prospectus, to explore "international union life, strikes, sabotage, revolution, ... wage movements, antisemitism as a sociological problem, Bolshevism and Marxism, party and mass, the cost of living. ..." (1–2). The point of this study would be to interact dialectically with practice, "taking living people as [both] subjects and objects" of praxis:

> Just as the theoretician in the field of empirical science needs continuous contact with the pulsating life of reality now more than ever, so too it has become impossible for the pure practitioner to obtain an overview of the intricate network of economic and social factors without cultivating the intellect and applying scientific results and methods.
>
> WEIL and GERLACH 1922: 1–2

No one, in the ensuing decade, would have portrayed the Frankfurt Institute as a luxury hotel for navel-gazing existentialists. The Institute's principals in the Weimar years shared a vision of a capital-free and despot-free world which they hoped to realize by revolutionary means. They and their co-thinkers, including Lukács in this phase, discovered or extended a host of critical concepts, ranging from reification and alienation to authoritarianism and the rarely discussed but pivotal Marxian concept of capital fetishism.

2   Weimar at Dusk

On April 7, 1931, Karl Korsch wrote to his friend and student Eiichi Sugimoto, who had hoped to gain access to the Institute library in Frankfurt but found it closed. Korsch, who was a controversial anti-authoritarian communist with a stormy history, replied reassuringly:

> I have Fräulein Dr. Hilde Weiss here with me now and she tells me that she will return to Frankfurt tomorrow and that my friend and comrade Dr. Kurt Mandelbaum will [also] return from his travels. I gave Comrade Weiss your address and ... Weiss and Mandelbaum will be able to give you

access to the Institute immediately. Even though the Institute remains closed to the public until the 13th, it is certainly open to the inner circle ...
KORSCH 1980: 380

The Institute, like Germany, was at a crossroads. Felix Weil, the Institute's founder, had written to the Culture Minister in 1929, reviewing the Institute's progress in its first half-decade. Weiss and Mandelbaum were both central to that report. Weiss, with Erich Fromm, was coordinating a survey of working-class attitudes of unprecedented scope and scale. Mandelbaum was leading an Institute study on the history of Social Democracy. Two of the Institute's senior associates had just published major books, *"Der lmperialismus" und seine Kritiker* by Fritz Sternberg (1929) and *Das Akkumulations- und Zusammenbruchsgesetz des kapitalistischen Systems* by Henryk Grossmann (1929). But seismic events – the start of the Great Depression, and the ensuing rise of National Socialism, which first registered on the electoral Geiger counter in 1930 – intervened.

Under the leadership of Max Horkheimer, who succeeded the ailing Carl Grünberg in 1930, the Institute began to change direction. Weiss and Fromm were able to complete only the torso of their massive study. Weiss soon found herself in European exile, far from the new center of Institute activities in New York. Korsch and Mandelbaum were also far away. What ensued is usually hailed as the Frankfurt School's classical period, a phase marked by the rise of a new inner circle and a new, deeper approach to theory. But, in fact, there was far more theoretical continuity between the two phases than is usually recognized. Many of the central achievements of the Frankfurt School in exile grew from seeds planted in the Weimar era.

The working-class study, which occupied Fromm's team for much of the 1930s and yielded reams of typescript analysis,[4] was the lineal ancestor of *The Authoritarian Personality* (1950) and directly inspired the idea of psychological authoritarianism, which Fromm elaborated in a series of seminal essays (1936a, 1937, 1995 [1937]). *The Dialectic of Enlightenment* by Horkheimer and Adorno (1947) was prefigured by the dialectical studies of Korsch and Lukács (1923). And as I contend, here and elsewhere, the Institute's earliest work remains

---

4   This study was promised in many Institute publications and appeared, in part, in *Studien über Autorität und Familie* (Horkheimer, ed., 1936), but full publication was delayed until 1980, when Wolfgang Bonss released a German-language version compiled from the unpublished typescript. That edition later appeared in English as well (Fromm [1937] 1984). Since many of the original manuscripts were written in crisp English, and since Bonss omitted some intriguing material, I am currently working to prepare a fuller, more exact version.

unsurpassed in many respects.[5] Interrupted by crisis and left tantalizingly incomplete, the projects Felix Weil, Karl Korsch, and their Institute colleagues undertook in the long Weimar decade remain exemplary.

Some of their achievements are well known, including the hotly contested 1923 books by Lukács (*History and Class Consciousness*) and Korsch (*Marxism and Philosophy*). The heresies that were to appear in these books, and their authors, were the center of attention at the *Erste Marxistische Arbeitswoch* in 1922, which inspired Weil to found the Institute. Over the course of the Institute's first six years, Korsch and Lukács both published their principal scholarly essays in the Institute's *de facto* journal, edited by Grünberg. So closely were they associated with the Institute that, between them, they contributed nearly 20 percent of the total pages in the five volumes of Grünberg's journal which appeared between 1924 and 1931.[6] In these seminal essays, Lukács and Korsch introduced themes of reification, alienation, and commodity fetishism which were to exert enduring influence. But the fact that these essays were written for Grünberg's journal, and that they sprang from and shaped Institute preoccupations, has received almost no attention. Nor have the contributions of other Institute figures in this period received the notice they deserve.

Viewed collectively, the Institute's Weimar studies came to the brink of breakthroughs revolving around two key themes – capitalist authority and workers' authoritarianism. Both of those themes had classically Marxian roots. The concept of capital fetishism had been most fully expounded in two of Marx's posthumous texts, in the section on the "Trinity Formula" late in Volume 3 of *Capital* (which appeared in 1894, edited by Engels) and in the two final chapters of Volume 3 of *Theories of Surplus Value*, which appeared in 1910, edited by Kautsky. The idea of authoritarianism was drawn from implications in the discussions of alienation and factory despotism in *Capital* and *The Holy Family*, and, in Fromm's case, from psychoanalytic theory. (Marx's Paris manuscripts, the *Economic and Philosophical Manuscripts of 1844*, did not appear in print until 1932.)[7] Neither of these themes had been carefully studied by Marx scholars before Lukács and Korsch, but the urgency of the early Weimar years – marked by a near revolution, a depression, history's worst hyperinflation, a

---

5 The present paper is a companion to my "Anti-Authoritarian Marxism" (2020), which focuses on the radical humanism of Erich Fromm and the neglected Hilde Weiss.

6 In all, of the roughly 1,700 pages of essays and review-essays which appeared in Grünberg's journal from 1925 to 1930, nearly 300 pages were contributed by Korsch and Lukács. Included among their contributions were Lukács' famous essays on Lassalle and Moses Hess (1925, 1926) and Korsch's most sustained critique of Marxist orthodoxy (1929). Besides their essays (seven in all) they also wrote many book reviews, including seven by Lukács in 1928 and 1929.

7 The editions of these works cited by Lukács, Korschd. appear in the references, below.

general strike, industrial "rationalization" and "socialization" campaigns, death squad murders, abortive *Volkish* putsches, and a failed attempt by the newly founded Communist Party (KPD) to take power – forced authority and authoritarianism into the *Zeitgeist*. Lukács, Korsch, and their co-thinkers were briefly swimming with the stream, not simply against it.

3   Weil, Korsch, and Grünberg

The Frankfurt Institute has been famous for so long that we could easily take it for granted. But the very idea of an official university institute which, from the outset, assembled an interdisciplinary body of scholars and graduate students for the express purpose of studying socialism and labor, with an openly Marxist outlook, remains surprising. There have been few other such institutes, and none with a matching record of collective ambition and achievement. That was already true in the 1920s, and it remained true for decades.[8]

The Institute's later years are well-documented, but the Weimar years remain obscure. That Karl Korsch was central to the Institute and its wider political and cultural milieu has barely been noticed. Even Ulrike Migdal, whose brief history of the Institute in the Grünberg years remains the fullest account of that period, mentions Korsch only in passing (1981). That his disciples – Weil, Weiss, and others – produced a sizeable body of literature on capital, capitalists, and authority has gone unremarked.

In the early 1970s, not long after Martin Jay published his groundbreaking Frankfurt School history, *The Dialectical Imagination* (1973), Henry Pachter wrote Jay a long, detailed letter in which, Jay reported,

> he scolded me for not having dealt in greater depth with the *Institut für Sozialforschung's* first decade, when its links with Weimar's organized Left, most importantly the Communist Party, were still strong. In particular, he wanted to impress upon me how vital Karl Korsch had been in the *Institut's* early years, a fact that surviving *Institute* members had downplayed in their interviews.
>
> JAY 1981: 25

---

8 The details of the chronicle below are drawn from myriad sources. To avoid burdening the published version of this paper with a groaning mass of source notes, I am appending those notes to a draft at my ResearchGate site (*https://www.researchgate.net/profile/David_Smith366*). Hence, below, only points that require brief substantive clarification will appear in the notes.

Pachter had belonged to Korsch's Weimar circle, and though he did not romanticize their shared history, he wanted it to be properly understood. My goal, in what follows, is to explore facets of this history. Given space constraints, I can discuss only a fraction of the important texts of that era. Later publications will review the contributions of Boris Roniger and Hilde Weiss, both of whom – especially Weiss, in *Abbe und Ford* (1927) – offer remarkable insights into capital fetishism and authority. Here, I can offer only a prolegomenon to their work by exploring the founding texts that preceded and inspired theirs. The authors of those texts are Felix Weil and Karl Korsch.

Readers who know the standard histories of the Frankfurt School might doubt the relevance of attention paid to Korsch and Weil. The latter is always mentioned, in passing, as the heir to a vast fortune whose wealth enabled him to finance the Institute, but beyond that little is said. A friend in the 1920s said that Weil despised his wealth, that it made him a kind of outcast, who was taken seriously only as a personification of his wealth. Scholars have viewed Weil similarly, calling him a "salon Bolshevik" and implying that he was, at bottom, a dilettante. The truth is quite different. Weil was a minor but very genuine scholar, who shared with Korsch a refined sensitivity to issues of class and democracy.

What Korsch and Weil shared when they met in the aftermath of the 1918 workers' and soldiers' uprising in Germany was a blend of revolutionary ardor, openness to Marxism – which they were both studying intently – and sympathy for workers' self-management. That attitude was widespread at the time, given the influence of the workers' council movement in post-war Germany, but Weil and Korsch both had pre-existing sympathies in that area. Korsch, who was 33, had lived in England for a time before the war, where he was influenced by the Fabian Society's concept of a kind of economic democracy which included, but went beyond, the syndicalist notion of worker-controlled factories. Weil, who was 21, was an Argentine citizen with a keen interest in syndicalist currents in the Argentine labor movement, which he discussed in a short book in 1923.[9]

Weil quickly fell under Korsch's influence, and they remained close friends and kindred spirits for decades. Weil's inaugural dissertation, on the movement to "socialize" industry in Germany – which was both a grassroots and an official campaign – offered a kind of aerial photograph of the entire field of discourse on socialization, which Korsch served administratively and which

---

9   Grünberg reprinted Weil's book in the 1925 issue of his journal. That version appears in the references, below.

he discussed in a widely-read booklet, "What is Socialization?" (1919). In 1921, Korsch published Weil's dissertation under the title *Sozialisierung* in his series *Practical Socialism.*

Not long afterwards, Weil and Korsch invited a group of like-minded intellectuals to join them at the *Erste Marxistische Arbeitswoch,* which they convened in the late spring of 1922 in Ilmenau, Thuringia, near the university in Jena where Korsch was on the faculty. Weil invited his friends Friedrich Pollock and Konstantin Zetkin while Korsch invited Lukács, Bela Fogarasi and an entourage of students, including Boris Roniger, Karl Schmückle and (it appears) Hilde Weiss.[10] In the sessions that followed, Weil spoke on socialization, Korsch joined Lukács in a colloquy on themes from their forthcoming books, and Fritz Sternberg and Karl Wittfogel lectured on their areas of expertise. It was during this stimulating week that Weil conceived the idea of the institute.

Weil reportedly wanted Korsch to direct the institute, but Friedrich Pollock objected, saying that Korsch was too much "the calvary officer" to play that role – that is, that he was too combative, too undiplomatic to tread lightly among the luminaries whose support the Institute would need to find a university home.[11] That was a fair assessment. Korsch had emerged as a leading KPD intellectual. In 1922 alone he had published three short books expounding a semi-syndicalist, radicalized Marxism. In October 1923, Korsch served as the justice minister in a regional workers' government which united the KPD with the Social Democratic Party (SPD). That government was soon ousted by the military and Korsch was briefly forced underground. In the spring of 1924, he re-emerged as the editor of the KPD's theoretical journal, *Die Internationale,* and he was elected to represent the KPD in the German *Reichstag.*

Korsch's days in the good graces of the party's Soviet patrons were short-lived. The version of dialectics that he espoused in *Marxism and Philosophy* proved discomfiting, and in June 1924 Korsch, like Lukács – and Korsch's friend and protégé, Boris Roniger – was denounced as an "ultra-leftist" from the podium of the Fifth Congress of the Communist International by the General Secretary, Grigorii Zinoviev. The charges against Lukács and Korsch were theoretical, even metaphysical, with only a hint of latent political content. But the charges against Korsch and "Comrade Boris" (who was criticized at length by the leading Soviet intellectual, Nikolai Bukharin), were far more overtly political. Korsch and Boris Roniger had published back-to-back articles critical of

10   Full details appear in Smith (2020) and Yagi (2011).
11   So Karl Wittfogel told Lewis Feuer in an interview. See Feuer (1980: 167, note 30).

the proposed Comintern platform in *Die Internationale,* and Roniger, in partic-ular, was overtly heretical, challenging central tenets of the 'Leninism' which was just then taking shape, five months after Lenin's death.

Details of Roniger's heresy – which was razor-sharp, intellectually rich, and fiercely anti-authoritarian – will be analyzed on another occasion. Suffice to say, for now, that Prof. Carl Grünberg, the director Weil had selected for the Institute, delivered the Institute's inaugural lecture at the University of Frankfurt just days after Korsch, Roniger, and Lukács had been denounced in Moscow. All three of them remained central figures in the Institute's milieu for the rest of the decade. No one published more extensively in Grünberg's journal than Korsch, who remained unrepentant. Lukács, who had officially accepted Zinoviev's censure, also chose Grünberg's journal as the venue for the essays he wrote after the controversy over *History and Class Consciousness.* Roniger was an Institute affiliate whose "quantitative and voluminous" treatise on *Trustkapitalismus* was featured by Weil in 1929 as one of the projected high-lights of the Institute's book series.[12]

It is perhaps unsurprising, given this history, that Korsch was expelled from the KPD in 1926. International communism, which was still just seven years old, had been torn from the start between rival impulses, which clustered around the iconic names of Rosa Luxemburg and Vladimir Lenin. Luxemburg, before she was assassinated by a right-wing death squad in January 1919, had long been recognized as a voice for radically democratic Marxism. Shortly before she was murdered, she wrote a friendly but unsparing criticism of the infant Bolshevik regime. That criticism, which she left unpublished at her death, said that Lenin and Trotsky would betray socialism if they were to make a virtue of the centralist methods that they had adopted to repel the white Russian mili-tary counterrevolution. The whole point of socialism, she insisted, is to ensure the fullest freedom for everyone, without exception – above all, for those who dissent. Intellectuals like Lukács and Korsch who hoped to reconcile the leg-acies of Lenin and Luxemburg were thus placed in a quandary when her lit-erary executor Paul Levi, who had recently clashed with Lenin, published her criticism of Bolshevism in 1922. It Before then it had already proven difficult to square the implicit tensions between Luxemburg's democratism and Lenin's bureaucratism, but now that tension was manifest.

Lukács, in one of the weakest essays in *History and Class Consciousness,* sided emphatically with Lenin. Korsch, by 1926, had made the opposite choice, which he made very clear and very public. With Roniger and others he formed

---

12   This description of Roniger's projected book is by Strzelewicz (1986: 154).

an anti-authoritarian alternative to the KPD, *Entschiedene Linke* (Intransigent Left), which forged links with similar tendencies in Russia, Poland, Italy and elsewhere. Weil, writing in 1928 in Grünberg's journal about Trotsky's critique of the doctrine of a transitional phase of Russian state capitalism, speculated about the likely fate of Korsch's ultra-left, which, he said, remained an open question. Weil also found and published in Grünberg's journal a stirring, final fragment of Luxemburg's criticism of Lenin (1929), which Levi had left unpublished.

All of this had a direct impact on the Institute. One of the first and most significant projects that Weil and Grünberg undertook was a coordinated effort, with David Riazanov's Marx-Engels Institute in Moscow, to archive and publish the complete works of Marx and Engels, the *Marx-Engels Gesamtausgabe* (MEGA). Riazanov and Grünberg were old friends, and Weil successfully persuaded the German Social Democratic Party to allow the Institute to photograph the whole of Marx's so-called *Nachlass* – amounting to roughly 150,000 pages of hitherto unpublished manuscripts – which they shared with Riazanov.

The early MEGA volumes, which Weil issued in German editions, included priceless discoveries, including Marx's late correspondence with Vera Zasulich. Several years later, *The German Ideology* and *The Economic and Philosophic Manuscripts of 1844* appeared as well. By then, however, the Soviet regime had broken its ties to the Institute, alleging, in 1927, that at least six of the MEGA's collaborators in Frankfurt were "Korschists."

In 1928, when Willy Strzelewicz joined the Institute as a student assistant, he found the students divided between Korschists and Communist loyalists. The latter, he recalled, were just beginning to be called "Stalinists" but were, in his case at least, "Lukácsians." This division within the Institute sparked predictable tensions but did not impede its work. Weil and Grünberg took pride in their non-sectarianism, and their journal was ecumenical in every way, featuring work by representatives of every left-of-center current, from the mildest (e.g., Rudolf Wissell) to the most radical (including, besides the Korschists, other communist dissidents who opposed Stalin such as Julian Gumperz and Franz Borkenau). Strzelewicz showed a similar ecumenical spirit when he went out of his way to praise the long-forgotten Roniger, whom he found "irritatingly stimulating."

Institutionally and intellectually, in other words, Karl Korsch's antiauthoritarian Marxism was a major influence on the Institute's early agenda. He was not wrong to assure Sugimoto in 1931 that, "if you have any wishes regarding the Institute, ... I will presumably always be able to have those wishes fulfilled very quickly. ..." (1980: 380). Until that point, that statement had always been true, and it undoubtedly remained true until Hitler's ascent to power scattered Korsch and the others to the four winds.[13] But did Korsch's influence on the Institute have significant *substantive* consequences? Was the Frankfurt Institute in the Weimar years already, in some sense, an embodiment of critical theory?

4   The Idea of Class Struggle

Conventional portraits of the Institute's early years often revolve around stereotypes about Marxist orthodoxy. Korsch and Weil were, in principle, far more "orthodox" in their Marxism than the reformists and Bolsheviks they criticized. They were intent upon restoring Marxism to what it had been in Marx's hands – a creative, unfinished doctrine of working-class self-emancipation, rescued, as Weil stressed, from dilettantes and party politics, with an empirical agenda of historical and sociological inquiry. But for most academics today the very word Marxism conjures up pale images of dusty tomes and dustier thinkers, forever meditating on the same weave of enchanted phrases: dialectics, historical materialism, praxis, proletariat, bourgeoisie.

Korsch did indeed take those dusty themes seriously. But he was anything but a walking stereotype. Like Lukács, he proposed a radical alternative to the inert materialism and lifeless dialectics of the previous generation, with its "Popes" and "temple guardians.". Just how radical, how disconcerting, that alternative Marxism could appear became vividly clear in debate between Werner Sombart and Carl Grünberg in late 1924.

Sombart and Grünberg were the leading Marx scholars of the day. Each had published major works before the turn of the century. Sombart had corresponded with Engels, who praised his review of Volume 3 of *Capital,* and later he polemicized against his colleague Max Weber over the *spiritus capitalisticus.* Sombart was also well known for his idealization of entrepreneurs, which made him a central foil for Hilde Weiss in her treatise on Henry Ford and Ernst

---

13   A May 7, 1931 typescript which lists the Institute's affiliates cites 22 *Mitarbeiter* in all, including the Institute's teaching faculty (Horkheimer, Fromm, Grossman and Pollock); Korsch and several of his close colleagues, among them Weiss, Mandelbaum, Rolf Katz, and Heinz Langerhans; and others such as Gumperz and Strzelewicz. Listed publications by these Institute affiliates include Korsch, *Marxismus und Philosophie;* Weiss, *Abbe und Ford;* Mandelbaum, *Die Erörterungen innerhalb der deutschen Sozialdemokratie über das Problem des Imperialismus 1895–1914;* and Katz (*Die deutsche Volkswirtschaftlehre als Spiegel der gesellschaftlichen Entwicklung*). See Institut für Sozialforschung (1931: File IX 5A).

Abbe. Grünberg, meanwhile, had been Sombart's counterpart in Austria, but with one decisive difference – namely, that Grünberg gravitated ever closer to Marx, while Sombart went in the opposite direction.

Grünberg had initially opposed Marxism from a left-Catholic standpoint. But as the leading student of socialism in Austria he taught the entire galaxy of "Austro-Marxist" scholars, of whom Max Adler, Rudolf Hilferding, Karl Renner and Otto Bauer were the best known. Ultimately, the educator was also educated – by his Marxist students.

Hence, when Grünberg met Sombart on the field of scholarly battle in September 1924 under the auspices of the *Verein für Sozialpolitik,* they were expected to offer clashing views. Those expectations were realized. Two years earlier, when Grünberg had attended the *Jubiläumstag* marking the *Verein's* semicentennial, he had been teased for his unreconstructed Marxism by a reviewer:

> ... [Professor] Grünberg, amiable, a hint malicious and not very convincing, presented the position of the "pure Marxist" (do these still exist?) ...
>
> GÜNTHER 1922: 519

The triumphalism of that snide comment – the complacent assumption that Marxism was now almost entirely passé among academics – was no longer easily maintained in September 1924, when Lukács and Korsch, both of whom Zinoviev had decried as "professors" just months earlier, had captured widespread attention among academics as well as socialists. One year earlier, at a session on revolution at the *Soziologentages* in Jena – which Grünberg and Max Adler addressed as representatives of Marxism – *History and Class Consciousness* was on everyone's mind.

Sombart had Korsch as well as Lukács in mind when he debated Grünberg at the *Verein* meeting in Stuttgart in 1924. The topic of the debate was "The Idea of Class Struggle," and Sombart, the first speaker, was eager to press the case that the current, radicalized idea of class struggle was something unhappily new. Yes, many socialists before Marx had advanced ideas of class struggle, and so too had the early Social Democrats. But all this, Sombart insisted, paled next to "the class struggle theory of the communists," which raised mass *Ressentiment* to exponential heights and, indeed, "absolutized" the class struggle:

> ... *revolutionary class struggle theory* ... has been so fully shaped under the pressure of revolutionary passion and [has] increased so [much] ... that it presents itself today as something essentially distinct.
>
> SOMBART 1924: 25

Sombart blamed Marx as well as his latter-day heirs for this absolutized world-view, which, he said, they also *ethicized*. "Only when I equate class rule with class *exploitation* [is it given] an ethical accent." Marx was wrong to malign the ruling class as "the exploiting class." (25) By doing so he had helped to swell a tidal wave of what Sombart, echoing Stahl, called "the slime of sin" – hubris, hatred, greed – which Sombart, like Stahl, held could be reversed only by a return to Christ and humility.

These comments left Grünberg was aghast: You say, he told Sombart, that "the class struggle worldview is based not on an idea but on resentment alone, the canaille's slime of sin." At this he threw up his hands: "What can one say about such statements?"

Sombart had said that Marxism reduces people to atoms of material self-interest. Grünberg denied that Marxism entailed that premise:

> It is admitted without further ado that there is an – as yet – unresolved remnant in historical materialism. In the interest of the "clarification" of ... spiritual phenomena I thus say ... *'Est deus in nobis.'*
> GRÜNBERG 1924: 32

This phrase, from Ovid's *Fasti,* VI, 5–6, affirms the creativity of the poet, and, by extension, all humanity:

> *Est deus in nobis; agitante calescimus illo: impetus hic sacrae semina mentis habet.* [*There is a god within us. When he stirs us, we are warmed. His impetus sows the seeds of sacred inspiration.*]
> GRÜNBERG 1924: 32

Sombart had said that the only true love is the self-abasing love of God. Grünberg answered that class solidarity is no less genuine:

> ... union workers or cartel members or employers' association members may not have the same kind of love as the early Christian communities, but [look closely at the unions:] What tremendous capacity for sacrifice, what dedication to a cause recognized as shared, what ... solidarity, what tenacity ... [Yes,] they were created for fighting purposes, but they fight, with love, for the sake of the *res communis!*
> GRÜNBERG 1924: 39–40

Sombart concluded with the charge that, in the hands of Marx and his most faithful and astute disciples – "So latterly Georg Lukácz" – the idea of class struggle had been *mythologized,* "a promise was made":

> ... the class struggle in the here and now was construed as the final strug-
> gle to be fought by the proletariat so that it could enter the realm of free-
> dom [and] achieve perfection in earthly life. ... The proletariat was thus
> raised to an army of saints ...
>
> SOMBART 1924: 29, 27

Grünberg replied sardonically. Sombart, alleging the *Schweinhund* nature of
the broad, resentful masses, repudiated in principle the idea that workers
could achieve altruism and heroism. And yet, at the same time, he professed
the optimism of faith, claiming that redemption would come when humanity stood, in the final hour, radiant with God's grace "on the golden ground of
transcendence" (86). Grünberg answered that solidarity, not saintliness, was
needed – and that it was *possible.*

> As far as I know, in the last 1924 years, God's grace appeared in some
> saints – e.g., in the apostolic history of the early church, perhaps tem-
> porarily in some small religious communities – but it did not extend to
> the great mass; and I am afraid that neither I nor many ... of you have yet
> shared in God's grace ...
>
> GRÜNBERG 1924: 34

But all was not lost, if we turned, not to theology, but to history and experience. "How often does history show us examples," Grünberg emphasized, "of
the purest devotion to interests other than our own and other than purely
material!"

> To take an example that is particularly evident to all of us: When a num-
> ber of men met in Eisenach in 1872 to counter the [free market] tendency
> which was then so powerful, and to found the *Verein für Sozialpolitik,* [it
> proved] that on the one hand there were intellectuals who found it to
> their advantage to stand with the rulers, with the mighty, while there
> were also those who dared to stand on the other side ...
>
> GRÜNBERG 1924: 33

This argument was echoed by Fritz Tarnow the chief of the timber workers
union and a leading figure in the German labor confederation:

> We are no longer supposed to fight, we should flee to God – that is the
> ultimate redemption Sombart offers us? ... I cannot accept your solu-
> tion. From the standpoint of the practical trade unionist ... the workers'

present standard of living can neither be maintained nor raised without struggle. And that struggle is the purest class struggle.

TARNOW 1924: 62

Sombart, holding his ground, closed the day with a spirited riposte to his critics – and he expressed incredulity when a discussant asked who in particular he had in mind. "I find this rather astonishing."

Are you unfamiliar with all the ... newer writings by Korsch, Lukácz, and Bukharin? ... [There, indeed,] you will find the point of view [that] I have characterized as ... absolute class theory.

SOMBART 1924: 82

5   Capitalists Are Capitalists Because Workers Are Workers

Just months after his debate with Grünberg, Sombart published the tenth edition of the volume on socialism and social movements which had first cemented his reputation as a Marx scholar (1897). He gave this edition a new title, *Der proletarische Sozialismus ("Marxismus")*, reflecting his emerging and increasingly narrow concern over "absolutized" revolutionary theory (1925).

Viewed as a whole, *Der proletarische Sozialismus* is a wild ride through Sombart's obsessions, an overstuffed Christmas goose in two massive volumes, full of invective, gossip, and *Volkish* antisemitism. But every so often (most notably, for our purposes, in the passages devoted to Lukács, who, like Korsch and Luxemburg, was among Sombart's *bêtes noir*), genuine scholarship appeared.

Sombart had carefully read *History and Class Consciousness*, and one of his criticisms stands out. Lukács had improved on established Marxian exegesis in many ways, most notably with respect to the concept of reification – that is, *Verdinglichung,* "thingification." This was a thread plucked from the tapestry of Marx's theory of commodity fetishism, which posited "social relations" between commodities and "thing-like" relations between their owners – that is, the fact that commodity sellers and buyers, interact through the mediation of the things (*Dinge, rei*) they have made.

Reification is the law of the market, and nowhere does it obtain more fatefully than in the market for labor power, where job candidates relate not only to capitalists, but to life's necessities, through the cash nexus. If they successfully become wage-earners they become bread-winners as well. But if they fail to get work, they are barred even from food and shelter. They must sell a product (in this case, labor power) to get other products, which, like all things produced in capitalist society, are "commodities" in Marx's sense – that is, they must be sold before they can be used.

Capitalists, of course, deal with workers both before and after they buy their labor power. In the market they enter into reified relations with workers as sellers of labor power. Subsequently, in the production process, they enter into instrumental relations with those same workers, whose labor, Marx says, they exploit for profit. Sombart rejects this conclusion, not substantively, but rhetorically, since he construes the term "exploitation" ethically while denying that it is unethical to profit from the labor of others .

For Marx, and Lukács, this criticism misses the point. Marx was no friend of the capitalist class – "I by no means paint the capitalist *couleur de rose*" – but he adapted the term exploitation from the natural sciences to make a scientific point, namely, that capitalism is fueled by surplus labor, extracted from workers, just as iron ore is extracted from the earth by those who exploit mineral resources. Marx often waxed indignant over capitalists' moral lapses –, but exploitation, he insisted, is integral to capitalism as a system.[14] It is not, in essence, a function of anyone's personal wishes.

Capitalists, too, are swept along by the profit imperative, independently of their will. If they decline to exploit their workers, they will be defeated by less sensitive competitors. They may *willingly* participate in exploitation, but the force that drives them, which gives them no *alternative* in the position they occupy, is the accumulationism inherent in the system. Capitalists, in word, *personify* capital. The forces that move them, Marx says, are blind, inhuman – impersonal. Ultimately, it is irrelevant whether any given capitalist enjoys exploiting workers, because the *role* is the source of exploitation, not the momentary will of the person who happens, for a time, to play that role.

Lukács quoted Marx to this effect in several places. In his essay on Moses Hess, he quoted a passage in *Theories of Surplus Value* in which Marx praised the working-class socialist Thomas Hodgskin for recognizing that the power of labor is routinely credited to things and thingified people. Hodgskin saw, Marx said, that "the effects of a specific social form of labor are ascribed to things, to the products of that labor; the relation itself is envisioned in *reified* form." This was true not only for commodities and money but, Marx says, "at a higher

---

14   This point, and the *"couleur de rose"* phrase, appears in English editions of the preface to the first German edition of *Capital.* In the original German this phrase is *"in rosigem Licht"* (1867: xi).

level," for capital. The efficacy of the labor process is ascribed to "things," to "the objective moments" of this process, "as if they had come to independently personify them against labor."

> ... they would cease to embody these effects if they ceased to confront labor in this *estranged* (*entfremdeten*) form. The capitalist as capitalist is merely the personification of capital, he stands opposed to labor as its creation, but endowed (*begabte*) with a will and personality of his own.
>
> H[odgskin] views this as a purely subjective delusion. ... He does not see how this way of seeing matters springs from the real relationship itself, how the latter does not express the former, but inverts it.[15]
>
> MARX [1864-65] 1910: 354, cited by LUKÁCS 1926: 46

Lukács adds that Hodgskin's "inability to recognize the reality-factor in the fetishistic forms of capitalist production" reflects the fact that he sees the result, the fetish, but not the process that creates it. The fetish is not simply an illusion. When people see a capitalist as the personification of their own alienated powers, they are not wrong – they are, rather, seeing an inverted reality without grasping its inversion. What they fail to see, Lukács add, is that "it is not a question of a 'thing' in the midst of the process, but rather of 'thingness' as being simply a manifestation of the process" (1926: 46).

Personifying the power of labor in this way, as a fetish to be idolized, is not an entirely happy fate. Workers are reified in the market and instrumentalized in the labor process, but capitalists, too, are reified in the market and reduced in investment and production to the personification of an impersonal force. Lukács extends this point, and Sombart resists. Genuine entrepreneurs, for Sombart, are heroic figures – innovators, creators. Calling them pawns in a blind game whose rules they can only obey, calling them agents of what Marx calls "self-valorizing capital," is sheer reductionism in his eyes. Lukács, affirming this point, is thus for Sombart a remarkable illustration of the "spiritual blindness" that afflicts even the shrewdest Marxist. Sombart faults him above all for endorsing and elaborating the following passage from *Capital*:

---

15   This was, and remains, a rarely cited passage. Google Books shows that the phrase "Der Kapitalist als Kapitalist ist bloss die Personifikation" appears in only two pre-1930 sources: *Theorien über den Mehrwert* and Lukács' essay (which is the source of the translation offered here). Lukács, in other words, may well have been the first commentator to cite this passage. It was subsequently cited in his book on *Der junge Hegel* (1948: 28) and by Jahn (1968: 361).

[Capitalism is] guided by no consciousness, driven only by its own immanent and blind dynamic, which in all its immediate appearance-forms reveals itself as the rule of the past over the present, as the rule of capital over labor; ... the 'laws' of the rigid, thingified reality of capitalism, in which the bourgeoisie is forced to live, can only assert themselves over the heads of the – apparently – acting bearers and agents of capital.

SOMBART 1925: 302-3, citing Marx from LUKÁCS 1923: 199

Sombart strenuously objects. The idea that capitalist "conduct could be 'determined' by something that does not form part of the entrepreneur's consciousness is altogether foggy," an example of Marx's mythologizing worldview (303). Capitalism, he insists, is the achievement of capitalists.

The rejoinder, from a Marxian and Lukáscian standpoint, is that Sombart's contention is itself a manifestation of fetishism –

"... thinking ... anchored in immediacy [and] clinging to ossified" social realities and habits of mind.

LUKÁCS citing MARX 1923: 199; cf. SOMBART 1925: 303

Capitalists are not demiurges. Seeing them that way, as Promethean figures, is a fundamental part of what Marx means by capital fetishism. In a crucial note in the first chapter of *Capital,* Marx explains the inversive logic of this kind of fetishized thinking.

Dieser Mensch ist z. B. nur König, weil sich andre Menschen als Unterthanen zu ihm verhalten. Sie glauben umgekehrt Unterthanen zu sein, weil er König ist.

[This man, e.g., is only King because other men relate to him as subjects. But they believe on the contrary that they are subjects because he is King.]

MARX 1867: 21

Marx's intent in this note was to clarify the logic of commodity fetishism by establishing a parallel in the realm of what I have called authority fetishism. The issue is the commodity's double nature, embodying both value and use-value. People in the grip of commodity fetishism see that duality as essential. They believe that labor products inherently embody value and must therefore sell, realizing that value in exchange, before they can be appropriated for use. Marx, on the contrary, regards value as entirely social, a transient social status which lasts only as long as people continue to sell their products rather than sharing them. Sharing, not selling, is Marx's ideal social relationship. But in order to realize that ideal, people would have to treat their products as use-values, cooperatively produced and held in common, rather than as values, produced and held privately.

Commodity fetishism makes that ideal seem utopian. Phrased in the language of Marx's note, above, the premise of commodity fetishism is the belief that producers are sellers because commodities are commodities – in other words, that products are inherently for sale. The truth, Marx says, is just the reverse, that products are only commodities because producers are sellers. If people chose to produce for use, not sale, products would *not* be dual in nature. They would have use, but not price.

Echoing Hegel, Marx calls fetishism an instance of "reflection-determination," or *Reflexionsbestimmungen*. This is an inversive logic, which inverts the world both in thought and, to the degree that people act on the basis of that logic, in practice. Remarkably, Marx applies this logic to the authority of the king as well as to the value of the commodity. No less remarkably, his application of this logic went unremarked in nearly the whole of the Marxian tradition before Lukács.[16]

Korsch, in 1930, said that before Lukács only Emil Lask had given the concept of commodity fetishism informed treatment.[17] In theses dating from the same period, Korsch stressed the centrality of the critique of fetishism to the nascent Marxist radicalism of the day:

> The *fetish*, upon whose theoretical and practical abolition (*Aufhebung*) the revolutionary Marxian critique of political economy hinges, has become the idol of Marxist scientific economists and a stumbling block and annoyance for Marx's bourgeois and reformist critics.
>
> KORSCH 1971: 70

---

16   The defining phrase (*Dieser Mensch ist z. B. nur König,* etc.) appeared in every German, French, English and Russian edition of *Das Kapital,* but it was quoted only three times: by Tomáš Masaryk (1899: 188–89) in a note; by Emil Hammacher (1909: 111) *en passant*; and in an anarchist tract by Francis Tandy (1896: 187). Even the term *Reflexionsbestimmungen* went virtually uncited, though it appeared in *Capital*, in Engels's *Anti-Duhring* and in excerpts from Marx's critique of Max Stirner which had appeared in a socialist reader edited by Eduard Bernstein (1904: 267, 369).

17   See Korsch's review-essay on books by Karl Renner and Evgeny Pashukanis in Grünberg's journal (1930a). Of the handful of scholars besides Lask who had devoted more than a few words to Marx's theory of fetishism before Lukács, Max Adler stands out.

In 1932, Korsch edited a new version of the second edition of *Das Kapital,* which had appeared precisely 60 years earlier and was the last German edition that Marx revised personally. His introduction to that volume, like his study *Karl Marx* six years later, showed that he was keenly interested in unearthing the psychosocial implications of value-theory – commodity fetishism above all. *Capital,* Chapter 1, he said, was "an absolute masterpiece of dialectical conceptual development,"

> ... a virtuoso feat (*Virtuosenkunststück*) unsurpassed even by Hegel, from the 'Value-Form' ... to the brilliant, and, for novices, correspondingly difficult section on the 'Fetishism of Commodities and Its Secret' ...
>
> Only here do we learn that 'value' itself, unlike corporeal commodities and their corporeal commodity owners, is neither physically real nor does it express, like the term *'use-value',* a simple relationship between a given or manufactured object and a human need. 'Value' reveals itself instead as an inter-personal relationship concealed beneath a reified exterior ...
>
> KORSCH 1932: 13

Value was the main topic of Korsch's correspondence with Sugimoto in 1931, a topic they were then debating with Pollock, Roniger and Mandelbaum. But none of those thinkers, or even Lukács, went beyond the water's edge with respect to capital fetishism *per se. History and Class Consciousness* was replete with the language of reflection-determinations and fetishism, but even Lukács discussed the "capital fetish" only in passing, in the passages I have cited and in just a few other places.

Capitalists are only capitalists because workers are workers. That much was clear to Korsch *et al.* But it was equally clear that workers thought they were workers because capitalists were capitalists – that is, that capitalists are job creators. That conviction was enshrined in the very language of class in Germany, which defined the capitalist as a "labor giver" (*Arbeitsgeber*) and classified the wage-earner as a "labor taker" (*Arbeitsnehmer*).

Capitalists differ in their personal gifts, and those qualities matter for the success or failure of their firms. But those qualities are not charismatic in Max Weber's sense, that is, gifts of grace that qualitatively transcend ordinary mortal capacities.[18] No capitalist is an island, or a solitary hero. Marx's Robinsonades were intended as thought experiments, not sociology.

If we define capitalists with Marx as those who invest their money in production, it is clear that no capitalist can succeed except by employing workers. Those workers contribute the vast majority of the effort needed for the

---

18   See Smith (2016, 2013, 2011).

firm – for the capitalist – to thrive. And yet workers often depend on capitalists psychologically as well financially. Only capitalists are felt to have the initiative and insight needed to guide production and satisfy basic needs. 'We are workers' they typically assume, 'because capitalists are capitalists.' The idea that labor power could be self-determining, possessed and shared collectively, without the patronage of a benefactor, remained foreign. The sociologist Leopold von Wiese, one of the discussants in Sombart's debate with Grünberg, said this in so many words:

> However production may be organized, one way or another, there will always be exploitation, and yet, even so, [a definite] spirit of community ... It will always be thus.
>   WIESE 1924: 68

Another discussant, Friedich von Gottl-Ottlilienfeld, was confident that the secret to that community spirit was already clear. Ever since the near revolution of 1918, hopes for lasting social reform without revolution had clustered around the idea of an *Arbeitsgemeinschaft,* a "working community" which would unite capitalists and workers in a spirit of harmony. Attempts to bring that hope to fruition were manifest in the innumerable "plant councils" (*Betriebsräte*) which had been legally mandated after 1918 as a central part of the effort to "rationalize" the struggling postwar economy. Over the course of the decade, one specific model of ostensible cross-class harmony had won growing influence. That was what was beginning to be called *Fordismus,* the experience, that is, of Henry Ford, the conveyor belt., and the '5 dollar day.' Gottl-Ottlilienfeld was an ardent Fordist, as he made clear in his remarks.

> I certainly appreciate that [Grünberg] remains true to himself. ... But it is tragic [to see him] lag behind the time. People are thirsting for something new, truly satisfying. I [favor] an 'ideology' [which] is not shaken from my sleeves, but read from something that plays out in the bright sunlight of American high capitalism, namely the work of Henry Ford!
>   GOTTL-OTTLILIENFELD 1924: 75–76

This, plainly, was capital fetishism of the highest order. Ford, the prophet, the oracle of the mechanized factory and the industrial work ethic, had come to save a world suspended between hyperinflation and depression, between wars. Nor was appreciation for *Fordismus* restricted to academics and capitalists. Fritz Tarnow, in 1926, traveled to the United States to see Fordism in action, and he returned in the seemingly chimerical form of a labor Fordist. Capitalism may have been shaken, roughly, by the tumult after the war, but capital fetishism was resilient.

Reflecting on this conundrum was a major part of what inspired Korsch and Lukács to probe class consciousness and, more generally, the "subjective factor" which traditional Marxism had neglected. This concern was at the heart of their critical theory. In 1930, Korsch looked back on the years which had elapsed since *Marxism and Philosophy* and *History and Class Consciousness* had appeared in 1923. He reaffirmed his intellectual solidarity with Lukács despite the political differences which now divided them. What had originally united them was their shared determination to take reification and class unconsciousness seriously, and for Korsch, at least, that resolve remained intact. Studies of class psychology like the one that Weiss had undertaken with Fromm coincided exactly with what he thought was most urgently needed: open-minded empirical research to resolve pressing unanswered questions.

Many questions remained unanswered about capital fetishism in particular. Hilde Weiss did not use that phrase as such in *Abbe und Ford* (1927), but it was audible as an undertone throughout. She was steeped in *Capital* and *Theories of Surplus Value* to an extent that rivaled Lukács, and she made Sombart, Tarnow and Gottl-Ottlilienfeld her theoretical foils. Grünberg was her dissertation advisor, and Korsch had been her original mentor (and remained her confidant).

Analysis of *Abbe und Ford* will appear later in another paper. Now, as a step on that path, I will conclude with a brief discussion of a neglected but notable contribution to the critique of capital and authority fetishism, Korsch's *Arbeitsrecht für Betriebsräte* (1922).

6   Capital Fetishism Is Contradictory

Weimar critical theory was forged in the aftermath of a near revolution, when intellectuals were a single current in a massive wave. The revolutionary hopes of Weil, Lukács, Korsch, Weiss *i tutti quanti* were taken very seriously, hence the sharpness of the criticisms directed against them by all and sundry – Sombart and Zinoviev, Social Democrats and Communists, academics and fellow activists. Unlike the Frankfurt School in exile, which convened in the melancholy shadow of fascism, Grünberg's colleagues were crafting a theory they hoped to unite with practice in the near future. The class struggle was "absolutizing" before their eyes. Their goal was to draw the lessons of that struggle and put their shoulders to the wheel to push it forward.

Grünberg was surprised that Sombart would give Marxists so much credit (that is, blame) for the sharpening of class tensions.

> Did the class struggle exist before theory, or was it, as Sombart suggests, caused by the theory? As far as I can tell, Sombart now really seems to believe that the class struggle is the work of revolutionary theorists ...
> GRÜNBERG 1924: 32

This belief was characteristic of Sombart, who saw devils and angels everywhere. But the reality was quite the reverse. Class struggle is elemental, Grünberg insisted. Marx and his true heirs – among whom Lukács and Korsch were pre-eminent, for Sombart at least – tried to grasp the shifting tectonics of history, with sensitivity to the spiraling, reciprocal influences of psyche and economy.

The electricity of change was apparent in all the works of this period. The upsurge of workers' councils across Europe and Russia, which yielded not only victorious Bolshevism but Soviet republics, with firefly lifespans, in Hungary and Bavaria, created new horizons for class politics. One of the main developments, Weil wrote in *Sozialisierung* (1921), was the spontaneous appearance of grassroots syndicalism. Prior to the war, only the Industrial Workers of the World in the United States and a few strands of Italian and French *ouvriérisme* had fought directly for the syndical ideal, workers' control of industry from below. Weil and Korsch saw this as an opportunity and a danger. The opportunity was the chance to bring syndicalist democratism into the socialist camp. The danger was that syndicalism would elbow socialism aside altogether.

The great virtue of syndicalism, for Weil, was that it called attention to the alienation of work and workers with unprecedented single-mindedness. Socialists, traditionally, had highlighted exploitation nearly to the exclusion of alienation. That was a one-sided mistake, which, unless it was remedied, would radically lessen the appeal of socialism – and Weil felt that socialism was necessary, if "socialization" was ever to be more than partial. Workers' control of factories and industries would be an immense step forward, but nothing essential would change until the whole of society was communal. Syndicalized enterprises would still produce and sell commodities. Socialism, in contrast, would replace selling with sharing.

Korsch amplified this outlook at length in *Arbeitsrecht für Betriebsräte*. Many aspects of this argument will sound familiar, but there are also elements that spring directly from the class tensions of the immediate postwar moment and call attention to capital fetishism not only in principle, but in their topical immediacy.[19]

Korsch begins with a strong statement of the case against alienated labor, calling "the unfreedom of workers in production the *economic* fundament of capitalist class society." (18) Echoing Lassalle's reply to Proudhon's famous slogan that "property is theft," Korsch emphasizes that, in capitalist society, where necessities are divided from producers by the barrier of price, most people experience property as something radically alien, subsisting in a domain all its own: Property is not theft but estrangement. (13).

Korsch's anti-capitalism is anti-authoritarian. He writes, in the spirit of Marx's texts on the Paris Commune: "In classless communist society," labor regulation will occur not in a "hegemonic labor regime that like of bourgeois society [but rather] in a superstructure of voluntarily cooperating communities."

> In place of the coercive political state, there will rise an association, in which the free development of each is the condition for the free development of all.
>
> KORSCH 1922: 21–22

Stressing unfreedom this emphatically was rare but not unknown among Marxists in 1922. Korsch, however, went much further, trespassing into the realm of reflection-determinations to challenge the very idea of the "job creator":

> ... in this *inverted capitalist world* the capitalist, who gets labor power from its natural owner, the worker, in return for wages and employs it for himself in his company, appears as the "labor-giver" (*die "Arbeitgeber"*) while the real labor-giver appears inversely as the "labor-taker" (*die "Arbeitnehmer"*). ...
>
> KORSCH 1922: 14

In this upside-down world, capitalists appear as patrons and benefactors, who show favor to supplicants in the labor market. Workers are clients, who owe their opportunity to work – and survive – to the job creator, the *Arbeitgeber.*

---

19   To my knowledge Korsch never discussed capital fetishism in so many words. But in an article in the left press accusing the industrialist Hugo Stinnes of exerting a malign influence over social policy (1921), he quoted at length a passage from Martin Luther which also appears, in the same form, with the same ellipses, in Marx's discussion of capital fetishism in *Theories of Surplus Value.*

Critique of this kind was rare.[20] But manifestations of fetishism were not rare in business circles. No sooner had labor legislation begun to be contemplated in Germany, Korsch noted, than corporate resistance appeared. He cited a protest by a business association against a *Reichstag* proposal for work regulations. This proposal, the association warned, would "alter the entire previous relationship between employers and employees."

> What was hitherto regarded as the employer's self-evident right is withdrawn from him and given to the worker. ... The worker is no longer the subordinate of the employer to whom he owes obedience, whose orders he must obey, whose punitive powers he acknowledges. ...
> KORSCH 1922: 29

In other words ... the sky was falling. Lujo Brentano urged the business association to take a less absolute stand, arguing that "the obedience owed by the worker to the employer can obviously only be strengthened if the orders [are] voluntarily obeyed," which is unlikely if the workers feel that their concerns are ignored. But it was not wrong, Korsch observed, for the business world to feel that regulating labor was, in fact, "an infringement of *capitalist* freedom." (29n.)

Far greater infringements of capitalist freedom were contemplated in the chaotic aftermath of the war. The anarchic spirit of the workers' and soldiers' councils of 1918–19 was soon deflected into safer channels, including the official socialization commissions and the official *Betriebsräte* legislation. Tarnow, in his reply to Sombart, pointed out that in 1918 the workers momentarily held the fate of German capital in their hands, but that they showed their willingness to accept less than absolute terms, to pursue what Sombart called a "relative" class struggle when they accepted the pact co-authored by the industrialist Hugo Stinnes and the union leader Carl Legien which established a kind of truce in the class war.

That truce, however, was shaky, and in the ensuing years a stream of conflicts spilled over into the streets. Korsch said that the prime impetus to those conflicts was a stiffening employers' offensive, in which Stinnes, the famous and famously belligerent "Steel King," was playing a central role. In four articles

---

20   It might seem unremarkable that Korsch cites a passage in *Capital* in which Marx ironizes about *"Freiheit, Gleichheit, Eigentum und Bentham"* at this point. But that phrase was not yet well known. Only Marianne Weber, writing about Fichte and Marx (1900), and a few other authors had quoted this phrase before Korsch: Ludwig, Gumplowicz, Lenin, Bernstein, and a pair of theologians. And none of those authors had concerned themselves with capital fetishism.

in regional KPD newspapers, Korsch offered popular versions of the case he was making more formally in *Arbeitsrecht für Betriebsräte*.

The crux of Korsch's argument was his claim, perhaps influenced by the Fabians, that the capitalist corporation is, in the most basic sense, a monarchy. And in fact, given the recent fall of Kaiser Wilhelm and Tsar Nicholas, actual monarchs at the level of the state suddenly had a diminished profile. Capitalists, who were increasingly monopolists and cartel members, were poised to fill the vacuum and they increasingly had the mentality to extend their dominion to realms beyond the economy alone. With apparent reference to an article by the director of the main German employers' association, Korsch offered this cautionary remark:

> Consider the celebrated words of the French king Louis XIV: '*L'état, c'est moi.*' *Arbeitgebers* today uphold a similar ideology, *Arbeitgebergedanken*, which they explain ... as the attempt 'to consolidate the employer's front,' to make ... German employers 'leaders in the German folk community,' ... to replace the political community which has sunk to [the level of] a mere 'formal state.'[21]
>
> KORSCH 1922: 29

I will discuss the many-splendored Stinnesien front and "employers' thought" in a later paper. But it suffices to say, for now, that Korsch was not ill-informed or exaggerating. Stinnes certainly put himself forward as a screen for fetishist projection. Films, novellas, and a vast occasional literature enveloped Stinnes in the class chaos of the early Weimar years. But to what extent was he actually fetishized? To what extent, in fact, can we say that capital fetishism reigned?

This brings us to a fundamental point – namely, that capital fetishism is contradictory. Confidence in capital or in specific capitalists is not a foregone conclusion. Fordist triumphalism and Stinnesien bravura can flicker and fade. So, the deeper question is whether inversive thinking, once shaken, springs back to life. Many workers and socialists in the early Weimar years had reached anti-fetishist conclusions, arguing, and organizing to prove, that capitalists are only capitalists because workers are workers. For 133 days in 1919, when Lukács

---

21   Korsch repeated this warning in "König Kapital und seine Hofnarren" (1971 [1922]: 336), in which he pronounced 'King Stinnes' the true ruler of a society with an eviscerated government. The phrase 'King Capital' may have come from a Fabian text by George Bernard Shaw, who was one of Korsch's favorite social gadflies. (He had published a witty essay by Shaw in his series on "practical socialism.") Only Shaw and a few others had used that phrase before Korsch.

was a central figure in the Hungarian Soviet Republic, the fate of authoritarianism was in doubt. When Korsch served in the *Arbeiterregierung* in Thuringia in 1923, authoritarianism was under assault.

It was hence no surprise that Sombart was shaken by nascent class absolution, and that, given the tint of his class spectacles, he blamed Marx, Luxemburg, Lukács, and Korsch. In a passage to which Sombart alluded, Friedrich Julius Stahl had given a similar feeling crystalline form in 1852. Revolution, Stahl wrote,

> ... founds the whole public estate on human will instead of God's order and ordinance. Revolution is thus, as the word says, inversion (*Umwälzung*); ... it elevates what eternal law has lowered. It makes man the origin and center of the moral world order. It makes subjects (*Unterthanen*) the masters of their superiors; it proclaims human rights without duties or calling. It makes the whole sin-slime (*Sündenschlamm*) of popular passion, which the authorities' power is supposed to suppress, rise up. – This is the revolution.
>
> STAHL 1852: 257

That revolution, plainly, is precisely what Marx and others envisioned, not only in 1848 – Stahl's point of reference – but in 1871 and later. Marx and Engels, in *The Holy Family,* had put this wish in a nutshell, quoting the banner motto of the newspaper, *Révolutions de Paris,* which had appeared in the earliest days of the French Revolution: "The great are only great because we are on our knees. Let us rise!"

No mention was made of "reflection-determinations" at this stage, nor did Marx deploy Hegel's vocabulary when, in one of his very final manuscripts, he criticized "the immense John Austin" and his disciple Henry Sumner Maine for arguing that true "Sovereigns" do not depend on their subjects, but rather that their subjects depend on *them*. Marx says that in this view, rulership "is taken as something which stands over the society, resting upon itself." But that, he says, is "... an illusion, since the state in all its forms is only an excrescence of society." The assertion that Austin's disciples "go very near to hazarding," namely "that the Sovereign person or group actually wields the stored-up force of society by an uncontrolled exercise of will, is certainly never in accordance with fact."[22]

---

22   These lines will appear in Marx (2022), in which manuscripts that Marx wrote in alternating German and English, with interpolations from other languages, will appear in English with an apparatus that makes clear when Marx is either speaking in his own voice or

Austin, like Sombart, was pledged to authority fetishism, genuflecting to the ruler's alleged superiority. But that fetishism was insecure, defensive. Very few people can sustain the ontological conviction that kings are so indelibly kings that they absolutely cannot be toppled. Figures like Sombart and Stahl think that God or nature *intends* monarchy. But that is at least partially a teleological belief, since they know that what they take to be God's will or natural law can be violated. Ontologically, however divine or natural, monarchs and King Capital *can* be overthrown. Awareness of that fact is the source of their fear and animosity towards the very idea of class struggle.

Sombart knew full well that, if Lukácsian or Korschist ideals were to prevail, the inverted order could itself be inverted. Subjects, realizing that monarchs are only great because they kneel before them, could rise.

7   **Authority and the Authoritarian Personality**

Whether authority fetishism proves resilient in any given instance is not simply a cognitive matter. Sombart was emotionally invested in the inverted world, Gottl-Ottlilienfeld was exuberantly invested in *Fordismus,* and many industrial sociologists and psychologists have shown that workers, too, are often profoundly psychically tied to authority.

That was the primary lesson, the dispiriting implication, of the critical study conducted by Hilde Weiss and Erich Fromm in the waning days of the Weimar Republic. It was that study, which was in full swing when "Fräulein Dr. Weiss" visited Korsch in Berlin in 1931, which inspired the concept of characterological authoritarianism.

Felix Weil held out high hopes for this survey. In his letter to the Culture Ministry in late 1929, near the survey's starting date, he stressed the importance of this survey to the Institute's identity. Of all the projects on the drawing board, none were as warmly endorsed as the Institute's plan to study the working class.

> Two major investigations are underway... One is trying for the first time to present the real situation of workers in the United States of North America on the basis of the vast and contradictory printed material

---

quoting one of the books he was excerpting. MEGA volume Abt. 4/27 will include this material as well. The idea for the original transcription of these manuscripts (1972) came from Korsch.

available.[23] The other study, the first stage of which we estimate will last five years or more, is designed to provide information about the material and spiritual situation of the main strata of blue- and white-collar workers in Germany. In that project we are not only using all existing [published] materials [but] also pursuing extensive surveys of our own, for which we have enlisted the assistance of leading workers' organizations and experts. ...

> WEIL 1929:1045

The Institute was also studying parties, unions, trusts, and other organizations. But Marxist hopes for the socialist future – and Weil stressed that he and Grünberg had always been candid about the Institute's Marxism – begin and end with the working class. Of all Marx's theoretical categories, few are as central to the socialist vision or as unfinished as the theory of class. The Weimar decade had proven decisively that history does not inevitably generate class consciousness. Contingency, not necessity, is the reality we face. And in no realm is that fact more fateful than in the field of class relations. The study of the German working class by Weiss and Fromm, Weil said,

> ... will cover psychological and ideological facts ... as well as questions of an economic nature ... [so that we can] form a new sociological taxonomy. With the help of that taxonomy ... we hope to gain new insights into the structure of society ... to further advance the strikingly incomplete theory of social classes.

> WEIL 1929:1045

The socialist scholar Robert Wilbrandt, with whom Weil studied in 1919 and under whom Korsch served in the early days of the Socialization Commission, published a book on the occasion of Marx's centenary in 1918 in which he said that Marx's theory of capitalism was far from complete. Henryk Grossman was just one of many who adamantly rejected Wilbrandt's thesis.[24] But Korsch and Weil defended the incompleteness thesis – which led them to hold that new inquiries are *essential* if Marxism is not to devolve into uncritical dogma.

In 1930, Korsch revisited the controversy over *Marxism and Philosophy* in an essay criticizing the dogmatic Marxism of both official socialism and

---

23   Weil refers here to the projected study "Die Lage der nordamerikanischen Arbeiter", by Julian Gumperz.

24   On this debate, see Maximilien Rubel (1981 [1968]). Weil, in his 1929 letter, cited disagreements of this kind as evidence of the Institute's open-mindedness.

communism. *"A fundamental debate on ... modern Marxism* has now begun,"
Korsch wrote,

> ... and ... the real division on all major and decisive questions is between
> the old Marxist orthodoxy of Kautsky allied to the new Russian or
> 'Leninist' orthodoxy on the one side, and all critical and progressive the-
> oretical tendencies in the proletarian movement today on the other side.
>
> KORSCH 1930: 1

Politically, "Kautsky and Lenin made a permanent virtue out of a temporary
necessity." They energetically defended the idea that socialism can only be
brought to the workers 'from outside', by bourgeois intellectuals who educate
the workers' movement (3).

This elitism was part and parcel of a vision of socialism which was itself
elitist. At the start of the 1920s, revolutionaries had awkwardly attempted to
combine insights from Lenin and Luxemburg. But the "Leninism" that took
shape in this decade became ever more obviously a doctrine of dictatorship
over the proletariat. It was thus becoming necessary once again to stress the
anti-authoritarianism which Rosa Luxemburg had said was the essence of
socialism, namely, that *"Socialism, both in its ends and in its means, is a struggle
to realize freedom"* (6).

This ringing affirmation could seem to be merely rhetorical. But Korsch, like
Weiss and Fromm, wanted to understand the obstacles that blocked the workers' freedom movement. That required inquiries which took subjectivity seriously. And that, too, required a break with the reigning orthodoxy, for which
"the Absolute," Korsch said, "instead of being called 'Spirit' is called 'Matter.' "

No one-sided doctrine, whether idealist or "materialist," could adequately
probe a reality which is dialectical in its essence. Only a research agenda which
took structure and superstructure equally seriously could understand either.

That shared premise had drawn Korsch to Lukács, leading him to republish
Marxism and Philosophy in 1925 with a brief afterword extolling *History and
Class Consciousness.* Korsch had learned by 1930 that he and Lukács were not
as close as he had originally thought. But he still believed that they were united
against those in the socialist and "Marxist-Leninist" camps who "drew a sharp
line of division between consciousness and its object' and 'treated consciousness as something ... fundamentally contrasted to Being and Nature' ..." (3).

How, then, could the struggle to realize freedom be more effectively conducted, after the chastening defeats and equivocal victories of the Weimar
years? That was the question Weiss was exploring, with Fromm, when she
visited Korsch in 1930. What she deduced from this research was not entirely

discouraging. "One general conclusion of my studies," she later wrote, "was that the workers did not restrict their thinking to a narrow party viewpoint."

> Many members of the Social Democratic Party, for instance, expressed just the same opinion as communists about war, the form of government they wanted and their estimates of most important personalities.
>
> WEISS 1939, in GARZ 2006: 62–63

What this showed, Weiss said, was that neither the socialist nor communist party leaders held full sway over the working masses. That was a hopeful sign. But over time the tenor of the workers' answers to the survey questions took a dark turn. As surveys arrived in 1932 and early 1933, it was ever easier "to recognize in them the reflection of the world crisis [which] started in 1929 and the growing political and social tensions which brought about the death of the ... Republic in the flames of the burning *Reichstag* at the end of February 1933."

> [Many workers] began to see no other way out [than] a strong hand, a man with absolute power. Bismarck, Napoleon, and Luther were [idealized more and more often] by National Socialist, Catholic, Social Democratic and even communist workers. They had never come to a confidence in themselves. Trust in the Republican form of government declined rapidly. (63)

This sobering realization informed Fromm's thinking about authoritarian personality traits and working-class authoritarianism. Since I have developed that point elsewhere,[25] I will refrain from repeating myself here. But one point bears repetition, namely, that besides learning that many workers were susceptible to the appeal of "great men" – industrialists, dictators, kings – and demagogic parties, Fromm and Weiss also discovered that relatively few of these workers were irredeemably authoritarian. An equal or even greater force, they found, was ambivalence. Those workers whom they described as *Ambivalenter* were torn. They cherished some liberties, but they were not democratic to the core.

The same was true with respect to capitalism. As history had repeatedly shown, workers felt ambivalent about capital and capitalists. It had been clear from the earliest days of industry that popular opinion divided capitalists into two antithetical camps: *schaffende* capitalists on one side (virtuous, productive) and *raffende* capitalists on the other (vicious, predatory). Industrialists

---

25   See, e.g., Smith (2020, 2017).

clustered at the positive pole while bankers appeared as their rapacious opposites.

Anti-bank sentiment, in turn, has often been suffused with anti-Semitism.[26] Finance capitalists have been routinely reviled as *raffende* Jews, as elders of Zion, while *schaffende* industrialists have been revered.[27] Henry Ford, who was a magnet for capital idolatry, was also one of the most effective purveyors of anti-financial anti-Semitism. It seems that ambivalence towards capital is often channeled towards different kinds of capitalists, and Ford took advantage of this bifurcation to enhance his standing as an industrialist.

Marx had noticed this antithesis, pointing out, in *Theories of Surplus Value* (1910 [1862–63]), that bankers are often seen as disconnected from production, active exclusively in the occult sphere of money and speculation. That makes them natural targets for bias and abuse. Capital's destructive consequences are blamed on destructive capitalists, and everything positive (innovation, job creation, etc.) is credited to productive capitalists.

This Manichaean dichotomy was central to *Volkisch* reaction in the Weimar era, and Werner Sombart joined the chorus, mixing his typical chemically-pure idolatry of industrialists with anti-Semitic invective against bankers and socialists. Friedrich Pollock, in the first Institute *Beihefte* in 1926, called attention to key themes in Sombart's *Der proletarische Sozialismus* which had not surfaced in his debate with Grünberg. Foremost among these were vitriolic anti-Semitism and an invidious contrast between 'true *Führers*' and mass demagogues which prefigured Sombart's ultimate Nazism. His jeremiads against *"jüdischer Geist"* ran the gamut from garden-variety slurs to *Volkisch* slogans against financial greed and Jewish communism, culminating in a sketch of the "bloodthirsty, bribe-dispensing" Rosa Luxemburg, in whom, Sombart said, we encounter the sum of all resentments, explosively united in a single person – the ideal-type of the subversive "as a woman, as a foreigner, as a Jew and as a cripple" (Pollock 1926: 55, citing Sombart, Bd. 1, 1925: 76).

Sombart's antitheses with respect to authority were equally Manichaean. Pollock turned these antitheses into a 10-point table of opposed traits. At the heart of this opposition was the contrast between the "foundational ideas" of

---

26   One of the best sources on this subject is still Paul Massing's *Rehearsal for Destruction* (1949), which appeared alongside *The Authoritarian Personality* in the *Studies in Prejudice* series edited by Max Horkheimer. Massing had been one of the Institute's students in the Weimar years and Felix Weil translated *Rehearsal for Destruction* into German.

27   On this see Smith (2009) and especially Worrell (2008).

the true *Führer* – "discipline, authority, subordination, piety, awe, willingness to serve, willingness to sacrifice" – and demagogic sermons about freedom and equality, which promise an "unfettered" individuality (24, citing Sombart 1925, Bd. 2: 269).

We are now on the terrain of authoritarianism as well as anti-Semitism. Authoritarian leaders expect subjection and even awe from their true devotees, while their opponents, professing freedom as their ideal, offer only poisoned bribes. Jews, for Sombart, refuse to recognize the charisma of true capitalists and *Führers* while they posed, fraudulently, as liberators. Jews, in short, were for Sombart the living embodiments of anti-authoritarianism. They threatened every inversive reality and ideal.

Investigating the entanglement of attitudes towards authorities, capitalists, communists, and Jews was part of what Fromm and Weiss tried to understand, and they broke new ground. Although they asked just three questions about Jews, they generated results sufficiently detailed and unique that modern social scientists, hoping to grasp the nettle of Weimar anti-Semitism, have used their findings as baseline historical data.[28] What they found with respect to class and authority was just as unique.

In *Abbe und Ford,* Weiss stressed that Henry Ford had an "autocratic personality."[29] It would not be surprising to learn that many of his admirers found this highly appealing. His autocracy was what enabled him to propel himself into the limelight. Henry Ford and Ford Motors became synonymous. His employees, even his principal executives, remained anonymous. The secret to success in the auto industry appeared to be personal. Weiss pointed out that General Motors, without a folksy patriarch at the helm, was nipping at Ford's heels, and she correctly predicted that GM would soon overtake Ford. But Ford's mystique, and Fordism, lived on.

Capitalists exert a gilded authority. This is true even when they are not personally extraordinary. They wield and embody the power of their capital. That can make even the least prepossessing figure appear masterful. Marx once said that money makes the ugly beautiful, the weak strong. That, it seems, applies doubly to the capitalist. The power of the persona, the personification, is not to be underestimated. The question that remains for critical theory is what that means now, at a time when investors of unparalleled wealth loom larger than ever on the cultural horizon – Gates, Soros, Buffett, Bezos.

Weimar critical theory, I believe, remains a resource for that task.

---

28   See e.g. Robert Smith's two papers (1998, 2010).
29   She quoted this phrase from an American labor newspaper.

References

Adorno, Theodor, Else Frenkel-Brunswik, R. Nevitt Sanford, and Daniel Levinson. 1950. *The Authoritarian Personality.* New York: Harper.

Engels, Friedrich. 1878. *Herrn Eugen Dühring's umwälzung der wissenschaft.* Leipzig: G enossenschaftsbuchdruckerei. (*Anti-Dühring*).

Feuer, Lewis S. 1980. "The Frankfurt Marxists and the Columbia Liberals," *Surveys* 25(3): 156–176.

Fromm, Erich. 1936a. "Sozialpsychologischer Teil." In *Studien über Autorität und Familie,* ed. Max Horkheimer, 77–135. Paris: Félix Alcan.

Fromm, Erich. 1936b. "Geschichte und Methoden der Erhebungen." In *Studien über Autorität und Familie,* ed. Max Horkheimer, 231–38. Paris: Félix Alcan.

Fromm, Erich. 1937. "Zum Gefühl der Ohnmacht." In *Zeitschrift für Sozialforschung,* Bd. 6, 95–119. Paris: Félix Alcan.

Fromm, Erich. 1984 [1937]. *The Working Class in Weimar Germany,* ed. Wolfgang Bonss, trans. Barbara Weinberger. Cambridge: Harvard University Press.

Fromm, Erich. 1995 [1937]. "A Contribution to the Method and Purpose of an Analytical Social Psychology." In *Wissenschaft vom Menschen – Science of Man. Jahrbuch der Internationalen Erich-Fromm-Gesellschaft,* Bd. 6, 189–236. Münster: LIT Verlag.

Garz, Detlef, ed. 2006. *Hilda Weiss – Soziologin, Sozialistin, Emigrantin.* Hamburg: Verlag Dr. Kovač.

Gottl-Ottlilienfeld, Friedrich von. 1924. *Fordismus?* Jena: Fischer.

Gottl-Ottlilienfeld, Friedrich von. 1924. Remarks, *Verhandlung des Vereins für Sozialpolitik in Stuttgart 24.-26. September 1924,* Bd. 170, *Schriften des Vereins für Sozialpolitik.*

Grossmann, Henryk. 1929. *Das Akkumulations- und Zusammenbruchsgesetz des kapitalistischen Systems.* Leipzig: C.L. Hirschfeld.

Grünberg, Carl. 1924. Remarks, *Verhandlung des Vereins für Sozialpolitik in Stuttgart 24.-26. September 1924,* Bd. 170, *Schriften des Vereins für Sozialpolitik.*

Günther, Adolf. 1922. "Die Jubiläumstagung des Vereins für Sozialpolitik in Eisenach," *Jahrbücher für Nationalökonomie und Statistik,* Folge 3, Bd. 64, 119(6): 516–521.

Hammacher, Emil. 1909. *Das philosophisch-ökonomische System des Marxismus.* Berlin: Duncker & Humblot.

Horkheimer, Max, and Theodor Adorno. 1947. *Dialektik der Aufklärung.* Amsterdam: Querido.

Horkheimer, Max, ed. 1936. *Studien über Autorität und Familie.* Bd. 5, *Schriften des Instituts für Sozialforschung.* Paris: Félix Alcan.

Institut für Sozialforschung a.d. Universität Frankfurt 1931. File IX 5A in the Max-Horkheimer-Archiv. Date-stamped 7 mai 1931.

Jahn, Wolfgang. 1968. *Die Marxsche Wert- und Mehrwertlehre in Zerrspiegel bürgerlicher Ökonomen.* Berlin: Dietz.

Jay, Martin. 1973. *The Dialectical Imagination.* Boston: Little, Brown.

Jay, Martin. 1981. "Remembering Henry Pachter." *Salmagundi* 52/53: 24–29.

Jay, Martin. 1982. "Misrepresentations of the Frankfurt School," *Survey* 26(2): 132–141.

Jeffries, Stuart. 2017. *Grand Hotel Abyss.* London & New York: Verso.

Korsch, Karl. 1919. *Was ist Sozialisierung?* Hannover: Freies Deutschland Verlagsgesellschaft.

Korsch, Karl. 1921. "Stinnes Kostgänger Staat," *Neue Zeitung* (19 September).

Korsch, Karl. 1922. *Arbeitsrecht für Betriebsräte.* Berlin: VIVA.

Korsch, Karl. 1922s. "Der 18 Brumaire des Hugo Stinnes," *Neue Zeitung* (17 March).

Korsch, Karl. 1922b. "Die spd. Die Entwicklung zur Stinnespartei," *Rote Fahne* (26 March).

Korsch, Karl. 1923. *Marxismus und Philosophie.* Leipzig: C.L. Hirschfeld.

Korsch, Karl. 1923a. "Die tote USPD und der lebendige Stinnes," *Neue Zeitung* (7 September).

Korsch, Karl. 1923b. "König Kapital und seine Hofnarren," *Neue Zeitung* (7 October).

Korsch, Karl. 1925. "Marxismus und Philosophie," *Archiv für die Geschichte des Sozialismus und der Arbeiterbewegung,* Bd. 11: 52–121.

Korsch, Karl. 1971 [1927/1931]. "Krise der Marxismus," in Karl Korsch *Die materialistische Geschichtsauffassung und andere Schriften,* ed. Erich Gerlach. Frankfurt: Europäische Verlagsanstalt.

Korsch, Karl. 1929. "Karl Kautsky und die materialistische Geschichtsauffassung," *Archiv für die Geschichte des Sozialismus der Arbeiterbewegung,* Bd. 14: 179–279.

Korsch, Karl. 1930. "The Present State of the Problem of 'Marxism and Philosophy'." At https://www.marxists.org/archive/korsch/19xx/anti-critique.htm.

Korsch, Karl. 1930a. Review, "Paschukanis, *Allgemeine Rechtslehre und Marxismus*" and "Renner, *Die Rechstinstitute des Privatrechts und ihre soziale Funktion,*" *Archiv für die Geschichte des Sozialismus und der Arbeiterbewegung,* Bd. 15: 301–10.

Korsch, Karl. 1932. "Die dialektische Methode im 'Kapital'." *Aufbau:* 144–150.

Korsch, Karl. 1933. "Über einige grundsätzliche Voraussetzungen für eine materialistische Diskussion der Krisentheorie," *Proletarier:* 20–25.

Korsch, Karl. 1938. *Karl Marx.* London and New York: Russell & Russell.

Korsch, Karl. 1972. "Introduction to Capital." In Karl Korsch, *Three Essays on Marxism,* ed. Paul Breines. New York: Monthly Review Press.

Korsch, Karl. 1977. *Karl Korsch: Revolutionary Theory,* ed. Douglas Kellner. Austin & London: University of Texas Press.

Korsch, Karl. 1980. *Gesamtausgabe: Briefe 1908–1939,* ed. Michael Buckmiller and Götz Langkau. Frankfurt: Europäische Verlagsanstalt.

Lukács, Georg. 1923. *Geschichte und Klassenbewusstsein*. Berlin: Malik-Verlag.

Lukács, Georg. 1971 [1923]. *History and Class Consciousness*. Cambridge: MIT.

Lukács, Georg. 1925. "Die neue Ausgabe von Lassalles Briefen," *Archiv für die Geschichte des Sozialismus und der Arbeiterbewegung*, Bd. 11: 401–423.

Lukács, Georg. 1926. "Moses Hess und die Probleme der idealistischen Dialektik," *Archiv für die Geschichte des Sozialismus und der Arbeiterbewegung*, Bd. 12: 105–155.

Lukács, Georg. 1948. *Der junge Hegel*. Zürich & Vienna: Europa Verlag.

Lukács, Georg. 1962. *Die Zerstorung der Vernunft*. Bd. 9, *Werke*, ed. Peter Christian Ludz. Nieuwied: Luchterhand.

Luxemburg, Rosa. 1922 [1918]. *Die Russische Revolution, eine kritische Würdigung*, ed. Paul Levi. Berlin: Verlag Gesellschaft und Erziehung.

Marx, Karl. 1904 [1846]. "Exerpte von Saint Max." In *Dokumente des Sozialismus, Bd. 4*, ed. Eduard Bernstein.

Marx, Karl and Friedrich Engels. 1902 [1845]. "Die Heilige Familie oder Kritik der Kritischen Kritik," in *Gesammelte Schriften von Karl Marx und Friedrich Engels, 1841–1850, Bd. 2*, ed. Franz Mehring. Stuttgart: Dietz.

Marx, Karl. 1932 [1844]. *Ökonomisch-philosophische Manuskripte aus dem Jahre 1844*, ed. David Riazanov. In *Marx-Engels-Gesamtausgabe*, Abt. 1, Bd. 3, 29–172. Berlin: Marx-Engels Archiv.

Marx, Karl. 1910 [1862–63]. *Theorien über Den Mehrwert, aus dem nach gelassenen Manuskript "Zur Kritik der politischen Ökonomie,"* Bd. 3, *Von Ricardo zur vulgärökonomie*, ed. Karl Kautsky. Berlin: Dietz.

Marx, Karl. 1894 [1864–65]. *Das Kapital, Bd. 3, Der Gesamtprocess der kapitalistischen Produktion*, ed. Friedrich Engels. Hamburg: Otto Meissner.

Marx, Karl. 1867. *Das Kapital, Bd. 1*. Hamburg: Otto Meissner.

Marx, Karl. 1932 [1872]. *Das Kapital, Bd. 1*, ed. Karl Korsch. Berlin: Kiepenheuer.

Marx, Karl. 1972. *The Ethnological Notebooks of Karl Marx*, ed. Lawrence Krader. Assen: Van Gorcum.

Marx, Karl. 2022. *Marx's World: Global Society and Capital Accumulation in Marx's Late Manuscripts*, ed. David Norman Smith. New Haven: Yale, forthcoming.

Masaryk, Tomáš. 1899. *Die philosophischen und sociologischen Grundlagen des Marxismus*. Duitsland: C. Konegen.

Massing, Paul. 1949. *Rehearsal for Destruction*. New York: Harper.

Massing, Paul. 1959 [1949]. *Vorgeschichte des politischen Antisemitismus*, Bd. 8, Frankfurter Beiträge zur Soziologie, trans. Felix J. Weil. Frankfurt: Europäische Verlagsanstalt.

Migdal, Ulrike. 1981. *Die Frühgeschichte des Frankfurter Instituts für Sozialforschung*. Frankfurt and New York: Campus Verlag.

Pollock, Friedrich. 1926. *Sombarts "Widerlegung" des Marxismus*. Leipzig: C. L. Hirshfeld.

Reijen, Willem van and Gunzelin Schmid Noerr, eds. 1988. *Grand Hotel Abgrund.* Hamburg: Junius.

Révolutions de Paris. 1789–90, ed. Elisée Loustalot.

Rubel, Maximilien. 1981 [1968]. "A History of Marx's Economics." In *Rubel on Karl Marx*, eds. Joseph J. O'Malley and Keith W. Algozin. Cambridge: Cambridge University Press.

Smith, David Norman. 2009. "Solidarity in Question: Critical Theory, Labor, and Anti-Semitism." *Critical Sociology* 35(5): 601–627.

Smith, David Norman. 2011. "Charisma and Critique: Critical Theory, Authority, and the Birth of Political Theology." *Current Perspectives in Social Theory* 29: 33–56.

Smith, David Norman. 2013. "Charisma Disenchanted." In *Current Perspectives in Social Theory* 31: 3–74. Somerville, MA: Emerald Group Publishing Limited.

Smith, David Norman. 2016. "Charisma and the Spirit of Capitalism." In *The Anthem Companion to Max Weber*, ed. Alan Sica, 67–116. London, New York & Delhi: Anthem Press.

Smith, David Norman. 2017. "Theory and Class Consciousness." In *The Handbook of Critical Theory,* ed. Michael Thompson, 369–424. London & New York: Palgrave Macmillan.

Smith, David Norman. 2019. "Authoritarianism Reimagined: The Riddle of Trump's Base." *The Sociological Quarterly* 60(2): 210–223.

Smith, David Norman. 2020. "Anti-Authoritarian Marxism: Erich Fromm, Hilde Weiss, and the Politics of Radical Humanism." In *Erich Fromm's Critical Theory*, eds. Joane Braune and Kieran Durkin, 131–165. London: Bloomsbury.

Smith, Robert. 1998. "Anti-Semitism and Nazism." *American Behavioral Scientist* 41(9): 1324–1362.

Smith, Robert. 2010. "Why Nazified Germans Killed Jewish People." *Current Perspectives in Social Theory* 27: 275–342.

Sombart, Werner. 1897. *Sozialismus und soziale Bewegung im neunzehnten Jahrhundert.* Jena: Fischer.

Sombart, Werner. 1924. "Die Idee des Klassenkampfes," *Weltwirtschaftliches Archiv,* Bd. 21, 1925: 22–36. Originally: *Verhandlung des Vereins für Socialpolitik in Stuttgart 24.-26. September 1924, Schriften des Vereins für Sozialpolitik,* Bd. 170: 9–26. München und Leipzig: Duncker & Humblot.

Sombart, Werner. 1925. *Der proletarische Sozialismus ("Marxismus"),* Bde. 1 & 2. Jena: Fischer.

Stahl, Friedrich Julius. 1852. "Was ist die Revolution? Ein Vortrag, auf Veranstaltung des Evangelischen Vereins für kirchliche Zwecke am 8. März 1852 gehalten," in *Siebzehn parlamentarische Reden und drei Vorträge von Stahl.* Berlin: Wilhelm Hertz, 1862.

Sternberg, Fritz. 1929. *"Der lmperialismus" und seine Kritiker.* Berlin: Soziologische Verlagsanstalt.

Strzelewicz, Willy. 1986. "Diskurse im Institut für Sozialforschung um 1930." *Ordnung und Theorie*, 1986: 147–167.

Tandy, Francis. 1896. *Voluntary Socialism*. Denver: Francis D. Tandy.

Tarnow, Fritz. 1924. Remarks, *Verhandlung des Vereins für Socialpolitik in Stuttgart 24.-26. September 1924, Schriften des Vereins für Socialpolitik*, Bd. 170.

Weber, Marianne. 1900. *Fichte's sozialismus und sein verhältnis zur Marx'-schen doktrin*. Tübingen: J. C. B. Mohr.

Weil, Felix and Kurt Albert Gerlach. 1922. *Denkschrift über die Begründung eines Instituts für Sozialforschung*. Max-Horkheimer-Archiv. At https://www.europeana. eu/en/item/2048618/data_item_ub_ffm_horkheimer_Na_1_656.

Weil, Felix. 1921. *Sozialisierung*. Berlin-Fichtenau: Verlag Gesellschaft und Erziehung.

Weil, Felix. 1925. "Die Arbeiterbewegung in Argentinien," *Archiv für die Geschichte des Sozialismus und der Arbeiterbewegung*, Bd. 11: 1–51.

Weil, Felix. 1926. Review, "Neurath, *Wirtschaftsplan und Naturalrechnung*" and "Trotzki, *Kapitalismus oder Sozialismus?*" *Archiv für die Geschichte des Sozialismus und der Arbeiterbewegung*, Bd. 12: 456–462.

Weil, Felix. 1928. "Rosa Luxemburg über die russische Revolution. Einige unveröffentlichte Manuskripte," *Archiv für die Geschichte des Sozialismus und der Arbeiterbewegung*, Bd. 13.

Weil, Felix. 2016 [1929]. Letter to C. H. Becker, November 1, in *Acta Borussica. Neue Folge, 2. Reihe: Preussen als Kulturstaat, Abt. II: Der preußische Kulturstaat in der politischen und sozialen Wirklichkeit*. Bd 9. Berlin: De Gruyter.

Weiss, Hilde and Erich Fromm. 1936. "Die Arbeiter- und Angestelltenerhebung." In *Studien über Autorität und Familie*, ed. Max Horkheimer, 239–71. Paris: Félix Alcan.

Weiss, Hilde. 1927. *Abbe und Ford: Kapitalistische Utopien*. Berlin: Prager.

Weiss, Hilda. 2006 [1939]. "My life in Germany Before and After January [30, 1933]." In *Hilda Weiss – Soziologin, Sozialistin, Emigrantin*, ed. Detlef Garz, 8–70. Hamburg: Verlag Dr. Kovač.

Wiese, Leopold von. Remarks, *Verhandlung des Vereins für Socialpolitik in Stuttgart 24.-26. September 1924, Schriften des Vereins für Socialpolitik*, Bd. 170.

Wilbrandt, Robert. 1918. *Karl Marx: Versuch einer Einführung*. Leipzig: B. G. Teubner.

Worrell, Mark P. 2008. *Dialectic of Solidarity*. Leiden: Brill.

Yagi, Kiichiro. 2011. "Was *Sozialforschung* an Aesopian Term?" In *The Dissemination of Economic Ideas*, ed. Heinz-Dieter Kurz et al., 315–336. Cheltenham: Edward Elgar.

CHAPTER 4

Mythology, Enlightenment, and Dialectic: Determinate Negation

Rudolf J. Siebert, Michael R. Ott, and Dustin J. Byrd

According to Max Horkheimer and Theodor W. Adorno, the bourgeois Enlightenment and revolution of the 18th century were *nominalistic* movements. In the view of the critical theory of religion and society (CTRS),[1] these nominalistic movements left behind themselves the Platonic, ontological principle of *universalia ante rem* ("universals before things"), which had been dominant in Antiquity, as well as the Aristotelian, ontological principle of *universalia in re* ("universals in things"), which had been important in the Middle Ages. The modern, bourgeois Enlightenment movement, however, concentrated completely on William of Ockham's nominalistic, ontological principle of *universalia post rem* ("universals after things"). This principle, which determines the thinking of Modernity, declares that universals, or general ideas, are merely contentless names that have no reality. Only particular objects exist, and their analytical categories, such as properties, numbers, and sets are thought of as merely features to consider the things that exist.

1 Nominalistic Movement

The CTRS was derived from the critical theory of society of the Frankfurt School. With Kant, Hegel, Marx, Freud, and the Frankfurt School, the CTRS understands Enlightenment to mean the full use of peoples' own reason, understood as analytical understanding and freedom of choice, which frees people from their superstitions, prejudices and fears as they become masters of their own fate. With Hegel and the critical theorists, the CTRS is critical of

---

1 CTRS is the acronym for the Critical Theory of Religion and Society. This is a special field of research created by Rudolf Siebert that is a part of the continuing development of the Critical Theory of the Frankfurt School. An excellent explanation of the history and purpose of the CTRS can be found in Siebert's latest book, *The Evolution of the Critical Theory of Religion and Society: Union, Disunion, and Reunion of the Sacred and the Profane (1946–2020)*. New Delhi, India: Sanbun.

the dialectic of Enlightenment as the vain elevation of analytical understanding over dialectical reason; as positivistic dogmatism; as eudaemonism that transforms the beautiful subjectivity of Protestantism into an empirical, utilitarian one; and as the abstract negation of venerable old religious and moral traditions.

The CTRS was inspired by Max Horkheimer's (1972) famous 1937 articulation of the *Critical Theory of Society,* which was always interested in dialectical social critique, not aiming to better the functioning of this or that particular social institution, but rather suspicious of the very categories of better, useful, appropriate, productive and valuable. While the Critical Theory did seek to transform the present crises, it did not and does not do so in a myopic spirit that bows positivistically to the immediate facts of the present. Rather, its critique is civilization-wide and world-historical, concerned with the totality of human existence in its particular social and political contexts (Horkheimer 1972, 1993; Horkheimer and Adorno 1972).

In the view of the CTRS, the modern nominalistic movement was already present in the Protestant Reformation, which occurred two hundred years before the bourgeois Enlightenment and revolution. As a result, according to critical theorist Jürgen Habermas, the discipline of philosophy was compelled to express the nominalistic anthropocentric point of view. However, in the 19th century, Habermas' greatest teacher, Georg W. F. Hegel, determinately negated all three ontological principles – *universalia ante rem, universalia in re, universalia post rem* – into his dialectical philosophy through the dialectical Notion, as the self-particularization and self-singularization of the universal. This movement of the Notion was Hegel's dialectical response to the nominalism of the bourgeois Enlightenment, which he discovered, criticized, and opposed over a century before Horkheimer and Adorno and their critical theory of society. Although Hegel's great disciple, Karl Marx, disliked his teacher's philosophical and theological "mountain melodies," he nevertheless continued Hegel's critique of the bourgeois political economics of Adam Smith, Ricardo, Says, etc., as he applied the determinately negated Hegelian trinitarian, dialectical logic and methodology throughout his entire work. Horkheimer and Adorno summed up Hegel's and Marx's dialectical method in the notion of

> determinate, specific or concrete negation: the antithesis, concretely negating the thesis, and the synthesis specifically negating the antithesis.[2]

---

2   See: Horkheimer (1947, 1985 [1970], 1972a, 1972b, 1974a, 1974b, 1974c, 1978, 1993), Horkheimer and Adorno (1972), and Adorno (1973, 1974, 1993, 1998).

2   Post-metaphysical Age

In Horkheimer's and Adorno's perspective, the nominalistic, bourgeois Enlightenment had consumed not just the religious and secular symbols, but also the universal concepts of their successors. It spared no remnant of metaphysics apart from the abstract fear of the collective, from which it arose in the first place. It thereby started the post-religious and post-metaphysical age. Mythological religion and rational metaphysics were abstractly negated by the bourgeois Enlightenment and revolutions from the Puritan Oliver Cromwell, through the deist Robespierre, to Abraham Lincoln and the American Civil War – the last bourgeois revolution, followed by socialist revolutions, and bourgeois, liberal and fascist counterrevolutions. Even if logical positivism allowed access to probability, *ethnological positivism* would put it into its place again. The vague ideas of chance and quintessence were pale shadows of this much richer notion: i.e., of the magical, or fetishistic substance. As an entirely nominalistic movement, i.e., *universalia post rem*, the bourgeois Enlightenment and revolution called a halt before the *nomen*: the exclusive, precise concept, the proper name.

However, it is the task of the CTRS to trace the history of religions from the ancient and medieval, original, relative union between the sacred (religious) and the profane (secular), through their modern disunion, toward their possible post-modern reunion (Siebert 2001, 2002, 2010a, 2019). The modern disunion between the religious and the secular also split religious communities into believers who strictly hold on to revelation and tradition, and believers who are open to modern Enlightenment movements and revolutions. It also separated Enlightenment communities into those who radically and abstractly rejected religion altogether, and those who were still open to religion, who through there radical critique of religion determinately negated it. The latter, in other words, criticized religion but also preserved and furthered the progressive contents of religion into new, concrete and secular forms, in their struggle toward the revolutionary promotion of a post-modern, more rational, humane, reconciled and peaceful future society; what the CTRS has named "alternative Future III."

3   The Myth of the "Fall"

In the views of Adorno and Horkheimer, Judaism, *the Religion of Sublimity*, expressed the Idea of the patriarchate as the concrete negation and destruction of the religious myth and of mythology. However, the bond between the

Universal and the Particular, the Name and Being, was still recognized in the religious ban on pronouncing the name of God – Yahweh, Elyon, Shaddai, Elohim – in some parts of the Hebrew tradition (Horkheimer and Adorno 1972).[3] Here, mythology means: *mythos* as representation in sensuous mode for subjective imagination and feeling; a faith not yet having fallen into disunion; picture thinking in a time when thought is still powerless; popular products of fantasy that contain as myth both divine and historical elements, which demonstrate the instinct of rationality and the pretense of philosophizing.

According to Hegel and his archenemy Arthur Schopenhauer, the archetype and prototype of all myths and mythologies was the *Story of the Fall*, or of *Original Sin*, that was present in many positive world religions. This story was the eternal mythos of humanity that expressed history in a mythical mode, and without which world history could not be understood. According to the dialectical philosopher and theologian Hegel, the Christian teaching of the original sin articulated that humanity as Spirit was a free being who could not let itself be determined by natural instincts and impulses. Humanity had to emancipate (i.e., determinately negate) itself as a natural, biological organism. The meaning and significance of the Christian teaching of original sin is that humanity had to free itself both individually and collectively from its immediate animality in terms of a concrete, determinate negation, which also preserved and sublimated what was negated in a new form. This negative and positive dialectical movement is expressed in the myth of Adam and Eve as the parents of all humanity and their disobedience of God; of their original sin of eating the forbidden fruit of the tree of knowledge of good and evil.

On the level of demythologized, dialectical thought or notion, as human beings, Adam and Eve had to disobey God and eat with internal necessity from this tree of knowledge of good and evil. Otherwise, people would not be human at all and would certainly not be in the image of God, but merely mindless animals, as they had been created. Not in its mythical form but on the level of dialectical, notional thought, the fundamental character through which humanity differentiated itself from the animal was that they now knew what was good and evil (Fromm 1966). Only through the fact that human beings recognized that they were thinking beings, through their becoming fully self-conscious, could they discern the difference between good and evil. In thinking alone lay the source of the evil and the good. Yet, in thinking as *transcending* also lay the cure for evil, which had been caused through thinking: the negation of negation leads to affirmation.

---

3   Genesis 1–3; Exodus 20; Psalm 91.

4   Education and Reconciliation

When Hegel determinately negated the mythological form of the Fall, and thus reinterpreted the consequence of this Hebrew myth of the Fall, namely, that all human beings are evil by nature, he had to say that human beings were by nature not what they *ought* to be, but humanity has within itself the Spirit and the destiny to become and thereby make real/for-themselves what they are in-themselves (Hegel 1948, 1956, 1967, 1969, 1971, 1984, 1985, 1987).[4] For Hegel and his friends, the concrete negation or supersession of the mere natural-ness of humanity was known as education through which the naturalness of humanity is tamed. Through Hegel's liberating notion of education, human-ity can become increasingly reconciled to its internal notion and to the good in general. Therefore, through such demythologization, through determinate negation, Hegel and the German idealists did not have to reject the content of the mythos of the Fall altogether but could also recognize the content in its truth. Mythos was thought in sensuous form. In the search for the higher, rational form of knowledge, Hegel did not negate the mythos abstractly, but it was negated determinately/concretely, i.e., criticized, as well as preserved, elevated, and fulfilled.

5   Will to Life

According to Max Horkheimer, the greatest teaching in Judaism as the *Religion of Sublimity*, and in Christianity as the *Religion of Becoming, Freedom and Manifestation*, was in the words of his great teacher Arthur Schopenhauer the mythos of the original sin. According to Horkheimer, informed by Schopenhauer, this mythos of the original and inherited sin had determined human history so far, and continued to determine the world for the thinking human being up to 1970. The CTRS may add that this historical determina-tion continues up to today in 2020. Horkheimer agreed with Schopenhauer's interpretation of the mythos, that what the first human did in Paradise was to commit this great sin based on which the whole history of humanity had really to be explained theologically. He also agreed with Schopenhauer (1958, 2004) that this teaching on original sin was one of the most significant theories in the history of positive religions, as it gave a brutally realistic description of the negativity of history, its empirical reality, its immeasurable evilness.

---

4   Genesis 3–4; Ecclesiasticus 21; Matthew 5–7:26–28; Luke 15:11–32; Romans 1–5; Corinthians 1–5.

For Hegel and Schopenhauer, as well as for Horkheimer and Adorno, demy-thologizing philosophy rescued the truth of the mythos in the form of thought. As such, Horkheimer (1972) thought the modern liberalization of religion would lead to the end of religion, as religion could not be translated into a bourgeois secularized form. Rather, the philosophical determinate negation of religion radically emphasized its truth core without any consoling decorations. From Plato to Hegel to Marx to Horkheimer, Adorno et al., art, religion, and philosophy present the same content, in different form (Horkheimer and Adorno 1972). Therefore, this very truth core of religion, namely, the "longing that the murderer shall not triumph over the innocent victims" (Horkheimer [1970] 1985), could only be rescued through its determinate negation and migration into secular form, while its inadequate, mythological form decayed (Adorno 1998).

6   Disenchanted World

According to Adorno and Horkheimer (1972), the disenchanted world of Judaism conciliated magic and fetishism, the beginning of religion, by determinately negating them in the Idea of God. It did not allow any word that would alleviate the despair of all that is mortal. Judaism associated hope only with the prohibition against calling on the false as God, against invoking the finite as the Infinite, lies as truth, or with ideology as the concrete negation of idolatry. The guarantee of salvation, or redemption, lay alone in the rejection of any belief that would replace it: it was critical knowledge obtained in the denunci-ation of illusion, or delusion. The critical theorists had to admit that the nega-tion of earlier religions and their mythologies by Judaism was not abstract and general, but rather concrete, and specific, and determinate. According to the CTRS, like the old Greek philosophers, at least since Heraclitus, Hegel knew and bequeathed to the critical theorists of society a double meaning of the negative, of nothing: there was a good, concrete nothing, *mae on*, or in Blochian terms, a possible humanization of the earth; and there was, in Hegelian terms, a flat, boring, and stupid, or in the terms of Jürgen Moltmann, a hard, evil, annihilating nothing, *ouk on* – absolute nothingness, of human finitude, tran-sience, malice, injustice and death (Bloch 1970, 1972, 2000; Hegel 1967, 1969; Moltmann 1967, 1974, 1996). The critical theorists gave expression mainly to the concrete *mae on*. They received their whole method of dialectic, or determi-nate, concrete negation, from their great teachers: from Hegel's *Phenomenology of Spirit* (1967) and *Science of Logic* (1969) and from Marx, who – following Feuerbach's (1986, 2004) lead – translated and concretely superseded Hegel's *a priori*, idealistic Notion dialectic into an *a posteriori*, materialistic, reality dialectic (Marx and Engels 1970 [1845]).

7   New Science

In the view of the CTRS, during what he called a *new fullness of time*, when the dialectic of the bourgeois Enlightenment made the dialectical Notion a need and a necessity, Hegel introduced a so-called new science in the Introduction to his *Phenomenology of Spirit*. According to Hegel, the completion of the development of the forms of human consciousness, which manifested themselves in the human potentials, or evolutionary universals of language and memory, work and tool, sexual and erotic love, struggle for recognition and community, was to be brought about precisely through the necessity of their advance and connection with one another (Hegel 1967, 1986; Habermas 1984). The series of shapes that consciousness traversed on this road were the detailed history of the process of training and educating of consciousness up to the level of the *Science of Logic* – which for Hegel, the philosopher and theologian, was the realm of theological Truth, as it was in and for itself. It was the Logic of God, the Creator, and of humanity. For Hegel, informed by Meister Eckhart, the eye, the logic, through which God saw humanity, human beings also saw God (Blackney 1941; Hegel 1971, 1984).

8   The Goal

In Hegel' s view, the goal of the whole dialectical process of the forms of consciousness was necessarily fixed, for both phenomenological knowledge and its dialectical succession (Hegel 1967, 1971). The *terminus* of the process was where phenomenological knowledge was no longer compelled to go further beyond itself, where it found its own self, and where the Notion corresponded to the object, and the object to the Notion. The progress of the forms of consciousness towards this goal of self-identity consequently was without a halt, and at no earlier stage or form of consciousness was satisfaction to be found. That which was confined to a life of nature, characterized by gravity, e.g., an organism, was unable to go beyond its immediate existence without being forced by something other than itself to go beyond that limit. Consciousness, characterized by rational freedom, however, was, in contrast to nature, to itself its own Notion. Thereby, consciousness immediately transcended what was limited. Such transcending belonged essentially to consciousness: thinking meant transcending. Therefore, consciousness transcended its own self. In the form of consciousness, along with the particular, there was at the same time set up the *beyond*, the universal. Thus, consciousness could find no rest on its way of determinate negation of one particular form of consciousness by the next on the way to the goal, until the final universal terminus was reached. In the view of the CTRS, here the crypto-Catholic Lutheran philosopher and theologian Hegel might very well have had in mind the famous statement of St. Augustine (1963: 17), informed by Neo-Platonism, the Hebrew Bible, and the New Testament:

Our hearts are restless until they rest in Thee.[5]

9   Method

According to Hegel, the exposition of what could alone be the true *method* of philosophical science, fell into the treatise and discourse of the science of logic, understood as *logos* theology, itself. This was because the method was the consciousness about the form of the internal self-movement of its content, of the Idea of God. In *Phenomenology of Spirit*, Hegel established an example of this dialectical method concerning a concrete (i.e., particular) object, namely, human consciousness – its development from sense perception through understanding and reason to spirit, which later on was followed by other concrete objects, such as the sun system, the human organism, the human subject, private right, personal morality, marriage and family, civil society, political state, world history, art, religion, and history of philosophy.

For Hegel there were forms of consciousness, each one containing internal contradictions, and dissolving itself at the same time in its realization through its own [determinate] negation. It thereby moved into a 'higher' form. The contradictory form dissolved itself not into abstract nothingness, but rather into the negation of its particular content, the negation of the determinate thing, and which thereby was determinate, or concrete, or specific negation: the result essentially contained that out of which it resulted. For Hegel, while the resulting form, the negation, was determinate negation, it had a content. It was a new notion, but a higher, richer notion than the previous one. The determinate negation had become richer because through the negation of the previous form it thus contained it, but also more than it, and was thereby the unity of itself and of its opposite. Thus, in the *Science of Logic*, Becoming

---

5   The Yahweh of Moses, or the father of Jesus of Nazareth.

contained Being and Nothing, or the Notion contained Being and Essence. In the *Philosophy of Right,* the State contained family and civil society, or the State itself contained internal and external state law, and history. In the *Philosophy of Religion*, the *Religion of Freedom* contained the *Religions of Nature* and the *Religions of Subjectivity*; in Christianity, the *Realm of the Spirit* contained the *Realm of the Father* and the *Realm of the Son*, and Enlightenment contained mythology.

For Hegel, in this logical way the system of notions had to form itself in general and had to complete itself in an irresistible course, which took nothing into itself from the outside. Because of this, Hegel knew that the dialectical method was the only true one, for this method was not something different from its object and content because the dialectic of determinate negation was derived from the content in itself, which it had in itself, and which moved it forward. Dialectics was/is the passage and course of the thing itself.

10   Image Prohibition

For Horkheimer and Adorno, informed by Hegel's concrete dialectical method of determinate negation, *mae on*, not abstract negation, *ouk on*, the abstract contesting of every positive form without distinction, e.g., the abstract stereotype of *vanity* – *"all is vanity"*[6] – arrogantly set itself above the prohibition against naming the Absolute in Judaism or in Kant's philosophy with names. Such abstract and vain negation set itself above the maxim just as far above and its contrary, pantheism or its caricature, bourgeois skepticism. In the view of the CTRS, the Third Mosaic Commandment – the prohibition against misusing the *name* of Yahweh – was a concrete or determinate negation, not an abstract or general negation, which was true of all of Judaism and of all positive religions, dead or alive.

Horkheimer and Adorno (1972), informed by the Hebrew Bible and by Kant, did not only point to the Third Mosaic Commandment, but also to the Second Mosaic Commandment – the prohibition of making any *images* of the Absolute. According to the Jewish *Dioscuri*, Horkheimer and Adorno (1972), in Judaism the image was determinately negated, i.e., the justness of the image was not only negated, but also preserved in the faithful pursuit of its prohibition. In their view, determinate negation rejected the defective ideas of the Absolute, the idols, which confronted them with the Idea to which they could

---

6   Ecclesiasticus 1.

not match. The dialectic of determinate negation interprets every image as writing or script and shows how the falsity of the image is to be read in the lines of its features; a confession which deprives the image of its power and allows for the appropriation of it for the truth. *Determinate negation* was the driving force of the history of religions as well as of world history. That, precisely, has been the main method of the CTRS, inherited from German idealism and German materialism, and from the critical theory of society of the Frankfurt School, in the past half century.

11   Death of God

As expressed by the Reformer Martin Luther, as well as by the philosopher Friedrich Nietzsche (1999, 2001), the theologian Paul Tillich (1952, 1967), and the Marxist Slavoj Žižek (Žižek and Milbank 2009; Žižek, Crockett, and David 2011; Žižek and Gunjevic 2012), Hegel (1967, 1977, 1987) also stated that God has died in Christianity.[7] For Hegel this is the most awful and terrible thought, that everything Infinite, and Eternal, and everything True was no longer. The negation itself was in God. God was in pain, in the monstrosity of the crucified Christ, not as paradox but as dialectic. With this negation in God was connected the highest pain, the feeling of complete hopelessness, and the giving up of everything higher. For the Christian Hegel, however, in contrast to Nietzsche and Žižek, God did not remain dead. The course of God's history did not remain standing still here with this terrible negation, Christ's death on the cross, but now the turnover happened, the negation of the negation: God maintains God's self in this process of negation, and it is merely the death of death. God rises to life again. The negative turns into its opposite: in resurrection, ascension, and the coming of the Spirit. The negation of the negation leads to affirmation.[8]

12   Triumph over the Negative

For the believer and philosopher Hegel, in his Christology from above this negation of the negation happens particularly in the resurrection and in the ascension of Christ. In Hegel's phenomenological and theological view, in

---

7   Matthew 26–28; John 1:18–20.
8   Matthew 26–28; John 1:18–20.

the Jesus narrative what was likewise present with Jesus' death was also this death of death, the overcoming of the grave, the triumph over the negative, and the elevation into heaven. In Horkheimer's words, the murderers have not triumphed over the innocent victim, at least not ultimately. However, for the humanist Hegel, the overcoming of the negative was not the taking off of human nature, but its highest proof even in death, in the face of the *ouk on*, the nasty nothing, and in the highest love: *Creatio nova ex nihilo.* The Spirit was only Spirit as this negative of the negative, which thus contained the negative in itself. Therefore, when the resurrected Son of Man ascends and sits on the right hand of the Father, there then comes the spiritual awareness in its highest manifestation that this is the elevation of human nature to its honor and its identity with God's nature and history.

13   The Death of Death

According to Hegel, the resurrection of Christ belonged as essentially to the faith as his death: Christ appeared after his resurrection only to his believing friends. The resurrection was not external history for the non-believers, but this appearance was only for the believers. The resurrection was followed by the ascension of Christ. The triumph of the elevation of Christ to the right hand of God closed his story, which for Christian consciousness is the explication of divine nature and history, which revealed itself partially in all positive religions and their mythologies, but manifested itself in all its *exitus-reditus* moments in Christianity as the *Religion of Manifestation*. When the phenomenologist and theologian Hegel comprehended in the first sphere of the trinitarian Divinity (the *Realm of the Father*) God in our thought, then things started in the second sphere, the *Realm of the Son*, with the immediacy of perception and with sensuous representation.

Now the process was that the immediate singularity of Jesus of Nazareth was concretely negated or superseded (*aufgehoben*). As in the first sphere, the Realm of the Father, the reserve of God ceased, and his first immediacy as abstract Universality, according to which he was the Essence of essences, was superseded, so was here now in the Realm of the Son, concretely negated the abstraction of humanity, the immediacy of the being singularity of Jesus of Nazareth: and this happened through his death on the cross. However, the death of Christ was the death of this death Itself: the negation of the negation as affirmation.

The same course and process of the explication of the nature and history of God took place in the Realm of the Father. Here, however, in the Realm of the

Son, the course and process happen in so far as it is an object of consciousness. This was because there was present the drive of the perception of the trinitarian, divine nature and history. In the third sphere, in the Realm of the Spirit, the Realm of the Father, and the Realm of Son were united and reconciled. Through the notion of determinate negativity, specifically, that of the sublation of religion and mythology – particularly that of the Christian narrative – to the level of reason and the dialectical Notion and Idea, Hegel revealed an element that distinguished the genuine Enlightenment from positivism.

However, neither in the *Phenomenology of the Spirit*, nor in the *Science of Logic*, nor in the *Philosophy of Religion*, nor anywhere else in the entirety of his philosophy and its dialectic of negation did Hegel make anything into the Absolute, and thus, contravene the Mosaic or Kantian name or image prohibition, and thereby lapse into idolatrous mythology. Hegel was as much committed to the not abstract but rather concrete negation of idols, or idolatry, as the Hebrew Bible, the New Testament, or the Holy Qu'ran, or, for that matter, Kant's subjective idealism, or Horkheimer's or Adorno's critical theory of society, or the CTRS. The Absolute, universal Spirit is as little a mere projection, absolutization, self-deification, or self-idolatrization of the finite human spirit in Hegel's dialectical philosophy and theology, as the Holy Spirit is in the Catholic or Protestant catechisms (John Paul II 1983, 1993, 1995; Küng 1992, 1993a, 1993b). Those positivists who blame Hegel's notion of the absolute Spirit for Auschwitz, forget that Jews, and Christians, and Muslims prayed to God (Spirit) in the camps.

14   Self-negation

According to Hegel's Notion- and reality-dialectical philosophy,[9] theology and Christology, in this determination of Christ's death of death in the resurrection, negation of negation as affirmation, in the negation of his infinite pain of self-negating, self-sacrificing love, lay the ground for the immortality of the human soul to become a determinate teaching in the Christian religion, more precisely in the Realm of the Spirit (Hegel 1967, 1984, 1985, 1986a; Küng 1987, 1995).[10] This self-negation of love was not abstract, but concrete. This self-sacrificing love meant rebirth, martyrdom, compassion, redemption, liberation, eternal life.

---

9   Hegel's dialectical philosophy of the Notion is unfolded through his "reality dialectic," which seeks to explains the Notion's dialectical movement in the realms of human consciousness, the family, civil society and the critique of capitalism, and history.

10   Matthew 2–5:26–28.

According to Hegel, in Christianity, the human soul, the singular subjectivity of the human being, had an infinite, eternal determination: to be a citizen in the kingdom of God. This is a determination, and a life, which is removed from time and transience. As it is at the same time opposed to this limited sphere of life on this earth, this eternal determination determines itself as a future, the *eschaton* and the *eschata*.

15 Radical Negativity

In the view of the CTRS, besides Jürgen Moltmann's (1967, 1974, 1996) theology of hope, the most advanced theology today, in 2020, is the new political theology of Johann Baptist Metz (1970 [1959], 1965, 1967, 1973, 1980, 1981, 1998), which also strongly influenced the liberation theology of Latin and Central America (Metz and Rendtdorf 1971; Metz and Wiesel 1999). In World War II, Baptist and I were both German soldiers (Siebert 1966, 1993). In the last desperate weeks of World War II in Germany, the 16-year-old soldier Johann Baptist Metz was sent by his commanding officer to the rear with a message for headquarters. When he returned, he found the other members of his unit, all as young as he, dead, wiped out in a sudden air and armored assault. Baptist remembered that he could only see dead and empty faces, where the day before he had shared childhood fears and laughter. He remembered nothing but a wordless cry. This is how he saw himself throughout his life, and behind this memory all his childhood dreams crumble away. Baptist asked himself, what would happen if one took this sort of thing not to the psychologist but into the church, and if one would not allow oneself to be talked out of such unreconciled memories even by theology, but rather wanted to have faith with them, and with them to speak about God? (Metz 1985, 1986, 1987).

In his later theological studies, Metz departed from Hegel, but also remained in continuity with him in terms of his reality dialectic. Baptist was a deep dialectician. He was informed by Karl Marx and Sören Kiergegaard, as well as by Adorno, Horkheimer and Walter Benjamin: in our discourses Baptist always recommended all five of these thinkers to me. Metz's new political theology is directed against the fascist political theology of Carl Schmitt, Hitler's jurist and political theologian (Schmitt [1921] 1928, [1923] 1925, 1985, 1996, 2008). During a meeting between the young theologian Metz and the old jurist Schmitt, in the former's small Bavarian village church, Schmitt called Metz's new political theology a Prometheus theology, and his own traditional theology an Epimetheus theology. While Schmitt's traditional political theology sided with the rulers, who appropriated the collective surplus labor of their slaves, serfs and wage laborers through the centuries, Metz's new political theology identified with the ruled who produce the collective surplus value, the wealth of nations.

The old Marxist Ernst Bloch was in a certain sense the mentor not only of the young Protestant theologian Jürgen Moltmann, but also of the young Catholic theologian Metz. When Baptist had a series of car accidents, Bloch psychoanalyzed him and came to the diagnosis and prognosis that Metz's Super-Ego punished him for his revolutionary thoughts by getting him into one accident after another. Moltmann was rather amused about the peculiar discrepancy in Baptist's life, between his being a country priest and pastor in his arch-conservative Bavarian parish, on one hand, and his radical, provolutionary, eschatological, new political theology, on the other. The Archbishop Joseph Ratzinger of Munich, on the Catholic Right, prevented Metz, Professor of theology at the University of Münster on the Catholic Left, from getting the very prestigious theology chair at the University of Munich, which had been occupied before by Metz's teacher Karl Rahner and by Romano Guardini. Metz never forgot this painful experience of the rejection of his new political theology as well as of the related liberation theology by Joseph Ratzinger, not only as Archbishop and Cardinal, and Inquisitor, but also as Pope Benedict XVI, not even when the latter once came to celebrate his birthday in Münster.

16   Negative Theology

According to the CTRS, the central themes of Metz's new political theology have been: the advent of God, Christian anthropocentrism, church in the world, evolving world and theology, reform and counter-reformation, liberating remembrance of Jesus Christ and his suffering as critique of a teleological-technological notion of the future, future out of the remembrance of suffering, redemption and emancipation, theodicy and hope after Auschwitz, faith in history and society, passion because of God, compassion for humanity, mystical-political dimension of Christianity, the actuality of monastic orders, movement beyond and departure from the bourgeois religion, the emergent church, time diagnoses, etc.

According to a summary of Metz's works at the occasion of his death in December 2019 by one of his most outstanding students, Edmund Arens (2019), Metz's new political theology is an elementarily negative theology. Its radical negativity has a practical-ethical character. It implies what Ernst Bloch (1970, 1986, 2000) and Herbert Marcuse (1964, 1969, 1972) called *the great refusal* to reconcile oneself with the horrible suffering in this world.

Metz's dialectical sticking and keeping to the radical, but nevertheless deter-minate, specific, concrete and not abstract negativity stands in solidarity with the Jewish and Kantian image – and name – prohibition. With Fyodor Dostoevsky's *The Brothers Karamazov*, and with Bloch's (1986) philosophy of hope, Metz insisted that the sufferings of the victims in history have not yet been repaid and satisfied. Horkheimer and Benjamin agreed that only after they had taken most seriously that history is closed, that the dead are really dead and that the murdered victims had really been murdered, they might say that history is also still open: that the murderer shall after all not triumph over the innocent victim, at least not ultimately. According to Metz, the pain, agony, and anguish of the forgotten and annihilated victims must never be *ad acta* – irrelevant and thus forgotten. The spine or sting of concrete negativity forbids believers to come to terms with, or to put up with, or to accept positivistically the given unjust conditions in antagonistic bourgeois or socialist societies. Determinate negation prevents the reconciliation with the falsity, falseness, wrongness, evil, and keeps open the hurting wound, and even opens the old wounds.

An abyss of negativity opened for Baptist with World War II, with Auschwitz and Treblinka, and with Hiroshima and Nagasaki. Like Adorno (1973), Metz recognized in the catastrophic tragedy of Auschwitz not only the monstrous crime of National Socialism, but also the failure of Christianity. According to Metz, Christian theology should no longer take place with people's backs turned toward Auschwitz. Theology that was disposed and structured in such a way that it remained untouched by Auschwitz, should no longer be done. Metz pushed the radical, determinate negativity up to a suffering concerning God, the God-passion and the missing of God. Thereby in his new political theology, Metz gave validity in a radical mode to the eschatological reservation against everything positive and every kind of positivism. Metz's friend Habermas' (2010) consciousness of that which is missing in the post-secular world is as painfully and fundamentally inscribed into the new political theology. It leads to the prophetic lamentation of and accusation against the passive tolerance of injustice, suffering and death: this passivity is to be sued for the lost victims before God and men. According to Metz's Jewish friend Elie Wiesel, prison-ers of Auschwitz put God on trial and found him guilty of having broken the Covenant with the Jewish people, who nevertheless went to the gas chambers with their hands on their heads, a sign of submission to Yahweh's will (Wiesel 1982, 1992; Metz and Wiesel 1993).[11]

---

11   Psalm 22.

17   Resistance and Interruption

Metz understood the emergent Church mainly as a remembering, narrating and hoping community. According to Metz, today the Church finds itself in an epochal transition from a culturally monocentric Church of Europe to a globally rooted, culturally and pastorally polycentric World Church. The new political theology was not a countercultural *Communio*. It rather pleaded for an *Ecclesia* that was fed out of the mystic, out of what Herbert Marcuse (1968) called *resistance and interruption*. This *Ecclesia* has to remember to make present, and to continue its ambivalent history of origin, its manifest history of guilt, and its interrupting departure history. With Metz, a subject-oriented understanding of the Church as the people of God makes itself strong for the long overdue subjectification or personalization in the Church, which has been long and well prepared by Luther, Hegel, and Kierkegaard. That subject-oriented understanding of the Church stands up for the recognition of others in their being other. It finds itself in the liberation struggles and experiences of those who are deprived of recognition for their subjectivities. Such a Church corresponded institutionally to the departure from the Western Church toward a World Church, in which tasks, burdens and hopes are divided and shared justly and in solidarity.

With Metz, compassion determines the reform program of the Church *ex memoria passionis*. It is reclaimed against the ecclesiastical self-privatization precisely in a pluralistic public. The Church of compassion recognizes the authority of those who are suffering. It preserves for itself a stock, or supply of insights, which are important and necessary for the survival of the Church, and which motivate and mobilize its social criticism as well as its public self-criticism. As do I, Arens wished that the God of the living and the dead, who calls all people into the subject-being before his face, may give to his great teacher Johann Baptist Metz the fullness of life. For Matthew Ashley, the systematic theologian at Notre Dame University in South Bend, Indiana, it was fitting that Baptist died on Dec. 2, 2019, the 39th anniversary of the murder of four U.S. women missionaries (one of whom was my student at Maryknoll, New York) and one lay woman, by the fascist Arena-Government in El Salvador. For Metz, both faith and theology achieved their full stature only in solidarity with the victims and as witnesses to hope against all hope. Likewise, it was fitting that Baptist died at the beginning of Advent, the season of hope.

In 2017, the organization Oxfam published a report that stated that the wealth held by the eight wealthiest people of the world is equal to the wealth of half of the world's population. In the perspective of the CTRS, informed by revelation *and* autonomous reason, since other global problems, like poverty, war and environmental issues, cannot be solved without the determinate negation of and departure from the contradictory modern social system of private appropriation of collective surplus labor, it is high time to move toward a post-modern social paradigm of collective appropriation of collective surplus labor: toward post-modern alternative Future III – the peaceful, reconciled society, which is opened in longing toward the theologically hoped-for New Creation of the totally Other.[12]

References

Adorno, Theodor W. 1973. *Negative Dialectics.* New York: The Seabury Press.

Adorno, Theodor W. 1974. *Minima Moralia: Reflections from Damaged Life.* London: NLB.

Adorno, Theodor W. 1993. *Hegel: Three Studies.* Cambridgessachusetts: The MIT Press.

Adorno, Theodor W. 1998. "Reason and Revelation" in *Critical Models: Interventions and Catchwords.* New York: Columbia University Press.

Arens, Edmund. 2019. "Gottespassion und Compassion. Zum Tod von Johannes Baptist Metz." In *Feinschwarz/3.* Dezember.

Augustine of Hippo. 1963. *The Confessions of St. Augustine.* New York: New American Library.

Bloch, Ernst. 1970. *Man on His Own.* New York: Herder and Herder.

Bloch, Ernst. 1972. *Atheism in Christianity: The Religion of the Exodus and the Kingdom.* New York: Herder and Herder.

Bloch, Ernst. 1986. *The Principle of Hope.* Vols. I, II, III. Cambridgessachusetts: The MIT Press.

Bloch, Ernst. 2000. *The Spirit of Utopia.* Stanford, California: Stanford University Press.

Feuerbach, Ludwig. 1986. *Principles of the Philosophy of the Future.* Hackett Publishing.

Feuerbach, Ludwig. 2004. *The Essence of Christianity.* Barnes & Noble Publishing.

Fromm, Erich. 1966. *You Shall Be as Gods: A Radical Interpretation of the Old Testament and Its Tradition.* Greenwich, CT: Fawcett Publications.

Habermas, Jürgen. 1984. *The Theory of Communicative Action. Volume One: Reason and the Rationalization of Society.* Boston: Beacon Press.

Habermas, Jürgen. 2010. *An Awareness of What is Missing: Faith and Reason in a Post-secular Age.* Polity.

Hegel, G.W.F. 1948. *Christianity: Early Theological Writings.* New York: Harper Torchbooks.

---

12 Horkheimer's (1985 [1970]) explanation of religion as "the longing for the totally Other" than "what is," is fundamental to Critical Theory and the CTRS.

Hegel, G.W.F. 1956. *The Philosophy of History*. New York: Dover Publications, Inc.

Hegel, G.W.F. 1967. *The Phenomenology of Mind*. New York: Harper and Row.

Hegel, G.W.F. 1969. *Hegel's Science of Logic*. New York: Humanities Press.

Hegel, G.W.F. 1971. *Hegel's Philosophy of Mind*. Oxford: Clarendon Press.

Hegel, G.W.F. 1984. *Lectures on the Philosophy of Religion. Volume I: Introduction and The Concept of* Religion, ed. Peter C. Hodgson. Berkeley: University of California Press.

Hegel, G.W.F. 1985. *Lectures on the Philosophy of Religion. Volume III: The Consummate Religion*, ed. Peter C. Hodgson. Berkeley: University of California Press.

Hegel, G.W.F. 1986. *The Jena System, 1804–5: Logic and Metaphysics*. Kingston & Montreal: McGill-Queen's University Press.

Hegel, G.W.F. 1987. *Lectures on the Philosophy of Religion. Volume II: Determinate Religion*, ed. Peter C. Hodgson. Berkeley: University of California Press.

Horkheimer, Max. 1985 [1970]. "Die Sehnsucht nach dem ganz Anderen. (Gespräch mit Helmut Gumnior. 1970.)" in *Max Horkheimer. Gesammelte Schriften, Band 7: Vorträge und Aufzeichnungen 1949–1973*. Frankfurt a.M: Fischer Taschenbuch Verlag GmbH.

Horkheimer, Max. 1972. *Critical Theory*. New York: The Seabury Press.

Horkheimer, Max. 1974a. *Notizen 1950–1969 und Dämmerung. Notizen in Deutschland.* Frankfurt a.M: Fischer Verlag.

Horkheimer, Max. 1974b. *Eclipse of Reason*. New York: The Seabury Press.

Horkheimer, Max. 1974c. *Critique of Instrumental Reason.* New York: The Seabury Press.

Horkheimer, Max. 1978. *Dawn & Decline: Notes 1926–1931 & 1950–1969*. New York: The Seabury Press.

Horkheimer, Max. 1993. *Between Philosophy and Social Science: Selected Early Writings*. Cambridge, MA: The MIT Press.

Horkheimer, Max & Theodor Adorno. 1972. *Dialectic of Enlightenment*. New York: The Seabury Press.

Küng, Hans. 1987. *The Incarnation of God: An Introduction to Hegel's Theological Thought as Prolegomena to a Future Christology*. New York: Crossroad.

Küng, Hans. 1992. *Theologie im Aufbruch: Eine ökumenische Grundlegung*. München: Piper Verlag.

Küng, Hans. 1993a. *24 Thesen zur Gottesfrage*. München: Piper Verlag.

Küng, Hans. 1993b. *Credo. Das Apostolische Glaubensbekenntnis–Zeitgenossen erklärt*. München: Piper Verlag.

Küng, Hans. 1995. *Christianity: Essence, History and Future*. New York: Continuum.

Marcuse, Herbert. 1964. *One-dimensional Man: Studies in the Ideology of Advanced Industrial Society*. Boston: Beacon Press.

Marcuse, Herbert. 1968. "Philosophy and Critical Theory" in *Negations: Essays in Critical Theory*. Boston: Beacon Press.

Marcuse, Herbert. 1969. *An Essay on Liberation*. Boston: Beacon Press.

Marcuse, Herbert. 1972. *Counter-Revolution and Revolt*. Boston: Beacon Press.

Marx, Karl, and Friedrich Engels. 1970 [1845]. *The German Ideology*. International Publishers Co.

Metz, Johann B. 1965. *The Church in the World*. New York: Paulist Press.

Metz, Johann B. 1970. *The Advent of God*. New York: Newman Press.

Metz, Johann B. 1973. *Theology of the World*. New York: The Seabury Press.

Metz, Johann B. 1980. *Faith in History & Society: Toward a Practical Fundamental Theology*. New York: The Seabury Press.

Metz, Johann B. 1981. *The Emergent Church*. New York: Cross Road.

Metz, Johann B. 1998. *A Passion for God. The Mystical-Political Dimension of Christianity*. New York: Paulist Press.

Moltmann, Jürgen. 1967. *Theology of Hope: On the Ground and the Implications of a Christian Eschatology*. New York & Evanston: Harper & Row Publishers.

Moltmann, Jürgen. 1974. *The Crucified God: The Cross of Christ as the Foundation and Criticism of Christian Theology*. New York: Harper & Row Publisher.

Moltmann, Jürgen. 1996. *The Coming of God, Christian Eschatology*. Minneapolis: Fortress Press.

Nietzsche, Friedrich. 1999. *Thus Spake Zarathustra*, ed. Thomas Common. New York: Dover.

Nietzsche, Friedrich. 2001. *The Gay* Science, ed. Bernard Williams. Cambridge: Cambridge University Press.

Pope John Paul II. 1983. *Codex Juris Canonici*. Rome: Libreria Editrice Vaticana.

Pope John Paul II. *Encyclical Letter: Veritatis Splendor*. At http://www.vatican.va/content/john-paul-ii/en/encyclicals/documents/hf_jp-ii_enc_06081993_veritatis-splendor.html.

Pope John Paul II. 1995. *Catechism of the Catholic Church*. New York: An Image Book Doubleday.

Schmitt, Carl. 1921/1928. *Die Diktatur. Von den Anfängen des modernen Souveränitätsgedankens bis zum proletarischen Klassenkampf*. München-Leipzig.

Schmitt, Carl. 1923/1925. *Römischer Katholizismus und politische Form*. München.

Schmitt, Carl. 1985. *Political Theology: Four Chapters on the Concept of Sovereignty*. Cambridgessachusetts and London, England: The MIT Press.

Schmitt, Carl. 1996. *The Concept of the Political*. Chicago and London: The University of Chicago Press.

Schmitt, Carl. 2008. *Political Theology II: The Myth of the Closure of any Political Theology*. Malden, Massachusetts: Polity Press.

Schopenhauer, Arthur. 1958. *The World as Will and Representation*. Vol. II. New York: Dover Publications, Inc.

Schopenhauer, Arthur. 2004. *The Wisdom of Life*. New York: Dover Publications, Inc.

Siebert, Rudolf J. 1966. "A German Experience," in *At the Cross Road*, 5 (2 and 3).

Siebert, Rudolf J. 1993. *Recht, Macht und Liebe: Georg W, Rudolphi's Prophetische Politische Theologie*, Frankfurt a. M: Haag and Herchen.

Siebert, Rudolf J. 2001. *The Critical Theory of Religion: The Frankfurt School.* Lanham, MD: The Scarecrow Press.

Siebert, Rudolf J. 2002. *From Critical Theory to Political Theology: Personal Autonomy and Universal Solidarity.* New York: Peter Lang Publishing.

Siebert, Rudolf J. 2010. *Manifesto of the Critical Theory of Society and Religion: The Wholly Other, Liberation, Happiness and the Rescue of the Hopeless.* (Vols.: I, II, III). Leiden: Brill Publisher.

Siebert, Rudolf J. 2019. *The World Religions in Idealistic and Materialistic Perspective: The Loss and the Rediscovery of the Idea.* New Delhi, India: Sanbun.

Siebert, Rudolf J. 2020. *The Evolution of the Critical Theory of Religion and Society: Union, Disunion, and Reunion of the Sacred and the Profane. (1946–2020).* New Delhi, India: Sanbun.

Tillich, Paul. 1952. *The Courage to Be.* New Haven & London: Yale University Press.

Tillich, Paul. 1967. *Systematic Theology.* (Three vols. in one.) Chicago: The University of Chicago Press.

Wiesel, Elie. 1982. *Night.* New York: Bantam Books.

Wiesel, Elie. 1992. *The Forgotten.* New York: Schocken Books.

Žižek, Slavoj and John Milbank. 2009. *The Monstrosity of Christ: Paradox or Dialectic?* Cambridge: The MIT Press.

Žižek, Slavoj, Clayton Crockett and David Creston. 2011. *Hegel and the Infinite.* New York: Columbia University Press.

Žižek, Slavoj and Boris Gunjevic. 2012. *God in Pain.* New York: Seven Stories Press.

PART 2

Psychoanalysis

∵

CHAPTER 5

The Dialectic of Unreason: Authoritarianism and the Irrational

Lauren Langman and Avery Schatz

1   Introduction

The project of modernity was about freeing knowledge from religious dogmas, myths, and superstition, to be based instead on logic and evidence, enabling social and scientific progress. Allegedly, this would eliminate ignorance, poverty, and tyranny, and would enable freedom, equality, and brotherhood (*liberté, égalité, fraternité*) for the newly emergent 'individual.' Yet if we look at the past century, notwithstanding unprecedented scientific advances, the adversities of rationality, capitalism, urban life and the division of labor (as noted by Marx, Weber, Simmel and Durkheim) have led to various social strains and crises that have fostered a variety of social, cultural and political movements.

In the past decade or so, in response to a cluster of crises and adversities (e.g., growing inequalities, economic stagnation, precarity, immigration crises, culture wars and political polarization, etc.), one major response has been the rise of a variety of right-wing populisms – reactionary antiestablishment mobilizations that generally promise to free and empower the 'victimized,' the 'real people' of the nation, who are said to be betrayed by weak, corrupt, indifferent elites.[1] Strong, authoritarian leaders, unfettered by democratic niceties, will return society to 'earlier times' that some believe were better, and punish those allegedly responsible for the demise of the 'real people.'[2] Today, after the socioeconomic implosions of 2008 and 2020 (the latter compounded by a global pandemic), as the old order collapses and the new has not yet arrived, there are a variety of what Gramsci would call 'morbid symptoms.'[3] Anger,

---

1   Echoes of Carl Schmitt might be heard (see Antonio, this volume).
2   And for some folks, these 'earlier' times were 'better,' unionized manufacturing jobs paid well and provided security and benefits, white privilege, male domination, and heteronormativity were unquestioned norms.
3   The COVID-19 pandemic has made visible many dysfunctions of the current neoliberal system, from growing social inequality in which vast populations of people are rendered expendable, to fossil fuel-based industrial production and transportation that promises species-threatening climate change.

anxiety, shame and *ressentiment* have led to a variety of reactionary populisms, ethno-religious nationalisms, neo-fascisms that involve aggression, bullying, Othering, etc.

One common feature of these movements is that they appeal to certain kinds of people; *reactionary ideologies and movements resonate with people who have underlying authoritarian character structures that willingly reject factual evidence and/or logic. Thus, they readily embrace a variety of clearly irrational beliefs.* While economic factors cannot be ignored, research has shown that most right populists are not economically distressed. Rather they are responding to social and cultural changes.

Hannah Arendt (1975: 80) inquired how authoritarian demagogues could get away with endless fabrications. She described "a curiously varying mixture of gullibility and cynicism with which each member ... in the movement, is expected to react to the changing lying statements of the leaders and the central unchanging ideological fiction of the movement."[4] Various cultural and/ or political 'understandings' that border on and often cross into delusions, prompt reactionary mobilizations which becomes a matter of life and death.[5] This was clearly evident in Germany when the crises of their post-WWI economy, together with a weak democratic government, gave rise to Nazi beliefs in an Aryan master race, that Jews were parasites or communists who stabbed Germany in the back at Versailles, and so on. These beliefs led to Hitlerism, WWII, and the Holocaust.

Today, the stresses and strains of modernity have led to what might be called a 'post-truth' society in which a variety of reactionary movements, typically right populisms, embrace views that move beyond credulity, without any substantive basis. This can be seen in various forms of conspiracy theories, rejection of science and distrust of mass media. As will be argued, modern capitalism has inherent tendencies for crises of legitimacy (Habermas 1975). In the face of such crises, authoritarian groups create, accept, and embrace various perspectives that some might think bizarre. These include 'explanations' for their hardships and victimization that includes targeting other social groups as blameworthy. A variety of right populist movements reject both democracy and objective evidence. As this essay is penned, the world faces a pandemic, but in some quarters, the 'explanations' range from God's

---

4 A more detailed explanation rooted in Frankfurt school studies of authoritarian leadership can be found in Lowenthal and Guterman (1949) and Adorno (1950).

5 One telling finding of the F- scale was the acceptance of astrology, which Adorno (1994) saw as fascism on the cheap (e.g. conforming to the stars), producing dependency, submission to authority and the status quo, with promises of love, prosperity and good health.

punishment for our sins, to even believing COVID-19 is a left-wing hoax to grab power. How do we unpack the reasons why many people steadfastly succumb to the most preposterous claims and beliefs – especially ones that are without any evidence?

2   The Rise of Modernity

Inspired by the increasingly rational basis of commerce and "new" scientific discoveries, a rising class of Italian merchants 'revived' Greco-Rome art, science, philosophy, identities, and values, spearheading the Renaissance. Two important consequences followed: 1) a revival of the spirit of critique, e.g., examining the difference of essence and appearance, and 2) the rise of humanism.[6] This paved the way for the Reformation as a critique of the Church – not just its corruption or its nepotism, but its 'irrationality,' e.g., its 'magical' beliefs and practices.

These political-economic and cultural changes led to the Enlightenment. Kant, its cheerleader, extoled Reason as man's emergence from his self-incurred immaturity and as 'freedom' from ignorance, superstition, and myth. Modernity was a moment of 'progress' qua Reason based on logic, evidence, efficiency, measurement, etc. Scientific rationality allowed and advanced sciences and technologies. 19th century metallurgy and chemical engineering enabled the explosive growth of industrial capitalism, which transformed the world. To secure their claims to leadership, the bourgeois classes and their philosophers decried dynastic rule as "tyranny." The new bourgeois states claimed legitimacy through enabling the voices of hitherto dominated peoples, now rendered citizens of nations, to elect their governments.[7]

As was clear to Habermas (1991 [1962]), with the rise of civil society, a bourgeois public sphere emerged in which the elites discussed and debated issues in situations free of 'distorted communication' to arrive at consensus. Today, the ideal of rational democracy based on reasonable debate to arrive at 'popular consensus' is quaint at best. In the early 20th century, with capitalist

---

6   As will be extremely important tin this essay, Marx attempted to critique appearances to reveal the actual workings of capital masked by ideology, while Freud revealed what was normally repressed.

7   There were of course tensions between dynastic rulers and the merchant classes, e.g., 1848, but by WWI, the pollical power of landed elites was over. There were of course constitutional monarchies in which the royalty had symbolic power and often became tourist attractions vide the dysfunctional royal family of England.

crisis, there was a combination of discontent and new mass media used for propaganda and charismatic leadership, that led to electoral victories for the Nazi party and Hitler. In the 21st century, we again see the emergence of a variety of authoritarian right-wing populisms, ethno-religions nationalisms and neo-fascisms. But, much like earlier iterations, these movements and governments are based on irrational fabrications, distortions, myths, scapegoating and conspiracy theories that find widespread appeal. As will be argued below, to understand these developments we need to consider the irrationality of Reason, informed by the Frankfurt School, who synthesized the ideas of Marx, Nietzsche, Weber, into a critique of domination, *The Dialectic of Enlightenment* (Horkheimer and Adorno 2002 [1944]).

3   Capitalism and Rationality

For Marx, the ideology, norms, values, and modes of understanding of every society, were controlled by the ruling classes. They functioned like a 'camera obscura' that rendered perceptions 'upside down,' masking the essential qualities of political economy, and thus sustaining class inequality. Dynastic rule was legitimated as 'God's will,' and endured for centuries.[8] Anticipating Weber's distinction between goal-oriented Reason (e.g. the logic of natural science) and *verstehen* (human understanding of the meanings of social action), Marx recognized the impasse of modern science when he claimed that "one basis for science and one for life is a lie" (1844). "The recognition by labor of the product as its own, and the judgment that it is separate from the conditions of its realization is improper, forcibly imposed" (1939). The weaknesses of the abstract materialism of the natural sciences, a materialism that excludes historical process, are immediately evident from the abstract and ideological conceptions of its spokesmen when they venture beyond the bounds of their own specialty (1887).

Sociology became an academic discipline carrying implicit assumptions that modernity and 'progress' were 'better' than feudalism, and that 'representative' democracy with meritocratic, bureaucratic administration was 'more rational' than dynastic rule. Weber was not so sanguine. Influenced by Nietzsche's critique of modernity as another form of domination thwarting the 'will to power' (Stauth and Turner 1998), *Weber clearly saw the irrationality of*

---

8   The analysis of "commodity fetishism," rendered the workers who produced commodities, not simply objects, but invisible.

Reason. Echoing Marx, (and even Adam Smith) he saw how new technologies of work (e.g., assembly lines) were dehumanizing and reifying, transforming subjects into objects and entrapping modern workers into the 'iron cage' of rationality (Sica 1988). Purposive, functional, goal-oriented rationality (a.k.a. Instrumental Reason) not only led to dehumanization, but according to Georg Lukács (1923), Reason, qua bureaucratic logic, was normalized and hegemonic, limiting and reifying the consciousness of the proletariat, thus, thwarting social transformation.[9] The commodity had become the "universal category of society as a whole" (1923a: 86). Work was more mechanized, specialized and rationalized as commodity exchange that fragmented social life and led to the erosion of the "organic, irrational and qualitatively determined unity of the product" (1923a: 88). The commodity form

> stamps its imprint upon the whole consciousness of man; his qualities and abilities are no longer an organic part of his personality; they are things which he can "own" or "dispose of" like the various objects of the external world. And there is no natural form in which human relations can be cast, no way in which man can bring his physical and psychic "qualities" into play without their being subjected increasingly to this rei-fying process.
>
> LUKÁCS 1971 [1923]: 100

Consequently, historically arbitrary capitalism, along with its bourgeois logic, was insinuated within language and culture; thus, dampening the potential for working classes to become aware of their class interests and critique or resist, attenuating the possibility of workers' self-understanding of themselves as a class for itself (Lukács 1971 [1923]). Bourgeois class domination was normalized.

Marx, Weber and Lukács informed the rise of the Frankfurt School/Institute of Social Research that was dedicated to developing an interdisciplinary Marxism for the 20th century. Their analyses focused on the cultural moments of late capital, especially nationalism, consumerism and the mass media of the 'culture industry'; these things offered "compensations," if not diversions from alienation and dehumanization by insinuating 'false needs' with ersatz gratifications, undergirding the *'One-Dimensional Thought'* that secured the

---

9 Sica (1988) has strongly argued that sociology, especially after Parsons' incorporation of Weber, has ignored the 'irrationality' of rationality, shifting such concerns to other disciplines. But the Frankfurt School remained consistent in its implication of interdisciplinary Marxism for the 20th century.

reproduction of the system by the erosion of critical thought as a basis of dissent (Marcuse 1964).[10]

4   Authoritarianism and the Frankfurt School

For Freud, beneath the seemingly rational conscious ego, lie powerful, irrational, unconscious drives that seek pleasure through release. The 'id,' beneath consciousness was a "seething cauldron where contrary impulses exist side by side, without cancelling each other out" (Freud 1933: 106). Civilization depended on the repression of these erotic and/or aggressive drives, which were held in check by guilt, so people might harmoniously join to work together (Freud 1930).[11] Hence the ego attempted to 'tame' desires for the sake of the 'reality principle.' While the superego, was the internalization of civilization's demands for renunciation, the repression of desires, that would supposedly 'control' the id, holding desires at bay and sublimating them to enable work, art, and beauty (Freud 1930).

It should be noted that ego formation was based on attachment to a caretaker as a defense against abandonment, which, for a child, evoked the fear of annihilation. The superego, however, was based on identification with the aggressor as defense against feared, potential aggression – castration anxiety. The superego could direct aggression to the person as guilt, and thus social control. It has been suggested that Freud could read the collective unconscious of the times and offered an explanation of the psychological basis of false belief systems such as religion [and political propaganda], what he called "illusions" (Freud 1990 [1927]). Freud's analysis of group psychology suggested that people would submit to powerful leaders who promised love in return for their obedience. The people's libidinal ties to the leader would foster ties between one another that would help them overcome feelings of isolation (Freud 1921). The powerful leader, as a collective 'ego-ideal,' provided a feeling of power for the powerlessness, a sense of community between the

---

10   It should be noted that the ink of ODM was hardly dry before Marcuse, reacting to protests of late 1960s, spoke of the 'great refusals' (Marcuse 1969).

11   His notion of 'harmonically' working together, ignored the oppressed working classes who might not think of class conflict, low wages, and tedious work as 'harmonious.' As Marcuse (1953) argued, Freud conflated civilization with its capitalist iteration that demanded 'surplus repression,' over and above what was needed to sustain civilization. However, to ensure the appropriation of surplus value, it depended on the necessary compliance for repressed, alienated workers, who were unlikely to resist their exploitation.

heretofore isolated followers, and framed other groups as blameworthy enemies of the people.

Writing as Fascism was dawning, Marxist psychoanalyst Wilhelm Reich (1933) drew upon Freud and argued that the repressive, strict, if not punitive childhood socialization practices of the petit bourgeoise, *especially the repression of childhood sexuality*, fostered a harsh, punitive superego. This was was not for the sake of harmonious social life but for the needs of capitalism. Capitalism needed to secure a diligent, compliant workforce in its factories and offices. Obedience/submission to socializers and conformity to norms resulted in a punitive, rigid superego, qua internalized socialization agents (role models). This left enduring emotional dispositions to submit to authorities (e.g. bosses), dominate subordinates (e.g. workers), and to express aggression toward perceived enemies. The result was a rigid, sadomasochistic, authoritarian character that was the basis of the 'mass psychology of fascism.'

As the Institute for Social Research was attempting to forge an interdisciplinary Critical Theory of society, Fromm, Adorno, Horkheimer and Marcuse, influenced by Freud and Reich, incorporated a psychodynamic perspective into the critique of capitalism and domination.[12] As Fromm (1947) argued, at times of political-economic and cultural transitions, increased freedom caused people to feel powerless, isolated, anxious, angry, and meaningless. This happened when feudalism waned and small-scale capitalism emerged. Furthermore, it occurred again when mass merchandising and industrialization displaced small merchants and artisans. To overcome these feelings, there were three intertwined mechanisms of 'escape from freedom': authoritarianism, destructiveness, and conformity.[13] As Fromm brought psychoanalysis into the critique of domination, the institute initiated a number of empirical studies on authority in German families, and (like Reich) found authoritarianism was most typical of the lower middle classes – the historical bearers of reaction.[14] But a number of the more affluent workers, often supervisors or foremen, also showed high levels of authoritarianism (as well as, the more repressive attitudes about sexuality Reich had noted).

During the Weimar era, Germany faced a number of crises – growing unemployment, hyperinflation, economic uncertainty, and legitimation (see

---

12 Reich had established a 'sex-pol' movement to provide sex education to young people that included hands on training. He thus wound up disdained by both Marxists and psychoanalysts, and it was not kosher to cite him and/or give him credit for his pioneering insights.

13 Fromm reinterpreted Freud's defense mechanisms into social terms.

14 This was clear for Marx who pointed out the support for Louis Napoleon came from the petit bourgeois peasant farmers.

below). The government could do little, and there was a great deal of anxiety and anger.[15] While most workers, intellectuals and artists supported socialist or communist parties, other sectors of the German population, especially the more authoritarian lower middle class, were psychologically prepared to embrace Hitler.[16] In times of crisis, such groups – given underlying predispositions for domination, subordination, conformity, and targeting aggression toward real or imagined enemies – had an 'elective affinity' with lies, falsehoods and conspiracy theories. These were essential aspects of Fascist propaganda. This projection of aggression into fabrications would be considered paranoia for an individual. Transformed into propaganda, it was an expression of collective irrationality. Hitler wrote that propaganda's "task is not to make an objective study of the truth, insofar as it favors the enemy, and then set it before the masses with academic fairness; its task is to serve our own right, always and unflinchingly."

The authoritarian leader articulates the conscious and unconscious feelings of his/her 'victimized' followers. Through transformations of discontents into grievances, he/she portrays the outer world as filled with enemies, and the media as an 'enemy' of the people. Thus, the rise of the Nazis was aided by traditions of anti-Semitism. They blamed allegedly subversive and treacherous Jews for the defeat of Germany in WWI. As well, they blamed the Jews for hardships and humiliations such as Versailles, and then for the economic Depression. Jews were cast as rat-like parasites and bankers seeking to control the world. They became targets for aggression. Thus, German fascism as an ideology and a movement assuaged the anxiety of the fearful, empowered the powerless, promised revenge, gave meaning to meaninglessness, and much like a religion, asked for individual sacrifices for the greater good.

Most commentators on their studies of authoritarianism have focused on sado-masochism and aggression toward outgroups. Yet also notable were the cognitive aspects of authoritarianism that disposed people to irrational illusions like Aryan racial superiority. Thus, the Frankfurt School pioneered psychoanalytic considerations of propaganda; clearly irrational beliefs appealed to authoritarians "based on psychological calculations rather than on the intention to gain followers through the rational statement of rational aims" (Adorno 1964). The adverse conditions that impacted authoritarian characters aroused powerful emotions and disposed them to accept what was clearly propaganda, containing irrational claims of victimhood, and injunctions to target

---

15   The crises of the 1920s and 1930s were later theorized by Habermas (1975), see below pp 19.
16   For Reich (1933) these more affluent segments of the working classes, especially in supervisory roles, were more likely to embrace the repressive bourgeois sexual morality.

aggression toward illusory enemies and follow a 'great' leader. In this tradition, Hartman (2000: 330–331) notes:

> ... propaganda depends on the comprehension of preconscious and unconscious aspects of human nature to hurt the morale of the enemy but also to enhance one's own group solidarity.

Adorno, Lowenthal, and Massing (see Sullivan, this volume)studied anti-Semitic Nazi propaganda as part of a larger study of anti-Semitism at Columbia University. They found that this propaganda won people over by playing on their unconscious conflicts rather than by logic. The propaganda was personalized and non-objective, substituted means for ends, and constituted an irrational wish fulfillment. They described propaganda as a regression to a ritualistic form of communication by which emotions are sanctioned by an agency of social control, an externalized conscience. Its purpose was to weaken the self-contained individual by 1) creating a dichotomy of friend and enemy and 2) promoting an indefatigable lone wolf, the innocently persecuted leader of the common people. The religious language and form of propaganda lends the impression of sanctioned ritual, as a cult is created. The cult is based on the premise that might makes right and what is established is right. Finally, the performance of a ritual sacrifice is needed to solidify the group. In Nazi Germany, the chosen enemy was the Jews and the slogan, *Judenblut muss fliessen* (Jewish blood must flow) (Hartman 2000).

With emotionally inspiring mass spectacles of power and the use of the new mass media of radio and film propaganda, endlessly disseminating diatribes against 'enemies' and promises of the restoration of 'greatness,' the Nazi party came to power. Hitler, the 'powerful leader,' represented the 'ordinary people' challenging the elites, while having the extraordinary power to affect social transformations; primarily, invigorating the economy and restoring a lost Germany that would alleviate their suffering (*Mach Deutschland wieder großartig*).[17]

In Adorno et al.'s (1950) F-Scale (F for "fascism") some telling items were:
- Science has its place, but there are many important things that can never be understood by the human mind.
- Every person should have complete faith in some supernatural power whose decisions he obeys without question.

---

17   Did the Frankfurt scholars anticipate Trump who has been described as working-class billionaire, a blue-collar president (Cf. Scaramucci, 2018)?

- Someday it will probably be shown that astrology can explain a lot of things.
- Most people do not realize how much our lives are controlled by plots hatched in secret places.
- The wild sex life of the old Greeks and Romans was tame compared to some of the goings-on in this country, even in places where people might least expect it.
- Thus, adverse economic, pollical, social and cultural conditions led authoritarians to accept what was clearly propaganda, blatantly irrational, resonating with their character, appealing to their emotions, indicating victimhood, at the hands of illusory enemies and following a great leader.

Authoritarianism has influenced a number of research agendas in social psychology. As well, some recent neuropsychology has suggested there are aspects of the brain that impact how events are perceived and evaluated.[18] Authoritarianism is associated with cognitive rigidity, dogmatism, rigid thinking (either/or, black/white, good/evil, etc. without any shades of grey), paranoia, stereotypy, intolerance of ambiguity, disdaining novelty or change, anti-intraception, and projection of one's aggression toward outgroups, accompanied by justification for it. (Adorno et al. 1950). We might note that authoritarians are more likely to be fearful and in turn see power and aggression as ways to deal with their fears. Authoritarianism, rooted in various aspect of fear, eroded the capacity for critical thought though constricted thinking-underpinning the reified nature of bourgeois thought as noted by Lukács (1923) and Marcuse (1964). Authoritarians, whose capacities for reflection and critique are attenuated, are more susceptible to mass mediated propaganda – specifically, through the increasing reactionary social media that systematically misinforms in order to stoke fear, anger, and support for reactionary leaders.

Further research, on dogmatism, motivated reasoning, and confirmation biases, shows that people interpret reality and events according to their own biases and pre-existing character structures (Rokeach 1960). We might also note he Dunning-Kruger effect, namely it takes a certain amount of expertise to judge certain claims and evidence. Many people, especially authoritarians, do not have the training and/or expertise to make informed judgments on medical issues, science, economics, and/or political realities.[19] To judge

---

18   This is not to suggest that political orientations are genetically based, but as will be noted, conservatives tend to be more fearful about the world and see authority and power as needed for protection and security.

19   The best description remains that of John/Cleese who simply stated, stupid people are too stupid to know how stupid they are. See https://www.youtube.com/watch?v=wvVPdyYeaQU.

COVID-19, one must have a background in virology or epidemiology. Expertise in global warming requires training in meteorology and geophysics. Trained experts and degreed scientists are seen as elites and thus authoritarian populists are against the establishment and distrust its experts, viewing them as 'enemies' of the people who are opposed to their interests.

Such folks are especially likely to believe there are 'miracle' cures for cancer, heart disease, Alzheimer's, diabetes, etc. They are also likely to believe that such things are sometimes mentioned in the Bible and that they are 'kept' from the 'real people.' American patriots, by big pharma's control of the lucrative market, their well lobbied representatives and greedy doctors who fear losing patients.[20] Meanwhile: The moon landings were staged. So were many school shootings. Hillary killed her lover Vince Foster and went on to organize a child porn ring from the basement of a pizza parlor. Can it get any worse? Following Trump, some were and ever remain convinced Obama was a Moslem born in Kenya, a socialist, terrorist, fascist or something else awful. Beware! The vaccine being developed by Bill Gates will include a microchip to track and terminate patriots. However, contact tracing is the basis for the coming of Soviet totalitarianism. Thus, we can now better understand how and why so many accept certain irrational beliefs because of psychological factors that shape perceptions of reality which are more typical of authoritarians (Cf. Mooney 2012).

For those of us in the real world, looking at the various "explanations" of reality, conspiracy theories and fabrications readily accepted as factual abound, whether it be the rejection of science about global warming, vaccines as dangerous, or COVID-19 either as a hoax or a biological weapon engineered in the Wuhan virology center to ruin America. Regardless, there are always evil doers that are responsible for one's suffering and/or victimization, also known as the 'paranoid style' (Hofstadter, 1964). Along with *ressentiment* (Nietzsche 1999 [1887]) toward 'evil elites,' non-conformists and subalterns, is the belief that they must be harshly punished. The shared paranoia and intense hatred toward imagined enemies can be considered what Erich Fromm (1955) called 'pathological normality.'

Authoritarianism does not in and of itself lead directly to reactionary politics. It is not an either-or character trait. Instead, it is more likely a bell-shaped distribution, where not all are fanatics, rather, certain factors may push people in certain directions. Yes, strict repressive socialization lays the foundation for

---

20   The history of snake oil "cures" dates back to the 19th C. when mixtures of cocaine and alcohol were sold as Chinese 'snake oil' and while yes, it makes people feel better, had NO curative powers whatsoever. But right-wingers spend a fortune on useless medication and vitamins, Alex Jones make a fortune peddling supplements.

authoritarianism and the likelihood of embracing conservativism, if not reactionary politics, that resonate with one's character.[21] But the levels and kinds of education people receive must also be considered. People who have college educations, especially in liberal arts, and specifically in sociology or philosophy are likely to have a more critical view and more liberal social and political outlooks. But we also need to locate geographies of meaning within larger political contexts. One's community has major impacts in several ways; rural and/or exurban people tend to reject the inclusive, tolerant cosmopolitan values of the city (Langman 2020).[22] Since world views and moral interests come from communities, people in small towns are more likely to have conservative views and value loyalty and conformity and conservative values that fit their moral outlooks (Haidt 2012). Finally, the rigidity, dogmatism and stereotyped thinking of authoritarians allows no critique and any criticism can only come from 'enemies.'

Furthermore, given neo-liberal globalization, cities, as nodal points in the global economy have thrived (Sassen 2014). Meanwhile, much of rural America has declined economically. Mines, mills, and factories have closed. Small businesses cannot compete with Walmart, Amazon, eBay, or Etsy. As many ethnographic studies have shown, if economic stagnation does not decline, along with political and cultural differences from more urban, cosmopolitan societies, it leaves many local people feeling 'left behind,' like political elites have ignored their interests. In Hochschild's (2016) parable, they feel like they stood in line working and waiting for the American dream, and that now other people – indeed often racialized Others – are jumping ahead of them, in part due to the nefarious policies of liberal elites whose moral interests are anathema to the 'people.' The rural conservativism of small communities is not simply economic, but also moral, rooted in conformity, loyalty, and tradition.

Wuthknow (2019) has claimed that in order to understand the anger of rural Americans, we must consider culture. Their anger is not simply about economics. Rather, they see government elites as indifferent to and threatening the very social fabric of their communities. They often see themselves as 'the real people,' now under siege, and that impacts character – fear and anger move many people to more authoritarian stances. History has shown

---

21   George Lakoff (2014) has made a similar argument, the 'strict father' socialization disposes a tough, independent, aggressive character with little capacity for empathy or sharing outside his/her own networks, Empathic parenting fosters caring, sharing and cooperation-disposing social welfare policies.

22   The author's city, Chicago, currently has an openly gay, African American woman as mayor, Lori Lightfoot.

that reactionary leaders frame their appeals to the ordinary people, the 'real people,' typically the lower middle classes who are ignored by the rich, powerful, and indifferent elites. Authoritarian leaders direct their appeals to the ordinary people who feel they have been victimized – and quite often, there is merit to such claims. But as the waning of racism threatens their privileged identities, their very authoritarianism limits their capacity to understand that it is capitalism that suppresses wages.

Sadly, we again see how the rapid social, economic, and cultural changes of recent history, compounded by crises of legitimacy (see below), have challenged heretofore entrenched world views. They have furthermore undermined established, seemingly eternal, status granting, valorized identities, and undermined morality, qua religious systems of meaning, thus fostering a "longing for yesterday." This resonates with the promises of reactionary ideologies and leaders. Louis Napoleon promised the return of the First Empire, Mussolini, who would restore the Roman Empire, Hitler would bring back Valhalla (Aryan supremacy), the Tea Party revived the American revolution at least the trichords, muskets and the Gadsden flag of the revolutionary whites. Trump would make American great again. To restore what has been lost, authoritarian populists target the corrupt and/or indifferent 'enemy elites' from the swamps above, as well as 'loathsome' subordinate scum, thugs and parasites from below; both must be challenged, punished and perhaps eliminated by authoritarian leaders.[23] The 'enemies' might need to be created, but authoritarian projection of aggression always 'finds' enemies to target. As Sartre once put it, if the Jews did not exist the Anti-Semites would create them. And even today, we see a resurgence of anti-Semitism from Budapest and Orban's castigation of Soros to Charlottesville, torchlight parades and chants of "the Jews shall not replace us."

5   Legitimation Crises

For Marx, capitalism was prone to a variety of crises such as class conflicts, overproduction, falling rates of profit, mass unemployment (that might kindle protest), and more recently, skyrocketing debt (Kuruma 1936). Such crises were thought likely to foster proletarian revolution. To forestall crises and revolution, capital disseminated hegemonic ideologies from rationalism to nationalism to

---

23   At this time, the extent to which Donald Trump names enemies, e.g. Mexicans, Moslems, protestors, and liberals as "scum," as thugs who need to be dominated, by "whatever means necessary." Much the same message was said by Hitler.

consumerism, and the escapist mass media of the culture industry, to limit class consciousness and assuage grievances. As early as 1872, Bismarck's government provided benefits and entitlements, slowing down rising wages, and limiting child labor.[24] By the early 20th century consumerism fostered acceptance of capitalism. Crises of social change rendered people isolated and powerless, with their meaning systems altered. This caused people to feel anxious, and thus they embraced authoritarianism to assuage their pains.

Habermas was born in 1929; the rise of Hitler happened when he was a child. Drawing upon, updating, and expanding on what Marx had said in the *Grundrisse* and *Das Kapital*, he would offer a theory of the 'legitimation crises' of late capitalism (Habermas 1975). Legitimation crises occur when the system's 'steering mechanisms' – i.e. the dominant social institutions of modern societies, namely the economy, the state, and the culture – fail, and disequilibrium follows. If State policies fail to save the economy and the State has exhausted all available options, then the State suffers a legitimation crisis and a rationality crisis. It loses the public's support and loyalty, as well as their willingness to embrace change.[25] The socio-cultural system is expected to provide shared meanings, social solidarity, loyalty to the system, and social integration. But what is essential for Habermas is that *crises at the level of the 'system' migrate into the 'lifeworld,' the realm of experience.* Thus, there arise crises of identity, intense emotions, etc. Motivational crises may be seen in civic privatism, the withdrawal of concerns with the system, or a waning work ethic.[26]

As will be seen, crises at the level of system, 'when things are no longer working,' are often experienced as various moral or emotional assaults on one's character and values. This occurs when the typifications and routines of everyday life including the economic and/or cultural sources of self-esteem and recognition are challenged if not assaulted. Generally, we see very strong emotional reactions such as anger, fear, and anxiety. As well, oftentimes there arise shame, humiliation, depression, etc. These are the types of feelings that

---

24   It was Bismarck who initiated these benefits, and no working-class movement has overthrown a State that provides unemployment, health care and retirement benefits.

25   As Offe (1984) argued, there is fundamental conflict between scoring capitalist economic growth and the welfare state's allocation of benefits and entitlements to the population that secure its legitimacy. NB. Many populist governments in Europe reject the 'individualism' of neo liberalism and secure their legitimacy as much through benefits as moral issues.

26   NB. Habermas was writing at the time of a growing counterculture who subordinated work to privatized hedonism, e.g. drugs and sex and rock n' roll. Today, the crises are not so much waning work ethic but the demises of well-paid work, job security and upward mobility as many youths, even with educations, join the precariat (Standing 2011).

evoke the more typically latent authoritarianism longings, disposing more people to authoritarian responses, both individually and collectively. Thus, in the face of the various crises of legitimacy – the humiliation of Germany in Versailles, capitalist crises, economic chaos, unemployment, hyperinflation, the weak Weimar government, and indeed the failure of modern rationality and 'democratic' government to deliver their promises of peace and prosperity – system crises migrated to the lifeworld. There was widespread fear, anger, and uncertainty that stoked the need for security and stability, and hence the authoritarianism of certain groups, who became disposed to embrace fascism. Did this prefigure the support for Trump and the contemporary American targeting of Mexicans as rapists, Muslims as terrorists, and Iranians, liberals, Hillary, and Barak as 'enemies'?

6   Identity and Extinction

Crises of the economy, polity, or culture evoke different understandings and reactions filtered and interpreted through character. The adverse economic consequences of global capitalism, liberal democracy, urbanism, mass migrations, secularism, and the growing embrace of inclusive cosmopolitanism as toleration of difference. As well, world citizenship has been anathema to the values and identities of many white authoritarians whose very identities and values, have been fostered as 'superior' to Others of color and had heretofore provided them with privilege, meaning, dignity, status, power, and respect that have been challenged and undermined. White power and privilege, ordained by God, has been under siege by uppity communists like MLK, who was pushing for equal rights and subsequently legislated by weak, 'girly men' in the Congress. But as the George Floyd protests have shown, most Americans support racial justice and equality. We might begin with the impact of globalization on the manufacturing sector that provided decent wages to [white] working class men. Increasingly, construction work has been taken over by many immigrants, especially from Mexico. Male power and privilege have been further 'undermined' by 'radical feminists,' i.e. college educated women workers who demand equality. Phallic aggressive masculinity has been challenged by such women – consider the #MeToo movement, wherein Cosby, Weinstein and Epstein were exposed. Heteronormativity has been contested by LGBTQ subversives who want dignity and unisex bathrooms.[27] One aspect of the anger

---

27   As this was written, SCOTUS ruled against abrogation of LGBTQ rights putting conservative's knickers in a twist.

regarding challenges to traditional, authoritarian identities can be seen in what was termed 'replacement' theory that 'explained' the French fear that Moslems would take over their country. As Mitchell (2020) described it:

> Its basic contours are this: "indigenous" white populations, and their cultures, societies, and institutions, are being replaced by a tide of racial others – Black people, Africans and Muslims. Moreover, this is happening not because of any natural demographic trend, but because enemies within have willed it, not only through weakness but through a suicidal, self-hating malice towards the civilization of which they are a part. (n.p.)

The result has been called 'extinction anxiety' by journalists such as Charles Blow and Chauncy de Vega. The term is used term to describe the fear of certain white people over changing demographics, namely higher birth rates and/or immigration of people of color. The fear is that whites will become a minority in America, losing power and privilege, and that the nation would be lost to people of color (the standby enemy), Jews, and even Muslim terrorists that seek to impose sharia law.[28] I would suggest that this concept of 'extinction anxiety' also applies to the various cultural changes and challenges to what had heretofore been 'privileged' identities based on gender, sexuality, region, ethnicity, religion, etc. The fear of death is one of the most powerful human motives (Becker 1973); like caged animals facing existential threats, authoritarians violently seek to defend their very selves, their hierarchical identities, their traditional values and cultures through right-wing populist social or political mobilizations. They are well armed and willing to use violence to fight what they regard as immoral, unnatural evils that must be eradicated through any means necessary. This may require the use of powerful weapons.

The expansion of democratic political practices has enabled the revolt of the right-wing 'people,' mobilizing to preserve their identities, values, lifestyles, powers, and privileges. Thus, we have witnessed economic, political, and cultural changes anathema to authoritarians. Various right populisms promise reattribution to the enemies responsible for the 'victimization' of the 'people' to restore a glorious past of the imaginary where their essentialist identities of privilege were unchallenged.

---

28   Many on the Right now resent major corporations supporting BLM (but not their own Black workers); Macy's is selling fashionable hijabs, while Costco offers halal meat-as well as kosher foods. The far-Right see this as the takeover of Sharia law rather than a marketing strategy.

To understand this, we see that notwithstanding political or economic factors, major cultural changes in which identities based on race, gender, religion, nation, etc. that sustain power and privilege are seen by authoritarians as 'fixed,' essential and unchanging. Moreover, these categories also provide a degree of comfort and ease of understanding the world – yet that world has changed, and so have these identities, especially for more urban, educated populations. In the meantime, there have been several challenges to notions of fixed and stable aspects of selfhood, now seen as social constructions. As noted, the civil rights movement challenged white supremacy, feminism challenged patriarchy, the sexual revolution (and the normalization of marijuana) challenged Puritanism, gay rights challenged heteronormativity and growing secularism challenged religion. *All that had been solid [of subjectivity] melted into thin air* – or at least as Bauman (2000) would claim, selfhood became liquid, fluid. Given the economic anxiety of late capitalism, many people seek to cling to these traditional, seemingly fixed, permanent pillars of selfhood as celebrated in various authoritarian populisms.

Given factors of class position, location, authoritarian character, economic uncertainty, intertwined assaults on their identities generate intense fear, anxiety, anger, *ressentiment* toward blameworthy elites, and aggression toward various different racial, ethnic or religious groups seen as despicable interlopers – 'enemies of the people.' For Nietzsche (1994), *ressentiment* had a specific meaning, not simply disdaining or disliking something or someone, but an intense visceral loathing and disgust toward the elites and the desire for revenge. *Ressentiment* is intertwined with a desire to have that which is disdained; repressed feelings and desires generate certain values that might be understood as 'Reaction Formations' (Cf. Scheler 2015 [1994].

Ressentiment is a state of repressed feeling and desire which becomes generative of values. The condition of *ressentiment* is complex both in its internal structure and in its relations to various dimensions of human existence. While it infects the heart of the individual, it is rooted in our relatedness with others. On the one hand, *ressentiment* is a dark, personal secret, which most of us would never reveal to others, even if we could acknowledge it ourselves. On the other hand, *ressentiment* has an undeniably public face. It can be creative of social practices, mores, and fashions; of scholarly attitudes, academic policies, educational initiatives; of political ideologies, institutions, and revolutions; of forms of religiosity and ascetic practices, etc.

The concept of *ressentiment* was first developed systematically by Nietzsche in his account of the historical emergence of what he terms 'slave morality' and in his critique of the ascetic ideal. To summarize and simplify, the once-powerful warrior-conquerors of Israel had themselves been conquered by

Roman warriors who personified and celebrated wealth, power, and wild sexuality. The now-subjugated Jewish priestly class were poor, powerless, and ascetic, and embraced a new morality that framed their condition as morally superior, in contrast to the Romans' superiority in wealth and power. This compensatory *ressentiment* provided an alternative basis of "status honor," and "moral superiority" rooted in envy and revenge.

Nietzsche's account of the conflict between the Roman warrior class and the Jewish priestly class is reminiscent of Hegel's master/slave dialectic and prefigures Freud's use of mythological models of conflict. Scheler's phenomenological approach to *ressentiment* aims at an understanding of the condition as a whole and in its constitutive elements. Scheler was concerned with grounding an *a priori* axiological ethics through a phenomenological typology of the field of affectivity. According to Scheler's schema, the Jewish priests did not simply resign themselves in humility to their inferior social position. Instead, they had a deep sense of self-esteem and pride, and this fueled a simmering rage at their situation and hatred toward their conquerors. An account of the heart would not be complete without an investigation of the corrosive condition of *ressentiment*.[29]

This *ressentiment* fuels conservative if not reactionary politics of blame and wrath, which demands punitive revenge. Indeed, sadistic punishments are dealt out to blameworthy elites who have sold the ordinary people out. Subalterns of race, ethnicity, gender, and gender identity face punitive revenge. *Ressentiment* provides powerful insights toward understanding authoritarian mobilizations as fearing demise of heretofore privileged identities. Hence, they react with anger, vitriol, and disdain toward 'establishment' elites, social policies that erode freedom, and/or inclusive cosmopolitan values. The desire for revenge provides compensatory self-esteem for various typically more rural/exurban less educated authoritarian populations who feel that they are being 'left behind,' and that their 'country' and former privileges as white and/ or Christian and/or male are facing a variety of challenges. (Hochschild 2016). What the 'illegitimate' elites see as 'good,' tolerance, inclusion, diversity and more flexible, pluralistic forms of selfhood and sexuality become cast as 'bad,' evils challenging the heretofore privileged identities. Reactionary politics of inclusion defends privileged identities based on fixed, essentialist notions of gender, racial/ethnic superiority, sacralized by authoritarian and patriarchal religions. This authoritarian *ressentiment* transforms unpleasant anxieties into gratifying aggression toward both corrupt elites and parasitic subalterns.

---

29   See Elizabeth Murray Moreli on "Ressentiment and Rationality" (n.d.).

Nietzsche strongly disdained equality and democracy, as especially evident in socialism and anarchism which he saw rooted in the spirit of revenge and hatred of the powerful typical of subordinated slaves thwarted in their 'will to power.' Authoritarian populisms would displace the weak and corrupt leaders with strong, powerful, and superior leaders embodying identities of racial and/or gender privilege. Such leaders serve as the ego- ideal of the followers (Freud 1923). *Ressentiment,* hatred of the corrupt elites and seeking revenge and punishment against these "enemies of the people" is an entirely negative sentiment. It rejects what is life-affirming, disdains what is different, what is 'outside' or 'Other'. *Ressentiment* is characterized by an orientation to the outside, rather than the focus of noble morality, which is on the self.

7   **Shame and Violence**

As Fromm (1941) noted, with the rise of capitalism, as people were "freed from the comforts" of a stable, cohesive, feudal society, they felt isolated. Their social ties were attenuated and anxious. Social status, heretofore based on birth, became problematic when based on markets that rendered people powerless against the caprice of markets. In contemporary society, income and possessions are markers of one's status and prestige. 'Conspicuous consumption' (Veblen 1899) advertises 'success' that is based on 'artificial needs' and may be quite ephemeral. Notwithstanding the fact that one's job, work or business may be subject to outside forces over which one has no control, people who lose jobs/fortunes often blame themselves and feel ashamed.[30] More importantly, when folks 'see' that Others are doing better than themselves, there is a degree of unconscious shame, especially when those Others are likely to have been stigmatized as 'inferior.' In the 1980's, as more and more women entered the work force, many men, especially blue-collar men, felt "shafted" (Faludi 1999). In turn they were angry and blamed feminism for challenging their power-when it was global political economy that required two incomes to support a family. We then saw a variety of celebrations of phallic aggressive masculinity, e.g., million-man marches, well-armed militias, and the popularity of WWE wrestling. As well, we saw the growing audience for white male condemnations of 'feminazis,' who were supposed to be ugly, man-hating lesbians who

---

30   Millions of people that lost homes in the housing crisis when their fraudulent lo-ball mortgages, collateralized by the banksters needed to be refinanced. But too many felt ashamed as losers to organize and demand the same bailouts given to the banks, Goldman Sachs, etc.

could not get laid. Similarly, many people could only process the "success" of subaltern 'inferiors' as being due to 'elite' politicians and policies that deprive the 'truly' deserving. Thus, Obama was seen as an unqualified Kenyan, an affirmative action student at Colombia, Harvard, and the *Harvard Law Review*, as well as an affirmative action hire at the University of Chicago Law School and even as President of the United States (POTUS).[31]

Thomas Scheff (1983) argued that unacknowledged, unconscious shame (qua denigration of self) led to violent aggression as a way of overcoming that shame. Salmelal and Von Scheve (2019) suggest that authoritarian mobilizations are characterized by repressed shame that transforms fear and insecurity into anger, resentment, and hatred against perceived 'enemies' of the precarious self. Shame is a pivotal emotion of contemporary societies where principles of competition and market exchange have spread from the economy to all domains of life (Bauman 1998). Here, shame emerges as an emotion about actual or anticipated losses for which individuals blame themselves. Anticipatory shame, or shame-anxiety, may not be as intense as actual shame, but it resembles the latter in its unpleasant hedonic quality and negative implications for the self. This is because it signals an expected loss rather than a possible loss or social exclusion (Miceli and Castelfranchi 2015; Neckel 1991).

In general, the more the domains of life in a society that operate on the principles of competition and market exchange, the more chances there are for failing to live up to the constitutive values of one's salient personal and social identities, and, consequently, for shame about this actual or anticipated incapacity, and for the repression of shame. For some it may mean limited income and/or mobility, for others, insufficient recognition. For academics it is not enough publications or citations. As argued by Scheff (1994) and Turner (2007a), the repression of shame can be considered part of a general emotional pattern of modern (Western) societies. Shame is culturally framed as deviant, despised, and socially undesirable, and therefore it is an inexpressible emotion. However, repressed shame does not disappear. It persists, becomes more intensive, and transforms into anger, hate, and *ressentiment* (e.g., Hoggett, Wilkinson, and Beedell 2013). The idea is that psychodynamic processes transform both the emotion (from shame to anger, hate, and *ressentiment*) and its intentional object (from self to other), with the purpose of protecting the vulnerable self. This mechanism is similar to Scheler's notion of *ressentiment* because the repression and transmutation of negative emotions, and the shift in their intentional direction, are central to that concept as well. Turner remarks that once

---

31   Hofstadter (1961) influenced by the propensity of authoritarian to project aggression, and
      the mass paranoia of McCarthyism, traced the history of paranoid thought in America.

shame is repressed, it can be manipulated by those with an interest in deflecting this anger onto chosen targets; typically this manipulation involves the symbols of one social identity and juxtaposes this identity through narratives about the evils of another social category or social identity.

TURNER 2007b: 521–22

Repressed shame therefore constitutes a social mechanism that may mediate between the emotional patterns of contemporary societies on the one hand and support for right-wing populist parties on the other hand. We suggest that the rhetoric of these parties is carefully crafted (a) to contribute to the repression of shame and (b) to deflect shame-induced anger and hatred away from the self and instead toward the political and cultural establishment and various Others, such as immigrants, refugees, and the long-term unemployed. If unconscious shame over lost or unobtained 'status' fosters aggression, then it becomes clear why the thwarting of 'genuine' self-fulfillment leads not just to authoritarian-based sadomasochistic aggression and the desire for revenge, but indeed to the kinds of necrophiliac love of death and destruction latent in so many. This is expressed in the many mass shootings in schools, churches, synagogues, mosques, shopping centers, and the mother of mass shootings: crowds at rock concerts (Fromm 1967).

As noted, rightwing populist mobilizations require a number of antedate factors. One such factor starts with authoritarianism that among other things, disposes the emotional foundation for acceptance of various mixtures of irrational myth, propaganda, conspiracies theory, clear cut lies, narratives of victimization and designations of the blameworthy. But there also needs to be a community that shares such beliefs and values. There needs to be a trigger or catalyst to mobilize people. As we have seen, between a deteriorating economy and weak government the Nazis came to power. Similarly, when Obama was elected POTUS, many white conservatives were shocked and horrified that an African Muslim atheist terrorist won the election. To this day, many still think so, notwithstanding his bailout of the banks and fostering a vibrant recovery. Thus, we need to consider legitimation crises evoking powerful emotions.

8 The Triumph of Unreason

As was clear to Reich in the 1930s, Fromm in the 1940s and Adorno in the 1950s, authoritarianism arose out of character structures that shaped the emotional basis of the way some people 'understood' the world. Authoritarian characters embraced what might only be called 'irrationality' – selective if not distorted logics of a 'sick society' – and acted upon that.[32] *Authoritarian irrationality was an inherent moment of modernity, not a residual of the past.* Thus, it must be understood psychodynamically, and for the authoritarian character, times of crisis, fear, anxiety, and anger undergird dogmatism, rigidity, paranoid styles, and the need for 'evil' enemies, often "explained" by various conspiracy theories. The critique of the 'Irrationality of Reason' was later articulated by Marcuse (1964) as 'one-dimensional thought' that thwarted the capacity for critical reflection. Moreover, resistance was truncated in a consumer society where the culture industries offered escapist distraction, insinuated 'artificial needs,' and encouraged 'repressive sublimation.' This promoted privatized hedonism, which, in Fromm's words, fostered the 'marketing personality' that valued 'having' over 'being' (Fromm 1947). But the promised rewards of greater wealth and cornucopias of goods proved pyrrhic, empty, and shallow. What became clear was that despite greater affluence, with consumerism there remained a great deal of anxiety and ennui. For many, the anxiety of loneliness and the meaninglessness of consumer society were evident, being clearly expressed in various strands of existentialism and/or the Beat generation writers. Advanced capitalist populations were pacified and distracted by consumerism and the culture industry. By the sixties, a variety of discontents were manifested in the various 'great refusals' – from civil rights, to feminism, to the various countercultural protests against mainstream conformity and Puritanism – as the hippies celebrated drugs and sex and rock n' roll. Ironically enough, what seemed 'radical' then is ordinary today-but these progressive cultural changes, fostered a variety of political backlashes as the right-wing agenda mobilized to maintain identities and values under assault.

9   To the Right – March!

The Golden Age of American Capitalism was the post-WWII era of economic growth when wealth was more equitably distributed and there was upward mobility and job security, at least for white men in unions or corporate offices. Admittedly, while seeking profits, corporations did create jobs, and as productivity increased, so did wages. This enabled a consumer-based lifestyle that

---

32   One telling findings of the F-scale was the acceptance of astrology, which Adorno (1994) saw as fascism on the cheap, e.g. conform to the stars, produces dependency, submission to authority, and conformity tot the status quo, and you will find love, prosperity and good health.

assuaged the alienation and dehumanization of rationalized work, whether factory production, construction, or the pink-collar jobs of salespersons, secretaries, etc. Notwithstanding the McCarthy era, ever since FDR's New Deal (and the alphabet of government programs, e.g. TVA, CCC, etc.) there were slow but sure movements toward a more progressive society. As well, the forces of the Right mobilized to thwart such "socialist" movements (exemplified through a planned coup to overthrow FDR and install a fascist government) (Archer 1973). With WWII, millions of women worked in the 'arsenals of democracy' providing them income, agency and empowerment that was thwarted after the war when the men returned to their homes. The military was desegregated in 1947. The GI bill enabled millions to go to college. The government then helped folks buy houses and built expressways to get them home.

At this time (the 1950s), there was a little social critique from poets and writers, modern jazz, and some Eastern religion, especially Zen Buddhism. Yes, there was C. W. Mills, but few paid much attention (Langman, in press). To be sure, this era of normalized racism, patriarchy, heteronormativity, and sexual repression persisted. But the seeds of agency had been planted that later fueled the discontents of subordination that would explode in the 60s. After many demonstrations and mobilizations following the widely televised brutality of Southern police, with growing political pressure the Civil Rights act passed. Later, the Vietnam War (a war of American imperialism) would lead to a number of massive antiwar movements, 'refusals,' and the rise of the 'New Left' (Marcuse, 1969). *These 'refusals' were progressive* and Marcuse was a hero to the 'New Left,' but between a legacy of "possessive individualism," growing prosperity, systematically biased mis-education, escapist mass culture/media and consumerism, there was still little explicit critique of capitalist political economy.[33] Then came feminism, the sexual revolution, and gay rights – all anathema to authoritarians. These progressive movements challenging the received wisdom, the status quo of conformity, and deconstructing essentialist identities, led to a backlash in 1968 when Tricky Dick, with the support of New Republican racists of the South (formerly Democrat racists of the South), along with some conservative (racist) blue-collar voters, was elected promising to support 'states' rights' – the dog whistle for keeping the now 'uppity' African Americans 'in their place' and establishing 'law and order' on the streets.

By the 1970s, more and more raw materials, steel, rubber, and chemicals, entered the country; followed by quality goods from cars to electronics. This

---

33 Critical Theory has often been critiqued for focusing on the *1844 Manuscripts* and less on the *Grundrisse* and *Das Kapital*. But in the 1960s, there was an upsurge of Marxist political economy.

led to what was called the 'deindustrialization of America,' as many American manufactures were unable to compete with forging goods. Some moved to the South and 'right to work' states, others to Mexico, and later to China. But in the ensuing years, the Keynesian economic policies that guided post-war growth began to sputter and faced crises, especially stagflation due to growing levels of outsourcing, automation, and robotic production. Thus, inflation rose. Prices rose, income did not, and Keynesian remedies did not work. In turn, there was an elite-inspired paradigmatic shift influenced by the classical liberalism of Frederick von Hayek and Milton Friedman. This shift included the control of monetary politics, laying the groundwork for globalized Neo-Liberalism, and hence leading to rapid economic growth that was unequally distributed. The bourgeois elites grew ever more prosperous, especially the top .01%, and especially in the financial sectors. The incomes of most people did not. Much of this wealth was used to support "friendly politicians" who voted to cut taxes and regulations, including overturning Glass Steagall. In the spirit of minimal fiscal regulation, part of this market fundamentalism was a pseudo-religious ideology celebrating rational self-interest.

These factors led to a variety of contradictions. A central moment of neoliberalism was financialization – 'casino capitalism' (leveraged buy outs, derivative markets, and currency speculation) that in turn fostered several debt-based crises, the Asian Tigers, Enron, the S & L crisis, the Dot.com crisis, and culminated in the 2007–8 housing implosion. These showed that capitalism hit the fan. Lehman Brothers and AIG went belly up. The 'freedom' of capitalism cloaked the criminal machinations of the banisters. The housing market implosion caused the worst economic crisis since the Depression, with massive unemployment, bankruptcies, collapse of the stock market, plummeting housing prices, etc.

What came next? Reactionary populism in the form of the Tea Party, a Koch brothers funded, AstroTurfed collection of the mostly older, white, racist, rural/exurban, lower middle class and religious men who saw themselves as the 'real people,' a moral community under assaults by indifferent, self-serving, liberal, indeed radical governments (Langman and Lundskow 2012). Many had been active in conservative causes; they were opposed to abortion, high taxes, social programs (assumed to go to racial minorities), feminism, and gay rights. As well, many were birthers (folks that believed Obama was a Kenyan Muslim terrorist schooled in madrassa who became an affirmative action student, then a professor, i.e. an elite intellectual, i.e. an atheist radical.

Like their original role models, these simulations were wearing tricorns, blowing fifes, and holding Gadsden flags as if they were in Boston Harbor when they deplored the corrupt. Back in the day, the corrupt consisted of

(British) elites, who imposed tariffs and taxes to support 'wasteful' government spending. Accordingly, the Tea Party opposed the social security they
collected and/or the Medicare that covered their health care, emphasizing
government spending saps individualism.[34] They feared that expanding government spending on health care would raise their taxes by subsidizing the
'undeserving poor' (a.k.a. racial minorities).[35] While they elected a number
of highly conservative representatives (the Freedom Caucus), the Tea Party
can be considered an opening shot of a move to authoritarian, reactionary
populism, a move to halt and indeed reverse a number of progressive political agendas and cultural trends that adversely impacted more authoritarian
segments of the society.[36]

As has been evident in many countries in Europe, Latin America, and Asia,
economic factors alone do not explain right wing mobilization. Rather, as
was central to the Frankfurt School, we need to consider the intertwining of
the political economy and the cultural/social psychological aspects of society. While the US media focused on the unemployed coal miners and industrial workers, many of these groups had long moved to the Republican Party
by the time Reagan was elected. The average white male Trump voter made
about $72,000/year and was perhaps anxious, but not actually economically
distressed. Rather, as has been argued, several social psychological factors,
beginning with authoritarianism. As Smith and Henley (2018) claim, 5 items
from the F-Scale had more predictive power than any other variables; income,
education, age, etc. This tells us why so many accept the alternative universes
of right-wing leaders and pundits, universes that arouse the fear and anger
of authoritarians. Otherwise said, capitalism in general, and especially late
capitalism's 'eclipse of reason,' (Horkheimer 1947) has led to the embrace of
'alternative facts' and magical 'solutions' – resting upon irrational beliefs – to
complex social and political questions that, while sustaining domination, are
contrary to the self-interests of most who embrace these ideologies.

---

34   Medical costs are the number one cause of bankruptcy in US.
35   Many did not really know that Social Security and Medicare were government programs.
36   These various movements, in the US as well as abroad, were not truly as totalitarian as
     the fascist movements of the 1930s in which the financial elites mobilized petit bourgeois
     and lumpenproletariat factions to fight left-wing parties. Further, with 'inverted totalitar-
     ianism' (Wolin, 2017) the populist icons of today, Orban, Modi, Bolsonaro, LePen, Wilders,
     and of course Trump, use populist rhetoric laden with "threats" to the prosperity, culture
     and identities of the besieged 'people,' readily embraced by authoritarians. However, in
     fact, these leaders could not care less about the people, indeed, their polices do no benefit
     the very people they celebrate.

10   Conclusion

One of the most important questions for epistemology was Locke's (1689) vs. Kant's (1781) view of the mind: Is it a blank slate, a *tabula rasa* (*Nihis in intellectu quod non prius in sensu*), or are there *a priori* forms of sensuous intuition and categories of the understanding which make experience possible? These *a priori* conditions, according to Kant, together make it possible to represent objects to the knowing mind. In this sense *the* a priori *structure of the mind actively frames our ability to understand the self and the world as they must appear to us.* Fair enough, but the extent to which underlying feelings and emotions impact perception and understanding was not developed. To update the theory of the active mind; the conscious ways people see, understand, and act upon the word are shaped by their character and in turn by their emotional structures.

If we look at the current worldwide protests over the widely viewed murder of Georg Floyd, an African American, by a white policeman, there are two views. For many young people, more liberal, tolerant, and inclusive than earlier generations, this lynching was the straw that broke the camel's back. To secure a more egalitarian, democratic, inclusive society, the progressive youth exercised constitutional rights to peaceful protest. But for older generations, especially authoritarian racists, these people were anti-American thugs, brainwashed by left-wing teachers and media, led by Antifa, who would like to turn America into a totalitarian Communist State. As I have tried to exemplify, political perceptions are based less on facts and evidence than on a person's underlying character structure, which operates as a template for emotionally based perceptions and understandings unfettered by any logic, facts, or evidence.

How and why does the rationality of modernity, celebrated in science, technology, and medicine, embodied in bureaucracies and law, also foster what has often been clearly irrational? This includes various 'irrational' sciences, e.g. Lysenko's genetics, eugenics, and the fabrications of anti-vaxxers and global warning deniers. At least we can understand that most who deny carbon emissions are well paid by – or well lobbied by – the polluting industries. But the current issue for the critique of domination has been the proliferation and ready embrace of clearly irrational ideas. These irrational ideas are often so clearly erroneous, and preposterous, that if it were expressed by a single individual, it might warrant a diagnosis of paranoid schizophrenia. But considering a number of Germans in the 1930s accepted Nazi propaganda, blamed Jews and Communists for hardships and humiliation, and elected anti-democratic, authoritarian leaders that promised collective retribution, we are reminded of what Fromm said about 'pathological normality' and 'sick society.' In this history of 'irrational fears,' eleven million people died in the camps and hundreds of millions more in WWII.

After WWII, a wave of hysteria swept across the US. Senator Joe McCarthy stoked hysterical fear that Communists had taken over the State Department, the military, the mass media (especially Hollywood), and the schools. Recently, we have seen a number of folks, 'birthers' whose racism was inspired by Trump, claiming that Barak Obama was an 'illegal' Kenyan, a socialist, fascist, terrorist Muslim who invited immigrants to come to the US and be given Green Cards, voter cards, health care and stipends upon crossing the border. Politics is supposed to be a contest between different views regarding the economy, social and civil rights, foreign policies, standards and regulations for workplace safety, commerce, medicines, and consumer goods. But today, political differences have led to such extreme polarization that political discourse is closer to propaganda. This has led to objective truths, facts or evidence having little value.

How and why have we seen a variety of right populist governments and leaders, themselves often quite antidemocratic, gain electoral victories through elections? The question informed the early Frankfurt School's studies of German workers, authoritarianism, and mass media, as well as their critiques of Instrumental Reason and anti-Semitism. The starting point is to understand the affinity of authoritarian characters to rightwing populism. Indeed, fascism is replete with the illusory claims typical of its demagogues. We need to understand, much as Freud did, why certain people are and were suffering, and that to deal with their genuine pain, they would use power to inflict pain on others. When children are raised in punitive and repressive families, super ego development is based on identification with the aggressor. In turn, such people not only inflict pain on others, a central aspect of authoritarianism, but insofar as sadomasochism is an integral aspect of authoritarianism and aggression, there is an enjoyment through inflicting pain, from name calling and humiliation to physical harm. Remember Trump thought the Central Park "rapists," African Americans, should be executed even when exonerated. He threatened tortures worse than waterboarding. Or, even more recently, consider the daily tweets of insults and denigrating 'nick names' from Trump, as well as his policies such as ICE raids, separating immigrant children from their parents and encouraging the Chinese to build concentration camps.

While authoritarians are more fearful, especially of being weak and powerless (as has been argued), what are the social conditions that mediate between character and the embrace of clearly irrational beliefs that dispose mobilization for rightwing populism? Hume (1739) famously asserted that *reason is a slave to the passions*. What people feel becomes 'rational' to them. Freud and Nietzsche echoed this perspective, and it had a major influence on Critical

Theory in attempting to understand the irrationality of modernity, especially perhaps in the form of anti-Semitism, which was pointed out by Horkheimer and Adorno (2002 [1947]).

Thus, we need also consider the actual fears that some people face when their identities, values and lifestyles are being challenged by long-term socio-cultural changes, demographic changes, and short-term legitimation cries. In the past sixty years, one legacy of the 60s was to catalyze a variety of progressive changes.[37] Feminism challenged essentialist notions of male 'superiority,' patriarchy in general and toxic masculinity in particular. Anxious about losing their status, more conservative men readily embraced "explanations" of docile women being brainwashed by "feminazis" to become radical man-hating lesbians. There were several male mobilizations. For example, the million-man march, which celebrated male power. Many men fearing the loss of their power, bought guns, the universal symbol of phallic power.[38] We might say much the same about homosexuality moving from a being considered a perversion or psychopathology to general acceptance by most Americans. We have an openly gay senator, and openly bisexual senator, an openly gay mayor of Chicago, massive Pride parades in most American cities, etc. But for certain authoritarians, homosexuality remains despicable, sinful, the various disasters of hurricanes (e.g., Katrina and Sandy) are signs of God's anger, and COVID-19 is another sign of displeasure over sexuality, pornography, and general sinfulness.

Over time, the USA has seen major demographic changes such that by 2050, white Americans will not be the majority, as African American, Latinx and Asian populations grow. The fear that this will mean a loss of white cultural and political power has created anxiety over 'replacement' – or as stated earlier, 'extinction anxiety.' Finally, we have also noted that the supposedly meritocratic individualism of capitalism leaves many people unconsciously ashamed when they seemingly fail and/or others seem to step ahead. This shame deposes violence to both corrupt elites and undressing subalterns.

---

37   This chapter was written at the time of the massive protests over George Floyd, an African American murdered by a white policeman. Thomas Edsel (2020) reviews a number of social scientists' research about the many values that were changing. America was moving to the left, and one aspect was the waning of racism by many, especially by young white Americans protesting the clearly visible racism captured in the video of the incident (police brutality went viral). At the same time, for older, conservative Americans like Trump or Ted Cruz, these youth were violent thugs and/or members of Antifa (which in reality is an ideology, not an organization).

38   Gun ownership may provide a psychological compensation for castration anxiety but think of the #MeToo movement which included the loss of jobs (Matt Lauer), jail (Bill Cosby and Harvey Weinstein), or even death (Jeff Epstein).

Besides the long-term demographic and cultural changes, neoliberal capital has shown itself prone to crises of legitimation that migrate from the system to the lifeworld, evoking intense emotional reactions. At such times, there comes a withdrawal of legitimacy to the system – people are ripe for change (but in which direction?). There are various sources of economic, political, and cultural strains of modernity, especially in its current iteration of neoliberal globalization. While many people have prospered, many have lost ground economically, politically, and culturally, and feel 'left behind.' They feel victimized, and they are. Yet such groups are little able to understand that their plight is due in part to the fact they support the very ruling class elites responsible for their circumstances. In any case, many people feel anger, fear, and anxiety, and seek to alleviate the discomfort. And so many people, especially those socialized in authoritarian families and found in particular social locations, embrace authoritarian responses. They become open to right populist ideologies and leaders that would empower the 'real people' who have been 'victimized' by 'enemies.' That these 'enemies' are really abstractions from automation, globalization, financializaton, and debt-based growth and collapse is not easily grasped by authoritarians, whose frameworks of understanding need to have specific enemies, such as corrupt, greedy politicians, left wing teachers, communists, socialists, Antifa, African Americans, Mexicans, Moslems, a radical left wing media dispensing 'fake news,' and the takeover of American colleges by radical Marxists, feminists and homosexuals. In addition, there are the old standby enemies, the Jews. The authoritarian leader, indifferent to facts, articulates the grievances of the 'people,' names the enemies to be punished, and targets *ressentiment* toward the evil elites above and the dangerous subaltern. S/he then provides an ameliorative agenda, that allegedly only s/he has the power to attain. The appeal of such leaders and agendas is that they resonate with underlying authoritarianism than undergirds various cognitive processes, from dogmatism to motivated reasoning to the Dunning Kruger effect. Therefore, authoritarians have an *elective affinity* to readily embrace various lies, falsehoods, and prevarications that support their biases. As Arendt (1975) said, they are cynical and gullible.

What is to be done? As Freud said, if rational explanations of one's troubles could be therapeutic, s/he could read one of his books and avoid therapy. Thus, when certain progressives raise the question of how to reach out to authoritarian right-wingers and educate them, from what has been said, this is an exercise in futility. What then must we do? We must organize, mobilize, and advance the "great refusals" that have in fact moved society toward a more progressive state. This is clearly seen among the young folks that have been in the streets so long advocating change. When masses of people find that a more collectively oriented society of caring, sharing, toleration, multiculturalism, diversity, and worker control, where being fully human is more important than having things, then as Fromm (1941) suggested, the processes of dynamic character change can be transformative, and capitalism can be transcend. Let us not forget that the very same forces that have mobilized the authoritarians have also impacted a variety of others to embrace a more progressive, democratic, humanistic society. While things may seem gloomy at the moment, the populations supporting progressive change have been growing and those embracing authoritarianism have been waning, leading the bulk of society in the middle to shift to the left. If rational capitalism has been a social construction that has produced various forms of irrationality, then the end product and vision of our 'great refusals' is to advance a different kind of society – a genuinely rational, sane, post-capitalist society, where discrimination, domination, exploitation, and alienation have fallen into the dustbins of history; where authoritarian populisms, ethno-religious nationalisms, and the myriad of neofascisms can only be found in history books.

References

Adorno, Theodor W. 1964. *The Jargon of Authenticity*. Northwestern University Press.

Adorno, Theodor W. 1950. *The Authoritarian Personality*. London: Harpo.

Adorno, Theodor W., and Stephen Crook. 1994. *The Stars down to Earth and Other Essays on the Irrational in Culture*. London: Routledge.

Arendt, Hanna. 1975. *The Origins of Totalitarianism*. New York: Schocken Books.

Archer, Dermont. 1973. "Philosophical Theology and Anthropology." *Irish Theological Quarterly*. https://doi.org/10.1177/002114007304000106.

Bauman, Zygmunt. 1998. *Globalization: The Human Consequences*. New York: Columbia University Press.

Bauman, Zygmunt. 2000. *Liquid Modernity*. Oxford, UK: Blackwell.

Becker, Ernst. 1973. *The Denial of Death*. New York: Simon & Schuster.

Edsall, Thomas. June 10, 2020. "How Much Is America Changing?" The New York Times. At https://www.nytimes.com/2020/06/10/opinion/george-floyd-protests-trump.html (accessed June 21, 2020).

Faludi, Susan. 1999. *Stiffed: The Betrayal of the American Man*. Crown Publishing Group.

Freud, Sigmund. 1921. *Group Psychology and the Analysis of the Ego*. Vienna: International Psychoanalytic Publishing House.

Freud, Sigmund. 1990 [1927]. *The Future of an Illusion*. New York: W.W. Norton.

Freud, Sigmund. 1930. *Civilization and Its Discontents*. New York: W.W. Norton.

Freud, Sigmund. 1933. *New Introductory Lectures on Psychoanalysis*. Vienna: International Psychoanalytic Publishing House.

Fromm, Erich. 1941. *Escape from Freedom*. United States: Farrar & Rinehart.

Fromm, Erich. 1947. *Man for Himself: An Inquiry into the Psychology of Ethics*. Taylor & Francis.

Fromm, Erich. 1955. *The Sane Society*. New York: Henry Holt and Company.

Fromm, Erich. 1961. *Marx's Concept of Man*. Frederick Ungar Publishing.

Fromm, Erich. 1967. *The Art of Loving*. Harper & Brothers.

Fromm, Erich. 1976. *To Have or to Be?*. Harper & Brothers.

Habermas, Jürgen. 1975. *Legitimation Crisis*. Cambridge: Polity Press.

Habermas, Jürgen. [1962] 1991. *The Structural Transformation of the Public Sphere an Inquiry into a Category of Bourgeois Society*. Cambridge: MIT Press.

Haidt, Jonathan. 2012. *The Righteous Mind: Why Good People Are Divided by Politics and Religion*. New York: Knopf Doubleday.

Hancock, Lynn, and Gerry Mooney. May 2012. "'Welfare Ghettos' and the 'Broken Society': Territorial Stigmatization in the Contemporary UK." *Housing, Theory and Society* 30: 46–64. https://doi.org/10.1080/14036096.2012.683294.

Hartman, John. 2000. "A Psychoanalytic View of Racial Myths in a Nazi Propaganda Film: Der Ewige Jude (The Eternal Jew)." *Journal of Applied Psychoanalytic Studies* 2: 329–346.

Hochschild, Arlie Russell. 2016. *Strangers in Their Own Land: Anger and Mourning on the American Right*. New York: New Press.

Hofstadter, Richard. 1961. *Academic Freedom in the Age of the College*. New York: Columbia University Press.

Hofstadter, Richard. 1964. *The Paranoid Style in American Politics*. New York: Knopf.

Hoggett, Paul, Hen Wilkinson, and Pheobe Beedell. 2013. "Fairness and the Politics of Resentment." *Journal of Social Policy* 42(3): 567–85. https://doi.org/10.1017/s0047279413000056.

Horkheimer, Max and Theodor Adorno. [1947] 2002. *Dialect of Enlightenment*. Stanford: Stanford University Press.

Hume, David. 1739. *Treatise of Human Nature Book II: The Passions*. Oxford: Clarendon.

Kant, Immanuel. 1781. *Critique of Pure Reason*. P.F Collier & Son.

Kuruma, Samezō. 1936. "An Overview of Marx's Theory of Crisis". *Journal of the Ohara Institute for Social Research* At https://www.marxists.org/archive/kuruma/crisis-overview.htm. *accessed July 14, 2020*.

Lakoff, George. 2014. *The All-new Don't Think of an Elephant!: Know Your Values and Frame the Debate*. White River Junction, VT: Chelsea Green Publishing.

Langman, Lauren. 2020. "The Dialectic of Populism and Authoritarianism." *Cosmopolitanism in Hard Times*. Leiden: Brill.

Langman, Lauren. (in press). 'History and Biography in the 21st Century. *C.W. Mills Revisited.* New York: Routledge Press.

Langman, Lauren and George Lundskow. 2012. "Down the Rabid Hole to a Tea Party." *Critical Sociology* 38(4): 589–97. https://doi.org/10.1177/0896920512437055.

Locke, John. 1689. *An Essay Concerning Human Understanding.* London: Penguin Classics.

Löwenthal, Leo, and Norbert Guterman. 1949. *Prophets of Deceit.* Tokyo: Tuttle.

Lukács, Georg. 1971 [1923]. *History and Class Consciousness: Studies in Marxist Dialects.* Cambridge, Massachusetts: The Mit Press.

Marcuse, Herbert. 1953. *Eros and Civilization: A Philosophical Inquiry into Freud.* Routledge.

Marcuse, Herbert. 1964. *One-Dimensional Man.* United States: Beacon Press.

Marcuse, Herbert. 1969. *An Essay on Liberation.* London: Allen Lane.

Marx, Karl. 1887. *Das Kapital.* Moscow, USSR: Progress Publishers.

Marx, Karl. 1939. *Grundrisse.* New York: Penguin Books.

Marx, Karl. 1982. *Economic and Philosophic Manuscripts of 1844.* Moscow: Progress Publishers.

Miceli, Maria, and Cristiano Castelfranchi. 2015. *Expectancy and Emotion.* New York: Oxford University Press.

Mitchell, Peter. June 10, 2020. "To the Far Right, Attacks on Protesters as Enemies of 'Western Culture' Are a Gift." The Guardian. At https://www.theguardian.com/commentisfree/2020/jun/10/attacks-protesters-enemies-western-culture-traction-far-right (accessed June 21, 2020).

Mooney, Chris. 2012. *The Republican Mind.* New York. Wiley.

Morelli, Elizabeth Murray. n.d. "Ressentiment and Rationality." *20th WCP: Ressentiment and Rationality.* At https://www.bu.edu/wcp/Papers/Anth/AnthMore.htm (accessed June 21, 2020).

Neckel, Sighard. 1991. *Status und Scham: Zur Symbolischen Reproduktion Sozialer Ungleichheit.* Frankfurt Am Main: Campus Verlag.

Nietzsche, Friedrich. [1887] 1999. *On the Genealogy of Morals.* New York, NY: Oxford University Press, USA.

Offe, Claus. 1984. *Contradictions of the Welfare State.* London: Hutchinson.

Reich, Wilhelm. 1933. *The Mass Psychology of Fascism.* Germany: Farrar, Straus and Giroux.

Rokeach, Milton. 1960. *The Open and the Closed Mind: Investigations into the Nature of Belief Systems and Personality Systems.* New York: Basic Books.

Salmela, Mikko, and Christian von Scheve. 2018. "Emotional Dynamics of Right- and Left-wing Political Populism." *Humanity & Society* 42(4): 434–54.

Sassen, SaSskia. 2014. *Expulsions: Brutality and Complexity in the Global Economy.* Belknap Harvard.

Scaramucci, Anthony. 2018. *Trump, the Blue-Collar President.* New York, NY: Hachette Book Group.

Scheff, Thomas J. 1983. "Toward Integration in the Social Psychology of Emotions." *Annual Review of Sociology* 9: 333–54. https://doi.org/10.1146/annurev.so.09.080183.002001.

Scheff, Thomas J. 1994. *Bloody Revenge: Emotions, Nationalism, and War.* Routledge.

Scheler, Max. 2015 [1994]. *Ressentiment,* trans. William W. Holdheim. Intro. Lewis A. Coser. Marquette, WI: Marquette University Press.

Sica, Alan. 1988. *Weber, Irrationality, and Social Order.* Berkeley: University of California Press.

Simmel E. 1978 [1946]. "Antisemitismus und Massen-Psychopathologie." *Psyche (Stuttg)* 32(5–6): 492–527.

Slaby, Jan, and Christian von Scheve. 2019. *Affective Societies: Key Concepts.* London: Routledge, Taylor & Francis Group.

Smith, David Norman, and Eric Hanley. 2018. "The Anger Games: Who Voted for Donald Trump in the 2016 Election, and Why?" *Critical Sociology* 44(2): 195–212. https://doi.org/10.1177/0896920517740615.

Standing, Guy. 2011. *The Precaria.* London, UK: Bloomsbury.

Stauth, Georg and Bryan Turner. 1988. *Nietzsche's Dance: Resentment, Reciprocity and Resistance in Social Life.* Oxford: Blackwell.

Turner, Jonathan H. 2007a. *Human Emotions: A Sociological Theory.* London: Routledge.

Turner, Jonathan H. 2007b. "Self, Emotions, and Extreme Violence: Extending Symbolic Interactionist Theorizing." *Symbolic Interaction* 30(4): 501–530.

Veblen, Thorstein. 1899. *The Theory of the Leisure Class.* United States of America: Macmillan.

Wolin, Sheldon S. 2017. *Democracy Incorporated: Managed Democracy and the Specter of Inverted Totalitarianism.* Princeton, NJ: Princeton University Press.

Wuthnow, Robert. 2019. *The Left Behind: Decline and Rage in Rural America.* Princeton: Princeton University Press.

Adorno and Freud Meet Kazuo Ishiguro: The Rise of the Far-Right from a Psychoanalytic Critical Theory Perspective

Claudia Leeb

1   Introduction

The interdisciplinary methodology of this chapter draws on the psychoanalytically inspired texts of Theodor W. Adorno, select psychoanalytic concepts of Sigmund Freud, and insights derived from Karl Marx, to show how economic factors interact with psychological factors to explain the rise of the far-right today. I explain the centrality of the psychoanalytic mechanisms of ego-ideal replacement, introjection, and narcissistic love, as well as the ways they interact with economic factors, to understand why millions of people respond to the failure of neo-liberal capitalism by voting in far-right leaders that further undermine their existence.

To illustrate the details and complexities of how the psychoanalytic mechanisms work, I turn to the British-Japanese novelist Kazuo Ishiguro, because a core theme in several of his novels is the subtle ways people become complacent with, and supportive of, regressive political forces. In particular, I engage with his novel *The Remains of the Day* (1988), because its main character Mr. Stevens, the English butler to Lord Darlington, allows me best to illustrate the ways psychological and economic factors interact in the rise of the far-Right.

Mr. Stevens gains his moral self-worth through his employer. The supposedly great deeds of his employer, via ego-ideal replacement (Freud 1989), generate his own view of himself as a "great butler." As a result, he fails to question his employers' exploitation of him and the unethical deeds of Lord Darlington's involvement with Nazi Germany, and actively contributes to such deeds by unconditionally serving him. Mr. Stevens' moral disengagement also results from the eradication of bodily moments of "uncontrolled mimesis" in capitalist societies (Adorno 2002).

My interdisciplinary approach echoes early Frankfurt School critical theory, which combined psychoanalytic insights and Marxist thought to study the rise of fascism in Europe and the potential for fascism in the USA. Furthermore, it echoes Adorno's turn to literature to explain complex concepts. Such an

approach is particularly important as members of and adherents to contemporary Frankfurt School critical theory (so-called "Habermasians") have, in contrast to the early Frankfurt School, largely abandoned Freud and Marx, as well
as literature; Habermasian approaches are less helpful when grappling with
the rise of the far-right today.

Furthermore, my interdisciplinary approach is important because even
scholars who draw on the early Frankfurt School to study the rise of the contemporary far-right (mostly Adorno) dismiss or fail to engage with Adorno's
texts that engaged with Freud.[1] Also, early Frankfurt School thinkers who were
trained as psychoanalysts, such as Erich Fromm and Alexander and Margarete
Mitscherlich, are today largely dissociated from the oeuvre of the early
Frankfurt School. While there is a culture industry around some of Adorno's
texts, such as *Negative Dialects* and *Dialectic of Enlightenment*, most contemporary political and social theorists do not engage with Adorno's texts on literature and rarely turn to literature in their own works. This leads to a certain
poverty of political theory and philosophy.

Current political theory literature that employs psychoanalytic theory
to explain the far-right suggests that the bond between leader and followers results from the followers identifying with the leader (Gandesha 2018).
However, if we take a closer look at Freud's *Group Psychology and the Analysis
of the Ego* (1989) it becomes clear that it is *not* identification, but rather introjection that establishes the bond between the leader and her followers.

In psychoanalysis, when a person identifies with another person, she molds
her own ego-ideal after the object she has taken as her role model (Freud
1989: 48). As a result, she has enriched her ego with the properties of the model.
In contrast, when one introjects another person, the ego is not enriched.
Rather, as Freud points out, the "ego is impoverished, it has surrendered itself
to the object, it has substituted the object for its own most important constituent," which is the *ego-ideal* (57).

Originally our ego believes itself to be fully self-sufficient. When the ego has
to contend with demands of the environment, which it cannot always meet, it
splits part of itself off – the ego-ideal, which represents the ideal view we have
of ourselves, or what we aspire to be like. Because the ego-ideal represents
what the ego ought to do and be like but is unable to accomplish, the ego-ideal
is in conflict with the ego. The split between ego and ego-ideal generates feelings of failure and frustration in the ego.

---

1   See, for example, contributions that draw on Adorno in recent publications on the far-right
    in *Logos* 16, no. 1–2 (2017), at http://logosjournal.com/.

As a result, the split between ego and ego-ideal "cannot be borne for long either, and has to be temporarily undone" (Freud 1989: 81). And insofar as "the ego-ideal comprises the sum of all the limitations in which the ego has to acquiesce ... the abrogation of the ideal would necessarily be a magnificent festival for the ego, which might then once again feel satisfied with itself" (Freud 1989: 81). There are several ways to undo the split between ego and ego-ideal and abrogate the ego-ideal, which all create a "magnificent festival" for the ego, which can get rid of nagging feelings of failure and frustration and feel satisfied with itself again.

In actual festivals and with jokes, the split between ego and ego-ideal is temporarily undone, which results in their cheerful character. In ego-ideal replacement, where followers replace their ego-ideal with a chosen leader (the one who fits best their ego-ideal), and which happens via introjection, the split between ego and ego-ideal is more permanently undone, which explains the uplifting character of far-right gatherings.

People who vote for far-right leaders do *not* identify with them or take them as their role model. Rather, they have introjected the leader into themselves, which means that they have replaced their ego-ideal with the leader, which allows them to feel satisfied with themselves again. The difference between introjection and identification is an important one, because the result of introjection is a mass of far-right followers with impoverished egos, who have uncritically *surrendered* their ego to the leader.

In "Freudian Theory and the Pattern of Fascist Propaganda," Adorno mainly draws on *Group Psychology and the Analysis of the Ego* to analyze the rise of fascism in Europe and proto-fascist elements in the USA. There, he points out that Freud's concept of ego-ideal replacement "clearly foresaw the rise and nature of fascist mass movements in purely psychological categories" (Adorno 2002: 134). However, Freud could not foresee that psychological mechanisms would interact with economic factors in the rise of the contemporary far-right.

Today, people frequently cannot live up to their ego-ideal, which comprises the standards of neo-liberal capitalist society, and which implies having economic success. They are furthermore confronted with neo-liberal capitalist ideology that paints them personally responsible for not being able to live up to its standard. By replacing their egos with that of the leader, by a process of introjection, millions of people left behind by the neo-liberal capitalist economy can escape feelings of failure and frustration.

Freud's distinction between mature and narcissistic love is another way to understand ego-ideal replacement. In narcissistic love, one chooses a love object not for its own merits, as in mature love, but because "the object serves as a substitute for some unattained ego-ideal of our own. We love it on account of the perfections which we have striven to reach for our own ego, and which we should now like to procure in this roundabout way as a means of satisfying our narcissism" (Freud 1989: 56).

Adorno, based on Freud's insights, says that narcissistic love plays a central role in the formation of fascist masses, because of the characteristic modern conflict between a rational ego and the continuous failure to satisfy the ego-ideal's demands. Such conflict results in strong narcissistic impulses that can be satisfied only through a partial transfer of narcissistic libido to the leader through idealizing her. As he puts it, "by making the leader [her/]his ideal [s/]he loves [her/]himself, as it were, but gets rid of the stains of frustration and discontent which mar [her/]his picture of [her/]his own empirical self" (Adorno 2002: 140–141).

The bond between leader and followers is akin to narcissistic love, where followers choose the leader as a substitute for their own unattained ego-ideal of "economic success." People "fall in love" with far-right leaders, because the leaders provide them with the illusion that they can become "great again," even if they can barely survive in neo-liberal capitalist society. The problem is that in the narcissistic love bond between leader and followers, "love is blind." The followers readily excuse any imperfections of their love choice. Because an alien object (the leader) is substituted for one's own ego-ideal, any reality orientation of the ego vanishes, and the followers blindly submit to the love object.

The present chapter is composed of five sections including the introduction and conclusion. In Section Two, titled "Exploited Labor," I outline the centrality of capitalist exploitation and show how sexually aggressive jokes can undo the split between ego and ego-ideal. In Section Three, titled "Ego-Ideal Replacement" I outline the ways in which Mr. Stevens introjects his employer to generate his view of a "great butler." In Section Four, titled "Mimetic Production of the Ego-Ideal," I outline the ways the eradication of mimesis contributes to Mr. Stevens' unethical deeds. In the conclusion, I provide some hints what we must do to counter the mechanisms that make people join far-right movements.

2   Exploited Labor

> Capital has only one life-drive, the drive to exploit itself, to create surplus-value, with ... the means of production, to suck the greatest amount of surplus work in. Capital is dead work that only enlivens itself through

the vampire-like sucking in of living work and that lives, the more it sucks in from it.[2]

MARX 1947: 247

Marx made the concept of "exploitation" accessible to us through the metaphor of capital as vampire. Capital, which Marx calls "dead work," can only enliven itself, if it sucks the blood out of "living work" (i.e. labor power, or the physical and mental capacities of the worker), which happens through the means of production (such as natural resources and machines), which are owned by the capitalist and from which the worker is separated.[3] Surplus-value, which is at the basis of capital accumulation, is generated by sucking in surplus work time (time the worker works beyond the necessary time she needs to sustain herself, yet for which she is not paid). Capital, in its quest to create surplus-value, aims to suck in the most life-blood possible from workers, their bodily and mental powers, in a 24-hour day. Marx also points out physical barriers (the worker needs rest to replenish her life-energy and satisfy her basic needs, such as eating and sleeping) and moral barriers (the worker needs time for the satisfaction of intellectual and social needs) to capitalism's quest for ever more blood. However, since "both barriers are of elastic nature" the capitalist can make her own interpretation about them, and even disregard them to generate more surplus-value (Marx 1947: 246–7).

Throughout Ishiguro's novel we encounter the ways in which the life blood of Mr. Stevens, the butler, as well as the other staff members employed in "Darlington Hall," has been sucked out by their employers, who disregarded physical and moral barriers to generate surplus-value. His current employer, the [US]American capitalist Mr. Farraday Ford, has downsized the staff from seventeen to four staff members. Thirteen staff members were thrown out into a precarious labor market, where it is increasingly difficult for them to get work – other employers of "distinguished households" had also downsized their staff, and often do not even have any full-time staff members anymore.

In this case capital enlivens itself and creates surplus-value by sucking in the most possible amount of work time of the four staff members left, which includes Mr. Stevens. The butler points out they all had to take on tasks "beyond

---

2   All Marx citations are from the original text and translated by the author.

3   As a result of a history of brutal violence that started with the expropriation of the means of production (land and tools) of farmers during the 15th and 16th century, which Marx vividly elucidates in the last chapters of *Das Kapital I,* the means of production are chiefly owned by the capitalist and "living labor" is separated from them, which is for Marx the precondition of capitalism.

their traditional boundaries," and all of their "workloads had greatly increased" (Ishiguro 1988: 9). Insofar as the four remaining staff members have to do the tasks and work of previously seventeen staff members, the vampire capital enlivens itself with what Marx detects as two core features of the capitalist blood-sucking enterprise: extending work hours and expanding the intensity of work (Marx 1947: 440).

Also, under their former employer Lord Darlington, Mr. Stevens and the other staff members had hardly any time or space to replenish their life-energy and satisfy their basic needs, because their employer aimed to suck out the last drops of blood from his staff members. Lord Darlington disregarded physical and moral barriers to exploitation – his household staff members got two days off every six weeks and were expected to really only take one day off and only take that day when there was "quiet time" (Ishiguro 1988: 170). They were not allowed to satisfy their social needs through partnerships or marriage – which secured that their mental and physical energies were solely available for the capitalist.

There was and continues to be no adequate space available for the staff members to satisfy their physical and social needs. They lived in small and stark rooms and the back-corridor, the backbone to the staff's quarters, was always "a rather cheerless affair due to the lack of daylight penetrating its considerable length" (78). Throughout *Das Kapital* Marx outlines the tragic consequences of capitalism's blood-sucking enterprise on the bodies of workers, such as chronic illness and premature death. Such consequences are salient in the novel via the example of Mr. Stevens' father, who was all of his life employed as a butler and had also trained his son.

Mr. Stevens' father served the industrialist Mr. John Silvers for 15 year as a butler, before he was dismissed. Now in his seventies, he finds himself without work and accommodation, and as a result of having his life-energy fully sucked out, he suffers from arthritis and other ailments. Here he finds employment below his rank, as an under-butler, with his son in Darlington Hall. However, due to the negative consequences of capital's life-sucking enterprise on his mental and physical energies he can only with great difficulty carry out the tasks of an under-butler, and repeatedly makes "mistakes and errors." Moreover, two years in his new job dies from a stroke. The doctor diagnosed death as the result of over-work (Ishiguro 1988: 51).

The consequences of capital's life-sucking enterprise are also salient in relation to Mr. Stevens, who, overworked and now advanced in age, akin to his father, repeatedly makes "mistakes and errors" when carrying out the required tasks of a butler. Such mistakes and errors expose that Mr. Stevens is increasingly unable to live up to his ego-ideal, in which the professional standards of a butler are concealed. This generates in him feelings of failure and frustration.[4] As he puts it, "(e)rrors such as these which have occurred over the last few months have been, naturally enough, injurious to one's self-respect, but then there is no reason to believe them to be signs of anything more sinister than a staff shortage" (Ishiguro 1988: 140).

This quote outlines that the butler is on some level aware that his errors impact his subjectivity, make him feel as a non-whole subject, and result from exploitation (although he does not term it as such). At the same time, he excuses and covers over such exploitation by drawing on capitalist ideologies that suggest retaining a large staff for the sake of tradition leads to a scenario where "employees have an unhealthy amount of time on their hands" (Ishiguro 1988: 7). Moreover, he hopes that once his other three staff members "got over their aversion to adopting these more 'eclectic' roles, they would find the division of duties stimulating and unburdensome" (Ishiguro 1988: 9).

His current employer, the capitalist Mr. Farraday, allows Mr. Stevens to undo the split between ego and ego-ideal through his joking behavior. When Mr. Stevens aims to unburden himself and the other staff members by bringing back his former housekeeper Miss Kenton, as to ameliorate the current staff shortage, his former employer responds to his request with what Freud calls a tendentious joke: "My, my, Stevens. A lady-friend. And at your age ... Keeps the spirit young, I guess. But then I really don't know it's right for me to be helping you with such dubious assignments" (Ishiguro 1988: 14). Here the capitalist employer, instead of addressing or redressing his downsizing that resulted in a heightened exploitation of his staff members, makes a joke out of it.

Adorno says the laughter produced by capitalism's "lighthearted" entertainment industry inscribes the violence of the capitalist order and trains the laughing audience to uncritically accept such violence. "[T]here is laughter because there is nothing to laugh at ... Fun is a medicinal bath. The pleasure industry never fails to prescribe it. It makes laughter the instrument of the fraud practiced on happiness" (Horkheimer and Adorno 2002: 140–1). Also, the employer's joking behavior aims to provide a "medicinal bath" for his exploited butler in a double sense -- to make him numb to his and his staff members' exploitation and to make him accept it uncritically.

Freud's critical theorizing of what he calls tendentious jokes, which are either hostile or sexually aggressive, outlines another dimension of the

---

4 I call these "mistakes and errors" in short "errors" and read them as a synonym for the moment of non-identity in the "whole (professional) identity" Mr. Stevens is striving for. These errors are key to grasping the core mechanisms of ego-ideal replacement and how they are connected to subjectivity and capitalist exploitation. They also deliver hints of how we can challenge such mechanisms, which I elaborate on in the conclusion.

exploiter's joking behavior. Tendentious jokes allow a temporary undoing of the split between the ego and the ego-ideal. This generates temporarily relief of the demands of the ego-ideal upon the ego (Freud 1989: 81) and leads to an increase in the listener's pleasure. This allows her to get rid of feelings of failure and frustration, but also makes her complacent to the agenda of the maker of the joke (Freud 2013: 137).

Mr. Stevens repeatedly, and as a result of heightened exploitation, fails to live up to the demands of his ego-ideal (the professional standards of a butler). This creates feelings of failure and frustration in him. The joking behavior of the capitalist exploiter temporarily undoes the split between ego and ego-ideal and creates pleasure in Mr. Stevens, which allows him (temporarily at least) to get rid of his nagging feelings of failure and frustration and experience himself as a "whole" subject again. But such joking behavior also makes the butler complacent to the agenda of the capitalist employer, who offers through his joking behavior a temporary relief of subjective feelings of failure, while the objective conditions of capitalism, that suck out the mental and physical energies of his employees, remain intact.

Furthermore, as Adorno in his *Aspekte the neuen Rechtsradikalismus*[5] points out, the concentration of capital means the possibility of a permanent declassing of those who are bourgeois in their subjective class consciousness and who want to hold on to their privileges and social status; and this creates the conditions for far-right extremism (Adorno 2019: 11). Also, Mr. Stevens, who was bourgeois in class consciousness (which all his talk about "professionalism" in the next section underlines), was threatened with the possibility of losing his class position at any time due to "downsizing," a fate his father and his current staff members already experienced. However, insofar as his former employer, Lord Darlington, allowed Mr. Stevens a more permanent undoing of the split between ego and ego-ideal, Mr. Stevens aimed to escape such treatment, making him at the same time an accomplice to fascism.

3   Ego-Ideal Replacement

Throughout Mr. Stevens' retelling of his employment for Lord Darlington before and during World War II, ego-ideal replacement becomes salient in his discussion "what makes a great butler," which stretches over several chapters.

---

5   This work of Adorno is the only one in which he discusses current forms of the far and extremist right. It was released in English in the summer of 2020.

First, a great butler is attached to a "distinguished household." And second, a "great butler" has "dignity in keeping with one's profession," meaning she remains calm and keeps her professional comportment through external and internal disturbances, which I will further elaborate in the next section.

In the first element of the definition, that a butler must be attached to a distinguished household, we can see how ego-ideal replacement is at work in this example. Such definition underlines an incentive for Mr. Stevens to view the person he is serving as "distinguished" no matter what that person does, so he can continue to experience himself as a great butler.

Mr. Stevens discusses the distinction between the older generation of butlers (the generation of his father), and his own generation of butlers. Whereas the old generation merely aimed to "climb a ladder" by serving old households, butlers today are more idealistic, he points out, insofar as they also are concerned with the moral status of the employer. Nowadays what makes a great butler is to serve "gentlemen who were, so to speak, furthering the progress of humanity," and those who made an "undeniable contribution to the future well-being of the empire" (Ishiguro 1988: 114).

Already in this definition we can see that the greatness of a butler lies in the (supposed) greatness of his employer. Mr. Stevens himself could not directly contribute to what he (uncritically) considers as "morally good" deeds – furthering the "progress of humanity" or the "future well-being of the empire." However, by replacing his ego-ideal with that of his employer, the butler himself could contribute via serving his employer to the creation of what he considers to be morally good deeds.

Mr. Stevens has not merely identified with his employer. He has introjected Lord Darlington by replacing his ego-ideal with that of his employer, whom he describes throughout the novel as a "great gentleman" who was "furthering the progress of humanity" so that he himself, via the introjected employer, can experience and define himself as a "great butler" (Ishiguro 1988: 114). He brings the aspect of ego-ideal replacement to the fore in his assertion that the "professional prestige lay most significantly in the moral worth of one's employer" (Ishiguro 1988: 115).

For Mr. Stevens it is not simply how well one practiced one's skills as a butler, but to *what end* one did so. As he puts it "each of us harbored the desire to make our own small contribution to the creation of a better world, and saw that, as professionals, the surest means of doing so would be to serve the great gentlemen of our times in whose hands civilization had been entrusted" (Ishiguro, 1988: 116). By introjecting his employer and replacing his ego-ideal with that of his employer, he can feel and claim that he himself contributed to the creation of a "better world."

Ego-ideal replacement also extends to the supposedly "great men and women" his employer gathered in his house during the pre-war years. Mr. Stevens rarely left the house he worked in, as he was only allowed two days off every six weeks, which he only took when there was no work to do, and as such has never seen much beyond the house that he served in. Despite this, he asserts that those in his profession, "did actually 'see' more of England than most, placed as we were in houses where the greatest ladies and gentlemen of the land gathered" (Ishiguro 1988: 4).

Serving a "great employer" who gathers "the greatest ladies and gentlemen of the land" allowed him, through ego-ideal replacement, to see himself as a "great butler," although he was indentured labor to Lord Darlington, and had to ask for permission to leave the house. Furthermore, when the "greatest ladies and gentlemen" gathered in Darlington Hall, he would gather with their servants in servant's hall, and states that "one witnessed debates over the great affairs preoccupying our employers upstairs" (Ishiguro, 1988: 18). The butler becomes "great" through the "great affairs" that preoccupy his employer and his guests upstairs (although he finds himself down below in the servant's quarters), and by making sure that the informal gatherings that happen in Darlington Hall run smoothly.

Mr. Stevens' bond to his employer can also be characterized as a love-bond. However, his love for his employer is not of a mature kind. It is purely narcissistic, insofar as introjecting his employer allows himself to feel like a "great butler." The difference between identification and introjection is important here. In mature love the critical ego maintains its functions, and one identifies only partially with the love object; one is thereby enriched with some of the love-object's qualities. By contrast, in narcissistic love the lover *introjects* the love object, meaning she substitutes an alien object for her own ego-ideal. As a result, the reality orientation and critical function of the old ego-ideal vanishes.

Insofar as Mr. Stevens' love for Lord Darlington is purely narcissistic, establishing and maintaining his view of himself as a "great butler," he carefully aims from the beginning and throughout the novel to uphold his view of his employer as a great gentleman who engaged in morally good deeds. However, little by little as the novel proceeds we learn that this Lord Darlington is a fascist. For some time, he belonged to a British fascist organization, and the "important conferences" held at Darlington Hall were but informal gatherings of British and German leaders through which his employer aimed to forge alliances of British and French leaders with Nazi Germany in support of Hitler.

For Mr. Stevens, "association with a truly distinguished household is a prerequisite of 'greatness.' A 'great' butler can only be, surely, one who can point to his years of service and say that he has applied his talents to serving a great gentleman and through the latter, to serving humanity" (Ishiguro 1988: 117). Insofar as the moral standing of his employer generates his own self as a "great butler," he cannot or does not want to see the ways his own work as a butler did not exactly serve humanity but did the exact opposite – advancing inhumanity. As an example, we learn that a core professional standard of butlers from Mr. Stevens' generation is perfectly polishing the silver set of the household. Such polishing is important because "no other objects in the house were likely to come under such intimate scrutiny from outsiders as was silver during a meal, and as such, it served as a public index of a house's standards" (Ishiguro 1988: 134). Mr. Stevens tells us proudly how his polishing of silver contributed to appeasing the English Lord Halifax, who was invited by Lord Darlington to meet Herr Bibentrop, the German foreign minister under Hitler, in Darlington Hall to forge and ease relations between England and Nazi Germany. Lord Darlington took Lord Halifax on a tour of the house to help him relax before the meeting, and when they came across the silver of the house he was delighted.

A few days later, his employer pointed out to Mr. Stevens that Lord Halifax was "jolly impressed with the silver the other night. Put him into a quite different frame of mind altogether" (Ishiguro 1988: 135). As such, the butler points out, his perfectly polished silver made a "small, but significant contribution towards the easing of relations between Lord Halifax and Herr Ribbentrop that evening," which shows that his work as a butler assisted in turning the world into a better one, and moreover contributed to the course of history (136).

Since Mr. Stevens' view of himself as a "great butler" is dependent on the "great moral deeds" of his employer, he cannot see how his work as a butler for Lord Darlington contributed to turn the world into a worse instead of a better one. Moreover, whenever the dubious affairs in which his employer was involved surface, the butler aims to keep them under the surface, by minimizing or covering his employer's fascist leanings and deeds. Here we can see that narcissistic love is blind; any reality orientation of the ego vanishes, and Mr. Stevens blindly submits to the love object.

As the early Frankfurt School and critical theorists Margarete and Alexander Mitscherlich – who, like Adorno, draw on Freud's *Group Psychology and the Analysis of the Ego* (1989) to grasp the rise of fascism – point out, in narcissistic love "every command of the idolized object, the leader, becomes ipso facto just, lawful, and true," which underlines that the love object has been put in place of the ego-ideal (Mitscherliches 1975: 60). No matter how many people expose Lord Darlington as a morally dubious figure, Mr. Stevens maintains that this is all "utter nonsense on an almost ignorance of facts" (Ishiguro 1988: 125–6).

Like the person in love, who finds herself in a state of fascination with the love object, the follower finds excuses for all the bleak imperfections of his love-choice. As such he has been ready to do anything to defend the "truths" proclaimed by his employer and to counter the "nonsense" spread about his employer. Mr. Stevens continuously rejects as "utter nonsense" remarks that his former employer played a dubious role "in great affairs ... Let me say here that nothing could be further from truth" (Ishiguro 1988: 61).

As an example, when his current employer Mr. Ford has visitors at Darlington Hall, Mrs. Wakefield asks the butler "what this Lord Darlington was like" as she thought he worked for him (Ishiguro 1988: 123). The butler responds: "I didn't, madam, no." Here he tells us that he certainly did not aim to deny that he worked for Lord Darlington, because he is "embarrassed or ashamed" of his association with him. Rather, his conduct is the result of "my wish to avoid any possibility of hearing any further such nonsense concerning his lordship; that is to say, I have chosen to tell white lies in both instances as the simplest means of avoiding unpleasantness" (Ishiguro 1988: 126). To uphold his view of himself as a great butler, he tells lies to not hear any critique of his former employer. He furthermore reiterates that Lord Darlington was a "gentleman of great moral status," who dwarfs all those who talk nonsense about him and assures us (and himself) that having served Lord Darlington during those years allowed him "to come close to the hubs of the world's wheel as one such as I could ever have dreamt ... and I am today nothing but proud and grateful to have been given such a privilege" (Ishiguro 1988: 126). The important element is here that shielding his employer from any criticism is purely narcissistic. Insofar as in his generation of butlers the "professional prestige lay most significantly in the moral worth of one's employer," any doubt of the moral worth of his employer threatens his view of himself as a "great butler" (Ishiguro 1988: 115).

As another example, when Mr. Stevens was still working for Lord Darlington, Sir David Cardinal – Lord Darlington's godson, who is publicly critical of his involvement with Nazi Germany, pays a visit to Darlington Hall because he has been tipped off that Lord Darlington is gathering the British Prime Minister, the Foreign Secretary, and the German Ambassador, to convince the British leaders to accept an invitation to visit Hitler. Cardinal engages Mr. Stevens in a conversation where he aims to open Mr. Stevens' eyes about his employer's unethical deeds, which aimed to support fascism. However, Mr. Stevens maintains: "I'm sorry sir, but I cannot see that his lordship is doing anything else other than that which is highest and noblest" (Ishiguro 1988: 225). He cannot "see" that what his employer does is morally wrong, because in narcissistic love one ceases to see anything wrong with the idolized object. As such, Mr. Stevens makes sure the gathering takes place without any disturbances and sees to it that the godson does not interfere with his employers' "important affairs."

At the end of the evening Mr. Stevens "has a deep feeling of triumph" that he served his employer unconditionally while "the most powerful gentlemen of Europe were conferring over the fate of our continent ... I have indeed come as close to the great hub of things" (Ishiguro 1988: 227). Insofar as Sir David Cardinal's presence and his attempt to open the butler's eyes about the twisted nature of Lord Darlington's deeds threatened his own view of himself as a 'great butler' who comes "close to the great hub of things," his feeling of triumph must also be understood as a triumph of narcissistic love, where the love object must remain great to uphold one's own greatness.

When Mr. Stevens discusses Lord Darlington's attitudes towards Jewish people, he aims to diminish and excuse his employer's salient anti-Semitism by suggesting that there were many Jewish people on his staff over the years and that they were never treated any differently, and that allegations about his employer's anti-Semitism are absurd, and merely the result of a "brief period" where he came under the influence of a member of a British fascist organization (Ishiguro 1988: 145). Only then did he hear his employer make unusual remarks about Jews, such as regarding a particular newspaper as being a "Jewish propaganda sheet" (Ishiguro 1988: 146).

As Freud explains, in ego-ideal replacement, "the criticism exercised by that agency is silent; everything that the object does and asks for is right and blameless ... in the blindness of love remorselessness is carried to the pitch of crime" (Freud 1989: 57). When Lord Darlington told Mr. Stevens to stop donating to a charity because the management is "more or less homogenously Jewish," he did so without any questioning, because he considered everything his employer does and asks for as right and blameless (Ishiguro 1988: 146).

Also, when his employer told him that they cannot have Jewish staff at Darlington Hall and that he needed to dismiss two Jewish housemaids, Mr. Stevens did so without questioning (Ishiguro 1988: 147). Here we can see that in blindness of love, Mr. Stevens carries his employer's commands out to the pitch of crime. However, to fully understand what allowed Mr. Stevens to carry out such crime, we must turn to the second part of the definition of "what makes a great butler."

4   Mimetic Production of the Ego-Ideal

Here I would like to take a closer look at the second aspect of Mr. Stevens ego-ideal, which implies that a great butler must have "dignity in keeping keep with her/his profession." Mr. Stevens points out at several occasions that his father as a butler best embodies such "dignity in keeping with his position." Insofar as he was trained by his father and started his butler career as a "footman" under his father's supervision, it was his father who generated this aspect of Mr. Stevens' ego-ideal (Ishiguro 1988: 35). He did so by repeatedly telling his son stories about how he "kept dignity" and maintained his professional comportment in taxing circumstances.

In "Elements of Antisemitism," Adorno and Horkheimer define "mimesis" as a dominant practice where one yields to outer and inner nature – outer nature to the extent that the subject loses herself in the surrounding world, and inner nature to the extent that the subject follows her natural impulses, such as when she helps someone in danger. With the advent of technical progress in capitalist societies, which aimed at the domination of outer nature via the subjugated working-classes, also inner nature and with that mimesis had to be dominated. Here mimetic behavior has become outlawed and with that suppressed in subjects, and rational practice (which is work) has secured its control (Horkheimer and Adorno 2002: 180).

In capitalist society, one finds remnants of uncontrolled mimesis in those moments when the subject is not wholly in control of her individual organs, such as when her heart stops beating, or her hairs stand up when she is in danger. However, as Adorno points out, "in the bourgeois mode of production the indelible mimetic heritage of all practical experience is consigned to oblivion." Here the subject experiences her own tabooed mimetic features in an *alienated* fashion, predominantly in certain gestures and behavior patterns which she encounters in other subjects, such as the "sweat which appears on the brow of the busy (wo/)man," which furthermore arouses her disgust (Horkheimer and Adorno 2002: 180).

The eradication of mimesis is also salient in the second aspect of the definition of what makes a "great butler," because it means that butlers must inhabit the professional role "to the utmost; they will not be shaken out by external events, however surprising, alarming and vexing. They wear their professionalism as a decent gentleman will wear his suit: he will not let ruffians or circumstances tear it off him in the public gaze" and he will only discard it when he is entirely alone (Ishiguro 1988: 43).

In "great professionals" any natural reactions to surprising, alarming and vexing events need to be eradicated, and she must have her ego under complete control, particularly in public settings. As Mr. Stevens further explains, "dignity of keeping with one's profession" implies "a butler's ability not to abandon the professional being he inhabits," whenever there is a provocation. It is the opposite of people who play the butler merely as a pantomime role, because here "a small push, a slight stumble, and the facade will drop off to reveal the actor underneath" (42).

Adorno points out that the severity with which leaders prevent the expression of mimesis in their followers and the subjugated working-classes expresses itself in the social banishing of actors (Horkheimer and Adorno 2002: 180). Similarly, a "great professional" eradicates the role of the actor in herself and strives to wholly embody the professional without play-acting or pantomime. Whenever mimesis does appear in the novel, it appears in an alienated fashion, such as when Mr. Stevens makes errors, and when his professional comportment is "out of control." However, instead of reading those errors as what they are – consequences of his physical and mental energies having been sucked out by vampire capital, which could lead to his anger at his exploitation and wanting to unite with other exploited butlers to change their work conditions, he feels embarrassed about them.

This happens several times in the novel, such as when Mr. Stevens aims to assure us that he had always lived up to this professional standard and took great pride in it, but admits that "a number of small errors have surfaced of late" and on several occasions he failed to perfectly polish the silver, which caused Mr. Stevens "genuine embarrassment" (Ishiguro 1988: 139). The professional standard of "polishing silver" is concealed in the ego-ideal of the butler. Not living up to the ego-ideal, which occurs in the moments where he makes errors, in the moment of non-identity, creates injuries to his self-respect, and generates feelings of embarrassment.

In other words, the errors leave him feeling non-whole as a subject. However, such errors are nothing else but bodily signs of exploitation, which outline that Mr. Stevens has reached the limits of physical and moral barriers to the exploitation by his capitalist employer. Insofar as his reaction to such "errors" are feelings of embarrassment instead of, for example, anger that he has been exploited all of his life and suffers now the consequences, we encounter here an alienated form of mimesis, which does not allow him to resist capitalist exploitation and contributes to his inability to resist when he is asked to perform unethical deeds under his former employer, Lord Darlington.

The eradication of mimesis is embedded in a gendered and racialized discourse that re-inscribes mind/body opposition, in which white British professional men are associated with the mind (professional comportment) and the rest as the lower uncontrolled body. Mr. Stevens points out that one finds great butlers who have dignity mainly in England, while in other countries one encounters mainly "manservants." As he puts it, "(c)ontinentals are unable as butlers because they are as a breed incapable of emotional restraint which only the English race is capable of." The Continentals, but also the Celts, and foreigners more generally, are unable to "control themselves in moments of strong emotion" and to maintain their professional demeanor in challenging situations. For him, they are "like a man who will at the slightest provocation, tear off his suit and his shirt and run about screaming" (Ishiguro 1988: 43).

The rendering of those men who cannot fully eradicate nature in themselves as effeminate and a "lower race," is a recipe for making willing servants who will ignore emotional cues that something is wrong with what they're being ordered to do. The problem is here that eradicating the bodily moment of non-identity – the moment of uncontrolled mimesis – to become a "whole professional" also eradicates our ability to make critical judgments and leads to what Adorno calls "paranoid judgments."

In such judgments, the insistence on the truth of a judgment, and not thinking about any inadequacies or contradictions within the judgment itself, leads to identity thinking – a blind subsuming of the particular under the universal, which eradicates the particular, and where the object is brutally identified with the stereotype (Horkheimer and Adorno 2002: 202). Because paranoid judgements are based on identity thinking, they suppress the bodily moment of non-identity, or uncontrolled mimesis, and this prevents the one who makes the judgement from having any feelings for the prospective victim.

When the former employer of Mr. Stevens told him that they cannot have Jewish staff at Darlington Hall and that he needs to let the Jewish staff members – two young housemaids named Sarah and Ruth – go "for the safety and well-being" of his guests, Mr. Stevens complied without any resistance (Ishiguro 1988: 147). He does point out that it was a difficult task to dismiss these housemaids, who were "perfectly satisfactory employees," but "my duty in this instance was quite clear, and as I saw it, there was nothing to be gained at all in irresponsibly displaying such personal doubts. It was a difficult task, but as such, one that demanded to be carried out with dignity" (Ishiguro 1988: 148).

Here we can see that "dignity in keeping with one's profession" leads to a paranoid judgment, because it demands the eradication of any moments of personal doubts, a mimetic reaction to the dismissal of two satisfactory employees under a dubious pretext, which does not allow Mr. Stevens to have any feelings for the prospective victims, and makes it easier to dehumanize them. By defining personal doubts as irresponsible, the irresponsibility of Mr. Stevens' paranoid judgement, that the Jewish housemaids had to be dismissed, disappears. In such judgement, Sarah and Ruth are subsumed under the general anti-Semitic stereotype that "Jews pose a potential threat," which eradicates the particular, and brutally identifies them with the stereotype. Such identity thinking eradicates any experience of contradiction or inadequacy in Mr. Stevens' judgement.

It is of no surprise then that he told the main housekeeper Miss Kenton, who supervised the two Jewish maids in a "concise and businesslike" manner, to dismiss the housemaids. Such "concise and businesslike manner," which has become a core manner of interaction in capitalist societies, contributes to eradicating uncontrolled mimesis, and thus assists in advancing his paranoid judgment. However, Miss Kenten challenges him, responding that she "cannot quite believe her ears" and that Ruth and Sarah have been members of her staff over six years and there is mutual trust between them. He responds that "we must not allow sentiment to creep into our judgement" (Ishiguro 1988: 148).

However, it is precisely the suppression of sentiment or feeling in judgement that leads to flawed judgement, because it prevents Mr. Stevens from having any feelings for the fate of the Jewish housemaids. This underlines how judgement is connected to both thinking and feeling. In *The Politics of Repressed Guilt* (2018), I develop the idea of "embodied reflective judgement," which is based on the insight that thinking and feeling are not only connected, but deeply entangled with each other. The way we think about something can prompt an emotional response, and that response can prompt further reflection necessary for critical judgment.

When Miss Kenton still does not give in, and she is outraged and cannot believe that they are dismissed on the grounds that they are Jewish, Mr. Stevens responds that "his lordship has made the decision and there is nothing for you and I to debate over," and later adds that their employer is better placed than themselves to understand "the nature of Jewry" and "to judge what is for the best" (Ishiguro 1988: 148). Here Mr. Stevens suppresses any sentiment in his judgement by displacing decision-making to his employer, which allows him to continue his moral disengagement.

Miss Kenton responds: had it occurred to him that dismissing the housemaids "on these grounds would be simply – wrong? I will not stand for such things. I will not work in a house in which such things can occur." Here Mr. Stevens tells her not to "excite herself and to conduct yourself in a manner befitting your position," and since his lordship wishes to let them go there is "little more to be said" (Ishiguro 1988: 149). Even when the following morning the two maids came sobbing to Mr. Stevens for a brief interview with him before they had to leave their employment, Mr. Stevens did not change his mind. Here the "dignity to keeping with one's profession," which means to suppress any sentiment and not to "excite oneself" in the face of unethical deeds, does not allow Mr. Stevens to show any sympathy for Sarah and Ruth. As a result, Mr. Stevens cannot resist, but instead contributes to fascist deeds.

5   Conclusion

Adorno, referring to Freud's *Group Psychology and the Analysis of the Ego* (1989), says there is a certain 'phoniness' of enthusiastic identification (or more precisely introjection) of fascist followers with the leader. And this increase in phoniness "may well terminate in sudden awareness of the untruth of the spell, and eventually in its collapse" (Adorno 2002: 153). Although Mr. Stevens maintains throughout that his employer was a "great gentleman," at the very end of the novel there is a moment where he admits to another butler whom he meets on the road that the path his employer took turned out to be mistaken and misguided: "You see, I trusted. I trusted in his lordship's wisdom. All those years I served him, I trusted I was doing something worthwhile. I can't even say I made my own mistakes. Really – one has to ask oneself – what dignity is there in that?" (Ishiguro 1988: 243).

His allowing of some criticism towards his employer, makes him, for the first time, also question his "dignity." However, after the other butler tells him that it is not advisable to dwell on the past and he should rather focus on enjoying himself, Mr. Stevens agrees and points out that "there is little choice other than to leave our faith, ultimately in the hands of those great gentleman at the hub of this world who employ our services." Furthermore, he maintains that he had made his contribution by sacrificing much of his life for "something true and worthy" which is "in itself, whatever the outcome, cause for pride and contentment" (Ishiguro 1988: 244).

Here we can see that the small opening, which could have allowed Mr. Stevens to further question his employer's and his own unethical deeds, was closed, because of his wanting to keep up his view of himself as a "great butler," which at the same time necessitates upholding the view of his former employer as a "great gentlemen." Only by "not dwelling on the past" can he remain in his narcissistic love relationship with his former employer. However, his "closing the books on the past" does not allow him to gain any insight into his former employer's and his own unethical deeds during the Nazi regime, which he might repeat in changed circumstances.

At the end, after Mr. Stevens learns that Miss Kenton has no desire to return to Darlington Hall, he gives up on thinking about avenues to ameliorate his and the other staff members' exploitation. Instead, he talks about how he could better his "bantering skills," which could allow him to respond with laughter to his current employer. Although such laughter might, temporarily at least, undo the split between ego and ego-ideal, and allow him to feel himself as a "whole butler" without errors, it also fully adjusts him to his and his staff members' exploitation.

Today, in neoliberal capitalist societies, the economic conditions for narcissistic love relationships between followers and idealized far-right leaders
remain intact. This underlines the importance of a methodological approach
that considers the interaction of psychological and economic factors in the
new global spike of the far and extremist right. Neoliberal capitalism created
a scenario of heightened exploitation of the raced and gendered working-
classes, as well as the threat to those identified with the middle-classes of losing their class position and privileges that go with it.

In this situation of heightened labor-precarity, people frequently cannot
live up to their ego-ideal, which in neoliberal capitalist ideology includes having "economic success," and they are made to feel that this is the result of their
personal failure rather than the neoliberal capitalist economy. Such a scenario
is fertile ground for the rise of a far-right leader, who, through psychologically
oriented techniques, can win over millions of people to her irrational aims that
conflict with these people's rational and material interests.

A core aim of the psychological technique of far-right leaders is to advance
ego-ideal replacement in their followers. This is very successful because it
allows them to get rid of feelings of failure and frustrations and feel themselves
as "great again."[6] However, such success is not the result of some pathological
psychic condition of the followers, but rather of economic factors that create
feelings of failure and frustration, which far-right leaders have a self-interest to
leave intact, because it makes followers more vulnerable to their psychological
technique.

The problem with a narcissistic love relationship is that the followers, to get
rid of feelings of failure and frustration and to uphold their own view of themselves as "great" (much like Mr. Stevens), do everything to defend their view of
having a "great leader." This makes them uncritical of any problematic deeds
of the leader, such as the implementation of policies that further undermine
their existence. The followers might even contribute (akin to Mr. Stevens) to
such deeds; here also the eradication of uncontrolled mimesis, which is far
advanced in neoliberal capitalism, assists.

The question is: How can the followers step out of this narcissistic love
relationship with the leader? Here *The Remains of the Day* offers some
hints. As the story unfolds, we can see that it is in those moments where Mr.
Stevens makes "mistakes and errors", where his attempt to become a whole
professional breaks down, which are connected to the bodily moments of

---

6   Such leaders also often use hostile and sexually aggressive jokes to further allow the followers
    to feel satisfied with themselves again.

non-identity as well as mimesis, where the possibility of resistance lies. We learn only gradually and later in the novel what the nature of Mr. Stevens' errors are. His admitting to his errors coincides with the gradual admitting of the fascist tendencies of his former employer Lord Darlington, and which makes it more and more difficult for him to uphold his fantasy of his (employer) and himself as "great."

It is then in these moments of error (which are the marks on the bodies of the exploited) that the followers might realize that after all the promises of the "great leader" they are still unemployed or exploited and can barely survive – the possibility of "falling out of love" with the idealized leader emerges. However, to begin with we must address the economic factors, as improving those in the long run might make people less vulnerable to the kinds of psychological techniques I have addressed in this chapter. Furthermore, we must challenge a capitalist culture that suppresses uncontrolled mimesis and with that renders people unable to feel for the fate of others. But in the short term we need to hasten the undoing of this spell the masses are under.

References

Adorno, T. W. 2002. "Freudian Theory and the Pattern of Fascist Propaganda." In *The Culture Industry*, ed. Jay Bernstein. London/New York: Routledge, 132–157.

Adorno, T. W. 2019. *Aspekte des neuen Rechtsradikalismus*. Berlin: Suhrkamp Verlag.

Freud, Sigmund. 1989. *Group Psychology and the Analysis of the Ego*. Trans. James Strachey. London/New York: W.W. Norton & Company.

Freud, Sigmund. 2013. *Jokes and Their Relation to the Unconscious*. Redditch: Read Books.

Gandesha, Samir. 2018. " 'Identifying with the aggressor': From the authoritarian to neoliberal personality." *Constellations* 25(1): 147–164.

Horkheimer, Max and Adorno, Theodor W. 2002. *Dialectic of Enlightenment*. Trans. John Cumming. New York: Continuum Press.

Ishiguro, Kazuo. 1988. *The Remains of the Day*. New York: Penguin Random House.

Leeb, Claudia. 2018. *The Politics of Repressed Guilt: The Tragedy of Austrian Silence*. Edinburgh: Edinburgh University Press.

Marx, Karl. 1947. *Das Kapital I, Kritik der politischen Ökonomie, Erster Band, Buch I: Der Produktionsprozeß des Kapitals*. In Karl Marx Frederick Engels Werke, Band 23. Berlin: Karl Dietz Verlag.

Mitscherlich, Alexander and Mitscherlich, Margarete. 1975. *The Inability to Mourn: Principles of Collective Behavior*. Trans. B. R. Placzek. New York: Grove Press.

CHAPTER 7

Marcuse and the Symbolic Roles of the Father: Someone to Watch over Me

Imaculada Kangussu

This essay employs psychological categories
because they have become political categories.
HERBERT MARCUSE, *Eros and Civilization*

∴

In *Eros and Civilization*, Herbert Marcuse presents a new reading of Sigmund Freud's philosophical theory (which he explicitly distinguished from his science), that can be very useful today to understand and critique authoritarian populism. This encounter with psychoanalysis opened new paths and provoked powerful resonances in contemporary philosophy.

Marcuse revisits Freud's statement that "happiness is no cultural value," claiming that Freud's own theory provides reason for rejecting the identification of civilization with unhappiness. If and when it is read within a historical key, it is possible to note that the interrelation between civilization and unhappiness results from a very specific historical organization of nature and human life. Historicizing the reality principle, Marcuse opens up the possibility – and designs the desire, that still exists – to go beyond it. The philosopher develops his reflections not against but with and beyond Freud's theories.

1   First Things First

According to Freud, the constraint of instinct is the precondition of civilization. The methodical sacrifice of libido is the price civilization must pay. The history of human beings is the history of their repression. They must be rigidly subordinated "to the established system of law and order," "to the discipline of work" and "of monogamic reproduction." "Happiness, said Freud, is no cultural value" (Marcuse 1966: 3).

The human primary objective is integral satisfaction and gratification at any moment. Civilization begins with renunciation of this primary objective, which transforms animal instincts into human drives. Through this fundamental transformation, the animal human becomes a human being – a transformation that affects the instinctual aims and changes the governing value system, from immediate satisfaction to delayed, pleasure to restraint, joy (play) to toil (work), receptiveness to productiveness, and finally from absence of repression to security. In "Formulations Regarding Two Principles of Mental Function," Freud describes this transformation as the step from the pleasure principle to the reality principle and uses these two principles as bases for interpretation of the mental apparatus. Ruled by the pleasure principle, the unconscious comprises "the older, primary processes, the residues of a phase of development in which they were the only kind of mental processes" (Freud 1950: 14).

The unrestrained pleasure principle guides the primary mental processes concentrated on gaining absolute and immediate pleasure. It is still present in the developed adult psyche as residue. Nevertheless, sooner or later the individual will feel the impossibility of full and total gratification. This traumatic moment introduces a new principle of mental functioning, the reality principle. It supersedes the older one, since human beings accept giving up immediate, momentary, and uncertain pleasure for restrained, delayed, safer and more assured pleasure. "Because of this lasting gain through renunciation and restraint, according to Freud, the reality principle 'safeguards' rather than 'dethrones,' 'modifies' rather than denies, the pleasure principle" (Marcuse 1966: 13). Pleasure is replaced by the reality principle but, in Freud's words, "this latter principle does not abandon the intention of ultimately obtaining pleasure, but it nevertheless demands and carries into effect the postponement of gaining satisfaction and the temporary toleration of unpleasure as a step on the long indirect road to pleasure" (Freud 2001: 10).

At first glance, it seems that the reality principle's function is serving the pleasure principle: this is not wrong, but things are more complex. By modifying its form and timing, the reality principle enforces a change in the very substance of pleasure. In turn, pleasure loses its former freedom. In order to overcome the incompatibility between instinctual pleasure and established rules and norms, pleasure itself must be transubstantiated by diversion or subjugation. The reality principle governs the mental apparatus towards reason's determinations. On the other hand, "the fact that the reality principle has to be re-established continually in the development of human beings indicates that its triumph over the pleasure principle is never complete and never secure" (Marcuse 1966: 15). The defeated pleasure principle, repressed by civilization, survives in civilization itself. Its full force remains alive in the unconscious.

Focusing on repression, Freud emphasizes the attraction exercised by what is primarily repressed upon everything with which it can establish a connection. The return of the repressed makes up the history of the individual and that of civilization as well.

Marcuse observes that Freud analyzes the birth and growth of the repressive mental apparatus at two profoundly interrelated levels: the ontogenetic, the development of the repressed individual from infancy to conscious adult existence; and the phylogenetic, the development of the repressed civilization from its archaic history to the civilized state. The center of Freudian metapsychology is, at the same time, biological and sociological. Soma and psyche, nature and civilization decide together, in an arena, the fate of the mental structure.

Since the earliest stage, Freud's theory considers the pleasure principle as the guide of primary mental processes. In *Beyond the Pleasure Principle* he declares:

> In the theory of psychoanalysis, we have no hesitation in assuming that the course taken by mental events is automatically regulated by the pleasure principle. We believe that the course of those events is invariably set in motion by an unpleasable tension, and that it takes a direction such that its final outcome coincides with a lowering of this tension, that is, with an avoidance of unpleasure or a production of pleasure.
>
> FREUD 2001: 7

It is clear that, in Freudian theory, the pleasure principle "does not refer to any kind of hedonistic searching and striving for pleasure," according to the cunning commentary of Alenka Zupančič, "but basically to seeking relief (from tension and excitation), to the 'lowering of tension,' in attempt to reach a homeostatic state" (Zupančič 2017: 98). According to Freud, the pleasure principle is a tendency to free the mental apparatus from excitation or, at least, to keep excitation as low as possible. "We have decided to relate pleasure and unpleasure to the quantity of excitation that is present in the mind but is not in any way 'bound'; and to relate them in such a manner that unpleasure corresponds to an increase in the quantity of excitation and pleasure to a diminution" (Freud 2001: 8).

There is no need to review all the history and the various stages of the Freudian theory of drives (*Triebelehre*): Marcuse considers that a brief summary may suffice. In Freudian theory, drive can be neither simply reduced to biological needs, nor totally separated from them. Freud presents his theory of drives as a kind of "mythology." "Drives are mythical entities [*Wesen*]; they are magnificent in their inaccuracy" (Freud 1968: 119). In the threshold between psyche and soma, drive is an internal impulse that cannot be ignored, contrary to what is possible to do with impulses whose origins are external to the organism. As it is well known, at the extremes the drives are two, but they are mixed most of the time and rarely found alone. They are Eros, the life drive (or life instinct, depending on how *Trieb* is translated), and Thanatos, the death drive (*Trieb*).

Freud's *Trieb* is translated into "instinct" in the first English translations, and into "drive" in the later ones. Laplanche and Pontalis consider it necessary to differentiate *Trieb* from *Instinkt* (the latter used by Freud solely to refer to non-human animals), to avoid confusing Freudian drive theories (*Triebelehre*) with psychological conceptions of animal instinct (Laplanche and Pontalis 1967). In both translations, "instinct" and "drive," there is a gain and a loss. According to Zupančič: "There is no doubt that what Freud discovered and named *Trieb* is not 'instinct' in the sense in which we usually speak of 'animal instincts' – as a kind of inborn survivalist autopilot aiming at self-preservation" (2017: 91). On the other hand, it would be going too far to consider "drive" as something completely different from animal nature. *Trieb* is neither only human, nor completely animal – neither all cultural, nor all natural. The prosaic formulation, according to which whenever an organism is hungry its instincts will look for food whereas its drives look for lasagna (the first natural and the latter cultural), is not always correct. For example, human sexual desires are not only cultural and not absolutely determined by procreative instincts ...

Well, in *Eros and Civilization*, Marcuse adopted the word "instinct," which may be explained by his choice of quoting Freud from the early English translations (between 1943 and 1950) in which *Trieb* was translated as "instinct." Had he used "drive" instead, English speakers would not have known what he was talking about. This is just a hypothesis ...

"Throughout the various stages of Freud's theory," Marcuse highlights, "the mental apparatus appears as a dynamic union of opposites: of the unconscious and the conscious structure; of primary and secondary processes; of inherited 'constitutionally fixed' and acquired forces; of soma-psyche and the external reality" (1966: 21–22). In the final formulation of *Triebelehre*, Eros and the death instinct are considered the basic instincts: but, ever and anon, Freud emphasizes a common nature of the instincts, prior to their differentiation. The relation between Eros and Thanatos remains obscure. "Eros is defined as the great force that preserves life" (27), although the destructive work of the death instinct – through socially permitted aggression – is also useful and necessary to self-preservation. Moreover, in *Beyond the Pleasure Principle*, Freud discovers the frightening convergence of pleasure and death, which he considers a "universal attribute of the instincts and perhaps of organic life in general." There is a sort of "inertia inherent inorganic life," an "organic elasticity," characterized as "a compulsion inherent" in all organic lives to restore a former state "which the living entity has been obliged to abandon under the pressure of external disturbing forces" (24). This compulsion is the substance of the primary process operating in the unconscious.

Freud says that *"inanimate things existed before the living ones"* and, at some point, "by the action of a force of whose nature we can form no conception," the attributes of life were evoked in the former inanimate matter ...

> [T]he tension, which then arose in what had hitherto been inanimate substance, endeavored to cancel itself out. In this way, the first instinct came into being: the instinct to return to the inanimate state. It was still an easy matter at that time for a living substance to die; the course of its life was probably only a brief one, whose direction was determined by the chemical structure of the young life. For a long time, perhaps, living substance was thus being constantly created afresh and easily dying, till decisive external influences altered in such a way as to oblige the still surviving substances diverge even more widely from its original course of life and to make even more complicated *detours* before reaching its aim of death. These circuitous paths of death, faithfully kept to by conservative instincts, would thus present us today with the picture of the phenomenon of life.
>
> FREUD 2001: 39

"Life is but a dream of the inanimate" (Zupančič 2017: 97). The pleasure principle, striving for the free outflow of excitation, is the mental equivalent to reducing the tension induced in inanimate matter by the emergency of life. It is analogous to the fundamental tendency of all life to return to the inanimate.

This way, the pleasure principle appears as an expression of the *Nirvana principle* – that is, the effort to reduce or keep the internal excitation constant – and this is the most compelling reason that led Freud to believe in the existence of the death instinct. Nevertheless, "the terrifying convergence of pleasure and death is dissolved as soon as it is established," notices Marcuse: "No matter how universal the regressive inertia of organic life, the instincts strive to attain their objective in fundamentally different modes. The difference is tantamount to that of sustaining and destroying life" (1966: 25). Eros, the life instinct, introduces new tensions, and "thus wins, against death, the 'potential immortality' of the living substance" (26). Sexual pleasure diverts instinct from its original procreative role, modifies the nature of natural needs and breaks up the return circle from organic to inorganic by introducing new desires.

The paradox of the death drive is that the return to a pre-organic peace, the goal of the Nirvana principle, would demand a greater effort by the psychic structure than the circular movement of the drive around the desired object. In a Lacanian contemporary interpretation of Freud's *Triebelehre*, Žižek stresses that the goal of Nirvana principle is false since it is false to consider the drive's goal (any drive's goal) as to reach an object. The true aim of the drive consists of reproducing its own circular movement around the void that provoked it (the drive) – by means of repeatedly missing its object, and not reaching it. In other words, the drive is about keeping on desiring. Realizing the desire is a kind of byproduct that opens space for a new desire – and not for a "pre-organic peace," for Nirvana. According to Žižek, "from the standpoint of libidinal economy, it is 'cheaper' for the system to repeatedly traverse the circle of drive than to stay at absolute rest" (2020: 294).

Eros' aim impels human beings away from the return to a former homeostatic stage. In "the classical Freudian stance," civilization is "sexually driven, 'motivated'" (Zupančič 2017: 97). According to Marcuse, "Eros is defined as the great unifying force that preserves all life. The ultimate relation between Eros and Thanatos remains obscure" (1966: 27).

2   The Father and the Archaic Heritage

The trauma of birth provokes the first expression of the death drive (*Trieb*), the drive to return to the comfortable womb and, according to Marcuse, such trauma "necessitates the subsequent controls of this impulse" (1966: 55). This traumatic experience is not individual but generic; it belongs to the genus. In *Moses and Monotheism*, Freud also perceives that some individual reactions could not be adequately explained by the individual's own experiences, and that only a phylogenetic event, an innate element, which is enrooted and still active in the psyche, could explain some little children's behaviors. This perception forces the analysis of the individual's mental structure into regressing to a time before early childhood, "from the prehistory of the individual to that of the genus" (56). It forces a link between conscious and unconscious, individual and collective history. Thus, Freud asserts that an *archaic heritage*, which includes dispositions, memory traces, and ideational contents of former generations, determine civilization. The idea of an archaic heritage is the most strongly rejected part of the Freudian theory, due to the difficulty of verifying it scientifically. Freud (1969) reveals the sources of his theory as

Darwin (*The Descent of Man*, 1871), Atkisons (*The Primal Law*, 1903), and Robert Smith (*Lectures on the Religion of the Semites*, 1889). Marcuse uses the Freudian anthropological hypothesis for its symbolic value. Regardless of the truth content of this theory, Marcuse gives it a cognitive value.

Marcuse says Freud's metapsychology "reveals the power of the universal in and over the individuals," and in doing so it "undermines one of the strongest ideological fortifications of modern culture – namely, the notion of the autonomous individual. Freud's theory here joins the great critical efforts to dissolve ossified concepts into their historical content" (Marcuse 1966: 57). Even Lacan, who did not accept the formulation of an archaic heritage psychologically transmitted, says the memories of former experiences of life are enrooted in language.

In *Moses and Monotheism*, Freud reconstructs the archaic history of humanity from the primal horde to civilization. In *Eros and Civilization*, Marcuse says "This phylogenetic hypothesis reveals that mature civilization is still conditioned by archaic mental immaturity." Going on with Marcuse's words, even though the archaic events stipulated by the Freudian hypothesis are beyond the possibility of anthropological verification, "the alleged consequences of these events are historical facts, and their interpretation in the light of Freud's hypothesis lends them a neglected significance, which points to the historical future. If the hypothesis defies common sense, it claims, in this defiance, a truth which common sense has been trained to forget" (60).

Freud's hypothesis is that, once upon a time, the first human community came to life. This primal horde was established by the absolute domination of one man over the others. This man is *the father* who possessed and monopolized all the desired women, produced offspring, and subjugated all group members to his power. The fate of the sons who disagreed with the father was death, exile or castration. In Marcuse's description:

> The burden of whatever work had to be done in the primal horde have been placed on the sons who, by their exclusion from the pleasure reserved for the father, had now become "free" for the channeling of instinctual energy into unpleasurable but necessary activities. The constraint of gratification of instinctual needs imposed by the father, the suppression of pleasure, thus not only was the result of domination but also created the preconditions for the continued function of domination.
>
> MARCUSE 1966: 61

Despite its cruelty, the archaic horde is sustained by a sort of order that can be considered rational; despite its despotism, it manages to preserve the group.

With Freud, Marcuse considers the primal father to set the model for the development of civilization. "Through enforced constraint on pleasure [...] he thus created the first preconditions for the disciplined 'labor force' of the future" (62). The patriarchal authority could be justified by the father's biological function, by his age, and – most of all – by his success in creating that order. An order that promotes security, protection, and a sort of love, a biological affection that accompanies hatred. Ambivalently, the sons not only desire to kill the father, but to be the father themselves.

In Freud's anthropological construction, one of the sons replaces the father after the latter's death and plays his role. The cycle of this old form of domination is only broken and transformed when the exiled sons' hatred leads them to gather their strength, murder the father collectively and in turn establish a brothers' clan. That is, after the parricide, the power goes not just to one son, who would impose himself as a new Father, but rather is shared by the collective of brothers. Freud tells the story:

> After the killing of the father, a time followed when the brothers quarreled among themselves for the succession, which each of them wanted to obtain for himself alone. They came to see that these fights were as dangerous as futile. This hard-won understanding, as well as the memory of the deed of liberation they have achieved together and the attachment that had grown up among them during the time of their exile, led at last to a union among them, a sort of a social contract. Thus there came into being the first form of a social organization accompanied by a renunciation of instinctual gratification; recognition of mutual obligations; institutions declared sacred, which could not be broken. In short, the beginnings of morality and law.
>
> FREUD 1969: 188

Freud says that after the father's murder and prior to the brothers' clan, the role of women grows and eventually leads to matriarchy. In his words: "A good part of the power which had become vacant through the father's death passed to the women; the time of matriarchate followed" (Freud 1969: 188–9). The end of patriarchal despotism makes way for erotic freedom and a low degree of repression, which according to Marcuse are both "traditionally associated with matriarchy" (Marcuse 1966: 65).[1] Freud notices that, even though his hypothesis concerning the primal horde cannot be precisely located in time, there is a

---

1   Even though these characteristics should not create a sort of generalization about all matriarchal societies, which can be conflictual too – Margaret Mead, in *Sex and Temperament in*

temporality: first the parricide, then the consequent liberation of power, next the sparkling moment of women's liberty, and then back to domination. Men recapture the power from female hands, which Freud considers a victory of intellect over sensibility.[2] It is the triumph of the idea over material perception. That is what happens every time the desired object does not coincide with the perceived object, i.e. most of the time.

In short, according to the Freudian hypothesis of the primal horde, civilization begins when the sons replace the father's tyranny by creating the brothers' clan: when domination by one – the patriarch, father and tyrant – is replaced by domination by many, and all members have to abide by the rules to maintain the group. The ruling brothers impose taboos, restraints, and repression to preserve the union. No one will ever enjoy unrestricted pleasures again.

However, as the sons who establish the brothers' clan desire the same as the father – long lasting satisfaction – this identity, allied to guilt, provokes the deification of the assassinated father. Freud attributes the beginning of monotheist religion to this moment. The parricidal rebels, in addition to turning the murdered father into a totem, impose self-domination to create a new and restrictive order.

Marcuse stresses that the development of the feeling of guilt is what most clearly differentiates the brothers' clan from the primal horde. The father would never feel any guilt. "Progress beyond the primal horde – i.e., civilization – presupposes *guilty feeling*: it introjects into the individuals, and thus sustains, the principal prohibitions, constraints, and delays in gratification on which civilization depends" (63).

The guilty feeling comes first because of parricide and then because of remorse for having reestablished the authority. Thus, the brothers suffer a double remorse: one for killing their father; another for creating a new authority. To make things even worse, this new authority must be obeyed by the whole clan; no one is above the law, no one has the absolute freedom the father once had. The price everyone must pay is the loss of a desirable absolute freedom experienced by the father alone. It seems that the guilt for having committed the crime is followed by the guilt of having suppressed absolute freedom and keeping everybody under the law again. In Marcuse's words: "The overthrow of the king-father is a crime, but so is his restoration [...] The crime against the reality principle is redeemed by the crime against the pleasure principle: redemption

---

Three Primitive Societies (1963) presents the two different situations) – they must not be dismissed. See Montagu (1992 [1952]), Turnbull (1981), and Horowitz (1994).

2 Maternity has clear evidence; "paternity is a hypothesis based on an inference and on a premise" (Freud 1969: 221).

thus cancels itself." The problem is that this second crime – the one against the pleasure principle – is not redeemed. "There is guilt over a deed that has not been accomplished: liberation" (68). Even though the new domination by the brothers' clan is self-imposed, and there is some degree of autonomy here, the promise of freedom is betrayed. Patriarchate replaces the matriarchal society.

However, as the "new fathers" in power never reach the same degree of omnipotence as the primeval one, the next step to stabilize the new order is the institutionalization of a religion that deifies and internalizes the figure of the father. The primal father, whose power is unlimited, returns as God – polytheism cedes to monotheism. The father and God represent both domination and security. Freud based his theory of religion on the parallel between God and the father.

Also, in *Totem and Taboo*, the possibility to ground a community appears through the murder of the father and the ensuing guilt bringing brothers together. Thus, in the individual unconscious, Freud believes there are always roots of a "floating anxiety."

> Freud assumes that the primal crime, and the sense of guilt attached to it, are reproduced, in modified forms, throughout history. The crime is re-enacted in the conflict of the old and new generation, in revolt and rebellion against established authority – and in subsequent repentance: in the restoration and glorification of authority. In explaining this strange perpetual recurrence, Freud suggested the hypothesis of the *return of the repressed*.
>
> MARCUSE 1966: 69

"Return of the repressed" is a movement Freud perceived in the analysis of the individual psyche and extended to the general history of civilization. Even though "in the course of thousands of centuries it certainly became forgotten that there was a primal father" – and his fate as well – there is an impression of this fact in unconscious memory traces that can be awakened by events and experiences that present similarity to repressed contents. "The decisive difference between the primal situation and its civilized historical return is, of course, that in the latter the ruler-father is normally no longer killed and eaten, and that domination is normally no longer personal" (Marcuse 1966: 74). Marcuse's description of the differentiation process – from the primal father to civilization – is well worth quoting in full:

> The function of the father is gradually transferred from his individual person to his social position, to his image in the son (conscience), to

God, to the various agencies and agents which teach the son to become a mature and restraint member of his society. *Ceteris paribus*, the intensity of restraint and renunciation involved in this process is probably not smaller than it was in the primal horde. However, they are more rationally distributed between father and son and among society as a whole; and the rewards, though not greater, are relatively secure. (75)

Freud's theory focused on the repeated cycle of domination-rebellion-domination. This dynamic repeats itself in the history of civilization. However, it is not simply repetition: domination becomes increasingly universal and impersonal. Domination by the primal father expanded into domination by society: "law and order are identical with the life of society itself" (Marcuse 1966: 91).[3] The restrained father resurrects more powerful in the administration of society and in the laws that preserve the administration. Thus, the father image becomes less and less decisive to society's adjustment, and gradually disappears behind institutions and mass media. Individuals become social atoms. "The antenna on every house, the transistor on every beach, the jukebox in every bar or restaurant are as many cries of desperation – not to be left alone, not to be separated from the Big Ones, not to be condemned to the emptiness or the hatred or the dreams of oneself" (Marcuse 1989: 237).

In "The Obsolescence of the Freudian Concept of Man," Marcuse defends that to be obsolete is not to be false, and that Freud's theory draws its strength precisely from its obsolescence: from its loyalty to individual potentialities and desires. Martin Jay considers that the theory of remembrance, constructed by Marcuse on a Freudian basis, gave him "a potent weapon in his attempt to find an Archimedean point for a Critical Theory no longer able to rely on the praxis of a revolutionary proletariat as its ground" (Jay 1988: 37).[4] Habermas goes further and stresses the fact that Marcuse keeps a place for an instinctual force that is still alive, and that poses a threat to the instruments of control and domination. Despite his perception that, after vanquishing the established power, revolutions failed not only because of outside forces, but also due to individual internal dynamics that deny a possible liberation – supporting and feeding counter forces – Marcuse believes that "we still may hope for the rebirth of rebellious subjectivity from a nature which is older than, and arises from below the level of, individuation and rationality. Marcuse has a *chiliastic* trust

---

3   See Alexander Mitscherlich, *Society without the Father*. New York: Schoken, 1970.

4   According to Jay, "From his earliest writing, beginning with *Hegel's Ontologie* in 1931, until the very last, *The Aesthetic Dimension*, in 1977, Marcuse returned again and again to what he saw as the liberating power of remembrance." Idem, *ibidem*; p.29.

in a revitalizing dynamic of instincts which works through history" (Habermas 1988: 9).

3   Marcuse's Hypothesis, a Biological Foundation for Political Practice

Marcuse reads Freud as presenting the "figures" of psyche as they appear in history, according to Freudian theories. The scheme of the *Triebelehre*, that establishes the relationships between the individual and the external world, is perceived as an unconscious substratum that continues to be effective in the history of individuals and, therefore, in that of civilization. This way, Marcuse holds in one hand an archaic scheme, whereas in the other, the current and temporal contents of this scheme. Human beings are determined by social structures, but not only by those presently existing – and, of course, not only by the archaic ones. Both the social structures and the individuals who create them change along history. Human beings must deal with a reduplication of the external world, that is, the one that lies outside them, and the one that once was external and now lies inside them as a constitutive element of their interiority. This dialectical movement between the individual's interior and the external world interweaves both in a time that is present and past, with a focus on an image of the future. Marcuse avoids objective essentialism – dogmatic ontology – and subjective relativism – the realm of contingent constructs; he deals with a sort of historicized ontology.

According to Freud, the pleasure principle remains unmodified in the most archaic and deepest unconscious processes. The reality principle substitutes it with promises of security and sustains the individual in the external world. A problem with Freud's theory is that it does not differentiate between biological necessities and socio-historical ones, and thus historical processes appear as natural ones. To overcome this limitation and express the difference between the repression necessary for survival and the socially necessary repression, Marcuse makes a distinction between "basic" repression (the modification of instincts necessary for the survival of the human race), and "surplus-repression" (the restrictions necessary for the maintenance of the social relations of domination). Marcuse also differentiates the reality principle, "which means that the struggle for existence takes place in a world too poor for the satisfaction of human needs without constant restraint, renunciation, delay" (Marcuse 1966: 35), from its prevailing historical form, the "performance principle." Poverty and scarcity are no longer necessary; now they are consequences of the social organization. In the Marcusean duplication of the concepts, Freud meets Marx. As Kellner observes, "the concept 'surplus repression' was inspired by, and functions analogously to, Marx's concept of 'surplus-value,' and the performance principle is connected with Marx's critique of capitalism and alienated labor" (Kellner 1984: 164).

Marcuse considers some repression to be necessary, but not surplus-repression. The same happens to the reality principle: its necessity does not imply the necessity of the performance principle. In short, there are possibilities of less repression, both for the psychic structure and for the external world. Remembering that the pleasure principle is at the root of instincts, the point is why the social organization develops new forms of control instead of a movement towards emancipation. The latter seems to be more adequate for the instinctual apparatus. Marcuse thinks the acceptance of domination originates from the long dependency of human infants on adults, most of the time on their parents. It is rooted in the helplessness of childhood when every human being, incapable of carrying out the actions required to fulfill his/her needs, must be taken care of. Compared to other animals' young, human offspring are more dependent on someone else's care, and for a longer time. According to Marcuse, "The autonomous development of the instincts is frozen, and their pattern is fixed at the child level. Adherence to a *status quo ante* is implanted in the instinctual structure. The individual becomes instinctually re-actionary – in the literal as well as the figurative sense" (1966: 33). The acceptance of domination is the price of security.

Freud considers this "original helplessness" (*anfangliche Hilflosigkeit*) as the primal source of all moral motives. It is also the source of the belief in Gods, of religions and of authoritarian populisms. So far, most people are more prone to endorse a religious or authoritarian populist political leader than to discuss rational arguments. Thus, the discontent of the exploited meets the false promises of authoritarian populism. The latter tantalizes people as it speaks directly to the unconscious remembrance of original care – that lies as mnemonic footprints deep inside every living person. Authoritarian populism sucks its energy from the social negativity present in every hierarchic social order. It obliterates the immanent social antagonism that traverses global capitalism with promises, hopes and dreams. It gives the people an occasion to not think, to go on sleeping, and just to redirect their free-floating desires according to the father's determination.

Atomized individuals depend on water, electricity, health care, laws; in short, they depend on a network they do not control. The ideal community is one where this network functions as invisibly and smoothly as the organs of a (healthy) body. Once again, the pleasure principle appears as an expression of the *Nirvana principle*. Remember the song: "Heaven is a place, a place where nothing, nothing ever happens" (Byrne 1979).

The well-known feeling of helplessness returns and grows in an omnipresent and impenetrable social structure. But so does the remembrance of being taken care of, an experience that every living human being has. Human life is regulated by mechanisms that in their totality are beyond representation – in the realm of the sublime. Established values become people's own values.

> Let's recall the basic premise of the Marxist analysis of capitalism: capitalism is a reign of abstraction; in it, social relations are permeated, regulated and dominated by abstractions that are not just subjective abstractions, abstractions performed by our minds, but 'objective' abstractions, abstractions that rule social reality itself, what Marx called *Realabstraktion*, 'real abstractions.'
>
> ŽIŽEK 2017: 259

Capitalist objective abstractions, rulers of social reality, also colonize the mental apparatus so that it should only accept the given. Everybody is enslaved in a structure whose powers are beyond one's control. Fear mobilizes the lowest instinct of self-preservation. Human beings' history, not nature, imposes the surplus subjugation of the instincts to repressive controls. "The primal father, as the archetype of domination, initiates the chain reaction of enslavement, rebellion, and reinforced domination which marks the history of civilization. But ever since the first," Marcuse stresses, "repression from without has been supported by repression from within: the unfree individual introjects his masters and their commands into his own mental apparatus" (1966: 16).

The "eternal primordial struggle for existence," according to Freud, sustains the repressive control of the instincts. Unfreedom and constraint seems to be the price we pay for life. In writings after *Eros & Civilization*, Marcuse historicizes this Freudian statement and shows that technological development and increased productivity make the possibility of a better life for all real, relieving the "struggle for existence." Achievements of the repressive civilization itself create the conditions for gradual abolition of repression. Scientific and technical achievements of existing societies could realize global elimination of hunger and poverty. The still prevailing misery in vast areas is due chiefly to the manner of distributing and utilizing natural and technical resources. The material facts responsible for this psychodynamic, which Freud unfolds as the dynamic of civilization, have changed. Scarcity, *Lebensnot, Ananke* can be objectively eliminated; the problem now is on the subject.

Even if the subject is more and more swallowed up by totalitarian society, Marcuse maintains the hypothesis of a less repressive development of the libido under the conditions of mature civilization. A specter of freedom is rounding civilization. "But the closer the real possibility of liberating the individual from the constraints once justified by scarcity and immaturity, the greater the need for maintaining and streamlining these constraints lest the established order of domination dissolve" (Marcuse 1966: 93). With the rationalization of the productive apparatus, domination assumes the form of administration, concentration of economic power increases with the impersonality and ano-nymity of laws. Progressive dissolution of the guarantees of stable traditional ways of 'earning a living' accelerate disintegration of the welfare state (a sort of brothers' clan) and provoke the awakening of father figures – embodied in religious leaders and authoritarian populist politicians.

On the one hand, technical objective capacities outgrow the framework of exploitation within which they are still confined; on the other hand, nature, people and cultures are destroyed on an accelerating and frightening scale. No more due to necessity, scarcity, *Lebensnot* or *Ananke*, but for so-called "profits." The human species is walking blind – like the living dead – towards the abyss, holding cell phones.

The corporate capitalist economy has created a second nature that ties human beings to the commodity form, libidinally. The need for consuming, eminently a stabilizing and conservative need, has become a biological need. Because the established values have become the people's own values, and mass media has adjusted the rational and emotional faculties to the market; unless the changes reach these patterns, this second nature, political and social trans-formations will remain self-defeating. When needs and desires reproduce a life in servitude, liberation presupposes changes in this inner dimension, in the drives that affect the mind as well as the body.

The situation now is more critical than at Marcuse's time, and surpris-ingly his alternative is still the only possibility of hope. What is at stake are the human values, desires and needs themselves. The advent of a new radical form of social organization requires a qualitative change in the infrastructure of individuals, which is in itself a dimension of the society's infrastructure. The condition *sine qua non*, according to Marcuse, is the emergence of different goals, dreams and aspirations "in the men and women who resist and deny the massive exploitative power of corporate capitalism" (Marcuse 1969: vii).

> The new direction, the new institutions and relationships of production, must express the ascent of needs and satisfactions very different from and even antagonist to those prevalent in the exploitative societies. Such a change would constitute the instinctual basis, which the long history of class society has blocked ... The rebellion would then have taken root in the very nature, the "biology" of the individual; and on these new

grounds, the rebels would redefine the objectives and the strategy of the political struggle, in which alone the concrete goals of liberation can be determined.

MARCUSE 1969: 4–5

For Marcuse, the political struggle must have roots in the individual organism that is no longer capable of tolerating the brutality and aggressiveness, a toleration required for well-being under domination. Such a change in human nature is only conceivable "because technical progress has reached a stage in which reality no longer need be defined by the debilitating competition for social survival" (5). Free from the framework of exploitation, technical capacities would propel human aspirations beyond those envisaged at the earlier stage, when "earning a living" through competitive performance – the "rat race" – was a kind of vital need. As did Nietzsche, Marcuse is thinking about a radical transvaluation of values ...

The construction of a different society presupposes a type of human being with a new consciousness and new sensibility: human beings, Marcuse wrote, "who have developed an instinctual barrier against cruelty, brutality, ugliness. Such an instinctual transformation is conceivable as a factor of social change only if it enters the social division of labor, the production relations themselves" (21). That is, radical change in consciousness is the first step in changing social existence: the emergence of a new subjectivity is just the beginning, a condition *sine qua non*, not a guarantee. The awakening of individual consciousness illustrates "the period of enlightenment prior to material change – a period of education, but education which turns into praxis: demonstration, confrontation, rebellion" (53). The emphasis toward subjective factors, "the development of awareness," assumes primary importance.

Awareness must replace alienation. New ecological patterns, workers' rights, control of banks, universal health care, and taxes on big fortunes must replace determinations now exerted by the global capitalist economy. Considering the contradictions between, on the one hand, possibilities of abundant goods and information; and on the other hand, banks and government monopolies keeping things private and scarce, it is not hard to perceive that the current system is against humanity and against Earth itself. Both are condemned to disappearing in a visible future, in a universal crime managed by capitalist organizations. To avoid the announced and already visible catastrophe, the only hope is the creation of a new paradigm. Billions, as we know then, are blood. If things are to change, it is necessary to traverse the savior father's fantasy, to replace patriarchate by sisterhood and, in the symbolic order of values, *to consider life before profit.*

Marcuse's reading of Freud can be useful to understand and criticize authoritarian populism because, through his writings since *Eros and Civilization*
(1955), he has made deep psychological realities emerge; realities that underlie
the whole symbolic structure of political and social edifices – just as plate tectonics underlie the ground we step on. He brings historical facts to the surface
and thus makes it possible to understand the factors behind current facts. The
problem is that the most perfect theory must find its expression in practice.
It must be accepted as correct and welcomed into the hive mind to change
the symbolic structure of the so-called "real world." In *An essay on Liberation*
(1969), Marcuse sort of revisits the Freudian theory of drives to present a possible "Biological foundation for socialism." It is possible to shorten this long
story stressing that Marcuse's bet on the life drive, on Eros, is a bet on hope.
That is what we now have in our hands to reconfigure the symbolic structure
on behalf of the survival of Earth and life.

Marcuse's emphasis on subjective factors, radical change in individual
consciousness, needs, dreams and desires assumes an incommensurable
importance in order to change the ongoing establishment. His reflections
reveal skills we need to analyze, decipher, and interpret the complex and
conflicting perspectives that surround us – and their emotional appeals as
well. The establishment's foundations and pillars are a symbolic structure
determined by the subjective vision of the objective world. The change we
want is, therefore, only possible through the change of the subjective vision.
These ideas stemming from Marcuse can be found in the contemporary philosophers of the "Slovenian School" – philosophers who have developed critical theories, adding Hegel and Lacan to Freud and Marx. Žižek, the most
renowned among them, quotes Marcuse's arguments in *The Metastases of
Enjoyment* (Verso, 2005) and *In Defense of Lost Causes* (Verso, 2011), among
other works.[5]

I would like to finish this essay with Marcuse's words, as if they were my own:

> For the world of human freedom cannot be built by the established societ-
> ies, no matter how much they may streamline and rationalize their dom-
> ination. Their class structure, and the perfect controls required to sustain
> it, generate needs, satisfactions and values which reproduce servitude of
> human existence. This 'voluntary' servitude (voluntary inasmuch as it is
> introjected into the individuals), which justifies the benevolent masters,

---

5   See Žižek, *The Year of Dreaming Dangerously* (Verso, 2012); *Living in the End Times* (Verso,
    2010); *First as Tragedy, then as Farce* (Verso, 2009); *The Sublime Object of Ideology* (Verso, 1989).

can be broken only through a political practice which reaches the roots of containment and contentment in the infrastructure of man.

MARCUSE 1969: 6

Translated by Sergio Penna

References

Byrne, David And Harrison, Jerry. 1979. "Heaven." In *Fear of Music*. New York: Sire Records.

Freud, Sigmund. 1968. "Angst und Triebleben." In *Neue Folge der Vorlesungen zur Einfuhrung in die Psychoanalyse*, Gesammelte Werke, Band 15. Frankfurt: Fischer Verlag.

Freud, Sigmund. 2001. "Beyond the Pleasure Principle." In *Standard Edition of The Complete Psychological Works of Sigmund Freud*, Vol. 18. London: Vintage Books.

Freud, Sigmund. 1969. *Der Mann Moses und die Monoteistiche Religion*. Gesammelte Werke, Band 16. Frankfurt: Fischer Verlag.

Freud, Sigmund. 1950. "Formulation Regarding the Two Principles in Mental Function." In *Collected Papers IV*. London: Hogarth Press.

Habermas, Jürgen. 1988. "Psychic Thermidor and The Rebirth of Rebellious Subjectivity." In *Marcuse. Critical Theory & The Promise of Utopia*, eds. Robert Pippin, Andrew Feenberg, and Charles P. Webel. London: Macmillan.

Horowitz, Gad. 1994. "Psychoanalytic Feminism in The Wake of Marcuse." In *Marcuse, From the New Left to The Next Left*, eds. John Bokina and Timothy Lukes. Lawrence: University Press of Kansas.

Jay, Martin. 1988. "Reflections on Marcuse's Theory of Remembrance." In *Marcuse. Critical Theory & The Promise of Utopia*, eds. Robert Pippin, Andrew Feenberg, and Charles P. Webel. London: Macmillan.

Kellner, Douglas. 1984. *Herbert Marcuse And the Crisis of Marxism*. Berkeley: University of California Press.

Laplanche, Jean & Pontalis, J.-B. *Vocabulaire de la Psychanalyse*. 1967. Paris: Presses Universitaires De France.

Marcuse, Herbert. 1966. *Eros And Civilization. A Philosophical Inquiry into Freud*. Boston: Beacon Press.

Marcuse, Herbert. 1969. *An Essay on Liberation*. Boston: Beacon Press.

Marcuse, Herbert. 1989. "The Obsolescence of Freudian Concept of Man." In *Critical Theory and Society. A Reader*, eds. Stephen Eric Bronner and Douglas Kellner. London: Routledge.

Mead, Margaret. 1963. *Sex and Temperament in Three Primitive Societies*. New York: Morrow.

Mitscherlich, Alexander. 1970. *Society Without the Father*. Trad. Eric Mosbacher. New York: Schoken.

Montagu, Ashley. 1992 [1952]. *The Natural Superiority of Women*. New York: Macmilllan.

Turnbull, Colin. 1981. "Mbuti Womanhood." In *Woman, the Gathered*, ed. Frances Dahlberg. New Haven: Yale University Press.

Žižek, Slavoj. 2020. *Sex and The Failed Absolute*. London: Bloomsbury.

Žižek, Slavoj. 2017. *The Courage of Hopelessness. A Year of Acting Dangerously*. Brooklyn, London: Melville House.

Žižek, Slavoj. 2011. *In Defense of Lost Causes*. Brooklyn, London: Verso.

Žižek, Slavoj. 2005. *The Metastases of Enjoyment. On Women and Causality*. Brooklyn, London: Verso.

Zupančič, Alenka. 2017. *What Is Sex?* Cambridge, MA: The MIT Press.

CHAPTER 8

"Variation within a Single Paradigm": The Latent Authoritarian Dynamics of the Culture Industry

Gregory Joseph Menillo

On August 13, 1969 a German audience heard the voice of Theodor W. Adorno broadcast over Hessian Radio for the last time; the great philosopher, sociologist, and cultural critic had died the week before.[1] It is ironic that the father of the "provocative and even notorious" (Jameson 1990: 139) concept of the culture industry would finally be memorialized by mass media, particularly radio, considering that Adorno spent his entire intellectual life developing a powerful (if incomplete) aesthetic theory that does not merely posit mass culture as art's darkening opposite, but takes it to be its deceitful inversion.[2]

Understanding Adorno's culture industry, however, requires not only a familiarity with his work in aesthetics but also his work on authoritarianism.[3] Both themes preoccupied him equally throughout his life, the "damaged life" of a composer-philosopher who witnessed first-hand the destruction of the Great War, the interwar depression years, and the rise of National Socialism.[4] It was

---

1　A discussion with Hellmut Becker, later transcribed and published as the titular essay in *Erziehung zur Mündigkeit: Vorträge und Gespräche mit Hellmut Becker 1959 bis 1969.* See Adorno and Becker 1983. Henry W. Prikford's preface to *Critical Models: Interventions and Catchwords* lends insight into Adorno's ambivalence to radio in the last decade of his life. See Adorno 1998b: vii-xii. For Adorno on radio as a tool for social education, see Parkinson 2014.

2　Following Kant (1987: 84), "*Beauty* is an object's form of *purposiveness* insofar as it is perceived in the object *without the presentation of a purpose;*" Adorno sees cultural commodities as inverting this aesthetic principle, presenting "purposelessness for purposes dictated by the market" (Adorno and Horkheimer 2002: 127–128). Resisting commodification and exchange valuation, authentic art opens up a space for authentic aesthetic experience contra the instrumental logic of the world. Its economic purposelessness enables its aesthetic purposiveness. Cultural commodities, however, are heteronomous. Governed by the logic of exchange, they present aesthetic purposelessness for the purposes of profit.

3　Although Horkheimer co-authored *Dialectic of Enlightenment*, G.S. Noerr convincingly argues that Adorno is predominantly responsible for "The Culture Industry: Enlightenment as Mass Deception," the chapter in which the term was first introduced. See Horkheimer and Adorno 2002: 217–247.

4　See Adorno's *Minima Moralia: Reflections from Damaged Life* (Adorno 2005b). Adorno's expatriation to the United States was unusually late: he and his wife arrived in New York

during his subsequent exile in the United States that this German intellectual, raised on Kant and Beethoven, also witnessed the rise of American consumer culture. His experience of many "double worlds" – old and new, pre-war and post, tonal and atonal, philosophical and sociological, German and American, authoritarian and democratic – afforded Adorno a unique perspective on a wide range of issues, especially that which concerns this discussion: resemblances between fascism and mass consumer culture, another "double" Adorno perceived not as opposites, but as two socio-historical expressions of the same antagonistic dynamics of modernity.

For Adorno, Nazism was neither an idiosyncratic phenomenon particular to Germany nor an historical accident, but rather a manifestation of latent authoritarian tendencies already present within modern capitalist society. He therefore feared that a fascist regime could arise again in *any* coercive society, regardless of its particular political structure; his abiding concern was the "survival of National Socialism *within* democracy," which he saw was just as possible in the United States as it had been in Germany.[5] Adorno's more provocative claim, however, which many of his penetrating critiques attempt to show, is that modern, mass consumer culture is animated by certain latent authoritarian dynamics, that a "fascist spirit" (Adorno 2001a: 373) haunts mass consumer culture, particularly the mid-century American consumerism he experienced first-hand. As Jameson noted, Adorno thus viewed the outcome of the Second World War not only as the Allies' victory over Germany, but also as the triumph of the culture industry over Nazism, which is perhaps better understood as a *"variation within a single paradigm*, rather than the victory of one paradigm over another" (Jameson 1990: 140).

An examination of his work on the social psychology of fascism can provide insight into the latent authoritarian physiognomy Adorno perceived in mass consumer culture. This chapter traces two key, closely related concepts – *standardization* and *pseudo-individualization* – in Adorno's work on fascism in order to show that these same mechanisms are at the core of his work on the culture industry. The first section focuses on the "authoritarian personality" as a standardized type, Sections Two and Three explore the concept of the historical decline of the individual and the psychological impact of the antagonistic social forces that engender this decline, and Section Four turns to Adorno's work on fascist propaganda and the authoritarian leader to demonstrate how

---

in February of 1938, a month before the Anschluss. All biographical details are taken from Wiggershaus 1995 and Müller-Doohm 2005.

5   "I consider the survival of National Socialism *within* democracy to be potentially more menacing than the survival of fascist tendencies *against* democracy" (Adorno 1998b: 90).

pseudo-individuality replaces a true, autonomous individuality under fascism. The discussion then pivots to Adorno's culture industry and considers how the conceptual framework previously discussed informs Adorno's interpretation of the latent authoritarianism he observes in modern mass consumer culture. The final section concludes with a conceptual schema for situating both authoritarianism and the culture industry in proper theoretical relation to one another.

1   Standardization of the Subject

> There is reason to look for psychological types because the world in which we live is typed and 'produces' different 'types' of persons.
>
> ADORNO et al. 2019: 747

The main concern of *The Authoritarian Personality,* as Adorno notes, is the "potentially fascistic individual," whose personality structure renders him "particularly susceptible to anti-democratic propaganda" (Adorno et al. 2019: 1).[6] In Adorno's understanding, while the opinions, values, and attitudes of people are highly variable, they nonetheless conform to certain general observable patterns.[7] Their personality traits are *"organized,* in the sense that the constituent parts are related in psychologically meaningful ways" (5) – essentially, as types. Adorno is fully aware of the controversial aspect of typology and maintains that "types" are useful insofar as they reveal significant patterns, so long as the particulars of the individual are not dominated by such potentially reductive concepts. However, Adorno sees the authoritarian personality – "in many respects characteristic of our time" (xliv) – as a peculiar exception in that it actually tends toward typification itself: "the more [individuals] are 'typified' themselves, the more they express unwittingly the fascist potential within themselves" (749). In other words, Adorno proposed that the personality structure of people who are more susceptible to fascism is itself a *more rigid structure,* as opposed to the personality structure(s) of people resistant to fascist deception, which appear more varied and fluid and therefore harder to generalize.

---

6   The choice of pronoun is intentional: while their interviewees included women, the most pronounced and characteristically authoritarian tendencies were observed among men.

7   While *The Authoritarian Personality* is a multi-authored work, I am referring only to sections authored by Adorno and sections otherwise consistent with what Adorno has written elsewhere.

In essence, *The Authoritarian Personality* indicates that Adorno does not understand the proto-fascistic type as just one of several personality types, but that *typification of individuals is itself an authoritarian phenomenon*. The poles of the spectrum from the authoritarian personality to its opposite range between "typified persons, individuals who are largely reflecting set patterns and social mechanisms, and ... persons who may be called types only in a formal-logical sense and who often may be characterized just by the *absence* of standard qualities" (749, fn. 2). This is the first noteworthy observation we can make about Adorno's work on the authoritarian personality: that the personality structure of the potentially fascistic individual tends toward uniformity, or *standardization*.

The "F-scale" was developed to examine the potentially fascistic individual after Adorno and his colleagues' previous efforts to measure the prevalence and intensity of anti-Semitism, ethnocentrism, and "political-economic conservatism" proved unsatisfactory.[8] The scale consists of standard "variables" understood as the foundational pillars of the authoritarian type: strong adherence to "conventional" values, uncritical submission to authority, aggression toward those who violate held values or otherwise appear weak, anti-interception, stereotypic thinking, viewing social dynamics as oppositions between strong and weak (and thus adopting a dominance-submission paradigm), cynical misanthropy, projecting inner turmoil onto the world, and even a heightened concern for "sexual goings on," or gossip (Adorno et al. 2019: 228). While none of the interviewees underwent psychoanalysis, Adorno's theoretical and interpretive framework is Freudian:[9] in essence, the potentially fascistic individual is a repressed person whose psychological needs are frustrated by an antagonistic society;[10] his repressed feelings are projected, often aggressively, onto others; he resists introspection because it would reveal the true internal nature of his frustrations, and strict conformity to dominant social conventions provides ego-security, which defends against repressed antagonisms within the self; his rigid binary opposition between

---

8   What they call "political-economic conservatism" is a type of pseudo-conservatism, a form of reactionary, proto-fascist politics. See Adorno et al. 1950: 153–178. They ultimately concluded that this and the other aforementioned traits were distinct expressions of an underlying authoritarian personality structure. See Adorno et al. 2019: 222–224.
9   However, not orthodox – although Freud's later typology is often used as a referent throughout the study, Adorno's reception of Freud is conflicted at best.
10   "The forces of personality are primarily *needs* (drives, wishes, emotional impulse) which vary from one individual to another in their quality, their intensity, their mode of gratification, and the objects of their attachment, and which interact with other needs in harmonious or conflicting patterns" (Adorno et al. 2019: 5).

strong and weak also reinforces his unstable ego, which is bolstered by membership in an actual or imagined authority structure, and legitimizes the dominance-submission paradigm that justifies his ambivalent relationship to said authority.

Whether or not *The Authoritarian Personality* wholly withstands criticism (see Christie and Jahoda 1954), what is most suggestive for our purposes is a second element of standardization: aside from the personality structure itself appearing as rigidly standardized, the potentially fascistic individual is characterized by the necessity to view the world in *rigidly standard terms*: self vs. other, strong vs. weak, leader vs. follower, etc. Although Adorno does not articulate his analysis in quite this way, *standardization* can be seen as the *point de capiton* (quilting point) around which all other variables of the authoritarian personality can be understood:[11] strict adherence to a *fixed, stereotypic worldview* as the governing norm for interpreting the world and guiding action. As Adorno notes, this way of thinking must constrain experience, leading to the reduction of complexities and of particularities and ultimately to the objectification of others, making this mentality particularly susceptible to fascist deception.

Before turning to *pseudo-individualization* for a more complete understanding of Adorno's social psychology of fascism, we must first deal with the problematic status of the autonomous individual itself, and also the socioeconomic conditions that, for Adorno, produce its historical decline.

2   Decline of the Individual

Individualism ... may ultimately become a mere ideological veil in a society which actually is inhuman and whose intrinsic tendency towards the 'subsumption' of everything ... shows itself by the classification of people

---

11   The *point de capiton* suggests the image of an upholstery button, an anchoring point that gives structure to the formless stuffing that fills a cushion. For Lacan's usage, see Lacan 1993: 258–270. Adorno was unaware of Lacan, but we can nonetheless understand that he sees *standardization* (along with *pseudo-individuality*) as such an anchoring concept that structures the fascistic individual, cultural commodities, and, broadly speaking, life in modern consumer society. Adorno's description of the conceptual 'constellation' is consistent with my suggestion a *point de capiton,* a kind of conceptual center of gravity: "Cognition of the object in its constellation is cognition of the process stored in the object. As a constellation, theoretical thought circles the concept it would like to unseal" which is revealed in its "monadological insistence" only in relation to the whole (Adorno 2007: 163).

> themselves ... large numbers of people are no longer, or rather never were, 'individuals' in the sense of traditional nineteenth-century philosophy.
>
> ADORNO et al. 2019: 747

Anticipating criticism to the proposal of an authoritarian personality type, Adorno admits that while "constructing types is itself indicative of that 'stereopathic' mentality which belongs to the basic constituents of the potentially fascistic individual," one cannot ignore that "people form psychological 'classes' inasmuch as they are stamped by variegated social processes" (746). Adorno's recently published "Remarks to the *Authoritarian Personality*" reinforces this position with an important assertion: "Individual psychology is largely an agency through which economic laws become operative in attitudes and behaviors without the individual's being aware of it" (li).[12]

Adorno claims that due to the alienating and objectifying forces of late capitalism,[13] the possibility for the development of the autonomous, bourgeois subject of the nineteenth century is foreclosed.[14] In contemporary society

---

12   Included in the recent edition of *The Authoritarian Personality*. See Adorno et al. 2019: xli-lxvi.

13   According to Jameson 1991, the term "late capitalism" originated with the Frankfurt School. He notes two central features: "1) a tendential [sic] web of bureaucratic control ... and 2) the interpenetration of government and big business ([i.e.] 'state capitalism')." (xviii) Under this rubric, Nazi Germany, the New Deal, and aspects of the Stalinist system would qualify them all as late capitalist systems. See also Pollack (1985).

14   Following Hegel, one's individual identity is actualized when one can experience their deeds "as their own" in the social world; one achieves full subjectivity when these deeds are undertaken in collaboration with others in mutual respect and recognition. Meaningful action therefore requires this reciprocal recognition within society, and it is dialectical in that the social world is already implicated in the formation and experience of one's individual deeds, intelligible and justifiable to both self and others as freely undertaken. As Robert Pippin explains, "Hegel argues that this can occur only in a state of social harmony ... [characterized by] a unity of subjective and objective freedom ... [wherein] the right sort of institutions will make it possible to experience – will educate us so that we can experience – other people and institutions as such a [sic] full realization of our own freedom rather than its sacrifice." Pippin continues, "in any just social and economic system, there must be the widest available social space for the expression of individual talents, psychological traits and so forth; for the possibility of the objective expression and recognition of variegated and contingent individual identities." Adorno endorses this view throughout his work and would agree with Pippin's conclusion that the late capitalism of his time (like ours) falls terribly short of this ideal: "What is now not viable in Hegelian terms is a form of capitalism that works actively to suppress and distort ... the depth of a mutual dependence that ought to be reflected in institutionalized forms of mutual respect and solidarity. ... for Hegel it is a form of capitalism, the chief marker of which is not just immiseration and material inequality, but humiliation" (Pippin 2020).

people undergo "the characteristic modern conflict between a strongly developed rational, self-preserving ego agency and the continuous failure to satisfy their own needs." This results in a "new type of psychological affliction so characteristic of the era which, for socio-economic reasons, witness[es] the *decline of the individual* and his subsequent weakness" (Adorno 2001c: 134).

What seemed like an historical inevitability in the dawn of the nineteenth century becomes impossible to defend in the twentieth: the idea of unlimited human progress, expanding freedom, and specifically the full realization of the bourgeois ideal of the autonomous, self-determining individual. Under the dominance of late-stage monopoly capital and modern, bureaucratic, administered society "people are reduced more and more to the status of functions" (Adorno 2006: 5). Freedom remains superficial, part of only private life, and "lacks substance as far as people's ability to determine their own lives" (5). When all social production is organized for profit, satisfying peoples wants and needs only indirectly, and when alienating and exploitative relations of production deny people the possibility of self-determination, the nineteenth century bourgeois notion of the autonomous individual persists only in an illusory, fetishistic form. The social and psychological ailments – e.g., fascism and the authoritarian personality – characteristic of the twentieth century are products of these antagonistic objective conditions, which negate the individual in order to integrate people into the prevailing socio-economic order.

The decline of the individual "is due to the total structure of our society or, to put it more sweepingly, to every basically *coercive* society" (Adorno et al. 2019: 1). This claim resonates in "Freudian Theory and the Pattern of Fascist Propaganda," where Adorno states that contemporary society in general "abolishes" the individual

> *through the perpetuation of dependence instead of the realization of potential freedom*, through the expropriation of the unconscious by social control instead of making subjects conscious of their unconscious ... In a thoroughly reified society, in which there are virtually no direct relationships between men, and in which each person has been reduced to a social atom ... the psychological processes, though they still persist in each individual, have ceased to appear as the determining forces of the social process.
>
> ADORNO 2001C: 151–152

Adorno contends that since the antagonistic dynamics of modern society have already repressed and atomized individuals, denied them the possibility of developing true subjective autonomy by perpetuating dependence on coercive institutions, fascism has only the simple task of exploiting these conditions by mobilizing the alienated "masses" already primed for authoritarian submission.

> [It] may well be the secret of fascist propaganda that it simply takes men for what they are: the true children of today's standardized mass culture, largely robbed of autonomy and spontaneity, instead of setting goals the realization of which would transcend the psychological *status quo* no less than the social one. Fascist propaganda has only to *reproduce* the existent mentality for its own purposes; it need not induce a change ... It relies absolutely on the total structure as well as on each particular trait of the authoritarian character which is itself the product of an internalization of the irrational aspects of modern society.
>
> ADORNO 2001C: 150

In this light we may understand Adorno's position that the collective regression of Nazi Germany was a product of the abnegation of the autonomous individual, the final result of alienating and reductive social processes that already compromised the individual's historical status. Germany fell under the spell of Hitler not due wholly to the seduction of fascist propaganda, or the cunning of the Nazi party, but the rise of Nazism should be broadly understood as a symptom of the irrational historical development of modernity. As both Horkheimer and Adorno concluded in *Dialectic of Enlightenment,* with Auschwitz as proof,[15] Enlightenment has turned into its opposite, is "sinking into a new kind of barbarism" (Horkheimer and Adorno 2002: xiv). The subjugation and ultimate renunciation of the self-realizing, autonomous, nineteenth century bourgeois subject, which entails the complete objectification and dehumanization of people, should be understood as its core.

It is important to note that Adorno does not see the Holocaust as the sole and inevitable result of the historical decline of the autonomous individual. Yet the fact that a such a large-scale, rationally calculated, bureaucratically administered mass genocide could come out of a modern, formally democratic Western society – particularly one with such a rich cultural history rooted in Enlightenment ideals – discredits the belief, generally accepted in "advanced liberal democracies," in unflagging human progress and universally expanding individual freedom. For Adorno, such an atrocity should not be

---

15   Also, the Manhattan Project: "No universal history leads from savagery to humanitarianism, but there is one that leads from the slingshot to the megaton bomb" (Adorno 2007: 320).

seen as an aberration but must be understood as part of modernity's trajectory. "Blindness" to this fact is itself a product of a socio-economic system that reproduces itself by suppressing individual autonomy and freedom in the pursuit of unending expansion and growth, the only type of inevitable 'progress' Adorno sees in modern Western society.

This blindness is a feature of the historical decline of the individual *"and his subsequent weakness,"* another symptom of the "new psychological affliction" that characterizes people under a repressive economic system that is intended, at least on its face, to provide the very things it denies. The modern promise of "freedom and spontaneity" is only an *"ideological veil"* which, when lifted, reveals society's true face, one that demands dependency and conformity. This "irrational aspect" of modern society, the alleged "harmony between society and the individual" – when the former actually dominates the latter – is the core social antagonism that the authoritarian character internalizes. The uneven dynamic that characterizes the antagonism between the interests of society and the interests of the individual (whom society supposedly serves) thus forms – or *deforms* – human psychology. Exploring just how Adorno sees these irrational aspects producing said psychological afflictions will bring us to a clearer understanding of how *pseudo-individualization* ultimately stands in for the individual under both fascism and mass culture.

3   An Irrational Totality

> The concept of the autonomous human subject is refuted by reality.
> ADORNO 2006: 7

Adorno suggests that when objective conditions cease to favor people, there arises a lack of *interest* in the development of autonomy and even a resistance to the possibilities of developing true freedom. For Adorno, modern socioeconomic reality achieves this by producing ego-weaknesses within individuals: the external powers which bear down on the ego ultimately overcome the countervailing internal forces to develop in distinction to these external pressures. As a result, the "internal and external powers do not reach a point of dialectic" (6). External social structures ultimately become permanent structures of authority as psychological development is arrested.[16] Without societal

---

16   "... the [socialization] process is such that children – Freud called this the normal development – generally identify with a father figure, i.e., an authority, they internalize it, appropriate it, and then in a very painful process that always leaves scars, they learn that

openings for the possibility of true individual development, the impulse toward freedom and autonomy are gradually degraded and enfeebled. For Adorno, people become so accustomed to the absence of true subjective freedom that they become dependent on the only semblance of freedom they are afforded in contemporary society, and to which they tightly cling – consumer choice.[17]

Given this social situation, the role of modern clinical psychology becomes problematic. Under what can be called an *irrational totality*, socialization can only be achieved by irrational means.[18] What clinical psychology claims to treat – aberrations within the subject, specifically unconscious, repressed drives – are really those lingering urges still resistant to the coercive demands of the totality. Understood this way, Adorno claims psychology itself becomes irrational in the twentieth century, and deceptive. By falsely locating the antagonisms of society in the individual, by assigning "the irrationality of the course of the world to individuals against their own reason" (Adorno 2006: 72), psychology therefore makes a mockery of the human subject as it sanctions an antagonistic world. Criticized here, although not by name, is Freud's "reality

---

the father or father figure does not correspond to the ego-ideal that they learned from him; and thus they break away from him. Only in this way do children become mature people. I believe the factor of authority is presupposed as a genetic factor in the process of maturation. But this fact must by no means be used to glorify and remain satisfied with this stage" (Adorno and Becker 1983: 106 – 107). For the relationship between education, *Bildung*, and the development of subjective autonomy, see also Adorno 1998b.

17   Adorno notes that in modern life people experience themselves as individuals only as consumers. Consumer choice stands in for individuation while, in actuality, people are reduced to objects of consumer society. As will be discussed below, Adorno views modern consumer culture as a "blocking device" barring people from developing autonomy and spontaneity outside of the working day, thus extending the chain of exploitation from labor time into "free" time until they eventually lose sight of fulfillment outside of the commodity system: "... all needs [are] presented to individuals as capable of fulfillment by the culture industry, they [are] set up in advance that individuals experience themselves through their needs only as eternal consumers, as the culture industry's object" (Horkheimer and Adorno 2002: 113).

18   Adorno takes Hegel's axiom – "The True is the whole" (Hegel 1977: 11) – and inverts it – "The whole is the false" (Adorno 2005a: 50) – to underscore the fact Hegel's apparent harmony is untrue, that history is not a progressive unfolding of the Absolute, the spirit of human freedom coming to know itself, as he had thought. Related is Hegel's notion of "what is rational is actual," which denotes that what is real is an instantiation of reason, or the Idea: "since reality (which is synonymous with the Idea) enters upon external existence simultaneously with its actualization" (Hegel 1967: 10). Adorno understands this in inverted form as well: modern society is not an instantiation of reason, but the societal structures developed with the alleged intention of emancipating people actually return to subordinate them, both materially and mentally. See especially "The Concept of Enlightenment" in Horkheimer and Adorno 2002: 1–34.

principle," that which enables the subject to recognize the society's requirements as opposed to his own urges and sublimate said impulses in socially
acceptable ways. While Freud sees this as natural, productive, and positive,
Adorno notes that in an antagonistic society the reality principle becomes a
mechanism for suppressing the subject, who must acquiesce to the world "as
it is."

Adorno's social world "as it is" is coercive: society "enacts sacrifices" from
people with the promise that they will be compensated for their suffering in
the future – a promise which is never kept. He describes this exploitation with
a Marxist analogy, as the extraction of "psychological surplus value":

> this fulfillment of the social promise in the future for what we sacrifice
> in the present by performing our social roles calls for a psychological
> surplus value to be squeezed out of us in addition to the ordinary, eco-
> nomic one. This psychological surplus value is the difference between the
> expectation of happiness in the long term that is always being held out to
> us and the actual satisfaction that we generally receive. (75)

In essence, Adorno sees Freud's reality principle collapsing *happiness promised*
into *actually existing happiness*, working at the behest of the forces of the status quo. Arising psychological antagonisms result from unconscious resistance
to the objectifying and overwhelming forces of social adjustment, which ultimately bring people to heel.

> People manage to come to terms with this phenomenon, with the reali-
> zation that their own rationality is irrational, and that they do not obtain
> what their rational behavior promises, only by making an irrational
> response. It is [sic] to accept the irrational course of the world, to identify
> with it and to make it their own. (76)

Identification with the world as it exists enables a collective Stockholm syndrome to take hold, making subjects wholly unable to effect the changes necessary to develop both themselves and society in a more "harmonious," dialectical fashion. It is not their hands that are chained, but their consciousness – in
truth, "the world which is hostile to human beings asserts itself against them
but [ultimately] with their approval ... with their conscious, self-destructive
acquiescence" (76). People's conscious acquiescence results from their unconscious identification with the existent, with "existing institutions, commodities, things and relations immediately familiar to them" that render them "incapable of perceiving their dependence on ... actual objective processes" (77).

Things "immediately familiar" to them comprise a permanent authority structure that dominates the psyche – whether in fascism or consumer culture, this
"social cement" functions the same way.

4 Pseudo-Individualization of the Masses

> We may conclude ... at the very moment when people believe they are
> most themselves and belong to themselves, they are not only the prey
> of ideology. We might even go so far as to say that they themselves have
> turned into ideology.
>
> ADORNO 2006: 78

We now turn to Adorno's understanding of how fascist propaganda "reproduce[s] the existent mentality for its own purposes" (Adorno 2001c: 150),
exploiting the psychological weaknesses of the modern individual, thwarted
and in decline. Drawing on Löwenthal and Guterman's (1949) *Prophets of
Deceit*, and his own research into fascist agitators (Adorno 2000), Adorno concludes that fascist propaganda is "based on psychological calculations rather
than on the intention to gain followers through rational statement of rational
aims" (Adorno 2001c: 132). Freud's *identification* is the key psychological mechanism Adorno sees at work. In Freud's analysis of Le Bon's "mass mentality"
in *Group Psychology and the Analysis of the Ego*, he finds that "the individual
gives up his ego-ideal and substitutes it for the group-ideal as embodied in the
leader" (Freud 1955: 129). Likewise, Adorno sees identification with the fascist
leader as an *ideal enlargement*, and ultimate displacement, of the thwarted
individual subject: the image of the leader becomes the "object [that] serves
as a substitute for some unattained ego ideal of our own" (Adorno 2001c: 140).
The subject then surrenders to the object of identification, "which it has substituted for its most important constituent" (140): true subjective autonomy.
   Subjective autonomy is lost, but the gain is psychologically invaluable: "by
making the leader his ideal he loves himself, as it were, but [also] gets rid
of the stains of frustration and discontent which mar his picture of his own
empirical self" (140). Fascism reinforces this by providing a seductive psycho-
narrative that feeds on the ambivalent, sado-masochistic aspect of the authoritarian personality, simultaneously sanctioning the status quo while offering
blame for its failure. In Nazi Germany, for example, it is the Jew, imagined as
the foreign usurper, both weak and pernicious, the corrupting agent (as las-
civious cosmopolitan, as Bolshevik conspirator, etc.), who has undermined an
otherwise "pure" German society. This hypothetical Jew – not existing social

conditions – is seen as responsible for the suffering of the strong, righteous *Völk*. Since this is not a rational explanation for their suffering, the aesthetic aspect of fascism – patriotic rallies, propaganda, etc. – must create a fantastic spectacle in order to mobilize people's "irrational, unconscious, repressive processes." Like the spectator of a Wagnerian music-drama,[19] the otherwise impotent citizen is engulfed in a grand *performance* of individuation, which comes with a cathartic release; but only in fascism does the spectator enjoy the *illusion of their own participation* as well as the illusion that the aestheticized spectacle *is* – not just reflects – unmediated political reality.

For Adorno, the fascist leader is a master showman; at rallies and through media he narcissistically projects his own ego-ideal (an ideal image with which he himself identifies), which is calculated to stir the unconscious frustrations of his would-be followers. He remains enough like the "average man" to appeal to their own narcissism, and in this way establishes an emotionally-based concord with them instead of presenting rational arguments which would encourage the kind of critical, reflective thought that risks breaking the spell of unconscious identification. The performance takes on elements of theater, sport, and ritual in order to gratify the follower, who accepts the ideology in the same way, as Adorno remarks, that 1940s housewives are compelled to buy the cleaning detergents advertised at the commercial breaks of soap operas – in an unconscious expression of gratitude for their cathartic release from the grievances and sufferings of repressive daily life. The fascist agitator is thus a "masterly salesman of his own defects" (Adorno 1991: 223) – he can successfully transform his own neuroses into a commodity to sell to a similarly afflicted public.

The "fictitious element" of the fascist performance is crucial, something Adorno didn't recognize at first: Adorno was initially unconcerned with Hitler, who appeared to him as a "caricature" of both "himself and of a real dictator ... a shady figure whose bizarre speech and gestures prevented him

---

19   Aside from being an admirer of Wagner's music, Hitler had an obvious affinity to Wagner's pro-Aryan, anti-Semitic thought, an ideological line that is connected through H.S. Chamberlin's *Die Grundlagen des neunzehnten Jahrhunderts* (1899), one of the most influential *Völkisch* racial histories of the nineteenth century. Chamberlin saw the composer as a great German genius and believed his art had redemptive power to restore the Aryan race to its rightful dominance. He penned a laudatory biography of Wagner in 1895 and settled in Bayreuth in 1907 where he married Wagner's only daughter, Eva von Bülow. After a meeting with Hitler in 1923, Chamberlin joined the Nazis and used his celebrity to bolster public support for the party until his death in 1927. See Köhler 2000. For the authoritarian character of Wagner's operas, see Adorno's *In Search of Wagner* (Adorno 2005a).

from being taken seriously" (Müller-Doohm 2005: 179). Adorno later realized that it is the very pretense of the fascist agitator that enhances his efficacy. In "Anti-Semitism and Fascist Propaganda" he insightfully remarks: "Hitler was liked not in spite of his cheap antics, but just *because* of them, because of his false tones and his clowning" (Adorno 1995: 225). The leader's "hysterical behavior" is thus part and parcel to the potency of fascist appeal. In expressing himself, the leader presents no inhibitions. He intentionally violates social norms and other taboos the acquiescent citizen cannot violate himself. The social risk of appearing extreme or foolish actually wins the agitator credibility; violating the norms of political and social discourse shows irreverence, daring, and strength that project an image of power particularly appealing to the authoritarian personality. Followers are gratified in having their "own minds expressed to them" with such "vigor and verbosity," and thus the fascist performance serves as an "institutionalized redemption" of their own political impotence and inarticulateness. This is the "ritual aspect" that characterizes collective regression under fascism: the leader performs a ceremonial role, becomes a "symbolic revelation of identity" for the de-subjectified masses who knowingly, even cynically, participate in his performance (225–226).

> [People] do not identify themselves with [the leader] but *act this iden-tification, perform* their own enthusiasm, and thus participate in their leader's performance. It is through this performance that they strike a balance between their continually mobilized instinctual urges and the historical stage of enlightenment they have reached and which cannot be revoked arbitrarily.
>
> ADORNO 2001C: 152

The fascist leader thus opens a space for the performance of individuation, a substitute for the space to truly develop subjective autonomy that is simultaneously promised and denied by modern society. For Adorno, this "fantasy of identification" with the leader hides the truth of the economically frustrated, politically impotent de-individualized subject. The fascist follower becomes an individual insofar as he submits to the personality of the leader – irreverent, erratic, but always strong and powerful – who performs subjective autonomy for him. The performance of identity, as opposed to the development of true individual autonomy, is in essence the *pseudo-individuality* of the otherwise dependent and coerced masses – it is individualism only as another *"ideological veil,"* an illusion of participation in the aesthetics of politics that hides the truth of submission.

5   The Latent Authoritarian Dynamics of the Culture Industry

> The culture industry intentionally integrates its consumers from above.
> ADORNO 2001a: 98

Before linking the foregoing discussion to the mechanisms of social integration in consumer society, we must first understand what Adorno takes the 'culture industry' to be. He offers a helpful clarification of his term in a late essay,
two decades after it first appeared in the *Dialectic of Enlightenment*:

> In our drafts we spoke of 'mass culture.' We replaced that expression with
> 'culture industry' in order to exclude from the outset the interpretation
> agreeable to its advocates: that it is a matter of something like a culture
> that arises spontaneously from the masses themselves, the contemporary
> form of popular art. From the latter the culture industry must be distin-
> guished in the extreme ... In all its branches, products which are tailored
> for consumption by masses, and which to a great extent determine the
> nature of that consumption, are manufactured more or less according to
> plan. The individual branches are similar in structure or at least fit into
> each other, ordering themselves into a system almost without a gap. This
> is made possible by contemporary technical capabilities as well as by
> economic and administrative concentration.
> ADORNO 2001a: 98

We see here that in the twentieth century, due in part to the development
of modern mass communication technology and techniques of mechanical reproduction, Adorno observed that for the first time "culture" was being
produced on an industrial scale for mass consumption: large corporate firms
managing large-scale production and distribution of "cultural goods" solely for
purposes of profit. This presented a monumental paradigm shift for Western
"culture," a new paradigm requiring a new conceptual framework for understanding the form and function of the content produced. Adorno's 'culture
industry' marks this shift in a broad sense. While the term often refers to the
industrial aspect of cultural production, typified by the big Hollywood studio
of the 1940s,[20] it is clear that it also encompasses any moment in the network

---

20   For example, the "Big Five" Hollywood film studios of the Golden Era: Fox, MGM,
Paramount, Warner Brothers, and RKO – large, vertically integrated corporations that
owned all moments of the cinema value chain; taken as a whole they represent an oligop-
oly that dominated the film industry until 1948. See Hesmondhalgh (2012).

of entities engaged in promotion and distribution of cultural commodities, in addition to the system as a whole.

Adorno well understood that when profit is the primary purpose, profitability becomes the governing logic of production – all other considerations of the object such as form, content, aesthetic merit, etc., become secondary, marshaled only to ensure its salability.[21] Under the culture industry a "cultural object" is no longer a piece of "culture," in the traditional sense, but a product, and its reception is no longer the perceptual engagement characteristic of the aesthetic experience of art, but that of an exchange – a purchase. What used to be a refuge from an increasingly rationalized modern world, has now been integrated into its dominating forces:

> Culture, in the true sense, did not simply accommodate itself to human beings, but it always simultaneously raised a protest against the petrified relations under which they lived, thereby honoring them. In so far as culture becomes wholly assimilated to and integrated in those petrified relations, human beings are once more debased. Cultural entities typical of the culture industry are no longer also commodities, they are *commodities through and through*. This quantitative shift is so great that it calls forth an entirely new phenomenon.
>
> ADORNO 2001a: 100

This "new phenomenon" is not merely the commodification of culture "through and through," but what happens to the totality of cultural life when the cultural commodity is the dominant form.[22] Adorno reveals this as having profound

---

21   This can be qualified: there is a spectrum of (pseudo) difference between shallow types of cultural commodities, engineered wholly for mass consumption and maximum profitability, and more subtle types that simultaneously resist as they conform to the dictates of the market. Adorno's rhetorical point is that the cultural commodity as a form requires profitability, by definition, and therefore aesthetic merit can never override the governing law of exchange.

22   The socio-psychological effect that arises when the commodity is the dominant form of social production is called *reification* – literally, "thingification," when an abstraction is mistakenly viewed as a material thing – a concept Adorno inherits from Lukács, who extends Marx's theory of commodity fetishism: "The commodity can only be understood in its undistorted essence when it becomes the universal category of society as a whole. Only in this context does the reification produced by commodity relations assume decisive importance for the objective evolution of society and for the stance adopted by men towards it. Only then does the commodity become crucial for the subjugation of men's consciousness to the forms in which this reification finds expression and for their attempts to comprehend this process or to rebel against its disastrous effects and liberate themselves from servitude to the 'second nature' so created" (Lukács 1971: 86).

consequences for not only the nature of the experience of the cultural commodity but also the nature of culture and experience in general.

Because the cultural commodity dominates cultural space, vying for consumer attention in a competitive culture market, Adorno contends that the faculties of cognition responsible for distinguishing among various sense impressions regress as they are conditioned by the specific demands of both the commodity form and its promotion. Instead of opening a space for the kind of active, critical engagement that characterizes authentic aesthetic experience, the cultural commodity "requires a quick, observant, knowledgeable cast of mind but positively debars the spectator from thinking" (Horkheimer and Adorno 2002: 100).[23] At the same time as it engenders inattention and distraction it also demands a type of "ingrained alertness" that represses the powers of imagination. In this way, the culture industry seeks to reproduce the facile habits of mind that enable the ready consumption necessary for fluid commodity exchange and quick realization of market value, instead of "developing autonomous, independent individuals who judge and decide [one could also add *create*] for themselves" (Adorno 2001a: 106).

This aspect of the culture industry was underscored during his exile in the United States, where Adorno noted striking parallels to the authoritarian culture he fled in the 1930s. Written in 1945, "What National Socialism Has Done to the Arts" (Adorno 2002b) outlines four "deeper-going" tendencies toward a potential survival of what he calls a "fascist spirit" in mass culture: a propagandistic tendency, a utilitarian tendency, a leveling tendency, and that which he calls the "freezing" aspect. As with fascist propaganda, Adorno observed that consumer culture similarly follows a set, repetitive ideological pattern in promoting a consumer lifestyle. The goal of advertising and even of the products themselves is to mold public taste in the direction of maximal, broad-based, repeated consumption. It is a utilitarian aim, orienting "free time" by funneling consumer attention toward activities profitable to the industry, heteronomously determining the possibilities for "spending" time outside of the working day almost as strictly as within it.[24] The leveling tendency can be

---

23   The tenor of much of Adorno's writing on the culture industry is undoubtedly polemical. He often articulates his critique in severe terms, such as this, which may be off-putting to some readers. I understand it as a necessary part of his dialectical approach, which attempts to hold out extreme oppositions for the purposes of revealing their contradictions.

24   Adorno makes an important distinction between leisure time and "free time": " 'leisure' (*Muβe*) denoted the privilege of an unconstrained, comfortable life-style" of the bourgeois class, which is qualitatively different from the free time people experience under late capitalism. "Free time depends on the totality of social conditions, which continue to hold people under its spell. Neither in their work nor in their consciousness do people

seen here, in the culture industry's function as social cement, whereby public wants, needs, and desires are mediated to conform to that which it profitably produces, but also in the averaging of consumer taste to the lowest common denominator. What results is a kind of arrested culture, a "freezing" of cultural standards, as opposed to an authentic, autonomous culture that resists the reductive logic of the exchange system by opening up possibilities for new cultural forms, expressions, and experiences.

Adorno draws this parallel further in "Freudian Theory and the Pattern of Fascist Propaganda":

> [Fascist propaganda's] effectiveness is itself a function of the psychology of the consumers. Through a process of 'freezing,' which can be observed through the techniques employed in modern mass culture, the surviving [particular] appeals have been standardized, similarly to the advertising slogans which proved to be most valuable in the promotion of business. This standardization, in turn, falls in line with the stereotypical thinking [of the authoritarian personality.]
>
> ADORNO 2001C: 148

We see here a clear correspondence between the arresting of cultural standards, manipulative techniques of promotion, and the standardization of the subject. This is perhaps taken to new extremes under the culture industry: while the socio-economic conditions of late capitalism determine people's material existence, objectifying them via the relations of production, the culture industry increasingly attempts to objectify people's "spiritual" existence as well:

> the culture industry undeniably speculates on the conscious and unconscious state of the millions towards which it is directed, the masses are not primary, but secondary, they are an object of calculation; an appendage of the machinery. The customer is not king, as the culture industry would have us believe, not its subject but its object.
>
> ADORNO 2002a: 99

---

dispose of genuine freedom over themselves." In truth, free time is only the shadow of work time, and becomes determined in relief. He notes that, under the culture industry, " 'free time' is tending toward its own opposite ... unfreedom is gradually annexing 'free time,' and the majority of unfree people are as unaware of this process as they are of the unfreedom itself" (Adorno 2001b: 187–188).

This occurs not only through promotion, but also in the objectification of culture when it is commodified. One can already anticipate how Adorno accounts for the apparent differences among standardized cultural commodities: what he calls the "veneer" of the particular is merely the *pseudo-individualization* of cultural forms, the illusion of difference among the ever same. Adorno ultimately understands both standardization and pseudo-individualization as the double-edged sword of the cultural commodity, with the latter masking the former. The pseudo-individualized aspect of the cultural commodity is little more than a "halo" of individuality that orients consumers by differentiating otherwise standardized products in the competitive culture marketplace.[25]

Adorno's analysis of this pseudo-individualization of the commodity is founded on Marx's theory of commodity fetishism. Marx observed that the commodity form has a "mysterious character," wherein what is essentially a relation between people takes "the phantasmagoric form of a relation of things" (Marx 1976: 165). Adorno develops this concept further:

> phantasmagoria [is] the point at which *aesthetic appearance* becomes a function of the character of the commodity. As a commodity it purveys illusions. The absolute reality of the unreal is nothing but the reality of a phenomenon that not only strives unceasingly to spirit away its own origins in human labor, but also ... stressing that this is authentic reality, that it is 'no imitation' – and all this in order to further the cause of exchange value.
>
> ADORNO 2005a: 79

This extension of Marx's fetish-character is subtle but crucial to understand. For Marx, the commodity appears as an object independent of human labor, hiding social relations of production: "the social character of men's labor appears to them as an objective character stamped upon the products of their labor" (Marx 1976: 164–165). For Adorno, this objective character also opens a space for a commodity *aesthetics*, enabling the culture industry to purvey

---

25   Adorno refers to this as "aesthetic barbarism" (Horkheimer and Adorno 2002: 103–104): with no resistant material to overcome, no internal aesthetic oppositions to be reconciled, the dialectical tension between form and content is negated – *pseudo-individuality* becomes the absolute stylistic standard of the culture industry in general and advertising in particular. This is the false consciousness of the commodity form; it presents only the *illusion* of a reconciled subject and object, when in truth the individual detail sacrifices itself to the totality in the heteronomous domination of the profit motive, much like the individual being sacrifices himself to the economic system.

highly stylized and deliberately cultivated aesthetic illusions in order to man-
ufacture the appearance of uniqueness, authenticity, and difference in each
product.[26]

The "phantasmagoric," enchanting aspect that Adorno sees in Wagner's
work – and fascist display – is preserved in the hyper-stylized objects the culture
industry proffers.[27] The primary "aesthetic" it employs to this end is what Adorno
calls "predominance of the effect" (Horkheimer and Adorno 2002: 99): the pre-
fabricated effectual detail of the cultural entity, not justified by an "immanent
formal logic" but stamped onto its form to induce a pleasurable unconscious
response, that is reinforced through repetition. Much like the sweeping gestures
of Wagner's music are calculated for their effect on the listener, the enticing
product of the culture industry is aesthetically calculated for its effect on the
consumer. The particular, characteristic image of the product reinforces an illusion of difference – Wagner's *leitmotiv* becomes the culture industry's advertising slogan, the labeling device functioning as a "trademark of identification
for differentiating between the actually undifferentiated" (Adorno 2002a: 446).
The hit song, for example, whose chorus, unabashedly referred to as a "hook," is
designed to do just that: hook the listener. The other elements of the song are
formally inconsequential, and serve as merely packaging for the unchanging,
intermittently returning melody, carefully composed to be immediately recognizable and quickly absorbed. In a sense, the song "becomes its own advertise-
ment," with the hook functioning like a product logo – the "ready-made cliché"
that detaches itself from the object to become a fetishized cultural signifier.

This type of cultural formula reduces perception from thoughtful, spontaneous engagement to mere recognition, requiring a whole apparatus of continual product repetition and reinforcement to become broadly accepted. The
simple "psycho-technique" advertising employs toward this end is the very
same as that used in fascist propaganda: "plugging," or the rigid, unceasing promotion that achieves the "transformation of repetition into recognition and
of recognition into acceptance" (Adorno 2001a: 452).[28] As it bars people from

---

26   The particular effectual detail never reaches the level of true individualization because it
     is governed by standardization itself: "standardization of the norm enhances ... standard-
     ization of its own deviation" (Adorno 2002a: 445).

27   For the phantasmagoric in Wagner and its relation to the commodity fetish see Adorno
     (2005a: 74–85).

28   Adorno's "theory about the listener" can be generalized to explain how familiarity
     becomes the acceptance of any product of the culture industry. There are five "moments"
     of the commodity experience: 1. Vague remembrance, in which the object seems famil-
     iar: whether or not the given object was previously encountered is irrelevant, standardiza-
     tion ensures that "new" cultural commodities resemble the "old," primarily in the attempt

making critical judgments, Adorno equates this technique to fascist manipulation: leaning on simplistic, repeated formulas to rally repressed urges rather
than reasoning with people through critical argumentation.

In essence, the phantasmagoria of consumer society similarly hides the
truth of the economically frustrated, politically impotent, de-individualized
subject. Under fascism, what *takes the form of* theater, sport, and spectacle
in order to gratify the follower, *is* theater, sport, and spectacle in the culture
industry. The latter offers the same substitute gratification – except in pur-
chasable form – for the space to truly develop the subjective autonomy that is
simultaneously promised and denied by modern society. Consumers become
individuals insofar as they submit to the mechanisms of the system, buying
their culture instead of developing it themselves. This purchase of identity,
as opposed to the development of true autonomy, is in essence the *pseudo-
individuality* of the otherwise dependent and coerced masses – individualism
only as another "*ideological veil*" that hides the truth of submission behind the
illusion of participation in the culture industry's spectacle.[29]

to replicate past success. 2. Actual recognition, or the momentary flash in which one says,
"I think I *know* this." 3. Subsumption by label, in which recognition immediately becomes
identification of the object according to its particular "social backing." This is the moment
when the product's social image (logo, slogan, brand, celebrity, lifestyle, etc.) stands in for
experience as such (i.e. the fetish character, the object's social valuation). 4. Self-reflection
on the act of recognition. This is marked by the satisfaction of being able to merely identify something among the barrage of commodities plugged from day to day, and also the
moment of "purchase" on the social fetish. It is a moment of "possession" in which experience becomes reified – "the hit becomes an object to the listener, something fixed and
permanent." 5. The last is a moment of psychological transfer, wherein this "gratification
of ownership" moves to the object, and the object *itself* is seen as possessing the pleasure
that arose out of its mere recognition. What often follows is a preference for the object,
even a predisposal to "liking" it (in a very constrained sense of the word), which is a far
cry from the critical and spontaneous aesthetic judgment both required and engendered
by authentic art. See Adorno (2002a: 452–457).

29   There is more to be said about the pseudo-individual under consumer society and its
      connection to the appearance of the fascist agitator. We recall that psychological iden-
      tification with the fascist leader happens similarly to how the consumer buys a prod-
      uct – by linking through association repressed urge gone unsatisfied by modern society
      to a particularized gratification offered. While the fascist leader commodifies his own
      personality, personality is readily and regularly commodified under the culture indus-
      try – in film, television, music, and news media personalities. In the move from person to
      personality, "the empirical person, just as he happens to be, is posited and transformed
      into a fetish" (Adorno 1998a: 162). While Adorno has the media celebrity in mind, this
      phenomenon is institutionalized in social media today. With the mediating mechanisms
      of social media platforms, 'people,' along Adornian lines, similarly become their own pub-
      licity, in a sense, and "travel as their own advertisements for themselves" (163). Under
      these conditions, what is sacrificed is the very thing that "personality" allegedly seeks to

It is here that we may observe an illuminating reversal, one that is evinced by the impossibility of discussing the culture industry without recourse to the terms of fascism. Interestingly, we've also already seen Adorno discussing fascism in culture industry terms – "the secret of fascist propaganda [is] that it simply takes men for what they are: the true children of today's standardized mass culture." The case can be made that Adorno is able to write in this way only given his experience of the culture industry in the 1940s. A more compelling conclusion, however, is that *Adorno's analysis of fascism cannot be sustained without recourse to the terms of the culture industry just as much as his analysis of the latter cannot be sustained without recourse to the former.* For Adorno, they are parallel tracks that lead in the same direction. Both speak with the same "rhetoric of dependency"[30] and trade in the same double-sided currency, standardization and pseudo-individualization, to coerce people into submitting to the antagonistic social totality.

As Leo Löwenthal, Adorno's lifelong friend and colleague, insightfully remarked, its authoritarian nature is revealed when mass consumer culture is understood as "psychoanalysis in reverse,"

> that is, as more or less constantly manipulated devices to keep people in permanent psychic bondage, to increase and reinforce neurotic and even psychotic behavior culminating in perpetual dependency on a "leader" or on institutions or products.
>
> LÖWENTHAL 1987: 186

If the point of psychoanalysis is to enable the patient to recognize and resolve repressed trauma, freeing them from the hold of the unconscious impulses that dominate their conscious life, Adorno's culture industry can be understood to not only reverse this, but invert these moments as well. Instead of recognizing and resolving their unmet wants, needs, and desires as self-actualized subjects, consumers are pacified and deceived by the culture industry, enticed to misrecognize the products it offers as satisfaction of their unmet social needs. By repeated consumption they further repress their unconscious resistances to the antagonistic social conditions that require them to "experience themselves

---

achieve: the appearance of a "true" person, an entirely authentic individual. One could argue that what Adorno sees happening with the mid-century movie star is now being universalized via Facebook, Instagram, and the like.

30   I have borrowed this term from Stephen Crook, who correctly notes that Adorno saw a "rhetorical and psychological continuum [extending] from 'everyday' products of the culture industry, through quasi-propaganda ... to frank fascist agitation" (Adorno 1991: 19).

through their needs only as eternal consumers, as the culture industry's object" (Horkheimer and Adorno 2002: 113), while the image of the autonomous, self-determining individual slips from historical memory. Freud's formulation, "Remembering, Repeating, and Working Through,"[31] can thus be submitted to a retrograde-inversion, a kind of transformation that Adorno would have recognized from his study of twelve-tone serial music: repressing, repeating, and forgetting.

6   Coda: A Dream of Remission

> ... one might refer to the fascist movements as the wounds, the scars of a democracy that, to this day, has not yet lived up to its own concept.
>
> ADORNO 2020: 9

A tacit assumption throughout this chapter is that the relationship between Adorno's culture industry and his work on the social psychology of fascism is best understood with a conceptual schema resembling the form of a Freudian dream. Not least of all because much of the literature in this area, by both Adorno and his commentators, frequently resorts to the dream metaphor explicitly, but also because a careful reading of Freud's theory of dream interpretation offers a helpful way to situate these two areas of Adorno's thought in proper relation to one another.

One should not see Adorno's culture industry as a type of fascism in disguise. This fallacy – essentially reducing analytic *interpretation* into mere *translation* from one psychic level to another – is often committed in discussions of Freudian dream interpretation. Freud does not say that the translation of dreams is the royal road to the unconscious, but "the *interpretation* of dreams is the royal road to a *knowledge* of the unconscious activities of the mind" (Freud 1953: 608). Latent "dream thoughts" and manifest "dream content" are not merely two versions of the same thing in different "languages," they are

---

31   "The first step in overcoming the resistances is made, as we know, by the analyst's uncovering the resistance, allow[ing] the patient time to become more conversant with this resistance with which he has now become acquainted, to *work through* it, to overcome it, by continuing, in defiance of it, the analytic work according to the fundamental rule of analysis. Only when the resistance is at its height can the analyst, working in common with his patient, discover the repressed instinctual impulses which are feeding the resistance; and it is this kind of experience which convinces the patient of the existence and power of such impulses" (Freud 1958: 155).

only "presented to us" as such. It is crucial to distinguish also the *dream-work* itself – the operations that transform the raw materials of the unconscious into the manifest dream – in order to understand the machinations of the psyche.[32] Confusing the latent content for the "truth" of the dream, when the *mechanisms of the dream-work itself* are most significant, is what we must avoid if our analogy should serve us.[33]

In this way, if we understand that Adorno saw the culture industry and fascism as two different "variations of a single paradigm" – or, perhaps, as two different dreams of the same dreamer – we can see that the same mechanisms are operating in both. The culture industry should not be understood as a latent form of fascism, but rather *both* are manifestations of the same antagonisms of modernity, both are social expressions of the same latent contradictions of late capitalist society. This schema can account for Adorno's frequently dramatic and polemical characterization of one in terms of the other, while preserving the insight that the "mechanisms of signification" – standardization and pseudo-individualization – are their common, underlying dynamics.

It would be helpful to at least consider Peter Gordon's illustrative remark in his discussion of *The Authoritarian Personality:*

> In [Adorno's] analysis, fascism becomes simultaneously truth *and* untruth: On the one hand, it holds out to the masses the promise of a collective release from the constraints of bourgeois civilization with its demand that all instinct (and perhaps especially violence) submit to a pathological repression ... On the other hand, it offers merely the *performance* of this release through the fantasy of an identification with a leader who offers *both* the experience of masochistic submission *and* the illusion that he is just like his followers. This is fascism's "social miracle,"

---

32 Consider the footnote Freud added to the 1925 edition of his *Interpretation of Dreams:* "I used at one time to find it extraordinarily difficult to accustom readers to the distinction between the manifest content of dreams and the latent dream-thoughts ... now that analysts at least have become reconciled to replacing the manifest dream by the meaning revealed by its interpretation, many of them have become guilty of falling into another confusion, which they cling to with equal obstinacy. They seek to find the essence of dreams in their latent content and in so doing they overlook the distinction between the latent dream-thoughts and the dream-work. At bottom, dreams are nothing other than a particular *form* of thinking, made possible by the conditions of the state of sleep. It is the *dream-work* which creates that form, and it alone is the essence of dreaming – the explanation of its peculiar nature" (Freud 1953: 506).

33 Freud's dream-work mechanisms are succinctly outlined in the 1917 *Introductory Lectures on Psychoanalysis.* See Freud (1963: 170–183).

which, like all miracles, serves as a *dream of redemption* without providing any actual transformation from the social conditions of unhappiness.
GORDON 2016

If fascism's "social miracle" was a "dream of redemption" – the illusion of
triumph over the antagonisms of modernity without providing an actual
transformation of its repressive social conditions – we might suggest that, for
Adorno, the culture industry represents a comparatively benign but equally
deluded "dream of remission" – the illusion that modern consumer society
has moved beyond fascism without transforming the same coercive mechanisms and treating the same socio-psychological ailments responsible for its
rise in the first place. The culture industry thus provides a collective escape
from the antagonisms of an administered, late capitalist society, only offering palliative panaceas for the ailments suffered by the de-subjectified individual in historical decline. It manufactures the highly profitable consumer
spectacle of modern "cultural" life, a phantasmagoria that ultimately serves
to distract the masses from the truth of their political impotence and social
subordination.

It is worth considering how Adorno's thought, forged in the cataclysm of
the first half of the twentieth century, resonates today. Had he lived longer he
would have seen the great transformation toward post-industrial, financialized
economies in the West. He would have grappled with neoliberalism's emancipation of capital, its spread of consumerism around the globe, and the further atomization and alienation it brought to Western societies (Harvey 2005).
Adorno would have also witnessed the coextensive development and expansion of mass media, with its requisite technologies, which has enabled the
culture industry to broaden its range of influence, becoming more intimately
enmeshed in modern daily life. His concept would have likely expanded given
these subsequent developments, but Adorno's model of the culture industry would remain strikingly current in the age of the soundbite, meme, and
tweet. Most distressingly, Adorno would also be disheartened to see the recent
rise of authoritarianism "within democracy," driven in no small part by social
media,[34] with the ascendency of right-wing populism in the United States and
across Europe.

Overall, Adorno's insights were incisive, perhaps even predictive. What his
prescient analyses indicate may have profound consequences for the possibility of opening up a space for the development of the truly autonomous

---

34 See Gounari (2018) and Fuchs (2018).

individual in the twenty-first century – or, as he rightly feared, the potential we might equally have for its extinction as we blindly slip into new types of barbarism.

References

Adorno, Theodor W. and Hellmut Becker. 1983. "Education for Autonomy." *Telos* 56: 103–110.

Adorno, Theodor W., Else Frenkel-Brunswik, Daniel J. Levinson and R. Nevitt Sanford. 2019. *The Authoritarian Personality,* intro. P.E. Gordon. New York: Verso.

Adorno, Theodor W. 1991. *The Stars Down to Earth, and Other Essays on the Irrational in Culture,* ed. Stephen Crook. New York: Routledge.

Adorno, Theodor W. 1998a. "Gloss on Personality." In *Critical Models: Interventions and Catchwords,* trans. H.W. Pickford, intro. L. Gohr, 161–165. New York: Columbia University Press.

Adorno, Theodor W. 1998b. "The Meaning of Working Through the Past." In *Critical Models: Interventions and Catchwords,* trans. H.W. Pickford, intro. L. Gohr, 89–103. New York: Columbia University Press.

Adorno, Theodor W. 2000. *The Psychological Technique of Martin Luther Thomas' Radio Addresses.* Stanford: Stanford University Press.

Adorno, Theodor W. 2001a. "Culture Industry Reconsidered." In *The Culture Industry: Selected Essays on Mass Culture,* ed. J.M. Bernstein, 98–106. London: Routledge.

Adorno, Theodor W. 2001b. "Free Time." In *The Culture Industry: Selected Essays on Mass Culture,* ed. J.M. Bernstein, 187–197. London: Routledge.

Adorno, Theodor W. 2001c. "Freudian Theory and the Pattern of Fascist Propaganda." In *The Culture Industry: Selected Essays on Mass Culture,* ed. J.M. Bernstein, 132–157. London: Routledge.

Adorno, Theodor W. 2002a. "On Popular Music." In *Essays on Music,* ed. R. Leppert, 437–469. Berkeley: University of California Press.

Adorno, Theodor W. 2002b. "What National Socialism Has Done to the Arts." In *Essays on Music,* ed. R. Leppert, 373–390. Berkeley: University of California Press.

Adorno, Theodor W. 2005a. *In Search of Wagner.* London: Verso.

Adorno, Theodor W. 2005b. *Minima Moralia: Reflections from Damaged Life.* New York: Verso.

Adorno, Theodor W. 2006. *History and Freedom: Lectures 1964–1965.* Cambridge: Polity Press.

Adorno, Theodor W. 2007. *Negative Dialectics,* trans. E.B. Ashton. New York: Continuum Press.

Adorno, Theodor W. 2020. *Aspects of the New Right-Wing Extremism,* aftwd. V. Weiss. Cambridge: Polity Press.

Christie, Richard and Marie Jahoda. 1954. *Studies in the Scope and Method of "The Authoritarian Personality."* Glencoe: Free Press.

Freud, Sigmund. 1953. *The Interpretation of Dreams.* In *The Standard Edition of the Complete Psychological Works of Sigmund Freud,* ed. J. Strachey, Vols. IV-V. London: Hogarth.

Freud, Sigmund. 1955. *Group Psychology and the Analysis of the Ego.* In *The Standard Edition of the Complete Psychological Works of Sigmund Freud,* ed. J. Strachey, Vol. XVIII, 67–143. London: Hogarth.

Freud, Sigmund. 1958. "Remembering, Repeating, and Working Through." In *The Standard Edition of the Complete Psychological Works of Sigmund Freud,* ed. J. Strachey, Vol. XVIII, 145–156. London: Hogarth.

Freud, Sigmund. 1963. *Introductory Lectures on Psychoanalysis.* In *The Standard Edition of the Complete Psychological Works of Sigmund Freud,* ed. J. Strachey, Vol. XV-XVI. London: Hogarth.

Fuchs, Christian. 2018. "Racism, Nationalism and Right-Wing Extremism Online: Austrian Presidential Election 2016 on Facebook." In *Critical Theory and Authoritarian Populism,* ed. J. Morelock, 157–206. London: University of Westminster Press.

Gordon, Peter E. 2016. "The Authoritarian Personality Revisited: Reading Adorno in the Age of Trump." In *Boundary* 2 (15, June 2016). At https://www.boundary2.org/2016/06/peter-gordon-the-authoritarian-personality-revisited-reading-adorno-in-the-age-of-trump/.

Gounari, Panayota. 2018. "Authoritarianism, Discourse and Social Media: Trump as the 'American Agitator'." In *Critical Theory and Authoritarian Populism,* ed. J. Morelock, 207–227. London: University of Westminster Press.

Harvey, David. 2005. *A Brief History of Neoliberalism.* Oxford: Oxford University Press.

Hegel, G.W.F. 1967. *Philosophy of Right,* trans. T.M. Knox. Oxford: Oxford University Press.

Hegel, G.W.F. 1977. *The Phenomenology of Spirit,* trans. A.V. Miller. Oxford: Oxford University Press.

Hesmondhalgh, David. 2012. *The Culture Industries.* Los Angeles: Sage Press.

Horkheimer, Max and Theodor W. Adorno. 2002. *Dialectic of Enlightenment: Philosophical Fragments.* Stanford: Stanford University Press.

Jameson, Fredric. 1990. *Late Marxism: Adorno and the Persistence of the Dialectic.* New York: Verso.

Jameson, Fredric. 1991. *Postmodernism: or, Cultural Logic of Late Capitalism.* Durham: Duke University Press.

Kant, Immanuel. 1987. *The Critique of Judgment,* trans. W.S. Pluhar. Indianapolis: Hackett Publishing.

Köhler, Joachim. 2000. *Wagner's Hitler: The Prophet and the Disciple.* Cambridge: Polity Press.

Lacan, Jaques. 1993. *The Seminar of Jaques Lacan, Book III: The psychoses (1955–1956),* ed. J.-A. Miller. New York: Norton.

Löwenthal, Leo and Norbert Guterman. 1949. *Prophets of Deceit: A Study of the Techniques of the American Agitator.* New York: Harper Brothers.

Löwenthal, Leo. 1987. *An Unmastered Past: The Autobiographical Reflections of Leo Löwenthal.* Berkeley: University of California Press.

Lukacs, Georg. 1971. *History and Class Consciousness: Studies in Marxist Dialectics.* Cambridge: MIT Press.

Marx, Karl. 1976. *Capital Volume I: A Critique of Political Economy.* London: Penguin.

Müller-Doohm, Stefan. 2005. *Adorno: A Biography.* Cambridge: Polity Press.

Parkinson, Anna. 2014. "Adorno on the Airwaves: Feeling Reason, Educating Emotions." In *Special Issue: West Germany's Cold War Radio: The Crucible of the Transatlantic Century, German Politics & Society* 32(1): 43–59. New York: Berghahn Books.

Pippin, Robert. 2020. "Capitalism at Dusk: Hegel and the Irrationality of Modern Economy." In *The Point* (15, April 2020). At https://thepointmag.com/politics/capitalism-at-dusk/.

Pollack, Freidrich. 1985. "State Capitalism: Its Possibilities and Limitations." In *The Essential Frankfurt School Reader*, eds. A. Arato and E. Gebhardt, 71–94. New York: Continuum Publishing.

Wiggershaus, Rolf. 1995. *The Frankfurt School: Its History, Theories, and Political Significance.* Cambridge: MIT Press.

CHAPTER 9

What Would Jesus Do?

Christianity as Wish Image and Historical Bloc

AK Thompson

An appropriate political initiative is always necessary ... to change the political direction of certain forces which have to be absorbed if a new, homogenous politico-economic historic bloc, without internal contradictions, is to be successfully formed ... Force can be employed against enemies, but not against a part of one's own side ... whose 'good will' and enthusiasm one needs.

ANTONIO GRAMSCI

As flowers turn toward the sun, by dint of a secret heliotropism the past strives to turn toward the sun which is rising in the sky of history. A historical materialist must be aware of this most inconspicuous of all transformations.

WALTER BENJAMIN

∴

For critical theorists, the moment of danger in which we now find ourselves has given rise to a troubling paradox. Indeed, even as scholars and activists have begun grappling with rightwing populism's role in reshaping the political field following the collapse of neoliberal hegemony, and even as efforts to devise a strategic orientation suitable to this terrain have yielded important insights (Mouffe 2018), there have thus far been few attempts to come to terms with the specific role that Christianity has played in consolidating this new populism at the level of its content, or of determining how Christianity itself provides opportunities for political realignment that may be of benefit to Left forces. Indeed, even as Christianity has shaped rightwing populism's cosmology and furnished a network of initiates ready to fulfill its profane, earthly tasks, the responses favored by the Left have tended to remain stuck at the level of smug repudiation (Hitchens 2008). Satisfying though it may be, this posture neglects to consider the strategic opportunities that arise from within Christianity itself.

In what follows, I offer a brief analysis of the relationship between Christianity and contemporary rightwing populism so that a more adequate response might be devised. Concretely, this means coming to terms with Christianity's role both as a central component of what Gramsci would have described as the historical bloc underwriting the Republican Party's current power *and* as an ambivalent Benjaminian wish image that stimulates desires that can't be resolved within the bounds of Christianity itself.

In Gramsci's analysis, historical blocs emerged through the struggle to consolidate leadership in social fields in which unity could not be presupposed. Correspondingly, struggles for revolutionary social transformation demanded both that the existing bloc be smashed and that a new one be constituted around a newly emergent core. According to Gramsci, fulfilling the latter task required that action be coordinated across a variegated field through the invocation of themes that might encourage people to proceed on the basis of a unity that, concretely speaking, had not yet come to pass. From the standpoint of constituted power, Christianity has served the function of consolidating today's historical bloc admirably well. It is my contention that insurgent forces might likewise take advantage of this possibility when working to devise a new bloc going forward. To understand why, it is necessary to consider how Christianity operates as a wish image.

For Benjamin, wish images arose when people became aware that their dreams of happiness might finally be fulfilled. Stimulated by transformations brought on by the development of material conditions, Benjamin proposed that people tended to recall the historically unresolved desires guiding their action while anticipating in wishful form the resolution of their lack. Because transformations in the present stimulate visions of future resolution by recalling the utopian longing embedded in the past, wish images are capable of provoking political action; however, because the means by which the future resolution is to be achieved are not made evident by the image itself, such visions remain politically ambivalent. The political legacy of Christianity attests to this, but it also makes clear why Left forces must orient to such images as a terrain of struggle.

For this reason, I will therefore conclude by outlining strategies for addressing Christianity's role in the consolidation of rightwing populism. These strategies highlight the possibility of fracturing the existing historical bloc and reconsolidating its elements around a new socialist core by *provisionally accepting* the desires that animated the initial wishful attachment. Moreover, they demonstrate how – through immanent critique, and at the level of its content – Christianity can be made to push toward Left conclusions. It is my contention that this maneuver might help us to "improve our position in the struggle against Fascism" (Benjamin 1968, 257) by providing a concrete resolution to potentially emancipatory desires that have hitherto remained trapped by the reactionary implications of the mythic resolutions to which they are currently cathected.

Methodologically speaking, this procedure requires that the important connection between Benjamin and Gramsci's projects be clarified. For while these figures are clearly bound at the level of biography (thus underscoring their importance for the moment in which we now find ourselves),[1] and while they are frequently paired in submissions to the literature in cultural studies or in the engagements with Western Marxism that proliferated following the publication of Perry Anderson's *Considerations* (1976), there have thus far been few efforts to reveal the extent to which Benjamin and Gramsci's intellectual and political projects are conceptually complementary and interlocking.

Nevertheless, when read in synthesis, these projects suggest a comprehensive political approach that clarifies the sometimes-enigmatic operational implications of Benjamin's thought while giving substance to Gramsci's more general comments regarding the animating power of myth (1971: 125–126). Whereas Gramsci's analysis of the historical bloc reveals the "how" (the means) of political alignment in fields shot through with contradictions, Benjamin's analysis of the wish image reveals the logic of the corresponding "why" (the end) that compels this "we" to gravitate toward such a resolution in the first place – or to shift its alignment should a more viable pathway to fulfillment present itself. Taken together, these elements are highly instructive for those seeking, not only to navigate, but also to constitute the political field in accordance with particular aims.

Before strategy must come analysis, however, and because the political thrust of this investigation must navigate the crossroads of critical theory and religion (and because it may be said that this spot is "bewitched," as Adorno

---

1   Although the roles they played in their respective contexts were different, both Gramsci and Benjamin confronted the challenge of building support for communism at a time when capitalism had attained a level of stability through liberal-democratic mass enfranchisement and the extension of consumer markets. For both thinkers, problems of consciousness came to the forefront as it became evident that the forms of materialist exposition upon which Marx had previously relied needed to be supplemented to address the new conditions (Benjamin 1968b: 217). This became especially true during the period of fascist ascent, in which what Benjamin called the "situation of politics which Fascism is rendering aesthetic" (1968b: 241) had prompted workers to enter into alliances that were – objectively speaking – contra their interests. Gramsci and Benjamin both died in the course of their struggle to address the fascist threat.

once proposed in a different but parallel context [2002]),[2] it is necessary at this point to clarify my orientation to the field. As is well known, Benjamin maintained that approaching history in a dialectically materialist fashion promised to reveal the degree to which *every moment* might become "the strait gate through which the Messiah might enter" (1968: 264). In this formulation, revolutionary transformations cannot be attributed to some abstract conception of progress. Instead, they arise from the fulfillment of opportunities that were always implicitly present but that needed to be *recognized* before they could be acted upon by the contemporaries of their "now" (261). Benjamin made the theological character of this reasoning explicit when he declared that his thinking was, in fact, "saturated" with it (2003: 471).

Although I feel a strong allegiance to this approach, I want here to highlight another tendency in Benjamin's work that suggests a distinct but complementary course. Concretely speaking, this involves subjecting the content of the theological tradition itself to analysis so that the struggle toward awakening in which it partakes can be brought into view. Rather than thinking about *politics* in theological terms, then, this approach invites us to perceive *theology itself* through the lens of politics by recognizing theology both as the content of "the political" and as a mode (or proto-mode) of political articulation in its own right. To be clear, the aim is not to reveal, as Carl Schmitt has already done, that every political category is itself derived from a prior religious one (2005). Instead, it is to recognize that, precisely by virtue of their correspondence, the theological always presses upon the political in much the same way that dreamers clamber toward awakening.[3]

One result of this correspondence is that both religious enthusiasm and the particular content of religious traditions have historically been susceptible to hegemonic capture and control by dominant political forces. Nevertheless, we should not imagine that this outcome exhausts their range, and it should not surprise us that religious convictions have often compelled subaltern groups to stage transformative confrontations with the status quo.[4] For this reason,

---

2 Adorno accused Benjamin of succumbing to Romanticism due to his "immediate" and "anthropological" approach to materialist reasoning, which deposited him "at the crossroads of magic and positivism." As far as Adorno was concerned, "that spot is bewitched" (2002: 129).

3 To provide but one example: in his analysis of "born again ideology," Arthur Kroker observed that the conception of the political that came to predominate during the reign of George W. Bush was not only a practical manifestation of the dispensational premillennialism to which Bush subscribed but also an effective remolding of modern statecraft in accordance with a new Protestant ethic (2007: 9).

4 Since I am speaking here of Christianity, many readers will feel prompted to recall the tradition of liberation theology and, prior to that, the legacy of Christian socialism or (still earlier)

it is wrong to presume that rightwing forces (whether culturally dominant or insurgent) are uniquely positioned to channel this energy, or that drawing on it to consolidate a new historical bloc is necessarily at odds with a materialist politics.

Christianity has played a powerful role in shaping American political culture. In order to wrest it from the Right, it is necessary to identify the fault lines within the historical bloc of which it is currently part. Combining Gramsci's insights with those advanced by Benjamin makes plain that these fault lines can be exacerbated by intensifying the desires (unresolved and unresolvable) bound up within Christianity itself. And as the current bloc fractures, the possibility arises for its fragments to be drawn together around a new socialist core. For this promise to be realized, however, it is necessary that the desires that prompted the initial attachment be genuinely understood so that they might be completed rather than invalidated or merely tolerated on opportunistic grounds.

∴

As a radical inspired by The Internationale (through which we learn that the wretched of the earth need "no condescending savior/no god, no Caesar, no tribune"), I will be the first to concede that my desire to rehabilitate Christianity by pushing it toward some point of profane reckoning may seem odd. I left the church at 18 following a misguided stint in a charismatic cult where feigned glossolalia gave proof to the presence of the Spirit in my life.[5] Unlike many of my compatriot weirdoes who were pushed out around the same time, however, I felt no strong urge to disparage my prior spiritual guides. Instead (and in keeping with an insight I would later glean from Frye's *Great Code* [2007]), I became

---

the antinomian tumult that gave a proto-communist cast to certain struggles during the English Civil War. But while the existence of such formations testifies to the affinity between Christianity and communism, my aim here is not to rehabilitate the Christian socialist tradition. Instead, it is to demonstrate how (at its logical conclusion) Christianity itself is fulfilled through communism, the profane form in which it finds sublation.

5   Much to my parents' dismay, I got caught up in the Charismatic Catholic Renewal. A Catholic apostolic movement launched in 1967, the Charismatics drew upon aspects of Pentecostalism (including glossalia, speaking in tongues) to foreground the importance of the gifts of the Holy Spirit within the catechism. In retrospect, I think what I liked most about the movement was that it seemed activist, congregant-led, and anti-clerical. Eventually, it became clear that I could not abide by its positions on abortion and queer sexualities; however, it was the accusation that I merely studied the Bible (as opposed to believing in it) that finally prompted me to leave.

fascinated by the persistence of Christian motifs in American culture. To be sure, these were often weaponized, and conservatives seemed to be running the show; however, a closer look revealed that the motifs themselves were ambivalent – and that they always threatened to spin off in unintended directions.

Occasionally, such ambivalence would become the subject of cultural productions themselves, as it did in Disney's scandalous 1996 adaptation of Victor Hugo's *Hunchback of Notre Dame,* or in Brian Dannelly's 2004 film *Saved!* In the latter case, Dannelly worked to save Christians from themselves by staging a confrontation between their deeds and the tenets of their faith. Despite its irreverent tone, Roger Ebert maintained that the film ultimately advanced a coherent religious vision of its own, arguing "not against fundamentalism but … intolerance." In this way, he thought, "mainstream Christian values" were not so much "overthrown, but demonstrated and embraced" (2004). Following from Ebert's observation (and in keeping with the legacy of critical theory), one might even say that Dannelly's exploration confirmed the idea that "the critical acceptance of the categories which rule social life contains simultaneously their condemnation" (Horkheimer 1995: 208).

But while I delighted in small breaches such as these, both my temperament and the legacy of misery to which the church remained bound seemed sometimes to beg for a more violent approach. Thus it was that I participated gleefully in disruptive kiss-ins at Catholic colleges where homophobic incidents had occurred, and I marveled when I learned about how ACT UP had once turned Saint Patrick's Cathedral upside down to confront Cardinal O'Connor and the church's hateful response to the AIDS crisis (Deparle 1989). Disruptions like these had been scandalous by design; however (even in their sacrilege), they seemed buoyed by the hunch that – somehow – they corresponded more perfectly with the Gospel truth than did the vain machinations of the church.

A little later, I learned about Daniel Berrigan and the spirit of resolve that led him and eight others to destroy, by one FBI agent's estimate, "at least 600 individual draft files" by setting them ablaze outside a Catonsville, Maryland army recruitment center (Berrigan 2004, xvii). Years later, Berrigan became a poet in residence at Fordham University, the school where I would teach sociology between 2014 and 2017. During my time on the Rose Hill campus, I helped to organize a union for adjunct faculty. As part of our campaign, we would invoke Berrigan's legacy, mobilize theological arguments to best opponents, and take every opportunity to point out the contradiction between the university's official commitment to Catholic social teaching and its chronically anti-labor stance.

After winning the union and leaving Fordham to assume my current role as a visiting professor of social movements and social change at Ithaca College,

I began adding Biblical texts to my syllabi. In my Social Change class, students would begin the semester by reading The Acts of the Apostles, where they encountered the insurrectionary temperament that defined Christianity at the moment of its inception. Through Luke's account of the apostles' struggle to spread the good news following the loss of their messiah, we would explore how a persecuted cult improved its chances by embracing collective living, engaging in confrontations with religious and political authorities (frequently leading to arrest, and to subsequent jailbreaks orchestrated by angels), planning extensive speaking tours, establishing networks of mutual aid, and (perhaps most important) encouraging those formerly deemed unclean to participate. That these commitments anticipate many of communism's defining features[6] is underscored by the fact that, in Acts, Luke informs us that "the faithful all lived together and owned everything in common; they sold their goods and possessions and shared out the proceeds among themselves according to what each one needed."[7]

Taken together, these experiences have led me to believe that radicals must devise an orientation to Christianity's significant social traction that goes beyond the repudiations to which many of us still cling.[8] Indeed, attending to Christianity's internal logic and its contradictory social implications is essential if we hope to reconstitute the political field by undermining the historical bloc now galvanized around the Republican Party.

∴

---

6   According to Karl Kautsky, early Christian communism had a coherent proletarian character. Nevertheless, it could be distinguished from what was to follow by the fact that – owing to the level of historical development characterizing the period in which it emerged – the apostles' interventions operated primarily at the level of consumption rather than at that of production (1972: 345–354).

7   Acts 2:44–45.

8   My first encounter with the Left's anti-religiosity came from punk music, where songs like "Religious Vomit" by the Dead Kennedys and "Faith Alone" by Bad Religion served as a contrarian rejoinder to Jerry Falwell's Moral Majority and the growing power of the Christian Right. This cultural stance was in keeping with the sensibility popularized by Auguste Blanqui a century earlier, when he insisted that proletarian struggle was autonomous and therefore required "ni dieu, ni maître." With the rise of anti-Muslim bigotry following the advent of the war on terror, radical Left responses to religion have become more strategic; however, these efforts have often struggled to clarify matters analytically. As a result, they have tended to succumb to opportunism or to reiterate liberal myths regarding the separation of private and public, church and state. For an example of current efforts to work through such impasses, see the Editorial to Upping the Anti No.20 (2019).

Despite official commitments to maintaining a separation between church and state, American politics (from their prehistory in colonial conquest, through the period of chattel slavery, and right up to our own era's insurgent fascism) remain bound inextricably to Christianity. The contours of this alliance as encountered today can be traced back to the refashioning of the American evangelical movement, which galvanized a multi-denominational force around shared opposition to abortion following *Roe v. Wade* in 1973 (Lewis 2017). Serving as a moral compass and a nurturing collective identity, this new evangelism welded Christians together by fostering a shared alignment on social issues with clear implications for electoral participation.

To get a sense of this bloc's enduring significance, it suffices to recall how, according to the Pew Research Center (2018), the percentage of "Protestants/Other Christians" (excluding Catholics) that cast ballots for Republican candidates during the 2018 midterm elections was 56%. When the sample is restricted to those who self-identified as "White Born-again/ Evangelical Christians" (a subset of "Protestants/Other Christians") however, this number rises to 75%. More partisan in their alignment, white evangelicals play a key role in getting the rest of the bloc to march in step with the Republican Party.

In 2018, the number of Catholics casting ballots for Republicans was just 49%. During the midterm elections of 2006, 2010, and 2014, however, Catholic voters alternated between slightly favoring either the Democratic or Republican candidate. Historically speaking, Catholic voter alignment with the Democratic Party can be attributed in part to Catholic social teaching and to the fact that Irish, Italian, and Latinx people's incorporation into whiteness was belated and, in some cases, remains uncertain. However, these factors have been insufficient to keep Catholics rooted in the Democratic camp, and abortion has served as a counterweight drawing them into the bloc galvanized by white evangelicals.

In terms of sheer numbers, "Protestant/Other Christians" made up 47% of all voters in the 2018 midterms, while "Catholics" and "White Evangelicals" each made up 26% of the total. Revisiting the findings of its *Religious Landscape Study* of 2014, the Pew Research Center reported in 2016 that 87% of respondents who identified as both Republican and evangelical were white. In contrast, among those evangelicals who identified as Democrats, 60% were nonwhite (Pew 2016). In addition to these deep racial and denominational divisions, a further schism within the Christian bloc can be detected by considering the generational split between the boomer evangelism of Jerry Falwell's era and the sensibilities of new formations like Hillsong, which have rebranded the tradition for a millennial demographic and (in the process) revised the manifest commitments of their theology.[9] Based on these findings, we might infer that, while a shared line on social issues has helped to galvanize this bloc and bind it to the Republican Party, its stability remains far from certain. Furthermore, by exacerbating the racial, generational, and denominational schisms that the bloc works to conceal, we might contribute to its destruction.

Given current demographic trends, some might wonder whether such a project is necessary. After all, the Democrats were able to win the House of Representatives in 2018 (though they lost ground in the Senate), and the number of adults in the United States who identify as Christian is shrinking, dropping from 78% in 2007 to just 65% in 2018 (Pew 2019). Based on this latter trend, journalist Nina Burleigh has proposed that, while white evangelicals have been key players in every election since 2000, the changing social landscape is "steadily diluting their outsize clout" (2018). Be this as it may, the problem of hegemony cannot be reduced to a numbers game. Indeed, the strength of the white evangelical bloc owes to more than its activist base and the missionary zeal with which it has clamored for power. Just as important has been its ability to devise resonant lines for coordinated action, and it is this skill that has allowed it to play a leading role.

In 2018, Jeff Sessions invoked St. Paul to justify Trump's policy of migrant detention and family separation (McMillan 2018). Although this policy seems antithetical to the Christian injunction to love one's neighbor,[10] the Attorney General's gloss on Romans 13 provided believers with a theological justification for the state's actions while underscoring the divine character of the state itself. Since Paul argued that earthly authorities could not exist unless sanctioned by God, it followed that anyone opposing the Trump regime was also logically in rebellion against heaven. In response, many commentators pointed out how inadequate Sessions' exegesis had been. But while the scriptural justification may have fizzled from a theological standpoint, what mattered most was the fact that Sessions had invoked biblical authority to justify a political position. In this way, he helped to preserve the historical bloc even as questions of interpretation remained unresolved.

Given the growing number of Americans who report "no religious affiliation" and align themselves with progressive positions on key political issues,

---

9   In its quintessentially neoliberal Vision Statement ("The Church I Now See," drafted by
     Brian Houston in 2014), Hillsong describes how it aims to be: "a church that loves God,
     loves people and loves life. Youthful in spirit; generous at heart; faith-filled in confession;
     loving in nature and inclusive in expression" (2014).
10   Mark 12:31.

it is clear that a new popular ideal is struggling to be born. Indeed, the fact that Trump was forced to declare during his 2019 State of the Union address that America "will never be a socialist country" reveals how far we've come. Still, this new sentiment is far from hegemonic, and even as the power of the historical bloc forged between Christians and Republicans begins to wane, we must suppress the urge to celebrate too soon or become mere spectators to the train wreck's ruin. As Gramsci observed, the disintegration of historical blocs tended to coincide with increased risks of authoritarianism (a tendency our own era confirms).[11] Such a threat clarifies the tasks that now fall to Left forces, and these include cracking apart the existing bloc so that we might reorganize the remnants of its base (not its leadership) by revealing how their desires might better be realized by other means.

To be sure, the ultimate aim of communism is to break people from superstition's allure by forcing a concrete reckoning with material reality and our place within it. Nevertheless, Marx maintained that the revolutionary transformation of consciousness needed to proceed, "not through dogmas, but by analyzing the mystical consciousness that is unintelligible to itself." Only then, Marx thought, would it "become evident that the world has long dreamed of possessing something of which it has only to be conscious in order to possess it in reality." If this is true, then revolutionaries must not be so preoccupied with prompting people to abandon their superstitions that we fail to demonstrate how – through profane and practical means – we might collectively go about *"realizing* the thoughts of the past" (cited in Benjamin 2003: 467). It is in relation to precisely this aim that the connection between Gramsci's analysis of the historical bloc and Benjamin's analysis of the wish image must be understood.

∵

In his *Prison Notebooks*, Gramsci took care to describe the means by which the political field was constituted. Advancing some initial, provisional ideas regarding the formation and character of historical blocs, he proposed that such blocs expressed themselves as a "unity of opposites and distincts" (1971: 137). By consolidating a historical bloc, dominant groups were able to

---

11   In his *Prison Notebooks*, Gramsci observed that, "as soon as the dominant social group has exhausted its function, the ideological bloc tends to crumble away: then 'spontaneity' may be replaced by 'constraint' in even less disguised and indirect forms, culminating in outright police measures and *coup d'états*" (1971: 60–61).

achieve the social cohesion that would underwrite their power. But while historical blocs produced unity across the social field, this unity remained more practical than actual. Consequently, for Gramsci, the role of the revolutionary was to reveal "the contradiction of the structure" and foreground "the objective conditions for the revolutionizing of praxis" (1971: 366). Seeking a concrete example through which to consider the means by which blocs were formed and might be taken apart, Gramsci turned naturally to the Catholic Church, which played a key role in consolidating political power in Italy. In his view, the church had achieved this aim historically by "preserving the ideological unity of the entire social bloc."

> The strength of religions, and of the Catholic church in particular, has lain, and still lies, in the fact that they feel very strongly the need for the doctrinal unity of the whole mass of the faithful and strive to ensure that the higher intellectual stratum does not get separated from the lower. The Roman Church has always been the most vigorous in the struggle to prevent the 'official' formation of two religions, one for the 'intellectuals' and the other for the 'simple souls.' (1971: 328)

In opposition to this approach, Gramsci proposed that communists needed to devise means for achieving unity that did not insist upon consensus but rather produced it through struggle. When approached in this way, the "complex, contradictory and discordant *ensemble* of the superstructures" (1971: 366) would become more apparent and thus more open to deliberate and practical intervention. Based on the distinction between these two postures, Gramsci concluded that "the position of the philosophy of praxis" could be nothing other than "the antithesis of the Catholic."

> The philosophy of praxis does not tend to leave the 'simple' in their primitive philosophy of common sense, but rather to lead them to a higher conception of life. If it affirms the need for contact between the intellectuals and [the] simple it is not in order to restrict scientific activity and preserve unity at the low level of the masses, but precisely in order to construct an intellectual-moral-political bloc which can make politically possible the intellectual progress of the mass and not only of small intellectual groups. (1971: 332–33)

How do these dynamics play out today? Considering the problem from the standpoint of constituted power, it's clear that the historical bloc binding Christians to Republicans has benefited from a preservation of doctrinal unity

at a relatively low level of development.[12] Indeed, through efforts to ensure
that the United States remains a "Christian nation," that abortion get outlawed, and that "family values" be restored, both Christians and Republicans
have ensured that the religion itself has become vulgarized, its mysteries
and paradoxes suppressed. For his part, Trump further stabilized the bloc
when, on January 24, 2020, he broke presidential norms and embraced the
Christians' primitive philosophy of common sense to speak at March for Life,
the anti-choice rally that convenes each year in Washington D.C. The effort
was well received, and rally participants returned the favor by chanting "four
more years" (Prasad 2020).

But while there has been broad agreement among evangelicals that, despite
his moral failings, the anti-abortion agenda justifies an ongoing alliance with
Trump, this position has not been unanimous. And as Christians are forced to
confront the implications of their Faustian bargain, opportunities for fracturing the bloc and reorienting its elements may arise. In the December 19, 2019
issue of the respected evangelical news magazine *Christianity Today*, editor
Mark Galli pulled no punches: "Trump Should Be Removed from Office," he
declared. Framing his arguments in terms of Christian morality, his reasoning
also underscored the problem of the historical bloc.

> Trump's evangelical supporters have pointed to his Supreme Court nom-
> inees, his defense of religious liberty, and his stewardship of the econ-
> omy, among other things, as achievements that justify their support of
> the president. We believe ... none of the president's positives can balance
> the moral and political danger we face under a leader of such grossly
> immoral character ... If we don't reverse course now, will anyone take
> anything we say about justice and righteousness with any seriousness for
> decades to come? Can we say with a straight face that abortion is a great
> evil that cannot be tolerated and, with the same straight face, say that the
> bent and broken character of our nation's leader doesn't really matter in
> the end? (2019)

---

12   On this point, it suffices to consider that, while Christians maintain that the Bible is
     somehow the word of God, a staggering number of believers admit to not having read
     their sacred text. For this reason, they only have a general understanding of its content
     and implications. From a theological standpoint, this situation is vexing and has even
     led the editors of the Christian magazine *Charisma* to proclaim that "Biblical Illiteracy is
     Killing Our Nation" (Stetzer 2014). Still, when considered from the standpoint of the his-
     torical bloc, this same illiteracy is central to the maintenance of those interpretive lines
     set out from above. In this respect, it seems that the original spirit guiding the Protestant
     Reformation may have lost its way.

Historically, radical forces have often gained ground by exposing their opponents' hypocrisy.[13] As Galli's editorial makes clear, however, factions within Christianity are themselves now concerned with resolving the hypocrisy inherent in their political alignment. To do so, they are returning to the tenets of their faith, which (though subordinated to conservative interpretations promulgated by church leaders) remain ambivalent at the level of their content. By paying attention to these moments of wavering, radicals have an opportunity to exacerbate the division between Christians and Republicans – and even to dissolve denominational alliances and break congregants from clerics so that they might be drawn into a new historical bloc.

If this is to be achieved, however, it will happen not by pointing out the obvious hypocrisy of current Christian alignments but rather by accepting the Christian desire for atonement at face value. By combining Gramsci's analysis of the historical bloc with Benjamin's insights into the role played by wish fulfillment in the struggle for freedom, it becomes evident that strategies based on the invalidation of existent forms are likely to be both insufficient and counterproductive. To break the impasse, we must provide a point around which the loosened fragments of the existent bloc might coalesce. When approached as a wish image, the motivation for this coalescence can be drawn out of Christianity itself.

∴

In the notes he collected for his project on the Paris arcades, Benjamin began to elaborate a materialist conception of Freud's observation that dreams constituted a form of wish fulfillment. For Freud, dreams provided a means for people to satisfy desires that could not be addressed (could often not even be acknowledged) in waking life (1921). Benjamin advanced this insight when he observed that material culture could itself be read as a manifestation of the dream work carried out historically within the unconscious of the collective. And while this dream work could alert the social analyst to the various forms by which the desire for absolution driving human development found expression across generations, it also revealed the extent to

---

13   According to James M. Jasper, the "citizenship movements" that arose during the nineteenth and twentieth century succeeded by pointing to the discrepancy between the formal claims made by nation states and the actual realities those states maintained. Since the founding documents claimed, "all men are created equal," for instance, movements could struggle for inclusion into the ostensibly universal category so that the rights and privileges associated with belonging might be enjoyed. (Jasper 1997).

which people strove toward awakening through practical activity in their daily lives.[14]

Benjamin's strategy for identifying and analyzing what, in "Paris, Capital of the Nineteenth Century," he called "wish-fulfilling images" (1978: 148) is invaluable to the study of material culture. And Benjamin was especially interested in the frequent correspondences he detected between commodities and ancient myths (2003). However, it is clear that his approach can be applied equally well to the direct analysis of *myths themselves*. By analyzing myths as modes of recollection that work simultaneously as forms of anticipation, one can detect the profane demands around which they circle – demands that remain unconscious right up until the moment when the practical means by which they might be resolved come into view on the historical stage. Applying Benjamin's approach to our current problem, it becomes possible to detect both the wish underlying people's identification with Christianity and the wishful content of the theological tradition itself. Here, historical variations in the manifest forms through which the wish finds expression correspond to the degree to which the latent desires underlying that wish have come into consciousness and (in the process) become profaned and political. Let us consider three distinct but interconnected levels at which this process plays out.

At the first level, the wish remains unconscious and the dreamer remains unaware of the connection between the dream's manifest content and the profane political demands it anticipates. To analyze this phase, one could do no better than to consider The Bible itself, and to approach it as an artifact of the collective dream work. At the second level, the wish congeals into concrete but still-mythical representations through people's intuited recognition of the correspondence between the desires underlying the dream and the profane demands of earthly politics. Here, evidence can be found in the conventions governing depictions of the divinity in art history. At the final level, both the content and the animating power of the wish are marshaled directly by political campaigns hoping to see them realized in concrete, profane terms.

---

14   Benjamin noted that the connection between these two registers (i.e. the intergenerational or phylogenetic and the biographical or ontogenetic) was especially clear in childhood. By his account, "every childhood achieves something great and irreplaceable for humanity. By the interest it takes in technological phenomena, by the curiosity it displays before any sort of invention or machinery, every childhood binds the accomplishments of technology to the old worlds of symbol. There is nothing in the realm of nature that from the outset would be exempt from such a bond. Only, it takes form not in the aura of novelty but in the aura of the habitual" (2003: 461). For Benjamin, the work of the analyst was to identify these correspondences and decipher their social significance from the standpoint of the struggle for actualization.

Considering the first level, and the narrative arc running from Genesis to Revelation, one immediately detects three key moments or stages in the biblical *telos*, which points ultimately toward absolution.[15] In the first, humans coexist with God in a state of innocence marked by an absence of alienation (when God brings the animals before the man, for instance, it is presumed that there should be a direct correspondence between what the latter names them and what they *are*).[16] However, this state is broken by the advent of knowledge. When Adam and Eve partake of the forbidden fruit, they develop consciousness and alienation ensues. Corresponding to this development is the direct confrontation with the world of labor, where Adam is thrown into agriculture and Eve is burdened with the pains of childbirth.[17] With the introduction of consciousness, alienation, and the subsequent expulsion from the garden, the first moment comes to an end.

Throughout the second stage of the biblical *telos*, God's people struggle to find their way back to the lost union. This struggle intensifies with Christ's appearance in The New Testament, where a novel strategy for resolving the conflict is introduced. The power of the divine mystery, in which Christ is cast as both man and God simultaneously,[18] arises from its promise to resolve alienation by providing a model of absolution. The problem of alienation persists, however, because logically speaking not everyone can be the Christ. And while believers are encouraged to find their way to God *through* Christ,[19] reliance upon a mediating figure ensures that the experience of alienation will persist.

The Book of Revelation marks the final stage in the elaboration of the biblical *telos*. In its pages, one detects how John's bewildering vision of the New Jerusalem collapses the interval between God and humanity so that they might once again exist on the same plane.[20] With the old earth and old heaven transcended, God and people are reunited, and the latter become "a son to

---

15   Teleological thinking maintains that the purpose or outcome of a given object or process is predetermined and that it can be discovered within the object or process itself. Marxists have often disputed this approach by highlighting its tendency to naturalize outcomes that are in fact consequences of purposive, volitional action carried out by humans operating under definite conditions. Nevertheless, Trotsky defended a certain conception of teleology by connecting it to Marx's discussion of the human labor process. By Trotsky's reckoning, politics itself was nothing so much as "embodied teleology" (2005: 98). Similarly, Benjamin maintained that "each epoch ... bears its end in itself and unfolds it – as Hegel already saw – with ruse" (1978: 162).

16   Genesis 2:19–20.

17   Genesis 3:16–19.

18   Corinthians 8:6.

19   John 14:6.

20   Revelation 21.

me" (thus assuming the role previously reserved for the Christ). In this way, Revelation foretells a return to the state of graceful absolution, which had been lost upon expulsion from Eden ("It is already done,' declares God, indicating that he is "the Alpha and the Omega, the Beginning and the End"); however, it's important to note that the situations are not identical. First and foremost, John's vision stages the reunification not in the garden but the city. Moreover, the inhabitants of this city, by virtue of their proximity to the absolute, have not lost consciousness of the preceding phase of estrangement. Alienation is overcome, not through a return to some prior innocence, but though absolute identification with God's power that leads to the collapse of former distinctions, on the one hand, and a polarized confrontation with the cowardly on the other.

Stripped of divine conceits so that its underlying logic might be laid bare, this *telos* suggests that Christianity may best be read as a premonition, a wishful anticipation of the scientific knowledge that would later be recounted by Marxists, and especially by Friedrich Engels in his *Origin of the Family, Private Property and the State* (1948).[21] Here, Genesis corresponds to the moment of primitive communism while Revelation anticipates communism proper (a phase that must still be recounted, both in The Bible and in daily life, in the mode of wishful anticipation). The intervening phase of struggle and alienation corresponds to our present, and there is little wonder that, as a stand-in for the promise of absolution, the image of Christ should be so compelling – or that Christians (who have committed themselves to *following*, and thus not to *being*, the Christ) should struggle so mightily with their faith. The impasse can be resolved; however, such a resolution would require that the theological material be approached, not from the standpoint of its manifest content, but rather from that of the latent desires to which it gives expression.

Considering the Christian wish image now from the standpoint of its second level of elaboration, in which people intuit the correspondence between religious themes and profane political forms, it becomes evident that the

---

21   When associations of this kind are made between Marxism and Christianity, it is often to disparage the former by casting it as a warmed-over version of the latter. The implication of this reasoning is that, by smuggling religion in through the back door (perhaps under the cover of Hegel's coat tails), Marxism fails on its own terms. The argument advanced here proposes the opposite: if there is a connection between Marxism and Christianity, it arises from the fact that the latter *anticipated* the former in dream form at a time when it was not yet possible to trace the course of human history scientifically. Provocative though it may seem, this thesis accords in every respect with Durkheim's canonical argument that humanity's knowledge of society first develops through its religious pursuits (1995).

FIGURE 9.1   Anonymous, *God the Father on his Throne*, late 15th c
             SOURCE: OIL AND GOLD ON OAK PANEL, 59,5 X 47 CM. WIKIMEDIA
             COMMONS, PUBLIC DOMAIN

myth's concrete manifestations have changed over time and that these changes
derive from (and thus can be indexed to) the historical developments to which
they correspond. Throughout the medieval era and into the Renaissance, for
instance, it seemed self-evident that God was a king. Consequently, representations guided by this perceived correspondence flourished (see Figure 9.1).

However, with the rise of the bourgeoisie at the end of the eighteenth century, mystics like William Blake would either consciously or unconsciously recall an idea set out in Proverbs (8:27) to begin reimagining God as an engineer or technician. This intuition would find concrete expression in Blake's *Ancient of Days* (see Figure 9.2), the canonical image he would produce for *Europe a Prophecy* in 1794 and would continue reproducing in various forms for the rest of his life. In this image, God (the "ancient of days" recounted in the Bible) and the figure of Urizen (who, in Blake's cosmology, served as a stand-in for the bourgeoisie's calculative rationality) become confused. Blake frequently depicted Urizen with a compass, which spoke to the latter's tendency both to create and to measure. According to Blake, such measuring ran the risk of destroying the life that circulated between discrete units prior to their calculative bisection. For this reason (and as was true for the Romantics more generally), he maintained that the bourgeois division between science and art needed to be resolved, and that their discrete contributions be synthesized. "Expel from among you those who pretend to despise the labours of Art & Science, which alone are the labours of the Gospel," he enjoined. "Is not this plain & manifest to the thought? ... That to labour in Knowledge is to Build up Jerusalem..." (1988: 232).

With the flourishing of vibrant socialist movements at the beginning of the twentieth century, however, Romanticism's critique of the calculative tendency in bourgeois reason was overtaken by visual representations that transposed the conflict, thus moving it from the epistemological realm to the field of profane political struggle. It is within this context that we can understand the work of José Clemente Orozsco, whose transfiguration of Christ gave him a directly proletarian form (see Figure 9.3). In Orozsco's depiction, which he worked out in three separate iterations over the course of his life, Christ manages through labor not only to free himself from persecution but also to disrupt the very eschatology that demands it.[22] In this way, Orozsco saved the mystical theme of redemption by providing it with a concrete, profane resolution.

---

22   "Eschatology" refers to the theological concern with resolution, which in Christianity –
      and especially among white evangelicals – is sometimes formulated in reference to the
      "End Times." It is important to note, however, that Christianity's eschatological concerns
      are both explicit in the Bible (hence John's vision in Revelation) and in the historical for-
      mation of the Church. The Nicene Creed, for instance, which outlines the articles of faith
      for believers, establishes a pattern of logical consequences that demands that the Christ
      play his sacrificial role so that "life in the world to come" might subsequently be assured. It
      is significant that, in Orozsco's depiction, Christ's destruction of the cross coincides with
      the immolation of sacred texts, thus suggesting that the story the church has been telling
      itself must be abandoned so that its aim might finally be realized.

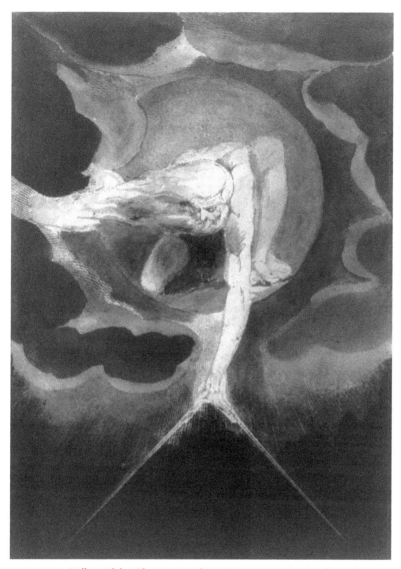

FIGURE 9.2   William Blake, 'The Ancient of Days Setting a Compass to the Earth,' 1794
SOURCE: FRONTISPIECE OF *EUROPE A PROPHECY*, METAL RELIEF ETCHING,
23.4 X 16.9 CM. LIBRARY OF CONGRESS, ROSENWALD COLLECTION, WWW.
LOC.GOV/ITEM/2005689083/

FIGURE 9.3   José Clemente Orozco, *Christ Destroying His Cross*, 1943
SOURCE: © 2020 ARTISTS RIGHTS SOCIETY (ARS), NEW YORK/SOMAAP,
MEXICO CITY

Considering these three images as a set, it becomes evident that, while each advances a different conception of the divine, they are all indexed to the political realities and aspirations that marked their emergence. When read in sequence, they suggest a growing awareness of the correspondence between the wish for absolution and the profane earthly sovereignty through which it would finally be fulfilled. For those who first envisioned them, medieval depictions that cast God as king posed no problem. By the time of Blake, however, struggles regarding God's nature had become impossible to ignore, and these struggles coincided not solely with the bourgeois usurpation of the feudal regime and its divine right of kings but also with the challenges arising from the split between positivism and metaphysics, science and art, within bourgeois conscious. Finally, with Orozsco, the problem is articulated consciously, and the tenets of Christianity themselves become the basis for its material sublation.

Considering the third level of wishful elaboration, in which political actors directly invoke the messiah to embolden their movements, it becomes clear that Christianity has furnished an impressive catalogue of resonant images. Significantly, Left forces have seemed more adept at citing this material than have movements on the Right. For even as images of Christ abound on the

Right, and even as initiates are enjoined to follow Christ's lead ("What Would Jesus Do?"), they remain unwilling to presuppose that, through the process, they will somehow become Christ, since commitment to Christianity's manifest content demands the maintenance of a formal distinction between messiah and believer so that the latter might find their way to God through the sacrifice of the former.

In contrast, the Left has demonstrated a willingness to cast people in struggle as the literal embodiment of Christ, thus demonstrating how the wish guiding Christian myth might finally, concretely, be fulfilled. And here we might recall *Guerrillero Heroico*, Alberto Korda's classic Christological photo of Che Guevara shot in 1960, or the montage of "Jesus Christ in Georgia," which the NAACP published along with an article by W.E.B. Du Bois in the December 1911 edition of *The Crisis* (Wood 2009: 188). Through the visual simile between Christ and Che established in Korda's image (a simile rendered visually through a kind of implied montage of superimposition), revolutionary commitment becomes the explicit means by which the promise of Christianity might be realized. In the NAACP image, lynching is brought into correspondence with the crucifixion. When pushed to its logical conclusion, this association makes plain that Black people themselves – through their organizing – become the literal embodiment of Christ.

At whatever level they find expression, examples such as these suggest that Christianity has been part of an active historical process of working through. The tendency toward concrete profanation expressed in successive iterations of the process, however, suggests that the search for absolution cannot be resolved within the bounds of Christianity itself. In order to resolve this impasse, the animating desire drawing people to Christianity must be affirmed even as the inadequacy of the posited object resolution is laid bare. Christianity's will to absolution anticipates the revolutionary process, which, for Benjamin, made the past "citable in all its moments" (1968: 254). However, this process must transcend its current wishful articulation if it is to be realized. If Gramsci's analysis of the historical bloc provides the conceptual tools required to break apart the Republican Party's current base, Benjamin's observations regarding wish images suggest a means of uniting that base's loosened fragments around a new socialist core.

.·.

How is this to be achieved, practically? Following Gramsci and Benjamin, a number of principles suggest themselves. First, and from a negative perspective, it's necessary to maximize the discord within the existing historical bloc by exacerbating the tensions that arise from the fact that its unity is more practical than actual. Second, it is necessary for Left forces to affirm the desires for salvation that draw people to Christianity while demonstrating that the content of the religious tradition is at odds with its current object resolution. On this basis, the connection between Christianity's latent content and revolution's profane objectives can be made clear. Finally, the animating desire might be parsed from its object resolution. At its threshold, this process makes it possible to demonstrate that believers don't want "Christianity" per se so much as they want absolution – and that this desire can only be realized concretely.

The point here is not to win over the Christian leadership or the hardened bigots that swell the ranks of the church. Instead, and through a provisional identification with Christianity's animating desire, it is to reveal that the posited object resolutions provided to believers are inadequate when measured against the longing that compels them to follow Christ in the first place. Recognizing both the legitimacy and the implicitly revolutionary force of those desires becomes the basis for new bonds to be forged. For radicals, this work can be carried out by pairing religious invocations with calls enjoining Christians to participate in the fulfillment of the profane earthly tasks to which they correspond. In this way, it shall become clear that – despite our irreligious temperament – Marxists are in fact better Christians than are the pastors who struggle to maintain the existing historical bloc.

References

Adorno, Theodor. 2002. "Letters to Walter Benjamin," *Aesthetics and Politics*. London: Verso.

Anderson, Perry. 1976. *Considerations on Western Marxism*. London: New Left Books.

Benjamin, Walter. 1978, "Paris, Capital of the Nineteenth Century," *Reflections*. New York: Schocken.

Benjamin, Walter. 2003. *The Arcades Project*. Cambridge: Belknap Harvard.

Benjamin, Walter. 1968. "Theses on the Philosophy of History," *Illuminations*. New York: Schocken.

Benjamin, Walter. 1968b. "The Work of Art in the Age of Mechanical Reproduction," *Illuminations*. New York: Schocken.

Berrigan, Daniel. 2004. *The Trial of the Catonsville Nine*. New York: Fordham University Press.

Blake, William. 1988. "Jerusalem: The Emanation of the Giant Albion," *The Complete Poetry and Prose of William Blake*. New York: Anchor Books.

Burleigh, Nina. 2018. "Evangelical Christians Helped Elect Donald Trump, but Their Time as a Major Political Force Is Coming to an End," *Newsweek*, December 13, 2018. At https://www.newsweek.com/2018/12/21/evangelicals-republicans-trump-millenials-1255745.html.

Deparle, Jason. 1989. "111 Held in St. Patrick's AIDS Protest," *New York Times*, Dec. 11, 1989. At https://www.nytimes.com/1989/12/11/nyregion/111-held-in-st-patrick-s-aids-protest.html.

Durkheim, Emile. 1995. *The Elementary Forms of Religious Life*. New York: The Free Press.

Ebert, Roger. 2004. "Reviews: Saved," *Rogerebert.com*, March 28, 2004. At https://www.rogerebert.com/reviews/saved-2004.

Engels, Friedrich. 1948. *The Origin of the Family, Private Property and the State*. Moscow: Progress Press.

Freud, Sigmund. 1921. *The Interpretation of Dreams*. London: George Allen and Unwin.

Frye, Northrop. 2007. *The Great Code: The Bible and Literature*. New York: Penguin.

Galli, Mark. 2019. "Trump Should Be Removed from Office," *Christianity Today* December 19, 2019. At https://www.christianitytoday.com/ct/2019/december-web-only/trump-should-be-removed-from-office.html.

Gramsci, Antonio. 1971. *Selections from the Prison Notebooks*. New York: International Publishers.

Hitchens, Christopher. 2008. *God Is Not Great: How Religion Poisons Everything*. Toronto: McLelland & Stewart.

Horkheimer, Max. 1995. "Traditional and Critical Theory." *Critical Theory: Selected Essays*. New York: Continuum.

Houston, Brian. 2014. "The Church I Now See," Hillsong. At https://hillsong.com/vision/.

Jasper, James. 1997. *The Art of Moral Protest: Culture, Biography, and Creativity in Social Movements*. Chicago: University of Chicago Press.

Kautsky, Karl. 1972. *Foundations of Christianity*. New York: Monthly Review Press.

Khan, Sharmeen et al., eds. 2019. "You Gotta Have Faith: Resolving the Unholy Alliance Between the Left and Religion," *Upping the Anti: A Journal of Theory and Action* 20. At https://uppingtheanti.org/journal/article/20-you-gotta-have-faith.

Kroker, Arthur. 2007. *Born Again Ideology: Religion, Technology, and Terrorism*. Victoria, BC: CTheory Books.

Lewis, Andrew. 2017. *The Rights Turn in Conservative Christian Politics: How Abortion Transformed the Culture Wars*. Cambridge: Cambridge University Press.

Luke. 1968. "Acts of the Apostles," *The Jerusalem Bible*. Garden City: NY, Doubleday.

McMillan, Keith. 2018. "Sessions cites Bible passage used to defend slavery in defense of separating immigrant families," *The Washington Post*, June 14, 2018. At https://www.washingtonpost.com/news/acts-of-faith/wp/2018/06/14/jeff-sessions-points-to-the-bible-in-defense-of-separating-immigrant-families/?arc404=true.

Mouffe, Chantal. 2018. *For A Left Populism*. New York: Verso.

Pew Research Center. 2018. "How Religious Groups Voted in the Midterm Elections," November 7, 2018. At https://www.pewresearch.org/fact-tank/2018/11/07/how-religious-groups-voted-in-the-midterm-elections/.

Pew Research Center. 2016. "Exit Polls and the Evangelical Vote: A Closer Look," March 14, 2016. At https://www.pewresearch.org/fact-tank/2016/03/14/exit-polls-and-the-evangelical-vote-a-closer-look/.

Pew Research Center. 2019. "In U.S., Decline of Christianity Continues at Rapid Pace," October 17, 2019. At https://www.pewforum.org/2019/10/17/in-u-s-decline-of-christianity-continues-at-rapid-pace/.

Prasad, Ritu. 2020. "Trump first president to attend anti-abortion rally," BBC News, Washington, D.C., January 24, 2020. At https://www.bbc.com/news/world-us-canada-51239795.

Schmitt, Carl, 2005, *Political Theology*. Chicago: Chicago University Press.

Stetzer, Ed. 2014. "Dumb and Dumber: How Biblical Illiteracy is Killing Our Nation," *Charisma*. At https://www.charismamag.com/life/culture/21076-dumb-and-dumber-how-biblical-illiteracy-is-killing-our-nation.

Trotsky, Leon. 2005. *Literature and Revolution*. Chicago: Haymarket Books.

Wood, Amy Louise. 2009. *Lynching and Spectacle: Witnessing Racial Violence in America, 1890–1940*. Chapel Hill: University of North Carolina Press.

PART 3

Human Subjects

∴

Mobilization of Bias Today: The Renewed Use of Established Techniques; A Reconsideration of Two Studies on Prejudice from the Institute for Social Research

Peter-Erwin Jansen

> Precisely the negative was the positive; this consciousness of non-partic-
> ipation; of refusal, the remorseless analysis of the status quo, this is really
> the core of critical theory.[1]
>
> LÖWENTHAL 1980

∴

In this essay,[2] I would like to turn our attention back to what was for its time (1944 to 1950) a pathbreaking research undertaking and five-volume series of publications: Studies in Prejudice.[3] The working group that coauthored these reports was organized by the American Jewish Committee (AJC) and located in California. Within it were scholars associated with the Institute for Social Research (Institute) or "Frankfurt School" that had been shut down by the Nazis in 1934, its members forced into exile.

In the first volume of this series, *The Authoritarian Personality*, Theodor W. Adorno (1950a) was primarily responsible for setting down the methodological and analytical guidelines. Max Horkheimer cowrote the foreword (with

---

1 See also Leo Löwenthal, *An Unmastered Past: The Autobiographical Reflections of Leo Löwenthal*, ed. Martin Jay (Berkeley: University of California Press, 1987, 62) for the following remark by Löwenthal: "I recall having heard in intellectual and personal conversations the reproach that one could not always be critical, that sometimes one should also be constructive. We were always scandalous troublemakers. You are familiar with the famous reproach to Eric Kästner: Herr Kästner, and what about the positive aspects?' Well, it is exactly the negative that was the positive: this consciousness of not going along, the refusal. The essence of Critical Theory is really the inexorable analysis of what is."
2 Previously published in *Radical Philosophy Review*, Volume 16, Issue 1, pages 169–186, 2013.
3 All five volumes of the Studies in Prejudice series are now available through the online archives of the American Jewish Committee. In addition, the archives also feature articles, press releases, correspondence, and other documents related to the series. http://www.ajcarchives.org/main.php?GroupingId=1380.

Samuel H. Flowerman, research director of the AJC) that outlined the basic research questions: Is there a mental disposition with definable attributes that predisposes people to react positively to an unscrupulous demagogue? May this condition also be the source of hostile attitudes, even violent behavior, against racial minorities? The series' fifth volume, *Prophets of Deceit*, written by Leo Löwenthal and Norbert Guterman (1949), emphasized that the demagogue must be understood concretely in the social context of contradictory economic and political conditions, as Herbert Marcuse (1970) stressed is his Foreword – added to the paperback, second edition of this volume.

In Germany, an incomplete translation of the entire series appeared first in a pirated edition published in Amsterdam in 1968. This was how I came across the "Foreword to Studies in Prejudice" by Horkheimer and Flowerman in which they asked:

> How could it be ... that in a culture of law, order, and reason, there should have survived the irrational remnants of ancient racial and religious hatreds? How could they explain the willingness of great masses of people to tolerate the mass extermination of their fellow citizens? What tissues in the life of our modern society remain cancerous, and despite our assumed enlightenment show the incongruous atavism of ancient peoples? And what within the individual organism responds to certain stimuli in our culture with attitudes and acts of destructive aggression?
>
> HORKHEIMER and FLOWERMAN 1950: V

Before, during, and shortly after World War II, numerous scholars, especially within the orbit of the American Jewish Committee, were absolutely astonished and exasperated to see that millions of American citizens, men and women, were *not at all disinclined* toward the National Socialist and fascist leaders in Europe (like Hitler and Mussolini). This was especially true for the decades between 1920 and 1940, which is to say the period before the outbreak of the war and before the systematically introduced deportation and killing of Jews in death/concentration camps.

Antisemitic propaganda, which could be identified very early on as an ideological partner to National Socialist politics, resonated in no small way even in the United States. The group that made the most powerful exertions to spread these ideas in the United States was the activist wing of the white supremacists, the Ku Klux Klan. The Nazis' "Aryan and antisemitic" propaganda served the white supremacist pathology perfectly. Many small, local groups were formed during this time in midsize cities, with new, local figures as leaders. Several of these figures turned up at informational gatherings about conditions in

Europe prior to the war where they distributed the antisemitic pamphlet, *The Protocols of the Elders of Zion*. This had been first published in 1903 by the white guards in Russia against the Bolsheviks, and, in German translation in 1920, it was widely distributed among the National Socialists. Klansmen and Nazi sympathizers in the United States warned about the ostensible dangers of a "worldwide Jewish conspiracy," which they saw as a threat to the United States as well as to Europe. Their spokesmen distributed commentaries sympathetic to Nazi politics via American newspapers and the radio. As Löwenthal and Guterman (1949: xv) emphasized in their preface to *Prophets of Deceit*, "Most of these openly expressed admiration for Hitler and Mussolini, were rabidly antisemitic, and indulged in intensive vituperation of our national leaders."

Americans quickly realized that they were confronted, not merely with the members of extremist groups, but with a large segment of so-called average citizens, who were, if not openly sympathetic, then possessed at least of an astonishing degree of indifference toward views that clearly violated human rights. Given this social context, antisemitism's "twin brother" – racism against African Americans – also intensified. So-called average Americans had a political mentality capable of significant sway, and, in certain crisis situations, they did not hesitate to adopt antidemocratic stances. In times of social duress, this mentality tended to follow leaders who focused attention clearly and simply on the presumed guilt of those who were said to have caused the crisis (i.e., a scapegoat), especially when promises were to be made about remedying the situation. Antisemitic propaganda has served, and still serves, as a key element of political scapegoating.

Antisemitic prejudice emanating from Europe thus acquired a new voice in the United States. The democratic tradition in the United States viewed itself as in competition with a hierarchically organized dictatorship of the sort that had been established in Germany. Reliance upon democratic politics began to fluctuate, and a demand for strong leaders intensified, as did the willingness to obey authority. This was a palpable change, even if not exhibited widely.

Some scholars became disturbed enough about these developments, however, that they began to wonder just how these dangerous changes had come about: whether there might be a particular sort of mentality that wanted to be led in an authoritarian fashion, whether an architecture of prejudice played a role, and how the nature of relationships between leaders and followers, the rulers and the ruled, may have contributed? How might a dictator or demagogue utilize propaganda, among those who were willing to obey blindly, to build what could possibly become a reliable following of violent extremists?

Given the experiences of the Nazi years, and the lack of social science study of prejudice as a phenomenon, the American Jewish Committee convened a

conference in May 1944 to focus on discrimination against minorities. Max
Horkheimer was one of the participants. The major upshot of the conference
was the formation of a group of social science researchers who undertook
an investigation of the questions raised above. This group was composed of
scholars from the University of California at Berkeley (UC Berkeley), Stanford
University, and the Institute for Social Research. By 1940, Horkheimer and
Adorno had already relocated from New York City to Los Angeles. There, as a
team, they had begun their research and writing on "Elements of Antisemitism,"
which became the concluding section of their highly regarded 1944 book,
Dialectic of Enlightenment. As they saw it:

> For some people today antisemitism involves the destiny of mankind; for
> others it is a mere pretext. The Fascists do not view the Jews as a minority
> but as an opposing race, the embodiment of the negative principle. They
> must be exterminated to secure happiness for the world. … The Jews
> today are the group which calls down upon itself, both in theory and in
> practice, the will to destroy born of a false social order.
>
> HORKHEIMER and ADORNO 1972 [1944]: 168

It is certainly not difficult to see the similarity here to the research goals of the
Studies in Prejudice series, which investigated the intricately interconnected
phenomena of societal distress, antisemitic prejudice, and techniques of propaganda. Löwenthal was also involved in formulating the chapter in *Dialectic
of Enlightenment* on antisemitism. He had written several short papers on
antisemitism that he discussed with Horkheimer and Adorno during his stay
on the West Coast. In one of these drafts, which also served as a foundation for
the antisemitism sections of the Studies in Prejudice series, Löwenthal made
a very interesting distinction: he differentiated between *nontotalitarian* and
totalitarian antisemitism. In the former, the Jew is considered an *enemy*. In the
latter, the Jew is considered a *victim*. "Traditional antisemitism treated the Jew
as a human being, albeit a hated human being" (Löwenthal 2000 [1930]: 98).
Modern (totalitarian) antisemitism is "streamlined"; however, "the Jew is
reduced to a passive object that can be manipulated for any purpose the particular political situation might require. This transformation of the Jew from
an enemy into a completely powerless victim" (98) eliminates the *mind* of the
Jew and regards him or her only as a material thing, a *body – with a number*.
With all the grisly details of the Nazis' apparatus of genocide before his eyes
and the eyes of the world, Löwenthal also wrote "Terror's Atomization of Man"
(Löwenthal 1946). The terror unleashed by National Socialism clearly demonstrated that human beings were reduced to passive objects. Human beings

were treated as items to be used and used-up. From his interviews with death camp survivors undertaken while serving in the US Office of War Information, Löwenthal knew how concrete individuals were degraded to anonymous numbers. These were then categorized as "useful" or "useless" and both entered into the annihilation apparatus never to be seen again.

Max Horkheimer had become acquainted with Nevitt Sanford, a professor of psychology at UC Berkeley, while working on "Elements of Antisemitism." He had visited him at Berkeley in May 1943. Sanford and his team had been working since the start of the 1940s on an empirical study of antisemitic attitudes and bigotry that, as it happened, was also being funded by the American Jewish Committee (AJC). Rolf Wiggershaus describes the goals of the project in the following terms:

> The central focus of the Berkeley group ... was the construction of a scale for the measurement of antisemitic attitudes and opinions and the discovery of the relationships possibly linking antisemitism to personality structure.
>
> WIGGERSHAUS 1986: 401

These were the very objectives that the Studies in Prejudice subsequently sought to pursue even more extensively.

By the middle of the 1940s, significant changes had also occurred in terms of the location and the structure of the Institute for Social Research. In retrospect, these developments turned out to be quite fortunate, if also rather happenstance. For example, financial constraints were compelling the Institute to develop partnerships with American research institutions. The relocation of Horkheimer and Adorno to southern California facilitated a closer working relationship with UC Berkeley and Stanford University. Löwenthal, Marcuse, and Franz Neumann relocated to wartime Washington, DC – Löwenthal to work with the Office of War Information, Neumann and Marcuse to work with the Office of Strategic Services (OSS). This facilitated contacts with numerous American scholars and opened up new directions for social research. Of especial importance is the fact that Löwenthal and Neumann had already begun to work with the American Jewish Committee on the framework for the AJC's proposed antisemitism project while in New York City. This happened because the AJC had become aware earlier of the work of the Institute through its 1936 study *Authority and Family*.[4] Here Horkheimer, Löwenthal, Marcuse,

---

4 *Authority and Family* is not yet available in English translation. Max Horkheimer, Erich Fromm, Herbert Marcuse, Hans Mayer, Karl A. Wittfogel, Paul Honigsheim, and Ludwig

Erich Fromm,[5] and other partners of the Institute had analyzed the rise of the National Socialist movement in terms also of an authoritarian mentality and upbringing. This was highly regarded in scholarly circles in the United States, and the AJC saw it as an important preparatory investigation into exactly what they intended to examine as the problem areas in their proposed Studies in Prejudice.

1   The Authoritarian Personality

I mentioned above that the first volume of the Studies in Prejudice series was *The Authoritarian Personality*. This came to involve Horkheimer, Adorno, Marcuse, and Löwenthal as well as two Viennese psychologists, Bruno Bettelheim and Marie Jahoda. There were, in addition, four Americans on the research team: psychologists Daniel Levinson and Nevitt Sanford as well as sociologists Norbert Guterman and Morris Janowitz. The team developed the project's own unique survey research instruments and its own charac-teristic interview methods. The scientific sample of the study represented a wide geographic and socioeconomic cross section of the US population. In an attempt to empirically measure subjective attitudes indicating antisemitism, a survey instrument and an "A-S Scale" were developed. This asked subjects the degree to which they agreed or disagreed [on a Likert continuum: +3, +2, +1, 0, -1, -2, -3] with statements such as the following: "Jewish power and control in money matters is far out of proportion to the number of Jews in the total population" (Levinson 1982 [1950]: 64). And, "Colleges should adopt a quota system by which they limit the number of Jews in fields which have too many

---

von Friedeburg, *Studien über Autorität und Familie: Forschungsberichte aus dem Institut für Sozialforschung* (Paris: Felix Alcan, 1936).

5   Two significant studies were undertaken during those years that were to have direct bear-ing on the larger US projects later. The first was by Erich Fromm, closely acquainted with Leo Löwenthal, and a member of the inner circle of the Institute of Social Research from its beginnings in the 1930s. Fromm's social-psychological contribution to *Authority and Family* was undergirded by his analysis of empirical research on the psychology of German work-ers conducted from 1929–30. The original research was subsequently published on its own as Erich Fromm (1984 [1929]). The second was an investigation by Siegfried Kracauer (1998 [1930]). Kracauer was also a close friend of Löwenthal and Adorno, and this book was also a study of the impact of social and cultural changes on the mentality of salaried employ-ees. Given the advent of techniques of scientific management during the Weimar period, a new type of employee developed, quite different from the industrial proletariat. On the tight friendship between Löwenthal and Kracauer, see Leo Löwenthal and Siegfried Kracauer (2003); also see Peter-Erwin Jansen (2003) and Martin Jay (2003).

Jews now" (65). The most valuable achievement of this project, celebrated yet today, was the extension of this work on antisemitism to the development of an "F Scale" that measured and assessed subjective tendencies toward fascism. The F Scale survey instrument synthesized items from the A-S Scale study with two other sets of items that had likewise been developed to gauge *ethnocentrism* [the E Scale] and *political-economic conservatism* [the PEC Scale] (Jay 1973: 241–44). An analysis of the Likert response data was facilitated by the use of well-defined and complex evaluation criteria, further extended and deepened through qualitative interviews and applied to formulate a characterization of "the authoritarian personality" (219–52).

Some later scholarship, reflecting back upon this first volume of Studies in Prejudice, criticized its survey instruments and methods as being too tightly tethered to the historical frame in which its investigations were undertaken. Valid in their particular context, the conclusions of *The Authoritarian Personality* were not regarded as valid in general. Other critics charged that the project was too rigidly and single-mindedly fixated on an ostensible authority figure: inevitably the father, who presided in the bourgeois family setting that the critical theorists were familiar with in 1936, but which had changed in the United States and was of limited relevance by the 1950s. In the United States, the role of the father had been significantly diminished, and other agencies of socialization, like the television (not to mention contemporary communications technologies and virtual social networks) had come (and were coming) into the foreground in the social development of young people.

It is true that *The Authoritarian Personality*, as a social-psychological study, was oriented primarily toward the form of fascism that spread in Europe. If Adorno saw this as a mass movement of the petty bourgeoisie, he nonetheless hypothesized that the appeal of fascist propaganda was not grounded in specific, rational, political, economic, or social interests as such (Adorno et al. 1950a: 8) Rather, "an individual's susceptibility to this ideology depends primarily upon his psychological needs" (3). In this regard, the researchers involved in the study wanted to understand something beyond the authoritarian personality structure: they sought insights into *potentially fascist* perspectives that are to be found in nontotalitarian, thoroughly democratic, social circumstances, and how, under changed conditions, these might become manifest in new ways. If one speaks of an authoritarian "character" here, this does not refer to an immutable quality that is ostensibly found among members of some social group or other. Adorno clearly indicates, instead, that a person's character is a dynamic structure that can certainly be altered under specific social conditions. An individual's opinions, views, attitudes, and values are established only amidst the reciprocally interrelated influences of one's

group memberships, biographical stages, and changing sociohistorical realities. One's character structure is, thus, not to be conceived as either inborn
or ethnically constituted. The authoritarian personality is formed through a
longstanding interaction with social authorities and institutions, and it can as
such be of great importance to the functioning of the society. It is clear that a
person's views and values can be manipulated into an authoritarian pattern
all the more easily if one has already armored oneself against the wider world
with stereotypes, narrow-mindedness, prejudice. Here prejudice and armoring
become matters of survival. Extreme identification with one's own "in-group"
protects one from the supposed threats of the out-group and/or the ostensible
threats to one's values. Prejudice provides easy explanatory power: it solidi-
fies a fictitious apprehension into an emotional crutch. "Why are they so easily fooled?" Adorno asks. "Because, it may be supposed, of their personality
structure; because of long-established patterns of hopes and aspirations, fears
and anxieties that dispose them to certain beliefs and make them resistant
to others" (10). Easy and irresponsible generalizations, against "the Jews" for
example, are never exclusively due to (negative) personal experiences; prejudice helps make these possible.

In spite of the fact that research on antisemitic stereotypes and racial prejudice comprises much of the study, Adorno emphasized that in the course of
the investigation the emphasis shifted.

> Our study grew out of specific investigations into antisemitism. As our
> work advanced, however, the emphasis gradually shifted. We came
> to regard it as our main task not to analyze antisemitism or any other
> antiminority prejudice as a social-psychological phenomenon per se,
> but rather to examine the relation of antiminority prejudice to broader
> ideological and characterological patterns. Thus antisemitism gradually
> all but disappeared as a topic of our questionnaire and in our interview
> schedule it was only one among many topics which had to be covered.
> ADORNO 1950b: 605

The dynamic phases of prejudice formation that political extremists make use
of are actually developed in a preliminary fashion through pressures toward
social conformity within the societal framework of capitalist competition.
Societal deprivations produce the threats to economic security individuals
experience along with the personal pain and suffering. They also produce
dissatisfactions so intense that individuals are willing to use violence against
minorities. In the *Prophets of Deceit*, Volume Five of the Studies in Prejudice
series, Löwenthal describes the political demagogue/propagandist as

"exploiting a state of discontent" yet having no interest in defining "the nature of that discontent by means of rational concepts. Rather does he increase his audience's disorientation by destroying all rational guideposts and by proposing that they instead adopt seemingly spontaneous modes of behavior" (Löwenthal and Guterman 1949: 6). The effectiveness of these "spontaneous modes" of action is said to hinge upon a clear identification of the action's targets. This becomes that much easier for the propagandist/demagogue if the appeal happens to fall upon the ears of individuals who tend toward the authoritarian personality type.

In addition to the insights just described, the Studies in Prejudice series indicates other features of the authoritarian personality that are equally important which I shall attempt to summarize: The authoritarian personality has an exaggerated conformist tendency. It is generally a middle-class phenomenon and is accompanied by a rigid sense of the prerogatives of property. In order to conserve the old and resist the new it humbles itself whenever confronted with authority and conforms to every expectation of the social context without hesitation. Rigid and possessed of only limited imagination, the authoritarian character is personified by the kind of individual who would give a piece of toast exactly thirty chews without question because a health professional said this was necessary. An experiment – carried out multiple times with multiple sample groups over the course of these investigations into prejudice – makes this clear: participants were given a well-defined problem and told to solve it in exactly the complex manner prescribed, even though much simpler solutions were readily apparent. Very few of the participants defied the instructions, prioritized the solution, and chose the simpler method.

The authoritarian personality is obedient to authority and fixated on conformity to the group. Hidden behind these traits is an exaggerated sense of identify with the group to which it belongs. This is sustained through a positive elevation and differentiation of its in-group from the negative evaluation it has made of the out-group. The authoritarian personality draws its own identity from its perception that the group to which it belongs is under siege. Out-groups are looked at only superficially, and its members are viewed primarily through prejudice. Prejudice aids the authoritarian personality in feeling assured that the out-group others are to blame for the difficulties it faces itself. The authoritarian personality believes itself always to be in the right. The out-group victims of even the most obvious wrongs are said to have only themselves to blame for the evils that have befallen them. Democratic procedures and democratic conduct are interpreted as weaknesses and viewed as the tyranny of the minorities: the authoritarian personality is antidemocratic.

2   Prophets of Deceit

The existence of the authoritarian mentality presupposes the existence of political propagandists and demagogues who will address it. Who are these? How does
this occur? How are the deceptions accomplished? Leo Löwenthal and Norbert
Guterman asked just these questions in *Prophets of Deceit*. I will discuss the major
conclusions of their study below, but first some brief remarks about the historical
context of this volume's publication.

Prophets of Deceit was intended as an investigation into the possibility of a
fascist takeover in the United States. At the time of its publication, Löwenthal was
confronted with an astonishing feature of the early 1950s. The former Allies, the
United States and the Soviet Union, had become rival political systems after the
war and struggled for supremacy in ideological and geopolitical matters. In
the United States, this led to a hitherto unimaginable hysteria against those with
nonconformist political ideas. US Senator Joseph McCarthy saw suspicious elements throughout American politics and culture, and he believed that domestic
Communists and Soviet sympathizers were eating away internally at the United
States. His US Senate position permitted him to interrogate political nonconform-
ists, journalists, scientists, particularly those who had immigrated to the United
States from Europe, regarding their political views. Löwenthal was not unscathed
by this process. He was investigated by the Federal Bureau of Investigation (FBI)
and members of McCarthy's committee as a coauthor of "Marxist-oriented"
scholarship produced by the Institute for Social Research and because of his
participation (also with that of Erich Fromm) in a socialist Zionist student organization during their studies at the University of Heidelberg. Even the subtitle
of *Prophets of Deceit* was used against him: "A Study in the Techniques of the
American Agitator." (Note that Löwenthal intended that 'agitator' should be read
here as synonymous with "Demagogue" or "Dictator.") Löwenthal was accused
of asserting that the political class in the United States was composed of Nazi
sympathizers and that the current American system was a preliminary stage of a
fascist social order. His work maintained that benighted radio commentators had
fascist tendencies. Such critical views could only be emanating from "an enemy"
or the perspective of a "socialist-Jewish mentality." Löwenthal reacted calmly to
these inquiries, and no appearance before McCarthy's committee occurred.

The volume itself found wide acceptance. Its authors had held numerous
lectures and presentations at prestigious conferences, even before final publication, reporting on the status of their research.[6] Individual chapters had

---

6 For example, a presentation was made at the sixteenth annual meeting of the Eastern
   Sociological Society, which was held on May 4–5, 1946, in New York.

also been published in professional journals by the end of 1948 (Löwenthal and Guterman 1948). As indicated earlier, a paperback edition was published in 1970 featuring an updated political foreword by Löwenthal's Institute colleague and longtime friend, Herbert Marcuse. This was written in August 1969, at the high point of student protest against the Vietnam War and in the wake of the 1968 campaigns of Richard Nixon and Hubert Humphrey[7] for the US presidency. George C. Wallace, who was serving as Governor of Alabama after being elected twice as a Democrat, became the chairman of the racist, right-wing, splinter party, the American Independent Party. With close contacts to the Ku Klux Klan, Wallace ran for US President as an ardent segregationist. He received 13 percent of the total popular vote after his many demagogic and racist speeches. Many in America were appalled at his showing, and the book by Löwenthal and Guterman appeared to be more relevant than ever. Marcuse captures this in his foreword.

> If we compare or contrast the agitator of the thirties and forties whom this book examines with the legitimate politicians of today, the shift in the target, tone, vocabulary seems slight. ... Today, we recognize some of the essential features of the agitator as those of the political Establishment. The social infrastructure, the mainsprings of agitation, the "background for seduction" are the same: exploitation of the prevailing frustration in ways which lead away from the roots of discontent and from its cure; a diffused appeal which is addressed to every American as a "potential follower" since every American is confronted with political and economic forces which operate behind his back, forces which he rightly suspects without being able to master them; and, finally, the enemy (national, and within the nation) who is everywhere and who threatens every American.
>
> MARCUSE 1970: v–vi

Just as Marcuse points out, Löwenthal understood political demagoguery as embedded in concrete socioeconomic conflicts. Demagoguery denounces ostensible enemies without ever furnishing evidence that can be critically examined. Such propaganda will reduce objective social problems and/or real social complaints to blameworthy individuals and then call for the elimination of these persons rather than for changes to the political structure that could eliminate the sources of the problem. In those circumstances where one should ask, "*what* is to blame for our misery?" the demagogue will always

---

7   Hubert Humphrey was vice president under US President Lyndon B. Johnson and was a proponent of the Vietnam War.

pose the rhetorical question, "*who* is to blame for our misery?" The prophets of deceit answer the loudest, "we know who is to blame, just let us at 'em." Such personification of the trouble detaches the discontent one has with actual conditions from rational argumentation and critical political analysis. Any thought of political causality fades into the background completely. In place of reasoned debate about the nature of the generative structures from which social problems emerge, one encounters opinions with a facile "insight" into those who are supposedly to blame. These views can be quickly picked up by all of us. It is at this juncture that propaganda conjoins the real dissatisfactions people have with their difficult social conditions with the will to power of the demagogue and his (or her) followers. The demagogue formulates a single-dimensional complaint with regard to societal circumstances that might go something like this: "People born in our country don't have enough to eat and are even committing suicide because refugee immigrants are taking away their jobs." This is exactly the kind of rationalization and/or lie that has accompanied the actions of NATO ships and the partially privatized, European border patrol, "Frontex," this year as they have driven back to the sea thousands of refugees from the rebellions in North African countries who sought refuge on islands in the Mediterranean. Nearly two thousand refugees have drowned since the first of the recent uprisings in Morocco and Tunisia.

The demagogue may claim to honor international agreements and treaties, but as Löwenthal was told more than sixty years ago: "We don't need any International Criminal Court or a United Nations, where a handful of Asians, Russians, Europeans, and Brits can tell us what to do."

Interpreting social reality through such appeals requires a specific psychological constitution: insecure individuals with an authoritarian personality structure. This kind of person is the product of a fear of losing their economic security, through mistrust, disillusionment, and dependency. The emotional background, Löwenthal adds, usually includes feelings of being shut out of opportunity and the feeling that one has been and will again be betrayed. The demagogue makes continual reference to the supposedly never-ending burden placed upon the American taxpayer. Furthermore, the taxes Americans pay don't do the taxpayer any good: "We're feeding the foreigners," says the demagogue, "who are derelict." So, the long-suffering American taxpayer is someone who never enjoys any benefit from taxes. The demagogue knows just how to employ social crisis situations for his or her own purposes: by mobilizing the anxieties that have long ago become routine in modern capitalist societies. Today, in spite of or because of "globalization," these techniques involve "desolidification" and "exclusion." These terms signify that in contemporary society only the economically privileged groups, the "global players" and their puppets, have access to and may participate in social and political life. According to the madness of neoliberalism, everyone participates in the public sphere acting upon a rational calculation of economic utility that is "morally neutral" and in which everyone prospers. This fails to acknowledge the forms of social disrespect, disregard, and discrimination as described, for example, by Axel Honneth (1996) in his "politics of recognition" – attitudes that are unmindful of the dignity of others are the source of the profound lack of legitimacy in modern society.

Löwenthal was aware that, given rapidly changing social conditions, the mobilization of fears and anxieties was a central strategy of propaganda. The demagogue must "dissolve away" the rust of passivity adhering to the discontented masses, splashing their surface with the oil of their disappointments and anxieties, in order to use them as tools to act against those who are said to be at fault. Thus, even legitimate complaints and worries that arise during periods of economic uncertainty become transformed into a single-minded hatred of those said to be to blame for their misery. The demagogue does not create the social difficulties, but he or she perpetuates and deepens them by closing off avenues of rational action that could lead to the removal of the real causes. An individual's disappointment at their society's betrayal of its promise of happiness and success is transformed into charges: (a) against others who supposedly lost faith in society's traditional values, (b) against degenerate culture, and (c) against fluctuations in social laws that were supposed to have the constancy of natural law. All of this can lead nowhere but into the abyss. The demagogue does not suggest real alternatives; instead there are pronouncements of decay, decline, and destruction.[8] The only alternative is an either/ or. The fundamental principle of all social life is reduced to "either you're with us or against us!" Of course, this is an unassailable constant in self-satisfied societies and a fundamental moral norm: this oppositional stance becomes a form of justifiable material action. According to Löwenthal and Guterman, really-existing social conflicts are persistently transfigured and reduced in this manner to individual experiences of humiliation. The demagogue knows just who is to blame and promises that the autocratic use of force will free people from their degradation and win the battle for survival. For this reason, the

---

8 Many intellectuals, particularly during the time of crisis between the first and second world wars, from Heidegger and Ernst Jünger to Oswald Spengler, made pronouncements of "the decline of the West" or the destruction of Western civilization. From an entirely different angle, for analyses of the policies of annihilation of National Socialism, see Karl-Otto Apel, *Diskurs und Verantwortung* (Frankfurt: Suhrkamp Verlag, 1988); and Dan Diner, *Zivilisationsbruch: Denken nach Auschwitz* (Frankfurt: Fischer, 1988).

construction of an image of an enemy is so important for purposes of political agitation. Hence the religiously different immigrants, the strangers, and the refugees are responsible for the decline in conventional morals and religion, for the disintegration of formerly prevailing cultural norms – just as neo-Nazi propaganda in Germany today tells us. I am reminded here of the recent case of racist mass murder by the Norwegian, Anders Behring Breivik (Mala and Goodman 2011). To him, "the Muslims" represented the threat of the destruction of Christian Europe and the West. But this was only possible in his estimation because of the greater tolerance of this "threat" brought about by the work of the multiculturalists and cultural Marxists, like Adorno and Marcuse, whom he explicitly named in his writings (Rehman 2011). His killings were intended to get out his message. With regard to Marcuse, the reactionary American journalist Pat Buchanan published similar statements in the United States in 2002.[9]

The demagogue develops a characteristic ruse. Utilizing the loaded language of bigotry, anxieties about some *thing* are channeled into a hatred of some *one*. Hand in hand with this hatred of one's 'enemies' comes a dehumanization of them. Treated as criminals, degenerates, uncivilized peoples, parasites, nonbelievers, they are repeatedly confronted with existing prejudice and face constant discrimination. The demagogue displays how "the enemy" is completely different from "those who suffer and shoulder the burden." No remnant of humanity may adhere to the enemy. The demagogue emphasizes that "the group of strangers" has no interest in integrating itself into a pluralistic democracy. Jews are a problem because they always seek their own interest at the expense of others. When the demagogue encounters assimilated Jews, they are either "cleverly hiding" their identity or "fundamentally conflicted" about it. Löwenthal makes clear through the use of textual excerpts from demagogic speeches that they are "double-barreled": they contain prejudiced descriptions and defamatory stigmatizations of Jews. Within this context, hostility and persecution comprise the "normality of exclusion." The demagogue avoids the term "exclusion" and instead uses words like "cleansing" or "cleaning house." The latter is supposed to sound as normal as everyday "house cleaning." The political demagogue not infrequently calls upon the discontented public in an incendiary fashion and suggests direct action to do away with the difficulties. Metaphors are employed: "to remove," "to throw out," "to throw away," "to eliminate," and these imply the necessity of one's own action. Only when those who are supposedly guilty are driven away, expunged, will the 'enemy' be defeated. Other excerpts Löwenthal examined include demands of the

---

9   See Buchanan (2002): 56, 80, 85–89, 91–93, 195, 216, 267, 280.

following sorts: all refugees must be returned to the countries from which they came; all foreigners, whether they arrived very recently or some time ago, must be deported. This sounds all too familiar, today, even though various rightwing demagogues have developed new rhetorical tools and the enemies are much more diverse. Today, the targets – in addition to blacks – are Hispanics, Jews, and now also Muslims.

No ideological one-sidedness should prevent us from recognizing that both right-wing and communist propaganda share many similarities, even if sometimes they make quite contradictory promises. Hannah Arendt's brilliant analysis of totalitarianism expresses the bottom line they have in common.

> The essence of totalitarian domination is to be found neither in the restriction or elimination of certain freedoms, nor in the obliteration of the love of freedom in the human heart; rather only in this: that human beings, just as they are, are violently encased within an iron cage of terror, such that any space for action – and this is the only reality of freedom – disappears.
>
> ARENDT 1988 [1951]: 958

In my opinion, Hannah Arendt's research into totalitarianism represents a deepening and widening of the critical theorists' analysis of the 1940s even if her work is sometimes quite different from theirs. The authoritarian personality considers conformity and accommodation to be important strategies for survival. It will "sacrifice" its freedom for some greater good. It wants to share in the salvation promised by the demagogue and views itself as belonging to the social sphere of the powerful. Diversity and difference are considered as threats to the nature of the society. Pluralism is not to be tolerated within it. Only those survive who fit themselves into a one-dimensional societal structure. All behavioral options disappear as they are channeled into predetermined patterns. What Arendt calls the "space for action" loses its authentically social quality: political action that has the potential to change society is replaced with promises that – with the help of a system of terror – all will be well, and this coercion will work to the "advantage of everyone."

The elimination of the political free space that is the "reality of freedom" is not in itself always sufficient. Mutual mistrust is fomented, images of the enemy furnished, empathy denounced, solidarity undermined, powerlessness produced. The ideology of terror becomes an end in itself in the individual's struggle for survival. In this, human beings are destroyed "for the sake of humanity." The victims are not only the "objective system opponents" but anyone who dares as a human being to act on one's own initiative in a way that would make new beginnings possible. The political system confronts such persons with its instruments of repression. Democratic societies are not the same as the terror systems (e.g., fascism and Stalinism) that Hannah Arendt investigated in order to elucidate the qualities of totalitarian domination. Nonetheless, a radical critique of society needs to analyze these threats (ever increasing in number) in a timely fashion.

One of the most disgusting stage personalities in the right-wing theatrics in Germany today is the formerly left-wing lawyer for the Red Army Faction, Horst Mahler, who has lately become the main propagandist for the NPD (the racist, right-wing National Democratic Party of Germany). Nothing is too out-rageous or coarse for Mahler to say; he utilizes neo-Nazi rhetorical flourishes like "*Umvolkung*," the Germanization or re-Germanization of a Germany that has supposedly become too multicultural. This is used as a political battle cry – "Germany for Germans only" – against the immigration of refugees to Germany. I shall conclude my presentation with some material that illustrates Mahler's type of right-wing invective pertaining to the attack on human rights and the World Trade Center in New York on September 11, 2001. The follow-ing quotation is taken from an essay by Alfred Schobert, who writes critically about it on the website of the Duisburg Institute of Linguistic and Social Studies. According to Schobert, Horst Mahler and cohorts Günter Maschke and Reinhold Oberlercher posted the following inflammatory screed, written by Oberlercher, to the website of their organization, Deutsches Kolleg [German Academy], in November 2001.

> Judeo-American *civilization*, representing *modernity* and therefore *bar-barism*, was struck at its political-economic core on September 11, 2001 with a major attack by the Islam of the middle ages. The attacks were carried out by resistance fighters and resurrected martyrs belonging to the jihadist culture of medieval Mohammedanism, who sacrificed themselves and ensured the deaths of the greatest possible number of enemies. *Holy War and its martyrs are the crown of Islamic culture.* The attack against civilization, the resistance to its cultures and the defeat of the United States, including its global apparatus that seeks to extend the influence of the Jews, and the elimination of the Jewish state itself, comprise the inseparable elements of a total agenda of the *anti-capitalist world revolution.* This seeks to establish a world order founded upon the successful elimination of *Western values* and a break from *Western norms and mores*, thus making possible the freedom and sovereignty of nations.
>
> OBERLERCHER 2011: 11

Here Horst Mahler's anti-Zionism leads him to embrace the goals of radical Islam, although other right wingers, like Anders Behring Breivik, regard all Muslims simply as foreigners who must also be eliminated. In both cases, the language and techniques analyzed by Löwenthal and Guterman in the 1940s are finding renewed currency as contemporary demagogues make their promises of deliverance. Images of the enemy have to be propagated toward those at home and those abroad. Sadly, the cult of the demagogue, built upon nationalist, ethnic, cultural, or religious paranoia and prejudice, is becoming more and more acceptable.

Translated by Charles Reitz

References

Adorno, Theodor W., Else Frenkel-Brunswik, Daniel J. Levinson, and R. Nevitt Sanford. 1950a. *The Authoritarian Personality*, Studies in Prejudice, Vol. 1. New York: Harper & Brothers, American Jewish Committee.

Adorno, Theodor W. 1950b. "Prejudice in the Interview Material." In Theodor W. Adorno, Frenkel-Brunswik, Levinson, and Sanford. *The Authoritarian Personality*, Studies in Prejudice, Vol. 1. New York: Harper & Brothers, American Jewish Committee. At http://www.ajcarchives.org/ajc_DATA/Files/AP19.pdf.

American Jewish Committee, 1950. Studies in Prejudice, a five volume series online. At http://www.ajcarchives.org/main.php?GroupingId=1380.

Apel, Karl-Otto. 1988. *Diskurs und Verantwortung*. Frankfurt: Suhrkamp Verlag.

Arendt, Hannah. 1988 [1951]. *Elemente und Ursprünge totaler Herrschaft* (München: Piper Taschenbuchverlag, 1988), 958. This book was originally published in English as Hannah Arendt, *The Origins of Totalitarianism*. Cleveland: World Publishing. At http://www.archive.org/stream/originsoftotalit00aren#page/n5/mode/2up.

Buchanan, Patrick. 2002. *The Death of the West: How Dying Populations and Immigrant Invasions Imperil Our Country and Civilization.* New York: St. Martin's Griffin Thomas Dunne Books.

Diner, Dan. 1988. *Zivilisationsbruch: Denken nach Auschwitz*. Frankfurt: Fischer.

Fromm, Erich. 1984 [1929]. *The Working Class in Weimar Germany: A Psychological and Sociological Study*, ed. Wolfgang Bonss, trans. Barbara Weinberger. Cambridge: Harvard University Press.

Honneth, Axel. 1996. *The Struggle for Recognition: The Moral Grammar of Social Conflicts.* Cambridge, MA: The MIT Press.

Horkheimer, Max and Samuel H. Flowerman, 1950. Forward to "Studies in Prejudice" v. At http://www.ajcarchives.org/ajc_DATA/Files/AP1.pdf.

Horkheimer, Max and Theodor W. Adorno. [1944] 1972. *Dialectic of Enlightenment.*
New York: Herder and Herder.

Horkheimer, Max, Erich Fromm, Herbert Marcuse, Hans Mayer, Karl A. Wittfogel,
Paul Honigsheim, and Ludwig von Friedeburg. 1936. *Studien über Autorität und
Familie: Fortschungsberichte aus dem Institut für Sozialforschung.* Paris: Felix Alcan.

Jansen, Peter-Erwin. 2003. Foreword to Leo Löwenthal and Siegfried Kracauer, *In steter
Freundschaft: Briefwechsel; 1921–1966.* Springe: zu Klampen Verlag.

Jay, Martin. 2003. Introduction to Leo Löwenthal and Siegfried Kracauer, *In steter
Freundschaft: Briefwechsel; 1921–1966.* Springe: zu Klampen Verlag.

Jay, Martin. 1973. *The Dialectical Imagination: A History of the Frankfurt School and the
Institute of Social Research, 1923–1950.* Boston: Little, Brown.

Kracauer, Siegfried. 1998 [1930]. *The Salaried Masses: Duty and Distraction in Weimar
Germany,* trans. Quintin Hoare. London: Verso.

Levinson, Daniel J. [1950] 1982. "The Study of Antisemitic Ideology." In Theodor W.
Adorno, Else Frenkel-Brunswik, Daniel J. Levinson, and R. Nevitt Sanford, *The
Authoritarian Personality.* New York: W. W. Norton. At http://www.ajcarchives.org/
ajc_DATA/Files/AP6.pdf.

Löwenthal, Leo and Siegfried Kracauer. 2003. *In steter Freundschaft: Briefwechsel; 1921–
1966,* ed. Peter-Erwin Jansen. Springe: zu Klampen Verlag.

Löwenthal, Leo. 1987. *An Unmastered Past: The Autobiographical Reflections of Leo
Löwenthal,* ed. Martin Jay. Berkeley: University of California Press.

Löwenthal, Leo. 1980. *Mitmachen wollte ich nie: Ein autobiographisches Gespräch mit
Helmut Dubiel.* Frankfurt: Suhrkamp.

Löwenthal, Leo and Norbert Guterman. 1949. *Prophets of Deceit,* Studies in Prejudice,
Vol. 5. New York: Harper & Brothers, American Jewish Committee. At http://www.
ajcarchives.org/main.php?GroupingId=6530.

Löwenthal, Leo, and Norbert Guterman. 1948. "Portrait of the American Agitator,"
Public Opinion Quarterly 12(3), Fall: 417–29.

Löwenthal, Leo. 1945–46. "Terror's Atomization of Man," *Commentary, A Jewish Review*
1(2): 1–8.

Löwenthal, Leo. [1943] 2000. "Das antisemitische Argument," published for the first
time in Peter-Erwin Jansen, ed., 2000. *Das Utopishe soll Funken schlagen: Zum hun-
dertsten Geburtstag von Leo Löwenthal.* Frankfurt: Vittorio Klostermann.

Mala, Elisa and J. David Goodman. 2011. "At Least 80 Dead in Norway Shooting," *The
New York Times,* July 22. At http://www.nytimes.com/2011/07/23/world/europe/
23oslo.html?_r=1&scp=10&sq=%22Anders%20Behring%20 Breivik%22&st=cse.

Marcuse, Herbert. 1970. Foreword to *Prophets of Deceit,* Studies in Prejudice, Vol. 5, by
Leo Löwenthal and Norbert Guterman. Palo Alto, CA: Pacific Books.

Oberlercher, Reinhold. 2011. "Der Untergang des judäo-amerrikanischen Imperiums
[The decline of the Judeo-American empire]." In Alfred Schobert, "Netze, Viren,

Ströme – Wurzeln und das Reich [Nets, Viruses, Tendencies – Roots and the Empire]." Duisburg, Germany: Duisburg Institute of Linguistic and Social Studies, Internet Library. At http://www.dissduisburg.de/Internetbibliothek/Artikel/ Netze%20Viren%20Stroeme.pdf.

Rehman, Jalees. 2011. "From Frankfurt to Utøya (Part 1): The Quest for Monoculturalism." In *Guernica: A Magazine of Art and Politics*, August 8. At http://www.guernicamag. com/blog/2955/jalees_rehman_from_frankfurt_t/.

Wiggershaus, Rolf. 1986. *Die Frankfurter Schule*. München: Deutscher Taschenbuch Verlag.

CHAPTER 11

From 'False' to 'Reified' Consciousness: Tracing the ISR's Critical Research on Authoritarianism

Daniel Sullivan

The Institute for Social Research (ISR) exemplified the method of 'critical research' in their program on authoritarian psychology in society. Notably, the 'three-wave' empirical program (Kramer 2011) – consisting of the 1930s studies of the Weimar working class and authority in the family, the 1940s U.S. 'exile' studies on anti-Semitism, and the 1950s *Gruppenexperiment* and *Betriebsklima* investigations in West Germany – paralleled developments in the theorizing of Horkheimer and Adorno. I hope to show that a theory of the transformation of the individual-societal relationship in the first half of the 20th Century, and corresponding methods for testing it, are available in the empirical reports and methodological writings of the ISR. The theory recognizes that social changes summarily referred to as the emergence of totally socialized society produced psychological effects that can be understood as 'reified consciousness.'[1]

My analysis does not fully contradict conventional narratives surrounding the inner circle of the early Frankfurt School (e.g., that they abandoned empiricism in later years in favor of pure theory). But it does seek to demonstrate that their late pessimism and philosophy both influenced and *was grounded in* their critical research to a greater degree than acknowledged by such conventional narratives. The benefits of acknowledging, and reconstructing in some detail, the early ISR's long-term project interweaving theory and research are two-fold. More proximally, the studies themselves are rich, offering a largely undiscovered corpus of data on 20th Century authoritarianism as well as innovative research methods that have only begun to be incorporated into a larger understanding of critical theory. But in a broader sense, the research program is a hidden font of inspiration, an obscured beacon for social theorists and researchers seeking a truly interdisciplinary, engaged response to the threat of nascent fascism in the neoliberal era. A model for how to critique authoritarian

---

1 Although various terms and translations have been employed to capture Horkheimer and Adorno's vision of late liberal, democratic-capitalist society, both by the authors themselves and secondary scholars, I prefer as a summative term this translation of *vergesellschaftete Gesellschaft*, used prominently in *Gruppenexperiment* (see Perrin and Olick 2011).

populism can be found in the ISR's ambitious but scattered and unfinished empirical works; it merely awaits comprehensive reconstruction. A review of the original program is the first step.

1   Epistemology of the Critical Research on Authoritarianism

The ISR constructed an outline of social science as critical research, a dialecti-cal endeavor characterized by the consistent attempt to interpolate elements and techniques typically kept separate: sociological theory and empirical research; qualitative and quantitative methods; and individual and societal levels of analysis. ISR methodology could be summarized as the effort to lever-age dialectical tension to unmask truths about society. As the Introduction (Morelock and Sullivan, present volume) provides an overview of ISR episte-mology, here I will only briefly review its three main elements.

First, the ISR sought a productive tension between interpretive philosophy and empirical social research, as an alternative to the technocratic research of contemporary sociology and social psychology (Adorno 1976; Horkheimer 1989 [1940]; 1972 [1937]). The data of empirical research served alternately as ending and starting points for the act of theoretical interpretation. The ISR's method involved dialectical movement between the focused investigation of concrete empirical phenomena and interpretations that illuminated those phenomena in light of a critical-historical understanding of society. The researchers were convinced that theory and research must be interwoven not only to overcome the limits of method, but the abstractness of philosophy.

Second, the ISR was concerned with the tradeoff between statistical generalizability and the concrete, historical data offered by a more ethno-graphic approach, and accordingly blended quantitative and qualitative tech-niques. Qualitative methods operate as a safeguard against naïve empiricism (Frankfurt ISR 1972 [1956]). The ISR asserted that interpretations of qualitative data permit researchers to go both "deeper" and "broader" than conventional empiricism, by probing psychological tensions and linking quantitative find-ings to broader social trends. By coaxing "webs of meaning" out from qualita-tive data, the ISR researchers could probe and problematize the picture pre-sented by their statistics, refracting the patterns through a broader social and philosophical frame.

Third, the ISR scholars emphasized the individual-social mediation, con-sistently combining sociological and psychological levels of analysis (Adorno 1967). The tension between the struggling individual and the alienating social environment was at the heart of the studies. The researchers wanted to understand how irrational social structures could be maintained through the irrational psychologies in which they were mirrored. Throughout their studies, the ISR progressively shifted their focus on various sites of mediating tension (e.g., culturally shaped attitudes; socialization in the family; group and organizational 'climates').

2   The Pivot in 'Inner Circle' Theorizing

The three-wave critical research program on authoritarianism was characterized by ambitious, innovative methods of data collection and analysis. The entire program could be summarized as an attempt to understand the circumstances under which false consciousness (ideology) overtakes rational class consciousness, as outlined already in the first study:

> A political doctrine can actually go against all common sense but, nevertheless, be of great significance because of its close ties with emotional needs. But in such cases, there must be some factors which prove emotionally irresistible, since the entire doctrine stands in opposition to the individual's immediate interests and, in its actual content, is apparently unable to convince him on a rational level. Political doctrine then becomes ideology, whose effectiveness is proportionate to the extent and intensity of its emotional appeal and its capacity to replace rational thinking with rationalization (Fromm 1984: 62).

Despite this consistent aim, there is a well-known transition in the way that the inner circle of the early ISR – Adorno and Horkheimer in particular – conceived of the nature of modern capitalist society, the category of false consciousness, and hence the nature of empirical social research. This transition took place largely during the ISR's U.S. exile, when Friedrich Pollock's state capitalism thesis, *Dialectic of Enlightenment*, and *The Authoritarian Personality* all appeared (e.g., Abromeit 2011; Wiggershaus 1994). Rather than discuss the pure theory in detail, my aim is to demonstrate the interdependence of the authoritarianism research with the transition in inner circle theorizing.

The conventional narrative is that Horkheimer and Adorno had simply become more pessimistic and interested in philosophy by the time they returned to Frankfurt, and hence empirical research was demoted. This narrative has always been overly simplistic, however, given the ISR's ongoing ambitious research efforts in the 1950s, as well as the importance Adorno continued to grant methodological issues not only in the 'positivism debate' but throughout his lectures of the 1960s (Adorno 2000 [1968]; Adorno [1964] 2019), and the fact that he continues to cite contemporary empirical studies in such otherwise densely philosophical works as *The Jargon of Authenticity* (2003 [1964]: 21). It is more accurate to say that the ISR's view of the nature of empirical research underwent a qualitative change paralleling their theoretical transition, than to say that it merely underwent a quantitative change in perceived importance.

Summarily, the pivot in inner circle theory can be described as a transition from a conventional Marxian theory of false consciousness in capitalist society to the post-*Dialectic* theory of reified consciousness in totally socialized society.

> To say that society is 'completely reified' [totally socialized] is to say that the domination of the exchange process has increased to the point where it controls institutions, behavior and class formation in such a way that it prevents the formation of any independent and critical consciousness. To say that consciousness is 'completely reified' is to say that it is capable only of knowing the appearance of society, of describing institutions and behavior as if their current mode of functioning were an inherent and invariant characteristic or property, as if they, as objects, 'fulfil their concepts.'
>
> ROSE 1978: 48

In other words, the totally socialized society and reified consciousness are mirroring phenomena. The totally socialized society (Schweppenhäuser 2009: 58–68) emerged out of a combination of historical forces, including the rise of "monopolistic" capitalism (with the trend of absorption of various middle into the lower classes, bifurcating society into the propertied and "mass of propertyless"), the increasing role of the state as an intervening force to protect and sustain the market (Cook 1998; Pollock 1989 [1940]), and mass media transitions facilitating the rise of the culture industry. The corresponding reified consciousness manifests in two interrelated aspects:

> On the one hand, as *concretism*, the restriction to the merely existent, and on the other hand *abstractism*, meaning the inability to have living experience ... and this inability to have experiences and the fixation on the mere objects of immediate exchange, which are affectively charged, idolized, and fetishized by people, are essentially the same thing.
>
> ADORNO 2019 [1964]: 48–49; emphasis added

Abstractism might be considered the deeper, more implicit level of consciousness through which the individual (fails to) experience reality in the totally socialized society, whereas *concretism* is the more explicit level of psychological reaction to this (failed) experience through compensatory processes of fetishization, personalization, etc.

The fulcrum point of the pivot is the alleged waning importance of the family under modern conditions. This fulcrum provides one key to understanding how and why the empirical research efforts of the ISR changed in the 1940s. The earliest conceptualization of authoritarianism, which characterizes the Weimar study and was essentially determined by Fromm (1998 [1936]), is as a failure of the patriarchal ego-ideal resulting in a punishing superego that generates sadomasochistic violence channeled through propagandized false consciousness. By contrast, the later conceptualization is as a success of the controlling superego directly bypassing (through culture-industrial techniques) and circumventing the development of an independent ego-ideal in reified consciousness (Hedrick 2018). In the early work, Frommian notions of "cultural lag" explained the mass of frustrated personality types seeking an outlet for aggression. In the late inner-circle works, social hyper-organization alters the socialization process such that individuals develop a group-oriented consciousness (Rose 1978). Hence, the pivot marks a transition toward understanding class conflict and consciousness primarily in terms of its absence in the contemporary "false classless society" (Cook 1998).

Additionally, the theoretical pivot explains why the ISR continually adopted new methods to investigate different sites of mediational tension between society and the individual. In their earlier works, *culture* (and cultural lag) often played this mediating role, viewed classically as a superstructure that committed individuals to irrational hierarchies because it satisfied psychological needs (Horkheimer 1972 [1936]). Hence, the earliest studies focused primarily on individual attitudes and content analyses of propaganda. In the Berkeley studies, the ISR moved toward a focus on *personality* as a tension site, investigated in terms of its formation via early experience in the patriarchal *family* (Horkheimer 1949). In their final years of active research, the ISR centered increasingly on the *group* and *organization* as mediating levels (Frankfurt ISR 1955; Pollock, Adorno et al. 2011).

3 The Critical Research Program on Authoritarianism

When Max Horkheimer assumed leadership of the ISR at the end of the 1920s, he steered it toward an ambitious empirical study of the proletariat in Weimar

Germany to determine whether they were in fact prepared to support a socialist revolution. This study, led in large part by Fromm, became known as *The Working Class in Weimar Germany* and pioneered the attempt to uncover latent, politically significant attitudes of the participants through indirect means. With the rise of Fascism in Germany, Horkheimer relocated the Institute and several affiliates, first to Columbia University and then Berkeley in the 1940s. During their exile, they first published *Studien über Autorität und Familie*, which acted as a summary document of the ISR theoretical positions and empirical efforts in Europe. With *Studien* as a blueprint, Horkheimer and his inner circle turned their empirical attention to the problem of authoritarian tendencies in the middle and working classes. The result was a lengthy and intense collaboration between Horkheimer, Adorno, Pollock, Leo Löwenthal, Paul Massing, A.R.L. Gurland, Else Frenkel-Brunswik, and colleagues in public opinion research at Berkeley. This marked the second wave of critical research on authoritarianism, producing the interdisciplinary five-volume series *Studies in Prejudice* (including *The Authoritarian Personality*), as well as the unpublished report "Antisemitism among American Labor." In 1950, Horkheimer re-established the Institute in post-war Frankfurt with Adorno and Pollock, where the third and final wave of the critical research program took place. It consisted of the development of a novel 'group experimental' method to investigate public opinion, the primary fruits of which were published as *Gruppenexperiment* (an investigation of attitudes toward democracy and secondary anti-Semitism in postwar Germany), and utilized in the industrial-sociological study *Betriebsklima*.

Since the ISR understood fascism as the most important contemporary instance of an irrational ideology to which false or reified consciousness might be bound, they attempted to pinpoint in their studies the extent to which the samples' political views and psychological dispositions were amenable to fascist versus anti-fascist ideology. The ISR was interested in comparative base rates of these different types, as well as associated demographic variables (e.g., political party, occupational group, clinical diagnoses, etc.). The analytic approach in these studies is remarkable – indeed, arguably unparalleled – in its integrated blending of quantitative and qualitative analysis. In each study, the researchers approach the data with concepts derived from Marxism and psychoanalysis but provide a comprehensive description of data which will inform and potentially contradict theory.

3.1   *The Working Class in Weimar Germany* (WCW)

For the *WCW* study – carried out 1929–1931 – a comprehensive survey was delivered to members of the working class from diverse strata (including the unemployed), from whom, in the end, 584 analyzable responses were obtained.

The sample constituted a reasonably diverse, if not completely representative, array of workers living in the Weimar Republic (Fromm 1984, hereafter *wcw*: 69). Importantly, the survey questions were open-ended, and did not force respondents to choose between particular responses.

The researchers attempted to uncover latent attitudes and authoritarian predispositions among the working class with a two-pronged methodological approach. First, they made both *interpretative* and *descriptive* classifications of the open-ended responses; in the case of the former, they used their knowledge of local culture as well as psychoanalytic defense mechanisms to discern situations in which a particular overt response likely rationalized an irrational, nonconscious motive (see *wcw*: 53–57). They felt this technique was well-suited for questions that did not touch directly on political themes but might nevertheless speak to politically relevant aspects of personality. Beyond psychoanalytic interpretation, quantitative correlations were a second means of uncovering latent conflicts; for instance, repressive tendencies were revealed when the researchers found participants at the highest relative income level were the most likely to suggest they did not lend to others because they had no money themselves.

Researchers further assigned responses labels along continua, e.g., "conventional, individual, or revolutionary response." The final outcome variables were percentage counts of response labels, stratified according to predictor variables of interest, such as demographics (primarily political party affiliation and income bracket) and personality type (derived from theory). What is remarkable is that all the percentages are derived from counts of labels that were painstakingly assigned to qualitative data through interpretive acts on the part of researchers.

The *wcw* study largely upset Marxist orthodoxy by suggesting that only 25% of workers in leftist parties had radical (socialist) personalities, while a nearly equivalent number displayed some level of authoritarian tendencies. Many workers in the leftist political parties apparently did not fully internalize the humanitarian ideals of socialism; they were able to parrot political slogans when called to do so, but, when probed by indirect, ostensibly non-political survey items, often failed to display moral enlightenment. Further, the ISR found that this disconnect between social goals and individual attitudes often resulted from the participants' divided inner natures. Important were the number of left-identified participants whose data classified them as "rebellious-authoritarian." These participants displayed "contradictory syndromes" of personality across the questionnaire, alternating between conservative ideals of submission to authority and radical commitment to drastic social change. Tellingly for their later research and theory, the ISR partly interpreted these findings as evidence that many working-class individuals had assimilated a middle-class ideology that conflicted with their objective interests (*wcw*: 62–63). From the vantage of theory, the alienation produced by capitalism and economic depression generated resentments in these workers, which (once projected outward) could be enlisted in the service of any political group promising social upheaval.

3.2   *Studien über Autorität und Familie*

There are many angles from which to approach and judge the importance of the voluminous *Studien über Autorität und Familie* (Frankfurt ISR 1936). On one hand, it was the only time that the ISR achieved – in a single sprawling document – Horkheimer's early vision for multidisciplinary scholarly output, i.e., the simultaneous inclusion of extended philosophical treatises with detailed empirical studies by specialists across disciplines. On the other hand, the volume was somewhat hastily constructed in the period of flight from Germany to New York (Abromeit 2011; Schad-Somers 1972), and also suffers from a "too-many-cooks" problem: because so many people were involved in separate projects, *Studien* rarely achieves the synthetic and dialectical passages, integrating research results with innovative theory, that characterize the ISR's later empirical reports. The empirical sections, in particular, tend to have more of the character of "pilot studies"; for instance, the treatment of the *wcw* study, which was in many ways the central empirical contribution of *Studien*, is a hasty sketch compared to the exhaustive manuscript later published by Fromm. Yet again, as Abromeit (2011) has convincingly argued, the *Studien* must be viewed as a pivotal foundation point for the intertwined development of later ISR research and theory for a number of reasons. The essays on authority, the family, bourgeois anthropology, and the sado-masochistic character by Horkheimer and Fromm set the stage for all subsequent ISR theorizing up to and including *Dialectic of Enlightenment*, and hence the volume is repeatedly referred to in articles and in *The Authoritarian Personality*.

In addition, the reported studies seem to have made several impacts on the developing research program. Methodologically, the foremost contribution of *Studien* is the emergence of the ISR's concepts of "typological" or "structural-statistical" analyses. At this stage, these analytic methods are still closely tied to the method of data collection Fromm referred to as the "interpretive questionnaire"; later, they would morph into the use of Likert-type scales (in *The Authoritarian Personality*) or factor and cluster analysis (in more mainstream research). But it is significant in the history of social science that Fromm's psychoanalytic theory of personality types fleetingly fused with Paul Lazarsfeld's burgeoning positivistic interest in quantifying typologies. Lazarsfeld greatly spurred the ISR's efforts by leveraging statistical methods to combine data from across a single questionnaire, rather than focusing on a spread of answers to individual survey questions.

This "structural-statistical" approach was applied thoroughly in a study of Swiss youth reported in *Studien* (Frankfurt ISR 1936: 353–456) and conducted by Lazarsfeld and Käthe Leichter. One-thousand surveys were collected from youth (majority ages 14–22) in a reasonably representative group of families living in Zürich, Basel, and Bern. Although the questionnaire was much shorter than that administered in *WCW*, it had similar aspects (e.g., asking about famous individuals who might serve as role models for the participants) and focused on authority relations within the family. Combining responses to items across the questionnaire for each participant, Lazarsfeld was able to construct an index that divided respondents into a "complete authority" and a "rebellious" type.[2] The former tended to report in the questionnaire that they were almost exclusively influenced by their parents, that they had few worldview conflicts with their parents, that they were occasionally physically punished, and that they attended church. The latter tended to report they had worldview conflicts with their parents, and that individuals outside the home had influenced their upbringing and career path (Frankfurt ISR 1936: 404). Interesting results included that authoritarian participants were more likely to report *not* having a particular role model, while rebellious participants were more likely to identify revolutionary figures as such; and, in response to a question about the meaning of life, authoritarians were more likely to report a 'bourgeois' ideal (i.e., preoccupation with work and worldly affairs), rebels a 'political' ideal.

Typological techniques were also applied in the ISR's first research endeavors after relocating to New York, which centered around investigations of attitudes toward authority and family amongst the unemployed. The ISR saw the Great Depression as an important 'natural experiment' that to an extent permitted the disentanglement of economic from cultural factors in determining patriarchal authority – if the father lost his breadwinner status, would he continue to be respected and feared? A very interesting study was briefly reported in *Studien*, in which Fromm's ideas about the matriarchal origins of culture were tested in a typological analysis of reactions of unemployed men to a reduction in their welfare benefits (Frankfurt ISR 1936: 463–469).[3]

---

2   Lazarsfeld (1937) articulated in greater detail the logical and statistical procedures behind this analysis in a subsequent *Zeitschrift für Sozialforschung* article.
3   Among other points of interest, the conclusions of this study remarkably anticipate John Bowlby's later articulation of attachment theory.

Mirra Komarovsky's (2004 [1940]) *The Unemployed Man and his Family* (co-designed with Lazarsfeld) was another study that emerged out of the *Studien* initiative but was published separately. Komarovsky reported on interviews with the jobless fathers, mothers, and children in 59 families in Newark. The major methodological significance of this study is that it presented a very careful explication of the interviewing procedure, which focused on questions about concrete family situations that had been impacted by unemployment, in order to permit subsequent extraction of psychological interpretations that would go beyond what family members were willing or able to report (Komarovsky 2004 [1940]: 16–22, 135–146). In this the study anticipated the later qualitative procedures and methods of Frenkel-Brunswik and Adorno.

Beyond heralding later methodological innovations, the *Studien* also played a role in the theoretical evolution of the research program. In particular, the empirical results doubtless influenced a re-conceptualization of the role of the family under capitalism. Two patterns of findings stand out in this connection. First, a rather striking conclusion is that Germany appeared relatively unique among European countries in the extent of disintegration of traditional family structure and authority (Abromeit 2011). Given historical events underway, this cross-cultural pattern encouraged a nuanced view of the family as not only a passive conduit for, but possibly a source of resistance to, broader forces of authoritarian socialization and consciousness. Second, and related, various findings from the typological investigations attested to Horkheimer's statement that "The social relations which the family helps to preserve and strengthen, themselves constantly reproduce it" (qtd. in Komarovsky 2004 [1940]: 3). It was perhaps not the economic position of the patriarch that was decisive, but rather the specific cultural milieu in which a given family was immersed. For example, in Lazarsfeld and Leichter's Swiss investigation, children in more secular households expressed more independence and political idealism. And in Komarovsky's Newark study, the Protestant, patriarchal individualism of the lower-middle class families ensured that only 22% of fathers lost their authoritative status in the family, and only 17% expressed any leaning towards class consciousness or socialist thought, as a result of unemployment. It is not surprising that Horkheimer began in the mid-1930s to think of the bourgeois family as a problematic but occasionally salutary bulwark against the onslaught of totally socialized society. Subsequent research efforts focused on identification of different patterns of socialization contributing to the genesis of different personality types that would be more or less amenable to fascism.

3.3 *Antisemitism among American Labor"* (AL).

Although it has never been fully published, the completed empirical report "Antisemitism among American Labor" (hereafter AL)[4] has received increased attention (Collomp 2011; Rensmann 2017; Worrell 2009). Originally to be a major part of the *Studies in Prejudice* project, the goal was to understand the extent and nature of anti-Semitic prejudice in the U.S. working class. Directed and written by Friedrich Pollock, A. R. L. Gurland, Paul Massing, and Leo Löwenthal, the study involved data collection done in 1944 by nearly 300 field workers who carried out 566 research interviews at sites in New York, New Jersey, Philadelphia-Camden, Detroit, Pittsburgh, Los Angeles, and California (AL Vol 1: 22–23). The sample consisted primarily of industrial laborers and shipyard workers in the defense industries (Collomp 2011; Worrell 2009: 69–75).

The major method – and innovation – of the study was the use of a 'screened interview' technique, what today might be called covert ethnography (Calvey 2017). Field research assistants would train factory workers to act as 'participant interviewers,' and these workers would then solicit information in casual conversation from their co-workers (the 'interviewees'), based on a detailed outline of questions, without ever revealing that what was going on was research (AL Volume 1: 19; Volume 4: 391–403). The participant interviewers would then write reports of the interviews and turn them in to the research assistants, who would check for thoroughness. This method was in keeping with the ISR's constant effort to achieve greater access to latent attitudes and minimize the problems of bias in controversial research.

The interview guide was a short series of questions designed to extract information relevant to the ISR's burgeoning theoretical conception of modern anti-Semitism:

> (a) General and traditional prejudice and fixed opinion ... (b) Prejudice in its more modern varieties, especially of the totalitarian type ... (c) Developmental features of the prejudice within the personality frame of the interviewee ... (d) Specific experiences with Jews as workers ... (e) The influence of the war [on anti-Semitism].
>
> AL Volume 4: 399

---

4 The five volumes of the unpublished report (Institute for Social Research 1945) have been digitized and made available in the Max Horkheimer Archive of Goethe Universität, Frankfurt am Main: http://sammlungen.ub.uni-frankfurt.de/horkheimer/nav/classification/10065106.

As in the other major ISR qualitative projects, a mixed-methods approach was taken to the copious data, with separate sections of the study devoted to detailed content analysis of major themes (particularly Löwenthal's contribution, Volume 3 Part 4, the only section to be independently published as "Images of Prejudice" in Löwenthal 1987), but the bulk of the analysis focusing on a quantitative reduction of the interview responses. The latter was achieved by iteratively developing a coding scheme, which eventually consisted of 50 main categories, to be used to classify answers to each of the questions from the interview guide (AL Volume 4: 407–411). Coders assigned labels to the responses in two primary ways: First, answers to questions such as "Are Jews different from other people? How?" or "How do you feel about what the Nazis did to the Jews in Germany?" would be broadly labeled as reflecting a positive, negative, or ambivalent attitude; second, specific common themes and categories were searched for and coded as present or absent in a given response (e.g., for "Are Jews different ..." – a scheme was employed consisting of common stereotypes about physique and traits).

Just as workers were classified in WCW as having radical or authoritarian personalities, one of the primary aims of AL was to summarily classify interviewees as being either blatantly anti-Semitic, non-prejudiced, or ambivalent. This was done by assigning an overall rating to every interview, which most strongly weighted the interviewee's attitudes toward Nazi atrocities (AL Vol 1: 162–165). The end result was that about 30% of the sample were classified as fascist or strongly anti-Semitic, 50% as non-prejudiced or anti-authoritarian, and 20% as ambivalent (AL Volume 1: 176; Worrell 2009: 87). Interestingly, the researchers invited comparison to the WCW results by stressing how one of AL's few significant demographic effects represented a reversal of the European situation:

> In countries like Germany, Austria, Poland, Hungary, it was the 'white-collar' workers, the office employees, the sales personnel that was the antisemitic group among labor ... In our sample, the picture is completely reversed. The least prejudiced occupational groups belong to the category of white-collar workers, the most prejudiced ones – next to that of supervisory personnel – belong to the category of manual workers.
>
> AL Volume 3: 163

AL marks the first appearance of a statistical technique that the ISR would later use to indicate the dominance of 'reified' over class consciousness. Specifically, in a dataset with a relative absence of demographic effects, the researchers would conclude that an ideological constellation had spread across occupational subgroups and obscured class differences (*AL* Volume 1: 181). Disheartening from a Marxist perspective, for example, was the finding that union membership did not seem to play any role in ameliorating anti-Semitism (*AL* Volume 3: 261). The thematic analyses of Massing and Löwenthal also make connections to the early analyses of reified consciousness Adorno was deploying in *The Authoritarian Personality*.[5] Massing similarly highlights the role of "ticket-thinking" in shaping U.S. anti-Semitism: people come to expect a "stand on 'the Jewish question'" as part of the slate of positions to be associated with a particular candidate and party platform (*AL* Volume 3: 248–250).

In Löwenthal's qualitative analysis of the particular attributions typical of anti-Semitism, he stresses how images of the Jew as "the parasite, the enemy of collectivity, and unbridled, excessive hedonist" constitute "a condensed, perverted, manipulated concept of all social conditions that [workers] resent or reject" (Löwenthal 1987: 236). He contends that worker anti-Semitism is misdirected aggression against life in totally socialized society taking the form of false projection (*AL* Volume 3: 301). At the same time that the stereotyped Jew is aggressed against, he is also unconsciously envied:

> Jews are resented as people who seem to have broken the inescapable circle of work and leisure ... Jews are seen as living in a paradise of pleasure ... These unconscious fantasies betray the deep longings of toiling humanity. They become perverted projections when they are consciously released under the label 'Jewish.' Pleasure becomes depravity; freedom from care, carelessness; freedom from conventional restraints, shameless offense against the accepted standards of morality.
>
> LÖWENTHAL 1987: 234

This unconscious envy translates at times into inadvertent physical mimicry, according to Löwenthal (1987); e.g., a laborer who stereotypes Jews as overly expressive gesticulating while she complains about them.

To whatever extent it might anticipate later analyses, *AL* nevertheless retains a more classically Marxist emphasis on the potential for the U.S. labor force

---

5   Indeed, in his *AP* chapter "Prejudice in the Interview Material", Adorno acknowledges that additional questions were added to some of the depth-psychological Berkeley interviews based on material from the screened interviews in *AL* (*AP*: 605). Adorno became deeply involved with the *AL* study at the write-up stage, and it is clear that his burgeoning ideas about methodology, and qualitative analysis in particular, were influenced in part by the *AL* material and procedures (Clavey 2020).

to break the false ideology of anti-Semitism. Despite their rather disturbing findings, the researchers point hopefully to the fact that education seems to play an important immunizing role against the cancer of prejudice (*AL* Volume 3: 167, 286–289). The fact that the *AL* study is probably the closest the early ISR came to "action" research is borne out by the concluding recommendations of the study. These include a call for more practical, local, and concrete forms of labor education against prejudice and propaganda, which could consist in part of the very methods and conversations used in the study (*AL* Volume 4: 593).

3.4   Studies in Prejudice

Of the published *Studies in Prejudice* conducted during their U.S. exile, the two which the ISR would later name as definitive for shaping their subsequent conceptualization of prejudice in modern society were *The Authoritarian Personality* (Adorno, Frenkel-Brunswik, Levinson, and Sanford 1950; hereafter *AP*) and *Prophets of Deceit* (Löwenthal and Guterman 1949). The goal of *AP* was to determine the personality structure of "the *potentially fascistic* individual, one whose structure is such as to render him particularly susceptible to anti-democratic propaganda" (*AP*: 1), while the goal of *Prophets* was "to discover the social and psychological strains of agitation [propaganda] by means of isolating and describing its fundamental themes" (Löwenthal and Guterman 1949: 5). The ultimate aim of the studies was to identify "not only the suscepti-bility to antidemocratic propaganda but the most dependable sources of resis-tance to it" (*AP*: 10).

In 1945–46 over 2,000 subjects primarily in the San Francisco Bay Area were recruited to complete questionnaires through which a series of scales were validated (*AP*: 72–83). The researchers also administered projective tests and received open-ended responses, and recruited 80 participants scoring high and low in ethnocentrism for intensive clinical interviews. The interviews were content-analyzed by Frenkel-Brunswik, with the goal of differentiating the personality and the typical familial history of 'high' and 'low' scorers; and they were interpreted by Adorno with the goal of connecting prejudicial tenden-cies to broader sociopolitical trends. Throughout the project, the interviews and quantitative measures supplemented each other, as initial interviews sug-gested items for inclusion in the scales, which were in turn used to select par-ticipants for interview (*AP*: 18).

AP marked the height of the ISR's empirical inquiry into unconscious motives. The resulting *F*-scale consisted of several items that ostensibly did not relate to one another or to ideology and prejudice, but which nevertheless demonstrated robust correlations with the manifest ethnocentrism measure (*AP*: 257–265), and which could be validated in clinical interviews of high- and low-scorers (AP: 295–300, 472–473). The interviews, for their part, also indirectly approached latent dispositions, using a method of 'manifest' questions specifically design to evoke 'underlying' authoritarian responses in the domains of family, religion, attitudes toward race, etc. (AP: 303–325).

The qualitative material in particular revealed an image of the authoritarian personality as one who idealizes a stern father from their youth yet fails to show true emotional connections to family or others. Unresolved childhood conflicts and hypostatization of authority produce an individual oriented to submit to powerful figures and to 'externalize' inner conflicts through aggression against others perceived as weak. A particular danger of this type is the tendency to project a rigidly-stereotyped, Darwinian worldview (the "world as jungle"; AP: 411) onto intergroup relations, leading to unquestioning affiliation with an ingroup and support for the containment or expulsion of 'inferior' outgroups. The "low-scoring" type, defined primarily in contrast to the authoritarian, was considered to be more cognitively flexible and to have a warmer and more trusting attitude toward interpersonal relations. A key observed difference was the relatively greater awareness and acceptance of ambivalence and inner tension among the "lows", facets that tended to be repressed through cognitive distortions by the "highs" (AP: 451–459), a tendency Adorno would later characterize as 'abstractism.'

The companion study Prophets of Deceit consisted of detailed analysis of the propaganda tactics in the radio speeches and pamphlets of "agitators." These figures – radio personalities and aspiring politicians such as Father Coughlin, Gerald L. K. Smith, and Joseph E. McWilliams – drew considerable audiences during the Great Depression with their anti-Semitic messages. A guiding assumption of the Prophets analysis is that the propaganda resonates with the "emotional substratum" of listeners assumed to suffer from a "malaise" that reflects

> Profound transformations taking place in our economic and social structure – the replacement of the class of small independent producers by gigantic industrial bureaucracies, the decay of the patriarchal family, the breakdown of primary personal ties between individuals in an increasingly mechanized world, the compartmentalization and atomization of group life, and the substitution of mass culture for traditional patterns.
>
> LÖWENTHAL and GUTERMAN 1949: 15

This malaise effects a profound sense of disillusionment in the average person, generating two psychological tendencies which the agitator turns to his persuasive advantage: a deep mistrust of conventional leaders, against whom the agitator can contrast his apparently more radical stance; and a barely latent desire for punitive retribution against those who appear better off, whom the agitator can scapegoat.

Many of the "*constants of agitation*" (Löwenthal and Guterman 1949: 5) identified support the hypothesis that the content of these messages was designed to appeal specifically to the authoritarian personality. The techniques are actually designed to stimulate and reinforce this type's irrational features, representing a propaganda strategy Löwenthal dubbed "psychoanalysis in reverse" (see Jay 1973). For instance, the agitator gratifies a masochistic urge for submission by simultaneously humiliating his audience and glorifying their humility. The agitator declines to offer a political program for practically addressing the political-economic sources of modern malaise: Instead, he amplifies resentment and channels it against "personalized" scapegoats. The agents of the alleged conspiracy against the listener are ultimately suggested to be Jews and other "aliens", who are routinely described as "creatures of the underworld" to stoke the listener's neurotic defilement anxieties. Finally, the agitator gratifies sadistic urges to aggressively externalize one's own insecurities by enacting a verbal "rehearsal for destruction" of the enemy (Löwenthal and Guterman 1949: 37).

Intensive study of the psychological effects of contemporary malaise and disillusionment forms the subject of Adorno's qualitative analyses in *AP*, the sections of the study most connected to the pivot toward theorizing reified consciousness. Adorno finds evidence in the interviews of a "cultural climate" which "transcends the boundaries" of "the dichotomy of high and low scorers" (*AP*: 655). Among other pieces of evidence, Adorno points to the degree of ignorance in political affairs displayed by the majority of participants, and their compensatory tendencies toward a characteristic form of psychological concretism dubbed "personalization": conflating socioeconomic issues with the personalities of celebrity politicians.

When *AP* is compared to *WCW* and *AL*, what stands out is the almost complete disappearance of an interest in demographic and socio-economic factors. The ISR had confined itself to the investigation of "the parent-child relationship in the establishment of prejudice or tolerance" independent of "the social and economic processes that in turn determine the development of characteristic family patterns" (*AP*: 972). This was in part because Horkheimer and Adorno were developing their "theory of modern society as a whole" (*AP*: 608), as a consequence of which the post-exile empirical efforts would move directly toward investigation of the "cultural climate" in totally socialized society.

3.5   *The Stars Down to Earth* (SDE)

Stars Down to Earth is an uncharacteristically brief psychoanalytic content analysis of an astrological column published in the *Los Angeles Times* 1952–1953, performed independently by Adorno (1994 [1957]; hereafter *SDE*) during a return visit to the United States. Adorno was interested in the astrological forecast as a product of the culture industry, one that has certain unique features due to its functioning as a vestigial form of "secondary superstition." The primary function of the column is to reinforce and exacerbate certain compulsive tendencies in its readership, strengthening their "identification with the aggressor" of totally socialized society while also acting as a diversionary pressure valve and appealing to their narcissism.

> The ideal of social *conformity* [is] promoted throughout the column and expressed by the implicit, but ubiquitous rule that one has to adjust oneself continuously to commands of the stars at a given time ... The column indulges in a symbolic expression and psychological fortification of the pressure that is being continuously exercised upon people. They are simply to have confidence in that which is anyway.
>   *SDE*: 56–58

The study occupies a unique, transitional place in the research program. Although not formally published until 1957 at the program's end, it provides insight into how the inner circle theoretical pivot influenced the categories and themes of the post-exile studies. Adorno characterized *SDE* as the missing link between the *Studies in Prejudice* and *Dialectic of Enlightenment*. Indeed, it is probably the one empirical study Adorno devoted entirely to the nature of contemporary reified consciousness.

Adorno identifies several techniques employed by the column that are also broadly representative of other culture-industrial products; for instance, "pseudo-individualization" (*SDE*: 52), the technique of "endowing cultural mass production with a halo of free choice or open market on the basis of standardization itself" (*SDE*: 124). Characteristic of contemporary "false classless society," Adorno notes that while the column is clearly written for a type he ironically calls the "vice president" – a middle manager with some power over others but mostly serving at the behest of greater authorities – it also caters to the fantasies of its readership by sometimes elevating their sense of importance (e.g., by assuming they are car owners, despite the fact that the total readership at that time likely included many non-car owners). Most important is a technique Adorno calls the "bi-phasic approach," namely, relying on fetishization of time as a means of reconciling readers to the fact that conflict-ing demands are made on them for industrious, isolating work and prosocial leisure. Straightforwardly, the column associates the morning hours with work and the afternoon/evening hours with leisure and relies on the astrological assumption that if problems arise in the reader's life, this is because they failed to do something at the right time (*SDE*: 67).

More generally, Adorno's primary concern is how products such as the column fill the void of 'cultural cement' left by waning traditional culture (e.g., declining institutionalized religion) and encourage psychological adaptation on the part of the reader to the demands of totally socialized society. For example, the bi-phasic approach reinforces the contemporary scheme of work and leisure as intertwined and interdependent. The column relies heavily on the technique Adorno called personalization: The unrelenting demands of the socioeconomic system are reduced to the immediate needs of 'higher-ups' with whom the reader interacts at work (*SDE*: 98). 'Higher-ups' are indeed the type of social relation referred to with the most disproportionate frequency in the column according to Adorno's quantitative analysis (*SDE*: 109), and they are frequently conflated with 'friends.'

> The rationality of business relations is transfigured into love relation-ships in which the same ones one has to fear are those who mean one's best and whom therefore one has to love.
>
> *SDE*: 104

At an even more general level of analysis, Adorno notes that all calamities are attributed to personal mistakes and conflicts, whereas "the objective forces beyond the range of individual psychology and individual behavior are exempt from critique by being endowed with metaphysical dignity" (*SDE*: 58). Secondary superstitious material – such as the astrological forecast or soap opera – play the role of theodicy in totally socialized society that was once the province of traditional cultural worldviews.

The *Studies in Prejudice* linked directly fascist propagandistic stimuli to the divided minds of potential radical authoritarians. In a similar but distinct way, *SDE* examines the indirectly totalitarian culture-industrial material typical of totally socialized society, as it relates to the reified consciousness of everyday authoritarians.

3.6   *Gruppenexperiment* (*GE*)

After completing the Berkeley studies, Horkheimer expressed the ISR's desire to transition

into areas of research in which the unit of study is the group, the institution, the community ... Fortified by a better knowledge of *individual*
dynamics, we are now concerned with achieving a better understanding
of *group* dynamics.

> AP: vii

They specifically wanted to understand how group dynamics in Germany had
allowed the Nazi disaster to occur, and whether they still might give rise to a
fascist revival. Upon returning to Germany, the ISR (Pollock, Adorno et al. 2011;
hereafter GE) developed a new 'group discussion' method to observe the *in situ*
emergence of public opinion in realistic social situations. When small groups
can be provoked into raw, spontaneous discussions of sensitive topics:

> The [revealed] collective opinions elevate themselves to 'social facts' in
> Durkheim's sense and are by no means identical with the opinions of
> all the individuals, nor even with that of the majority, but instead corre-
> spond to the real or imagined mind (*Geist*) of the larger group with which
> each of the speakers identify.
>
> ADORNO and HORKHEIMER 1960: 6-7; my translation

For their first study employing this new technique, working in 1950–1951 from
research centers in Hesse, Bavaria, and Northern Germany, the ISR organized
semi-formal discussion groups of 8–16 unacquainted participants who met in
public places (e.g., clubs, cafeterias) accompanied only by an ISR research assistant and a tape recorder. Participants were given pseudonyms and assigned
to groups based on sociological categories of interest (e.g., college graduates,
older adults, farmers, clerks, housewives). Data were collected from roughly
1,800 participants, resulting in 121 discussion transcripts (over 6,000 pages).
The rich data were processed through content analysis, starting with a "coding key comprising hundreds of categories" (GE, p: 48) and resulting, through
iterative coding rounds, in close statistical consideration of seven key themes
or "attitudes."

The ISR used their qualitative data to probe defense mechanisms in public
speech, to document how "people virtually speak two languages" (GE: 51).

> In the language of their profession and of daily contact, they are able to
> express themselves rationally ... When they are confronted with highly
> emotionally charged problems, however, this language fails them, and
> they are forced to resort to a second one, which has in common with
> language only the use of words. Actually, it is stammering ... The conflict

situation appears to destroy language; it reduces the ability for meaningful, intelligible expression. By doing just that, however, it unearths the real psychological layer. The irrational, whose expression the speaker unconsciously tries to prevent, emerges in the structure of the second language.

GE: 51

The 'conflict situation' was the question of German guilt for World War II and the Holocaust. Latent attitudes toward this issue were examined through the organization of the group discussions around a carefully constructed stimulus, the 'Colburn letter," which was read at the beginning of each session. Ostensibly written by a U.S. soldier stationed in occupied Germany, the letter critiqued German society and touched on the highly sensitive topics of collective guilt and German submissiveness to authority. This stimulus was designed to provoke the emergence of latent attitudes and a preformed ideology – lingering after the apparent eradication of Nazism – that participants normally hid but would enact to defend their "collective narcissism" (GE: 149).

Just as in the anti-Semitism study, researchers assigned individual statements in the group discussions labels, e.g., "approving, ambivalent, or disapproving attitude." The content analysis involved coding statements based on their relevance for identified focal themes. As in the Weimar study, the final outcome variables were percentage counts of labels assigned to the qualitative statements, stratified according to social group (gender, age, occupation, and levels of education and military service).

Results revealed that a preponderance of German citizens showed lingering remnants of a fascist ideology. Only a disconcerting minority of participants displayed an unambiguously positive attitude toward Western democratic ideals. Many were openly apologetic for National Socialism and refused to acknowledge German collective guilt or to absolve Jewish citizens of any responsibility for the atrocities they suffered. Of course, these disturbing attitudes were to a large extent evoked by the threat of the clearly impactful stimulus letter. Yet notable beyond the number of clearly anti-democratic remarks was the ambivalence displayed by many participants, chronicled extensively in Adorno's (2010) separate qualitative analysis. Individuals sometimes oscillated between condemnation of Nazi crimes and anti-Semitic remarks without awareness of their self-contradicting statements. In their summary of the quantitative results, the ISR reported that "only about one-sixth of the speakers have a positive attitude (16%) [towards topics such as democracy, remilitarization, and German guilt], but almost three times as many have a negative one (44%) and more than twice as many an ambivalent one" (GE: 106).

Despite the fact that some of the demographic groups (e.g., farmers) displayed remarkably deviant (and authoritarian) attitudes (GE: 102–104), the researchers interpreted the overall pattern as evidence of a consistent public opinion that emerged spontaneously across the discussions (GE: 108).

Perhaps most interesting are the detailed analyses of the typical group dynamics that generated this public opinion. Groups often displayed a dynamic of artificial solidarity: over the course of the discussion the members gradually moved toward conformity and a climactic point during which they would compete with each other to echo stock phrases (see GE Appendix B). The researchers interpreted the discussions as satisfying the participants' "drive for expression, the wish to have an audience, but also the desire to be part of an audience"; yet they were quick to point out that this did not imply individuals gained control over the social field. Rather, a dynamic process occurred through which individual behavior gave rise to social facts which in turn exerted dominion over the participants:

> At first, liberation of the individual takes place in the formation of a group insofar as fears are alleviated and controls (taboos of strangerhood) are removed. While the individuals in this phase seem to try to shape the group according to their will and their aims, regression soon sets in. The individuals then submit to new controls (group norms); they delegate their own will to a certain degree again to the group, and the group for its part gains power over its elements.
>
> GE: 146

This "regression" was repeatedly observed as the artificial solidarity, once established, would then quickly fade into exhaustion, with each individual retreating from conversation.

Participants drew on culturally standardized, rationalistic defenses to address accusations of guilt in the stimulus letter. As Adorno (2010) observed, the indoctrination of the German populace by Nazi propaganda left a trace in their arguments and expressions. Interestingly, many of these rationalizations echoed those employed by U.S. laborers during the war, as documented in the anti-Semitism study. Earlier, Massing pointed out that U.S. workers disbelieved stories about the Holocaust because it was psychologically simpler to imagine them too horrible to be true (AL Volume 3: 172); similarly, Adorno (2010: 56–67) found that post-war Germans often denied or qualified the idea that they actually knew about the atrocities as they were occurring. Massing found cases of U.S. workers rationalizing Nazi actions with the "just-world" logic that if such terrible things were being done, the victims *must* have been in some way responsible (*AL* Volume 3: 170); disturbingly, even among Germans after the Holocaust, Adorno (2010: 134–136, 152–156) still observed instances of such victim-blaming perversity. One of the most common defense mechanisms in the *GE* data, however, was a form of fatalistic submission to the status quo that served as a defense mechanism for those unwilling to admit complicity. "It is significant for the problem of guilt that individuals are not only actually dependent, but regard themselves from the very beginning as dependent chess pieces, identify with the situation, and in the process strengthen it even more" (Adorno 2010: 101). Although the majority of the participants were not Nazi exterminators, they still felt compelled to defend themselves against charges of collective guilt: they sometimes exonerated themselves by pointing to the immediate threat of the Nazi military, but just as often gestured toward the inexorable hand of history and the eternal recurrence of war in the face of which the commoner is powerless. Aided by such stereotyped defenses, with few exceptions, the *GE* participants failed to achieve either critical self-consciousness or genuine interdependence in the groups.

For the ISR, German Fascism was a prototype of the processes they believed to be occurring in totally socialized society everywhere: the decline of the individual in the face of powerful, anonymous economic forces, and the infiltration of group-based consciousness through the propagandistic culture industry. The interpretations of the *GE* data move the research program at its end away from the typologies employed in the earlier studies. Gone is the polarizing focus on understanding the individual psychology or social background of authoritarians and egalitarians. In its place is a microscopic examination of the process through which ideology emerges and feeds reified consciousness. In their final studies with small groups, the ISR achieved a methodological perspective on society that matched the pivot in inner circle theorizing. The unique combination of a controlled social setting with detailed transcription of individual statements allowed the researchers to document the social construction of ideology as it occurred, and to observe how the pressures of anomic social interaction give rise to individual acts of ambivalent conformity.

3.7   *Betriebsklima*

The group discussion method was employed again by the ISR in their research on the *Betriebsklima* or 'workplace climate' of five German factories, funded as an internal study by the Mannesmann company (Frankfurt ISR: 1955). The method was indeed appropriate, insofar as the ISR conceived of workplace climate as an essentially social-psychological construct, an organizational ideology that fluidly intertwined static and dynamic elements of the industrial process, as well as subjective (worker attitudes) and objective (political-economic conditions) factors (von Friedeburg 1963: 14–15, 18–19). In addition to carrying out individual interviews with nearly 12,000 employees, researchers conducted 55 group discussions in response to the stimulus of a fictional conversation between two workers ("Karl" and "Jupp") conveying, on the one hand, the belief that better worker representation in high-level decision-making is important, and, on the other, that improved and secure terms of employment are sufficient (Frankfurt ISR 1955: 95–96, 107–109). The study was led by Ludwig von Friedeburg, who would write a *Habilitation* thesis (1963) that built on the results with more critical-theoretical exposition (Eichler et al. 2010: 166–170; Wiggershaus 1994: 480–489).

The fact that *Betriebsklima* represented the last concentrated empirical effort led by the central members of the early ISR is emblematic of the inner circle shift toward studies of reified consciousness. Indeed, given that the published report of the study is the closest the ISR came to 'administrative' as opposed to critical research – facilitating the Mannesmann company's control over its workers – one could take issue with the idea that the work belongs to the broader program on authoritarianism, and even see it as a direct contribution by the ISR to the *production* of reified consciousness (Wiggershaus 1994). The published report makes little reference to the group discussions, focusing instead on average results of quantified responses to the interview questions. The major, somewhat paradoxical finding was that, at a conscious level, workers tended to express that adequate pay was the most important factor determining their job satisfaction; however, when using more indirect questions or statistical techniques, wages were a less important determiner of climate than social factors such as job security and relationships with bosses (von Friedeburg 1963: 48; Wiggershaus 1994: 483).

Despite the apparently administrative quality of the research, the results were interpreted through a critical lens by the ISR on multiple occasions. In fact, Horkheimer (1985 [1955]) characterized the study as a documentation of dramatic changes in the consciousness of contemporary workers that had taken place since the World War I era, inviting interpretation of *Betriebsklima* as an empirical bookend to the original Weimar investigation. Building from the contradiction between what workers believed influenced workplace climate (wages) and the factors that objectively did (humanization of the workplace), von Friedeburg (1963: 48–51, 73–74) stressed how the ideologically-charged atmosphere in a firm could act as a breeding ground for reified consciousness reproducing status quo conditions.

> The conflicts of interest between management and the workforce man-
> ifest in symptoms [e.g., the symbolically inflated importance of wages]
> that simultaneously mask them, because a particular moment pretends
> to be the whole. Concretism and personalization allow the dissolution of
> an objective clash of interests in the phenomenon of workplace climate.
>
> VON FRIEDBURG 1963: 51; my translation

For his part, Adorno also interpreted these data in terms of concretism and
personalization, and he returned to them repeatedly in discussions of reified
consciousness. He used the *Betriebsklima* findings as the basis for a 1964 lecture on the "system-immanence of the proletariat, or the so-called integration of the proletariat, from the perspective of the proletarian consciousness"
(Adorno 2019: 33). Adorno essentially argued that because the interviewed
workers failed to report much concern with system-level factors or desire
for higher-order participation – focusing instead on 'concrete' factors such
as organizational identification and immediate relationships with bosses –
a potentially historically extant class consciousness had been replaced by
a reified mode of thought. Adorno discussed the tendency for employers to
exploit organizational ideologies to weaken class consciousness and warned
about "the moment of apathy [in post-war Germany], developing in several
aspects, where no fundamental democratic conditions are in place" (Frankfurt
ISR 1955: 16; my translation). In an unpublished afterword written for the study
concerning "Workplace climate and alienation" (Adorno 1955), he further
traced the workers' concretism to several political-economic factors, including
the apparent improvement of living conditions through the rise of consumer
society, the mediatized up-playing of international conflicts (i.e., with Russia),
and the general discrediting of political thought by the implosion of the Nazi
propaganda machine.

Interestingly, at the very end of the research program, Adorno also continued
to emphasize the lingering occasional importance of social class in determining
consciousness. When discussing *Betriebsklima* (e.g., Adorno 2017 [1958]: 122–
123), he would often highlight a fact obscured in the report, namely that among
the types of workers interviewed, miners were especially likely to personalize
their bosses and treat them as scapegoats. Adorno interpreted this finding in
light of the fact that miners felt they still labored under relatively strenuous
and dangerous conditions and were being left behind and stigmatized through
general social-technological progress. Because personalization is a psychological defense mechanism against the anxiety of helplessness in totally socialized
society, miners were especially motivated to invoke this defense.

4   The Critical Research Program in Hindsight and Prospect

What are we to make of the reconstructed, 30-year empirical program on authoritarianism of the early ISR? I think three conclusions are clearly warranted. First, it was a remarkably vibrant and productive example of the interplay between theory and research. The ideas of Horkheimer and Adorno about the nature of contemporary authoritarianism changed dramatically during this period, but their empirical methods kept pace. Continual reference to study findings even in their later theoretical works suggests this was not a one-way street, but rather an ongoing dialogue. Certainly, the pivot in theorizing influenced the nature of the questions asked and the methods used in the later studies, but this does not thereby invalidate the results. Indeed, the ISR's willingness to devise new methods on the basis of changing theory represents a remarkable approximation to idealized prototypes of the scientific method – a certainly ironic state of affairs given their reputation as pseudoscientists or 'mandarins.'

Second, and related, the empirical program is a richly extensive documentation of authoritarianism in diverse geographical and historical contexts. Even if different scholars take issue with some of the theoretical interpretations, there is no denying that the massive effort behind the studies bequeathed a wealth of historically valuable information about the psychology of labor and anti-Semitic prejudice. Secondary scholars have only recently begun to realize the potential for theory refinement or new theory-testing by direct 'digging' through these data. For example, the report of the anti-Semitism study is digitally available from the Max Horkheimer archive and contains a wealth of information on prejudice among U.S. workers at the time, which has only begun to be reconstructed and re-examined in secondary sources (Rensmann 2017; Worrell 2009; Ziege 2012). The mass of data from the *Gruppenexperiment* is currently housed in the archives of the contemporary ISR, and secondary researchers Lohl and Winter (2019) have, for instance, used the raw data to test the Mitscherlichs' (1975) thesis about psychodynamic and affective complexes in postwar Germany. The data from the Mannesmann company used in the *Betriebsklima* study are available for purchase and download from the Gesis archive of the Leibniz Institute for Social Science at Köln. Although more archival work would certainly improve the accessibility of the Frankfurt School data for a wide audience of researchers, the mass of well-documented but largely undiscovered information on authoritarianism in the 20th Century could keep scholars and historians busy for a long time.

Third, arguably more important than the data themselves, or the conclusions the inner circle drew from them, are the *methods* the group constructed for probing the interplay between unconscious individual and mass-sociological factors in the emergence and sustentation of authoritarianism. With the exception of the scale construction techniques used in *AP*, these methods are also only now being fully appreciated by a new generation of social scientists struggling to combat totalitarian ideologies, in efforts such as the present edited volume. It is worth pausing for detailed reflection on how many of these methodological innovations anticipated, but might also improve upon, the contemporary social science of authoritarianism, prejudice, and other topics.

A consistent goal was the revolutionary attempt to capture latent attitudes of the participants. The 'interpretative questionnaire' method pioneered by Fromm and collaborators for the Weimar study warrants revisiting. It was most effectively used decades later in Fromm and Maccoby (1996 [1970]), a study that integrated the qualitative method with quantitative factor analysis to produce a typology of peasant participants which could then be related to social and economic factors. The screened interview and group discussion methods are also highly innovative ways to elicit attitudes that might otherwise be disguised or distorted. At the same time, the 'Colburn letter' presented as a stimulus at the beginning of the *GE* sessions was an innovation that predates two broad empirical literatures on politics, prejudice, and intergroup conflict in contemporary social psychology, namely terror management theory (Pyszczynski, Solomon, and Greenberg 2015) and social identity theory (Postmes and Branscombe 2010). These theories share, along with many other contemporary psychological theories, the hypothesis that prejudice is often a response to a threatened cultural worldview or social identity. *GE* followed a similar logic, assuming that latent prejudices of postwar German participants could be elicited through a threat to the already fragile status of their national identity.

The ISR also anticipated the importance of true experimental methods in contemporary social psychology. They had in fact planned to conduct experiments with U.S. community samples in which a video stimulus would be shown with different conditions depicting a schoolyard altercation between a Jewish and a Gentile boy (Horkheimer and Adorno 1941). Although the plan was never executed due to insufficient resources, it was remarkably prescient, particularly in the researchers' recognition that the assessment of responses to a controlled, fabricated stimulus would permit examination of attitudes that might otherwise be censored. The plan pre-dated the first comparable 'experimental' study of prejudice in social psychology (Allport and Postman 1945) and might have had a major influence on the field if it had been carried out. Despite their understanding of the experimental method, prominently lacking throughout the early ISR studies are unequivocal statements regarding the outcome of hypothesis tests and multivariate comparisons highlighting the most 'significant' causal factors. The reports always rely on comprehensive presentation of numerous percentages stratified by the predictor variables. In a surprising update to the positivist dispute between Popper and Adorno, this complex analytic style – which was already becoming unfashionable in U.S. social psychology of the 1950s – anticipates the 'new statistics' approach currently being recommended, which advocates for comprehensive descriptions of the data over simple null-hypothesis significance tests (Cumming 2014).

Also highly prescient was the attempt to carry out multilevel analyses that considered the interplay between individual attitudes and cultural products – e.g., in the *Studies in Prejudice* approach of concurrently investigating personality factors and propagandistic stimuli. While this had arguably been attempted before in social science research, it had never been done on such an extensive and systematic scale.[6] This methodology anticipates an entire contemporary subfield referred to as cultural psychology, in which the 'mutual constitution' of individual psyches and cultural institutions and products is assumed and examined (Markus and Kitayama 2010; Morling and Lamoreaux 2008). More recently, the importance of propaganda analysis for understanding a current epidemic of authoritarian populism has been rediscovered, often by researchers not fully aware of the ISR's programmatic efforts.[7]

Beyond these positive conclusions concerning the legacy of the empirical program and its prospects for future revitalization, the preceding review of the reconstructed body of work also permits defense of the early ISR against some common misguided accusations. The popular but ridiculous accusation levied by many contemporary social psychologists that the ISR reduced prejudice and authoritarianism to "mere personality" clearly stems from a lack of serious engagement with the body of research. It is true that, within mainstream social psychology, the ISR is exclusively remembered for the *F*-scale, which was initially widely popular but fell into disfavor as its factor structure proved

---

6   By contrast, for example, the related work of the Institute for Propaganda Analysis in the
    1930s reads more as the output of a kind of "fact-checking" service arming the public against
    propaganda without deeply considering its psychological appeal (Lee and Lee 1939). The
    most sophisticated multilevel work was being done contemporaneously (and to some extent
    in collaboration with the ISR) by Lazarsfeld and his associates at Princeton and Columbia
    (see Barton 1979; Jennemann 2007).

7   For instance, in a large sample of U.S. residents surveyed prior to the 2016 election, Morgan
    and Shanahan (2017) found support for a statistical mediation model in which greater hours
    spent watching Fox News predicted greater personal authoritarianism, which in turn pre-
    dicted greater intentions to vote for Donald Trump. Similar effects were found among spe-
    cific viewers of *The Apprentice* by Gabriel et al. (2018).

unreliable and the 'situational' perspective of Milgram and Zimbardo rose to prominence.[8] But consideration of the research program shows that the study of the authoritarian personality was only one aspect of the ISR's much broader dialectical approach. After the Berkeley studies, the GE project was an unparalleled attempt to observe how group-based consciousness gives rise to a noncritical public opinion in concrete social situations.

It is also far too simple to state that the inner circle abandoned research in their twilight years. What the ISR increasingly rejected was not empiricism per se, but rather the kind of technocratic empirical work (ascendant in the 1950s) that abandoned the search for comprehensive and philosophically critical views of social reality. The ISR were hostile towards theoretical developments which have only gained influence up to the present, including approaches that positioned authoritarianism and prejudice as universal aspects of psychology and not as historically situated actions rooted in material social forces. Contemporary researchers like Milgram and Sherif, and later Tajfel and Zimbardo, abstracted conformist behavior from its sociological context, explaining the 'power of the situation' in largely evolutionary-psychological terms. The classic social psychological experimentalists suggested that humans in all societies developed an adaptive commitment to authority structures which made them susceptible to a conformist shift under the influence of situational pressures. This trend toward universalizing, norm-based explanations continues basically unabated in 21st Century frameworks for understanding authoritarianism. Social psychologists routinely ignore cultural-historical variation by implying that people's innate social cognitive tendencies – rather than the situated experience of life in late capitalist society – make them either endlessly malleable pawns of the situation, or reducible to a few 'good' and 'bad' types. These developments have been directly traced to historical changes in the methodology of mainstream social psychology (e.g., towards controlled lab experiments and methodological individualism) which the ISR critiqued (Greenwood 2004).

Adorno sought to differentiate the findings of critical research from these universalizing social psychological interpretations as they were already taking shape. He was concerned that evolutionary-psychological discussions of problems like the human tendency toward ingroup bias mistook manifestations for true causes in the study of prejudice.

---

8   A fairly ironic course of events, given that the F-scale was in fact among the *only* individual difference measures that explained meaningful variance in participant behavior both in Milgram's paradigm *and* the Stanford Prison Experiment (Elms and Milgram 1966; Haney, Banks, and Zimbardo 1973).

Such assumptions frequently lead to a neutralization of scientific issues permitting phenomena which are intrinsically related to concrete property and power relationships, to appear as being due to the existence of organized society as such. In spite of the emphasis on 'social factors,' current sociological explanations thus assume an air of 'naturalness' which makes prejudice seem harmless – a necessary evil of organized society – and perennial ... [This approach] would hypostatize the congealed effect of material social forces and make them, in turn, responsible for tendencies of which they themselves are mere results. This leads to a superficial common sense attitude that ... [cannot] conceive the idea of a social change through which this threat may disappear.

ADORNO 2019 [1948]: liv

It is true that Horkheimer and Adorno's cynical analysis of the pressures of totally socialized society led them to believe that reified consciousness would become increasingly prevalent, prompting them to all but abandon the more optimistic attempt to overcome false consciousness that characterized their early studies. But standard accounts to the contrary, the ISR never completely lost sight of the possibility that some individuals might retain the strength to resist these pressures. The qualitative analyses of Frenkel-Brunswik (AP: 409–411) and Adorno (Adorno 2010: 170–179) converge on the insight that the least authoritarian and most open-minded individuals in contemporary society are those who can empathetically understand the contexts in which others find themselves, and who have at least some grasp of the role of broader social and historical forces in shaping our daily lives – in other words, those who have not lost the capacity for experience in abstractism, and who refuse to invoke the defensive postures of concretism. To the end, the ISR's struggle against positivism was that between a view of science as a tool for historical reflexivity in the hands of individuals striving for a better society, and as a tool for describing the social world as it is in generalizable, parsimonious formulae. Quantitative social scientists working today would do well to revisit this epistemological struggle.

5   Toward Deep Interdisciplinarity and the Integration of Theory and
        Research

Over the course of the 20th Century and into the 21st, divides between the humanities and the social sciences, between qualitative and quantitative methods, between philosophy and empirical research have deepened and been – dare one say – reified. It is all too difficult for scholars today, on either side of these aisles, to project themselves back into the mindset of ambitious possibility that characterized the early work of Horkheimer, Fromm, and their collaborators. It is all too easy to forget that the study of the Weimar working class was one of the first large-scale sociological surveys with a psychological emphasis, outside of administrative efforts at consolidating biopower (Smith 1998). When Horkheimer wrote his critical theory essay, and when Adorno engaged in the positivist dispute, it was still possible to believe that critical theory and research were the correct and viable modes for social science, that logical positivism and Popper's fallibilism were temporary distractions, and that eventually *mainstream* research would be ensconced in Marxist and psychoanalytic frameworks. Today, most of us working with critical theory inherit what automatically feels like a secondary and reactionary vantage point: Positivist social science was victorious, and we struggle in the dark to keep the flame alive.

But like most narratives about the early Frankfurt School, this one is too simple. It was always a struggle, even for them. Thus, at a time when authoritarian populism is again ascendant, and the scholarly resources for combatting it seem fragmented, we would do well to reflect on the unique constellation of factors that allowed the early ISR to pursue their integrative program of theory and research. If we understand what it took for the original work to be done, perhaps the Frankfurt School's model can not only be reconstructed but resurrected.

First, the researchers of the ISR were remarkably collaborative and open-minded. Horkheimer recognized from the beginning that expertise in multiple disciplines would be required to pursue the project. But not only did the ISR assemble a stellar 'internal' team of scholars united by an interest in Marxism and psychoanalysis; they also willingly collaborated with and learned from, on multiple occasions, their positivist 'opponents,' such as Paul Lazarsfeld. More so than many contemporary theorists, the early ISR recognized that it was essential to engage with concrete data derived from advanced empirical methods; and moreover, that engagement should be substantive, requiring collaboration, education, and experience. One cannot really critique a method until one has mastered it. It is one thing to engage in the hard work of collaboration and apprenticeship in methods; it is still more difficult to keep a truly open mind about the interplay of empirical methods and philosophy. The emergence of 'lazy pragmatism' in contemporary social science (see Morelock and Sullivan, present volume) attests that the easy road is to simply practice either philosophy or empirical research and tolerate the other field with indifference or polemically try to write it out of existence. Maintaining a balance between these different modes of human inquiry requires a pragmatic openness about method that is cognitively very difficult to sustain. But Horkheimer, Adorno, and Fromm – each in their own way – recognized the importance of this and offer examples we might emulate.

Second, the ISR had a consistent, driving vision of research as a socially engaged and crucial effort independent of careerist and mediatized concerns. Their studies were massive efforts involving extensive research teams and large samples – and despite this, the researchers consistently note in their reports that the data always fell short of their original ambitions. Such efforts were only possible because the studies engaged the most pressing socio-political issues of the time, and the researchers involved believed what they were doing was crucially important to society. In the isolating cages of today's academic 'rat race,' researchers can easily lose sight of such a big picture and console themselves with positivist rationalizations about epistemic humility – best to be a functioning cog if it puts food on the table. If the deep interdisciplinarity of the early ISR is to be recovered, a key component will be the rekindling of an inspiring vision of what social research can do to achieve social goals, such as the fights against fascism and inequality.

But such considerations bring us to the third factor behind the ISR's program, one that is perhaps the most unique and circumstantial yet played a pivotal role in both the successes and failures of the program. This is the relatively autonomous nature of the ISR in terms of both research 'inputs' (funding) and 'outputs' (publication). The program would have never gotten off the ground without the highly fortuitous support of Felix Weil, and over the subsequent decades Horkheimer proved repeatedly resourceful in marshaling continued support and organizing independent publication outputs. On the one hand, this autonomy allowed the ISR to pursue its alternate vision for theory and science in ways that would not have been possible if they were competing for standard funding sources and publication through traditional presses and journals. On the other hand, it undoubtedly contributed to their "outsider" status, and the containment of their ideas, outside the walls of mainstream social science. The prejudices of positivists can only be blamed to such an extent; aside from the intrinsically difficult language and scope of the ISR reports, many of them were never actually published or translated.

At least this relatively minor stumbling block is now being cleared, through the recent translation efforts of scholars like Jeffrey Olick and Andrew Perrin, as well as the archival work of secondary scholars such as Mark Worrell, John Abromeit, and Lars Rensmann – building, of course, on the earlier foundations of Martin Jay, Wolfgang Bonß, Douglas Kellner, Gillian Rose, Susan Buck-Morss, the staff of *Telos*, and many others. The present volume is another milestone in the long but profitable enterprise of reconstructing – and, in many ways, attempting to complete – the innovative model of integrated theory and research proposed by the early Frankfurt School. When these relatively simple literal translation efforts are complete is when the comparatively difficult work of figurative translation begins. How will we marshal the vision and the talent to bring this model of deep interdisciplinary scholarship to bear on the ruptures of current global society? How will we once again foster the spirit of intensive and open collaboration between philosophers and empirical researchers? How will the funding be generated to support intense empirical investigation of large samples of human subjects, across typical disciplinary boundaries and in opposition to the technocratic aims of research agencies?

The road will be long and hard, but the map bequeathed to us is being pieced together at last and recognized for what it was. And as the founders of the Frankfurt School would have stressed, the price paid for foregoing the journey would be dear. To the last, the ISR faulted both their study participants and fellow social scientists for the denial of history and for fatalistic acceptance of the present as an instantiation of allegedly universal, recurrent processes. And, to the last, they retained hope that a critical sociology might cast light on the way out.

> The inheritance of philosophy that has been taken over by sociology is not exhausted in the self-reflection of society. Without thoughts of resistance against the descent into totalitarianism, of the preservation and expansion of the powers of freedom, sociology will not be able to find its way out of the labyrinth of social machinery, however unclear this way is in the dark.
>
> HORKHEIMER 1959: 34; my translation

References

Abromeit, John. 2011. *Max Horkheimer and the Foundations of the Frankfurt School.* New York: Cambridge University Press.

Adorno, Theodor W. 1955. "*Betriebsklima* und Entfremdung." In Theodor W. Adorno, *Gesammelte Schriften, Vol. 20.2: Vermischte Schriften II*, 674–684. At https://soth-alexanderstreet-com. Accessed October 30, 2019.

Adorno, Theodor W. 2010. *Guilt and Defense*, trans. Jeffrey K. Olick and Andrew J. Perrin. Cambridge: Harvard University Press.

Adorno, Theodor W. 2017 [1958]. *Introduction to Dialectics,* ed. Christoph Ziermann, trans. Nicholas Walker. Cambridge: Polity Press.

Adorno, Theodor W. 2000 [1968]. *Introduction to Sociology*, ed. Christoph Gödde, trans. Edmund Jephcott. Cambridge: Polity Press.

Adorno, Theodor W. 1976. "Introduction" and "Sociology and empirical research." In *The Positivist Dispute in German Sociology*, ed. David Frisby, trans. G. Adey, 1–86. London: Heinemann.

Adorno, Theodor W. 2003 [1964]. *The Jargon of Authenticity*, trans. Knut Tarnowski and Frederic Will. New York: Routledge.

Adorno, Theodor W. 2019 [1948]. "Remarks on *The Authoritarian Personality*." In Adorno et al., *The Authoritarian Personality*. Brooklyn: Verso.

Adorno, Theodor W. 2019 [1964]. *Philosophical Elements of a Theory of Society*, eds. Tobias ten Brink and Marc Phillip Nogueira, trans. Wieland Hoban. Cambridge: Polity Press.

Adorno, Theodor W. 1967. Sociology and psychology. *New Left Review* 46: 67–97.

Adorno, Theodor W. 1994 [1957]. "The Stars Down to Earth: The *Los Angeles Times* Astrology Column." In Theodor W. Adorno, *The Stars Down to Earth and Other Essays on the Irrational in Culture*, 46–171. New York: Routledge. [Abbreviated *SDE* in this chapter].

Adorno, Theodor W., Else Frenkel-Brunswik, Daniel J. Levinson, and R. Nevitt Sanford, et al. 1950. *The Authoritarian Personality*. New York: Harper. [Abbreviated *AP* in this chapter].

Adorno, Theodor W. and Max Horkheimer. 1960. "Vorwort." In Werner Mangold, *Gegenstand und Methode des Gruppendiskussionsverfahrens: aus der Arbeit des Instituts für Sozialforschung (Frankfurter Beiträge zur Soziologie, Vol. 9)*, 5–8. Frankfurt am Main: Europäische Verlaganstalt.

Allport, Gordon W. and Leo J. Postman. 1945. "The Basic Psychology of Rumor." *New York Academy of Sciences: Section of Psychology*. November 19.

Barton, Allen H. 1979. "Paul Lazarsfeld and Applied Social Research: Invention of the University Applied Social Research Institute." *Social Science History* 3: 4–44.

Calvey, David. 2017. *Covert Research: The Art, Politics, and Ethics*. Thousand Oaks, CA: Sage.

Clavey, Charles. 2020. "Inhuman Methods for an Inhuman World: Adorno's Empirical Social Research, 1938–1950." In *A Companion to Adorno*, eds. Peter E. Gordon, Espen Hammer, and Max Pensky, 153–172. New York: John Wiley.

Collomp, Catherine. 2011. "'Anti-Semitism among American Labor': A Study by the Refugee Scholars of the Frankfurt School of Sociology at the End of World War II." *Labor History* 52: 417–439.

Cook, Deborah. 1998. "Adorno on Late Capitalism: Totalitarianism and the Welfare State." *Radical Philosophy* 89: 16–26.

Cumming, Geoff. 2014. "The New Statistics: Why and How." *Psychological Science* 25: 7–29.

Eichler, Lutz, Hermann Kocyba, and Wolfgang Menz. 2010. "Gesellschaftstheoretischer Anspruch und die Beharrlichkeit des Besonderen: Theorie und Empirie in den industriesoziologischen Arbeiten des Instituts für Sozialforschung." In *Industriesoziologische Fallstudien: Entwicklungspotenziale einer Forschungsstrategie*, eds. Hans J. Pongratz and Rainier Trinczek, 163–201. Berlin: Edition Sigma.

Elms, A. C. and Stanley Milgram. 1966. Personality characteristics associated with obedience and defiance toward authoritative command. *Journal of Experimental Research in Personality* 1: 282–289.

Frankfurt Institute for Social Research. 1972 [1956]. *Aspects of Sociology*. Trans. J. Viertel. Boston: Beacon Press.

Frankfurt Institute for Social Research/Institut für Sozialforschung. 1955. *Betriebsklima: Eine industriesoziologische Untersuchung aus dem Ruhrgebiet* (*Frankfurter Beiträge zur Soziologie, Vol. 3*). Frankfurt am Main: Europäische Verlaganstalt.

Frankfurt Institute for Social Research/Institut für Sozialforschung. 1936. *Studien über Autorität und Familie*. Lüneburg: Dietrich zu Klampen Verlag. At https://ia800504. us.archive.org/29/items/HorkheimerEtAlAutoritatUndFamilie/Horkheimer%20 et%20al-%20Autorita%CC%88t%20und%20Familie.pdf.

von Friedeburg, Ludwig. 1963. *Soziologie des Betriebsklimas: Studien zur Deutung empirischer Untersuchungen in industriellen Großbetrieben* (*Frankfurter Beiträge zur Soziologie, Vol. 13*). Frankfurt am Main: Europäische Verlaganstalt.

Fromm, Erich. 1998 [1936]. "Social Psychological Aspect." Unpublished translation by George Lundskow. In Frankfurt ISR, *Studien über Autorität und Familie*. Lüneburg: Dietrich zu Klampen Verlag.

Fromm, Erich. 1984. *The Working Class in Weimar Germany*, ed. Wolfgang Bonβ, trans. Barbara Weinberger. Cambridge: Harvard University Press. [Abbreviated *WCW* in this chapter].

Fromm, Erich and Michael Maccoby. 1996 [1970]. *Social Character in a Mexican Village: A Sociopsychoanalytic Study*. Englewood Cliffs, NJ: Grove Press.

Gabriel, Shira, Elaine Paravati, Melanie C. Green, and Jason Flomsbee. 2018. "From *Apprentice* to President: The Role of Parasocial Connection in the Election of Donald Trump." *Social Psychological and Personality Science* 9: 299–307.

Greenwood, John D. 2004. *The Disappearance of the Social in American Social Psychology*. New York: Cambridge UP.

Haney, Craig, Curtis Banks and Philip Zimbardo. 1973. Interpersonal dynamics in a simulated prison. *International Journal of Criminology and Penology* 1: 69–97.

Hedrick, Todd. 2018. *Reconciliation and Reification: Freedom's Semblance and Actuality from Hegel to Contemporary Critical Theory*. Oxford: Oxford University Press.

Horkheimer, Max. 1972 [1936]. "Authority and the Family." In Max Horkheimer *Critical Theory: Selected Essays*, 47–128. New York: Seabury Press.

Horkheimer, Max. 1949. "Authoritarianism and the Family Today." In *The Family: Its Function and Destiny*, ed. Ruth Nanda Anshen, 359–374. New York: Harper.

Horkheimer, Max. 1985 [1955]. "Menschen im Großbetrieb." In Max Horkheimer, *Gessamelte Schriften: Vorträge und Aufzeichnungen 1949–1973, Vol. 4: Soziologisches*, 95–105. Fischer Verlag.

Horkheimer, Max. 1989 [1940]. "Notes on Institute Activities." In *Critical Theory and Society*, eds. Stephen Eric Bronner and Douglas Kellner, 264–266. New York: Routledge.

Horkheimer, Max. 1959. Soziologie und Philosophie. In *Soziologie und moderne Gesellschaft: Verhandlungen des 14. Deustchen Soziologentages vom 20. bis 24. Mai 1959 in Berlin*, ed. A. Busch, 27–38. Stuttgart: Ferdinand Enke.

Horkheimer, Max. 1972 [1937]. "Traditional and Critical Theory." In Max Horkheimer *Critical Theory: Selected Essays*, 188–243. New York: Seabury Press.

Horkheimer, Max, and Theodor W. Adorno. 1941. "Research Project on Anti-Semitism." *Studies in Philosophy and Social Science* 9: 124–143.

Institute for Social Research. 1945. *Antisemitism among American Labor*. Unpublished report, 5 vols. At http://sammlungen.ub.uni-frankfurt.de/horkheimer/nav/classification/10065106 Accessed April 10, 2020. [Abbreviated *AL* in this chapter].

Jay, Martin. 1973. *The Dialectical Imagination*. Berkeley: University of California Press.

Jenemann, David. 2007. *Adorno in America*. Minneapolis: University of Minnesota Press.

Komarovsky, Mirra. 2004 [1940]. *The Unemployed Man and his Family*. Walnut Creek, CA: AltaMira Press.

Kramer, Helgard. 2011. "The Epistemological Fate of the Authoritarian Character Studies of the Frankfurt School: A legacy for the study of Racism, Antisemitism, and Fascism?" *Current Perspectives in Social Theory* 29: 3–31.

Lazarsfeld, Paul F. 1937. "Some Remarks on the Typological Procedures in Social Research." *Zeitschrift für Sozialforschung* 6: 119–139.

Lee, Alfred M. and Elizabeth Briant Lee. 1939. *The Fine Art of Propaganda*. New York: Harcourt Brace.

Lohl, January and Sebastian Winter. " 'Deutschland ... ist ja das letzte Bollwerk': Ein psychoanalytisch-sozialpsychologischer Beitrag zur Mentalitätsgeschicte der westdeutschen Nackriegszeit." In *Kritische Socialpsychologie: Dichte Interpretation*, ed. J. König et al., 191–223. Wiesbaden: Springer Fachmedien.

Löwenthal, Leo. 1987 [1945]. "Images of Prejudice." In Leo Löwenthal, *False Prophets: Studies in Authoritarianism*, 189–245. New Brunswik, NJ: Transaction Books.

Löwenthal, Leo and Guterman, Norbert. 1949. *Prophets of Deceit: A Study of the Techniques of the American Agitator*. Palo Alto, CA: Pacific Books.

Markus, Hazel Rose and Shinobu Kitayama. 2010. "Culture and Selves: A Cycle of Mutual Constitution." *Perspectives on Psychological Science* 5: 420–430.

Mitscherlich, Alexander and Margarete Mitscherlich. 1975. *The Inability to Mourn: Principles of Collective Behavior*. New York: Grove Press.

Morgan, Michael and James Shanahan. 2017. "Television and the Cultivation of Authoritarianism: A Return Visit from an Unexpected Friend." *Journal of Communication* 67: 424–444.

Morling, Beth, and M. Lamoreaux. 2008. "Measuring Culture outside the Head: A Meta-analysis of Individualism-Collectivism in Cultural Products." *Personality and Social Psychology Review* 12: 199–221.

Perrin, Andrew J., and Jeffrey K. Olick. 2011. "Introduction." In Friedrich Pollock and Theodor W. Adorno et al., *Group Experiment and Other Writings*, xv-lxi. Cambridge: Harvard University Press.

Pollock, Friedrich. 1989 [1940]. "State Capitalism: Its Possibilities and Limitations." In *Critical Theory and Society*, eds. Stephen Eric Bronner and Douglas Kellner, 95–118. New York: Routledge.

Pollock, Friedrich, and Theodor W. Adorno, et al. 2011. *Group Experiment and Other Writings*, trans. Andrew J. Perrin and Jeffrey K. Olick. Cambridge: Harvard University Press. [Abbreviated *GE* in this chapter].

Postmes, Tom and Nyla R. Branscombe. 2010. *Rediscovering Social Identity: Key Readings*. Washington, DC: APA Press.

Pyszczynski, Thomas, Sheldon Solomon and Jeff Greenberg. 2015. "Thirty Years of Terror Management Theory: From Genesis to Revelation." *Advances in Experimental Social Psychology* 52: 1–70.

Rensmann, Lars. 2017. *The Politics of Unreason: The Frankfurt School and the Origins of Modern Antisemitism*. Albany: SUNY Press.

Rose, Gillian. 1978. *The Melancholy Science: An Introduction to the Thought of Theodor W. Adorno*. New York: Macmillan Press.

Schad-Somers, Susanne P. 1972. *Empirical Social Research in Weimar Germany*. The Hague: Mouton.

Schweppenhäuser, Gerhard. 2009. *Theodor W. Adorno: An Introduction*, trans. James Rolleston. Durham: Duke University Press.

Smith, David Norman. 1998. "The Ambivalent Worker: Max Weber, Critical Theory, and the Antinomies of Authority." *Social Thought & Research* 21: 35–83.

Wiggershaus, Rolf. 1994. *The Frankfurt School: Its History, Theories, and Political Significance*. Cambridge: Polity.

Worrell, Mark P. 2009. *Dialectic of Solidarity: Labor, Antisemitism, and the Frankfurt School*. Chicago: Haymarket Books.

Ziege, Eva-Maria. 2012. "Patterns within Prejudice: Antisemitism in the United States in the 1940s." *Patterns of Prejudice* 46: 93–127.

CHAPTER 12

Franz Neumann's *Behemoth* and Trumpism: Comprehending the Beast of Bad Government

Dan Krier

As the Trump administration enters its fourth year, it is time to return to comparisons that abound in popular commentary between Trumpism and National Socialism.[1] These comparisons are apt. Though Donald J. Trump was a *rentier* capitalist, television personality, and dilettante politician, he obtained the presidency by adopting themes, policy positions, and rhetorical styles reminiscent of National Socialists. Trump's ethnic nationalist campaign promised to "Make America Great Again." This was to be accomplished by cleansing the nation of "illegal immigrants," building a wall on the southern border with Mexico, excluding visitors from Muslim countries, locking up his political opponent, strengthening the military, and waging an enhanced war on terrorism. Trump further promised an "America First" economic policy that would repatriate manufacturing jobs by renegotiating trade deals and by establishing a regulatory and tax environment favorable to U.S. capital. During the general election campaign, Trump's campaign rallies drew larger, more effervescent crowds who chanted slogans of symbolic violence in response to Trump's increasingly strident rhetoric. Comparisons to National Socialism intensified in the years following the election as Trump appointees with ties to the "Alt-Right" and European ethnic nationalist movements assumed prominent positions in his administration.

So, is Trump a new Hitler, and is Trumpism a new form of Nazism as suggested by many critics? Rather than making simple assertions about similarities and differences between these two illiberal movements, this chapter approaches these questions with a (re) reading of the most detailed analysis of the rise of Hitler, the Nazi Party and the Nazi state: Franz Neumann's (1944) *Behemoth: The Structure and Practice of National Socialism, 1933–1944*. Neumann, a labor lawyer, Marxist political scientist, and associate of the exiled Institute for Social Research, analyzed National Socialism as

---

1   This chapter is an updated version of Dan Krier's "Behemoth Revisited: National Socialism and the Trump Administration" from *Logos*, Volume 16, Issues 1–2, 2017, http://logosjournal.com/2017/behemoth-revisited-national-socialism-and-the-trump-administration/.

a contradictory structure of four "machines:" the machinery of the Nazi party, the apparatus of the bureaucratic-administrative state, the military, and industrial corporations in cartels, trusts and other monopoly capital forms. Tensions between these four machines were mediated by the Fuhrer or Leadership principle and by anti-Semitic "racial proletarian" ideology, both of which broke up class formation and class consciousness, atomizing workers into easily controlled and manipulated mass formations. As a social system, Nazism blocked workers from unifying against capital, preventing class solidarity and egalitarian democratic rights. Workers masochistically submitted to "leaders" while sadistically identifying as a racial *Volk* superior to degraded, internal enemies.

Parallels abound between National Socialism and the Trump administration's positions and ambitions. National Socialism and Trumpism shared a distrust of liberalism and fear of working-class solidarity that might challenge or overthrow capital. Both had an ambivalent relationship to the state, glorifying military power, hierarchy and obedience, and National Socialism further promoted an ideal of society "fused into the army" (Neumann 2009 [1944]: 6). National Socialism sought to invert liberalism's strong civil society/weak state by reasserting a particular form of state power over civil society. To Neumann, "the imperialism of German monopoly capitalism" had destroyed the economic foundation for bourgeois civil society that had depended upon small capital, handicraft industries and competitive trade. Monopoly capital had centralized, cartelized, and concentrated industry, forcing out small business and liberal civil society based upon it, leaving behind a "network of authoritarian organizations" (14). National Socialism did not seek to restore competitive small capital and civil society, but rather embraced the economic efficiencies that resulted from rationalization, concentration and bureaucratization. Politically, monopoly capital dramatically expanded the pool of undifferentiated labor as small capitalists, craftspeople and tradesmen were displaced by big business. Enormous firms of great complexity yielded high efficiency, but reduced workers to an undifferentiated mass underneath highly technical administration.

The fallen or displaced middle-classes were one core constituency of National Socialism. But there were many others, including "the most diverse social strata ... never hesitating to take in the dregs of every section, supported by the army, the judiciary, and parts of the civil service, financed by industry, utilizing the anti-capitalist sentiments of the masses and yet careful never to estrange the influential moneyed groups" (33). No single, stable ideology could tie these groups together. Neumann describes the ideological writings of National Socialists as "abominable, the constructions confused, the consistency nil. Every pronouncement springs from the immediate situation and is abandoned as soon as the situation changes" (37). Underneath "a mass of irrelevant jargon, banalities, distortions, and half truths" lay ongoing promotion of imperialism and the interests of monopoly capital (38). Neumann's description of Nazi ideology mirrors contemporary analysts of Trump's confused pronouncements: the ideas are "constantly shifting," promoting "certain magical beliefs," including "leadership adoration ... [and] the supremacy of the master race" but without system or consistency (39). Like contemporary analysts of Trump's supporters, Neumann asserts that only a minority of Germans was ardent Nazi's. For most, its ideological message left them cold.

Both National Socialism and Trumpism were illiberal and critical of the weak political leadership of the "night watchman's" liberal democratic state" (42). Following Carl Schmitt, both reject the basic principles of liberal parliamentarianism: deliberation and debate, separation of powers, and universal law. To Schmitt, "rigid party discipline" meant that "debate is a fraud" and that "secret committees" made decisions behind closed doors so that the "publicity of the debate is a sham" (43). Since monopoly capitalism eroded the essential features of civil society (freedom of speech, assembly press, association), and since parliamentary procedures were ineffective, the desire for rapid decision, efficiency, and strength led to a glorification of executive power: hence, "all power to the president" (44). Trumpism clearly shares such a desire for executive sovereignty along the lines of Carl Schmitt.

1   Schmitt's Decisionism, the Enemy, and the State of Exception

Carl Schmitt's "decisionism," the dominant political philosophy of National Socialism, grounded sovereignty in power to declare a "state of exception" while placing the friend-enemy distinction at the center of politics (Schmitt 1985, 1996; Agamben 1995, 2005). In this philosophy, politics is organized by an existential struggle against enemies "who must be exterminated physically" (Neumann 2009 [1944]: 45). The political emerges when opponents, competitors, outsiders, subordinates, and challengers were defined as 'enemies' who could neither be tolerated nor accommodated but must be destroyed (Schmitt 1996: 26, 49; Schmitt 2004: 64–6).

The Nazi state was more authoritarian (hierarchical rule of leader over subordinates) than totalitarian (identity between ruler and ruled). Hence, hierarchical leadership was rooted in superior rank that was "valid against the people's will" (Neumann 2009 [1944]: 48). Nazi's viewed the state as the "form of life of the racial people" that provided "unconditional authority" while maintaining (limited) autonomy for monopoly capitalism (50). To Schmitt, sovereignty emergences in the capacity to declare and inhabit a "state of exception," a charismatic claim that sets aside rational-legal and traditional forms of law so that sovereignty is absolute, unlimited (Schmitt 1985: 5; Schmitt 2006b: 13–4). Hitler famously assumed emergency powers that were sustained throughout the entire Nazi period: the Nazi state was in a perpetual exception, a non-ending state of emergency that provided Hitler supreme sovereign power.

> Adolph Hitler is top leader. He combines the functions of supreme legislator, supreme administrator, and supreme judge; he is the leader of the party, the army and the people. In his person, the power for the state, the people, and the movement are unified.
>
> NEUMANN 2009 [1944]: 84

Hitler was "sole legislator" whose will was the law, an embodiment of the executive, legislative and "infallible" judicial function, as well as supreme commander of armed forces, whose "power is legally and constitutionally unlimited" (Neumann 2009 [1944]: 84). A full appreciation of the nature of sovereignty and the absolute consolidation of power in the hands of Hitler as Fuhrer emerges from a review of the oath of office required of every soldier in the army: *"I swear this holy oath to God; that I shall give unconditional obedience to Adolf Hitler, Leader of the Reich and the people, supreme commander of the army ..."* Similar oaths were sworn by all cabinet members and civil service office holders: *"I swear that I shall be true and obedient to Adolf Hitler, the Leader of the German Reich and the people, that I shall obey the laws and fulfill my official duties conscientiously, so help me God"* (84–5). These oaths of fidelity and loyalty to the person of Hitler contrast strongly against those sworn by U.S. soldiers: *"I do solemnly swear (or affirm) that I will support and defend the Constitution of the United States against all enemies, foreign and domestic; that I will bear true faith and allegiance to the same; and that I will obey the orders of the President of the United States ..."* (Oath of Enlistment n.d.).

National Socialism was constituted by full Schmittian sovereignty, supreme leadership of a personal, idolatrous, *charismatic* kind that was unconditioned by rules, laws, regulations or universal law. The U.S. elevation of constitutional law to the position of sovereignty that could not (in ordinary times) be overridden or suspended by persons has been a crucial defense against Nazism. This is what makes a "state of exception" so dangerous: the temporary suspension of the rule of law consolidates absolute sovereignty in the charismatically justified hands of a single person. Liberal democracies, including the U.S., have been rooted in deliberative decision-making, dismissed by Schmitt as "government by discussion" (Sorrell 2003: 227), as well as the separation of powers, and judicial review. Sovereignty is further divided by the distribution of governance in a nested, multi-form array of jurisdictions (federal, state, local) that are inefficient and problematic from the standpoint of decisionism, but that serve as crucial circuit breakers against consolidated Nazi-like power. As Neumann reports, Hitler dissolved the power of individual states within the Reich to maintain state-level legislatures or to elect state officials. The Reich usurped all authority formerly possessed by states and municipalities so that authoritarian control was "complete from top to bottom" (Neumann 2009 [1944]: 55). While it is difficult to imagine Trump (or his successor) in possession of sufficient sovereign power to remove all state governors and replace them with appointees under his control. However, the Republican party has been surprisingly successful in securing judicial appointments for deeply conservative, highly partisan jurists.

Trump's rise to office occurred in the context of an almost non-existent legislative function in the United States. Lawmaking, such as it was, during the 21st century, has been accomplished primarily through executive orders or, in the language of Neumann and Schmitt, decree (Schmitt 2014b: 7–9). The Schmittian state of exception similarly depowers the legislative function so that the executive absorbs lawmaking: Neumann describes the Nazi-era Reichstag as a "mere ornament." Under Trumpism, the U.S. legislature has almost ceased to function as a lawmaking body. Congress and the Senate pass few laws of note, and their co-equal status in the separation of powers has been severely eroded under Trumpism. Republican partisans have largely overridden congressional oversight of executive action, including powers to review administrative and judicial appointments, to investigate the administration, or to impeach the president.

Nazi criticisms of parliamentary deliberation and debate are strangely applicable to the U.S. situation under Trump. Though congressional and senate rules of evidence and procedure were nominally designed to facilitate high-quality debate and to optimize collective decision, such legislative debate has all but vanished. Party leaders in consultation with and command of corporate owners formulate public issues and policies privately, without public deliberation. The Tax Cut and Jobs Act of 2017, for example, was crafted outside of public view and without opportunity for public input. The law was and entirely partisan affair: the law was shaped exclusively by Republicans and passed into law without any votes from outside the party. The legislative branch in the United States no longer debates issues in an open forum, and few legislators change their minds or consider the words and viewpoints of colleagues outside their own party. Party discipline that aggressively punishes dissent prevents independent exercise of legislative judgment. Therefore, actual law making has shifted to the executive branch: the office of the president serves as "lawmaker in chief" through executive decree.

2 The Party over the State

Like contemporary Republicans in the U.S., Nazi's were primarily attached to and pursued the interests of party rather than country. As Hitler noted, "the state is not our master; we are the masters of the state" (Neumann 2009 [1944]: 65). Neumann characterized changing conceptions of the relationship of the Nazi party to the Nazi state by describing National Socialism both as a "movement state" and using Carl Schmitt's phrasing, a "tripartite state," in which state, movement, and people (nation as racial *Volk*) remain distinct from each other. The Nazi party as the dynamic element (movement), provided leadership to the other parts of state, mediating between, dominating, and uniting them (66). Neumann notes that in the USSR, the Communist party completely dominated the state; in Italy, the fascist state completely dominated the party; while in Germany, the Nazi state remained in tension with the party, united together by the leadership principle ("Adolf Hitler, who is both leader of the party and chief of state. …").

The charismatic nature of Nazi party power brought it into contradiction with the "rational bureaucracy" of the administrative state. The state was saturated with the characteristic traits specified in Weber's famous ideal type concept of bureaucracy: "precision, permanency, discipline, reliability … rationality … impersonality … [action] without hate or passion … duty … without regard to person, with formal equality for everyone" (80). Charismatic authority operates on an entirely different logic – magical, emotional, unsystematic, vanishing -- hence the party and its leaders by necessity rejected and attacked the administrative state because rational law and formal order were contrary to charisma. Decisionism, the supreme power of a sovereign under charismatic authority, depends upon the state of exception, which is by definition a suspension of bureaucratic, rational-legal authority. It would seem that the fantasies of the Trump administration were fully aligned with its Nazi predecessor, as highlighted by Steve Bannon, one-time Chief Strategist of the Trump White House, when he stated that a primary objective of the Trump administration was the "deconstruction of the administrative state" (see below).

The Nazi party as a bureaucratic structure was autonomous from the Nazi state to a remarkable degree, with its own party courts, its own party sources of revenue, freedom from state taxation and from state control. Yet, by the 1930s, the party had grown so large that it had itself become a massive bureaucracy with thousands of officials in leadership positions in both the party hierarchy and state bureaucracies, a paramilitary organization that rivaled many standing armies, massive youth organizations and leadership control over most of associations in civil society. Compared to Hitler, who was the most important architect and developer of the Nazi party and who was fully identified with the party as its leader, Trump's relationship to the Republican Party that he now leads was haphazard, even laughably accidental (he was registered as a Democrat in the early 2000s). Hitler's party had bureaucratic durability, despite its charismatic claims. At the time of his election, Trump had built no formal party at all, but had called forth spontaneously assembled mobs of spectators with weak ties to formal party leadership. Hence, Trump's authority originally rested upon the unstable footing of charisma and should he have failed to prove his charismatic claims, there was little institutional structure to fall back upon. Charismatic leadership is always a vanishing phenomenon, and when Trump's term ends, or should he quit, or become enfeebled, a "crisis of succession" will almost certainly arise.

Has Trumpism become a partisan movement in a manner similar to National Socialism? This question leads to a consideration of Schmitt's "theory of the partisan." In line with his conception of the tri-partite state, Schmitt views parties as dynamic, charismatic forces that emerge to lead a traditional, racial *Volk* and to dominate and disrupt the legal-state apparatus. Schmitt defines friend-enemy distinctions at the center of politics and affirms Clausewitz's famous dictum that warfare is an extension of politics by other means. To Schmitt, partisans are spontaneously-ordered, non-uniformed, irregular warriors who remain distinct from bureaucratically-organized, uniformed, regular soldiers. Partisans form paramilitaries, people's armies, and militias. Partisans struggle against enemies as guerillas, co-combatants, or freedom fighters in a spontaneous, autonomous fashion without a "duty to obey" military command (Schmitt 2004: 22). Schmitt identifies four criteria characteristic of partisans: 1. Irregularity: autonomy from formal military command, 2. Mobility of combat: guerilla resistance tactics, sabotage, and terror, 3. Intense political commitments: does not fight on his own account but in advance of an existential cause not personal gain, 4. Tellurian character: fight in defense of "patch of true home soil" in order to preserve the way of life of a spatially-rooted, autochthonous *Volk* (13–4, 50). Partisan warfare violates many of the core categories of classical martial law, eliding distinctions between war/peace, combatants/non-combatants, and enemies/criminals. Partisan warfare is not a "contained" war between states but "real enmity" between existential enemies: partisan struggles do not result in peace treaties or return to normalized co-existence.

They are uncontained, totalized, wars – such as civil wars or colonial wars – with intensive commitments to "resistance to the end" and complete "annihilation" of real, existential enemies (6–7). Schmitt emphasizes that partisans played decisive roles as irregular, non-uniformed, resistance fighters in wars since Napoleon (8–9). Modern wars are partisan wars whose outcomes are determined by charismatically qualified, irregular resistance fighters called forth from a traditional *Volk* who defensively combat an enemy's bureaucratically disciplined regular soldiers in an existential struggle to the death.

Schmitt's conception of the partisan contrasts sharply with classical liberalism, in which political parties are opponents who engage in parliamentary debate in search of compromise (a sort of peace treaty) rather than annihilation of enemies. Schmitt's equation of partisanship with guerilla warfare accounts for many features of National Socialism. For example, paramilitaries appear as uniquely important agents within National Socialism throughout Neumann's book. The S.S. and S.A. remained under the command of party leadership and were autonomous from and immune to the state bureaucracy and the directives of the official military (Neumann 2009 [1944]: 69–71). As irregular partisans, paramilitaries unleash all the lethal violence of formal armies, but without their constraining rules, formal regulations and disciplinary controls. Germany had a long tradition of paramilitaries (militia) that served as retention structures for officers, soldiers, and munitions suppliers between formal military deployments. Paramilitaries such as the *Freikorp* mustered routinely, maintained discipline, traditions and systems of honor and were heavily involved in the extra-legal civil war after the end of WWI (Theweleit 1989; Amidon and Krier 2009). Trump's support was especially strong among gun enthusiasts and Second Amendment activists, including those with strong rebel-authoritarian tendencies and psychological attachment to myths of American outlaw biker gangs, badass militia, moonshine running stock car racers, and other cultural forms of anti-establishment rebellion (Krier and Swart 2016: 150–82). Post-election analysis provides convincing evidence of his appeal and popularity in red states, areas of stagnation, who were most vulnerable to his appeal to bring back jobs, creating new wealth and prosperity in the rust belt, coal mining and other industries that have migrated to other low production cost countries (Oberhauser, Krier, and Kusow 2019).

Trump has even called upon his supporters to function as a paramilitary, asking them to harass and violently silent protestors at rallies and to ride Harley-Davidson motorcycles as a defensive shield against protestors at his inauguration. The Trump administration has granted broad powers to Immigration and Customs Enforcement (ICE) officers and has hampered congressional and journalistic oversight of their activities. Though employed by the state and uniformed, ICE officers are under unconstrained command of the Trump administration, and function closer to irregular partisans than regular soldiers. During the coronavirus pandemic, the Trump administration has called upon partisans to conduct armed, disruptive protests of pandemic response policies in states governed by 'enemies' of the administration. The Trump administration has called upon supporters to act as partisans in retaliation against other "enemies," including journalists, late-night talk show hosts, congressional leaders, and celebrities. At this date, it remains difficult to envision gun toting, Second Amendment defending supporters of Trumpism forming either a party-directed standing militia or a people's army with sufficient strength, discipline and acumen to pose a threat to regular, uniformed, armed forces (try to imagine a random collection of his aging, out-of-condition rally attendees marching in uniform, rifles at attention, vigorously goose-stepping in disciplined formation). Despite their admiration for Nazi militia, it remains unlikely that Trump supporters could function as a party-directed paramilitary equivalent to the S.S. In part, this is due to the purely personal quality of Trump's following: the strongest adherents of Trumpism are loyal to Trump the man not Trump the leader of the Republican Party. Like Trump himself, supporters of Trump lack intense political commitments that Schmitt viewed as essential to distinguish partisans from mere thieves, criminals, and pirates whose "bad deeds ... aim at private theft and profit" (Schmitt 2004: 10). Trump rarely displays intensive political commitments but often fights on his own account, engaging in twitter battles against imagined personal foes rather than political enemies. Trump's preoccupation with politically irrelevant *ad hominem* attacks is not entirely inconsistent with fascist propaganda (Adorno 1982: 118), but these struggles are outside the conceptual bounds of Schmittian partisanship.

3   Anti-Semitism and the Racial Volk

As a Marxist, Neumann analyzes National Socialism's "all-pervading anti-Semitism" as an ideology that disrupted working class solidarity and class-consciousness. Rather than identify as a proletariat vis-à-vis capital, anti-Semitism encouraged German workers to identify as a racial people (*Volk*) vis-à-vis an exploitative, racialized enemy: "racism and anti-Semitism are substitutes for the class struggle" (Neumann 2009 [1944]: 125). The emphasis upon racial identity integrated German (Aryan) workers into a racial state while negating class struggles against capital. Anti-Semitism substituted the "Jew" for "capital" as the Schmittian political enemy that organized politics and society along racial, rather than class, lines (Arendt 1976). Jews were "held in readiness as a scapegoat for all the evils originating in the socio-political system" (Neumann 2009 [1944]: 125; Žižek 2008: 140–4). Racial identity was not only implicated in definition of an internal political enemy, but also in the definition of external enemies and the project of German imperialism, defined as conquest of subordinate racial peoples. Together, anti- Semitism and racial identity supplanted class struggle with civil and imperial war (Neumann 2009 [1944]: 199). The social psychology of National Socialism, following Fromm, was sadomasochistic: insignificant, isolated persons forced to submit to leaders with compensating discharge of sadism directed at internal and external enemies. Liberal democracies thrive when democratic characters embrace equality, spontaneity, and free development. National Socialism, on the other hand, was fully hierarchical. Anti-Semitism provided the white working class with social ascendancy over racialized others. The racial *Volk* and the Nazi movement-state were strong when traditional, racial hierarchies were rigidly maintained and enforced. Nazis formed a reactionary middle-stratum fighting on two fronts: outwardly toward external enemies and downward to suppress internal enemies. Fueled by out-hating and down-hating, this reactionary middle stratum never fought "up" against elites, but masochistically embraced their domination while sadistically kicking down against enemies below.

The racial ideology of Trumpism is eerily similar. Racism in many forms (anti- Semitism, anti-Muslim, anti-Latino, and anti-Black) is rampant in Trump's ethno-nationalist rhetoric and has been encoded in the policies of the Trump administration. Such ethno-nationalist appeals, replayed and rekeyed from time-worn tropes, indicate that the authority of Trumpism is not only charismatic but also traditional, rooted in "folk aesthetics" and conservation of racial and gender hierarchies (Krier 2019; Krier 2020: 140–1). Blacks, Mexicans, Muslims have rotated in turn as Schmittian enemies that are intensely down-hated by Trump supporters to psychologically elevate themselves in the social hierarchy. These groups have also rotated as external enemies out-hated by Trump supporters to purify and defend the racial people (*Volk*). Metonyms for racial enemies appear frequently, including "liberal," "terrorist," and "criminal." Trumpism is held together by the perpetual ignition of Schmittian friend-enemy distinctions based upon traditional racial coding, augmented by the charismatic power of fear, hatred and aggression. The social psychology is more than just authoritarian or sadomasochistic, but destructive or necrophiliac in Fromm's specific meaning (Fromm 1973; Kellner 2015). When linked to partisan warfare, as in National Socialism, racial friend-enemy distinctions can feed into decisions regarding and death that constitute a regime of *thanatopolitics* (Foucault 2003; Esposito 2008).

4   Space: The Final Frontier

Antisemitism and other ethnonationalist elements in National Socialism were fundamentally linked to what Schmitt called the *nomos* of the earth, elemental structures of autochthonous normative and ordering principles organically rooted over long duration in specific spatial territories (Schmitt 2006: 73–50). Following in the footsteps of avowedly racist and imperialist geographer Halford Mackinder, Schmitt contrasts the *nomos* of the earth (agrarian settlement, cultivation, and racial connection between "blood and soil") with the *nomos* of the sea (maritime commerce, trade, industry, and rootless mobility) (Schmitt 2006, 2014a). The land and sea distinction is fundamental to Schmitt's late thought and, in general, land-based cultures linked to illiberal continental empires (Russia, Austria, Prussia) receive positive valuation while sea-based cultures linked to liberal maritime nations (Western Europe, England, United States) receive negative valuation. Many of Schmitt's core categories (friend-enemy distinction, tripartite state, sovereign dictator, the partisan, the *Volk*) and many of the policies of National Socialists can be located within the land and sea distinction (Meyer, Schetter, and Prinz 2012). Take partisanship for instance: one core defining trait of the partisan was a "tellurian character" (Schmitt 2004: 13–14). The partisan fights to defend a particular piece of land occupied and ordered by habitation and cultivation of long duration. The other three traits follow from this mystical, racial attachment of "blood and soil." The partisan is not a professional soldier but remains rooted to the homeland and fights irregularly in its defense, deploying guerilla tactics, terrorism and the like. The partisan is animated by intense political commitment precisely because the enmity in partisan warfare threatens the partisan's existence. To Schmitt, the mystical connection between blood and soil is entirely absent from sea cultures and the very concept of Reich is etymologically linked to the connection between the blood of a *Volk* (the *Mannring* of warriors who form a fence/wall as the original defensive political structure) and the soil they cultivate (Hutton 1999: 100–1). Though outside the scope of this chapte, the land-sea distinction was not only incorporated into National Socialism but also resonates in political theories of the contemporary Far-Right, including factions within Trumpism. Trump's valorization of traditional, illiberal "red states" in the American "Heartland," disdain for liberal, coastal "blue states," intentional disturbance of international treaties, alliances, and organizations (NATO, G7, UN, Paris Accord), and "America First" economic populism repeats the folk aesthetics of National Socialism.

5   Death of Civil Society and the Destruction of the Administrative State

Neumann highlights how bourgeois civil society (in a Weberian not a Marxist sense) was a barrier to the rise of National Socialism. The Nazi party sought to evacuate civil society, disrupt spontaneous social life, and overwrite free association with regimented administration. Liberal democratic society (autonomous civil rights, voluntary association, free assembly, free speech) was the enemy of the Nazi state. To weld atomized masses to the Nazi order, civil associations were broken apart and replaced with party-controlled substitutes. The forced atomization of classes into masses was one of the reasons why Neumann viewed German people as largely indifferent to Nazism. They were not fervently bonded to Nazi structures but were prevented from associating outside of them, always subject to party oversight, surveillance and control. Of course, a strong, vibrant civil society might have been a barrier to the rise of Trumpism, but civil society has been in decay in the U.S. for many decades (see the massive literature on community decline associated with Putnam's *Bowling Alone*). In the contemporary US, churches remain as almost the sole voluntary association in civil society, a potential resource for left resistance.

However, the largest "fast-growth" churches in the U.S. are firmly aligned with the cultural right and frequently function as right-wing mobilizing structures, herding their flock toward nationalist, neo-liberal and neo-conservative candidates using a variety of hooks and crooks (abortion, gay marriage, gender). Outside of work, most Americans are tied to the wider world through the glowing screens of spectacle, which often places them in streams of data that confirm rather than challenge nationalist, capitalist and conservative views.

National Socialism's hostility to the bureaucratic state was linked by Neumann to its charismatic party structure: the rules, regulations and universal law of the state generated a "Big Other" that mediated conflicts through a stabilized symbolic structure. The bureaucratic state stood between individuals, establishing a normative order. Without the triadic function of the state, parties in conflict must engage in dyadic struggle of a zero-sum variety. The Big Other of the state enables aspirants and contenders to compete without destruction, generating win-win social surpluses.

By taking over the state, the Nazi party captured such social surpluses, enriching and empowering its members at the expense of the underlying society. The leadership principle and the massing of workers contributed to this exploitative situation. Leaders throughout the Nazi regime acted by arbitrary decision (decree) not by rational law. The power of the leader was unconstrained and unchecked to such a degree that law itself vanished. At the end of the book, Neumann argues that National Socialism was not a state because the power of law did not exist, only arbitrary decision of the Fuhrer (Neumann 2009 [1944]: 452).

National Socialism's supreme sovereignty attacked all agents of the Big Other that mediated disputes and settled questions of truth: the judiciary, science, disciplined scholarship, investigative journalism. All information that remained was propaganda (which Neumann defined as "violence against the soul") that advanced the interests of the Nazi party. The Trump administration has made similar moves for similar reasons. Trump advisor Steve Bannon's desire to destroy the administrative state targeted institutional agencies of the Big Other that made "triadic" decisions based upon analysis of data. Science, public schools, environmental agencies, labor department, health and human services, interior department, state department all have been identified for severe budget and staff cuts. The government departments that have escaped intact are those associated with "hard power," such as the military, police, and prison administration. Trumpism aims to remove these triadic structures that mediate between differentiated interests, thus reducing all action to dyadic friend-enemy extermination or zero- sum conflict. In the administration's response to the coronavirus, scientific experts were frequently sidelined and contradicted by political operatives concerned about the stock market, election optics, and approval ratings. Under Trumpism, the judiciary is also under siege, in part because it has been a safeguard of the rule of law, civil rights, and universal justice. In Trumpism, the judiciary is just another forum for friend-enemy struggle. Rather than providing impartial judgment of the Big Other, courts are being transformed into arenas for humiliation, defeat, and struggle between small others. Courts are not about justice, in this worldview, but "winning."

The Trump administration also seeks to "complete" the neoliberal project pursued by conservatives at least since Reagan, gutting social services, repealing health care, cutting minimum wage and labor protections, removing collective bargaining protections, and forthcoming cuts to social insurance coupled with removal of civil rights protections for those who protest or resist the regime. The Trump administration also refuses to submit to international authority or collective agreements and has already weakened U.S. support for multi-national associations like NATO, the G-20, and even the United Nations. This is, again, an attempt to remove the triadic function of universal law, a Big Other, such that all nations are placed upon a single plane of dyadic struggle for power and "negotiation." In such a system, the military and economic might of the U.S. will be leveraged to cut better "deals" in one-on-one bargains.

Both National Socialism and the Trump administration insisted upon preserving social and economic hierarchies while removing any triadic institution to serve as a "Big Other" that mediates between players in never ending friend-enemy dyadic struggles. Trump himself – a multi-billionaire by his own reckoning -- refuses to pay and legally attacks small contractors, small political actors, and even small children as enemies that must be annihilated. This is the mark of a Lacanian psychotic psyche: structure is missing, hence paranoid insecurity lets one be defeated and displaced from the social order.

Trumpism, ultimately, is historically conditioned by the waning of post-Fordism and neoliberalism. Fordism – the relatively egalitarian regime of stabilized mass production and mass production, coupled with social democratic redistribution of income to ensure full employment – was already in full retreat in the early 1970s. Post-Fordism – explosive growth in income and wealth inequality resulting from the globalization of industry, deregulation and destruction of the social democratic state – is now in its fifth decade. Fordism has been in decay longer than it was in construction. There is already little actual memory of what life was like under Fordism. It is no longer a memory, merely a myth, and a pastoral for the 21st century. National Socialism arose during Fordism. As Neumann noted: "National socialism is built on full employment. That is its sole gift to the masses ... unemployment must be prevented so as to retain this one link that still ties the masses to its ruling class" (Neumann 2009 [1944]: 431). National Socialism, unlike Trumpism, actually provided employment, social insurance, old age benefits, health and accident insurance to the working (Aryan) masses. Compared to Nazism, Trumpism provides its supporters equal levels of sadomasochism and racial hatred, but far fewer economic benefits.

6   Conclusion

6.1   *So, Is Trump a New Hitler?*

After nearly four years in office, Trump remains at best a political dilettante, an outsider to the political process, who parlayed the display value of celebrity into incessant media attention and votes. By comparison, Hitler spent decades as a political operative, building the Nazi party and its extensive bureaucratic and paramilitary apparatus. Trump is approaching his mid-seventies, a narcissistic libertine accustomed to incredibly soft living and sycophantic adoration from those he pays to be near him. Hitler was in his early forties when the Nazi's seized power in Germany and had already bitten his cyanide pill at fifty-six. Given his age and lack of political commitment, it seems too late for Trump to personally forge Trumpism into any kind of lasting movement or to completely reform the Republican Party in his ethnic nationalist image. Trump's sophomoric rhetorical skills and political ineptitude stand in marked contrast to almost any political leader. He has no obvious successor to replace him; his followers are heterogeneous and lack institutional stability. Given that charisma is always a vanishing form of domination, it remains possible that Trump will fail to prove his charismatic claims at some point and enough of his followers will cease to recognize his authority. He will appear to them – as he does to most of his non-supporters -- as a comic buffoon rather than a great political leader.

6.2   Is Trumpism a New Form of Nazism?
But the problem of Trumpism is larger than the person of Trump, and Trumpism exhibits many features that Neumann found in National Socialism. Both movements unite disparate, even contradictory "machines" into a single system: Nazism united a party apparatus, the military, the bureaucratic state and monopoly capital with a powerful racial ideology and charismatic leadership. Upon the election of Trump in 2016, Trumpism lacked such a party apparatus. In the early years of his presidency, the Republican Party was temporarily on loan to the Trump administration, but payment could be demanded at any point. However, by the time that Trump signed tax cuts into law in December of 2017, opposition to Trump within the Republican Party all but vanished. The Republican Party and Trumpism cross-pollinated: key notes in the folk aesthetics of Trumpism -- economic nationalism, ethno-nationalism, nativism, cronyism, unhidden corruption – became widespread themes in 2018 Republican election campaigns. The Republican Party backed the Trump administration strenuously to render ineffective both the investigation into Russian collusion and impeachment. At this point, the Trump administration is approximating Hobbes's characterization of parliamentary rule during the English civil war: a Behemoth of bad government, a "non-state, a chaos, a situation of lawlessness, disorder, and anarchy." (see Hobbes 1889; see also Springborg 1995). This quote and the one that follows are taken from the frontispiece to the first English edition of Neumann's *Behemoth*: "Since we believe National Socialism ... has swallowed the rights and dignity of man, and is out to transform the world into a chaos by the supremacy of gigantic land masses, we find it apt to call the National Socialist system the Behemoth."

The parallel here between Neumann and Schmitt's *nomos* of the earth is striking (Mastnak 2010). The new hybrid formed by Trumpism-Republican Party has created a system that bears many of the features of National Socialism. A tripartite state structure has emerged in which the constitutional, bureaucratic U.S. state has been challenged by a partisan movement leading a newly energized ethno-nationalist *Volk*. This "movement-state" has come into control of administration (including the regular military) and has enriched many factions of capital. Though Trump's charismatic leadership has been inept and bumbling, partisan leaders have been effective in their propagation of racialized ideologies that appeal to "heartland." As Neumann noted, Nazism was grounded in a strong form of Schmittian decisionism, with a powerful unitary executive bypassing the legislature. The Trump administration, supported by the Republican partisans, has overridden constitutional separation of powers, neutered the legislative branch, stacked courts with partisan functionaries, and eliminated offices with the power to oversee and investigate administrative action. Once in power, National Socialism consolidated power by the declaration of a state of exception, strong friend-enemy distinctions deployed consistently and aggressively to sustain charismatic political power under the *Fuhrer* principle. Trumpism, though grounded in a charismatic movement, has likewise sought to erode the rule of law through (limited) states of exception, and has sought to define opponents (Democrats, the Press, Celebrities) as enemies with great force in an effort to increase political power. Due to Trump's erratic, undisciplined pronouncements and the highly personal transference relationship between Trump and his avid supporters, the *Fuhrer* principle has so far been much less effective than under National Socialists, despite the best efforts of broadcast and social media affiliated with Trumpism-Republicanism.

In the early years of the Trump administration, despite an obvious desire to subvert norms of political civility central to liberal democracy, Trumpism was not able to suspend the rule of law in its entirety in a manner similar to National Socialism. The Trump administration's executive orders have been partially negated by judicial review, and legislative processes and inquiries were instituted that partially constrained and controlled attempts to increase executive authority. While National Socialism developed a strong, partisan, paramilitary apparatus to override and dominate the state (including the regular military), the Trump administration has had less success and lacks a partisan paramilitary enabling domination of the administrative state and military.

Finally, Nazism was fundamentally tied to the historical moment of Fordism and delivered to its (Aryan) adherents full employment and a basic array of social insurance and welfare protections. Trumpism is tied to the historical moment of waning post- Fordism and neoliberalism, and despite nationalist rhetoric promising to bring manufacturing jobs back to America, the administration seems primarily focused upon completing the neoliberal project of dismantling the social insurance, welfare, regulatory and taxation systems. While National Socialism provided jobs and benefits to adherents, Trumpism enters its fourth year in power with massive unemployment, a record budget deficit, and no clear plan to provide jobs or prosperity to even its most fervent ethnic nationalist supporters.

By comparing the Trump administration to Neumann's portrait of National Socialism, it is apparent that the aging, clownish, dilettante Trump is a rather pathetic Fuhrer. Because his moment on the world stage will soon pass, our attention and concern focus much more upon comparisons between Trumpism and National Socialism. In less than four years, the new hybrid Trumpism-Republican party has followed the National Socialist playbook closely and has laid the groundwork for a complete "movement state" in the Nazi manner. The US may be only a single "state of exception" away from the transformation of the U.S. into something approximating National Socialism.

References

Adorno, Theodor W. 1982. "Freudian Theory and the Pattern of Fascist Propaganda." In *The Essential Frankfurt School Reader*, eds. A. Arato and E. Ghebhardt, 118–37. New York: Continuum.

Agamben, Giorgio. 2005. *State of Exception*, trans. K. Attell. Chicago: University of Chicago Press.

Agamben, Giorgio. 1995. *Homo Sacer: Sovereign Power and Bare Life*. Stanford, CA: Stanford.

Amidon, Kevin S. and Daniel Krier. 2009. "On Rereading Klaus Theweleit's *Male Fantasies*." *Men and Masculinities* 11(4): 488–496.

Arendt, Hannah. 1976. *The Origins of Totalitarianism*. New York: Harcourt Harvest.

Esposito, Roberto. 2008. *Bíos: Biopolitics and Philosophy*. Minneapolis: University of Minnesota Press.

Foucault, Michel. 2003. *"Society Must be Defended:" Lectures at the College de France, 1975–6*. New York: Picador.

Fromm, Erich. 1973. *The Anatomy of Human Destructiveness*. New York: Henry Holt.

Hobbes, Thomas. 1889. *Behemoth, or the Long Parliament*. London: Simpkin Marshall.

Hutton, Christopher M. 1999. *Linguistics and the Third Reich: Mother-Tongue Fascism, Race and the Science of Language*. London and New York: Routledge.

Kellner, Doug. 2015. "Donald Trump as authoritarian populist: A Frommian analysis," *Logos: A Journal of Modern Society and Culture* 15 (2/3): n.p.

Krier, Dan. 2020. "The Repressed Returns: Mann's Doctor Faustus and the Fugue of Capital." In *Capital in the Mirror: Critical Social Theory and the Aesthetic Dimension*, eds. D. Krier and M.P. Worrell, 123–45. Albany, NY: SUNY Press.

Krier, Daniel. 2019. "Shakespeare's Plays of Deranged Authority: The King's Three Bodies." *Fast Capitalism* 16.2.

Krier, Daniel, and William J. Swart. 2016. *NASCAR, Sturgis and the New Economy of Spectacle*. Leiden: Brill.

Mastnak, Tomaz. 2010. "Schmitt's Behemoth." *Critical Review of International Social and Political Philosophy* 13 (2–3): 275–296.

Meyer, Robert, Schetter, Conrad, and Janosch, Prinz. 2012. "Spatial Contestation? The Theological Foundations of Carl Schmitt's Spatial Thought." *Geoforum* 43: 687–696.

Neumann, Franz. 2009 [1944]. *Behemoth: The Structure and Practice of National Socialism, 1933–44*. Chicago: Ivan R. Dee.

Oath of Enlistment, U.S. Army. N.D. Accessed January 15, 2017. At https://www.army.mil/values/oath.html.

Oberhauser, Ann, Krier, Dan and Kusow, Abdi. 2019. "Political Moderation and Polarization in the Heartland: Economics, Rurality, and Social Identity in the 2016 U.S. Presidential Election." *The Sociological Quarterly* 60(2): 224–244.

Schmitt, Carl. 2014a. "The Planetary Tension between Orient and Occident and the Opposition between Land and Sea." *Política común* 5: n.p.

Schmitt, Carl. 2014b. *Dictatorship: From the Origin of the Modern Concept of Sovereignty to Proletarain Class Struggle*. Tr. M. Hoelzl and G. Ward. Cambridge, UK: Polity Press.

Schmitt, Carl. 2006. *The Nomos of the Earth in the International Law of the Jus Publicum Europaeum*. New York: Telos Press.

Schmitt, Carl. 2004. *The Theory of the Partisan: A Commentary/Remark on the Concept of the Political*. Michigan State University Press.

Schmitt, Carl. 1996. *The Concept of the Political*. Chicago: University of Chicago Press.

Schmitt, Carl. 1985. *Political Theology: Four Chapters on the Concept of Sovereignty*. Chicago: University of Chicago Press.

Sorrell, Tom. 2003. "Schmitt, Hobbes, and the Politics of Emergency." *Filozofski vestnik*. XXIV(2): 223–41.

Springborg, Patricia. 1995. "Hobbes's Biblical Beasts: Leviathan and Behemoth." *Political Theory*, 23(2): 353–75.

Theweleit, Klaus. 1989. *Male Fantasies*. Minneapolis: University of Minnesota Press.

Žižek, Slavoj. 2008. *The Sublime Object of Ideology*. London: Verso.

CHAPTER 13

Donald Trump and the Stigmata of Democracy: Adorno and the Consolidation of a Religious Racket

Christopher Craig Brittain

The success of Donald Trump's 2016 presidential election, and the subsequent support he was able to maintain while in office, has baffled many commentators. Wendy Brown, Peter Gordon, and Max Pensky suggest that Trump's rise, along with that of other contemporary right-wing populist movements, do not fit "received categories of political analysis" (Brown, Gordon and Pensky 2018: 2). Chief among the puzzles that Trumpism represents to such observers is its lack of ideological coherence. Commentators have also been struck by the seemingly contradictory support Trump has received from white Evangelical Christians, and to a lesser degree, from white Roman Catholics. These Christian communities have traditionally demanded that the political leaders they support share not only their views but also serve as examples of a moral life. Few supporters of Trump suggest he represents a successful model of the latter, but even after over three years in office, this has had little impact on the support white evangelicals are prepared to offer the President.

This chapter draws from sociological studies of right-wing populist movements that were conducted by Theodor W. Adorno in the 1940s, 50s, and 60s to help explain the attraction Trump has among those who vote for him. It demonstrates that Christian support for Trump is appropriately described as a religious "racket" that functions as "social cement." As market capitalism began to erode the nation state and undermine the security it had offered to the majority of its citizens, Adorno drew on the analysis of colleagues who discerned the emergence of gang-like oligarchic cliques, which reorganised the social order into rival tribal groups gathered around strong authoritarian leaders. Adorno's perspective analyses how rhetoric like that employed by Trump supports such a development. Trump's speeches can be understood to serve as a form of ideological "massing," whose power is achieved by overwhelming his audience with information, rather than by its content. The ongoing contemporary relevance of Adorno's general approach is demonstrated with reference to a dispute within the evangelical movement over an editorial published in *Christianity Today* in early 2020. The resulting analysis stands in contrast to scholarly literature that emphasises cultural over economic factors to explain support for Trump. The chapter argues that Adorno's basic approach to analysing of right-wing populism remains relevant, particularly for the way in which it interprets the phenomenon as being rooted in the general socio-economic conditions of society. This position is supported with reference to emerging ethnographic studies conducted among white evangelicals and Roman Catholics who have continued to support Donald Trump since 2016.

1   Interpreting Trump's Success among White Christian Voters

It is established that 81% of white Evangelicals voted for Donald Trump in the 2016 Presidential election (Pew 2020). Less attention has been given to the fact that 60% of white Roman Catholics (and 56% of all Catholics who attend church weekly) also voted for Trump (Gayte, Chelini-Pont and Rozell 2018: 4–5). Mark Rozell suggests that, because Trump received more Catholic support than previous Republican contenders like Mitt Romney, John McCain, or George W. Bush, "it is reasonable to argue that the Catholic vote played the most substantial role in the 2016 presidential campaign outcome" (Rozell 2018: 5). On this point, however, it is noteworthy that Trump also received greater percentage of votes from white evangelicals than the three preceding Republican candidates. Strikingly, this support among white Christians has remained strong over President Trump's first term, with 69% of white evangelicals continuing to approve of his performance after three years in office – although support among white Catholics slipped to 44% (Schwadel and Smith 2019).

Recent studies of white Christian voters offer various interpretations for such widespread support: the formation of conservative Christianity into a right-wing political identity (Miller 2019), a reactionary collapse of American religion into white nationalism (Gorski 2017), the product of negative partisanship (Margolis 2020), a reaction against social stigma (Silva 2019), or a response of a threatened sense of identity (Whitehead, Perry and Baker 2018). Such interpretations are characterised by a shared conviction that the explanation for Trumpism's success must go "beyond class-based" approaches (14) in order to attend to the power of affect and cultural identity that fuel Trump's support. Alan Abramowitz (2017), for example, argues that racial resentment on the part of whites, not economic discontent, was the strongest predictor motivating voters to choose Trump over Clinton. Henry Giroux (2017) similarly emphasises how white supremacy and militarism nurtured a "war culture" and an authoritarian ethos, which enabled Trump's rise. Gary Jacobson (2017) highlights the extent to which disdain for Hillary Clinton drove many to vote

Republican in 2016. Read together, such recent articles point to an assortment of seemingly non-economic factors that combined to enable Trump's victory, including racism, sexism, right-wing populism, fear of Islamic terrorism, xenophobia, and nostalgia.[1]

The reason why many interpreters of Trump's support emphasise culture and identity over economics is relatively clear. Studies of the demographics of those who vote for him emphasise the extent to which they offer support because they share his prejudices and respond to his rhetoric, not because they were financially stressed (Smith and Hanley 2018). Moreover, media coverage of "the white working class" has been criticized for lumping together a broad range of differing groups and social positionings (Walley 2017). Some dismiss best-selling accounts of the white underclass like J.D. Vance's *Hillbilly Elegy* (2016), which portrays life in poor Appalachia. For Angela Denker (2019), such depictions offer oversimplifications and adopt a paternalistic attitude towards Trump's supporters, akin to Hillary Clinton's "basket of deplorables" remark. Thus, Denker concludes that Vance's account serves only to reinforce crude stereotypes and "soothe liberals' wounds" (197).

While such contributions offer useful insights and correctives regarding the complex assemblage of issues giving rise to support for Trump, they generally focus solely on describing various dynamics that fuel Trumpism, rather than on offering explanations for these developments. If racism and xenophobia are key motivating factors, why have these particular dynamics come to the fore in the current historical moment? Why was Clinton such a figure of disdain? What lies underneath white Christian resentment over feeling stigmatized and marginalised?

Such questions are significant, not only to achieve deeper understanding of the dynamics being observed, but also if effective strategies to challenge right-wing populism are to be developed. Denker's journalistic study is a case in point. After summing up the diverse reasons she encountered for evangelical support of Trump – "some because they wanted to overturn *Roe v. Wade*, some because they hated Hillary, and many because they felt Trump was talking directly to them and speaking for them" (292) – she suggests that this divide in American society could be healed if people would only talk to each other across the divide; "If given the chance, we can accept one another, learn from each other, and build an entirely new country built on justice and freedom for all" (295). Here nuanced thick description of individual perspectives comes at

---

1   Compare the similar list of factors discussed by Gorski (2017: 339), Silva (2019: 3), and Whitehead, Perry and Baker (2018: 149).

the expense of attention to the wider social conditions they inhabit, so that the political response advocated for is reduced to sentimentality. As significant as individual conversations and relationship may be, what needs to be better understood are the structural barriers and impediments that frustrate such interactions.

Moreover, despite the emphasis made in many studies on the diverse factors and interests found among Trump supporters, they generally also gesture toward some shared concern or attitude. For example, Denker writes, "Red State Christians were more afraid of losing than they were afraid of Trump." She suggests that her informants collectively expressed a sense of being "besieged" or of having lost the "culture war" (150). In other studies, a common general theme that is identified is rage against those perceived to not be paying their dues or waiting their turn – "line cutters" – be they recent immigrants, latte-drinking urban liberals, women, or others perceived to be threatening the "traditional" American way of life. Arlie Hochschild (2016a) describes how one informant described his frustration against people perceived to be "cutting in line;" "After a while, the people get fed up, and form their *own* line with their *own* leader" (686). Elsewhere, Hochschild (2016b) reports that many of those she spoke with, feeling betrayed by the existing system to the extent that they could no longer feel pride in American society, resolved that they would "have to feel American in some new way – by banding with others who feel as strangers in their own land" (4).

2 Banding Together – Trump's "Religious Racket"

It is the widespread sense of grievance or fear, as well as this desire for a leader who will band the group together, that requires more sustained attention and analysis than is offered in the above accounts. For what gets lost as the diversity found amongst Trump's supporters is overly emphasised in these various studies is the dynamics that result in shared support for Trump. Andrew Arato (2013) has observed that the absence of a real identity or ideology in a populist political movement is "made up for by affective, libidinal ties, 'love' for the leader and love for all those whom the leader supposedly loves" (160). It is such libidinal, affective, bonds that serve to draw Trump's diverse supporters together into a common movement that merit more scrutiny by scholars if greater understanding of the dynamics that are driving linger support for Trump is to be achieved.

Arato's concern to link authoritarian populism, societal pressures, and psychological factors resonates with the studies of right-wing radicalism and authoritarianism conducted by the Institute of Social Research ("The Frankfurt School), first in the early 1930s in Germany, and subsequently in the 40s and 50s in the USA and West Germany. Indeed, scholars like Peter Gordon (2017) have observed that the findings of a study published in 1950, *The Authoritarian Personality*, with which Theodor W. Adorno was heavily involved, offers insights that are strikingly relevant in the wake of the emergence of contemporary right-wing populist movements. Moreover, Adorno's perspective is also relevant for the way in which it recognises a significant overlap between religion and authoritarian populism.

In his remarks in an appendix of *The Authoritarian Personality*, Adorno reports that reference to the Christian religion was common among those interviewed by his research team. Adorno (1964) argues that these religious aspects of his informants' discourse (including a rigid dualism between good and evil, and emphasis on individual conscience) congealed as a "social cement" that bound their right-wing movement together (730). He argues that, "the more this cement is needed for the maintenance of the status quo and the more dubious its inherent truth becomes, the more obstinately is its authority upheld and the more its hostile, destructive and negative features come into focus."

Elsewhere, Adorno (2000) links this understanding of religion as a social cement to the notion of a "racket." In his study of the radio addresses by the right-wing Christian broadcaster Martin Luther Thomas in the 1940s, Adorno argues that Thomas' use of Christian rhetoric amounts to "racketeering in religion" (89). Here Adorno draws upon a theory of rackets developed by his colleagues Max Horkheimer and Friedrich Pollock. As they studied the rise of National Socialism in Germany, Horkheimer and Pollok observed how charismatic leaders established their own private instruments of power from outside of established mechanisms of democratic institutions.[2] As such oligarchic groupings developed new forms of economic concentration, gangster-like behaviour ensued. Socially necessary services (like energy and water) became privatised, and narrow, pragmatic associations replaced prior forms of social organisation, such as labour unions. The group came to compensate for the perceived limitations of the individual and general society.

Adorno (2000) points to the way in which Thomas claimed to stand for "living faith" over against institutional religion as an example of religion functioning as a racket (88). This appeal is to immediate and subjective emotional experience, based as it is on charismatic rather than bureaucratic authority.

---

2   For a fuller description of this theory of rackets, see: Stirk (1992: 131–154).

Adorno observes, "the individual must think of God and his own immediate relationship with God, rather than of the Church to which he belongs" (90). He argues that this emphasis on the believer's direct and immediate personal relationship with God is stressed by the leader to "exclude any interference from outside agencies." The individual's relation to God is mediated through the appeal of an authoritarian leader, rather than an institutionalised tradition.

Adorno suggests that the concept of a racket captures the function of Christianity in Thomas' radio addresses. He writes, "religion, while being used as a net to ensnare a certain group of the population, is also transformed into a technique of political manipulation" (98). Adorno describes how this functions as follows, "[t]he complete cynicism with which [Thomas] handles Biblical stories shows that he is actually concerned only with the residues of religious prestige and authority."

Contemporary developments support the concerns Adorno raises about the oligarchic forces that he calls "rackets." Mark Weiner (2013) has compared the tensions emerging in the Twenty-First century to those of competing tribes: "All of these new clans, from extended families and gangs to churches and corporations, offer a wide range of goods and services previously furnished by the state or dispersed under its watchful guidance. The various functions of the state continue to be discharged" (202). Like Adorno, Weiner stresses the distinction between how the nation state previously provided goods to individuals as individuals, whereas the emerging collective groupings serve only their members. There are clear indications of a pattern of political forces encouraging individuals to attach themselves to a collective racket, rather than work to bolster the liberal welfare state and its related concept of individual subjectivity. The undermining of labour unions, public health care, equal access to education, and ever-more-rigid immigration policies all serve to fuel these trends. To the extent that these forces continue to shape socio-economic life, Adorno's analysis of the loss of culture's autonomy to political and economic structures remains a relevant theoretical perspective. Indeed, as Arato has highlighted in his analysis of right-wing populism, "conflict has to be institutionalised if it is not to mean dualistic friend-enemy relations" (Arato 2013: 155). The erosion of democratic institutions, therefore, reduces political life to contestations between rival tribes, each of which seeks to constitute themselves as the true expression of 'the people.'

Elsewhere, I have elaborated further on the relevance of Adorno's concept of a "religious racket" for explaining the dynamics surrounding Trump's successful 2016 presidential campaign (Brittain 2018). In what follows, I focus on the ways in which this perspective illuminates subsequent ongoing support on the part of conservative evangelicals.

3   Holding One's Nose before King Cyrus

"He drives me crazy but he'll get my vote." This statement by a resident is offered by journalist Chris McGreal (2020) to summarise the tone of his interviews with citizens of Howard county, Iowa, prior to the 2020 presidential primaries. Like this Iowan farmer, increasingly, evangelical leaders have tended to acknowledge that Trump is an "imperfect vessel," exhibiting unattractive traits and behaviour. To explain why they remain willing to support him, many have compared him to the Persian King Cyrus in the Hebrew Bible (Isaiah 40–55), who liberated the Jewish people from their Babylonian captivity – a powerful political outsider who nevertheless served God's purposes in the world (Gabatt 2020). Some, like energy secretary Rick Perry, have instead compared Trump to flawed (and adulterous) biblical heroes like King David. Survey data suggests that such attitudes towards Trump are widespread among his religious supporters. It is noteworthy, for example, that one study found that 72% of conservative evangelicals consider the performance of immoral acts to be irrelevant to the question of whether an individual can hold public office (Rozell 2018: 9).

While some observers have puzzled over how to explain this discrepancy between traditional evangelical emphases on the need for leaders to live moral lives, and this willingness to ignore Trump's flagrant immorality, such a pattern was identified by Adorno in his studies of right-wing authoritarian movements. Moreover, he observes ways in which the message delivered by leaders of such movements serves to deflect such contradictions by flooding their audience with a wave of messages that redirects their attention and focus.

In a lecture from 1967, Adorno describes a curious aspect of the rhetorical strategy deployed by right-wing leaders of populist movements, "This propaganda is less about spreading an ideology, which is already too thin, than it is about massing it" (Adorno 2019: 41).[3] Adorno notes that authoritarian-inclined leaders often present a wide range of factual claims and statistics to support their position, which cannot be rendered clear and consistent because "it is too difficult to control," yet "because of its uncontrollability, it lends a special kind of authority to those who bring it forward" (44). The audience is not won over by convincing them of a position based on argumentation; instead they are swept away by a massed wave of collected quasi-factual claims, anecdotes, and accusations. Adorno describes the strategy as nurturing an "appeal of concreteness." Offering a wide range of data and statistics, accompanied by "fantastic stories," such speeches combine to create an emotional response that

---

3   Quotations from this text are my translation.

feels rooted in reason and evidence, but which is in fact an inconsistent assemblage based largely on fiction and exaggeration. These observations by Adorno clearly resonate with more contemporary critiques of what is now known as "Fake News" (Fuller 2018). Adorno (2019) adds that this "salami method" of propaganda adds layer upon layer of stories and statistical figures whose power to influence the audience is based solely upon the weight of the massed amount of information, rather than on its content (45). Moreover, the vast array of different issues and concerns raised is intended to resonate with as broad a constituency as possible.

For a case in point of precisely this kind of rhetorical strategy, it is instructive to turn to a recent controversy within the evangelical movement over support for Trump, which erupted in the wake of the 2019 impeachment process initiated by the Democratic Party.

4 The Christianity Today Dispute

In the autumn of 2019, a process to impeach President Trump was initiated in the House of Representatives, which was launched following revelations over his attempt to pressure the President of Ukraine to provide compromising information about the son of Democratic rival Joe Biden. In December, the editor in chief of the flagship evangelical magazine *Christianity Today* published an editorial that suggested that, "Trump Should be Removed from Office" (Galli 2019). Mark Galli advanced this argument on the basis that the President had attempted to coerce a foreign leader to discredit a political opponent, which "is not only a violation of the Constitution" but "profoundly immoral." The commentary was offered in the face of the fact that 80% of white evangelicals opposed the impeachment process (Washington Post-ABC News 2019).

Although the editorial received significant attention in mainstream media (Green 2019), the reaction by Christian supporters of Trump was dismissive and intense. Galli and *Christianity Today* were quickly labelled out of touch and irrelevant. Jack Graham, a member of Trump's "Religious Advisory Council," articulated three common defences of the President. First, the view that he had "delivered" on evangelical priorities by appointing two conservative Supreme Court justices, by defending "religious freedoms," by advancing "pro-life policies [that] are more wide-reaching than any of his predecessors," and by achieving a strong domestic economy. Second, Trump had stood up against the enemies of evangelicals, in the form of socialism and secularism. Finally, Graham paints the President's critics as small-minded and cruel, because they focus on Trump's limitations rather than his major achievements: "Our critics seem to have a theology with so little grace [that] they fail to recognize that someone with an unrighteous past can still make righteous decisions on behalf of those they lead."

Note the way in which a range of very different claims are 'massed' together here to defend Trump, even though the different 'slices' have little to do with each other. First there is a general *ad hominem* attack on *Christianity Today* – it is simply accused of being "out of touch." This is followed by a list of specific achievements that the President is said to have delivered – some of them concrete (Supreme Court) and others vague (opposes "secularism"). The subsequent move is to portray Galli as un-Christian for his lack of forgiveness of sinners like Trump. The scope and weight of the rhetoric is what gives this criticism its power, not its content. The layering of additional arguments on top of each other intends to overwhelm any sympathy for the concerns raised by Galli, if one does not pause for any significant amount of time to reflect on the details of the claims being made.

Other evangelical leaders followed a similar pattern in response to the *Christianity Today* editorial. Michael Brown (host of a nationally syndicated radio program) noted that "despite his shortcomings, [Trump] has been a Godsend." He argues that "We can support the president for the very real good he does do" (M. Brown 2019). While Brown adopted a rhetorical tone that allowed for some minor consideration to be granted to the concerns raised by Galli's editorial, John Grano and Richard Land (2019) displayed no such inclination. *Christianity Today*, they wrote, offers "words of elitists who look down on opponents as inferior human beings who need to be controlled." By the time that more prominent leaders like James Dobson ("Focus on the Family") publicly criticised Galli's editorial (Dobson 2019), and Ralph Reid (executive director of the Christian Coalition) appeared on Fox News to declare that the magazine should change its name to "Christianity yesterday" (Fox News 2019), it had become clear that there would be little shift in white Evangelical support for Trump.

Two weeks later, as if to ritually symbolise this rebuke of *Christianity Today*, Cissie Graham Lynsch, a granddaughter of Billy Graham (the founder of the magazine), appeared on stage with Trump at a rally in Miami and vowed to help him win re-election (Medina and Habermann 2020). As the crowd chanted, "four more years," Trump proclaimed, "Evangelical Christians of every denomination and believers of every faith have never had a greater champion, not even close, in the White House, than you have right now." He was defending religion, he told the crowd, "which is under siege." During the rally, Evangelical leaders laid hands on the President and prayed for him. The chief pastor prayed that Trump would fulfil his role as a new King Cyrus, while Paula White asked God to defend him against the demonic forces seeking to undermine his presidency (Fea 2020). The message delivered by Trump to his audience was, essentially, that the impeachment was not so much an attack on him, but an attack on them.

Even when one recognises the extent to which these rhetorical defences of Trump can be described as "massing" ideology, or what Adorno describes elsewhere as a "flight of ideas technique" (Adorno 2000: 33), this is not to deny that some of his Evangelical audience very much appreciate a number of Trump's policy decisions, be it his nominations to the Supreme Court, or his emphasis on defending "religious freedom." It is conceivable that critics might argue that the fact that Trump's rhetoric resonates with concrete policy concerns on the part of his white Evangelical audience contradicts Adorno's suggestion that right-wing populist rhetoric provides only a "movement trick" – merely evincing an attitude of being *against* some opponent, rather than standing *for* something concrete (31).

Trump's claim to fight for "religious freedom" offers a lens into this question. It is noteworthy that his defence of the freedom of religion does not represent any specific policy initiative; rather, it is a vague assertion of religious identity against the spectral enemies of secularism and socialism. It is, thus, a stance against a perceived danger, not a positive plan for something concrete. Yet in a sample survey conducted by political scientists Ryan Burge and Paul Djupe (2019), 60% of white Evangelicals reported believing that atheists would not permit them First Amendment rights and liberties if they took power. 58% said that same would be true if the Democrats were "in Congress." Trump's speeches are geared to resonate with such fears. As Adorno argues in his analysis of Thomas' radio addresses, "a feeling of impotence is turned into a strength" (Adorno 2000: 44).

5   From Subjective Opinion to Objective Social Conditions

Key to Adorno's interpretive approach to authoritarian populist movements is his emphasis on the idea that the objective conditions of society play a decisive role in the formation and content of subjective opinions. He argues that individual opinions of the sort gathered by survey data or interviews "are in truth highly derivative and mediated" (Adorno and Pollock 2011: 25). On the question of an individual subjective political opinion, he continues, "While it is borne by the individuals and based on their thinking and feeling, it is not built up from their individual opinions." Instead, Adorno concludes that subjective opinions are intertwined with what he calls the "objective antagonisms" of society.

In the polemical atmosphere surrounding the *Christianity Today* dispute, however, such a reading of Trump's followers will have to tread cautiously if it is to avoid falling prey to accusations of "elitism" or to a tendency to regard Trump's followers from a paternalistic vantage point. For this reason, prior to drawing any further from Adorno's perspective, this chapter will first engage with some emerging ethnographic work on the phenomenon under consideration. Moreover, the recent trend among some scholarly studies of Trump's support to emphasise cultural identity over economic factors is another reason to proceed with care while engaging with Adorno's provocative approach to such movements. Indeed, the fact that many emphasise the extent to which the American economy is booming under Trump (Wolf 2019) might be taken to falsify Adorno's argument that authoritarian impulses are rooted in the economic conditions of society. For these reasons, it is necessary to linger at greater length on some nuanced field work among Christian Trump supporters.

6   The View from God Land

The freelance journalist Lyz Lenz (2019) is one of many writers who have spent a considerable amount of time interviewing supporters of Donald Trump, particularly in the "Red States" dominated by Republican voters. As a former evangelical church-planter, Lenz's ethnographic perspective approaches her Midwestern subjects as an insider, which is to say that her account lacks any hint of an "elitist" dismissal of a "basket of deplorables." Instead, she offers empathetic, if critical, analyses of her research subjects, who she clearly feels sympathy for and often appears to enjoy spending time with.

This is not to suggest that Lenz describes carefree and easy-going conversations with her informants. Anger and fear are the primary themes encountered in her interviews. She writes, "In 2016, 75 percent of Trump voters were angry at the way the government was operating, compared to 18 percent of Clinton voters. A CNN poll in December 2017 showed Americans are still angry" (142). Lenz describes how what she heard from her informants resonated with this general survey:

> I see it in the farmer who voted for Trump despite the fact that he had his best years under Barack Obama. I see it in the pastor's wife who told me that city values are sinful. I see it in the women who volunteer in their churches, but are silenced in the decision-making process. I see it in the people of color tired of fighting and having no one listen. ... We are all

tired. We are all angry. ... The anger is a fire outside that has been brought inside (143).

It is precisely such an anger at an external fire, which ignites an internal fire, that Adorno's analysis seeks to illuminate and explain. Yet it is instructive to linger at greater length with Lenz's ethnographic accounts prior to returning to Adorno's critical theory, since she helps brings into view two features discussed more theoretically by Adorno: the social roots of this anger and fear in economic circumstances, and the way in which these dynamics are expressed in religious terms by white evangelicals in the American Midwest.

Several people Lenz interviewed are rooted in farming and agriculture. She highlights how, in a country that is largely urban and post-industrial, this already encourages a sense of being distinct and an outsider. Moreover, Lenz describes what she calls a "rural mentality" or an "agrarian worldview," which, shaped by the unpredictable forces of nature, has come to redefine success, not in terms of advancement, but as survival (37). The narrative Lenz hears from farmers, such as in the case of someone she calls Mark, is one of "making do." She writes, "It's a discourse of loss and a fatalistic language of survival," of "barely holding on." This theme of survival is interspersed with a deep nostalgia – for an age resembling the period when Mark's father was a farmer, when "Things were hard, but life was good. Easier somehow." Here it is clear that, however "booming" the American economy is reported to be, many Midwestern Americans express a deep insecurity, and a sense that life is not as it should be.

Drawing from the work of Jennifer Sherman (2009), Lenz notes that this nostalgic dimension among her informants has a strong moral dimension; it has to do with a vision of how things should be, and how communities should operate (even if they have never actually functioned or existed in such a manner). According to Sherman, "rural morality is not about actual morality, but about defiance and opposition. About setting themselves apart from the 'other' " (Lenz, 39). Resisting an identity felt to be imposed upon them by more urban Americans, individuals in the rural Midwest construct a sense of themselves that is taken to be morally and socially superior to that 'other' America. This dynamic is not merely to do with identity, since it is rooted in a particular social environment. For those living in places lacking in resources available elsewhere, morality – understood in terms of worldview and general way of life – comes to serve as social capital. As Lenz describes, "Appearing 'good' unlocks jobs and community resources" (104).

Lenz establishes an intimate link between the socio-economic location of her informants and their religious identity, observing how they interweave conservative Christian dispensationalism and a "rural discourse of loss" (38). She describes this as "an ideology that says the world is bad, so I tend to my own garden and just have faith in Jesus." Although this religious self-understanding is wrapped in pious language, Lenz observes how this perspective seeks to make sense of a feeling that one's fate is beyond one's control, and that it encourages a withdrawing into the self and abandoning any significant sense of obligation to care for the well-being of one's neighbours.

In Angela Denker's (2019) ethnographic work in Appalachia, she observes a quite different ethos among her sample of Trump supporters than Lenz encountered among those she studied in the Midwest. Yet Denker also emphasises the socio-economic roots of the attitudes she encounters. Unlike in some other "Red State" contexts, Denker observes, "their primary concerns are not conservative social issues but rather the economy, political corruption and mistrust" (202). In such a context, Trump's emphasis on national pride and patriotism has a particular resonance, as does his criticism of "troublemakers" and "whiners" (206). Resentment against those so perceived has a clear class dimension – at least as much as it has to do with a cultural identity, "They have all this money, and they're whiners. ... I work harder than them, and I will never have that money." Here Denker's observations resonate with Hochschild's findings on the extent of anger against those perceived to be "cutting in line" that she encountered among Trump supporters.

7   Adorno on the Social Roots of Authoritarianism

The sociological research conducted by Adorno in the 1950s and 60s sought to make sense of similar populist discontent, expressed through right-wing politics. Like Lenz and Denker, he observes significant socio-economic factors embedded in the more general moral and cultural issues voiced in such movements. In his study on Martin Luther Thomas, Adorno argues that modern authoritarianism, "feeds upon the lack of emotional gratification in an industrial society" (Adorno 2000: 7). The drift towards a populist conservative politics, which eschews the procedures and compromises of democratic negotiation, and replaces them with the values of the family and the market, is, according to Adorno, rooted in a sense of resentment and vulnerability in the face of perceived (or feared) changing social circumstances. This interpretation resonates with the themes that emerge out of the ethnographies of Lenz and Denker.

Like Lenz and Sherman, Adorno argues that the religious identity of supporters of far-right leaders like Thomas is interwoven with deep anxiety over socio-economic security, and anger against those perceived to be benefit-ting from the dominant economic order. Adorno suggests that conservative Christians are influenced "on a deeper, more unconscious level" by their reli-gious heritage, particularly in the way they express resentment over a sense of declining status in modernity (Adorno 1964: 728). Although Christianity remains a significant cultural presence in the USA, its political influenced has been gradually eroding in the face of declining membership. As religion is increasingly relegated to the private sphere, to the status of "leisure," this generates frustration and insecurity among many adherents.

In a study of new radical right-wing populist groups in Germany in the 1960s, Adorno further developed this link he sees between such movements and socio-economic anxieties and frustrations. Even for those holding down decent jobs, he notes, there emerges significant fear for the future. In an indus-trial economy in which automation increasingly raises production levels using fewer human resources, Adorno observes that, "the people involved in the production process already consider themselves as potentially superfluous – to actually feel like a potentially unemployed person" (Adorno 2019: 12). This lingering sense of vulnerability, Adorno continues, wears down an individual's sense of worth, but also any allegiance to society's institutions.

Wendy Brown notes that Herbert Marcuse advanced a similar reading of authoritarian politics, which he argues offers a "non-liberatory release of instinctual energies" (Brown, Gordon and Pensky 2018: 29). Brown develops this perspective in relation to the emergence of white supremacy, which she interprets not exclusively in terms of economic decline, but also "as lost enti-tlement to politically, socially, and economically reproduced supremacism" (25). This is to say that, even though white people may continue to have high levels of employment in periods of economic prosperity, what has changed in recent decades is a sense that their traditional secure status is no longer guar-anteed – for two reasons. The most immediate challenge is the emergence of new rival minorities groups for the same jobs, but the deeper, not fully articu-lated issue, is the feeling that one's role in society is becoming redundant and expendable. As such, right-wing "outbursts carry the specific resentments and rage of aggrieved power."

It is for reasons such as these that Adorno argues that right-wing populist movements "can be called the stigmata or scars of democracy, which do not fully live up to its own concept" (Adorno 2019: 18). This summation captures both the fear and anger that Lenz observes among Trump supporters, as well as their nostalgia for a lost idealized past. What democratic society is supposed to "feel like" eludes such people, and thus they lament that the "American Dream" is dead. Adorno describes such a state of being as embodying a "feeling of social catastrophe" (19). It is for such an audience that Trump's slogan, "Make America Great Again," has such resonance and power. William E. Connolly (2017) draws from another scholar associated with the Frankfurt School, Fran Neumann, to establish a similar connection between structural strains within democratic political systems and the rise of authoritarian radicalism, "Fascism twists and distorts democracy while retaining its imperative to seek a mass basis. It mobilizes and organises the popular support it needs, and it seeks to render the lines between consent and imposition blurry" (8).

The key issue for Adorno is that this understandable fear and anger get misdirected and misinterpreted. He observes that "These groups ... shift the guilt of their own potential declassification, not on the apparatus that does this, but to those who have been critical of the system in which they had status" (10). Adorno argues that those caught up in such movements continue to uphold the promises and values of democracy, such as freedom and equality, but they no longer have any confidence that the social order can sustain them. As such, anxiety and frustration are directed at scapegoats who serve as easily targets for the symptoms of this failure of society. In this manner, anger over the failure of neoliberal free-market capitalism gets redirected and vented against those who are critical of that very system. Fearful of the collapse of a system that formerly was experienced as protective and preferential, right-wing movements react against those who they understand to be weakening the crumbling system still further.

Lenz provides an example of this very dynamic in her study of evangelical megachurches in the USA. She charts a history of ways in which "the mix of capitalism, industrialism, and corporate culture permeated America, making us believe in the power of bigger is better" Lenz 2019: 112). She describes megachurches as "Big-box religion," built around moral sameness and a sense of belonging. Essentially serving as "conservative cultural centers," Lenz argues that megachurches promote a brand of corporate Christianity, often focused on lamenting that America and its values are under attack and blaming anything deviating from neoliberal economics or conservative Christianity as the source of the nation's problems. Kevin Kruse (2015) notes that conservative Christianity emerged as a political force in the USA in opposition to the New Deal. Lenz develops this observation, highlighting how Billy Graham, the most prominent American evangelical in the Twentieth Century, blamed decline of American cultural norms and economic struggles on socialists, communists, and atheists (Lenz 2019: 113).

Several other scholars identify significant resonances between contemporary conservative Christianity and right-wing free market ideology. Linda Kintz (1997), for example, identifies shared patterns of belief between American religious and secular conservatives. She argues that both groups are "loosely joined under the umbrella of a remarkably clear and comprehensible cosmology" (5). Kintz supports this view with reference to writings of leaders such as Newt Gingrich, Pat Robertson and Elizabeth Dole, and by analyzing organizations like the Christian Coalition and the Heritage Foundation. She demonstrates that the political agenda promoted in this material constructs a rigid conception of the traditional family and gender roles, privileges private property and the free market, and advances aggressive conceptions of patriotism and national exceptionalism.

William E. Connolly (2008) develops this analysis along similar lines. He suggests religious and political conservatives in the USA, who previously had been thought to have little in common, share a common "spirituality." This is characterized by resentment of alternative worldviews, a strong defense of capitalism, and a rejection of the concept of class. Connolly argues that this development emerged as capitalism generated increasing levels of diversity (or "nomadism"), which fragmented a general sense of a unified society into a collection of ever-increasing minority groups. What the spirituality of the capitalist-Christian "resonance machine" enables in the wake of this dynamic is the nurturing of a political position in which the capitalist system is exempted from criticism while the minority groups it generates are defined as problematic (28–29). In right-wing American rhetoric, Connolly continues, Christianity functions as a prominent device to establish the distinction between legitimate and illegitimate forms of nomadism. As Connolly puts it, "the advocates of different creeds – secular in some cases, theological in others – are drawn together despite creedal differences because of affinities or complementarities of spirituality" (40).

Despite aligning so profoundly with the dominant political and economic order of American society, at the same time, many conservative Christian leaders also preach a theme of being under constant attack – by the very social order they reinforce with their religious rhetoric. For example, at the rally at the Florida megachurch in January 2020, which was held in the wake of the *Christianity Today* editorial dispute, Trump himself raised the spectre of the persecution of Christians by the state, "Faith-based schools, charities, hospitals, adoption agencies, pastors were systematically targeted by federal bureaucrats and ordered to stop following their beliefs" (Luscombe 2020). True to his general procedure, no evidence is offered to support these claims, thus amounting to what Adorno might describe as Trump's "appeal to concreteness" through a "salami-method." It nonetheless resonates with views often espoused by several prominent white evangelicals.

In Denker's interviews with pastors in Florida, she encounters leaders like Pastor Allen, an advocate for gun ownership and fiercely critical of Hillary

Clinton and the Democratic Party, "Guns are not for sport but serious protection, needed in an age when Christians are under siege. We need to protect our people" (Denker 2019: 73–74). Among white Catholics in New Hampshire, Denker engages with supporters of Trump who rage against a liberal agenda bent on eliminating free speech in the USA, "Today, if you want to be freethinking and value thought, you are a conservative. ... You saw during the Kavanaugh trial[4] that the Left does not allow for free thought or freedom of the individual. ... The Left no longer tolerates any idea of its own" (239). This sense of being the true expression of American values, while at the same time being under constant threat of attack from external enemies, echoes throughout various studies of contemporary conservative Christianity.

Lenz highlights the way in which megachurches are a prime example of this development. She recognises how they serve to provide a network for like-minded people longing for community in a shifting social environment. Megachurches offer "familiar safe harbour in a lonely, modern, and dangerous world" (Lenz 2019: 111). However, she also argues that "megachurches have a way of distilling that tribal identity and weaponizing it." For Lenz, these institutions function as the "epitome of white privilege." When such large-scale, largely homogeneous congregations function in this manner, they coincide with Adorno's description of religion as a "racket."

In this section of her book, Lenz writes in a very personal tone, describing her own growing sense of dis-ease over the extent to which leaders in her church advocated support for Trump because he promised to defend them from "attacks" on Christianity (116–17). Seeking to discuss her concerns with some fellow church members over dinner – regarding the overly political and fearful tone of the preaching at the church – the friends respond, "We hadn't even noticed."

8   Guilt and Defence

This failure of recognition captures the principal concern raised by Adorno's approach to sociological research, and on this point his analysis probes more deeply than the ethnographic studies summarised in this chapter. In an essay he wrote as part of a "Group Experiment" conducted with Friedrich Pollock in 1955, which involved a study of latent Nazi sympathies within West Germany,

---

4   This refers to the contested congressional hearings that considered the nomination of Brett Kavanaugh for Associate Justice of the Supreme Court in 2018.

Adorno analyses ways in which guilt over the past is repressed and masked by many Germans, yet it persists under the surface of their daily lives. Describing the intentions of this study, he wrote, "Our study is more concerned with intellectual supply than with intellectual demand. ... The central interest of the study is therefore not directed towards subjective opinions at all, but rather to those elements of consciousness which are objectively predetermined and prescribed and disseminated socially."[5]

What Adorno is after here is greater precision and understanding of the basic observation that Denker offered above, "Red State Christians were more afraid of losing than they were afraid of Trump" (Denker 2019: 153). At the same time, he also intends to capture the dynamic the Lenz observes among individuals caught up in such religious rackets – that they "hadn't even noticed." Adorno's approach to the study of right-wing authoritarian movements explores the root causes of such behaviour and existential perspectives. As such, his methodology contrasts with much of the emerging scholarly literature on Trumpism. Although such perspectives are correct to identify the diverse range of issues and concerns that Trump's supporters offer as reasons for their sympathy for his agenda, Adorno's method argues that these differing surface rationales are rooted in the dominant conditions of society. He views the most common reasons that members of populist movements offer for their support of their leader as "a ready-made stock of arguments" in which "individual judgement seems to play only a secondary role" (Adorno 2010: 51). His analysis seeks instead to identify what he variously describes as an "overarching collective moment" or a "collective narcissism" that fuels the movement (22–23). This is because Adorno argues that right wing authoritarianism nurtures and shapes a "cultivated reaction as opposed to a stated preference" on the part of the members of its racket (15).

This is to say that Adorno's intention is to achieve more than a general Diltheysian understanding (*Verstehen*) of the reasons that individuals offer in order to explain their support of Trump. Instead, he argues that critical social research must "be able to investigate subjective issues objectively instead of subjectively" (Adorno and Pollock 2011: 20). He seeks to discern the socio-economic roots that encourage and shape the views being expressed, and which reinforce the rhetorical power of right-wing political rhetoric. Adorno understands the emergence of an authoritarian ethos in this manner; "While it is borne by the individuals and based upon their thinking and feeling, it is not built up from their individual opinions. Rather, it confronts every

---

5   Quoted in Wiggershaus (1994: 439–40).

individual as something already preformed, solidified, and often overwhelm-
ingly powerful" (25).

9   Conclusion

Although a fuller analysis of the socio-economic conditions in the contemporary Unites States is beyond the scope of this chapter, it is clear from emerging ethnographic data derived from interviews with evangelical supporters of
Donald Trump that, despite the many reasons offered for such support, what
they share in common is a fear over the potential loss of their current social
status, and anger against anyone perceived as a threat to their cultural security.
These dynamics can be better understood and accounted for by drawing upon
Adorno's analysis of right-wing populist movements in the 1950s and 60s. From
a perspective informed by his work, the support of evangelicals for Donald
Trump is explained by the ways in which his rhetoric and persona call upon
his followers to jettison their individual subjectivity and merge into his religious racket. Adorno's critical theory illuminates how Trump's "racketeering
in religion" disregards the content of Christianity, while tapping into the evangelical movement's energy and social discontent. Adorno's methodology helps
explain this development as being the result of structural changes in society,
which increasingly fragment large-scale national institutions, leaving people
to associate themselves with competing rackets at the price of their individual
subjectivity.

   This chapter also suggests that, although some aspects of Adorno's theoretical reading of society have become dated as capitalism has taken on new
dynamics (Brittain 2018), his approach to analysing authoritarianism remains
relevant and, in many ways, distinct from more dominant attempts to understand contemporary right-wing populism. In the wake of President Trump's
mishandling of the Covid-19 pandemic in the USA, which was ongoing at the
time of the final editing of this chapter, commentators and media coverage
continuously expressed bewilderment at Trump's disinterest in scientific
data and medical advice, his xenophobic nationalism, and egotistic self-
promotion through fake-news. Less attention was given to the reasons that
his supporters continued to express loyalty to him, and even when such questions were asked, the answers rendered were generally reduced to cultural
issues. Attention to what Adorno calls the objective social conditions behind
the subjective fears and prejudices uttered by Trump's followers seldom
received sustained analysis. This suggests that the study of emerging authoritarian movement requires not only close observation and ethnographic

study, but that this important work needs to be accompanied by analysis of the more general social and economic conditions that structure and shape the motivations and concerns expressed by followers of such movements. This is Adorno's principal contribution to the future study of radical right-wing political movements.

References

Abramowitz, Alan I. 2017. "It Wasn't the Economy, Stupid: Racial Polarization, White Racial Resentment, and the Rise of Trump," *Trumped: The 2016 election that Broke all the Rules*, ed. Larry L. Sabato, Kyle Kondik & Geoffrey Skelley. Lanham, MD: Rowman & Littlefield, 202–210.

Adorno, Theodor W. 2019. *Aspeckte des neuen Rechtsradikalismus*. Frankfurt: Suhrkamp.

Adorno, Theodor W. 1964. *The Authoritarian Personality*, 2 vols. New York: John Wiley & Sons.

Adorno, Theodor W. 2010. *Guilt and Defense*, trans. & ed. Jeffrey K. Olick & Andrew J. Perrin. Cambridge: Harvard University Press.

Adorno, Theodor W. 2000. *The Psychological Technique of Martin Luther Thomas' Radio Addresses*. Stanford, CA: Stanford University Press.

Adorno, Theodor W. and Friedrich Pollock 2011. *Group Experiment and Other Writings*, ed. & trans. Andrew J. Perrin & Jeffrey K. Olick. Cambridge: Harvard University Press.

Arato, Andrew. 2013. "Political Theology and Populism." *Social Research* 80(1): 143–172.

Brittain, Christopher Craig. 2018. "Racketeering in Religion: Adorno and evangelical support for Donald Trump." *Critical Research on Religion* 6(3): 269–288.

Brown, Michael. 2019. "A Response to Christianity Today's Call for the Removal of Trump from Office," *The Stream* 20 Dec (accessed 17 February 2020). At https://stream.org/a-response-to-christianity-todays-call-for-the-removal-of-trump-from-office/.

Brown, Wendy, Peter E. Gordon and Max Pensky. 2018. *Authoritarianism: Three Inquiries in Critical Theory*. Chicago: IL: University of Chicago Press.

Connolly, William E. 2017. *Aspirational Fascism: The Struggle for Multifaceted Democracy under Trumpism*. Minneapolis: University of Minnesota Press.

Connolly, William E. 2008. *Capitalism and Christianity, American Style*. Durham, NC: Duke University Press.

Denker, Angela. 2019. *Red State Christians*. Minneapolis: Fortress Press.

Djupe, Paul A. and Ryan Burge. 2019. "White evangelicals fear atheists and Democrats would strip away their rights. Why?" *Washington Post* (December 23). At https://www.washingtonpost.com/politics/2019/12/23/white-evangelicals-fear-atheists-democrats-would-strip-away-their-rights-why/(accessed December 17, 2020).

Dobson, James. 2019. "Opinion." *Christian News Wire* (December 20). At http://www.christiannewswire.com/news/4551683350.html?fbclid=IwAR0vE3cUiImoyE5Oceu9bwPKgIzpVBkszOgBfyFVpkjOAFPaZTBh45vhhg (accessed February 16, 2020).

Fea, John. 2020. "Evangelicals for Trump." *USA Today* (January 11). At https://www.usatoday.com/story/opinion/2020/01/11/donald-trump-evangelicals-rally-stunning-sad-unprecedented-column/4421150002/(accessed February 17, 2020).

Fox News. 2019. The Ingraham Angle (December 21). Athttps://video.foxnews.com/v/6117465995001#sp=show-clips (accessed February 17, 2020).

Fuller, Steve. 2018. *Post-Truth: Knowledge as a Power Game*. London: Anthem Press.

Gabbatt, Adam. 2020. "Unparalleled privilege: why white evangelicals see Trump as their savior." *The Guardian* (January 11). At https://www.theguardian.com/us-news/2020/jan/11/donald-trump-evangelical-christians-cyrus-king?CMP=Share_iOSApp_Other (accessed 18 February 2020).

Galli, Mark. 2019. "Trump Should be Removed from Office." *Christianity Today* (December 18). At https://www.christianitytoday.com/ct/2019/december-web-only/trump-should-be-removed-from-office.html (accessed February 17, 2020).

Gayte, Marie, Blandine Chelini-Pont and Mark J. Rozell, eds. 2018. *Catholics and US Politics After the 2016 Elections*. Cham, Switzerland: Palgrave Macmillan.

Giroux, Henry A. 2017. "White nationalism, armed culture and state violence in the age of Donald Trump." *Philosophy and Social Criticism* 43(9): 887–910.

Gordon, Peter. 2017. "The Authoritarian Personality Revisited: Reading Adorno in the Age of Trump." *Boundary 2* 44(2): 31–56.

Gorski, Philip. 2017. "Why Evangelicals Voted for Trump: A critical cultural sociology." *American Journal of Cultural Sociology* 5(3): 338–354.

Grano, John and Richard Land. 2019. "Christianity Today and the problem with 'Christian elitism,'" *Christian Post* 23 Dec. At https://www.christianpost.com/news/christianity-today-and-the-problem-with-christian-elitism.html (accessed February 17, 2020).

Green, Emma. 2019. "How Trump Lost and Evangelical Stalwart," *The Atlantic* (December 19). At https://www.theatlantic.com/politics/archive/2019/12/christianity-today-trump-removal/603952/?utm_content=edit-promo&utm_term=2019-12-20T04%3A46%3A04&utm_medium=social&utm_campaign=the-atlantic&utm_source=facebook (accessed February 17, 2020).

Hochschild, Russell. 2016a. "The Ecstatic Edge of Politics: Sociology and Donald Trump." *Contemporary Sociology* 45(6): 683–689.

Hochschild, Arlie Russell. 2016b. *Strangers in their own Land: Anger and Mourning on the American Right*. New York: The New Press.

Jacobson, Gary C. 2017. "The Triumph of Polarized Partisanship in 2016: Donald Trump's Improbable Victory." *Political Science Quarterly* 132(1): 9–41.

Kintz, Linda. 1997. *Between Jesus and the Market: The Emotions that Matter in Right-Wing America.* Durham, NC: Duke University Press.

Kruse, Kevin. 2015. *One Nation Under God.* New York: Basic Books.

Lenz, Lyz. 2019. *God Land: A story of faith, loss, ad renewal in Middle America.* Bloomington, IN: Indiana University Press.

Luscombe, Richard. 2020. "He was sent to us." *The Guardian* (January 4). At https://www.theguardian.com/us-news/2020/jan/03/trump-florida-evangelical-rally-king-jesus. (accessed April 30, 2020).

Margolis, Michele F. 2020. "Who Wants to Make America Great Again? Understanding Evangelical Support for Donald Trump." *Politics and Religion* 13(1): 89–118.

McGreal, Chris. 2020. "Swing Voters on Trump." *The Guardian* (January 13). At https://www.theguardian.com/us-news/2020/jan/13/swing-voters-donald-trump-crazy-but-will-get-my-vote-us-election-2020-iowa?CMP=Share_iOSApp_Other (accessed February 18, 2020).

Medina, Jennifer and Maggie Habermann. 2020. "In Miami Speech, Trump Tells Evangelical Base: God Is 'on Our Side'." *New York Times* 3 January (accessed February 17, 2020). At https://www.nytimes.com/2020/01/03/us/politics/trump-miami-rally-evangelicals.html?smid=nytcore-ios-share.

Miller, Daniel D. 2019. "The Mystery of Evangelical Trump Support?" *Constellations* 26: 43–58.

Pew Research Centre. 2016. "How the Faithful Voted" (November 9). At http://www.pewresearch.org/fact-tank/2016/11/09/how-the-faithful-voted-a-preliminary-2016-analysis/(accessed February 17, 2020).

Rozell, Mark J. 2018. "Donald J. Trump and the Enduring Religion Factor in U.S. Elections." *God at the Grassroots 2016*, eds. Mark J. Rozell and Clyde Wilcox. Lanham, MD: Rowman & Littlefield.

Schwadel, Philip and Gregory A. Smith. 2019. "Evangelical approval of Trump remains high, but other religious groups are less supportive." *Pew Research Center* (March 18). At https://www.pewresearch.org/fact-tank/2019/03/18/evangelical-approval-of-trump-remains-high-but-other-religious-groups-are-less-supportive/(accessed February 17, 2020).

Sherman, Jennifer. 2009. *Those Who Work and Those Who Don't.* Minneapolis: University of Minnesota Press.

Silva, Eric O. 2019. "Donald Trump's discursive field: A juncture of stigma contests over race, gender, religion, and democracy." *Social Compass* 13(12): 1–13.

Smith, David Norman and Eric Hanley. 2018. "The Anger Games: Who Voted for Donald Trump in the 2016 Election, and Why?" *Critical Sociology* 44(2): 195–212.

Stirk, Peter. 1992. *Max Horkheimer: A New Interpretation.* Hemel Hempstead: Harvester Wheatsheaf.

Vance, J.D. 2016. *Hillbilly Elegy: a memoir of a family and culture in crisis.* New York: Harper.

Walley, Christine J. 2017. "Trump's election and the 'white working class': What we missed." *American Ethnologist* 44(2): 231–236.

Washington Post – ABC News. 2019. "Telephone poll." (October 27–30). At https://docs.google.com/spreadsheets/d/1LHZOvmGxA31NQboKQeaqHii1YoClJ-DWQtbIK-QwyjY/edit#gid=0 (accessed February 18, 2020).

Weiner, Mark S. 2013. *The Rule of the Clan.* New York: Farrar, Straus & Giroux.

Whitehead, Andrew L., Samuel L. Perry and Joseph O. Baker. 2018. "Make America Christian Again: Christian Nationalism and Voting for Donald Trump in the 2016 Presidential Election." *Sociology of Religion* 79(2): 147–171.

Wiggershaus, Rolf. 1994. *The Frankfurt School*, trans. Michael Robertson. Cambridge: MIT Press, 1994.

Wolf, Zachary B. 2019. "The strong US economy is Trump's safety blanket." *CNN.com* (July 5). At https://www.cnn.com/2019/06/01/politics/trump-economy-inequality-2020/index.html (accessed February 18, 2020).

PART 4

Media Discourse

∴

CHAPTER 14

Siegfried Kracauer and the Interpretation of Films

Jeremiah Morelock

In order to investigate today's society, one must listen to the confessions of the products of its film industries. They are all blabbing a rude secret, without really wanting to.[1]

SIEGFRIED KRACAUER

∴

In *From Caligari to Hitler: A Psychological History of the German Film*, Kracauer (2019 [1947]) analysed popular German film during the Weimar era as displaying how Nazi sentiments developed in the popular German mind in the years leading up to Hitler's reign. In the preface to his book, Kracauer voiced the "contention that through an analysis of the German films deep psychological dispositions predominant in Germany from 1918 to 1933 can be exposed – dispositions which influenced the course of events during that time and which will have to be reckoned with in the post-Hitler era." He further proposed "the use made here of films as a medium of research can profitably be extended to studies of current mass behavior in the United States and elsewhere" (2019 [1947]: li). His work became very known and influential in the history of film studies. Its basic tenets are still useful, and the book is especially pertinent in the current era when authoritarian populism is again surging, today on a much larger scale than in Kracauer's time.

In this chapter I outline an approach to film analysis stemming initially from the early work of Siegfried Kracauer and stretching to the recent work of Douglas Kellner. The core of the approach is in analyzing films as cultural artifacts which reveal sentiments – fears, longings, emotional and psychological dispositions – rampant within the population at the time and place they were produced and released. Sometimes these underlying sentiments are expressed directly, but there is a lot that is couched in metaphor. This basic approach – looking at the manifest content of films as metaphorically expressing latent attitudes – largely mirrors Freud's theory of dream interpretation.

---

1 From Kracauer's 1927 essay "The Little Shopgirls go to the Movies," in *The Mass Ornament* (Kracauer 1995).

Yet there are at least two major differences between the dream from a Freudian perspective and the film-as-dream from a Critical Theory perspective. First, unlike dreams, films are created and experienced by multiple people, and the audience of any given film is almost always made up of mostly different persons from the film's authors. This makes the film much more of a social phenomenon than the dream, in the sense that it concerns the latent attitudes of many different persons – an open-ended collection of persons, in fact. Second, Freud's interpretations of latent meanings stayed at the level of individual lives and psychologies, such as sexual and aggressive desires, interpersonal resentments, and so on. By contrast, film-as-dream interpretations of latent meanings focus on the collective mind, in political and sociocultural terms.[2]

I begin with a basic outline of Freud's theory of dream interpretation. Next, I provide a brief analytical outline of film-as-dream approaches, with special attention paid to Kracauer's seminal early work on Weimar film. Next, I propose three basic principles for film-as-dream methodology. Finally, I provide a brief example of this sort of analysis, applied to the film *The Last Man on Earth* (1964).

1   Freudian Interpretation of Dreams

> I contrast the dream which my memory evokes with the dream and other added matter revealed by analysis: the former I call the dream's *manifest content*; the latter, without at first further subdivision, its *latent content*. I arrive at two new problems hitherto unformulated: (1) What is the psychical process which has transformed the latent content of the dream into its manifest content? (2) What is the motive or the motives which have made such transformation exigent. The process by which the change from latent to manifest content is executed I name the *dream-work*. In contrast with this is the work of analysis, which produces the reverse transformation.
>
> FREUD 2001 [1914]: 19

For Freud, all dreams express some sort of a wish. Some dreams – more common for young children than for adults – are obvious in these terms. In this

---

2   Relatedly, Fredric Jameson (2013) famously coined the term 'political unconscious' in outlining a methodology of psychoanalytic Marxist cultural interpretation.

case, the distance between the latent and manifest content is small. The dream has little "dream-work" to do to get from one to the other. In other cases, the distance is greater, the dream harder to decode, and the wish harder to discern. The dream-work is more involved in this case.

Dream-work contains two key mechanisms connecting the latent content (or 'dream thoughts') to the manifest content (or 'dream elements'): *displacement* and *condensation*. Displacement concerns the relationship between a desire and an object. In the original dream thought, there is a kind of desire (it could be positive or negative) in relation to a kind of object (literally a physical object, but it could also be a person, place, and so on); but in the dream-work, a new, unrelated object is substituted for the original one. Then in the manifest content of the dream, the force of the desire remains, but the object it is pinned to is different. Condensation refers to a) a single dream element expressing multiple dream thoughts, and b) multiple dream elements expressing a single dream thought.

With the above, we have a complex landscape of metaphor, metonymy, and multiple meaning. Freud believed that a good psychoanalyst – via extensive knowledge of and extended dialogues with the patient – could decode dream elements back into their dream thoughts of origin. It is easy to see how tricky this would be. Our minds are labyrinths of defense mechanisms. Considering the open-endedness of condensation and interpretation in general, even sticking within Freud's framework it is reasonable to doubt the possibility of uncovering singularly true meanings or wishes beneath dreams. Yet it is very possible to make reasonable guesses at parts of the multiplicity of latent meaning. The key to avoiding arbitrary guesses is by informing them with prior knowledge of the patient. Could these interpretations plausibly reflect real-life issues from the patient's present or past? This is the starting point.

2   A Brief History of the Film as Dream

One of the exciting innovations of the early Frankfurt School is their extension of Freud's ideas beyond his individualist approach. Combining Freud with Marx and Hegel (among other thinkers), the early Frankfurt School focused a lot on looking beyond the taken-for-granted level of bare facts, bringing to the surface buried – 'immanent' – meanings of culture and artistic artefacts, studying them as forms of ideology in the Marxist sense.[3] As early as the

---

3 By "ideology in the Marxist sense" I mean elements of consciousness that serve to mask or excuse class oppression.

1920s – even before the Frankfurt School thinkers discovered psychoanalysis – Kracauer compared films to dreams, and was formulating notions about
a mass unconscious that was expressed through the film as dream (Kracauer
1995; Schlüpmann and Gaines 1991; Petro 1983). In his early essay "The Little
Shopgirls go to the Movies," Kracauer says: "Stupid and unreal film fantasies
are the *daydreams of society*, in which its actual reality comes to the fore and
its otherwise repressed wishes take on form" (1995: 292).

In Kracauer's film interpretation, just as in Freud's dream interpretation,
the interpreter needs to read manifest content as expressing displaced latent
thoughts and desires. Like a good psychoanalyst, he never takes the said,
overt, or even consciously intended, at face value. It is precisely the unsaid,
covert, unconscious conveyances, which interest him. In his early essay "The
Mass Ornament," Kracauer said that when attempting to diagnose a society, the interpreter should not complacently accept an "epoch's judgments
about itself. Since these judgments are expressions of the tendencies of a
particular era, they do not offer conclusive testimony about its overall constitution" (Kracauer 1995). Kracauer's most sustained, direct application of
the film-as-dream analogy is in his analysis of Weimar's "stabilized period"
(1924–1929), a time when he diagnosed German film as expressing a "widespread inner paralysis" (Kracauer 2019 [1947]: 137). "A number of films of this
group divulged their messages in the manner of dreams. It is as if they were
the confessions of someone talking in his sleep" (153). One group of films
during this period – 'street films' – "are dreamlike complexes of images con-
stituting a sort of secret code" (159). Regarding his interpretation of *The Man
Who Murdered* (1931) – from the "pre-Hitler period" (1930–1933) – Kracauer
observes:

> Here, as in other cases, the objection presents itself that undoubtedly nei-
> ther the film-makers nor the German audiences were aware of such par-
> allels. Yet these parallels exist, and that they passed unnoticed increases
> rather than invalidates their significance. (255)

Similarly, Adorno noted that political sentiments expressed at the latent
level may be more revealing than those expressed at the manifest level.
This is because the manifest level will always contain messages that are
socially acceptable enough to be expressed directly and could be tied back
to displaced latent desires. In other words, they might be revealing, but they
also are likely to be shallow and/or misleading about the political desires
that really drive the appeal of the film. "Totalitarian" proclivities are often
more prominent at the latent levels, says Adorno. He never completed any

substantial studies of film,[4] yet in 1954 he outlined a critical psychoanalytic approach to analysing television, where he distinguished between overt and hidden layers of meaning.[5] As such, his essay fits well within the 'film-as-dream' approach.[6]

Taking influence from Kracauer,[7] feminist author and women's rights advocate Barbara Deming employs the notion of the film as dream.[8] On the first page of her *Running Away from Myself; A Dream Portrait of America Drawn from the Films of the 40's*, Deming says: "It is not as mirrors reflect us but, rather, as our dreams do, that movies most truly reveal the times" (Deming 1969: 1), and footnotes Kracauer's book on German film. Albeit briefly, she introduces by name the Freudian notion of wish-fulfillment. She emphasizes that the wish of the film-as-dream can be understood as a wish to escape from a resonant problematic scenario.

> The truth is that the spectator always knows very well – in essence – the dramatic situations in which these screen figures are placed [as they] act out the predicament in which we all find ourselves – a predicament

---

4   Walter Benjamin also never completed significant studies of film, but various of his writings touch upon the subject. In various ways he employed similar concepts to Kracauer, Demming and Adorno, albeit with different implications. In his uncompleted, posthumous opus The Arcades Project (1999) he articulated a 'dreaming collective' enraptured with consumerist delusion; and in the first and second editions of his famous essay "The Work of Art in the Age of its Technological Reproducibility," he compared films to shared psychotic experiences, suggesting a therapeutic, discharging function to the collective laughter-at-cruelty that film audiences would participate in when watching cartoon characters such as Mickey Mouse (Benjamin 2008; Hansen 2012). Adorno was of a similar but darker opinion, associating audience laughter with 'bourgeois sadism' (Adorno and Benjamin 1999, 130) and charging that Donald Duck "receives his beatings so that the viewers can accustom themselves to theirs" (Horkheimer and Adorno 2002 [1947]: 110).

5   Sociologist Albert Bergesen (2016) draws a different distinction between two layers of the cinematic text: the 'foreground' and 'background.' The foreground is what happens in the film. The background comprises cultural assumptions, values or understandings required of the audience for the foreground to have import (or coherence). The foreground is the literal, surface level of the film, and the background is the contextual and taken-for-granted that frames the foreground. Regardless whether a film carries more explicitly conservative or oppositional themes, "the analyst's task is the same: note what is happening and then ask, 'What background understandings are in existence, or challenged, to make this legitimately happen?' " (Bergesen 2016: 594).

6   See also Wood (2018).

7   See Bordwell (1991).

8   Hortense Powdermaker employs the dream metaphor in her seminal work about the film industry of the 1940s: *Hollywood, the Dream Factory* (1979), and so do Nimmo and Combs (1990) in their work on films as fantastic expressions of popular political sentiments.

from which the movie-dream then cunningly extricates us. But the mov-iegoer need never [...] admit what that condition really is from which he is being vicariously relieved. (2)

Some films, of course, speak explicitly to socio-political issues, while others only refer to the socio-political on the latent level. Deming distinguishes "top-ical" films from "entertainment films" – acknowledging there is considerable overlap – saying of the latter:

> [B]ecause they are in the nature of day dreams, [they] bear the same relation dreams do to events of the day [...] The focus here is on those films which above all mean to serve the public as daydreams. It is in a wide selection of a time's most popular film daydreams that the historian will find evidence of issues and of attitudes not talked of, not professed, but felt in the bones. From a study of these films, together with the top-ical films, he will be able to learn much about the equilibrium existing between deep-felt attitudes and verbalized attitudes, and from this will be able to deduce something of the state of health of the culture as a whole. (1946: 19-20)

More recently, drawing a distinction like Deming's concerning 'topical' and 'entertainment' films, Haas et al. (2015) propose a quadripartite typology along two axes – political *content* and political *intent* – in order to classify movies as differently political. The highly populated quadrant of films low in political content but high in political intent

> suggests films in which political meaning is imparted – perhaps artisti-cally – without overt reference to obvious political imagery. Instead, such films may typically invoke symbolism and other artistic devices to trans-mit their politically charged messages. (12)

In other words, one of Deming's 'entertainment' films might have a low politi-cal content, but a high political intent, and so still be reasonably considered a political film despite its lack of overt political discussion or imagery.

Largely abandoning the dream metaphor but still working much in the spirit of Kracauer, media studies scholar Douglas Kellner has written a vari-ety of analyses of popular films using 'diagnostic critique,' a methodology he explicitly attributes to the influence of the early Frankfurt School (Kellner, Leibowitz, and Ryan 1984; Kellner 2002, 2004, 2010). Kellner explains this approach as involving "a dialectic of text and context, using texts to read

social realities and events, and using social and historical context to help situate and interpret key films [to] provide privileged insight into how people
behave, look, and act in a particular era, as well as their dreams, nightmares,
fantasies, and hopes" (2010: 35). Kellner concurs "sometimes the political
ideologies of films are implicit, while at other times they are quite explicit"
(Kellner 2010: 2).

3   Who Are the Players?

In Freudian dream interpretation, the analyst might help the patient discover the meaning of the dream, but the analyst does not invent the meaning.
Meaning comes from people, and so the meaning behind the dream comes
from the dreamer. Using the film-as-dream framework, there is the question of
who the various players are, or who the various dreamers are. One major difference between a dream (while sleeping) and a film is the distance between
author and audience in either case. When analysing an individual's dream as
part of psychoanalytic practice, the latent meanings of the dream could only
be found – if anywhere – within the psyche of the dreamer. In other words,
they do not *go* anywhere. The author of the dream is also the audience of the
dream. In the case of the film, the author and audience are primarily different
persons, albeit possibly inhabiting similar cultural milieus. The meanings of
the film travel from author to audience. This distance opens a great sphere of
ambiguity.
    Deming says:

> If the dreamers are unaware of what it is they dream, the men who
> contrive these dreams know little more than they do. They consciously
> indulge the public [but] their cunning at providing blind comfort is,
> itself, largely blind. (1969: 2-3)

Adorno's 'culture industry' model proposes a unidirectional flow of meaning.
It is not from 'author' to audience per se, so much as from system to audience,
in other words *from* the interests of the ruling class and the perpetuation of
the present order, *to* the passive, more or less duped audience. For Stuart Hall,
however, the distance between author and audience means that audiences
have some weight in interpreting meaning. In Hall's (2001) terminology, the
author 'encodes' meanings, the audience 'decodes' meanings, and the two sets
of meanings may or may not match up. While all signs carry denotative (literal)
and connotative (associative) 'levels' of meaning, most mismatches between

encoded and decoded meanings happen on the level of *connotation* rather than denotation.[9]

> The level of connotation [...] is the point where already coded signs intersect with the deep semantic codes of a culture and take on additional, more active ideological dimensions. [...] The so-called denotative level of the tele-visual sign is fixed by certain, very complex (but limited or "closed") codes. But its connotative level, though also bounded, is more open, subject to more active transformations, which exploit its polysemic values. Any such already constituted sign is potentially transformable into more than one connotative configuration.
>
> HALL 2001: 168–169

Hall maintains – and I will *emphasize* – that the process or circuit of encoding and decoding is not entirely about conscious will. Intended meanings as well as unintended meanings are sent and received, along a spectrum of awareness on both sides. As in Barthes' (2001) famous declaration of the 'death of the author,' meanings are assembled and conveyed, interpreted and reinterpreted, to such a complex degree that in some sense it is more accurate to view the 'author' as a semi-aware medium through which culture transmits its multiplicities. Some signs used by the author will be borrowed from the customary cultural lexicon, which will carry certain metaphors and metonymies regardless of the author's conscious or unconscious meanings. This is inevitable simply in the use of any language to convey meaning – a person cannot say anything without simultaneously participating in what Foucault (2012) called 'discursive formations.' To say *anything* is to participate discursively in sets of valuated associations, regardless whether this discursive context is 'intended' or not.[10]

---

9   Although Hall notes that the distinction between these levels is analytic rather than objective.

10   There is also the question of not just what meanings are in the films, but how the films may have *influenced* audiences, feeding into social trends and popular discourses of the times. While it is "common sense" that to some extent popular films must shape the persons who are exposed to it, to date it has been exceedingly difficult to prove this, and even more elusive to prove exactly how and how much Hollywood influences whom. Hence this remains an important area of future investigation. However, studies have shown that political messages on the metaphorical level are more effective at influencing people than are political messages on the literal level. If this is extrapolated to the politics of racism and Othering, it suggests a disturbing pattern. Even if overt representations of racism and ethnocentrism have become more taboo, and even if the simplistic us-vs.-them narratives in the post-9/11 renditions of *I Am Legend* and *Day of the Dead* are largely there for the strategic purpose of catering to a new, younger audience combined with the need

Psychoanalytic methods have been applied to the individual mind as well as to culture as a system of signs. In principle, the 'implicit' or 'hidden' or 'unconscious' or 'latent' or 'connotative' level, however we are to label it, can be analysed across two overlapping, analytically (but probably not objectively) distinct dimensions: (1) the individual or intrapersonal, and (2) the cultural or extrapersonal. Neither can be empirically identified, but both are – at least theoretically – intrinsic layers of experience and understanding. A text can then be analysed on one or both dimensions, (among others), and at one or both ends of the communication: (1a) what meanings might the author have encoded in the text, spanning the continuum from conscious to unconscious intent, (1b) what meanings might the viewer decode from the text, from conscious to unconscious reception, (2a) what meanings are intrinsic to the historical and cultural context within which this text was produced, and (2b) what meanings are intrinsic to the historical and cultural context within which the text was received.

A great theoretical challenge to the psychoanalytic methodology of analysing the meaning of film is determining *who* exactly is dreaming the film as dream. The challenge is complex, and the answer can carry significant implications. To answer it definitively requires determining: (1) who is constructing the dream, and (2) who is experiencing the dream. Broadly as a medium of communication, this means determining who is sending the message (the speaker) and who is receiving the message (the interpreter). In more specific terms, this means who is the 'author' of the film and who are its 'audience.'

4   Situational Complexity in Author and Audience

> [F]ilms address themselves, and appeal, to the anonymous multitude.
> Popular films – or, to be more precise, popular screen motifs – can therefore be supposed to satisfy existing mass desires.
>
> KRACAUER 2019 [1947]: 5

Kracauer was convinced that films (in a capitalist society) are at bottom produced in the interests of making profit, and so they will be contoured to fit

---

for Hollywood to continuously outdo itself; one result in that these Diseased Other stories have evolved to carry an increasingly amoral and violent Othering metaphor, where tribal resentments are indulged and transmitted, and may have greater influence on American attitudes than messages on the overt level (such as Will Smith talking admiringly in 2007 about Bob Marley's anti-racism).

what most people want to see. Because the dictates of the mass and of capital are so heavy,

> films are the mirror of the prevailing society ... Society is much too powerful for it to tolerate any movies except those with which it is comfortable. Film must reflect society whether it wants to or not.
>
> KRACAUER 1995 [1963]: 291–2

His unit of analysis 'society' was dictated two-fold. First, he was thinking in terms of the nation-state. His *Caligari* study was about German films, as reflective of the German mentality (Kracauer 1947). Of course, national populations are not homogeneous – people differ by race, gender, class, and so on. Kracauer was not blind to this fact:

> It is always possible that certain screen motifs are relevant only to part of a nation, but caution in this respect should not prejudice one against the existence of tendencies affecting the nation as a whole. They are the less questionable as common traditions and permanent interrelationship between different strata of the population exert a unifying influence in the depths of collective life. In pre-Nazi Germany, middle-class penchants penetrated all strata; they competed with the political aspirations of the Left and also filled the voids of the upper-class mind. This accounts for the nation-wide appeal of the German cinema – a cinema firmly rooted in middle-class mentality. (2019 [1947]: 8)

Hence the second aspect of his unit 'the prevailing society' is rooted his ideas about the nation in his analysis of the middle-class 'salaried masses' (Kracauer 1998), which he saw as culturally dominant, inferred they were a reliable enough representation of national psychology as a whole (Gilloch 2015). To whatever degree these two inferences may have reasonably applied or not to Weimer Germany, they are certainly suspect when applied to America today.

Kellner (1995) suggests taking a 'multiperspectival' view of film. A plural reading, speaking to different views from different social locations, promotes more robust understanding. Kellner further suggests that "[C]ontemporary Hollywood cinema" as a whole "can be read as a contest of representations and a contested terrain that reproduces existing social structures and transcodes the political discourses of the era." Multiple perspectives are not only to be assumed by an audience of multiple subject positions, but the political messages that make it into popular films are cast out by a variety of players and mix and mingle to produce a wide array of political encodings.

> [W]hile some Hollywood films articulate in aggressive fashion contemporary liberal, conservative, or radical ideologies, and thus intersect with current public controversies, other films are complex, multilayered, and open to multiple readings ... while many are simply incoherent.
>
> KELLNER 2010: 2

Haas et al. concur with Kracauer's claim that popular films (and their political meanings) are dictated by 'public desires' (Kracauer 2019 [1947]: 5). Hollywood is primarily profit-driven, thus "it is probably safe to say that most, if not all, contemporary American movies are not intended to send any particular political or ideological message" (Haas et al. 2015: 8). This is a rather ambivalent description though, differing from Kracauer, who believed a coherent dominant set of meanings could be discerned in Weimar Germany, middle-class tastes determining films' content. Haas et al. are closer to Kellner's assessment about 'contested terrain' in American film. They claim that consumer-drivenness is paramount, but this does not mean films are devoid of political meanings. Rather, political meanings are often diluted, buried and unintentional. Taking a strong, clear political position can alienate many American viewers (and perhaps colleagues in the film industry),[11] who are socially and politically heterogeneous, and most of whom prefer light entertainment.

The mass media, such as the film industry – adds layers of complexity at both ends – author and audience. In accordance with the view that social location dictates or at least strongly influences authors' perspectives and in turn the meanings encoded in their works, it would be necessary and sufficient to analyse the demographics and social locations of authors in order to properly interpret films in terms of their authors. Unfortunately, this is not entirely possible, for the simple reason that there are typically many players on the encoding (production) side of the film. Generally speaking, it is not entirely possible to determine precisely who has influence, how much influence they have, and in what particular ways they have influence over the film, beyond their designated role titles (writer, producer, director, and so on). As Janet Wasko points out, some films are particularly studio-driven, even at the writing stage. "After securing the rights to an idea or the movie rights to an existing literary property, a studio may hire a writer to prepare a script or at least, a first draft, often with the guidance of the studio's development staff" (Wasko 2003: 27).

---

11   Deming says: "One can speak also of political instinct here. Films that open no eyes stir up no trouble. The film industry, like many another, is not without its stakes in maintaining the status quo. Within Hollywood ranks one can find a variety of political opinion; yet all, more than they would like to admit, involve themselves in this conspiracy" (1969: 2, fn. 2).

Karsten Grummitt (2001: 4), the managing director of Dodona Research,[12] has commented:

> The often-complex transactions involved in bringing a film to market make analysis of the production industry difficult. Without detailed inside knowledge it can be impossible to determine the actual producer of a film.[13]

As Kracauer (2019 [1947]: 5) emphasized,

> [F]ilms are never the product of an individual ... Since any film production unit embodies a mixture of heterogeneous interests and inclinations, teamwork in this field tends to exclude arbitrary handling of screen material, suppressing individual peculiarities in favour of traits common to many people.

Because finished films embody the influences of a variety of people, they must be understood as collectively generated, and so reflecting a conglomeration of minds.

We are left with more than a little muddiness. To make matters even more opaque, we must assume that successful authors *cater* to audiences to some degree. Because of this, we have the conundrum: In what ways, if at all, can we assume that popular films reflect predicted audience perspectives rather than simply the perspectives of authors? And to what extent, if at all, can authors 'accurately' reflect perspectives of persons from different social locations? We are now drowning in mud.

Just as it is difficult to determine who exactly has what influence over the content of films, it is also difficult to discern how much of a film's content speaks to the values of its author(s), and how much is calculated to speak to the desires of its predicted audience. A writer can hypothetically write anything into a script, but in practice the scripts that are purchased for production are chosen by studio executives based on their predicted market value.

---

12   "Dodona Research tracks cinema markets worldwide, following expansion and the penetration of new technologies, cinema admissions, ticket prices and box office. We interest ourselves in audience demographics, and ancillary revenue sources for cinemas such as refreshment sales and on-screen advertising. Our global approach allows us to carry insights from one market to another, and to assess the comparative strengths and weaknesses of national film and exhibition sectors" (Dodona Research 2019).

13   Quoted in Wasko (2003: 27).

Screenwriter William Goldman (1989) and producer Thom Taylor (1999) both attest to the overwhelming power of the bottom line in the selection of scripts for production (Wasko 2003). According to Martin Scorsese, "there is one iron rule that has never changed: every decision is shaped by the moneymen's perceptions of what the audience wants" (Scorsese and Wilson 1997: 20).[14] Political scientist Daniel Franklin (2016) argues:

> Commentators from both the Left and the Right assume that the ethnic, political, and class backgrounds of the production side of the movie industry constitute a slam-dunk case for a particular bias in entertainment content. But it would probably make more sense to assume that because the film industry is a business that Hollywood movies are largely product, not art. [...] It wouldn't be accurate to say that the personal backgrounds of journalists and filmmakers make no difference at all in the content of films, entertainment, or the news. But it could be more than plausibly argued that the influence of their personal backgrounds is overrated because of the influence of a much more powerful force – capitalism. (69-71)

These testimonials to the commodified nature of popular films support the claims of Kracauer and Deming, that "in the long run public desires determine the nature of Hollywood films" (Kracauer 2019 [1947]: 6) and "the role most filmmakers choose [is] that of giving the public 'what it wants'" (Deming 1969: 2). They point toward the importance of the intended audience in the shaping of the content – and perhaps by extension the meanings – of popular films. Following this logic then, several questions require answers. First, who are the intended audiences of popular films? Assuming that film production companies are informed by – at minimum – the best available data on what demographics are the largest consumers of popular films, then knowing this information might give an indication as to whose dreams popular films are at least *intended* to be. Second, is there reliable data on what different demographics gravitate toward what different types of films? And can we know to what extent these different types of films then come closer to *reflecting* the discourses and values of their audiences back at their audiences?

These are not easy questions to answer, even if only because there is little publicly available representative demographic data on individual movie ticket sales. For years, the Motion Picture Association of America has produced

---

14   Quoted in Franklin (2016: 73).

annual reports on the film industry that include general information such as what demographics visit movie theaters most; so, some general impressions can be drawn. However, the data does not lend itself to clear-cut conclusions. In 2018, for example, per capita movie theater attendance was 4.0 for men and 3.7 for women, 3.3 for Caucasian, 4.7 for Hispanic, 3.7 for African American, 4.5 for Asian and 4.0 for 'Other.' Age shows the most discernible pattern, showing something of a right-skewed distribution curve in the MPAA 2018 report, jumping from 3.0 per capita for 2–11 year-olds up to a peak at the 12–17 and 18–24 age groups at 5.1 movie theater visits per capita. The arc of the curve is not all that drastic on the right side, however. The 25–39 and 40–49 age groups are 4.3 per capita. 50–59 are still at 3.2 per capita, and 60+ are 2.5 per capita. To some extent, this suggests that the most active – although certainly not the only active – market for theater visits is among teenagers and young adults. Note, however, that the age groupings of the study are nominal, not ordinal; for example, the age range of 25–49 (those at 4.3 per capita) is twice as large as the 12–24 age range (those at 5.1 per capita). It is probably safe to assume that overall, production companies gear their products more – but by no means exclusively – towards a vaguely 'younger' market. While this is somewhat telling, it is not clear-cut enough to inform any reliable sweeping judgements (MPAA 2018). To complicate matters further, the majority of American film industry revenue currently comes from other countries (Franklin 2016).

The impossibility of reliable sweeping judgments does not, however, indicate that the audience is properly understood as a melting pot where individuals share the same spectator experiences and interpret films the same ways, rendering the issue of positionality moot. Feminist standpoint theorists articulated the theory of 'situated knowledges,' that the perspective of the interpreter (or knower) is always partial, as it is situated within and conditioned by her social location (Smith 1987; Haraway 1991; Harding 1986; Wood 1992). Ultimately, feminist postmodernism and feminist standpoint theory landed in the conclusion that standpoints are not inherent, nor are they absolute, and that people can transcend their situatedness and understand others' perspectives through exposure (Haraway 1991; Anderson 2020). Regarding the historical and cultural context, contemporary standpoint theory – especially of the intersectional variety – teaches us that it is always multiple. Different social locations – such as notably race, class, and gender – generally engender different experiences and understandings, even of the same empirical events.

Yet divisions between identity groups are not ontological absolutes. They are constructed or constituted, and they all leak. Disparate identity groups are overlapping and interpenetrating, and individual persons are better understood as occupying complex positions within a shifting landscape of articulated identities. Because we participate in social networks that directly or indirectly to us cross intro other identity groups, however, our networks expose us to standpoints from identity groups other than our own. One way to think about this is through meme theory. Richard Dawkins invented the notion of "meme" to refer to bits of ideas and culture that act in an analogous way to genes, that is, through evolutionary processes involving virus-like behavior, i.e. replication and diffusion via human carriers (Dawkins 2016 [1976]; Dennett 2017).

Our 'webs of group affiliations,' as Simmel calls them, require that every person occupy a stance of multiplicity, and especially in a multicultural and global information society, this means our [in]direct social influences are more likely to be demographically heterogeneous. And even when it is invisible, we gain exposure to the echoes of other groups removed once, twice, and so on from our direct involvement, as well as reverberations from remote networks which others key us into without anyone's awareness or intention. Demographics influence, but do not *determine*. Individuals are shaped but are not *contained*. We can detect broad regularities but cannot reliably assume them *a priori* in any individual case. A sober assessment of the issue can only lead to the conclusion that there is no clear answer.

5   How to Watch Movies

Considering all the above, one could very reasonably question whether popular films can be legitimately interpreted, due to the impossibility of demarcating the boundaries of a unit of analysis to ground interpretation. If author and audience are thus both 'dead' in a Barthesian sense, there are no anchor points besides the interpreter's own predispositions. According to this reasoning, film-as-dream analysis would be like holding up a mirror: the analyst just writes their own meanings as if they are in some sense objective or at least widely held. I will suggest that there are credible ways around this problem, although one needs to preserve a respect for speculation and lack of precision. Basically, the analysis is sounder to the extent that it is anchored in history, and that it deals with broad themes that are *so* prominent in the films that they are arguably next to impossible *not* to read into them. And if 'society' – which comprises multiple subject positions, standpoints, and perspectives – is being diagnosed, then the analysis is sounder when the broad themes are wide enough that they can metaphorically refer a variety of latent 'dream thoughts' that may be separately pertinent to diverging socio-political identities. Here are a few principles which can sum this up. They are not offered to suggest a hardened schematic for doing this sort of analysis. These are not boxes that must be checked for every film-as-dream interpretation. Instead they are offered as useful guideposts. They should be oriented around and experimented with, rather than 'Fulfilled.'

5.1   Form

The most important elements of the film to notice are those which are impossible to miss. Identify overarching trends, central relationships, and very prominent or recurring objects of narrative importance. Move from content to form. Details matter – content composes the form. But do not get overly concerned with the precise interpretation of a given moment, word, image, object, etc., unless the object is very pronounced and/or enduring or repeated in the film. This last statement diverges from Kracauer in that he analysed specific material objects at times – 'visible hieroglyphs' – and made no claims about their minimum qualifications of frequency, prominence, etc. to be theorized (Kracauer 2019 [1947]: 7).[15] In his essay "The Mass Ornament," Kracauer (1995: 75) says

> The position that an epoch occupies in the historical process can be determined more strikingly from an analysis of its inconspicuous surface-level expressions than from that epoch's judgments about itself.

The word 'inconspicuous' is important here, in that it is precisely by virtue of the seeming insignificance of these "surface-level expressions" that they are likely to be bereft of conscious insight or socio-political intentionality; and because of this lack, the censorship and deformation of conscious filters is more likely absent (Gilloch 2015).

As much as possible, forms should be articulated as *relations* or existential conditions rather than particular objects or persons. In *From Caligari to Hitler*, a central preoccupation for Kracauer is how German films of the Weimar period indicated various emotional positions surrounding the felt alternatives of 'tyranny' and 'chaos.' When analysing individual films, he does not always stay on this abstract level, but he always returns to it. For example, in his discussion of the film *The Cabinet of Dr. Caligari* he interprets circles to represent chaos, and a psychiatrist's descent down a large staircase to emphasize unapproachable power. He indicates many characters represent 'tyrants,' but he never says a character represents a *specific* tyrant, nor does he discuss the portrayal of Jewish characters or anti-Semitic insinuation. Even Kracauer's analyses of specific moments or objects are always rooted within a larger claim

---

15   My suggestion to err away from this is not meant as a hard and fast rule; nor is it because I assume such interpretations to be wrong. Rather, I assume them to be more easily dismissed as only unfounded projections of the interpreter.

about these major emotive-existential conditions in the 'collective soul,' with an eye toward their political implications.

5.2   *Condensation*

This principle diverges from Kracauer's approach. In taking the German middle-class mentality to represent the national mentality, Kracauer did not see the need to look for multiple latent 'dream thoughts.' Rather, he sought a singular significance in each instance, a singular film-as-dream thought displaced into the film-as-dream content. Extrapolating Freud's theory of condensation – where multiple latent thoughts can be simultaneously displaced onto a singular object of manifest dream content – to a pluralistic social subject, the standpoints or perspectives from multiple subject positions can be condensated into a singular object of manifest film content. Assume overarching forms are *overdetermined*, meaning that they can speak meaningfully to people from multiple, even contradictory identity groups. Rather than looking for one true meaning to a form, try to see it as overdetermined, as referencing a condensated array of possible meanings. The 'collective soul' can meaningfully be one and many simultaneously.

5.3   *History*

The condensated possible meanings should have independent, discernible logics that are relatable – in the sense of how Weber emphasized *verstehen* – to divergent identity groups during the moment in history when the film was produced and released. As Kellner (1995) emphasizes, use a "multiperspectival" approach that anchors various meanings within prominent social, cultural and political developments around the time of the film's release (in the year of the film's release and in the years leading up to it).

6   Example: The Last Man on Earth

To take an example from early biological horror and science fiction, consider *The Last Man on Earth* (1964), a film adaptation of Richard Matheson's novel from 1954, *I Am Legend.* The story marks the beginning of the modern zombie genre, which has since then risen to enormous popularity. A significant and memorable element in the story is that the protagonist hides inside a boarded-up house, which the zombies[16] threaten to invade. There are two

---

16   Technically, the creatures in the story are vampires, but they function much more recognizably today as akin to zombies. In addition, George Romero credits *The Last Man on*

elements here that I will argue can be read as signifying overdetermined forms. One is the nature of the zombie threat. The other is the significance of the boarded-up house.

6.1   The Zombie Threat

This element consists of four interlocking parts: contagion, hordes of Others, absorption, annihilation. Regarding contagion, the threat of pandemic illness is an ongoing one in human history, and at least in principle it could strike anyone. Hence the threat of the zombie virus can function very literally, and (perhaps partly because of this) it is an effective signifying carrier of other, condensated fears. The relationship between disease, difference, medicine, and Othering is an involved one with many internal pathways. Sometimes ill persons are ostracized as Other. Sometimes epidemics and pandemics are blamed on Others. Both were the case with HIV/AIDS in the 1980s and 1990s, being associated with Africa, homosexuality, and intravenous drug use. Sometimes disease metaphors – such as cancer – are used to describe subpopulations, either ethnic or political, which are thus framed as a threat that must be cast out if not exterminated. Also consider the rise in hate crimes against Asian Americans in the face of the COVID-19 pandemic. The mixing of Othering and radical measures of medical control came together in Nazism in Germany and forced sterilization in the United States. The fear that deviant behaviours and ideas can spread like a disease throughout the population and turn people into Others, is also common, for instance in anti-communist discourses (Wald 2008). Likewise, consider the fear of groupthink, of the 'madness of crowds' and the mindless horde. Gustav Le Bon even identified emotional 'contagion' as an element of crowd behaviour. And lastly, of course, death is a universal threat, like contagion – but the zombie phenomenon collapses the boundaries between death, absorption into the horde of mindless Others, and infectious disease. The zombie is a complex condensation of this landscape of threat.

The phenomenon of anti-Communism is an important element considering the general timing of these stories. The 1950s saw McCarthyism and the Second Red Scare. The treat here of groupthink could be felt on the Right and the Left alike: on one side, the groupthink of Communists, on the other side, the groupthink of anti-Communists. Hence the threat of the mindless horde, of their contagious nature, and so on, had immediate political resonance for two very opposed and urgently felt political platforms, both of which feared the

---

Earth with providing him a huge amount of influence in developing his *Night of the Living Dead* (1968). For simplicity's sake, I refer to them here as 'zombies.'

authoritarianism of the other. In these terms, the zombie metaphor had great potential to be compelling for a wide and diverse swath of the population. And yet there is more. The 1950s was an era of stifling conformity for many, and 1960s saw much youth rebellion against conformism. While young people saw conformism as a threat, for the more conservative the youth movement was an encroaching threat to traditional values and ways of life (Jancovich 1996). The Civil Rights movement spanned both decades, threatening to overturn white-dominated society, and the women's movement rose in the 1960s, which was a threat to patriarchal family culture. One could view the situation from either direction as the threat of the mobs: the conservative mobs rigidly conforming to their unjust and stultifying institutions; or the progressive mobs naively tearing apart cherished institutions. Finally, although there are no African American characters in the film, the mob seeking to capture and execute the Other echoes the form of lynching. In this respect, the threat of the mob touches upon the standpoint of the black community during the Civil Rights era. *All* of this can be read as condensated into a general form.

6.2   The Boarded-Up House

Generally speaking, it is the last sanctuary of quasi-normalcy for our protagonist(s). The zombie hordes want to break through the walls, invade, and destroy that island of normalcy. No doubt the relevance to conservative fears of the 1950s and 1960s fit very well here, especially considering the suburban feel of the house. It was the home that our protagonist lived in with his wife and daughter before they were overtaken by the contagion. Now, the protagonist hides in his home and preserves the remnants of his normal life there, but he is very much *alone*. His clinging to his humanity, his retaining of his individuality, his resistance to the mass, his defending of his tenuous fortress of rationality – all these things come along with a terrible, crushing sense of social alienation. In a sense, our protagonist is both a lonely nonconformist, and a die-hard traditionalist suffering from the alienation endemic to modern suburban life, but also due to a changing world that seems to have left him and his way of life behind. *All* of this also can be read as condensated into a general form.

Kracauer and Adorno especially were interested in unearthing latent meanings that spoke to pre-fascist tendencies, in other words to social currents which upon further reflection or hindsight have the chance to feed into authoritarian movements. This could be a direct indication of authoritarian longing, but it could also be various states of social unrest which in history or in theory have been shown to precede authoritarian uprisings. In the examples of the zombie hordes and the boarded-up house, clear connections can be drawn. Depending on the viewer, the nightmare could speak to the fear of aggressive mobs of authoritarian populists, to the desire to fend off chaos through authoritarian measures, or a contradictory mixture. Stepping back from the right-wing vs. left-wing interpretations above, consider the general forms: Our protagonist must defend himself against the hordes of infected subhumans who threaten to tear down the boundaries of his ordered and human world. They would invade and kill or somehow absorb him into their mindless, inferior mass, if they could. He must protect himself and his superior ways which are in danger of disappearing completely, by barricading himself inside night after night, as the hordes try to push their way in and destroy what remains of his world.

References

Anderson, Elizabeth. 2020. "Feminist Epistemology and Philosophy of Science." *The Stanford Encyclopedia of Philosophy* (Spring 2020 Edition), ed. Edward N. Zalta. At https://plato.stanford.edu/archives/spr2020/entries/feminism-epistemology/.

Dawkins, Richard. 2016 [1976]. *The Selfish Gene*. Oxford: Oxford University Press.

Deming, Barbara. 1969. *Running Away from Myself: A Dream Portrait of America Drawn from the Films of the Forties*. London: Penguin.

Dennett, Daniel C. 2017. *From Bacteria to Bach And Back: The Evolution of Minds*. New York: W.W. Norton & Company.

Franklin, Daniel P. 2016. *Politics and Film: The Political Culture of Television and Movies*. Lanham, MD: Rowman & Littlefield.

Freud, Sigmund. 2001 [1914]. *On Dreams*. New York: Dover.

Gilloch, Graeme. 2015. *Siegfried Kracauer: Our Companion in Misfortune*. Malden, MA: Polity.

Haraway, Donna, 1991. "Situated Knowledges." In *Simians, Cyborgs, And Women*. New York: Routledge.

Harding, Sandra, 1986. *The Science Question in Feminism*. Ithaca, NY: Cornell University Press.

Jameson, Fredric. 2013. *The Political Unconscious: Narrative as A Socially Symbolic Act*. New York: Routledge.

Jancovich, Mark. 1996. *Rational Fears: American Horror in the 1950s*. Manchester: Manchester University Press.

Kellner, Douglas. 2010. *Cinema Wars: Hollywood Film and Politics in the Bush-Cheney Era*. Malden, MA: Blackwell.

Kracauer, Siegfried. 2019 [1947]. *From Caligari To Hitler: A Psychological Study of The German Film*. Princeton, NJ: Princeton University Press.

Kracauer, Siegfried. 1995 [1963]. *The Mass Ornament: Weimar Essays*. Cambridge, MA: Harvard University Press.

Kracauer, Siegfried. 1998. *The Salaried Masses: Duty and Distraction in Weimar Germany*. New York: Verso.

Matheson, Richard. 1995 [1954]. *I Am Legend*. New York: Tom Doherty Associates.

Morelock, Jeremiah. 2017. "Authoritarian Populism Contra *Bildung*: Anti-Intellectualism and The Neoliberal Assault on The Liberal Arts/Populismo Autoritário Contra *Bildung*: O Anti-Intelectualismo E O Assalto Neoliberal Contra as Artes Liberais." *Cadernos CIMEAC* 7(2): 63–81.

Morelock, Jeremiah. 2018a. "Changing Politics of Tribalism and Morality." In *I Am Legend* and Its Remakes. *The 'M' In Citams@30: Media Sociology*. Bingley, UK: Emerald Group Publishing.

Morelock, Jeremiah, Ed. 2018b. *Critical Theory and Authoritarian Populism*. London: University of Westminster Press.

Nimmo, Dan D. and James E. Combs. 1990. *Mediated Political Realities*. London: Longman.

Popper, Karl. 2002. *The Poverty of Historicism*. London: Psychology Press.

Scorsese, Martin and Michael Henry Wilson. 1991. *A Personal Journey with Martin Scorsese through American Movies*. New York: Hyperion.

Popper, Karl. 2005. *The Logic of Scientific Discovery*. New York: Routledge.

Smith, Dorothy E. 1987. *The Everyday World as Problematic: A Feminist Sociology*. Toronto: University of Toronto Press.

Sontag, Susan. 1965. "The Imagination of Disaster." *Commentary*, October, 42–48. At https://www.commentarymagazine.com/articles/susan-sontag/the-imagination-of-disaster/.

Sontag, Susan. 1989. *Illness as Metaphor and Aids and Its Metaphors*. New York: Picador.

Wald, Priscilla. 2008. *Contagious: Cultures, Carriers, and the Outbreak Narrative*. Durham, NC: Duke University Press.

Weber, Max. 1978. *Economy and Society: An Outline of Interpretive Sociology*. Berkeley, CA: University of California Press.

Wolff, Kristina. 2007. "Strategic Essentialism." *The Blackwell Encyclopedia of Sociology* (2007). Hoboken, NJ: Wiley-Blackwell.

Wood, J. T. 1992. "Gender and Moral Voice: Moving from Woman's Nature to Standpoint Epistemology." *Women's Studies in Communication* 15: 1–24.

Wood, Robin. 2018. *Robin Wood on the Horror Film: Collected Essays and Reviews*. Detroit: Wayne State University Press.

CHAPTER 15

How to Mediate Reality: Thinking Documentary Film with Adorno and Horkheimer

Stefanie Baumann

The responsibility lies with the How, not with the What.

THEODOR W. ADORNO, Prologue to Television: 53

•••

To deny the reality of film in claiming (to capture) reality is to stay "in ideology" – that is, to indulge in the (deliberate or not) confusion of filmic with phenomenal reality.

TRINH T. MIN-HA, Documentary Is/Not a Name: 90

•
• •
•

When Robert Kramer wrote, in 1991, that "[p]ower is the possibility to define what is real,"[1] he was referring to the complex political and ideological potency of documentary formats. A documentary filmmaker himself, he was well aware of the political element of perception and the persuasive force of films claiming to address reality directly. And indeed, documentaries, especially those that are transmitted through official channels, are commonly considered as serious, trustworthy productions. Allegedly based on facts, they are supposed to document, explain, reveal that which matters in the actual state of the world – the real world, the one that we share with those that appear in the films and in which "issues of life and death are always at hand," as Bill Nichols puts it (Nichols 1991: 109). Therein lies the additional value and characteristic seriousness of documentary. And therein also lies its assumed authority: its direct association with the factual world grants it with a specific credibility

---

1   Translated from French by the author.

likely to become ideology when it remains unquestioned. Thus, documentary formats are particularly susceptible for authoritarian instrumentalization, all the more so if they take on a neutral, affirmative stance and conceal the fact that the empirical reality captured by the camera necessarily goes through the subjective mediation of the filmmaker.

It was such authoritarian tendencies that Kramer detected both in American news coverage and official journalistic reports. As a critical response, he co-founded the New York Newsreel collective in 1967 in order to counter the alleged authority of official representations as sole suppliers of truthful information. Through independent experimental works, the members of the collective aimed to disrupt the consensual appearance of reality. They opposed subversive forms to the normalized standards of image production, so as to open up a space for discordant voices and emancipatory perspectives. Evidently, Kramer and the New York Newsreel collective were neither the first, nor the only filmmakers who engaged critically with the mediatic representations of reality delivered by the reigning institutions of society. Many independent artistic productions, activist videos, and essay films were and continue to be driven by the idea to challenge the hegemonic legitimacy claim of authorized versions – either by questioning the ideological impact of media, their subliminal strategies and the appearance of immediacy on which they rely; or by problematizing reductionist or misleading representations, and using documentary films to give a visibility to subjects and objects that "must be represented" (Rabinowitz 1994). However, such critical works are usually available only through specialized festivals, art galleries, more or less private circuits or the internet, and require insider knowledge to be found.

During the last decades, commercial productions have appropriated critical issues in order to convert them into "culinary"[2] entertainment products. Alongside with documentaries praising the beauty of allegedly 'authentic' nature, narrating the fascinating biographies of celebrities, exposing the newest technological inventions, ancient civilizations, or impressive discoveries, the offer of popular documentary formats featuring serious content is overwhelming. Hence, documentaries of all shapes are nowadays omnipresent in the sphere of what Theodor W. Adorno and Max Horkheimer have called, since the 1940s, the culture industry. When the two philosophers first problematized the potency of culture industry, the permissible content of media formats was still largely subjected to legal constraints. Political campaigns against fascism, communism or, on the other side of the iron curtain, capitalism, as well as

---

2   This expression, often employed by Theodor W. Adorno, stems from Bertolt Brecht.

moral restrictions as the (in)famous Hays Code in the USA, significantly limited the topics that could be raised in the public sphere. Meanwhile, the media landscape has been widely liberated from direct political and moral censorship, at least in those countries that have adopted the Western model of neoliberalism. Consequently, the situation of documentary film has radically changed. Besides officially authorized documentary formats on the one hand, and their subversive counterpart, independent productions, on the other, we are nowadays confronted with a great diversity of films that present themselves, as it were, as their popular synthesis. Claiming to be critical visions of reality, they nevertheless rely on documentary's persuasive agency, while being entertaining enough to suit for mass consumption.

Hence, big commercial productions like *An Inconvenient Truth* (dir. Davis Guggenheim 2006), *Leaving Neverland* (dir. Dan Reed 2019), *Blackfish* (dir. Gabriela Cowperthwaite 2013), *Fahrenheit 11/9* (dir. Michael Moore 2018), *Citizen 4* (dir. Laura Poitras 2014) or *Inside Job* (dir. Charles Ferguson 2010) are released in multiplex cinemas, available on public tv programs, internet platforms such as YouTube and Vimeo, or payable streaming services such as Amazon Prime, Hulu, or Netflix. More often than not, they disclose shocking scandals (be they political, economic, social, or ecological), uncover illicit practices or humanitarian atrocities, and constitute by themselves an intervention in the debate in question. Covering a wide range of miscellaneous subjects, documentary films present themselves nowadays as critical consciousness of societal evil and watchdog of ongoing or forthcoming crises. They are considered as an appropriate medium to address virtually any issue of contemporary society, including failures of state management or even the bias of media coverage – as long as it is spectacular enough to raise public interest, and thus promising enough to turn into a box-office success. Climate change, racism, the global financial crises, devastating wars, the malfeasance of capitalism, communism or the evangelist church, the Cambridge Analytica affair, the viciousness and egocentrism of the American or the North Korean president, the danger of terrorism and extremist groups, worldwide sex trafficking and horrifying abuse cases – broaching severe societal problems through compelling non-fiction formats has become as common a cultural praxis as watching action movies, soap operas, or quiz shows.

Admittedly, this does neither mean that everything shown under the sign of mainstream documentary is nowadays critically motivated, nor that truly every topic has since then come into the focus of the public sphere. Nevertheless, the broadened diversity of topics embraced in the media, together with their compelling presentation, affect the societal perception of reality significantly. The public exhibition of seemingly every issue nourishes not only the impression that virtually any aspect of the global society was potentially in the reach of everyone's grasp, but also the assumption that a comprehensive understanding of a respective topic in particular – or even a critical attitude in general – could be attained simply by watching the right films. The problem is not only that it becomes more and more difficult to discern whether a documentary representation is based on thorough research, populist interests, or pure market orientation, but also that the idea of critique as something that could be smoothly consumed is misleading. What is more: such an idea hides in its folds signs of what Adorno et al. called an authoritarian character trait (Adorno et al. 2019). By inherently claiming to show "reality as it is," many commercial documentaries feed such an attitude, and thereby incite the viewer to subordinate herself to the authority of the provided information and its explanation rather than leaving space for her own interpretation and critical assessment. A critical behavior, on the contrary, requires "the ability to distinguish between what is known and what is accepted merely by convention or under constraint of authority" (Adorno 2005a: 282). Thus, it is fundamentally different from the compelling media treatment of a sensitive topic and its passive consumption.

This is not to say that popular documentary films inciting to adopt a genuine critical attitude rather than conformist faith cannot or do not exist beyond the margins of the public media space. It does not mean either that simply by watching conformist films, one necessarily loses the capacity for critical thinking. However, in order not to succumb to a relation of pure belief, it is important to understand how contemporary documentary films deal with the authority attributed to them, how they produce and legitimate certain effects of reality, how they relate to society as a whole, and how the forms through which contents are mediated shape and orientate our perception. The critical theory of Horkheimer and Adorno can therefore provide a productive starting point. For even if they never addressed the authoritarian agency of documentary films directly, their insights on the representation of reality through the culture industry and its intimate relationship with authoritarian tendencies touch upon the genre in a particularly acute manner. This chapter aims at problematizing certain recurrent features of documentary films through the lens of the critical theory of the early Frankfurt school, in order to open up a critical space for the understanding of documentary formats today.

1   Dividing the Real: The Common Ground of the Culture Industry
       and Positivism

As already mentioned, the authority attributed to documentary films is related to its allegedly direct association with the objective world. The reason why they appear as truthful is that the representation of reality they provide is not only thought to be accurate because of the direct recording through a camera, but also because the complementary information is supposedly based on factual truth. Just as positivistic tendencies in the sciences, such documentaries thus adhere to the "cult of fact" (Adorno and Horkheimer 2002: 119), which pervades the entire sphere of the culture industry. Both, positivistic science and the products of the culture industry, rely on the uncritical belief in the factual as an objective, neutral, detachable realm, and the conviction that this realm could be approached empirically, without relating it to the historically developed society from which it stems and in which it is imbedded. This underlying idea that factual truth equates truth *tout court* seems to be taken for granted. Horkheimer and Adorno vehemently criticized this assumption, and urged to scrutinize its social, political and epistemological implications. A short consideration of their argument might help to understand what makes an uncritical faith in the veracity of a documentary representation susceptible for authoritarian behavior.

The elective affinity between the culture industry and positivism consists in their tacit agreement upon the existence of two distinguishable spheres: the objective one understood as the real world of hard facts, and the subjective one encompassing sensations, experiences, personal opinions, and individual biases. This division is presupposed to be naturally given. In science, it translates into an intentional exclusion of everything that is thought to be subjective, and a rigid definition of what is supposed to be relevant – the cold facts –, combined with an accurate system of classification which anticipates a specific category for any given element. In the case of the culture industry, this separation is already apparent in the categorization of its products into different genres, some of which are considered as serious because they address the objective realm (like the news and documentary forms), while fictional formats are usually associated with trivial entertainment (e.g. romances, comedies, dramas or action movies) that appeals to feelings such as love, hope, aggression, or distress. "These types have developed into formula," writes Adorno, "which, to a certain degree, pre-establish the attitudinal pattern of the spectator before he is confronted with any specific content and which largely determine the way in which any specific content is being perceived" (1954: 226).

Accordingly, many commercial documentaries not only claim to depict the factual real in its immediacy but also legitimate this allegedly direct link through their conventional formal constitution, which has become so familiar that its constructedness all too easily falls into oblivion. Yet, it is exactly because mainstream documentaries rely on generalized patterns and standardized approaches that they are taken to be credible. "Each statement, each piece of

news, each thought has been preformed by the centres of the culture industry,"
writes Adorno in *Minima Moralia*. "Whatever lacks the familiar trace of such
pre-formation lacks credibility, the more so because the institutions of public
opinion accompany what they send forth by a thousand factual proofs and all
the plausibility that total power can lay hands on" (2005b: 108). Through mechanisms such as the use of authoritative voice-over, talking head interviews
with experts, victims, or other people who are directly or indirectly concerned
with the respective topic, impressive 'authentic' media footage, participatory
interventions, graphic depictions of alleged proofs, statistic data, or scientific
diagrams, documentary films have adopted characteristic shapes making them
recognizable as genuine sources of evidence. Contemporary commercial documentaries further link their claim to truthfulness with depictions of powerful
emotional responses to the factual events, e.g. through dramatic testimonies
of victims, often accompanied by a dramatic music score – a stylistic means
already criticized by Adorno in *Composing for the Film* for its stimulation of
artificial inwardness when employed uncritically (Adorno and Eisler 1974).
However, those different aspects are usually kept separated in contemporary
documentary films. Each is associated with a particular function: while the
factual data accounts for the veracity of the representation, the subjective
add-ons appeal to the spectators' emotions and thus communicate its impact
through an adaptation to the subject. Rather than dialectically relating subjective and objective moments, this division exacerbates their separation even
further. The alleged authority of the representation is thereby endorsed: it fills
all the voids, appeals comprehensively, but on different levels, to the viewers'
emotions and discernment, without however leaving any space for personal
interpretation or subjective experiences.

What is problematic in the division between an objective and a subjective
sphere is that it fails to address the complex ways through which those spheres
are interrelated. Knowledge cannot be reduced to isolated contents and is thus
not merely a matter of methodological analysis, verification, and proof alone.
For contents only become meaningful when they are dialectically related to
the experiences and forms that mediate them. Neither content nor form are
ahistorical, neutral, independent givens: both have been historically developed and continue to evolve with regards to each other, both are products of
society, just as both affect, in turn, the actual constitution of this society. What
is ignored by both, positivism and the culture industry, is thus, as Horkheimer
puts it, that "[t]he facts which our senses present to us are socially preformed in
two ways: through the historical character of the object perceived and through
the historical character of the perceiving organ. Both are not simply natural;
they are shaped by human activity" (2002: 200). Therefore, "[t]he very concept

of 'fact' is a product – a product of social alienation; in it, the abstract object of exchange is conceived as a model for all objects of experience in a given category" (Horkheimer 2004: 56). Far from being a neutral conception of the objective world, far from being as disinterested as it is presented by those who dogmatically rely on it, the idea of the factual, the social practices it engenders and the cultural productions that rely on it, are part of the reigning ideology.

Institutionalized science in a positivistic sense and its divulgation through popular formats are thus indeed related to all the other layers of society. Adopting an authoritarian stance by considering themselves as actual providers of knowledge – the only ones able to do so, as it is them defining the conditions for knowledge production – they are perfectly integrated in the reigning power structures of society. They perpetually reproduce the capitalistic principle of division of labor, consolidate its implicit value structure, and impose a worldview in which individuals are considered as passive receivers of information and its accurate interpretation rather than subjects capable of experiencing on their own. Through the products of the culture industry, "[e]xperience – the continuity of consciousness in which everything not present survives, in which practice and association establish tradition in the individual – is replaced by the selective, disconnected, inter-changeable and ephemeral state of being informed which, as one can already observe, will promptly be cancelled by other information" (Adorno 1993: 33). Rather than instigating the development of a critical awareness, many entertaining documentaries, even when they deal with serious topics, thus feed a consumerist attitude that is perfectly adapted to capitalism.

2   Becoming Cliché: The Homogenizing Agency of Culture Industrial Production

The problem we are faced with when we question the agency of commercial documentary film is thus wide-ranging: it is a matter of how perceptual habits are shaped and perpetually endorsed through the standardization of cultural expressions in modern capitalism. It is this normalization of the perception which facilitates that authoritarian presentations are not only established, but also pass almost unnoticed. Obviously, technically produced images and sounds play thereby an important role. Combining indexical images that seem to be exact copies of the empirical world, with the repetitive use of stereotyped patterns, frozen genres and rigid forms, films are likely to generate the internalization of benchmarks and thereby to endorse the normalized values which underlie the current state of society. For the culture industry's "inherent tendency to adopt the tone of a factual report" (Adorno and Horkheimer, 2002: 118) operates to blur the boundaries between reality and its replication. This is true for any product of the culture industry, but especially decisive when it comes to documentaries. What makes the appearance of the artificial world of the culture industry as immediate reflection of reality so strong is that its clichéd imagery imposes a strong and all-encompassing scheme which assimilates any element of the empirical world by converting it into a recogniz-able commonplace. "Reality becomes its own ideology through the spell cast by its faithful duplication," writes Adorno in *The Schema of Mass Culture*. "This is how the technological veil and the myth of the positive is woven. If the real becomes an image insofar as in its particularity it becomes as equivalent to the whole as one Ford car is to all the others of the same range, then the image on the other hand turns into immediate reality" (2001b: 63).

What Adorno articulated, prophetically, in the 1940s, has in the meantime become reality: nowadays, events, situations, objects, individual appearances or memories are often said to be akin to films or photographs. It is telling that many contemporary feature-length documentaries or serials, as well as var-ious hybrid forms such as docudrama, true-crime stories, reality tv and the like, have meanwhile converged with their fictional counterparts on many lev-els: like fiction films, they display intriguing characters and fascinating circum-stances, rely on thrilling, often spectacular narratives and are provided with intense soundtracks and special effects, while keeping the aura of the factual intact. In the late 1980s, the recourse to fictional strategies and Hollywood-aesthetic in a non-fiction film like Errol Morris' *The Thin Blue Line* (1988) was still an extraordinary, subversive stylistic device with a strong, very concrete political impact.[3] Since then, it has developed into a widespread formula in documentary film-making. It seems as if the reality-effect of fiction films had superseded even reality itself – as if "real life" happened where the drama is and, in order to be recognized as such, required specific patterns that stand for its significance.

The problem is that when reality is automatically associated with the ubiquitous images that command the way of perceiving it, this very reality, in turn, appears as if it was as flat, consistent and univocal as the products of the culture industry pretend it to be, even if it takes on a spectacular look in their representation. For through their dazzling appearance, the products of the culture industry obscure the persisting antagonisms and structural

---

3   Morris' film depicts the conviction of Randall Dale Adams for the shooting of a police officer. The documentary discloses serious inconsistencies of the official investigation, which led to the liberation of the accused one year after the film was released.

contradictions of society by upholding an imagery in which it appears as coherent in itself. Rather than critically assessing conflicts in their substantial social and political dimension, they are treated in a particularistic manner, dissociated from their manifold imbrications with other layers of society, and isolated from the structurally related problems which facilitate their emanation. Documentaries today widely reproduce this pattern. It is particularly visible, for instance, in nature films such as *March of the Penguins* (dir. Luc Jacquet 2005) or series such as *Our Planet* (prod. Netflix 2019) which present savage animals as authentic creatures of nature completely disconnected from the global society. The occasional remarks about the precariousness of their living environment because of human destructiveness are thoroughly overshadowed by the stunning images of their intact surroundings and the moving stories of their peculiar ways of living, peppered with stirring soundtracks.

But this pattern is also visible, to a certain extent, in documentaries that aim at addressing critical issues. Recently, for example, a feature-length film about the Hollywood-mogul Harvey Weinstein (*Untouchable,* dir. Ursula Macfarlane 2019), accused of severe and repeated sexual abuse on women at his mercy, resonates in several ways with a such a figure that Adorno already criticized in the mid 20th century as "the spurious personalization of objective issues" (1957: 485) – a figure that corresponds to one of the patterns analyzed in the comprehensive study on the *Authoritarian Personality.*[4] Adorno's (fictional) example relates to the representation of a dictator as "nothing but a bad, pompous, and cowardly man," while his wife is depicted as warmhearted, helpless victim and those who defend her and the "right cause" are "personally idealized." In *Untouchable,* several of the abused women and other people in Weinstein's surroundings disclose terrifying situations of harassment, abuse of power and rape, and describe him as fascinating, but power-hungry and perverse, while physically unattractive and vulgar. However, by focusing on the personage and presenting him as an evil, all-mighty perpetrator, while the witnesses appear as his vulnerable targets, the film ratifies the stereotypical representation it aims, at the same time, to overcome. Rather than problematizing the structural conditions of the Hollywood-system, based on hard, merciless, misogynic business which not only perpetually reproduces stereotyped representations, but also generates both the unquestioned desire to become a star and the aura of those in power, in relation to the fact that this very system serves as a blueprint for society as a whole and is at the same time its glossy

---

4   In Chapter XVII (written by Adorno), "Ticket Thinking and Personalization in Politics," personalization is mentioned as one of the formal constituents of fascist approaches to political thinking.

reflection, the film concentrates on one exceptional individual who seemingly degenerated and became a monster. This is not to say that the 'real' affair – which opened a huge critical debate about women's vulnerable position in society and triggered the world-wide #MeToo movement – was itself nothing but another repetition of a recurrent media scheme. Even if it is surely characteristic of contemporary society that such a subject gains attention precisely when it touches those who are already in a privileged position, it is still an emancipatory move to problematize the conditions of those who are subjected to the power of others. However, its coverage through a film like *Untouchable* reduces its impact to a Hollywood-like drama about Hollywood itself.

Another aspect of Adorno's statement, which is intimately linked with the elaborations above, touches upon the fact that through the culture industrial standardization of the perception of reality, any singularity is immediately superseded by familiar tropes, associated with generalized features, and thus absorbed by reproduceable patterns. Instead of appearing in its particularity, its irreducible otherness and complexity, any singular being or event is converted into that which makes it comparable with allegedly identical others. Even the most exotic feature thus loses its uniqueness, turns into a cliché and gets thereby associated with preconceived ideas. Any remote tribe turns into an example of savageness or, inversely, of respectful unison with nature similar to many others of the like, when shown through the ever-same formal devices; any individual history becomes ordinary when narrated in a conventional, stereotypical way.

This reduction to attributed traits also appears in many documentaries with humanitarian aspirations. In her book *Immediations,* Pooja Rangan (2017) demonstrates comprehensively how certain aesthetic strategies used in documentary in order to produce the impression of immediacy, authenticity, urgency, and commitment, rely on an authoritarian projection of consensual ideas onto their subjects that remain unquestioned. One of her examples is the award-winning film *Born into Brothels* (dir. Zana Briski and Ross Kauffman 2005) about a group of children raised in an Indian red-light district. The filmmaker documents how she teaches them to use a camera in order to help them emancipate themselves from their social condition. Yet, she thereby reproduces not only the trope of "feral innocence" – the stereotyped representation of children as pure "figure[s] that exist[...] outside mediation and political economy" (Rangan 2017: 27), as opposed to the sheer cruelty of their mothers and the context into which they were born. She also reinforces the colonial fantasy of the superior humanitarian moralism of the Western subject over Third World barbarism. Rather than challenging the perception of these children in relation to the generalized context of exploitation of late capitalism, the film upholds the hegemonic world view of domination and thus sanctions the status quo.

Such an ambiguous dimension can also be found in the example given above, in which Harvey Weinstein himself, despite the focus on his personae, appears as the perfect stereotyped image of a repulsive, power-obsessive, very rich man. However, the message is double: the film suggests that such individuals are evil, but at the same time, they are well-off and thus remain societal models to follow in a society in which success largely determines the value of a person. Likewise, the representation of his victims in the film makes them resemble each other in their expressions and the way they tell their experiences, and thereby conform to the socially established way how victims are supposed to behave. Moreover, their physical appearance as shown in the film also sets the beauty standards of contemporary society; their objectified bodies thus serve as ideal irrespective of the history they have gone through. Adorno calls this dimension of the culture industry its "hieroglyphic script" (2001b: 93), akin to the appearance of value as hieroglyphic in Marx's Capital[5] (Marx 1976: 167, cf. also Behrens 2003: 76), which is supposed to instill messages in a subliminal way that affect the spectator on a more unconscious level and are thus all the more powerful as they remain undetected. Adorno goes as far as to claim that "the hidden message may be more important than the overt since this hidden message will escape the controls of consciousness, will not be 'looked through', will not be warded off by sales resistance, but is likely to sink into the spectator" (1954: 221).

These underlying messages are all the more efficient because the overarching presence of all kinds of images that are, despite their apparent disparity, aligned through normalized patterns, does not leave much space for subjective appropriation, genuine experience, and the development of awareness. For it generates the spontaneous association of any image with a meaning, an emotion, a value, which supersede any deviant instinctive reaction. Hence, the problem raised by Horkheimer and Adorno is a structural one. It touches upon society as a whole, its self-understanding and the perceptional conventions it continually reproduces. The culture industry – understood as a principle of standardization based on market criteria rather than an ominous god-like power controlling the market – is thus much more than a mere means to

---

5   In Capital, Marx writes: "Value, therefore, does not have its description branded on its forehead; it rather transforms every product of labor into a social hieroglyphic. Later on, men try to decipher the hieroglyphic, to get behind the secret of their own social product: for the characteristic which objects of utility have of being values is as much men's social product as is their language." (167).

sell entertainment products to the masses. The problem is that it provides an all-encompassing schema in the Kantian sense of the term,[6] which directly links images with more or less inflexible ideas. "Kant intuitively anticipated what Hollywood has consciously put into practice: images are precensored during production by the same standard of understanding which will later determine their reception by viewers." (Adorno and Horkheimer 2002: 65) Thus, a normalized perception of society as a whole and of any of its respective elements is generated, which directly associates reality with unquestioned, seemingly consensual values. Yet, this consensual, inflexible view is problematic in itself. Claiming to represent 'realistically' the society as such, it facilitates authoritarian tendencies by cutting down the ability to develop critical awareness of society. As Horkheimer puts it with regards to the critical attitude he defends, "it is suspicious of the very categories of the better, useful, appropriate, productive, and valuable, as these are understood in the present order, and refuses to take them as nonscientific presuppositions about which one can do nothing" (2002: 206). Documentary formats which adopt the recurrent normalized schema intrinsically validate its pretention to represent the real, as if the association between specific contents with predetermined moral and political implications was a natural given rather than a socially formed, historically developed construction. But when the standardization of allegedly accurate forms automatically validates a representation as truthful, the mere application of such forms, in turn, facilitates the instrumentalization of such a representation for any political, ideological or populistic trend, as long as the underlying schema remains intact. Whence the importance to develop a sensitivity for the agency of forms, and to approach them through an immanent critique.

3   Non-identical Forms: That which Resists the Schema of Culture Industry

A thorough examination of that which distinguishes the products of the culture industry from their antipode – genuine artworks – can help grasp how different mediations of content through form correspond to different attitudes towards reality, and how critical approaches hold the potential to subvert authoritarian truth claims. Both, the products of the culture industry and

---

6   Briefly said, for Kant, a (transcendental) schema is that which relates non-empirical concepts to sensory perception (cf. Kant 1999, Book 2 Chapter 1).

genuine artworks, are according to Adorno social facts,[7] both emanate from the same historically developed society and mediate it through artistic forms, and both address it in one way or another. As both are intimately linked with the society and thus subject to its perpetual transformations, Adorno refuses to provide any formal, material or topical criteria supposed to be eternally valid for either of them. "Because art is what it has become, its concept refers to what it does not contain," he writes in *Aesthetic Theory*. "Art can be understood only by its laws of movement, not by any set of invariants" (1997: 3). Hence, the fundamental divergence between genuine art and the products of the culture industry lies not in their aesthetic appearance as such, but in the stance they take on towards the social reality, its underlying power structure, and its conventionalized perception. This stance is expressed through their relation with their own material. While artworks follow their material as strictly as possible in order to carve out its inner truth content through a thorough formal construction, the products of the culture industry subordinate their material to the intentional purpose of producing effects, as we have seen previously. Thus, they are likely to adopt any fashionable form, regardless its relation to the content it mediates.

Genuine artworks, by contrast, are only able to deploy their critical potential by resisting through their formal arrangement to their total integration into the codes of society. "The unsolved antagonisms of reality return in artworks as immanent problems of form," writes Adorno. "This, not the insertion of objective elements, defines the relation of art to society. The complex of tensions in artworks crystallizes undisturbed in these problems of form and through emancipation from the external world's factual façade converges with the real essence" (7). Only by not conforming to conventionalized forms and formats that would immediately orient the meaning, only by subverting perceptual habits and frustrating the normalized expectations towards a given matter, can an object still be perceived, through its artistic mediation, in its singularity, instead of being seized through established criteria and thus absorbed in the realm of the return of the ever same. In order to allow contradictory elements to unfold in their dialectical movement, artworks must wrest their appearance from the veil of familiar consistency imposed by the culture industry. As Adorno, puts it: "Form works like a magnet that orders elements of the empirical in such a fashion that they are estranged from their extra-aesthetic existence, and it is only as a result of this estrangement that they master the

---

7   Adorno grasps genuine artworks through their double constitution "as both autonomous and
    fait social" (1997: 7).

extra-aesthetic essence" (309). It is precisely in their unassimilable otherness that lies the autonomy of artworks and thus their utopian moment which foreshadows the possibility of a not yet fathomable, different social reality.

Accordingly, Adorno also insists on the fact that art is opposed to communication. Contrary to most products of the culture industry, art's inherent protest is all but a message: this is why Adorno rejects not only all kind of propaganda and advertising, but also the various shapes of artistic realism and committed art. "The notion of a 'message' in art, even when politically radical, already contains an accommodation to the world: the stance of the lecturer conceals a clandestine entente with the listeners, who could only be rescued by refusing it," he writes in *Commitment* (1974: 193). While the products of the culture industry consist of images meant to dissolve into signs associated with an accommodated signification, artworks, as "imageless images" (Adorno 1997: 379), immanently protest against the reality principle shaped by the societal logic of capitalism, in which every meaning is already determined in advance. The meaning of artworks eludes categorial prehension and defies unilateral interpretation; therein lies their singular enigmatic character.

Concerning films, Adorno was primarily critical about the medium and its potential as an artform because of its representational character and its perfect adaption to the culture industry. However, he also saw the possibility of emancipating film from its direct association with the tropes of mass production (cf. Adorno 2001c; Hansen 2012). And indeed, the works of many independent documentary filmmakers resonate strongly with his critical elaborations. Instead of taking the indexical material as evidence of reality and concentrating exclusively on the content, they consider their artistic material to be the genre's inherent tension between its seemingly direct relationship with the empirical world on the one hand, and its aesthetic configuration through which it acquires its meaning, on the other – a tension already stressed by John Grierson in the 1930s when he famously defined documentary as "creative treatment of reality" (2016: 216). While many mainstream productions exploit the fact that the artistic mediation is all too easily overshadowed by the film's appearance as immediate, artistically exigent documentary films unfold their form while taking heed of the complexity of their medium. Alexander Kluge for example – Adorno's disciple and friend – challenges in his hybrid films the "pseudo-realism of the culture industry" (Adorno 2005b: 141) by merging fictional elements, paintings, heterogeneous music scores, subjective narration, archival material and direct intervention into real situations, in order to produce a multiplicity of interrelations and contexts that refuse any unilateral interpretation. Mingling not only different modes, but also temporalities and perspectives, Kluge's films critically deconstruct the recurrent representation of reality through mainstream formats, re-inscribe it in its history and deploy heterogeneous layers of sense at the same time. Rather than stipulating a meaning by declaring it as truth, films like Kluge's interrupt the habits of perception and destabilize conventional preconceptions.

In a similar manner, the filmmaker Trinh T. Min-ha writes that in films addressing the real, "[m]eaning can [...] be political only when it does not let itself be easily stabilized, and when it does not rely on any single source of authority, but, rather, empties or decentralizes it" (1990: 89). Hence, she refuses to provide clarifications on the people or situations appearing in her films, and develops an approach of "speaking nearby" her subjects rather than taking on an authoritarian perspective. Examples for artistic strategies to open up questions through formal devices rather than presenting contents as factual evidence are multifold. Some filmmakers disrupt the impression of conclusive coherence in their films by refusing to harmonize sound and images, or by abstaining from imposing a comprehensive narrative. Others undermine the appearance of immediacy of the images by taking on a reflective stance and exposing their materiality as such, or discursively disclose the precariousness of their own position. And still others problematize the ideological force of images by alienating them from their initial context and editing them together anew. For example, Angela Ricci Lucchi's and Yervant Gianikian's compositions of colonial film material (e.g. *Pays Barbare* 2013, or *Images d'Orient – Tourisme Vandal* 2001) or Susana de Sousa Dias' arrangements of propaganda films made during the Portuguese dictatorship (e.g. *Natureza Morta/ Still Life* 2015) bear a strange compelling quality. With the slow rhythm and the absence of comments, the spectator is encouraged to sense that which hides in the folds of representation. For despite their link with a political agenda, those films make transpire a "mark of [the] society" (Adorno 2001c: 182) from which they originate, which exceeds the intentions of the filmmaker – Adorno alludes to this potential of medium in his text *Transparencies*. There are lots of independent films that carve out such a truth content of already existing images by recomposing them, estranging their initial aim and configuring them in subversive ways – Harun Farocki's critical filmic essays on the use of images in military or penitentiary contexts are particularly strong examples in this regard (cf *War at a Distance* 2003, *Images-War* 1987, *Prison Images* 2000). Other artistic devices proceed for example through a radical change of focus which betrays the sclerosed stereotypical embedding of their subjects (e.g. Roberto Minervini's docu-fiction *The Other Side* 2015, portraying a group of drug-addicts in Louisiana, Wang Bing's *Till Madness Do Us Part* 2013 focusing on patients in a mental asylum; or Sergei Loznitsa's *Factory* 2004, about a working day in a factory), or disrupt the common connotations of a representation through subversive formal intercessions. Marie Voignier's film *International Tourism* (2014) for example features videos she made during her visit in North Korea with a group of tourists. The images show what all traveler films of the otherwise inaccessible country show: captures of carefully selected tourist attractions, geographical sites, mass spectacles approved by the authorities in order to produce a specific image, as opposed to the demonized representations of the West. *International Tourism* neither tries to corroborate the official views, nor to present an alternative reality. Instead, the film interrupts the flow of perception through a thorough reconstitution of the soundtrack, which features all the environmental sounds but cuts off the voices, thereby producing a strange distance which reverberates the spectator back on her own gaze. Otherwise disorienting is Lucien Castaing-Taylor's and Véréna Paravel's film *Leviathan* (2012), a documentary featuring a fish trawler by night. The film is constituted by a strange composition of immersive images produced by cameras attached on different objects, without any associated spoken comment. Here, the difficulty to identify what is shown by the images subverts even the understanding of what documentary film might be.

What such artistic documentaries have in common despite the heterogeneous formal devices through which they operate is that they challenge the normalized perception of reality by wresting the images out of their immediacy and undoing their direct association with a specific meaning. However, this subversive force can only deploy itself as long as the forms retain their unfamiliar particularity which marks them as artistic rather than mainstream productions. For as both artworks and the products of the culture industry are intimately linked with the society in which they are embedded, their agency always depends on their position in and vis-à-vis the actual historically developed reality. And just as society is in constant transformation, so are the conventions on which its perception is based. The perceptive habits and schemes of the reality that artworks seek to challenge are molded by the products of the culture industry, while the latter strives to assimilate autonomous artworks and typecast their particularity as yet another pattern. Hence, the products of the culture industry as affirmative expressions of society and their subversive counterpart, genuine artworks, are also permanently mediated one through the other. Rather than two distinct spheres, they constitute opposed, but dialectically interconnected poles.

Therefore, autonomous artworks are likely to lose their subversive potential when they "age" (cf. Adorno 1988), when their formerly unique, idiosyncratic form turns into a generalized design applied on indifferent topics and integrated in the canon of the culture industry as yet another trendy novelty. While a documentary film as *Silverlake Life: The View from Here* (dir. Peter Friedman and Tom

Joslin 1993) showing the disturbing intimacy between a couple of two men suffering of AIDS and their camera until one of them dies still provided an unsettling
account of private life in the 1990s, self-representations though reality television
and documentary formats have become the norm today and largely provide
material for mass consumption. At the same time, home-made video material
and its large diffusion on the internet also facilitates that otherwise prohibited
representations reach international audiences, as non-professional films made
during the Arab revolutions comprehensively show for example. Once again, the
problem needs to be faced dialectically with regards to society as a whole.

Not every documentary film shown on big screens is *per se* ideologically suspicious, and not every independent production necessarily subversive. What
needs to be stressed is that "[d]ocumentary is always about something more
or other than what it depicts," as Jonathan Kahana puts it (2009: 7). Rather
than blindly believing or straightforwardly rejecting what passes as immediate
reality, as objectively real or undoubtedly true through documentary formats,
the recourse to the critical theory of Adorno and Horkheimer leads us to question how a meaning is constructed, embedded, and mediatized in society. Only
by considering the multiple mediations through which a content acquires its
meaning, a form appears as trustworthy, and a societal issue as worthy to be
addressed, can a critique of the documentary realm become at the same time
an immanent critique of the historically developed society in which it acquired
its significance, by which it is informed, and which it addresses.

References

Adorno, Theodor W. 1997. *Aesthetic Theory*. Minneapolis: University of Minnesota Press.

Adorno, Theodor W. 1974. "Commitment." *New Left Review* 87–88: 75–89.

Adorno, Theodor W. 2005a. "Critique." In *Critical Models. Interventions and Catchwords*,
    trans. Henry W. Pickford, 281–288. New York: Columbia University Press.

Adorno, Theodor W. 2001a. "Culture Industry Reconsidered." In *The Culture Industry.
    Selected essays on mass culture*, ed. J. M. Bernstein, 98–106. London and New York:
    Routledge Classics.

Adorno, Theodor W. 1954. "How to Look at Television." *The Quarterly of Film Radio and
    Television* 8(3): 213–235.

Adorno, Theodor W. 2005b. *Minima Moralia: Reflections from Damaged Life*. Trans. E.
    F. N. Jephcott. New York: Verso.

Adorno, Theodor W. 2005c. "Opinion Delusion Society." In Critical Models. *Interventions
    and Catchwords,* trans. Henry W. Pickford, 105–122. New York: Columbia University
    Press.

Adorno, Theodor W. 2005d "Prologue to Television." In *Critical Models. Interventions and Catchwords*, trans. Henry W. Pickford, 49–57. New York: Columbia University Press.

Adorno, Theodor W. 1988. "The Aging of the New Music." *Telos: Critical Theory of the Contemporary* 77: 95–116.

Adorno, Theodor W. 1993. "Theory of Pseudo-Culture." *Telos: Critical Theory of the Contemporary* 95: 15–38.

Adorno, Theodor W. 1957. "Television and the Patterns of Mass Culture." In *Mass Culture. The Popular Arts in America,* ed. Bernard Rosenberg and David Manning White, 474–488. New York: The Free Press.

Adorno, Theodor W. 2001b. "The Schema of Mass Culture." In *The Culture Industry. Selected Essays on Mass Culture,* ed. J. M. Bernstein, 61–98. London: Routledge Classics.

Adorno, Theodor W. 2001c. "Transparencies on Film." In *The Culture Industry. Selected Essays on Mass Culture*, ed. J. M. Bernstein, 178–186. London: Routledge Classics.

Adorno, Theodor, Else Frenkel-Brunswik, Daniel J. Levinson and R. Nevitt Sanford. 2019. *The Authoritarian Personality.* New York: Verso.

Adorno, Theodor W. and Hanns Eisler. 1994. *Composing for the Films*. London, Atlantic Highlands, NJ: Athlone Press.

Adorno, Theodor W. and Max Horkheimer. 2002 [1947]. *Dialectic of Enlightenment: Philosophical Fragments*, ed. G. S. Noerr and trans. by E. Jephcott. Stanford: Stanford University Press.

Behrens, Roger. 2003. *Die Diktatur der Angepassten. Texte zur kritischen Theorie der Popkultur.* Bielefeld: transcript.

Grierson, John. 2016 [1933]. "The Documentary Producer." In *The Documentary Film Reader. History, Theory, Criticism,* ed. Jonathan Kahana. 215–216. New York: Oxford University Press.

Hansen, Miriam Bratu. 2012. *Cinema and Experience. Siegfried Kracauer, Walter Benjamin, and Theodor W. Adorno.* Berkeley, CA: University of California Press.

Horkheimer, Max. 2004. *Eclipse of Reason*. London, New York: Continuum.

Horkheimer, Max. 2002. "Traditional and Critical Theory." In *Critical Theory. Selected Essays*, trans. Matthew O'Connell et.al., 188–251. New York: Continuum.

Kahana, Jonathan. 2008. *Intelligence Work. The Politics of American Documentary.* New York: Columbia University Press.

Kant, Immanuel. 1999. *Critique of Pure Reason.* Trans. Paul Guyer and Allen W. Wood. Cambridge: Cambridge University Press.

Kramer, Robert. 1991. "Être ou ne pas être dans le plan?" At http://derives.tv/etre-ou-ne-pas-etre-dans-le-plan/(accessed May 27, 2020).

Marx, Karl. 1976. *Capital. A Critique of Political Economy*. Vol. One. Trans Ben Fowkes. New York: Penguin.

Nichols, Bill. 1991. *Representing Reality: Issues and Concepts in Documentary.* Bloomington: Indiana University Press.

Rabinowitz, Paula. 1994. *They Must Be Represented: The Politics of Documentary.* New York: Verso.

Rangan, Pooja. 2017. *Immediations: The Humanitarian Impulse in Documentary.* Durham, NC: Duke University Press.

Trinh T. Minh-Ha. 1990. "Documentary Is/Not a Name." *October* 52: 76–98.

CHAPTER 16

One-dimensional Social Media: The Discourse of Authoritarianism and the Authoritarianism of Discourse

Panayota Gounari

1   Introduction

In his graphic novel *Unflattening* artist and sociologist Nick Sousanis creatively reimagines forms of scholarship and counteracts "flatness, a contraction of sight, a narrowing of possibilities" that promotes "one-dimensional thought and behavior" (Sousanis 2015: 6 [see Figure 16.1]). "Unflattening" means to add dimension to our thinking, to start thinking about what we see and how we come to see it.

In this chapter, I argue for the 'unflattening' of the universe of discourse; I make the case that the analysis of right-wing authoritarianism as manifested through language and discourses, in its contemporary iteration in social media, has a lot to gain from revisiting Critical Theory (CT) from the Institute of Social Research (*Institut für Sozialforschung*) also known as the Frankfurt School. More specifically, Critical Discourse Studies (CDS) analyzing authoritarianism in social media can find important theoretical, conceptual, and analytical tools in Theodor Adorno et al.'s *The Authoritarian Personality* (Gounari 2018; Wodak 2015) but also in Herbert Marcuse's work, particularly his discussion on "The Closing of the Universe of Discourse" in his 1964 seminal book *One-Dimensional Man*. While Critical Discourse Studies have drawn heavily on Max Horkheimer and Theodor Adorno (from the first generation of CT), and particularly on Jurgen Habermas (from the second generation), Marcuse's work has been largely unexplored in the CDS field.

Below, I explore existing connections in the bibliography between the Frankfurt School's CT and CDS, particularly the discourse-historical approach (DHA) that explicitly draws on CT. I then discuss Marcuse's work related to discourse in order to draw theoretical, conceptual, and analytical tools that can support and enrich inquiry into right-wing authoritarian discourses. My method is to read Marcuse's theoretical work from a linguistic/discursive perspective; to form a frame of reference where authoritarian discourse can be analyzed and understood, based on Marcuse's discussion and; to further build

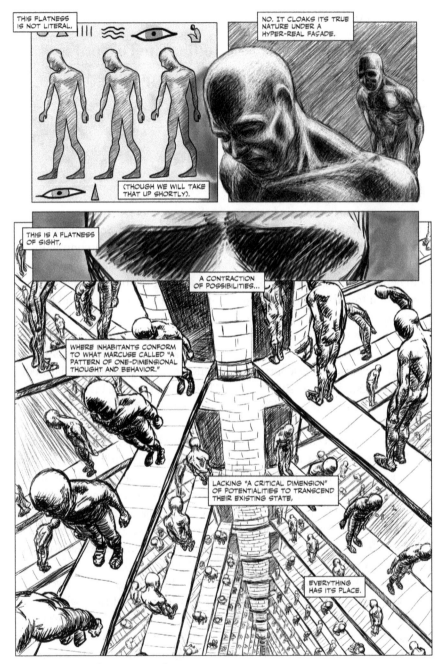

FIGURE 16.1   Nick Sousanis, *Unflattening*, 2015

on it so as to create a framework that will address current needs for scholars who work on authoritarianism in social media. My aim is not to provide a closed "grand theory" for CDS as this would be antithetical to the core of CT that held an aversion to all closed systems (Jay 1996). I am rather revisiting work that was borne out of a historical moment of authoritarian triumph (as embodied in German fascism at the time) and transposed to the United States of the 1950's "where ideological conformity and the introjection of domination in the form of false needs were 'advanced' over anything" (Agger 1988: 324) in order to cast some light on contemporary right-wing authoritarian populism in the current aggressive capitalist context. Finally, I present the ways in which this analysis is most appropriate for social media as a site of authoritarian discourses.

2   Critical Theory and the Institute for Social Research

The influence of Frankfurt School Critical Theory on Critical Discourse Studies is far-reaching and cannot be overstated. This section briefly presents the Institute for Social Research and the main themes emerging from Critical Theory that are relevant to the study of discourse. It further explores the CDS bibliography that explicitly draws on the Frankfurt School.

The Institute for Social Research (*Institut für Sozialforschung*) was established on February 3, 1923 as an intellectual organization at Goethe University in Frankfurt, Germany (Jay 1996). This was a crucial time for the history of Germany and the entire world, considering that Nazis assumed power on January 30, 1933. Critical Theory coming out of the Institute was applied to the most pressing problem of the time: the rise of European fascism. Members of the Institute had an early interest in studying problems of authority, even before their forced migration because of Nazism (Fuchs 2018; Gordon 2019).

Critical Theory "has as its object human beings as producers of their own historical form of life" (Horkeimer 1993: 21). Core Critical Theory themes encompass the critique of positivism, instrumental reason and rationality; rejection of "traditional theory"; critique of modernity and capitalist society; and the proposition for immanent critique. It is a social theory oriented toward critiquing and changing society as a whole, in contrast to traditional theory oriented only to understanding or explaining it: "a critical sociology which saw society as an antagonistic totality, and which had not excluded Hegel and Marx from its thinking, but rather saw itself as their heir" (Wiggershaus 1998: 1). Critical Theory must meet three criteria: "it must be *explanatory*, *practical*, and *normative*, all at the same time." That is, it must present and explain the problems/

ills of current social reality, identify the actors to change it, and "provide both clear norms for criticism and achievable practical goals for social transformation" (Bohman 2019: para. 3). In order to meet these three criteria, CT should a) be directed at the totality of society in its historical specificity, and b) improve the understanding of society by integrating all major social sciences, including economics, sociology, history, political science, anthropology and psychology (Wodak and Meyer 2009).

From the vantage point of 1964, with experience from the Weimar Republic, Herbert Marcuse identified a kind of authoritarianism deeply ingrained in advanced capitalist societies. He introduced a theory of advanced industrial society where "changes in production, consumption, culture and thought have produced an advanced state of conformity" (Kellner 1991: xii). More importantly, he identified crucial linkages between political economy and culture that brought about the explosive emergence of domination. His work aligned with the Frankfurt School's general critique of more rigid Marxist economism, where "culture (including language) [is] a mere reflection of the economy" (Collin 2015: 2). The power of culture as a political tool emerged as a central concept in Marcuse's work, and it included the power of "mass media." One-dimensionality was, thus, intended to explain what happens when advanced capitalist political economy utilizes culture and personality to reproduce alienation in the spheres of both work and leisure (Agger 1998).

In *One-Dimensional Man,* he critiqued new forms of domination and oppression and elaborated on what he saw as the tension between one-dimensional individuals, thought, discourse, and politics on one hand, and a critical, dialectic, historical dimension on the other. He challenged "the repression of all values, aspirations and ideas which cannot be defined in terms of the operations and attitudes validated by the prevailing forms of rationality" and he discussed one-dimensional discourse as instrumentalist, ahistorical, repressive and authoritarian, a phenomenon he termed the "closing of the universe of discourse" (Kellner 1991: xii). The fusion of cultural critique with political economy made up Marcuse's one-dimensional society, a society where reality is thought to correspond to reason (Agger 1988). This one-dimensional society is dominated by one-dimensional discourse. Marcuse importantly saw the manifestations of this discourse as precursors of fascism.

3   Critical Discourse Studies: Influences from Critical Theory

Critical Discourse Studies (CDS) see language as a social practice (Fairclough and Wodak 1997) always embedded in a social and historical context. It explores how discourses are both embodied in diverse social practices and how, in turn, these social practices generate, shape, inform, structure or distort discourses. CDS examine language in use in order to identify, uncover, problematize and challenge power and ideology nested in discourses through the investigation of semiotic data (written, spoken or visual). CDS are interested in "studying social phenomena which are necessarily complex" (Wodak and Meyer 2009: 2) and therefore call for a multidisciplinary, multitheoretical, and multi-methodical critical and self-reflective approach (Wodak 2001; Wodak and Meyer 2009). As Kress stressed, CDA has "from the beginning had a political project: broadly speaking that of altering inequitable distributions of economic, cultural and political goods in contemporary societies" (1996: 15). Critical Discourse Analysis has viewed discourse "as one element that shapes and is shaped by other 'social elements' such as power relations, institutions, and social identities" (Fairclough 2014: 9). CDA does that dialectically, what Collin (2015) calls a "back-and-forth movement as the analyst asks how a text's content and form shape and are shaped by the text's economic, social, cultural, and political contexts" (3–4). Clearly, the goals of the CDS program align with the core of Critical Theory.

The influence of the Frankfurt School on the critical program of what started as Critical Discourse Analysis (CDA) is uncontested and widely acknowledged in the literature (Anthonissen, 2001; Chouliaraki 2008; Chouliaraki and Fairclough 1999; Collin 2015, 2011; 2018; Forchtner and Tominc 2012; McKenna 2004; Wodak and Meyer 2009). This holds particularly true for the discourse-historical approach (DHA) pioneered by Ruth Wodak and the Vienna School of CDA that explicitly "adheres to the socio-philosophical orientation of critical theory" (quoted in Forchtner 2011: 3) differing from other approaches to CDA (Fairclough and Wodak 1997; Reisigl and Wodak 2001, 2009; Wodak 1996, 2001; Wodak and Meyer 2009). Forchtner confirms the inextricable theoretical connection between DHA and critical theory stressing that "a series of specific propositions concerning its understanding of critique [...] are linked to the Frankfurt School" (2011: 3).

Overall, the literature in CDS that acknowledges a theoretical debt to CT, has relied mostly on Horkheimer and Adorno, in particular *Dialectic of Enlightenment* (Reisigl and Wodak 2001, 2009; Fairclough and Wodak 1997) or *The Authoritarian Personality* (Reisigl and Wodak 2001; Wodak 2015; Forchtner 2018). For instance, Wodak's *Politics of Fear* (2015) draws on Adorno's *Authoritarian Personality* to articulate an analysis of right-wing populist politics (Reisigl and Wodak 2001, Wodak, 2015).

On the other hand, from the second generation of Critical Theory scholars, it is Jürgen Habermas' work that has had a more profound impact on the field (Chouliaraki and Fairclough, 1999; Collin 2015; Forchtner 2018; Reisigl and

GOUNARI

Wodak 2009; Wodak and Reisigl 2001). This can be illustrated in the work of Chouliaraki and Fairclough (1999) who have argued for a systematic consideration of the shifting place of communication and language within modern societies. In this context, they present Habermas' work as indicative of a critical theory of modern social life that also focuses on language: "Language is seen as an important part of modern social life, and social analysis is correspondingly oriented towards language to a substantial degree" (74). Similarly, Forchtner (2011) marks clear connections between Habermas' language philosophy and the critical study of language and encourages a more engaged study of his work for CDS scholars. Along the same lines, he strengthens the existing connection between CDS and the work of the Frankfurt School and proposes a more in-depth engagement that would address accusations that DHA lacks theoretical principles by more consistently grounding CDA in the work of the Frankfurt School (Forchtner 2011). Habermas' impact on CDS, important as it is, falls outside the scope of this chapter.

While Herbert Marcuse is the only scholar from the first generation who explicitly discusses the workings of language in advanced industrialized societies, raises linguistic questions and even presents his concept of "one-dimensional discourse," his work does not seem to have found its way into CDS. There are few exceptions; van Leeuwen (2018) has a brief mention of the "functionalization of language", McKenna (2004) quotes Marcuse in his discussion of technologies and technocratic control, and a few other scholars draw on his work when applying CDA in media studies (Carvalho 2008; Santos and Ndlovu 2015). The heavy focus on the role of culture in the reproduction of the capitalist order, the critical scrutiny of all social forms and norms, the rejection of positivism and the bridging of the social with the individual, and the role of historicization in understanding and analyzing social phenomena; borne out of Marcuse's work, are recurring themes in CDS literature. It follows, then, that Marcuse's work can serve as an appropriate, useful and rich theoretical home for Critical Discourse Studies.

4 One-dimensional Discourse, Authoritarianism and Mediatization

4.1 What is One-dimensional Discourse?

> The ritual-authoritarian language spreads over the contemporary world, through democratic and non-democratic, capitalist and non-capitalist countries.
>
> MARCUSE, *One-Dimensional Man*, 1964: 102

One-Dimensional Man is eerily relevant and timely in 2020, as is most of Marcuse's work, at a time of global capitalist crises, increasing authoritarianism, right-wing populism and the explosion of social media – an embodiment of technological rationality. As Andrew Robinson (2010) has astutely observed, *One-Dimensional Man* (written in 1962) reads as if it could have been written today:

> the flattening of discourse, the pervasive repression behind a veil of 'consensus', the lack of recognition for perspectives and alternatives beyond the dominant frame, the closure of the dominant universe of meaning, the corrosion of established liberties and lines of escape, total mobilization against a permanent Enemy built into the system as a basis for conformity and effort ... It was product of a previous period of downturn and decomposition, similar in many ways to our own (para. 1).

Much in the way that Marcuse identified new forms of social administration that closed off possibilities for radical change, and dispelled the myth of freedom in advanced capitalist consumer societies, similarly he and his Frankfurt School counterparts saw language and power to be organized "around economic and political structures of domination" with the relationship between meaning and power taking "the form of ideological domination" (Chouliaraki 2008: 680). Even though scholars in the Institute were not linguists, language was part of their theoretical preoccupations in terms of its function within authoritarian advanced capitalist societies, often referred to as "affluent" or "sick" societies. They engaged with the role of language in social life with important contributions "to the study of mass popular culture and the emergence of consumer and media culture in capitalist modernity" (Chouliaraki 2008: 680). In *One-Dimensional Man*, Marcuse is preoccupied, among other things, with discourses in advanced capitalist industrialized societies (documented in great detail in Chapter 4 "The Closing of the Universe of Discourse"), as well as with answering more philosophical questions about language and critiquing the empiricism of linguistic analysis (in Chapter 7 "The Triumph of Positive Thinking: One-dimensional Philosophy").

"The Closing of the Universe of Discourse" is appropriately positioned under the "One-Dimensional Society" section of the book that immediately establishes the connection between social issues and discourses. Here, while identifying discourse as a fundamental element of analysis, he presents a compelling account of the role of language in a totalitarian industrial capitalist society that has been commodified, and where human beings have been losing their freedom, autonomy, and their basic critical function. This state of affairs, he claims, is mostly unknown to them as the one-dimensional society survives and proliferates exactly because people do not recognize the totalitarian character of the system. In this one dimension, not only are humans complicit in their unfreedom, but they actively participate in their subjugation, maintaining the illusion that this is actually a choice that liberates them. "Totalitarian" for Marcuse, is "not only a terroristic political coordination of society, but also a non-terroristic economic technical coordination which operates through the manipulation of needs by vested interests" (3). "Totalitarian" is an economy and culture that effectively control people's thinking, needs and desires; a feature deeply ingrained in the fabric of advanced industrial capitalist societies, embodied in positivism, instrumental reason, and one-dimensional thought and discourse. Accordingly,

> the new reality of domination, rooted in the instinctual structure of individuals, is more difficult to dispel than was previous economic exploitation; domination covers exploitation in the illusions of false harmony and material abundance, but it does not eliminate it.
>
> AGGER 1988: 315

In this dystopian reality, the prevailing forms of social control are also technological, and by technological, I also refer here to the digital world, as the "very embodiment of Reason for the benefit of all social groups and interests" (Marcuse 1964: 9). All this is operationalized and embodied in the *Language of Total Administration*: a "rational" language, permeated by magical, authoritarian and ritual elements, deprived of mediations, a functionalized language that has fully integrated conformism, unfreedom, even opposition; a language that "militates against a development of meaning" where concepts are absorbed by the word: "the thing is identified by its function"; and where "transgression of the discourse beyond the closed analytical structure is incorrect or propaganda" (88). In this language, the prevailing mode of freedom is servitude, equality is superimposed inequality, war is peace. The closed universe of discourse unifies the opposites in a perfect harmony. The constitution is unconstitutional, breaking the law is legal, democracy is oligarchy, science is unscientific. The working class invest politically their future in an administration that advocates welfare for plutocrats. Marcuse claims "the loaded language proceeds according to the Orwellian recipe of the identity of opposites: in the mouth of the enemy, peace means war, and defense is attack, while on the righteous side, escalation is restraint, and saturation bombing prepares for peace. Organized in this discriminatory fashion, language designates a priori technological aggression and satisfaction" (1968: 196).

4.2   (Social)Mediatization

The most relevant place to look for ideology in the world of culture is online. (Salehi 2017: para. 5)

We live in the era of extreme mediatization. Mediatization colonizes every realm of private and public life to an unprecedented degree. This has "broad consequences for everyday life and practical organization (social, political, cultural, economic) of media" (Couldry and Hepp 2013: 191). Our lives are now lived between the material and digital, an "online-offline nexus" where the two "can no longer be separated and must be seen as fused into a bewildering range of new online-offline practices of social interaction, knowledge exchange, learning, community formation and identity work" (Blommaert 2019: 1). We can understand the role and function of social media in the context of what Marcuse (1968: 248) calls "affluent society." Its characteristics are:

> (1) an abundant industrial and technical capacity which is to a great extent spent in the production and distribution of 'unproductive goods and services': luxury goods, gadgets, waste, planned obsolescence, military equipment (2) a rising standard of living, which also extends to previously underprivileged parts of the population; (3) a high degree of concentration of economic and political power, combined with a high degree of organization and government intervention in the economy; (4) scientific and pseudoscientific investigation, control, and manipulation of private and group behavior, both at work and at leisure (including the behavior of the psyche, the soul, the unconscious, and the subconscious) for commercial and political purposes.

At the same time, media exercise "growing authority over the organizing principles of our every-day lives" (Higgins 2017) as they shape and impose rules on how politics should be conducted, and not the opposite (Corner and Pels 2003; Higgins 2017; Mazzoleni and Schultz 1999; Flew 2017). John Corner (2018) differentiates between "politicized media" as an imbalance in the direction of a circumscribed media system, and "mediatized politics" as a situation where politics has "become colonized by media logics and imperatives" (4). While mediatization has existed since the time of black and white TV and print newspapers, what is new about our mediatized era is not the fact that the media dictate rules of political engagement, but rather that "media" *are* political engagement. They are embodied in different sites, genres, discourses, communication tactics, modes of delivery and content creation. This extreme mediatization aligns with Marcuse's argument that in advanced capitalist societies, technological rationality colonizes everyday life, imposing rules for thinking and living that prevent individuals from exercising their critical capacity. He also makes the point that the role of the media is essentially to "mediate between the masters and their dependents" (85).

I want to build on this line of thinking to suggest that a) contemporary "media" cannot be understood *outside* and are dominated *by* "social media." Social media serve as the new technological rationality and tool of control, domination and exploitation (Fuchs 2016) in an authoritarian capitalist context, and b) in social media, contemporary mediatization is reconfiguring language use and discourse in ways that still need to be explored. Aggression and control are digitized, and this digitization also crosses through language and other semiotic signs. Mediatization erases mediation, understood as an important "stage in the cognitive process that does not exist anymore" where "language tends to express and promote the immediate identification of reason and fact" (Marcuse 1964: 85). The closed language does not demonstrate and explain – it communicates decision, dictum, command. It is, according to Barthes, a language proper to all authoritarian regimes. Language not only reflects the controls set by the system. It becomes itself an instrument of control, "even where it does not transmit orders but information; where it demands not obedience but choice, not submission but freedom" (Marcuse 1964: 103).

At a time of post-truth, fake news, conspiracy theories, online trolls, and what has been referred as a "Twitter presidency," it is challenging to define "media" and to identify exactly who produces content, on behalf of whom and for whom. Social media should naturally be included in our definition of media. Social media are "social" because they "enable and are means of sharing, communication, community and collaboration" (Fuchs 2016: 113). The "shared" aspect should be problematized, since media still function in the context of what Jodi Dean (2009) terms "communicative capitalism": "The proliferation, distribution, acceleration, and intensification of communicative access and opportunity [that] result in a deadlocked democracy incapable of serving as a form for political change" (22). In the context of this democracy, social media are "deeply embedded in capitalism's commodity logic, and therefore reflect individual private property, individualism and structures of exploitation and domination" (Fuchs 2016: 113–114). This point is often lost in the hype of social media as the great equalizer, or as alternative open space for oppositional voices, and as an indicator of massive political involvement.

What is missed in understanding the commodity character of social media is the fact that they are the product of massive corporations who have total control over content, audience, and market. Seymour (2019: 22) makes the case that,

> [w]hile some platforms are about enabling industry to make its work pro-cesses more legible, more transparent and thus more manageable, data platforms like Google, Twitter and Facebook turn their attention to con-sumer markets. They intensify surveillance, rendering abruptly visible huge substrata of behavior and wishes that had been occulted, and mak-ing price signals and market research look rather quaint by comparison. Google accumulates data by reading our emails, monitoring our searches, collecting images of our homes and towns on Street View and recording our locations on Google Maps. And, thanks to an agreement with Twitter, it also checks our tweets.

4.3   Critical Discourse Studies and Mediatization

There is a well-established connection in the Critical Discourse Studies liter-ature between the rise of right-wing populist parties, authoritarianism, alt-right groups and mediatization (Bartlett 2014; Chilton 2017; Enli 2017; Enli and Rosenberg 2018; Forchtner, Krzyzanowski and Wodak 2013; Gounari 2018; Kreis 2017; Montgomery 2017; Ott 2016, 2017; Reisigl 2013, Wodak 2017; Wodak and Krzyzanowski 2017). Kreis (2017) notes that "Right-wing populist politicians seem to have been particularly successful in adopting social media for cam-paign purposes and have used them as a strategic communication tool and as an instrument of power politics" (2) while Wodak and Krzyzanowski (2017) insist that the mediatized and individualized model of right-wing populism is best exemplified by "Trumpism" (474). With the explosion of social media, in addition to the more traditional political communication genres (such as speeches, press conferences/interviews, rallies and print/online political material), political parties and candidates have been turning more and more to digital media (Forchtner, Krzyzanowski and Wodak 2013), online commu-nication, and online communities, and use novel tools for political influence, including memes, trolling subcultures, etc. (Seymour 2019). J.M. Berger, who analyzed 30,00 Twitter accounts that self-identified as alt-right or followed someone who did, powerfully argues that "Trump is the glue that binds the far right" (2018). Alt-right signs have effortlessly penetrated mainstream imagery, as is the case of the appropriation of trolling icon "Pepe the Frog." Pepe has long been a "react" meme on 4chan message boards, but was more recently adopted by the alt-right, "associating it with white-supremacist ideology"

(Seymour 2019: 33). Pepe was subsequently depicted as Adolf Hitler, as a member of the Ku Klux Klan, and as Donald Trump. Trump is notorious for using memes (including alt-right inspired ones), and presidential candidate Mike Bloomberg paid social media influencers to post memes and other messages that make him look "cool" (Derysh 2020).

As I argued earlier, the rise of right-wing authoritarian populism is strongly connected to mediatization and social media (Blommaert 2019; Forchtner, Krzyzanowski and Wodak 2013). Social media power is so pervasive that it even led some researchers to claim Donald Trump would not be (and remain) the US President had it not been for Twitter (Ross and Caldwell 2019). To that point, Blommaert (2020) adds that Trump appears to move from a "Twitter presidency" to "Twitter governance": "Twitter here is no longer just the vehicle for communicating the president's political "message" – it has become an instrument for formal bureaucratic procedures regulating the communication between the president and other branches of government" (para. 5).

Extremist ideologies and alt-right politics find fertile ground and free space to develop and flourish in online fora under the "anonymity" of digital technology. There is a wealth of online communities that attract far-right, neo-Nazi users and these include the more innocuous Facebook and Twitter, but also more "specialized" sites such as Gab, a censorship-free alternative to Twitter. Thanks to a massive data dump leaking in 2019, the infamous violent white supremacist site Iron March was fully uncovered. Iron March numbered 1,653 members, bringing together a number of fascist groups from different countries in its nine years of operation: Vanguard America, Action of Serbia, Casa Pound of Italy, Golden Dawn of Greece, Antipodean Resistance of Australia, Skydas of Lithuania, Azov Battalion of the Ukraine, among others (Hayden 2019).

In our highly mediated communications environments, social media now embody the new technological rationality in that they produce one-dimensional thinking and discourse. Under the pretense of unlimited freedom, massive participation, access, participatory practices and democratic processes, mediatization builds the new unfreedom of our times: "We believe in the potential of people when they can come together" claims the Facebook motto (https://about.fb.com). "When they come together to do what?" is a fair question. Who brings them together and for what purposes? What is to be said about privacy concerns, sharing personal information and online activity with third parties? There has never been in human history a time where people have voluntarily provided so much personal information to the market. There has never been a time in history where so many know so much about so many others. And there has never been a time in history where this information was monetized to the last cent.

5   Features of One-dimensional Discourse and Social Media

> Magical, authoritarian and ritual elements permeate speech and language.
>
> MARCUSE 1964: 85

> The noun governs the sentence in an authoritarian and totalitarian fashion, and the sentence becomes a declaration to be accepted. (ibid. 87)

So far, I have established the connection between Critical Discourse Studies, Critical Theory and Herbert Marcuse's concepts from *One-Dimensional Man*, with mediatization in advanced capitalist industrialized societies. The proliferation of authoritarian right-wing populist discourse in social media, and its constant shifting and appropriation of different registers and genres calls for more conceptual and analytical tools. Drawing on Marcuse's work on one-dimensional thought and discourse, I propose exploring the discursive features of the *language of total administration* as an embodiment of authoritarianism and conformity, and to draw parallels with the discourse of social media. Concerns around surveillance, privacy, the role of bots and trolls and the degree to which social media monitor and control user information makes it a *par excellence* control device – a closed universe that is tightly monitored and controlled – and it does so under the veil of freedom, when in fact it is by and large the epitome of "democratic unfreedom." Here, I do not want to make a totalitalizing claim that social media only produce and reproduce one-dimensional discourse, or that they are the absolute medium of control. I rather want to suggest that because of their commodity character and their functioning in conditions of violent capitalism, they are important sites for the production of authoritarian discourse, and they have powerful potential for total control. Social media platforms are not owned by 'the people.' A case in point is that Facebook reported a total revenue of over $55 billion dollars for 2018 (an increase of 37% compared to 2017), thanks to its ability to monetize content that users willfully shared. Three companies tower above all others in counts of combined monthly active users of the social media platforms they own. Facebook also owns WhatsApp, Facebook Messenger and Instagram, Google owns YouTube, and Tencent owns QQ, WeChat and QZone (Internet health report 2018).

Social media, as tools for producing and consuming different kinds of texts in the context of "communicative capitalism" (Dean 2009) are fertile sites for the production of *one-dimensional discourse* as the "materialization of ideals of inclusion and participation in information, entertainment, and communication

technologies in ways that capture resistance and intensify global capitalism"
(Dean 2009: 2).

5.1   *Five Features of One-dimensional Discourse for Analyzing Authoritarianism*

As I have argued elsewhere (Gounari 2018), we can distinguish six specific features
of one-dimensional discourse that can be applied to the critical analysis of social
media discourse in the context of authoritarian capitalist societies:

5.1.1   Dehistoricization

A core feature of discourses produced in social media is the erasure of the historical context and the apotheosis of the present – the here-and-now. One-
dimensionality works as a celebration of the present, rendering the historical dimension invisible or, worse, irrelevant. While there is around-the-clock
exposure, constant access, and immediacy (all content is immediately available for reading and commenting), the message is often decontextualized and
largely depends on the "reading" of it by different audiences and individuals.
The context is always that of-the-moment, limiting broader interpretations,
connections and exploration of ramifications. There is a planned obsolescence
in social media, as the next tweet, the next post, the next photo, or the next
story will now draw even more attention, commentary, visibility, and currency;
and possibly even cancel out the previous one. A news story just breaking will
often only draw from a limited temporary understanding and coverage since
what matters is speed and not the quality of information; there is no time to
dig in, verify sources and investigate background.

The lack of historical dimension can also be attested in the multiple distorted versions of "history" that circulate in social media and the selective
use of them to legitimize politics of fear and hatred. The revival and legitimation of neo-Nazi and authoritarian politics largely owes its existence to social
media and the networks created therein, as the story on the Iron March data
dump mentioned earlier shows. More importantly, this constructed capitalist
universe of social media discourse closes itself against any discourse not in
its own terms, blocks intertextuality (the way texts are linked to other texts
synchronically and diachronically)[1] and literally serves as the antithesis of historical thinking.

---

1   Synchronic and diachronic views (Saussure 1916) are two ways to conduct linguistic analysis.
    A synchronic view considers language at a particular moment, a given point in time, while a
    diachronic view considers language historically in its development through time.

Technological rationality as embodied in the new digital technologies becomes the great vehicle for better domination, creating a truly totalitarian universe. In this universe, meanings are contained, fragmented and dehistoricized, and language serves as an ahistorical social bond that connects people based on who their enemy is. This is antithetical to critical theory's refusal to eternalize the present (Jay 1996: 78). Dehistoricized discourses suppress the development of critical consciousness and historical thinking about the social world. A historical-discourse analysis of social media with its focus on the historical dimension can uncover the multiple layers of synchronic and diachronic histories that shape discourses and discursive practices.

5.1.2   Operationalism/Instrumentalism

Marcuse makes the case for the *language of total administration,* a language that serves as an instrument of control. It is fragmented and decontextualized and it "tends to express and promote the immediate identification of reason and fact, truth and established truth, essence and existence, the thing and its function" (Marcuse 1964: 85). Names are indicative of their function and concepts are absorbed by the actual word. Everything that is ideologically contrary is fake news. The leader is a very smart person. He knows the "best words." This is a central characteristic of the "closing of the universe of discourse" where language, neutralized and purged of its historical meanings and significations, is operationalized in the service of capitalist significations (Marcuse 1964). The content authored on social media promotes this development of meaning as "natural" and "neutral."

In the current authoritarianist revival, operationalist language is used in official political discourse. Operationalist language expresses a very high degree of familiarity (so close to everyday language and yet so far from everyday people's issues), a familiarity that can be linked to Fairclough's (2010) conversationalization of public life or what Montgomery (2017) terms "vernacular folksiness." Repetition as a rhetorical device is another characteristic of operationalism. This device is very often used by Trump in speeches, rallies and tweets. Repetition asserts self-righteousness, imposes conviction, closes down discussion, and is frequently combined with appeals to authority (Wodak 2015). Repetition is also attributed as a characteristic to "publicity and information practiced by the mass media." Permanent repetition means

> the same commercial with the same text or picture broadcast or televised again and again; the same phrases and clichés poured out by the purveyors and makers of information again and again; the same programs and platforms professed by the politicians again and again [...]

Hitler knew well the extreme function of repetition: the biggest lie, often enough repeated, will be acted upon and accepted as truth. Even in its less extreme use, constant repetition, imposed upon more or less captive audiences, may be destructive: destroying mental autonomy, freedom of thought, responsibility and conducive to inertia, submission, rejection of change. The established society, the master of repetition, becomes the great womb for its citizens.

MARCUSE 1968: 12

5.1.3   The Language of Digital Aggression

In his 1968 essay on aggressiveness in advanced industrial societies, Marcuse makes the case for the *language of aggressiveness* and how the impact of great technological advances initiates "new modes of work and of leisure and thereby affect all social relationships and bring about a thorough transvaluation of values" (192). Marcuse talks about the "brutalization of language and image" to refer to the ways media present violence as commonsensical, factual and even humorous, reducing it "to the level of natural events and contingencies of daily life" (1968: 195): "a specific vocabulary of hate, resentment, and defamation is reserved for opposition to the aggressive policies and for the enemy. The pattern constantly repeats itself."

President Trump's Twitter account is notorious for not only degrading Trump's opponents, but also openly inciting violence against them. One need simply to look at Trump's treatment of the media, immigrants and Democrats, and the nouns he has been using to characterize them; or his posting of a video with graphic violent footage targeting Democratic Representative Ilhan Omar. Kellner (1991) claims that the destructiveness unleashed in advanced industrialized societies is more lethal and it "finds a mass base of approval in those who have been conditioned to approve of aggression. Aggressive behavior thus provides a social bond, unifying those who gain in power and self-esteem through identifying with forms of aggression against shared objects of hate" (xxxviii-xxxix). Aggression (both discursive and material) as a social glue that holds together groups is very much an element of current right-wing populist regimes (e.g., of Trump, Bolsonaro, etc.) that thrive on hatred, dehumanization of the other and the creation of "shared objects of hate." Trump's rallies are vivid examples of discursive aggression: His followers are unified against a common enemy, and through his discourse and discursive strategies he legitimizes and promotes aggression. Aggression also serves as political glue that holds together very different people with different individual and collective experiences and diverse relations to the means of production.

5.1.4   Discourse as Commodity

Cultural commodities consist of signs – they are semiotic (Chouliaraki and Fairclough 1999); they are the communicative aspect/layer of material commodities; they embody the material object, its production, decoding and consumption. The vast majority of social media content are cultural commodities branded, sold and consumed (fashion, law, public opinion). Central themes include beauty, leisure, travel, pets, etc. Politics are glossy and gossipy. Social media, as products of the capitalist culture industry and illustrations of technological progress, "are deeply embedded in capitalism's commodity logic and therefore reflect individual private property, individualism and structures of exploitation and domination" (Fuchs 2016: 114). Digital media, as tools of the capitalist imaginary, "are modes of reification and therefore expressions of instrumental/technological rationality" in that they "reduce humans to the status of consumers of advertisements and commodities" while as cultural commodities they are "produced by cultural wage-workers that are bought by consumers and audience commodities that the media consumers become themselves by being sold as an audience to capitalist media's advertising clients" (Fuchs 2016: 132).

In this sense, politics also becomes a highly valued commodity in social media. Authoritarianism permeates and shapes all layers of the culture industry and this includes discourse. Social media even produce fascism as a commodity, to be consumed by specific groups of people. Fascism online uses specific language and other semiotic signs coming across communicatively as "friendly fascism" (Gross 1980).

5.1.5   The Self as a Brand

"We are possessed by our images, suffer our own images" (Marcuse 1964: 250). One of the most valued commodities on social media, as it emerges in capitalist societies, is now the *self*. The trend of influencers on Instagram – the photo-sharing application, and other social media is the most glorious example. As of June 2018, Instagram had reached one billion monthly users with 50 billion plus pictures shared to date (Clement 2019; TechCrunch 2018). In 2018, there were approximately 3.7 million sponsored influencer posts on the platform. Influencer culture is inextricably connected to consumerism and the rise of social media: "The term is shorthand for someone (or something) with the power to affect the buying habits or quantifiable actions of others by uploading some form of original – often sponsored – content to social media platforms like Instagram, YouTube, Snapchat, or, god forbid, LinkedIn" (Martineau 2019). The financial stakes are high. Influencers with smaller followings (also known as "nanoinfluencers") can make between $30,000 and $60,000 a year, micro-influencers can make anywhere from $40,000 to $100,000 while for celebrities the figures can be astronomical (Lieber 2018).

Self-branding takes place in multiple semiotic ways and most importantly, it can be monetized. Even users who create content without being associated with a brand, paid to advertise, etc., are still deeply engaged in creating a certain profile for themselves, as reflected in their semiosis. The "politics of the self," are further illustrative of a "promotional culture" (Fairclough 2010). Wodak (2015) succinctly notes that one of the salient elements of right-wing populist politicians' success is their well-crafted strategic frontstage performance in traditional and new media including social media, in election rallies, press conferences and speeches, always oriented towards a specific audience.

Frontstage performance, a strategy often employed in branding populist right-wing leaders, is also widely used by individuals in social media. In the case of right-wing populism, the populist leader (as a brand) develops his own discourse and discursive strategies, always finds the right register to speak to his voters, articulating a specific authoritarian discourse. His (sic) branding includes marketing/marking and indexing his recognizable political stance and identity for all listeners and viewers that might identify (Wodak 2015). The populist leader's discourse is characterized by the use of simple, impoverished language, the kind that Umberto Eco notes can be found in Nazi or Fascist schoolbooks: "an impoverished vocabulary, and an elementary syntax, in order to limit the instruments for complex and critical reasoning" (Eco 1995: 8).

5.1.6   Discourse of Amusement

Marcuse's "happy consciousness" sums up his idea of what an unfree, authoritarian society does to consciousness. In the state of happy consciousness individuals are happy in their ignorance because they have lost their autonomy, critical capacity and ability to understand. For Marcuse, however, "euphoria is unhappiness." This kind of euphoria is produced in social media as part of the culture industry, since social media are marketed as entertainment – an entertainment that is accessible 24/7. The ideology behind this type of "amusement" is hardly new. Facebook, Twitter and other sites serve as "the prolongation of work" that is "sought after as an escape from the mechanized work process, and to recruit strength in order to be able to cope with it again" (Horkheimer and Adorno 1994: 137). Social media are now the new prolongation of work relegating people to a hypnotic state, "an effective aggression against the mind in its socially disturbing, critical functions" (Marcuse 1968). Marcuse notes that this inertia may well reduce the stress of intelligence, the pain and tension which accompany autonomous mental activity – thus it may be an

effective aggression against the mind in its socially disturbing, critical functions (Marcuse 1968).

"Effective aggression against the mind" is achieved through the fetishization of technology where "autonomous mental activity" is severely inhibited.
Doing politics on social media is essentially creating content to be consumed.
This content ends up being "mere contributions to the circulation of images,
opinion, and information, to the billions of nuggets of information and affect
trying to catch and hold attention, to push or sway opinion, taste, and trends
in one direction rather than another" (Dean 2009: 24). This content is often
funny and created as amusement – think political memes. However, as Salehi
(2017) notes: "No amount of memes can ever really unify the fragmented cor-
ners of our personalities. The enormous breadth of community and information online will always carry the risk of letting young, frustrated people retreat
into subcultures that divert their energy" (para.49).

6   Unflattening

I started this chapter with the notion of "unflattening": the cognitive, intellectual, social and emotional activity of experiencing the world in more than one
dimension; unflattening is the antithesis of one-dimensional society and discourse. I tried to show that authoritarian discourse produced in social media
is a type of one-dimensional discourse and I presented six features as a tool
to analyze it. The six features discussed make up what Marcuse called "ritual
authoritarian language", a language that unsettles the boundaries "between
different domains of social use of language", leading to a "pervasive discoursal
hybridity", that is, the mixing of discourses and genres (Chouliaraki and
Fairclough quoted in Wodak 2015: 161). Exploring this discoursal hybridity along
the six features can help us somewhat grasp the "elusive and complex nature of
(right-wing) populism" (Wodak and Krzyzanowski 2017) and the mechanisms
at work in producing and reproducing right-wing authoritarian discourses
in social media; and in turn, how these discourses shape specific ideological
positions for individuals. In the shadow of increasing authoritarianism worldwide, the closing of the universe of thinking and discourse and the imposition of one-dimensionality are steppingstones towards a new totalitarianism
where social media would function as an Orwellian machine. Dissenting from
Marcuse's and the Frankfurt School's pessimism, there are many radical rays of
light in the capitalist abyss gaining force from social movements, unions, and
other collectives. There is also an antagonistic discourse developing against

the language of total administration. The struggle over discourse is real and it has real material consequences and ramifications.

References

Adorno, Theodor, Else Frenkel-Brunswik, Daniel Levinson, and Nevitt Sanford. 2019. *The Authoritarian Personality.* London: Verso.

Agger, Ben. 1988. "Review Essay: Marcuse's 'One-Dimensionality:' Socio-Historical and Ideological Context." *Dialectical Anthropology* 13(4): 315–29. At https://www.jstor.org/stable/29790288?seq=1.

Anthonissen, Christine. 2001. "Critical Discourse Analysis: A methodological Discussion for Analysis of Editorials on the State of Emergency, die Kerkbode 1986–1989." *Scriptura* 76: 17–31.

Bartlett, Jamie. 2014. "Populism, Social Media and Democratic Strain." In *European Populism and Winning the Immigration Debate*, ed. Clara Sandelind, 99–116. Stockholm: Fores.

Berger, J.M. 2018. "Trump is the Glue that Binds the Far Right." *The Antlantic,* October 29, 2018. At https://www.theatlantic.com/ideas/archive/2018/10/trump-alt-right-twitter/574219/.

Blommaert, Jan. 2019. "Political Discourse in Post-Digital Societies." *Tilburg Papers in Culture Studies.* Paper 236. At https://www.tilburguniversity.edu/research/institutes-and-research-groups/babylon/tpcs.

Blommaert, Jan. 2020. "Twitter Politics: The Next Stage." *Diggit Magazine*, January 14, 2020. At https://www.diggitmagazine.com/column/twitter-politics-next-stage.

Bohman, James. "Critical Theory." In *Stanford Encyclopedia of Philosophy.* Stanford University. Article published March 8, 2005. At https://plato.stanford.edu/archives/win2019/entries/critical-theory.

Carvalho, Anabela. 2008. "Media(ted) Discourse and Society." *Journalism Studies* 9(2): 161–177. https://doi.org/10.1080/14616700701848162.

Chilton, Paul. 2017. 'the people' in Populist Discourse." *Journal of Language and Politics* 16(4): 582–594. https://doi.org/10.1075/jlp.17031.chi.

Chouliaraki, Lilie. 2008. "Discourse Analysis." In *SAGE handbook of cultural analysis,* eds. Tony Bennett and John Frow, 674–698. London: Sage Publications.

Chouliaraki, Lilie, and Norman Fairclough. 1999. *Discourse in Late Modernity: Rethinking Critical Discourse Analysis*. Edinburgh: Edinburgh University Press.

Clement, J. 2019. "Number of Daily Instagram Stories users from October 2016 to January 2019." *Statista*, January 8, 2020. At https://www.statista.com/statistics/730315/instagram-stories-dau/.

Collin, Ross. 2015. "Introducing Jameson to Critical Discourse Analysis." *Critical Discourse Studies* 13(2): 158–173. https://doi.org/10.1080/17405904.2015.1042393.

Corner, John. 2018. "Mediatization": Media Theory's Word of the Decade. *Media Theory.* At http://mediatheoryjournal.org/john-corner-mediatization/.

Corner, John, and Dick Pels. 2003. *Media and the Restyling of Politics.* London: SAGE.

Couldry, Nick, and Andreas Hepp. 2013. "Conceptualizing Mediatization: Contexts, Traditions, Arguments." *Communication Theory* 23(3): 191–202.

Dean, Jodi. 2009. *Democracy and Other Neoliberal Fantasies: Communicative Capitalism and Left Politics.* Durham: Duke University Press.

Dean, Jodi. 2005. "Communicative Capitalism: Circulations and the Foreclosure of Politics." *Cultural Politics* 1(1): 51–73.

Derysh, Igor. 2020. "Mike Bloomberg is Paying Social Media Influencers to Post Fake Messages to Make Him Look "Cool"." *Salon*, February 14, 2020. Athttps://www.salon.com/2020/02/14/mike-bloomberg-is-paying-social-media-influencers-to-post-fake-messages-to-make-him-look-cool/.

Eco, Umberto. 1995. "Ur-Fascism." *The New York Review of Books*, June 22, 1995. At http://www.nybooks.com/articles/1995/06/22/ur-fascism/.

Enli, Gunn. 2017. "Twitter as Arena for the Authentic Outsider: Exploring the Social Media Campaigns of Trump and Clinton in the 2016 Presidential Election". *European Journal of Communication* 32(1): 50–61. https://doi.org/10.1177/0267323116682802.

Enli, Gunn, and Linda Therese Rosenberg. 2018."Trust in the Age of Social Media: Populist Politicians Seem More Authentic." *Social Media + Society* 4(1): 1–18. https://doi.org/10.1177/2056305118764430.

Fairclough, Norman. 2014. *Language and Power.* London: Routledge.

Fairclough, Norman. 2010. "Discourse, Change and Hegemony." In *Critical Discourse Analysis: The Critical Study of Language,* ed. Norman Fairclough, 126–45. Harlow: Longman.

Fairclough, Norman and Ruth Wodak. 1997. "Critical Discourse Analysis". In *Discourse as Social Interaction*, ed. Teun van Dijk, 258–284. London: Sage.

Feldman, Max. "Seductive Fascist Style." *Verso* (blog). September 6, 2019. At https://www.versobooks.com/blogs/4430-seductive-fascist-style.

Flew, Terry. 2017. "The 'Theory' in Media Theory." *Media Theory* 1(1):43–56.

Forchtner, Bernhard. 2018. "Critical Discourse Studies and Social Theory." In *The Routledge Handbook of Critical Discourse Studies*, eds. John Flowerdew and John Richardson, 259–271. London: Routledge.

Forchtner, Bernhard. 2011. "Critique, the Discourse–Historical Approach, and the Frankfurt School." *Critical Discourse Studies* 8(1): 1–14. https://doi.org/10.1080/17405904.2011.533564.

Forchtner, Bernhard and Ana Tominc. 2012. "Critique and Argumentation: On the Relation Between the Discourse-Historical Approach and Pragma-Dialectics." *Journal of Language and Politics* 11(1): 31–50.

Forchtner, Bernhard, Michal Krzyzanowski, and Ruth Wodak. 2013. "Mediatization, Right-wing Populism and Political Campaigning: The Case of the Austrian Freedom

Party." In *Media Talk and Political Elections in Europe and America*, eds. Mats Ekström, and Andrew Tolson, 205–228. Basingstoke: Palgrave Macmillan.

Fuchs, Christian. 2016. *Critical Theory of Communication: New Readings of Lukács, Adorno, Marcuse, Honneth and Habermas in the Age of the Internet*. London: University of Westminster Press.

Fuchs, Christian. 2018. "Authoritarian Capitalism, Authoritarian Movements and Authoritarian Communication." *Media, Culture and Society* 40(5): 779–791. https://doi.org/10.1177/0163443718772147.

Gordon, Peter. 2019. "Introduction." In *The Authoritarian Personality*, eds. Theodor Adorno, Else Frenkel-Brunswik, Daniel Levinson, and Nevitt Sanford, xxxiii–xl. London: Verso.

Gounari, Panayota. 2018. "Authoritarianism, Discourse and Social Media: Trump as the 'American Agitator'." In *Critical Theory and Authoritarian Populism*, ed. Morelock Jeremiah, 207–228. London: University of Westminster Press. At https://www.uwestminsterpress.co.uk/site/books/10.16997/book30/.

Gross, Bertram. 1980. *Friendly Fascism*. Boston, MA South End Press.

Gruber, Helmut. 2008. "Analyzing Communication in the New Media." In *Qualitative Discourse Analysis in the Social Sciences*, eds. Ruth Wodak and Michael Krzyzanowski, 54–74. New York: Palgrave Macmillan.

Hayden, Michel Edison. 2019. "Visions of Chaos: Weighing the Violent Legacy or Iron March." *Southern Poverty Law* (Februrary 15, 2019). At https://www.splcenter.org/hatewatch/2019/02/15/visions-chaos-weighing-violent-legacy-iron-march.

Higgins, Michael. 2017. Mediatisation and Political Language. In *The Routledge Handbook of Language and Politics, edited by Ruth Wodak and Barnhard Forchtner*. 383–397. London: Routledge.

Horkheimer, Max. 1993. *Between Philosophy and Social Science*. Cambridge: MIT Press.

Horkheimer, Max, and Theodor Adorno. 1994. *Dialectic of the Enlightenment*. New York: Continuum.

Internet Health Report. 2018. "Social Media Giants Facebook, Tencent, Google Reign." At https://internethealthreport.org/2018/social-media-giants-facebook-tencent-google-reign/.

Jay, Martin. 1996. *The Dialectical Imagination*. London: University of California Press.

Kellner, Douglas. 1991. "Introduction to the Second Edition." In Herbert Marcuse *One-Dimensional Man*, xi–xxxix. Boston: Beacon Press.

Kreis, Ramona. 2017. "The 'Tweet Politics' of President Trump". *Journal of Language and Politics* 16(4): 1–12. https://doi.org/10.1075/jlp.17032.kre.

Kress, Gunther. 1996. "Representational Resources and the Production of Subjectivity: Questions for the Theoretical Development of Critical Discourse Analysis." In *Texts and Practices*, eds. Rosa Carmen Caldas-Coulthard, and Malcolm Coulthard, 15–31. London: Routledge.

Lieber, Chavie. 2018. "How and Why Do Influencers Make so Much Money?" *Vox*, November 28, 2018. At https://www.vox.com/the-goods/2018/11/28/18116875/influencer-marketing-social-media-engagement-instagram-youtube.

Lowenthal, Leo, and Norbert Guterman. 1949. *Prophets of Deceit: A Study of the Techniques of the American Agitator*. New York: Harper & Brothers.

Marcuse, Herbert. 1968. "Aggressiveness in Advanced Industrialized Society." In *Negations: Essays in Critical Theory*, with translations from the German by Jeremy J. Shapiro. Boston: Beacon Press.

Marcuse, Herbert. 1968. "Philosophy and Critical theory." In *Negations: Essays in Critical Theory*, with translations from the German by Jeremy J. Shapiro, 134–158. Boston: Beacon Press.

Marcuse, Herbert. 1964. *One-Dimensional Man*. Boston: Beacon Press.

Martineau, Paris. 2019. "The WIRED Guide to Influencers." *Wired* (December 6, 2019). At https://www.wired.com/story/what-is-an-influencer/.

Mazzoleni, Gianpietro, and Winfried Schulz. 1999. "Mediatization of Politics: A Challenge for Democracy?" *Political Communication* 16(3): 247–261.

McKenna, Bernard. 2004. "Critical Discourse Studies: Where to From Here?" *Critical Discourse Studies* 1(1): 9–39. https://doi.org/10.1080/17405900410001674498.

McKenna, Bernard and Neal Waddell. 2006. "Technologizing Inhumanity." *Critical Discourse Studies* 3(2): 211–228. https://doi.org/10.1080/17405900600908129.

Montgomery, Martin. 2017. "Post-Truth Politics? Authenticity, Populism and the Electoral Discourses of Donald Trump." *Journal of Language and Politics* 16 (4): 619–639. https://doi.org/10.1075/jlp.17023.mon.

Ott, Brian. 2016. "The age of Twitter: Donald J. Trump and the Politics of Debasement." *Critical Studies in Media Communication* 34(1): 59–68.

Reisigl, Martin and Ruth Wodak. 2009. "The Discourse–Historical Approach." In *Methods of critical discourse analysis*, eds. Ruth Wodak and Michael Meyer, 87–121. London: Sage.

Reisigl, Martin and Ruth Wodak. 2001. *Discourse and Discrimination. Rhetorics of racism and anti-Semitism*. London: Routledge.

Robinson, Andrew. 2010. "In Theory – Herbert Marcuse: One-dimensional Man?" *Ceasefire* (October 22, 2010). At https://ceasefiremagazine.co.uk/in-theory-6-marcuse/.

Ross, Andrew, and David Caldwell. 2019. "'Going Negative': An APPRAISAL Analysis of the Rhetoric of Donald Trump on Twitter." *Language & Communication* 70: 13–27. https://doi.org/10.1016/j.langcom.2019.09.003.

Salehi, Kumars. 2017. "What Would Frankfurt School Think of Social Media?" *Verso* (Blog) (October 2, 2017). At https://www.versobooks.com/blogs/3417-what-would-the-frankfurt-school-think-of-social-media.

Santos, Philip and Khulekani Ndlovu. 2015. " 'Democratic Unfreedom' on Facebook in Zimbabwe." *African Journalism Studies,* 36(4): 145–163. https://doi.org/10.1080/23743670.2015.1119496.

Saussure, Ferdinand. 1916. *Lecons de Linguistique Générale.* Paris and Lausanne: Payot.

Seymour, Richard. 2019. *The Twittering Machine.* London: The Indigo Press.

Sousanis, Nick. 2015. *Unflattening.* Cambridge: Harvard University Press.

Van Leeuwen, Theo. 2018. "Moral Evaluation in Critical Discourse Analysis." *Critical Discourse Studies* 15(2): 140–153. https://doi.org/10.1080/17405904.2018.1427120.

Wiggershaus, Rolf. 1998. *The Frankfurt School: Its History, Theories, and Political Significance Studies in Contemporary German Social Thought,* trans. Michael Robertson. Cumberland: MIT Press.

Wodak, Ruth. 1996. The genesis of racist discourse in Austria since 1989." In *Texts and Practices,* ed. Rosa Carmen Caldas-Coulthard, and Malcolm Coulthard, 107–12831. London: Routledge.

Wodak, Ruth. 2001. "What CDA Is About – A Summary of Its History, Important Concepts and Its Developments." In *Methods of Critical Discourse Analysis,* eds. Ruth Wodak and Michael Meyer, 1–13. London: Sage.

Wodak, Ruth. 2017. "Discourses About Nationalism." In *Handbook of Critical Discourse Analysis,* eds. John Richardson and John Flowerdew, 403–421. London: Routledge.

Wodak, Ruth. 2015. *The Politics of Fear.* London: SAGE.

Wodak, Ruth and Michael Meyer. 2009. "Critical Discourse Analysis: History, Agenda, Theory and Methodology." In *Methods of Critical Discourse Analysis,* eds. Ruth Wodak and Michael Meyer, 1–33. London: Sage.

Wodak, Ruth, and Brigitta Busch. 2004. "Approaches to Media Texts." In *Handbook of Media Studies,* eds. John Downing, Denis McQuail, Philip Schlesinger, and Ellen Wartella, 105–123. New Delhi: Sage.

Wodak, Ruth, and Michał Krzyżanowski. 2017. "Right-wing populism in Europe & USA: Contesting Politics & Discourse Beyond "Orbanism" and "Trumpism." *Journal of Language and* Politics 16(4): 1–14. https://doi.org/10.1075/jlp.17042.krz.

CHAPTER 17

Applying and Extrapolating *Prophets of Deceit*: Heuristics of 'Agitator' Identification through Löwenthal and Guterman's Analysis

William M. Sipling

1 A Summary of Löwenthal and Guterman, Their Analysis, and Introduction to Agitators

This examination focuses primarily on *Prophets of Deceit*, a critique of 20th century American political 'agitators' by Löwenthal and Guterman, investigating their methodology to construct identification criteria for today's virulent and anti-social political activists on digital media. Context will first be given regarding the authors and their backgrounds, followed by an introduction to their methodology, and concluding with a summary of their use of the term "agitator."

1.1 *The Authors and Their Work: Löwenthal, Guterman, and Prophets of Deceit*

Leo Löwenthal (1900–1993) lived in Germany at the time of the Weimar Republic, born into a family with a complicated relationship to Orthodox Judaism; though later in his life, Löwenthal would subscribe to a Jewish political identity (Löwenthal 1987: 17–18). Affiliated with the Institute for Social Research at Goethe University in Frankfurt, he escaped to America in the wake of Hitler's regime, pursuing a lengthy academic career in media studies, psychology, and literary criticism, serving his last post as emeritus professor of sociology at UC Berkeley (Bogart 1993: 1). Norbert Guterman (1900–1984), of Hasidic heritage, was a student of psychology and philosophy, and a professional translator of German, Latin, French, Russian, Hebrew, Polish, and English texts. He worked closely with the Frankfurt School, being invited by Max Horkheimer to participate in the Institute's research (Jacobs 2014: 94–95).

Their combined critical theory culminates in *Prophets of Deceit: A Study of the Techniques of the American Agitator*. The title invokes denouncements from the Hebrew Bible's Prophet Jeremiah – "Yea, they are prophets of the deceit of their own heart" (Löwenthal and Guterman 1970: xxx) – perhaps an indication of the work's kerygmatic nature concerning national crises and social deterioration, and certainly an appropriate reference to the Christianity-laced language common to populist American pundits, particularly independent radio hosts. An expansion of the shorter 1948 article "Portrait of the American Agitator" in the political science journal *The Public Opinion Quarterly* (Löwenthal and Guterman 1948: 417), this book-length version, across ten sections and twenty-one themes, contains the authors' outline for descriptively analyzing characteristics of these aggressors.

1.2   Methodology: Qualitative Content Analysis
Though theoretical and rhetorical interpretations of written texts, radio speeches, and other media from extreme political voices were often research interests for the two writers – Löwenthal especially (Hardt 1991) – *Prophets of Deceit* sought a more practical goal: a generalizable methodology. They state their objective is in the spirit of *Egoismus und Freiheitsbewegung* (Horkheimer 1982), wherein Horkheimer traces an "anthropology" of the egoistic "authoritarian personality," creating a heuristic for categorizing traits and affects which tend toward or quintessentially are that of demagoguery (Worrell 1998). The goal of building such identification criteria is the general extrapolation of the framework into qualitative content analyses of various media and influencers (Löwenthal and Guterman 1970).

Löwenthal and Guterman's qualitative content analysis does not claim to be a 21st century evidence-based, positivistic approach to agitator identification. It is a social philosophy, something more interpretive or suggestive than 21st century mainstream sociological methods (Wiggershaus 1994). *Prophets* is not to politics what the *Diagnostic and Statistical Manual of Mental Disorders* is to clinical psychology, nor is it Freudian psychoanalysis, the counseling/therapeutic tradition of their day which they inherit and reference throughout their work (Wells 1950). The writers describe their interpretive methodology as related to the examination of "surface material of deeper social and psychological currents," that it is "frankly experimental," that it requires "a certain degree of probability for conclusions about latent content," and ultimately that their "approach may pave the way for an empirical exploration of the psychology of the agitator and for field work on his actual effects upon audiences" (Löwenthal and Guterman 1970: xvi).

None of this means, however, that their work should be considered invalid or insignificant, or their methodological approach non-indicative. There are over 500 references, quotations, and allusions to speeches, literature, and periodicals analyzed in their text, indicating very close engagement with their source materials (Löwenthal and Guterman 1970). They went so far as to recruit "skilled court stenographers or trained reporters" to create multiple-years' worth of transcripts of audio content (150).

Communications researchers, media professionals, and social theorists, in their usage of Löwenthal and Guterman's analysis, should be aware of the intended range and application of their work (Zygmunt 1972) – not only in terms of "experimental" versus "empirical" science, but regarding the conclusions that a *Prophets*-based examination may draw. The Frankfurt School theorists' anti-authoritarian impulses were unapologetically strong, and they were more than willing to polemically critique political actors and regimes. At the same time, researchers and theorists today should note that the "suggestive" nature of qualitative content analysis allows for a more flexible *pathos* as opposed to a binary "either/or" *propositio*. That is to say, this method allows theorists to identify agitator *behavior*, not necessarily *agitators themselves*. The advantages here are at least twofold: first, this approach may be interpreted as less accusatory and less *ad hominum* (and perhaps less reifying) because presenting behaviors are what are being analyzed; second, looking for behaviors and tendencies rather than discrete figures or persons may allow researchers to identify agitators in unexpected places – perhaps serving as a check if such agitator behavior incarnates itself under the blind spot of a theorist's own biases (or daresay, their own ideologies).

1.3   *Defining Terms: An Introduction to the Analysis of the Agitator*

At the time of *Prophets*, which followed the rise and fall of the Nazi regime, the primary topics of public critique in America concerned firebrand figureheads and populist presenters who were known for extremist and conspiratorial ideologies, rabid anti-Semitism, and "indulgence in intensive vituperation of our national leaders" (Löwenthal and Guterman 1970: xv). Essentially, they were comparable to anti-global "locker room talk," speaking about topics that perhaps were unacceptable for polite company (such as the myth of Aryan supremacy), but allowable in the right circumstances and through the right channels. Such channels (media), including newspapers, journals, and radio stations, provided platforms for these "self-appointed popular spokes[men]" self-proclaimed as "advocate[s] for social change"(xv, 6) – these expressions summarize how these Frankfurt School writers use the term "agitator."

According to some, and accurate to a limited degree from Löwenthal and Guterman's perspective, agitators rise to power because they engage in media-driven populist demagoguery, which has rhetorical power for audiences; 1) because of expressive relief features, and 2) via the protection of plausible deniability (Vitolo-Haddad 2019).

Regarding expressive outlet, frustrated audiences mitigate personal tension by vicarious association with central polarizing characters. Individual audience members might perceive such personas as more extreme than themselves, and therefore be able to self-identify as comparatively "not as bad as" these agitators. Further, agitators are labeled as truth-speakers who say "just the facts" and are not arrested by negatively-perceived social prerogatives, such as openness to immigration or differing religious ideologies (Löwenthal and Guterman 1948: 422–23). Agitators allow subscribers to be appeased-via-association with statements or ideologies for which they themselves would normally suffer social consequences. Some examples could include conspiracy theory, denial of history, and racism or xenophobia. In common parlance, a listener harbors tension because they are not allowed to "say the quiet part out loud," but they can listen intently as an agitator does.

This leads to the second point, regarding plausible deniability. From the perspective of those "outside of the know," these individuals form protective boundaries or social plausibility deniability for subscribers. This is because agitators have "crackpot" characteristics (Löwenthal and Guterman 1970: xv), and therefore lack general credibility in some parasocial informational front (Madison et al. 2018), though their rhetorical power flows out of this. Statements that wider social circles consider to be too extreme can be hand-waved away by apologists claiming that they are just "provocateurs" or that it is simply performance. They "suggest a quack medicine salesman," with "many characteristics of a psychological racket: they play on vague fears," and yet, "they give their admission-paying audience … a kind of act – something between a tragic recital and a clownish pantomime – rather than a political speech." This allows agitators to "get away with" extremist "jokes to doubletalk to wild extravagances" because they navigate in a "twilight zone" spectrum between "the respectable and the forbidden" (Löwenthal and Guterman 1970: 4–5).

Both of these characteristics of their social power may be true – certainly both of these behaviors are popularly cited as what is both attractive and dangerous about these infamous personas. However, if the essence of the social power of these people were from this alone, their spheres of influence could be mitigated by deplatforming or education. Of course, today such deplatforming and anti-fake facts or fake news initiatives have mixed results. This is perhaps because there is more to agitators' appeal; more lies under the surface. Löwenthal and Guterman state that over the obvious or popular explanations for these individuals' rise to influencer-ship, agitators further call upon "unconscious mechanisms to build instruments" for audience manipulation – the obvious/popular explanations are only "surface manifestation[s] of deeper and social psychological currents" (xvi).

The difference between the agitator and the non-extremist political leader is not one of taxonomy (they are both "public influencers"), but rather of degree. An ordinary leader may have a calling to civic or social concerns, whereas the agitator follows an "innate predestination" (118). Both work in systems with steep learning curves and profound nuance, but the agitator's communication style includes furthering logical incoherence. The agitator uses direct insult, with insensitive and offensive language towards both allies and adversaries. To a more graphic extreme, the agitator employs violent or sadistic language to incite and provoke their listeners.

They carefully craft their origin stories, contextualizing family ties or educational backgrounds which could be taken as 'elite' or overly privileged to a simple or ordinary audience (the agitator's perception of their target market). Agitators rarely identify with diversity, multiculturalism, or non-dominant religions, preferring the "humility" of the "common folk" as a run-of-the-mill "old-fashioned Christian American" (124). They also have a flair for the dramatic and choose to burden their audience by sharing their paranoia – realized in concocted death threats, musings emerging from martyrdom syndrome, or deluded grandiose conspiracy theories.

2 Understanding Agitator-Identification Criteria Categories

In this section, the background of what causes audience and agitator to be disposed to one another will be explored, followed by five agitator communication categories: 1) narrative discourse, 2) adversarial discourse, 3) anti-Semitic discourse, 4) in-group-ing discourse, and 5) concealment discourse. The broad categories serve as easily identifiable criteria for extrapolation, though in the following sections, more specific explanations as utilized by Löwenthal and Guterman will be added.

2.1 *Setting the Stage: The Groundwork of a Susceptible Audience*
2.1.1 The Role of Seduction and Dis/Belief
There is a causality dilemma in the origins of agitators and their audiences, considering they appear to arise from the same primordial cultural factors. Meeting at the right place and time, a communicative and social serendipity allow for a coming together of two minds, compared by Löwenthal and Guterman to a dance of flirtation and seduction (4). With hints of a grave crisis, loss of identity or some other self-conception is promised to be replaced by the unrelenting attention of the agitator. Therein develops an unspoken relationship, an "unconscious complicity or collaboration."

Suspension of disbelief is required from the audience to overcome "obvious incongruities" in the agitator's discourse. With little regard to continuity or rhetorical argument, agitators are able to link threats – from "secret formulae and technical instructions" to impending "violent Death" – for Americans who have not awoken to the lurking danger-of-the-day, which ranges from Communism to people of color to Judaism (8). As in some intimate relationships, the "red flags" of the agitator begin to go unnoticed at a certain point by the audience as they commit to the agitator's explanations. In the face of bad press or poor reviews, the agitator appeals to the heart of the audience, playing the victim and "tak[ing] on paranoiac overtones" (9). They may direct the audience to identify others' claims as immoderate, without cause, or simply unable to compete with the agitator's own veracity.

2.1.2   Tapping into the "Catalogue of Grievances"
Forces that instigate the audience to join the agitator's side have to do with an appeal to activating events or a catalogue of grievances, linked primarily to a "specific condition of discontent" (11). Discontent is not necessarily a state originating from class struggle, poverty, or some other ill, but rather (and perhaps more efficacious for the agitator) things normally identified as innocuous, now coded by the agitator as grievances. Previously, such things may have otherwise not been in the audience's awareness as negative, or even as things that could affect the audience in any way. Now they are made to be top-of-mind and perhaps even described as the greatest problems facing the audience. The fact that is audience is unaware (or perhaps, made to be unaware by deleterious social forces) could be used by the agitator as a rhetorical point.

Grievances are tailor-made for their audiences, and come in a variety of forms, including economic, political, cultural, and moral. From immigration to globalism to entertainment to moral panics, the agitator is able to find (or create) the issues that underlie a particular thread in the audience's identity, to shape passionate messaging around a potential threat for the sake of their social movement.

Grievances often center on the individual's placeless-ness in the grand scheme of governmental conspiracies, potential widespread diseases, and institutions supposedly crumbling under the weight of non-dominant cultures. In the 40's (and in the 21st century) it may be that one's "sense of isolation, his so-called spiritual homelessness, his bewilderment in the face of the seemingly impersonal forces of which he feels himself a helpless victim" at the hands of "gigantic industrial bureaucracies, the decay of the patriarchal family, the breakdown of primary personal ties between individuals in an increasingly mechanized world" have led to modernity's hyper-awareness and potential openness to the coding of issues as personal hazards (15). However, this internal sense of chaos is enhanced by conspiracy, and then yoked to an agitator's messaging, which likely does nothing to truly alleviate the perception of turmoil. The "malaise" of a truly "oppressive situation" is pressed into service for the agitator, and thus the audience potentially increase their anxiety if/when they begin to notice the numerous incongruences in the agitator's *weltanschauung*.

Like scratching an itchy sore from a bad rash, engaging with an agitator's discourse may provide a sense of immediate gratification and relief. Yet it causes scarring and the further spread of infection. This scratching, this revolt against grievances, takes the form of romanticism, "ritualistic fetishes," or vague heroism, and causes one to believe that "something has gone astray in modern life [and] also [be] strongly convinced that he lacks the power to right whatever is wrong ... the individual lives in a sort of eternal adolescent uneasiness" (17–18). In this social adolescence guided by the peer pressure of an agitator with an older-wiser persona, the audience must account for their problems; and these have now been coded as the results from some broken system. Now typical social awareness is replaced with a "phalanx of repressed impulses that storm the gates of the psyche" (18).

2.2   Five Categories of Agitator Communication
2.2.1   The Volatile and Unfulfilled Inverted Hero's Journey: Narrative Discourse

To summarize the first of the five agitator communication categories, agitators create for audiences a narrative of the world that inverts the hero's journey – there is no rescue or redemption from a "permanent conspiracy." There is no happy ending, only the "perpetual expectation of apocalyptic doom" (20). The audience member is characterized as in danger of being duped (or looking stupid or silly, fooled by higher powers), victimized by conspiracies, alienated from opportunities or safety, disaffected from normalizing institutions, and vulnerable to inevitable catastrophe (see also Horkheimer and Adorno 2016).

Regarding the danger of being duped: the agitator credits hostility – at being sidelined away from power and humiliated by "the man" – as part of the audience's identity (Löwenthal and Guterman 1970: 20–21). Perhaps counterintuitive, agitators do not use flattery or appeals to the intelligence of the audience. For example, an agitator "denounces Communist slogans as 'catch-phrases to obtain power over ... dupes.'" This agitator highlights the dunce-like nature of his post-war audience because they fail to recognize the conspiratorial signs of Communist agendas in their news, local and state politics, or workplace environments. They are pitiable, innocently-naïve individuals who did not know any better – they need a faithful leader who has the virtue to deal with their "plain ordinary sincere sheeplike" behavior (21), and who has the intelligence not to be duped by the powers-that-be. This further highlights the fortitude and bravery of the agitator, the true hero of this narrative, who is able to fight against social deceit while carrying the dead weight of his loyal throng – and the agitator is quick to remind them of this fact.

The presence of grand, ubiquitous conspiracies are evident in the storytelling, in that duping is not simply from a boss, a governmental agency, or a circle of friends. Rather, it is the individual against the world – except for the generous agitator and anyone who follows them. This reconstructs the self-perception of the audience. In terms of narrative, the agitator and the audience are against enormous evils engaged in fateful battles – at stake is nothing less than "the existing order," "Western civilization," the "American way of life" or "the Church" (25).

These disenfranchised audience members require exodus from being under the thumb of missed opportunities, the "forbidden fruit" of the wealthy, the privileged, and especially those of Semitic background. Outsiders (coded in the story as "the enemy") insidiously take away jobs and luxury from red-blooded Americans (coded as sub-characters of the agitator-protagonist), and these outsiders in turn use their undeserved influence to further their conspiracies. There is something incoherent, however, about this appeal – "even when the agitator denounces the 'society world of snobbery and fraud' ... he is not proposing to the audience a way for it to increase its share of wealth and pleasure" (29). Rather, he simply aggravates the audience's anxiety by pointing out the direct losses that result from their situation.

In the audience's journey, their guide is the agitator, who begins to take authority over institutions which the agitator and the audience previously identified with. Their mission, their commissioning, is to soak in disaffection. Unlike in standard monomyth, dramatic choice between "good and evil" is removed from the script; instead, lines are blurred between ideals and loyalties. In one sentence, the agitator will speak in strong support for their president, ideal society, or other authority, citing the glories of democracy and justice that come from said association. Then in the next sentence, they may speak in a condemning way towards politicians, voting blocs, or systems in general (29–30).

There is no great "last stand," dénouement, or ultimate boon awaiting the audience, but rather the "possibility of total disaster" wherein a "positive alternative to the threat ... is either totally lacking or suggested only in the vaguest form" (33). Alarmism is presented as the logical response to the revelation of such apocalyptic crises; helplessness is the only cure to such hopeless eschatology. There is again a counterintuitive strategy to total despondency – it is to make "original fear [that is, what existed before the agitator began their influence] ... thinner, less urgent, and compelling," replaced with "an enhanced imaginative reality – fear is transformed into a morbid nihilistic expectation, perhaps even hope, of total destruction" (35–36). They become desensitized to actual or real issues, enraptured by the excitement of the agitator's theatrics.

2.2.2   Identifying the Self against Other: Adversarial Discourse
After establishing the audience's place in the world, the agitator turns to the enemies who surround them, shining the spotlight on specific groups (or characteristics of groups) who are claimed to be the sources of danger and destruction – Communists, plutocrats, the government, and foreigners.

Communists, or communism, though never defined beyond broad platitudes, characterizes all political movements which are against (also not defined) the spirit of good American citizens. Distinctions or definitions are rare in the invocations or accusations of Communism, as any movements deemed outside the agitator's orthodoxy are "lumped together into an undifferentiated revolutionary threat" (39). Though what makes a Communist is not entirely clear (outside of the agitator's label), what is clear is the communists pose a real and present danger; no grey area exists regarding the evils of their supposed end goals, from media confusion to world domination. Further, the communist threat is often simply the "sheep's clothing" around a Jewish wolf – nonsensically, agitators claim that the true evil behind Communism is Hebraic influence.

Regarding plutocrats, subtle distinctions creep into what is normally black-and-white thinking. Criticisms regarding the rich center not on issues of capitalism or personal success (these critiques could be interpreted as Communist), but rather on the individuals behind the wealth, depicted as Medieval landlords, hoarders of material goods such as gold ingots, and often of Jewish heritage. Though the keepers of filthy lucre are antagonized, credit is given to CEOs, industrialists, or those who embody the ideals of hard work and labor. Similar but reverse distinctions are made concerning the government, wherein only corrupt individuals are criticized and never the underlying system. For example, the values of free speech are venerated, but the antagonism highlights those who seek to limit free speech. Similarly, American democracy is held in high regard, but congressmen and senators who supported the New Deal are regarded as disloyal anti-patriots. Finally, foreigners, without the spark of the Founding Fathers, the colonial/pioneer spirit, or Western religious standards, carry with them something new and supranational, not able to be shaped by the dominant culture's norms. Refugees are especially suspicious.

They are viewed as volatile or unstable, carrying with them strange habits and the baggage of totalitarian regimes, the trauma of some other nation they fled.

Counterintuitive reasoning is a consistent theme in adversarial discourse. It is strategic to refer to enemies as lurking parasites or degenerate animals, because such depictions communicate distaste or fear, and also something sub-human or inferior. Notwithstanding, the regular reminders of impending doom, the agitator may provide some level of comfort by pointing out the weaknesses or inferiority of these political pests.

To summarize, the agitator's strategy requires them not only to rewrite the audience's story – that is, their own self-conception – but also to redefine the groups and power dynamics which surround them. In some cases, some nuance is introduced, but only for the sake of clarifying which concepts are aligned with the agitator and which concepts supply further evidence of the presence of perceived political opponents.

2.2.3   The Fetish of a Hyper-Disparaged Target: Anti-Semitic Discourse

Within the previous two criteria categories, there is a particular emphasis on an ethnic and religious group upon whom agitators have traditionally cast blame – those who have Jewish heritage.[1] Jewish identity, for the agitator, is inclusive of many of the negative stereotypes of adversarial figures (Löwenthal and Guterman 1970). Jews are seen as suspicious refugees having endured generational persecutions and geographic exile, and as perhaps deserving this fate (Herf 2012). Further, the worst of the bankers and ruling classes are identified with Judaism, identified in parodies by their ethnic appearances, religious garb, and luxury or money. Jewish populations are accused of rejecting cultural assimilation, living in mockery of dominant (Christian) religious practice, engaging in unseemly social ladder-climbing, and being culturally cliquish (Löwenthal and Guterman 1970). Because of these things, they are seen to be mysterious at best, surreptitiously dangerous at worst.

Though the Jewish people are identified with historical persecution (it would be difficult to simply ignore this historical fact), the agitator makes a point to reshape the public's perception of the silver lining of anti-Semitism: they argue that even if Jewish people were mistreated, they exploited this for the sake of bringing about their own hordes of wealth, crony capitalism, or communism,

---

1   Löwenthal and Guterman do not present their own history or theory of anti-Jewish bias – *Prophets* itself is one volume in the series *Studies in Prejudice* which explores anti-Semitism (Jurczak and Massing 1950). Also, this topic is covered in other Frankfurt School works (Horkheimer and Adorno 2016), and further, it is outside of the focus of *Prophets'* content-focused qualitative goals of building able-to-be-extrapolated diagnostic criteria.

and though hamstrung by history, have managed to clumsily or accidentally maintain control of political and social power. Their uncanny ability to have cultural staying power despite regular conquests and captivity can only be credited to conspiratorial means. Despite the propagandizing of agitators via popular media, Jewish people are said to maintain control of radio stations and film studios. Obliquely (and offensively), this counterintuitive "persecution complex" applies to more than the communication and banking industries; agitators claim that the terrors of concentration camps were nothing more than PR stunts carried out by Jewish people themselves:

> It IS necessary that Jews be persecuted. If they were not, their whole international system would collapse. This is why it was necessary that Hitler be made to kill so many before the United States would destroy Germany. By Jewish reports, Hitler killed every Jew in Germany about six times. (83)

2.2.4   Social Realignment and Reconstruction: In-Group-ing Discourse
Despite contradictory accounts over various issues – e.g., who truly has political power, the realistic possibility for recovering particular traditionalist values, the impossibility of the total repudiation of Communism – the agitator does present some comfort in the creation of an audience community, a "home for the homeless" (90), built upon shared mission and values. In outline, this community creation from the agitator:

1.   Descriptions of the values and ideals that are to replace the rejected values and ideals.
2.   Formulations of goals which contain some assurance that the factors leading to present frustrations will be eliminated and that a situation will be created in which frustrated needs will be fully gratified.
3.   Descriptions of the methods of realizing these goals – a practical program of action.
4.   References to the character of the movement's adherent as contrasted with the character of the enemy. (90)

Regarding the first point, the agitator has to engage in his own public policy ambitions and PR, to present [at least the appearance of] viable economic or educational plans. This is essentially a custom-designed party, wherein the agitator and the audience stand against the all-encompassing dangers from the "united front of Jewry" or the "Talmudic philosophy of Europe-Asia-Africa" or "Red godless Communism" (93–94). Drama is created between the agitator and the world, but the agitator sets the scene, engaging with the audience in a way that appeals to a deep-seated sense of traditionalism or Americanism. The agitator is the holder of normative values, instead of essentially everyone else. This absolutist either/or language requires the audience pick a side.

The second point within the agitator's communication is almost medical, taking on the role of a doctor against the pathologies that they see within culture. The agitator can promise some relief against the irritations caused by the diseased world around them. The goal, temporarily, is to follow the teachings of the agitator; and at some point, some issues may enter remission. At least, decreasing symptoms of the crumbling of society, or preservation or conservation of last bastions, may be expected outcomes. This creates the environment for nationalism and protectionism to develop – if one cannot change the globalist and multicultural direction of the modern world, one must turn in an insular direction.

Third, the agitator enjoys getting down to business, setting up plans mostly without logistical support. For instance, they scheme up marches, protests, and community organizing, seeking to stir up the audience's awareness into a tangible show-of-force; they speak highly of military demonstrations, but without the logistical familiarity to manage them. Finally, they pick descriptive metaphors for portraying their movement versus the general population. Of particular note (perhaps for its psychoanalytic appeal) are comparisons made regarding smells – for example, the dingy odor of greedy Wall Street is paralleled to the hardworking, honest smells of rural America.

2.2.5   Protectionism and Rules for Followers: Concealment Discourse

In concealment discourse, the agitator seeks to help the audience identify themselves within the chaos of the world. These threats are a grand scale, and salvation is only possible through commitment to the truths of the agitator's community. However, for their own protection or because of their own limitations, this community cannot know the true innerworkings of either the enemy or the agitator, so discourse must be limited or concealing to some degree. This is ensured by appeals to simplicity, anti-intellectualism, and selective watchfulness.

Contradictory incoherences play a part again. Though the agitator gives the impression that most "simple Americans" are duped or able to be duped, the agitator also claims that the voice of this *hoi polloi* truly matters (107) – majority opinion is often invoked as an appeal to authority. With broad-brush statements, they claim that "90% of average, hardworking people" innately understand the agitator's appeals, contrary to the machinations of the 'elites.'

Anti-intellectualism serves as concealment and is appropriate considering the audience's simplicity. The agitator feigns ignorance regarding global politics and economics and tells the audience these sorts of things are only smoke and mirrors, in any case. Suspicion is cast towards progressive ideas or innovative science, especially of a psychological nature. The common person, with common sense, has no need of high-and-mighty pleonastic verbiage.

Selective watchfulness requires the audience to "wake up," or be alert for either the subtle shibboleths or the obvious signaling of new regimes (112). This selective attention operates historically as well, when an agitator invites listeners to think nostalgically about "good old days" before the influence of the adversaries. The audience is further taught to ignore the fact that though agitators attempt to remove themselves from under the thumb of the elites, the audience is shuffled away from the agitator's green rooms as well.

3 Addenda: Setting the Stage for Extrapolating Agitator-Identification Criteria and Categories into Today's Time

By utilizing the five summarized agitator criteria categories – narrative, adversarial, anti-Semitic, in-group-ing, and concealment discourse – various insights can be drawn in attempting to make sense of today's agitators. Certainly many palpable examples of digital demagoguery may be found in Donald Trump (Gounari 2018), Alex Jones (Mercieca 2019), or the Alt-Right (Dozono 2018).

Since the Frankfurt School's inception and the time of the Institute's "first generation," digitally-mediated platforms – from Patreon, to Facebook, to podcasts – have brought on drastic changes in communication theory. Today's digital media is a "mind industry" of incredible ubiquity and reach (Wayne 2012: 120), yet it can still be examined through the agitator identification criteria in *Prophets*. However, much more vigilant anti-agitator work should be carried out; researchers can critique 21st century "Father Coughlins" by this 20th century criteria and may investigate new media communication formats (such as memes or image macros) through *Prophets*. Löwenthal and Guterman's analysis contains much timeless material and calls to be applied in various ways across modern digital media. This section lays groundwork for applying their work in the age of instant-access social and digital media.

3.1 *Puzzles and Challenges of Applying Agitator Categories in Digital Media*

3.1.1 Issues from Convergence Culture: Lessened Barriers to Entry and Niche Communities

In the post-war era, to have a voice in emerging media required television or radio stations, broadcasting equipment, broadcasting crew, contracts with corporate sponsors, and potentially governmental approval from agencies such as the FCC. The first-generation Frankfurt School writers did not have anticipate the industry transformation stemming from democratized and independent media, with influencers who require only YouTube or a podcasting feed to reach listeners. These lessened barriers to entry, which have led to the creation of niche communities, can be referred to as "media convergence," or the "flow of content across multiple media platforms, the cooperation between multiple media industries, and the migratory behavior of media audiences who will go almost anywhere" to find their preferred content (Jenkins 2006: 2).

Because broadcast syndication can happen through services such as iTunes rather than public radio, agitators who may have been filtered out by well-meaning executives or advertisers of previous generations are now free to start their own media empires on content-sharing websites. Further, an agitator is not bound by the synchronous nature of being live in a studio (unless they are "livestreaming"), since their material can be created and shared, for audiences to watch on-demand. Agitators have the potential to "go viral" on the proverbial front pages of social networks.

Modern agitators are not bound by the need to censor their language or their content to appease a mainstream audience. If they happen to be removed from particular platforms for inflammatory or offensive behavior, they can simply instruct their audience to converge upon another media-sharing service. This was the case for Milo Yiannopoulos, who was removed from various social media platforms and lost speaking and writing contracts, but directed his audience to his own new eponymous media company (Mildenberger 2017).

3.1.2 Issues Emerging from New Definitions of Reach and Influencer-ship

Because of convergence media, it can be more difficult to apprehend generalized audience and agitator sentiment. In a previous generation of media, the "expert" was easily identifiable as the television presenter, radio host, or member of a panel that was researched and filtered by producers and screeners. With the sheer mass of varied internet forums, "subreddits," and Discord servers, almost anyone can become an agitator or audience member of a custom hyper-niche – there is a loss of the credentialed authority who can be fairly critiqued (Derksen et al. 2017). Especially when combined with the issue of online anonymity (Keum and Miller 2018), this can cause difficulty when attempting to critically examine discourse among particular audiences. In short, Löwenthal and Guterman had a relatively narrow bank of sources from which to draw their critique; digital researchers today are in a different situation, even if they limit their research to one social network or subreddit. Though reach is much more limited and harder to measure when investigating hyper-niche audiences (such as on the Dark Web), these communities are still capable of anti-social and dangerous behavior. For example, before committing his crime, the 2019 Christchurch mosque shooter posted a manifesto online to 4chan to be shared and commented on by supporters (Peacock 2019; Ludemann 2018).

3.1.3 The Practicality and Helpfulness of Löwenthal and Guterman, Specifically

Though the communication highways have been drastically renovated, repaved, and re- and de-constructed since the post-war era, Löwenthal and Guterman's critique specifically may be helpful for today's theorists and researchers. Both their methodology and categorical approach provide frameworks for critical analysis of today's popular platforms and provocateurs.

Regarding their methodology, the socio-psychoanalytic perspective of these theorists provides an intuitive framework – several of their criteria, such as plausible deniability, shibboleths, and dog whistles, are all clearly used by agitators, and yet may be hard to codify using a more empiricist approach. Their analytic perspective reaches past a "participant's" presenting behavior, and toward the *geist* of an agitator's appeals. It dives deeper than laundry lists, seeking what lies underneath the surface of checkmarks and survey responses. For example, the "Intellectual Dark Web," may meet certain standards of diversity on paper (for example, some listings of IDW members include non-white, LGBT, non-Christian members) (Harris 2019), and yet may share some conspiratorial tendencies with alt-right or radical right agitators. Another advantage of psychoanalysis is the posture towards intuitive interpretation of human behavior. For instance, a theorist allowing their criteria to include the Freudian "fight or flight" response may be able to bring helpful interrogative tools to the table – tools that require speculation beyond observable facts. In the case of voices on some radical media outlets calling for retribution towards actors they believe to have originated the COVID-19 virus, a theorist using Löwenthal and Guterman's perspective may ask questions such as "is this agitator looking for a scapegoat to blame, or are they engaging in some process involving wish-fulfillment in attempting to take on the archetype of a prophet?"

Using their categorical approach, researchers and theorists can easily interpret agitators' expressions due to the analogical nature of the categories. Though intuition is helpful, it is not always active. Having heuristics to map agitators' language according to pre-defined categories may allow theorists to filter out misplaced judgements or to uncover agitator behavior otherwise unidentifiable, imperceptible to themselves based on their own experiences or inexperience, or simply forgotten about – that is to say, without intuition, it can be easy to forget the steps to identify an agitator, and having a formula such as Löwenthal and Guterman's may be elucidating. In any case, walking through their categories allows one to make a weighted case for identifying someone as engaging in agitator-like communication. People high in the "anti-Semitic language" category almost always give themselves away as engaging in the harmful, habitually antagonistic discourse of agitators. Alternatively, such categories could be applied in situations that are not as clear cut. For instance, narrative discourse, in-group-ing discourse, or concealment discourse categories could be applied to the actors in the ping-ponging narrative of the January 2019 Lincoln Memorial confrontation between Covington High School students and a Native American activist. The categories could even be used to uncover potential agitator-like tendencies in the sustained #MeToo accusations against Associate Justice of the United States Supreme Court Brett Kavanaugh or former US Vice President Joe Biden (Pogrebin and Kelly 2019; Sullivan, Lee, and Bradner n.d.).

Engaging with history and psychology and investigating closely the rhetoric of demagogic orators and dissenting activists, are *all* relevant in today's time. New media – social and anti-social – operates within an already-existing media landscape of partisan politics and radicalizing ideologies. Löwenthal and Guterman developed a system that, though likely outside of their imaginary, has been and will continue to be extrapolated for use in the world of clickbait and the attention economy.

References

Bogart, Leo. 1993. "In Memoriam: Leo Löwenthal, 1900–1993." *The Public Opinion Quarterly* 57(3): 377–79.

Derksen, Christina, Anna Serlachius, Keith J. Petrie, and Nicola Dalbeth. 2017. "'What Say Ye Gout Experts?' A Content Analysis of Questions about Gout Posted on the Social News Website Reddit." *BMC Musculoskeletal Disorders* 18(1): 488. https://doi. org/10.1186/s12891-017-1856-y.

Dozono, Tadashi. 2018. "The Fascist Seduction of Narrative: Walter Benjamin's Historical Materialism Beyond Counter-Narrative." *Studies in Philosophy & Education* 37(5): 513–27. https://doi.org/10.1007/s11217-018-9612-9.

Gounari, Panayota. 2018. "Authoritarianism, Discourse and Social Media: Trump as the 'American Agitator.'" In *Critical Theory and Authoritarian Populism*, ed. Jeremiah Morelock, 207–27. London: University of Westminster Press.

Hardt, Hanno. 1991. "The Conscience of Society: Leo Löwenthal and Communication Research." *Journal of Communication* 41(3): 65–085. https://doi.org/10.1111/j.1460-2466.1991.tb02324.x.

Harris, Uri. 2019. "Is the 'Intellectual Dark Web' Politically Diverse?" *Quillette* (blog) (April 17, 2019). At https://quillette.com/2019/04/17/is-the-intellectual-dark-web-politically-diverse/.

Herf, Jeffrey. 2012. "'Dialectic of Enlightenment' Reconsidered." *New German Critique* 117: 81–89.

Horkheimer, Max. 1982. "Egoism and the Freedom Movement: On the Anthropology of the Bourgeois Era." *Telos: Critical Theory of the Contemporary* 1982 (54): 10–60. https://doi.org/10.3817/1282054010.

Horkheimer, Max, and Theodor Adorno. 2016. Dialectic of Enlightenment. Brooklyn, NY: Verso.

Jacobs, Jack. 2014. *The Frankfurt School, Jewish Lives, and Antisemitism.* New York: Cambridge University Press.

Jenkins, Henry. 2006. *Convergence Culture Where Old and New Media Collide.* New York: NYU Press.

Jurczak, Chester A., and Paul W. Massing. 1950. "Review of Review of: Prophets of Deceit, by Leo Löwenthal and Norbert Guterman." *The American Catholic Sociological Review* 11(1): 50–51. https://doi.org/10.2307/3706927.

Keum, Brian TaeHyuk, and Matthew J. Miller. 2018. "Racism on the Internet: Conceptualization and Recommendations for Research." *Psychology of Violence* 8(6): 782–91. http://dx.doi.org.ezproxy.stthomas.edu/10.1037/vio0000201.

Löwenthal, Leo. 1987. *An Unmastered Past: The Autobiographical Reflections of Leo Löwenthal.* Berkeley, CA: University of California Press. At http://ark.cdlib.org/ark:/13030/ft8779p24p/.

Löwenthal, Leo, and Norbert Guterman. 1948. "Portrait of the American Agitator." *The Public Opinion Quarterly* 12(3): 417–29.

Löwenthal, Leo, and Norbert Guterman. 1970. *Prophets of Deceit: A Study of the Techniques of the American Agitator.* 2nd ed. Palo Alto, CA: Pacific Books Publishers.

Ludemann, Dillon. 2018. "/Pol/Emics: Ambiguity, Scales, and Digital Discourse on 4chan." *Discourse, Context & Media* 24: 92–98. https://doi.org/10.1016/j.dcm.2018.01.010.

Madison, T. Phillip, Emily N. Covington, Kaitlyn Wright, and Timothy Gaspard. 2018. "Credibility and Attributes of Parasocial Relationships with Alex Jones." *Southwestern Mass Communication Journal* 10(10): 1–17.

Mercieca, Jennifer R. 2019. "Dangerous Demagogues and Weaponized Communication." *Rhetoric Society Quarterly* 49(3): 264–279. https://doi.org/10.1080/02773945.2019.1610640.

Mildenberger, Florian. 2017. "Milo Yiannopoulos: Dangerous." *Sexuality & Culture* 21(4): 1238–1239. https://doi.org/10.1007/s12119-017-9464-4.

Peacock, Colin. 2019. "The New Zealand Mosque Massacre: 2. 'End of Innocence' for Media and Nation." *Pacific Journalism Review* 25(1/2): 18–28.

Pogrebin, Robin, and Kate Kelly. 2019. "Brett Kavanaugh Fit In With the Privileged Kids. She Did Not." *The New York Times*, sec. Sunday Review (September 14, 2019). At https://www.nytimes.com/2019/09/14/sunday-review/brett-kavanaugh-deborah-ramirez-yale.html.

Sullivan, Kate, MJ Lee, and Eric Bradner. n.d. "What We Know about Tara Reade's Allegation against Joe Biden." *CNN*. At https://www.cnn.com/2020/05/02/politics/tara-reade-allegation-joe-biden/index.html (accessed May 2, 2020).

Vitolo-Haddad, C.V. 2019. "The Blood of Patriots: Symbolic Violence and 'The West.'" *Rhetoric Society Quarterly* 49(3): 280–296. https://doi.org/10.1080/02773945.2019.1610641.

Wayne, Mike. 2012. "Hans Magnus Enzenberger and the Politics of New Media Technology." In *Revisiting the Frankfurt School: Essays on Culture, Media and Theory*, ed. David Berry. London: Routledge. At http://ebookcentral.proquest.com/lib/unistthomas-ebooks/detail.action?docID=4500771.

Wells, Charles A. 1950. "Review of Review of: Prophets of Deceit, by Leo Löwenthal and Norbert Guterman." *The Journal of Genetic Psychology* 77: 321–22.

Wiggershaus, Rolf. 1994. *The Frankfurt School: Its History, Theories, and Political Significance*. Cambridge: MIT Press.

Worrell, Mark P. 1998. "Authoritarianism, Critical Theory, and Political Psychology: Past, Present, and Future." *Social Thought & Research* 21(1/2): 3–33.

Zygmunt, Joseph F. 1972. "Movements and Motives: Some Unresolved Issues in the Psychology of Social Movements." *Human Relations* 25(5): 449–67. https://doi.org/10.1177/001872677202500506.

Dialectical Images and Contemporary Times: Thinking Critically about Authoritarian Populism

Mariana Caldas Pinto Ferreira

> The whole problem is born of the fact that we have come to the image with the idea of synthesis ... an image is an act and not a thing.
>
> SARTRE, *L'Imagination*, 1936

1 Introduction

Much has been said concerning Walter Benjamin's works, especially in transitional justice, cultural studies of memory and political theory. Dying prematurely, Benjamin never actually participated as an active academic in the Institute of Social Research, but his work on History[1] and culture were influential to Frankfurt School thinkers. In particular at providing an alternative reading of history taking into account Kantian and Hegelian traditions of thought amid the technological and cultural changes of the 20th century.

Benjamin insisted on the role of the thinker in his/her times. Critical thinking is not only about discussing theories of History, politics and culture, but also taking responsibility for consequences this theorization might lead to. In other words, thinking critically means being aware of one's embeddedness in the present time, realizing that thinking *per se* also implies material and political consequences. Ultimately, revisiting Benjamin requires not applying his method straight away to social phenomena, but acknowledging *how we explain events in our daily lives*, and how this relates to the way we describe our past and projections we make towards the future, observing how our lived experience shapes the way we understand the world in common.[2]

---

1 In this chapter, I will use "History" with a capital letter to indicate a traditional narrative of the events. This is helpful to contrast the idea of History, as we are used to, to Walter Benjamin's conception of history, which looks for hidden and small narratives not told in the sequence of the events.

2 By "world in common," I mean the space in between we share when living among others – creating meanings and common grounds to understand the world and its events.

One can ask: Why insist on dealing with different times while theorizing about social and political events? Benjamin argues it is because the present carries within itself elements from the past and, as thinkers, we should be able to grasp these elements to find continuities and discontinuities in our social narratives. It is not about praising the past for being exactly as it was but finding what past components still inform how we deal with political events. Therefore, to discuss how authoritarianism and far-right movements have been rising everywhere in the world, a "Benjaminian" attitude is to take a step back, grasping which elements were already hidden in our social relations. Moreover, to be aware of which narratives are set in dispute within our present time.

Benjamin introduces a concept of History based on what he calls 'constellations,' where past and future come together with the present. By constellation, he suggests an image that crystallizes all periods, known and unknown, in the present time. Once one realizes this constellation, it breaks with the order of the things – one becomes aware of the social gaps society has. Critical theorists, especially Frankfurt School scholars, will emphasize that the role of critical thinking is to identify the injustices and gaps of society in order to find paths to its transformation, and ultimately its emancipation. So, when Benjamin advocates looking carefully at how we perceive our present and its social dynamics, he is emphasizing the role of criticizing the present in developing awareness of conditions for resistance and change, transformation and political.

This is different from traditional approaches to history. Here, conceptions of past and future are not static – they operate within a dynamic that changes how we live in our own present time. Benjamin argues that identifying the present as a constellation of images helps us see history by " 'telescop[ing] the past through the present (Benjamin 2002: 471) This would allow " 'the past to place the present in a critical condition' " (Buck-Morss 1989: 338). In this sense, Susan Buck-Morss advances a "dialectics of seeing." This dialectical movement means to become aware of historical conditions, considering this past in the order of things, with its continuities and discontinuities. A dialectics of seeing means "[that] historical images will turn visible philosophical ideas, which came in a discontinuous way" (Buck-Morss 1989: 55).

Today's worldwide surge of populist and authoritarian discourses introduces us to new challenges, theoretically speaking but mostly politically speaking. In 2016, Trump's election crystallized the spread of these discourses over the globe, but this movement had already been prominent in countries such as Brazil, Germany, and others. Overall, many of these discourses hold a hard criticism of liberal norms and human rights, proposing a conservative agenda very disrespectful of differences. To understand all these recent phenomena in consultation with Benjamin's works, one should be attentive to how these authoritarian expressions happen in culture, media, and information exchange because this informs a "constellation," i.e., an image of our times.

Among those countries today where authoritarian populism comes to play a leading role, each country differs in how authoritarian populism comes to reach political amplitude. Yet social media is a common characteristic. *WhatsApp* messages, *Twitter* and *Facebook* posts, uploading and circulation of hate speech videos – these are some of the elements that authoritarian populism has been using to achieve its popularity, especially in populations unhappy with their living conditions and distrustful of political representation. Technology plays a different role than the one discussed by the first generation of Frankfurt School thinkers. Indeed, technological improvement was an essential matter of analysis for them. Still, none predicted how simple electronic devices and new ways of communication would have such an impact on shaping subjectivities and altering ethical standards.

No one insists as much as Benjamin in the relevance of the intellectual in his or her period (Gagnebin 2014). What could we, then, ask him? Of so many lessons we learn from the Frankfurt School, a crucial one is that each generation must reconcile themselves with their embeddedness in History. An appropriate engagement with Benjamin's work takes the presentness of our times seriously, in its limits and potentialities. My aim in this chapter is straightforward: to introduce Benjamin's discussion of the dialectical image, and to suggest how it might shed light on what we have been thinking lately about our present time.

Culture (and artistic expression) is grounded aesthetically: today, much of it transmits through technological devices, social media and other forms of communication. Benjamin's method highlights culture as a crucial area that we can problematize to help us become aware of our relationship towards our present. In other words, examining culture helps us to think critically towards our own times, to look for social gaps and potentialities for transformation, to challenge authoritarian populist discourses, and to enlarge perspectives and embrace other possible daily narratives and voices. In this way, Benjamin's writing helps us to find ways to become conscious of the dangers of authoritarian and populist discourses, to react and even resist them.

Since thinking critically towards the present requires thinking about history, and, as Benjamin argues "History decays into images, not in stories" (Benjamin 2002: 476), we can grasp a sense of our times by looking at transmitted historical and contemporary images, observing how they create a sense of what was and is. Images show us crystallizations of historical and political moments, and therefore, as thinkers, we should pay attention to what we see.

An introduction (such as this) to Benjamin's concept of the dialectical image must include an analysis of how this concept is akin to a methodology for thinking about History. It demands discussing how culture, beyond expressing heritage and remembrance, also facilitates strategies to react to the emergence of authoritarian populism. Benjamin, for example, wrote most of his work during the rise of Nazism. For him, effective political action against totalitarian movements would come from the cultural realm, and in historical vision. While most cultural dynamics take place outside academia, Benjamin knew that artistic expression holds within itself the potential to enlarge thinking – bringing a critical attitude towards the present.

I divide my chapter into three sections. First, I analyze how Benjamin conceived the dialectical image as part of his reaction against the philosophy of History, and his will to find alternative grounds for a different historiography. Next, I discuss briefly the Adorno-Benjamin debate, especially concerning aesthetics. Finally, I conclude with some considerations on the development of authoritarian populist aesthetics, and on political action nowadays.

2   "History Decays into Images": History through Image

Benjamin advances a concept of criticism intimately bound to history and time. History, in its turn, is best understood through its cultural expressions. When Benjamin started writing *The Arcades Project* (2002) he wanted to understand the emergence of modernity as expressed in the proliferation of mercantile galleries in Paris during the mid-nineteenth century. He used the new kind of architecture there as a sort of "artefact" of the period. To Benjamin, history is deeply connected to images, since visual objects inform modes of perception of a particular period. In other words, we only become aware of how a specific object carries within itself modes of perception inhabiting other historical moments when we become self-conscious of the present. In this awareness, we observe how forms and ornaments seem to come from specific times and places (Jennings et al. 2008: 7).[3] Still, objects of the present become legible as such only at a later moment, when they pass into history. This is not to say that images hold unique meanings; on the contrary, the point is to bring out how

---

3   This is why Benjamin's studies of Parisian nineteenth-century galleries are not ordinary. Benjamin realized that a specific cultural expression would have a close relationship with later political updates as if the former were both an artefact of this period and a material condition of the possibility for future events. *The Arcades Project* turns to Parisian galleries because they relate to how capitalism develops along with technological improvements.

our perceptions of time struggle with other cultural expressions, which will reveal hidden aspects of how we see and interpret the world around us.

The moment of revelation of hidden stories, narratives and subjects is integral to what he called the "dialectical image;" it is the moment when one awakes to historical consciousness by taking into account other perspectives. A good and practical example of this is to look at Memorials and Museums that honor victims of human rights violations. These spaces enlarge our capacity to imagine and be sensitive to other forms of being and even suffering. This moment of historical awareness is a moment of thinking enlargement because we see different perspectives by becoming aware of social struggles. Thus, we are not yet referring to a clear definition of what "dialectical image" means, but one can observe that this image is intimately connected with Benjamin's concept of History.

Concerning Benjamin's historiography, he reads Hegel's (2004) philosophy of History with criticism, because Benjamin wants to emphasize the role of small stories, namely, the lived experiences that disappear when the Great History is told. For that, Benjamin offers an alternative methodology to the idea of time as progress. In his work, past and future are not only stages with a linearity of events, but a challenge for imagining politics otherwise.

> Articulating the past historically does not mean recognizing it 'the way it really was.' It means appropriating a memory (*Erinnerung*) as it flashes up in a moment of danger. Historical materialism wishes to hold fast that image of the past which unexpectedly appears to the historical subject in a moment of danger.[4] The danger threatens both the body the content of the tradition and those who inherit it. For both, it is one and the same thing: the danger of becoming a tool of the ruling classes.
>
> BENJAMIN, *thesis VI* 2010: 391

The following are some of the divergences between Benjamin and Hegel's readings of time and History. First, Benjamin introduces an alternative idea of time. While Hegel affirms that History observes temporal standards, Benjamin

---

4 Benjamin uses the words flash and danger very often, especially when discussing dialectical images in *The Arcades Project*. The use of the term flash is particularly interesting because Benjamin makes a direct correspondence with photography devices – a dialectical image appears as if a photo was taken, we just see a "flash," very quickly. This is relevant because we suddenly became aware of injustices or victims of violence in a quick way, so the danger is twofold: one is how some aspects of violence and injustice can still exist in social bonds; the second is the danger of forgetting theses injustices for a second time.

highlights how this History has interruptions in its chronological flow. This is relevant because focusing on disruptions, as an analytical method, might provide a consciousness of our embeddedness in History. Hegel, on the contrary, says that this awareness happens when one looks at History's process (progress). Second, for Hegel, History should not take into account all events, objects, and individuals, since every historical moment overcomes a previous one. In this way, History has a linear progression. Benjamin says this linearity might turn invisible some alternative versions of History, especially from victims and minorities. For him, these forgotten aspects of History contain expressions of concrete historical moments (Seligmann-Silva 2007: 108). In other words, they reveal other historical subjects, stories, events. This awareness of forgotten accounts of History happens when one stops paying attention to the dominant Historiography to consider other possible explanations for the present time (Buck-Morss 1989; Löwy 2005; Pensky 2004: 192).[5] It is not about taking into account every detail that happens in History. It is about understanding other perspectives when dealing with events, especially in our daily lives.

To be fair, Hegel advances a concept of time in which the past continues to exist within the present. He posits History as a progression towards the realization of human freedom. The individual, when pursuing freedom in his/her existence, improves societal institutions until society achieves the realization of freedom. Contradiction is part of the process of the development of modernity[6] (Douzinas 2002: 383). Historical changes maintain within themselves the [superseded] historical contradictions of the past, including alternative perspective from the past – which were necessary parts of historical change – that are hidden in the present. However, Benjamin highlights the importance of looking back to these hidden aspects of History to make visible some aspects of the present.

As this awareness of History comes in *flashes* (i.e., very quickly), Benjamin's notion of image is key to his historiography (Ross 2015: 201). For Benjamin, "the image that is read [...] bears to the highest degree the imprint of the perilous critical moment on which all reading is founded" (Benjamin 2002: 463 [Arcades, N3,1]). In other words, the dialectical image presents itself as a moment of *awakening*. It is a moment of consciousness both of historicity and

---

5   For instance, a concrete example is to look at indigenous narratives to enlarge our comprehension of colonization and territorial expansion in the Americas.

6   Hegel proposes a system in which positive and negative aspects of thought integrates into a boost in the movement of the Universal Spirit (*Sittlichkeit*) in historical progress. So, the individual is both part of the Spirit and unique because his uniqueness is fully realized when he integrates organically with the Moral Spirit (Hegel 1977: 12–18).

of danger of what is coming (Benjamin 2002: 463 [Arcades, N3, 1]), since "the materialist presentation of History leads the past to bring the present into a critical state" (Benjamin 2002: 471 [Arcades, N7a, 5].

In Benjamin's words:

> It's not that what is past casts its light on what is present, or what is present its light on the past; rather, image is that wherein what has been come together in a flash with the now to form a constellation. In other words, image is dialectics at a standstill. For a while, the relation of the present to the past is a purely temporal, continuous one, the relation of what-has-been to the now is dialectical: is not progression but an image, suddenly emergent. – Only dialectical images are genuine images (that is, not archaic); and the place where one encounters them is language.
>
> BENJAMIN 2002: 462 [*Arcades*, N2a, 3]

The concept of dialectical image plays an essential role in Benjamin's *Arcades Project* [*Das Passagen-Werk*].[7] Despite being the methodological heart of Benjamin's alternative historiography, however, there is no straightforward definition of what this "image" is. It is difficult to understand how dialectical images "were to be related to the agency of the critical historian" (Pensky 2004: 178). According to Rolf Tiedemann (1989: 294), the term "dialectical image never achieved any terminological consistency." Thus, the dialectical image, which was supposed to shed new light on looking at History, turned into a theoretical black hole (to quote Max Pensky's words).

As stated in the literature, the reasons are, overall, twofold: First, as the concept of "dialectical image" was meant to be both a new theoretical framework of materialist historiography and a practical tool for political intervention, it is unclear how this methodology was supposed to be used (Pensky 2004: 178; Ross, 2015: 102; Tiedemann 1989: 294). Second, Benjamin's lack of explanation for the concept, notwithstanding his frequent use of it (Buck-Morss 1989: 67; Pensky 2004: 178), makes it difficult to connect the applications of the methodology of the dialectical image *per se* developed in *Arcades* with "the critical

---

7 In a letter to Scholem on January 20th, 1930, Benjamin states that the Arcades Project "was to embody a theory of the consciousness of History." Although leaving more gaps than answers, Benjamin, meant to put in motion alternative historiography by proposing a phenomenological approach to History by using images. It worth reading this work along with his "Thesis of History." Written days before Benjamin's suicide, these enigmatic fragments help shed light in what it wanted to do in Arcades Project's essay (Löwy 2005).

perspective Benjamin's early writing takes on the hermeneutics of the image" (Ross 2015: 103).

It is also worth stressing that throughout his work Benjamin does not fully enclose the conceptions he uses. As Pensky argues, elaborating a closed theory demands introducing "a subjective intention on the structure of historical time," stabilizing it and, thus, pacifying how phenomena should be read. Benjamin was interested in an epistemology that would allow him not to define events, but rather to interrupt any stable comprehension of them. In this sense, Benjamin did not want to enclose a theoretical framework because he tried to advance an alternative method of History (Pensky 2004: 199); especially to be "more persistent in his attack against the myth of automatic historical progress" (Buck-Morss 1989: 80). As a philosophy of History like Hegel's holds a very limited method to explain events, Benjamin wanted to advance a methodology that would open room for other perspectives and ways of thinking.

In other words, to understand what a dialectical image is and its relationship with the now, one must consider History not as a sequence of events, but a *dispute* of them in which past and future are matters of political struggle in the present. Thus, culture, media and works of art are not the products of an epoch *per se*, so much as elements of the superstructure, in Marxist terms. Benjamin realized that the transformation of cultural products into commodities directly informs how the current period understands (and uses) the past (Gagnebin 2014: 199).

> It seems, then, that Benjamin hoped that readers of his essay on the work of art would become aware not only of the political and epistemological potentialities of forms of art made possible utilizing new technologies of production and reproduction, but also of their correspondence to the artefacts and modes of perception inhabiting other historical moments, and thus of the particular – and particularly endangered – character of our own embeddedness in History.
>
> JENNINGS 2008: 6

If we use the dialectical image as a concept that explains his methodology and objectives, we can understand his version of historical materialism. For Benjamin, cultural products, works of art and informal media inform how we perceive the present. Culture is not only a product, but mainly, as Nietzsche says, an extemporaneous (*unzeitgemäss*) sign. Consequently, it is also an anticipatory sign of another time – as Bloch (1986) advances (Gagnebin 2014: 199).

In sum, the dialectical image implies enlarging the way we look at events. Benjamin proposes a conception of time characterized by lived experience and disruption. The dialectic, to him, works such that images of the past (remembrance) inform historical consciousness. This remembrance opens the possibility for intervention in the present. Nevertheless, this awakening promise never fulfils its commitment – this historical consciousness is always in danger of not working well. Plus, Benjamin was dealing with a political aesthetic expressed by fascism in his time. Culture is at the core of his philosophy because ways of seeing inform ways of understanding our times. Benjamin knew that the openness of the dialectical image, this awakening, was also a dispute of culture.

3   Dialectics in Discussion: Adorno and Benjamin

The letters exchanged between Adorno and Benjamin offer a rich overview of their aesthetic and philosophical debates in the thirties. Both were discussing the role of technology within artistic production. Nevertheless, these conversations are well-known for their disagreement, especially regarding Adorno's criticism of Benjamin's inclination to think about materialism along with theology and mythology,[8] as I shall discuss below. When the Institute for Social Research refused Benjamin's article on Baudelaire due to Adorno's substantial criticisms and stipulations[9] – their theoretical divergences became evident.

To meet some of Adorno's criticisms, Benjamin revised his essays on the reproducibility of the work of art and his never-finished work *The Arcades Project*. The revisions mostly surrounded Benjamin's ideas about "aura"[10] and

---

8   As Susan Buck-Morss highlights, the concept of dialectical images as proposed by Benjamin resembles very much what Gershom Scholem "describes as 'theological symbols' in which even the most insignificant phenomena are understood and explained about redemption" (Buck-Morss 1989: 245).

9   Adorno's comments on the essay were about a lack of more analytical explanation of the terms. In Adorno's view, Benjamin was so restricted to the accumulation of period details that he misses the relevance of historical materialism and relies too much upon mysticism. The article's refusal to be published is primarily accredited to Adorno. Some commenters acknowledge "the correct course for the *Zeitschrift* [Institute for Social Research's journal] was, surely, to publish the manuscript and then proceed to a critical discussion of it in the journal" (Adorno et al. 1980: 105).

10 Aura is a characteristic and effect of objects being uniquely present in time and space. As the concept refers to authenticity, the work of art reproduced cannot be fully presented anywhere, while the original one loses its uniqueness. As a result, objects lose their authenticity along with their authority. Within a mass society, the loss of aura happens when the masses are constantly seeking to bring things closer. Notwithstanding, the work of art, traditionally, is experienced through distanced contemplation. In this

the relevance of art as a tool to intervene in the present. The sharpness of Adorno's comments are evident in a letter to Benjamin on August 2nd, 1935, in which Adorno states that "the notion of a collective consciousness was invented only to divert attention from true objectivity and its correlate, alienated subjectivity" (Adorno et al. 1980: 113). Adorno was sceptical of the attainability of a historical awakening in Benjamin's terms. He says, "it is up to us to polarize and dissolve this 'consciousness' dialectically between society and singularities, and not to galvanize it as an imagistic correlate of the community character" (Adorno et al. 1980, 113). In other words, Adorno was unconvinced that dialectical images, in a growing mass society, would be enough for political transformation.

Furthermore, according to Adorno, the dialectical image is actually undialectical. He stresses Benjamin's sentence that 'every epoch dreams its successor'; the dialectical image concept is grounded in this undialectical sentence and lacks a theoretical explanation of its use (Adorno et al. 1980). Adorno explains that this sentence is undialectical because it poses a development where each epoch is self-contained, looking to the future as a sort of Utopia. To Adorno, this oversimplifies dialectics, taking away the social movement and contradiction that true dialectical thought holds. As he suggests:

> If you transpose the dialectical image into a consciousness as a 'dream' you not only take the magic out of the concept and render it sociable, but you also deprive it of that objective liberating power which could legitimize it in materialistic terms. The fetish character of the commodity is not a fact of consciousness; instead, it is dialectical, in the eminent sense that it produces consciousness. This means, however, that consciousness or unconsciousness cannot merely depict it as a dream, but responds to it in equal measure with desire and fear. But it is precisely this dialectical power of the fetish character that is lost in the replica realism of your present immanent version of the dialectical image.
>
> ADORNO et al. 1980: 111

The dialectical image lacks a common ground that works in both theory and practice. For Adorno, this concept is too theological, and by consequence it empties what the dialectic is. Adorno also says that the relationship between the past and what is new/actual is "of utopian reference to a 'classless society'"

---

modern society, in which every aesthetic form can be enlarged; photographs, shows, films are displayed in an imperative and dynamic way to the viewer.

(Adorno et al. 1980: 112). In his opinion, when Benjamin states that past and present exist at the same time, he is not taking into consideration the role of social classes in these temporal dynamics. The dialectical image implies historical consciousness but understanding if and how this consciousness would arise is far too complicated for Benjamin's concept. Also, Benjamin's understanding of a historical period is too general. The concept of the dialectical image is interesting as a description of a force, but it lacks a dialectical sense, namely, a movement of contradiction within social relations. Taking the dialectical image's concept seriously, Adorno says, it is not easy to observe its contradictions, and nothing is left but mythical thinking: faith that an image might reveal everything. A dialectical image would not be enough to provide a historical synthesis as expected in a dialectical movement, and most likely it would not be capable of irrupting a class-consciousness (Adorno et al. 1980: 110–120).

The dialectics debate leads Adorno and Benjamin to different conclusions, becoming a source of disagreement between them. To Benjamin, dialectical images represent a methodological constellation, which means that different times coexist in the present, forming an image, a frame through which the world and its social relations are revealed. Adorno, in his turn, argues that dialectics is supported by a dialectical argumentation, i.e., finding contradictions within discourses that lead to significant historical change (Buck-Morss 1989: 67).

However, far more interesting is to read this discussion considering how these authors are both looking at subject construction and possibilities for resistance with the transformation of productive conditions (Gagnebin 2014: 100). Adorno and Benjamin agree there is a sort of exhaustion in how the bourgeoisie produce art and define the modern subject in autonomous terms. This exhaustion informs not only how we aesthetically apprehend the things we see around us, but also the construction of subjects.[11] The transformation of

---

11   Here, it is essential to highlight the remarkable text *Experience and Poverty* from Benjamin, which aims to illustrate the problematic conditions of communication in modern times, caught by technological development and speed. "Where do you still hear words from the dying that last, and that pass from one generation to the next like a precious ring?" asks Benjamin. Benjamin compares how there is a sort of lost treasure transmitted to each generation to the next one and, in this way, the present is woven like a thread of the past. It is not to praise a past which is no longer here; on the contrary, Benjamin reflects upon the conditions for subject construction within fragmented time, considering how his ability to narrate an event might achieve a reconciliation with the world we share with other subjectivities. In this way, the construction of shared meaning to provide the conditions of political belonging happens. However, within the material and ideological conditions, the transmission is somehow impoverished with the advancement of technology and reproducibility.

society towards modernity presents some consequences. Politically speaking, it opens new paths for totalitarianism. Besides, both authors recognize that the idea of the subject as an autonomous entity is no longer reliable to advance for the struggle for freedom in modernity (Gagnebin 2014: 102).

In the essay "Little History of Photography," Benjamin (2008) discusses how artistic vanguards interrupt traditional transmission of representation. This notable shift translates into a change in world perception. According to Benjamin, the gaze towards the world ceases to be contemplative, turning into a consumerist way of looking that needs to own the object seen. To a certain extent, both Adorno and Benjamin understand that the tension between traditional production of works of art and new tools of expression expresses a long-term transformation in perception.

The Adorno and Benjamin exchange, impressive as it is, shows that their divergence was because they were mobilizing different comprehensions of art and dialectics, leading to a sort of deafness. Especially regarding Adorno's criticism, some commentators will argue that Adorno reads Benjamin's drafts imposing a rigorous conception of dialectics. Fredric Jameson observes that "there is a disturbing note of willed insistence on certain of Adorno's ideas [...] at the expense of complete respect for the autonomy of Benjamin's concerns" (Adorno et al. 1980: 105).

Benjamin believes that the dynamics of attention and distraction would open the path for historical consciousness through dialectical images (Benjamin 2008). According to him, distraction means to get lost in thoughts. Certainly, when one discusses mass societies, distraction appears as a problematic feature, since these masses are not aware of reality itself. However, Benjamin uses distraction as an attitude of absorbing the work of art freely. To do so, he compares distraction to contemplation which, for him, is a sort of domination by the author, while distraction allows another form of incorporating the work of art. This compares to the activity of getting lost in a city, being open to finding things one did not expect before, such as a new library, building, sculpture, and so on. It is the same with the dialectical image: distraction allows us to be open to other possibilities. The dialectical image appears very quick, when one is not paying attention to anything else – when one is distracted.[12] In this regard, Benjamin highlights distraction

---

12   In a sense, Benjamin's argument relied a lot on readings from Simmel and Kracauer. Kracauer argues that the life and work conditions of workers do not allow them access to traditional works of art and not because they are difficult to understand (Kracauer 1977). This work influenced Benjamin to advance a conception of art not as sublime or superior; but rather as culture that reflects life conditions.

as an interruption within time and space, which matters to him since he is looking at disruptions in History. Adorno will come back to this discussion thirty years later in his work *Aesthetic Theory* but arguing that distraction is an alienated trap of the culture industry (Adorno 2002: 244–246; Gagnebin 2014: 113).[13]

Nevertheless, Benjamin's framework leaves us with two points that are worth considering today. Benjamin, following Brecht, believes dialectics should be supported by a comic exposition of reality, expressing how living conditions are fragmented. This will lead subjects, laughing at what they see and recognizing themselves, to acknowledge their alienation (Gagnebin 2014: 116). This is not to say that the only legitimate cultural expressions that awaken dialectical images are comedies. Perhaps there is a branch of cultural activities (significantly including comedies) that make the subject aware of himself – a disclosure.

Moreover, Benjamin faces the reproducibility of cultural expressions as the end of the "aura"[14] of works of art. It is not as bad as it seems though, because when art ceases to be used for ritual and ceases to be exclusive to elites, it opens new paths of perception. The new cultural expressions create possibilities for understanding and transmitting differently. Certainly, Benjamin is not naïve: there is always the danger of being coopted by the culture industry, but there is a hope of finding branches for political intervention in the present (Gagnebin 2014: 118–119).

---

13   For instance, in Adorno's words: "Shudder, radically opposed to the conventional idea of experience [*Erlebnis*], provides no particular satisfaction for the I; it bears no similarity to desire. Rather, it is a relic of the liquidation of the I, which, shaken, perceives its own limitedness and finitude. This experience [*Eifahrung*] is contrary to the weakening of the I that the culture industry manipulates. For the culture industry, the idea of the shudder is idle nonsense; this is probably the innermost motivation for the deaestheticization of art. To catch even the slightest glimpse beyond the prison that it is, the I requires not a distraction but rather the utmost tension; that preserves the shudder, involuntary comportment, incidentally, from becoming regression" (Adorno 1997: 245).

14   According to Benjamin: "What disappears during the era of technical reproducibility of work of art is its aura. This process is symptomatic, and its consequences extend beyond the realm of art. The technique of reproduction delineates what was reproduced and what was produced under the scope of tradition. By reproducing the same work multiple times, it replaces the unique existence of a work of art by a serial one. So, to the extent that reproduction allows the recipient to access the work under any circumstances, it updates it constantly" (Benjamin 2008: 15). Regarding this, the cinema would configure the technique of art that would be most damaging to tradition, in the sense that it redefines and impoverishes the human experience of reality – intensifying it (and, hence, the reason of Benjamin's critique on totalitarianism and mass movements).

Hence, the Adorno-Benjamin debate reveals what is most promising and frustrating concerning cultural transmission in modern times, especially when considering recent political and social trends. Indeed, these thinkers were concerned with their epoch. Nowadays, the culture industry and communication technologies have developed new methods of expression. However, the *problemátique* remains the same: What are the conditions of possibility for critique, namely historical consciousness, today? What is the role of the new technology in formatting our perceptions of the world? How does cultural production, both in a broad sense and specifically considering social media communication, shape the construction of subjectivities?

Benjamin was quite aware of the fire alarm of his period: the emergence of fascism and its use of culture to expand its political influence. Lately, debates about populism in Europe and the Americas speculate on the conditions of possibility for the rise of such authoritarian discourses in the general culture, especially after a democratic ode in the 1990s with the fall of the Berlin Wall, the fall of the Soviet Union, and the expansion of the human rights agendas. In this sense, Benjamin's advancement of the dialectical image, asking for a critical attitude towards the subject's times, is urgent for identifying the cultural projections we are seeing. This follows what Buck-Morss (1989) advances in *The Dialectics of Seeing*. It implies being aware of how today's politics are grounded in specifics understandings of what is legitimate and what is not, which is expressed culturally through various forms of communication (Buck-Morss 1989: 4). Thus, discussion of populism should include how culture is expressed and transmitted, creating meaning in the world in common. Through culture, we may find a glimpse of collective historical imagination, and identify tensions and possibilities for political transformation.

4   Populism Decays into Images (and Social Media)

"Everything is genuine. And there is no tendentious commentary for the simple reason that there is no commentary at all. It is History – pure History" was Leni Riefenstahl's defence when arguing that her movies were not Nazi propaganda (Sontag 1981: 82). Her movie *Triumph of the Will* (1935) is well-known for being a paradigmatic example of the intimate relationship between art and politics as pursued by fascist elites. She frames monumental sequences aiming to strengthen what she called the "heroic" spirit of the regime. This documentary represents "an already achieved and radical transformation of reality: History become theatre" (Sontag 1981: 83). After what happened, Susan Sontag advances

Anyone who defends Riefenstahl's films as documentaries, if the documentary is to be distinguished from propaganda, is being ingenuous. In Triumph of the Will, the document (the image) not only is the record of reality but is one reason for which the reality has been constructed, and must eventually supersede it.

SONTAG 1981: 83

Riefenstahl provides an experience of politics as sublime[15] – and Benjamin is quite aware of the political implications. Large pictures of soldiers reunited in Nazi Party Commissions produce a particular perception of the world, implying a specific aesthetic[16] and experience; namely, the ability to apprehend reality as it supposedly is. It is worth stressing that when Kant discusses the sublime experience at the moment of contact with the work of art, he is considering the ability of this work to be further than representation, becoming a reality itself. With the sublime, "there is no room here for the subject of History and politics, the subject of differential cultural experience" (Jabri 2006: 821). Hence, being in contact with the sublime implies capturing the historical subject, since "it is assumed to belong to a realm that is beyond contestation [...] of the public arena" (Jabri 2006: 821). When Benjamin denounces the aestheticizing of politics, it is how Riefenstahl (among others artists) frames reality as "History – pure History"; and this is why Benjamin aspires to find fissures within late modern society, so History can find its redemption. To Benjamin, politicizing art means seeing how aesthetic experience of the world in common disrupts its boundaries as the boundaries of the historical subject.

Art is an expression of economic conditions, i.e. the materiality of the social world, which informs spatial and temporal ways of perceiving the world (Benjamin 2008; Buck-Morss 1989; Jabri 2006: 821; Jennings et al. 2008; Gagnebin 2014: 100–113). In this way, Benjamin worries how fascism mobilizes aesthetics in a mass society experiencing a crisis both of the emancipated subject and the Philosophy of History. A crisis because, according to the "natural"

---

15   The sublime experience happens when one looks at a work of art, according to Kant. Kant in his *Critique of Judgment* analyses how we create opinions and taste towards works of art. The sublime, in particular, is a moment when one encounters beauty itself, as if there are no possible words to describe it. It is a moment of suspension.

16   It is essential to note that the etymological origin of the word "aesthetic" derives from the Greek word *Aisthitikos*, which means "perceived by sensation" (Buck-Morss 2015: 175). Aesthetics is the sensory experience of perception, and therefore its materiality comes not from art, but from reality itself. The experience addresses the capacity to create a meaning to an event. In other words, it refers to the construction of meaning in the world in common that politically connects us as subjectivities.

laws of Philosophy of History, as we saw previously, humankind walks toward its emancipation. Benjamin's historical moment revealed an alienated mass society, unaware of what was happening around. We are not, however, living in an emergence of Nazism as it was in the twenties and thirties.

Nevertheless, Benjamin's attempt to advance an alternative historiography is still important today. As political beings, we are continually dealing with the construction of perceptions that represent the world. Benjamin helps us to enlarge our perspectives on how contemporary populism, spreading all over the globe, develops a specific aesthetics. Being aware of how History produces images, through culture, helps us find ways to deal with new authoritarianism. Moreover, Benjamin asks us, as political and historical subjects, to be aware of possible spaces in society that allow political expansion and inclusion. In other words, Benjamin's ideas are is relevant to the current urgency of thinking critically towards our own times in order to act in the present.

As discussed previously, the dialectical image appears at the instant of danger, as if the past left us a hidden message looking for redemption.[17] Putting it simply, one recognizes their present once they become aware of the meanings the present gives to the past. One irrupts with so-called "historical truth", in the sense of a unique version of History and events (as I discussed in the first section of this essay). However, this awakening can only happen when the subject is aware of being situated in relation to History. In this sense, redemption means a sort of enlightenment of the dialectical process that configures the present (Didi-Huberman 2008).

Significantly, Benjamin uses the example of photography to illustrate this change of perception along with technological. Turning back to his *text Little History of Photography*, what is relevant is that photography contains a History

---

17   Benjamin will use the term "redemption" as a moment in which the past gains its emancipation in the present. This means that the hidden narratives, or invisible victims of History, when acknowledged, become free, as a goal of History. It is not exactly a final stage of History, but it is a moment that they are taken into account as part of the order of things. It means to embody different stories and untold perspectives. The term is particularly more developed in "Thesis on History." When he uses the term "redemption," Benjamin implies theology. In this respect, it is worth noting that Benjamin points to two implicit conceptions: remembrance (*Eingedenken*) and messianic redemption (*Erlösung*). Both concepts relate on how the past affects the present in an innovative and revolutionary way (Löwy 2005: 44). Specifically, the concept of *Erlösung* relates to how the individual conceives the redemption of his own past to achieve personal fulfillment – something like a reparation for the lost suffering and pain of previous generations (Löwy 2005: 49).

in itself because it is reproducible.[18] This ability to be printed many times breaks with the unique ("auratic") character of the work (Benjamin 2008; Burck Morss 1989); from the twentieth century onwards, any work of art can be reproduced. Because of this, photography can express history – the work is no longer self-contained in a certain period or epoch, but rather demands a gaze sensitive towards the past. Until technological improvements, works of art "were closed [...] at a particular time and place, making the work into an object of contemplation rather than use" (Caygill 1998: 92). In this regard, Benjamin argues that photography facilitates an openness to the future because it provides an optical unconscious in which "a space informed by human consciousness gives way to a space informed by the unconscious" (Benjamin 2008: 284). According to Caygill, "a space free of consciousness is charged with contingency if it is open to the future and to becoming something other than itself" (Caygill 1998: 92).

Indeed, photography reveals a significant achievement in terms of technological apparatuses of transmission – especially concerning the cinema as technique and reproducibility of sound and image. Conversely, Benjamin looks directly at the alignment between fascist monumental art, aestheticism and historicity (Caygill 1998: 92). Coming back to politics as theatre, as Susan Sontag criticizes, Caygill states:

> Yet the monumental condition of the auratic work of art is deceptive since every work of art undergoes change as a condition of its existence. The auratic work of art which pretends to be immune to the passage of time is in truth only a particular way of negotiating finitude, that is, by denying it. Such works, as monumental, literally refuse their future, since time is arrested in their claims to uniqueness and duration.
>
> CAYGILL 1998: 103

Thus, when Benjamin writes about the dialectical image, he is worried that an aestheticization of politics[19] leads to an experience of the sublime that

---

18   No doubt that all metaphors to describe dialectical image relates to the use of the photographic camera. As Susan Buck-Morss observes "dialectical images are represented by Benjamin in modern metaphors: the 'lightning flash' of cognition they provide is like illumination from a camera flashbulb; the images themselves – 'dialectics at a standstill' are like camera shots, that 'develop' in time as in a darkroom (Buck-Morss 1989: 250).

19   In this regard, see Sontag's point concerning Riefenstahl: "the force of her work being precisely in the continuity of its political and aesthetic ideas, what is interesting is that this was once seen so much more clearly than it seems to be now when people claim to be drawn to Riefenstahl's images for their beauty of composition. Without a historical

suspends critical thinking. Benjamin introduces the crucial link of technology, "since [for him] fascism was a response to a crisis which was both social and technological" (Caygill 1998: 103) – as we saw in the Adorno-Benjamin debate. As perception changes, it also changes how we think about ourselves concerning place and time in History, so technological apparatuses have a crucial role in this mediation. Technology affects this process either by leading to constant innovation (in terms of the construction of the subject or reality), or by imposing a distance between object and subject, creating the sublime, the monumentality.

This link between technology and experience is important to consider when dealing with the present time. Specifically, social media informs our meanings, how we explain History, how events happen, and the relationships between all of these things. Populism and far-right movements arise today in a moment of deep social crisis, clearly expressed with scepticism towards public institutions and promises of political representation. It is notable in authoritarian discourses that content is less important than the way things are said – for instance, politicians rely very often on their private Twitter accounts to state short but shocking sentences (Solano 2018). The present era witnesses major political declarations happening online within 280 characters.[20] Thus, social media is a proper arena of theatrical gesture, updated daily. It expresses new ways of communicating and making sense of the world.

Particularly more severe, the disclosure between content and image, appearing as sublime, does not open room for thinking critically. The circulation of information on social media has been one of intensifying a sensation of shock. When looking at recent political images, such as from migration centres, violence, or even from political campaigns, the viewer feels shocked, and this feeling provides an interruption of thinking. It is not the same feeling as a distraction as I was demonstrating before, because shock implies a suspension and a physical state of defence. To overcome this suspension, political discourse has the capacity to provide an in-between space between individuals, in which they might discuss shared political concerns and tensions. However,

---

perspective, such connoisseurship prepares the way for a curiously absentminded acceptance of propaganda for all sorts of destructive feelings – feelings whose implications people are refusing to take seriously" (Sontag 1981: 97).

20   A recurrent phenomenon is populist politicians going on social media, such as Twitter, to make official statements concerning their government. They use it not only to advocate for their platforms, but also as a legitimate space of expression, alternative to traditional news media. In Brazil, all recent political debate concerning the Federal Policy competencies and its relationship to the current leaders happened through videos, messages, apps, and the president's Twitter account.

the problem with shocking and inflammatory fake news, for example, is that we are not feeding space for politics as a mediator – common space in which difference is welcome and civil disagreements are possible. Thus, one could argue that our stoked worries lead us in a direction where no truth matters; but only the great gesture of saying things – an image that reveals much of our political concerns (Solano 2018).

As an example, the researcher Esther Solano conducted interviews to analyse the rise of authoritarian discourses during the 2018 Brazilian elections, concluding that the point was not precisely *what* authoritarian orators were saying, but *how* they were saying it (Solano 2018). She inquired into the reactions of supporters of authoritarian candidates, mostly young and upper-middle class, by showing them the candidates' public speeches. Surprisingly, their primary reaction was to say that "he actually did not mean it" or "it's just the way he is, not a big deal" (Solano 2018). She realized that even when confronting the use of violent and racist words, her interviewees would state that it was not too serious. Then, the authoritarian orators are highly praised by the way they perform – a displacement of political energy from the message's content to the act of speaking itself.

Hence, what Benjamin left us is a courageous methodology to dare to investigate our constellations, how images operate within them, and what struggles they expose us to. Didi-Huberman (2008: 182) argues that "the question of images is at the heart of the great darkness of our time." The point is to find theoretical tools that could help us to open these images in order to provide opportunities for political action; a different attitude than looking at them and experiencing shock and sublimity. Images, understood as an expression of how we apprehend the world around us, can help us to find gaps for enlarging critical thinking. With this, we can act politically upon the world, questioning authoritarian discourses and expanding political understanding. And it seems that Benjamin offered a suggestion how.

The aesthetic offered by authoritarian populism is indeed compelling; it is easy to understand and to operate through its grammar. Although trying to pin down Benjamin's dialectical image concept generates more doubts than answers, his broad theoretical proposal can be sensed. It relies on the metaphor of the experience of awakening from a dream. This awakening is to be understood as the development of a new kind of critical attitude and a new conception of images within historical time (Buck-Morss 1989: 188). Furthermore, we are not only passive receptacles of cultural dynamics; we also produce them daily, creating and informing perceptions and ways of understanding events. A critical methodology implies a political attitude towards the present – not only looking at culture and image communication nowadays but considering as well our roles at producing culture and images. In this sense, no one can escape from dialectical images because no one can escape from their own times. Benjamin offered a methodology for using cultural artefacts to understand History, and how we give meaning to our past, present and future. Contemporary authoritarian populism aims at suspension of thought and dialogue. Benjamin's approach has the capacity not only to make us aware of the complexities and violence of authoritarian populist policies, but also to find ways to resist them. Dialectical images might provide the conditions for awareness of the dangers of our present time. Benjamin has shown that we should pay attention to them.

References

Adorno, Theodor. 2002. *Aesthetic Theory*, eds. Gretel Adorno and Rolf Tiedemann. London: Continuum.

Adorno, Theodor; Benjamin, Walter; Lukács, et al. 1980. *Aesthetics and Politics*. Aftwd. Fredric Jameson. London: Verso.

Benjamin, Walter. 2010. *Selected Writings, v. 4 – 1938–1940*, trans. Edmund Jephcott and others, eds. Howard Eiland and Michael W. Jennings. Cambridge, MA: Harvard University Press.

Benjamin, Walter. 2008. *The Work of Art in the Age of Its Technological Reproducibility and Other Writings on Media*, eds. Michael Jennings, Brigid Doherty, and Thomas Y. Levin. Cambridge, MA: Harvard University Press.

Benjamin, Walter. 2002. *The Arcades Project*, ed. Rolf Tiedemann. Cambridge, MA: Harvard University Press.

Bloch, Ernst. 1986. *The Principle of Hope*. Cambridge, MA: The MIT Press.

Buck-Morss, Susan. 2012. "Estética e Anestética: uma reconsideração de 'A Obra de Arte' de Walter Benjamin." In: *Benjamin e a Obra de Arte: técnica, imagem, percepção*, organized by Tadeu Capistrano, trans. Marijane Lisboa and Vera Ribeiro, 172–222. Rio de Janeiro: Contraponto.

Buck-Morss, Susan. 1989. *The Dialectics of Seeing: Walter Benjamin and the Arcades Project*. Cambridge, MA: The MIT Press.

Caygill, Howard. 1998. *Walter Benjamin: the colour of experience*. London: Routledge.

Didi-Huberman, George. 2008. *Images in Spite All: four photographs from Auschwitz*, trans. Shanne Lillis. Chicago: University of Chicago Press.

Douzinas, Costas. 2002. "Identity, Recognition, Rights or What Can Hegel Teach Us about Human Rights." *Journal of Law and Society* 29(3): 379–405.

Gagnebin, Jeanne-Marie. 2014. *Limiar, Aura e Rememoração: Ensaios Sobre Walter Benjamin*. São Paulo: Editora 34.

Hegel, Georg Wilhelm Friedrich. 1977. *Phenomenology of Spirit.* Oxford: Oxford University Press.

Hegel, Georg Wilhelm Friedrich. 2004. *The Philosophy of History.* Courier Corporation.

Jabri, Vivienne. 2006. "Shock and Awe: Power and the Resistance of Art." *Millennium* 34(3): 819–839.

Jennings, Michael; Doherty, Brigid and Levin, Thomas. 2008. "Introduction." In Benjamin, Walter. *The Work of Art in the Age of Its Technological Reproducibility and Other Writings on Media,* eds. Michael Jennings, Brigid Doherty, and Thomas Y. Levin 1–19. Cambridge, MA: Harvard University Press.

Kracauer, Siegfried. 1977. "Kult der Zerstreuung." In *Das Ornament der Masse.* Frankfurt: Suhrkamp.

Löwy, Michael. 2005. *Walter Benjamin: aviso de incêndio.* São Paulo: Boitempo.

Pensky, Max. 2004. "Method and time: Benjamin's dialectical images." In: *The Cambridge Companion to Walter Benjamin,* ed. David Ferris, 177–198. Cambridge, UK: Cambridge University Press.

Ross, Alison. 2015. *Walter Benjamin's Concept of the Image.* London: Routledge.

Seligmann-Silva, Márcio. 2007. "Quando a Teoria Reencontra o Campo Visual: passagens de Walter Benjamin." *Concinnitas* 2(11): 103–114.

Solano, Esther. 2018. "Crise da Democracia e Extremismos de Direita." In *Friedrich Ebert Stiftung Analysis* 42(May) – São Paulo, SP.

Sontag, Susan. 1981. "Fascinating Fascism." In: *Under the Sign of Saturn,* 73–83. New York: Vintage.

Tiedemann, Rolf Tiedemann. 1989. "Dialectics at a Standstill: Approaches to the *Passagen-Werk.*" In *On Walter Benjamin,* ed. Gary Smith, 261–291. Cambridge, MA: The MIT Press.

Afterword

Douglas Kellner

With the election of Donald Trump in 2016 and rise of rightwing authoritarian governments throughout Europe, authoritarian populism threatens democracies and public safety throughout the world. With authoritarian populism accompanied by the COVID-19 pandemic, people throughout the world are struggling with dual viruses threatening the health of democracy and the polity, as well as human life. The Introduction to Jeremiah Morelock's *How to Critique Authoritarian Populism: Methodologies of the Frankfurt School* correctly states that: "Far from disappearing, authoritarian populism has been reinvigorated, and the scope of its appeal far surpasses its spread in the inter-war era. If social science is intended to help society, then any social scientist should be aware today of the pressing need to understand authoritarian populism, to help society overcome it."

With this challenge confronting us, Morelock and his various contributors present a wealth of perspectives that demonstrate how the Frankfurt School provide powerful analyses of authoritarian populism that capture its complexity, evolution, and dangerous future trajectories. The studies collected show how Frankfurt School critical theory provides powerful research methods and critical analysis of authoritarian populism with well-documented research into its various manifestations. These studies demonstrate the continuing relevance of Frankfurt School theories and research methods, which combine critical social science research with substantive research projects into crucial sociopolitical issues of the day like authoritarian populism.

The Frankfurt School developed theories of the authoritarian personality which were used to characterize the personality structures and sociopsychological dynamics that described the authoritarian movements of the 1930s, and Morelock and his contributors demonstrate that these methods and theories are of great use and relevance today in analyzing, contextualizing, and critiquing the current forms and dynamics of authoritarian populism. The studies demonstrate that authoritarian populism involves masses submitting to a leader's authority, suggesting a continuity between the fascism and mass movements of the 1930s with today's global profusion of authoritarian leaders and movements. Just as the 1930s authoritarian movements led to war, economic and political chaos, and massive human tragedy, today's authoritarians are bringing wide-spread human chaos, political oppression and division, and economic crisis and uncertainty that is cascading throughout the globe.

The introduction and the studies collected in this volume put on display how the Frankfurt School's theories of the authoritarian personality, mass society and political movements help illuminate the rise of autocrats and authoritarian movements, and the ways that demagogic autocrats in conjunction with mass movements and the mass media, help produce a massification of public opinion and demagogic authoritarian political leaders who present themselves as saviors of the people. "I am the One," the authoritarian leader proclaims, and the masses follow in obedience. The autocratic leader seeks a monopoly on political truth and action and attacks the media, the judiciary, political organs and representatives, and any person or institution that does not follow his way, that opposes him, or that he cannot control. The autocrat's propaganda requires and elicits obedience and loyalty, and disdain for voices and institutions that oppose the Leader and his followers.

Hence, the autocrat is necessarily an enemy of democracy and democratic institutions, while mobilizing masses to follow his rule and dictates as he attacks democratic forces that oppose him. The autocrat is a demagogue who lies to the people and who attacks the very norms of truth, rational political discourse, and reason, truth, and science itself. While truth depends on curiosity and debate, the autocrat insists on conformity to his dictates and complete loyalty to his person. He claims to represent the people and the nation and mobilizes mass movements and supportive mass media to trumpet his every word and dictate.

The people identify with the leader who expresses their grievances, resentments, hates, and prejudice. The authoritarian leader attacks privilege and institutions that represent privilege, even though he may be part of the elite himself. The autocrat uses his office to promote his own interests, often at odds with the people's or public interests, violating political norms and often engaging in outright criminality.

Authoritarian populism often leads to and produces violence, as an enraged leader or group stigmatize and take out their grievances on minority groups who they blame for their own problems. This leads to demagoguery, outrage and hate which produces societal division and violence. The autocrat chooses an "Other," who his followers see as an "enemy," dividing the society and polis into "Us" and "Them."

While the studies in this volume document that ways that authoritarian populism threaten democracy and democratic values, they also show how authoritarian populism may generate resistance. The institutions, groups, and individuals that the autocrat attacks, and that his followers are led to demonize and hate, may fight back, mobilizing individuals against the autocrat and

his anti-democratic forces in newspapers, books, mass media, public demonstrations and oppositional movements.

We cannot see where our current plague of authoritarian populism will take
us, where the rising resistance movements will go, or what impact global pandemics and ecological crises will play in our crisis-infected future. It is clear,
however, that authoritarian populism has created crisis and political oppression throughout the globe that threatens democracy, civility, and human
life. It is also clear that global opposition movements are rising to challenge
authoritarian populism and the key question we face – as many times before –
remains: Which Side Are You On?

Index

CPSIA information can be obtained
at www.ICGtesting.com
Printed in the USA
JSHW021906100222
22654JS00003B/3